Paul Schalow—
January 15, 2000
Rutgers University

Cartographies of Desire

Cartographies of Desire

Male-Male Sexuality in Japanese Discourse, 1600–1950

GREGORY M. PFLUGFELDER

University of California Press

BERKELEY   LOS ANGELES   LONDON

University of California Press

Berkeley and Los Angeles, California

University of California Press, Ltd.

London, England

© 1999 by
The Regents of the University of California

Library of Congress Cataloging-in-Publication Data

Pflugfelder, Gregory M., 1959–

   Cartographies of desire : male-male sexuality in Japanese discourse,
      1600–1950 / Gregory M. Pflugfelder.

         p.   cm.

   Includes bibliographical references and index.

   ISBN 0–520–20909–5 (alk. paper)

      1. Homosexuality—Japan—History.   2. Homosexuality and
literature—Japan.   3. Legal literature—Japan—History and
criticism.   4. Medical literature—Japan—History and criticism.
5. Love in literature.   6. Homosexuality in literature.   I. Title.

HQ76.3.J3P35   1999
306.76'6'0952—dc21   98–20632
                                                              CIP

Printed in the United States of America
9   8   7   6   5   4   3   2   1

For my parents and grandparents

Contents

Acknowledgments   ix

Note   xi

Introduction   1

1. AUTHORIZING PLEASURE: MALE-MALE SEXUALITY IN
   EDO-PERIOD POPULAR DISCOURSE   23

   Finding the Way   23
   Youths, Lovers, Brothers, and Others   29
   Contextualized Pleasures   44
   The Boundaries of *Shudō*   63
   The End of the Way   82

2. POLICING THE PERISEXUAL: MALE-MALE SEXUALITY
   IN EDO-PERIOD LEGAL DISCOURSE   97

   Divine Pleasures/Devilish Pursuits   97
   Outrageous Spectacles   105
   Dangerous Liaisons   124
   The View from Above   142

3. THE FORBIDDEN CHRYSANTHEMUM: MALE-MALE
   SEXUALITY IN MEIJI LEGAL DISCOURSE   146

   The Origins of Civilization   146
   Anal Violations   158
   Enacting the Obscene (Or, Napoleon in Japan)   168
   Penile Servitude   182

4. TOWARD THE MARGINS: MALE-MALE SEXUALITY IN MEIJI
POPULAR DISCOURSE   193

    Forgetting Edo   194
    Encompassing the Margins   203
    Roughnecks and Smoothies   212
    Beautiful Boys   225

5. DOCTORING LOVE: MALE-MALE SEXUALITY IN MEDICAL
DISCOURSE FROM THE EDO PERIOD THROUGH THE EARLY
TWENTIETH CENTURY   235

    Healing Passions   235
    The Nature of the Unnatural   240
    Dichotomies of Love   251
    Dissecting the Past, Diagnosing the Present   277

6. PLEASURES OF THE PERVERSE: MALE-MALE SEXUALITY
IN EARLY TWENTIETH-CENTURY POPULAR DISCOURSE   286

    The New Language of Love   286
    The Pervert Speaks   291
    Ero-Guro Nanshoku   311
    War and Aftermath   326
    Coda: Historicizing Male-Male Sexuality in Japan   333

    Bibliography   337

    Index   371

Acknowledgments

Since beginning to gather materials for this project in or around 1981—so long ago that I do not remember precisely—I have incurred many and various debts, all of which it would be impossible to acknowledge, much less to repay. To those individuals and institutions whom I may have omitted to mention here, I offer my sincerest apologies and heartfelt, if silent, gratitude.

Publication of this book provides a welcome opportunity to pay tribute to the wise mentors and warm colleagues whom I have encountered in my academic career. During my years as a graduate student at Waseda University (1981–1987), Kano Masanao exemplified in innumerable ways the humanity to which I hope many historians may continue to aspire. I remain forever in his debt. My knowledge of Japanese history also owes much to the training that I received in those years from Yui Masaomi and Anzai Kunio. During a later stay at Waseda in 1993–1994, Izumi Masato furnished priceless assistance reading Edo-period legal documents. At Stanford University (1988–1996), Peter Duus was an ideal dissertation adviser, trusting my lights to guide me yet always ready to supply his wisdom when needed; Jeffrey Mass taught me the virtues of casting one's historical net across a broad expanse of time; James Ketelaar opened up entire new intellectual worlds to me; Harold Kahn awakened me to the joys of writing in English—a particularly agreeable discovery after I published my first book in Japanese;* Estelle Freedman aided and abetted my still heretical interest in the history of sexuality; and Paul Schalow, a visiting lecturer at nearby Berkeley, shared with me unstintingly his rich knowledge of Edo-period erotic culture. I am grateful also to my fellow graduate students Robert Eskildsen,

---

Gregory M. Pflugfelder's first book was *Seiji to daidokoro: Akita-ken joshi sanseiken undōshi* (Domesu shuppan, 1986).

James Orr, Mark Ravina, and Martha Tocco for their companionship, intellectual and otherwise. At Columbia University, where I have been teaching since 1996, I could not have wished for more cordial and generous colleagues than my fellow Japan historians Carol Gluck and Henry Smith, nor benefited from a more stimulating group of graduate and undergraduate students. My associates in Columbia's Department of East Asian Languages and Cultures, Department of History, East Asian Institute, and Institute for Research on Women and Gender, too numerous to name individually, have helped to create a congenial environment for my intellectual pursuits, for which I am greatly thankful.

Financial assistance during the different stages of this project has come from the Mabel MacLeod Lewis Memorial Fund, the Japan Foundation, the Social Science Research Council, the Department of History of Stanford University, and the East Asian Institute of Columbia University. The generosity of these benefactors within a political climate not always supportive of such research as I have chosen to undertake is deeply appreciated.

Various versions of this manuscript have been enriched by the thoughtful responses of Kim Brandt, Peter Duus, Robert Eskildsen, Estelle Freedman, Carol Gluck, David Halperin, Gustav Heldt, David Howell, Kano Masanao, James Ketelaar, Mark Ravina, Luke Roberts, Donald Roden, Julie Rousseau, Paul Schalow, Henry Smith, Janice Stockard, Martha Tocco, Tomiko Yoda, Ueno Chizuko, the participants in my spring and fall 1996 and spring 1997 graduate seminars on Japanese history at Columbia, and the manuscript readers for the University of California Press. Naturally, I remain responsible for all errors of fact and interpretation.

Finally, I would like to thank Laura Driussi, Sheila Levine, and Scott Norton, of the University of California Press, along with my copy editor Carl Walesa, for their skillful guidance in shepherding this manuscript through the various stages of publication.

Gregory M. Pflugfelder
Tokyo
September 1998

Note

Japanese names in this book appear family name first (when known), followed by personal name or pen name (*gō*), except in citations of Western-language writings, where Japanese names follow the order given in the text cited. I use the family name alone in subsequent references (e.g., Minakata for Minakata Kumagusu, Mori for Mori Ōgai), with the exception of Ihara Saikaku (Saikaku) and Matsuo Bashō (Bashō), whose pen names seem all too well entrenched. In some instances where individuals share a family name, as with members of the same household or dynastic rulers, I have used personal names alone (e.g., Ieyasu for Tokugawa Ieyasu) in order to avoid confusion.

Unless otherwise noted, the place of publication for all works cited is Tokyo. In citations of Japanese-language sources, angle brackets (<>) indicate supratitles (*tsunogaki*; literally, "horn script"), which in the original texts usually precede the main title in smaller characters, and are analogous to the subtitles of Western-language books and articles.

Introduction

If "cartography" is understood to mean the study and production of maps representing geographical and other spatial configurations—those charts, atlases, and globes that so fascinate us in childhood and continue to serve us faithfully as adults—then this book is not about cartography in its conventional sense. I evoke the image of mapmaking in the title, if only metaphorically, out of a belief that human understanding involves a continual mapping and remapping, not just of physical but also of social reality. Maps of the latter variety are not necessarily tangible, but they are no less instrumental than the conventional sort in orienting us to our environments. Which person is more lost, one might ask: the foreign tourist in an unfamiliar city who carries no guide to its transportation system, or her fellow traveler who does not comprehend the notion of "foreignness" or of "travel"—of her embeddedness, in other words, within new social circumstances—to begin with? Even the use of a conventional map requires an understanding of what those artifacts we call maps are and do, of certain relationships among objects, places, and people that they presuppose, that is nowhere visibly expressed on the surface of the map itself. It is only because we have internalized some of the basic principles of contemporary mapmaking, such as the rule of proportion or the use of a "bird's-eye" (rather than, say, a "mole's-eye") perspective, that we do not ordinarily stop to consider the arbitrary nature of these conventions or to imagine other possible arrangements. We assume that the forms and symbols on the map correspond unproblematically to the external reality that they are supposed to represent, and continue on our merry ways.

The specific terrain whose mapping concerns me in this study is that of sexuality. Historians and other scholars have spilt much ink over the past two or three decades in arguing that sexual constructs and categories, like national borders and even geological continents, are perpetually shifting.[1] Even within a particular cultural tradition, sexual meanings may register profound transformations over time, as Michel Foucault has memorably shown in the case of Western cultures from classical Greece to ancient Rome to post-Enlightenment Europe.[2] Such scholarship demonstrates that the systems of sexual knowledge and categorization prevailing in contemporary society cannot be assumed to hold any more authority, or be destined for any more lasting permanence, than their historical predecessors. And this perspective bears not only a scholarly but also a political weight. As the emergence of such fields as lesbian and gay history vividly illustrates, a recognition of the human suffering that the authority of various sexual knowledge systems has produced in bygone ages as well as in the present era—witness the persecution of "sodomites," for example, in the European Christian tradition—can serve as a potent motivating force for historical research.[3] The continuing criminalization of consensual male-male sexual acts as "sodomy" stands on shakier rhetorical foundations when it is realized that this sexual category, far from being a biblical construct, represents the historically much more recent invention of Church theologians and other latter-day authorities, who did not and do not always agree upon its meaning.[4] Yet it would be naive to overestimate the positive influence that historians and other academics have thus far been able to exert on the overall tenor of public debate.

In illuminating the historicity of sexual categories, recent scholarship on sexuality has at the same time raised some profound, and for many persons

---

1. On the historicity of sexual categories, see Robert A. Padgug, "Sexual Matters: On Conceptualizing Sexuality in History," in *Hidden from History: Reclaiming the Gay and Lesbian Past*, ed. Martin Bauml Duberman et al. (New York: NAL, 1989), 54–64.

2. Michel Foucault, *The History of Sexuality*, trans. Robert Hurley, 3 vols. (New York: Vintage, 1980–1988). The designation "Western" is, of course, inherently problematic, since it lumps together a variety of cultural traditions possessing distinct understandings of sexuality as well as significant commonalities. Throughout this study, I use "West" and "Western" as a convenient shorthand for European and (non-indigenous) North American societies.

3. For a collection of essays representative of the chronological and geographical diversity of scholarship in lesbian and gay history, see Duberman et al., *Hidden from History*.

4. The literature on the construction of "sodomy" is now quite extensive. I have found especially provocative John Boswell, *Christianity, Social Tolerance, and Homosexuality: Gay People in Western Europe from the Beginning of the Christian Era to the Fourteenth Century* (Chicago: University of Chicago Press, 1980); Jonathan Goldberg, *Sodometries: Renaissance Texts, Modern Sexualities* (Stanford: Stanford University Press, 1992); Mark D. Jordan, *The Invention of Sodomy in Christian Theology* (Chicago: University of Chicago Press, 1997).

troubling, questions about the nature of "desire" itself. The human record suggests that not only sexual understandings but erotic desires themselves are less uniform across time and space than most people ordinarily suppose. The biologistic reasoning that informs much of late twentieth-century thinking on sexuality insists, to the contrary, that sexual desire, and perhaps even sexual "orientation," are inscribed in the very deepest structures of the human body (for example, in our hypothalamuses or in our genes). In this formulation, which derives cultural authority from various contemporary institutions of medicine and science, the transformation of biological givens or "imperatives" into actual practices of sexuality and in turn the representation of these practices through language (which inevitably involves sexual categories) are epiphenomenal to the essentially presocial and prelinguistic, hence pre-historical, reality of sexual desire itself. Even those who recognize that designations for various forms of sexuality differ according to place and speaker—just as "Germany" appears in certain atlases as "Deutschland" and in others as "Allemagne," or is sometimes shaded in yellow, sometimes in red—seldom consider that the underlying geography of desire is anything but universal.

A growing body of scholarship on the history of sexuality challenges this biologistic view. One of the premises of the present study, like others that follow an interpretive tradition commonly labeled "constructionist," is that desire, sexual or otherwise, is not a constant or a given, but is shaped in crucial ways by the very manner in which we think and speak about it.[5] As David Halperin has put it, there is "no orgasm without ideology."[6] From such a perspective, mappings of sexuality do not reflect an unchanging reality so much as participate centrally in its construction, helping to engender the very desires and subjectivities that they purport merely to represent. In this sense, maps of the conventional and metaphorical variety are in the end not so very different, for few would deny the crucial role that

5. For introductions to and critiques of constructionism, particularly in its relation to male-male sexuality, see David M. Halperin, "'Homosexuality': A Cultural Construct (An Exchange with Richard Schneider)," in *One Hundred Years of Homosexuality and Other Essays on Greek Love* (New York: Routledge, 1990), 41–53; Edward Stein, ed., *Forms of Desire: Sexual Orientation and the Social Constructionist Controversy*, Garland Gay and Lesbian Studies, no. 1 (New York: Garland, 1990); Carole S. Vance, "Social Construction Theory and Sexuality," in *Constructing Masculinity*, ed. Maurice Berger et al. (New York: Routledge, 1995), 37–48.
6. David M. Halperin, "Historicizing the Subject of Desire: Sexual Preferences and Erotic Identities in the Pseudo-Lucianic *Erôtes*," in *Foucault and the Writing of History*, ed. Jan Goldstein (Oxford: Blackwell, 1994), 34.

cartographers and surveyors play in determining the boundaries and thereby maintaining the integrity of such an artificial entity as "Germany," or "Japan," or any other nation-state. Indeed, if political borders were physically inscribed on the earth's surface for all to see and recognize, many wars might never have been fought.

This study, then, is a constructionist analysis of sexual cartographies. Put another way, it offers a personal mapping of other people's mappings. Specifically, I investigate in this book the construction of erotic desires and practices between males, referred to here as "male-male sexuality." In Japanese as in Western cultures, male-male erotic relations have been a key site over which sexual meanings have been contested, albeit in historically distinct ways. The salience of male-male erotic behavior within Japanese cultural ontology is illustrated by the fact that literally hundreds of categories and signifiers have emerged around it in the native languages over the centuries.[7] This book will consider some of the most influential of these constructs, examining their shared assumptions as well as their mutual differences, and will trace the historical processes by which certain forms of understanding have gained ascendance over, or been superseded by, others. Although I do not deal in any depth with female-female, male-female, or other modes of sexuality, it is my hope that the analysis will help to illuminate and to raise productive questions regarding the larger landscape of sexual knowledge in Japan and its historical changes. At the same time, the specific focus on male-male sexual relations will prove useful to those who are interested in cross-cultural comparison, given the wealth of literature that has become available in recent years on the construction of male-male sexuality across a wide range of social and historical contexts.[8]

In speaking of sexual desires and practices between males, I use the term

7. Much work remains to be done on the construction of male-male sexuality in the Ryukyuan and Ainu languages and cultures also indigenous to the Japanese archipelago. The most detailed lexicon of Japanese (i.e., *Nihongo*) terms relating to male-male sexuality—along with various Chinese expressions that would have been familiar to many educated Japanese up until the present century—that is currently available is "Nanshoku ishōshū," which appears as an appendix (273–371) in Iwata Jun'ichi, *Honchō nanshoku kō* (Toba: Iwata Sadao, 1974), and contains close to two hundred entries. However, Iwata does not include, among other things, the vast number of neologisms coined by Japanese sexologists of the late nineteenth and early twentieth centuries, which alone would multiply this total by several figures.

8. Broad-ranging cross-cultural studies of male-male sexuality include Duberman et al., *Hidden from History*; David F. Greenberg, *The Construction of Homosexuality* (Chicago: University of Chicago Press, 1988); Gilbert Herdt, *Same Sex,*

"male-male sexuality" rather than the more familiar "homosexuality" for deliberate reasons. To begin with, as I explain in chapter 1, inhabitants of the Japanese archipelago before the last century did not usually draw a conceptual link between male-male and female-female forms of erotic behavior. Thus, to adopt the term "homosexuality," which implies an inherent connection between the two, is to accept uncritically the effects of a discursive process whose very emergence demands historical accounting. Since one aim of this book is to provide precisely such a genealogy, anachronistic use of this term would obscure a central element of my narrative. Even after Japanese in the late nineteenth and early twentieth centuries coined a host of words in their own language, including the now standard "same-sex love" or *dōseiai*, to translate Western notions of "homosexuality," the precise connotations and nuances of the resulting vocabulary continued to differ in significant respects from their Euro-American analogues, taking on, as it were, a life of their own. I have thought it best to avoid the word "homosexuality" entirely, except when referring specifically to a Western cultural milieu, and even then only after the mid–nineteenth century. To impose such categories as "homosexuality" and "bisexuality" upon a society or conceptual universe, whether non-European or pre–nineteenth century, in which they would not have been understood in the same sense that they are currently understood, if indeed at all, and in which behavior often followed patterns quite different from those we associate with them in our own societies, is unwittingly to hide from view the experience of those very historical subjects whom we seek to comprehend.[9]

Even the word "sexuality" invites misinterpretation, so clarification is in order. By "sexuality," I do not mean a fixed sexual orientation, as late twentieth-century speakers of English tend to do, for instance, when they refer to a particular individual's "sexuality"—meaning that person's place within the currently canonical trinity of "homosexuality," "heterosexuality," and "bisexuality." For much of the period examined in this study, the notion that each individual possesses a deeply rooted personal identity based

---

Different Cultures: Gays and Lesbians across Cultures (Boulder, Colo.: Westview, 1997). Studies that focus on a particular cultural or historical context are far too numerous to list.

9. It is partly for this reason that I have criticized the analytic strategy pursued in Gary P. Leupp's otherwise valuable *Male Colors: The Construction of Homosexuality in Tokugawa Japan* (Berkeley: University of California Press, 1995), which argues that a "bisexual" norm prevailed among urban Edo-period males. See my review of Leupp's work in *Monumenta Nipponica* 53 (1998): 276–280.

on the biological sex of the preferred sexual object or objects (and specifically whether it is the same as or different from her or his own), and the tripartite taxonomy of sexual types that has resulted from this construction, held no currency in Japan, nor had they yet emerged even in the West.[10] Rather, I use the term "sexuality" to designate a broader realm of behavior and understanding, more or less interchangeably with "eroticism." Since what is defined as "sexual" or "erotic" varies culturally and historically, it is important to acknowledge that "sexuality" and "eroticism" are relatively porous signifiers, designating a shifting set of practices and desires without a constant or easily identifiable center.[11]

How sexuality has been constructed in that region of the globe today called "Japan" has been more often remarked upon than rigorously studied.[12] No less imposing a scholar than Foucault was content to assert vaguely that Japanese "civilization"—like that of China, India, ancient Rome, and the Is-

10. For a brilliant essay on the historical emergence of this taxonomy, see David M. Halperin, "One Hundred Years of Homosexuality," in Halperin, *One Hundred Years of Homosexuality*, 15–40.

11. The adjective "sexual" will refer in this study to questions of sexuality rather than biological sex. I have discussed the complex interrelation of the categories "sex," "gender," and "sexuality" as represented in a twelfth-century Japanese work of fiction in my "Strange Fates: Sex, Gender, and Sexuality in *Torikaebaya Monogatari*," *Monumenta Nipponica* 47 (1992): 347–368.

12. As I suggested in the discussion of cartography, "Japan" is by no means a geographically self-evident or historically stable entity. To give an example, the Ryukyu islands (Okinawa) have moved in and out of "Japan" several times during the period of this study, variously forming an independent kingdom (until 1609), a tributary of Satsuma domain and simultaneously of the Chinese court (1609–1871), a domain and later prefecture under national administration by Tokyo authorities (1872–1945), and a territory under U.S. military occupation (through 1972). The extent to which "Japanese" meaningfully characterizes the cultural traditions of these islands is therefore open to question, despite the fact that present-day world maps color them the same shade as their immediate neighbors to the north. Much the same may be said of the island of Hokkaido, which came fully under central "Japanese" control only in the latter part of the nineteenth century. From the late nineteenth to the early twentieth century, "Japan" also formed a colonial empire, militaristic ventures planting the national flag in places as far afield as Burma, the Aleutians, and New Guinea. Yet the indigenous resident of colonial Korea during the 1920s, for example, did not necessarily stand in the same relationship to the knowledge systems introduced in the following pages as a Tokyo native, even though both may have carried a "Japanese" passport. Although my analysis cannot fully encompass these multiple dimensions of "Japan," I feel it necessary at least to acknowledge their existence. I will refrain from using "Japan" in this study to refer to anyplace outside the current political boundaries of the archipelago (disputed though even these may be).

lamic world—was characterized by an *"ars erotica,"* in contrast to a *"scientia sexualis"* that he viewed as unique to the postclassical West.[13] Foucault's simple dichotomy of *ars erotica* and *scientia sexualis* is clearly inadequate to describe the differences that exist among and within sexual knowledge systems in these diverse societies, and, in typically Eurocentric fashion, makes little allowance for historical change outside the West. As the following chapters will detail, popular elaborations of the "way of youths" (*shudō*) in Japan until the nineteenth century embodied a pleasure-centered and initiatory understanding of sexuality that is in many ways akin to Foucault's notion of *ars erotica*, yet coexisted with other, contending regimes of sexual truth—among them a formidable array of juridical mechanisms for regulating male-male erotic behavior. Likewise, the "Western" knowledge constituted by Foucault's *scientia sexualis* found its way to Japan within decades, if not years, of its articulation by Euro-American authorities (often through translations of those very sources—Krafft-Ebing, Ellis, and so forth—whom Foucault repeatedly cites), leading to a rapid popularization of a medico-scientific model of sexuality no less characteristic of twentieth-century Japan than it is of twentieth-century North America and Europe. Only in recent years has the orientalizing vision of Foucault given way to more-nuanced Western-language accounts of the historical construction of sexuality in Japan.[14]

If Western scholars have only begun to explore the Japanese historical archive for what it reveals about the construction of sexuality, they do not lag far behind their Japanese colleagues. In Japanese academic circles, as in Western ones, the idea that sexuality has a history—much less one that historians may respectably talk about—is a recent, and for some an unset-

---

13. Foucault, *History of Sexuality*, 1:57–58. In a later passage (1:70–71), Foucault concedes the possibility that "since the nineteenth century, the *scientia sexualis*—under the guise of its decent positivism—functioned, at least to a certain extent, as an *ars erotica*," creating "its own intrinsic pleasures"—an interpretation, I would argue, that applies at least as aptly to Japan since the nineteenth century as to the West.

14. Recent Western-language books that explore the history of sexuality in Japan include Sabine Frühstück, *Die Politik der Sexualwissenschaft: Zur Produktion und Popularisierung sexologischen Wissens in Japan, 1900–1941*, Beiträge für Japanologie, no. 34 (Vienna: Institut für Japanologie, Universität Wien, 1997); Sumie Jones, ed., *Imaging/Reading Eros: Proceedings for the Conference, Sexuality and Edo Culture, 1750–1850* (Bloomington: East Asian Studies Center, Indiana University, 1996); Leupp, *Male Colors*; Cecilia Segawa Seigle, *Yoshiwara: The Glittering World of the Japanese Courtesan* (Honolulu: University of Hawaii Press, 1993).

tling, proposition. It is not too many years ago that a senior Japanese scholar could offer the advice, after hearing me read a paper in which I addressed the "history of sexuality" (*seiaishi;* literally, "history of sex and love"), that such an expression might be too indiscreet for a public forum, and was better substituted with the "history of conjugal life" (*fūfu seikatsushi*). To point out that the two are not identical only begins to scratch the surface of the problem. For the polite fiction that they are one and the same has historical roots in Japan dating back at least as far as the late nineteenth century, when a code of "civilized morality" bestowed legitimacy upon the view that sexual behavior outside the bounds of male-female marriage should be dealt with in silence or euphemism rather than with public acknowledgment. Yet in Japan as well, the work of Foucault and others has begun to make a noticeable impact, with the result that shelves labeled "Sexuality" now appear in bookstores and a younger generation of scholars produce pathbreaking research, with much more presumably on the way.[15]

Rather than sexual practice, this book is a study primarily of sexual discourse. I am concerned here, in other words, less with the sorts of sexual acts that people engaged in than with how they wrote and spoke about these acts and the meanings that they attached to them. For historians of sexuality, the relation of actual behavior and its discursive representation is a critical one, since to a large extent the historical traces of sexuality lie in the written word. Yet written accounts should not be assumed to encode in any transparent fashion the realities of the behavior that they represent. The discursive process is a complex negotiation of knowledge, practice, and power, whose work lies precisely in obscuring the ontological gap that separates reality, in all its multiplicity and polysemy, and its representation, whose effect is to close off certain forms of meaning in favor of others. All of this is a rather complicated way of saying that readers of this book should not

---

15. Recent Japanese works on the history of sexuality that I have found illuminating include Fujime Yuki, *Sei no rekishigaku: Kōshō seido dataizai taisei kara baishun bōshihō yūsei hogohō taisei e* (Fuji shuppan, 1997); Kawamura Kunimitsu, *Otome no shintai: Onna no kindai to sekushuariti* (Kinokuniya shoten, 1994); Kawamura Kunimitsu, *Sekushuariti no kindai*, Kōdansha sensho mechie, no. 86 (Kōdansha, 1996); Ujiie Mikito, *Bushidō to erosu*, Kōdansha gendai shinsho, no. 1239 (Kōdansha, 1995); Ujiie Mikito, *Fugi mittsū: Kinjirareta koi no Edo*, Kōdansha sensho mechie, no. 88 (Kōdansha, 1996); along with a number of the essays collected in Inoue Suguru et al., eds., *Sekushuariti no shakaigaku*, Iwanami kōza gendai shakaigaku, no. 10 (Iwanami shoten, 1996). Furukawa Makoto's forthcoming social history of male-male sexuality since the Meiji Restoration is also eagerly awaited.

assume that sexual behavior actually took place, in all instances and for all individuals, in the way that written texts describe it. Let us ourselves hope that future generations will not judge what we do in bed, or who we are as people, simply on the basis of the portrayals in our fiction, the proscriptions in our law codes, or the diagnoses of our physicians and psychiatrists.

The Japanese discourse in my title covers a vast territory. I have narrowed the range of the investigation, therefore, to three particular realms or registers of discourse: the popular, the legal, and the medical. Of the three modifiers, "popular" is without a doubt the most slippery. Academics speak of "popular thought," "popular culture," and so forth, but all too often fail to specify the parameters of this designation. For the purposes of this study, I employ a working definition that, while perhaps idiosyncratic, is more or less clear-cut. My interpretation of the "popular" hinges upon commercial factors.[16] "Popular discourse" refers specifically in this study to the system of utterances and silences that is to be found in written texts bought and sold upon the commercial market, consisting in material terms chiefly of books and periodicals.[17] Although this criterion of commodification does not figure (at least explicitly) in most common definitions of the "popular," it provides a measure of analytic precision, since commercial texts are easily distinguished from their noncommercial counterparts. More fundamentally, the mediation of market mechanisms offers an indication, imperfect though it may be, that the texts under consideration were intended for consumption by a relatively broad audience to whom the terms of their discourse were, if not already familiar, at least readily intelligible. The composition of this audience might vary from text to text and period to period, and was inflected in significant ways by differences of class, gender, age, and region, yet may nonetheless be meaningfully construed as "popular" in that it was not narrowly confined to any single social constituency.

Such a definition of "popular" makes sense only in a society where a com-

16. I have benefited here from Peter Nosco's suggestion (*Remembering Paradise: Nativism and Nostalgia in Eighteenth-Century Japan*, Harvard-Yenching Institute Monograph Series, no. 31 [Cambridge: Harvard University Press, 1990], 16) that "popular culture is culture that pays for itself."

17. The broader realm of visual representation, although similarly implicated in market mechanisms from around the seventeenth century and often, as in the case of book illustrations or woodblock prints, interdependent with the written word, lies outside the scope of the present investigation, whose focus is on linguistic and in particular written representation. For an exploration of male-male sexuality in the Japanese visual field, see Tan'o Yasunori, "Honchō nanshoku bijutsu kō," *Hikaku bungaku nenshi* 26 (1990): 164–188.

mercial market for written texts existed, as in Japan after 1600. The phe-
nomenal growth of the publishing industry in Japan from around this time
had profound consequences for the organization of knowledge, including
the ways in which sexual meanings were created and disseminated. The
large-scale production of written texts and their consumption across an expanding range of regions and classes is one of the features, I would argue,
that gives Japanese history over the past four centuries an underlying continuity. This conspicuous spread of written publications brought with it not
only new degrees of shared understanding among Japanese (indeed, it may
be said to have brought that discursive community called "Japan" and the
"Japanese" into being), but—and this is perhaps the most important shared
understanding of all—it elevated the printed page (as opposed to simply the
written word) into a privileged site for the cultural production of meaning.
Within this new structure of knowledge, published texts came to provide a
powerful arena for negotiating and contesting the significance of, among
many other things, male-male sexuality. Because of the sustained vigor of
the publishing industry since the seventeenth century, historians possess a
continuous and extensive record of written materials relating to the popular construction of male-male sexuality in Japan that enjoys few parallels
in world archives, although researchers have yet to take full advantage of
its wealth of resources. Chapters 1, 4, and 6 of the present study are devoted
entirely to this realm of popular discourse, tracing the changes and continuities in its representation of male-male sexuality over a period of far-
reaching social and cultural transformations.

In contrast to popular discourse, with its diverse authorship, legal discourse
emanates by its very definition specifically from political authorities. An examination of laws, therefore, and of the various mechanisms through which
they have been implemented, provides a useful sense of how male-male sexuality was constructed in official ideology. Before 1600, male-male sexuality seldom appeared as an explicit object of legislation in Japan. The regulation of male-male erotic relations by governing officials receives extensive
codification only from around the beginning of the seventeenth century with
the restructuring of political authority that attended pacification of the country under the hegemony of the ruling Tokugawa house. Since that time, Japanese lawmakers, both in central and in local seats of power, produced a vo-
luminous corpus of proscriptive as well as prescriptive legislation dealing with
male-male erotic behavior. Orientalist tendencies to imagine that legal strictures on such behavior were culturally specific to the Judeo-Christian West
and unlikely to coexist with an elaborate "*ars erotica*" have all too often ob-
scured this fact. On the contrary, from the seventeenth century legislators

in Japan, no less than popular writers, were highly assertive in attempting to demarcate the limits of proper and improper male-male sexual behavior, although the two did not always agree in their definitions.

I have divided my discussion of legal discourse into two chapters in order to take into account a fundamental reorganization of political power that occurred in Japan midway through the nineteenth century. Before the Meiji Restoration of 1868, political authority in the archipelago was distributed in a complexly multilayered fashion, the Tokugawa house standing as a *primus inter pares* among numerous regional lords or daimyo. Historians such as Mark Ravina have aptly described Japan under Tokugawa hegemony as a "compound" state.[18] In examining the legal construction of male-male sexuality during these more than two and a half centuries, it is therefore necessary to consider the pronouncements of lawmakers not only in Edo (today's Tokyo), where the Tokugawa shoguns established their political base, but also in the hundreds of self-governing domains (han) and tens of thousands of peasant villages that dotted the landscape, each of them enjoying a significant measure of legal autonomy. As chapter 2 shows, this complicated geography of power embraced an equally variegated system of sexual legislation, its very diversity emblematic of the period.

With the so-called restoration of imperial rule in 1868, Japan began its rapid transformation into a centralized nation-state along the lines of the Western imperialist powers who, through their growing intrusion into the region of East Asia since the early nineteenth century, had come to threaten its sovereignty. This political change involved not only new governmental and civic institutions, but also a reconfigured regime of sexual regulation to help sustain a newly national order. Legislated into being for the first time was a sexual subject who was "Japanese" before he or she was a resident of a certain region or locality or a member of a particular class, in contrast to the situation prior to 1868 (and for several years thereafter), in which no such nationally authoritative standards for sexual behavior existed. Chapter 3 will consider in detail the emergence of this new sexual regime, tracing the evolution of a legal system for regulating male-male and other forms of sexual behavior that remains fundamentally in place even today.

By "medical discourse," I refer not to any particular school of medical knowledge or practice, but rather to a broader spectrum of discourses dealing with human sickness and health. Such terms as "health" and "sickness" take on meanings only within specific structures of knowledge concerning

18. Mark Ravina, *Land and Lordship in Early Modern Japan* (Stanford: Stanford University Press, forthcoming).

the human body and mind, each of which may define their desirable state and "normal" functioning differently. Over past centuries in Japan, male-male sexuality provided a significant site of contestation among medical authorities. The relationship of male-male sexual behavior on the one hand, and health and health professionals on the other, was construed in remarkably diverse ways. Positions ranged from the view, common as late as the nineteenth century, that medical knowledge and medical specialists should aid those who pursued male-male erotic relations to fulfill their desires, or even encourage such desires for health-related reasons, to the more recent understanding that such desires were by definition pathological. The shift over time was quantitative as well as qualitative: medical authorities since the nineteenth century devoted far more attention to male-male sexuality than their predecessors, according such matters an unprecedented degree of prominence within their overall constructions of bodily and mental health.

Because of this burgeoning of medical interest in the late nineteenth and particularly during the early twentieth century, I have reserved discussion of medical discourse for a relatively late point (chapter 5) in my chronological narrative. The pathologization of male-male sexuality in Japan must be understood against the backdrop of a larger restructuring of medical institutions and knowledge. What are commonly thought of as "Western" science and medicine were familiar among limited circles of Japanese as early as the seventeenth century, but it is only from the late nineteenth century, owing to a wide range of legal, institutional, and intellectual changes, that their distinctive framework of knowledge concerning "nature" and the body came to enjoy a degree of cultural authority that would allow many Japanese of later times to regard them as "medicine" and "science" plain and simple.[19] The historical timing of this restructuring of knowledge is significant, for it was during the same period in the late nineteenth century that male-male sexuality, under the rubric of "homosexuality," began to receive attention from medical and scientific authorities in the West. The reconfiguration of medical knowledge in Japan was thus linked from the outset to new interpretations of male-male erotic behavior, providing a basis of institutional

19. For basic introductions to the history of medicine in Japan, see James R. Bartholemew, *The Formation of Science in Japan: Building a Research Tradition* (New Haven: Yale University Press, 1989); John Z. Bowers, *When the Twain Meet: The Rise of Western Medicine in Japan*, Henry E. Sigerist Supplements to the Bulletin of the History of Medicine, n.s., no. 5 (Baltimore: Johns Hopkins University Press, 1980); Fujikawa Yū, *Nihon igakushi* (Nisshin shoin, 1941); Sakai Shizu, *Nihon no iryōshi* (Tōkyō shoseki, 1982); Kōseishō, *Isei hyakunenshi*, 3 vols. (Kōseishō imukyoku, 1976).

authority for the dissemination and popularization of the "same-sex love" (*dōseiai*) construct that remains influential to the present day.

The medico-scientific model of sexuality that took root in Japan after the late nineteenth century constituted one form of Foucault's *scientia sexualis*. The orientalist temptation of narrating its development in terms of "East" and "West"—a romantic narrative in which the naive charm of the former inevitably succumbs to the virile strength of the latter—must be resisted, however, because such geographical markers do not do justice to the global dimensions and local complexities of the knowledge system in question. Not only did the medico-scientific model of understanding sexual behavior achieve cultural prominence at virtually the same point in historical time in Japan, Europe, and North America, but the flow of knowledge across geographic borders was by no means unidirectional. Japanese sexologists should not be seen as handmaids to what is sometimes nostalgically imagined as the corruption of pure and innocent native traditions merely through their act of introducing Western sexual science into Japan, but rather as engaging in an ongoing and creative dialogue with their non-Japanese colleagues, active participants in a global network of sexual knowledge in which they were not only tutees but mentors as well.[20] It is due in part to the international authority of this medico-scientific model and its pretensions to universal truth that the understanding of sexuality it entailed was able to gain enormous influence within Japan over a relatively short period of time. By the same token, it must be recognized that "Western" medical theories concerning male-male sexuality circulated within their Japanese contexts in forms and with meanings that often varied considerably from their counterparts in Europe and North America, so that such designations as "Western" have limited descriptive value.

The three realms of discourse outlined above were not discrete entities operating in isolation from one another. Rather, all were implicated in a broader process of contestation over the cultural significance of male-male and other modes of sexuality, and it is precisely the nature of their interaction that interests me here. One sign of this interaction was the emergence of various hybrids at those points where different discursive interests converged. Prominent examples include such fields of knowledge as forensic pathology, which linked the realms of legal and medical discourse, and popular sexology, which straddled the medical and the popular domains. A single individual might serve, in the case of forensic pathology, simultaneously

---

20. On the international dimensions of sexology, see also Frühstück, *Politik der Sexualwissenschaft*.

as a health professional and as a vital component in the state apparatus for regulating sexual behavior, while in popular sexology, professional expertise concerning the human body generated not only patients for the clinic but also profits in the marketplace for commercial publications. The emergence of such discursive hybrids stands as testimony not to the breakdown of heterogeneous categories but rather to the deeper interconnection of their parent domains, and in this sense exchanges among the different discursive realms are as significant to this history as what occurred within each.

Finally, it is important to note that in all three realms of discourse, enunciative authority belonged almost exclusively to males. The bulk of my materials consists of men writing about men (or about other cultural categories of males, such as boys and youths). This book is thus properly regarded as a study of how male-male sexuality was constructed in masculine discourse. Although women (and girls) were undoubtedly among the consumers as well as discursive objects of the texts and utterances to be considered in the following pages, how female subjects wrote, spoke, and thought about male-male sexuality remains a topic for future research. It should be added that the historically male-centered bias that has governed textual production and preservation in Japan, as in so many places, makes the existing source materials for such an inquiry significantly more limited than those available in the case of males.[21] It is also necessary to point out that although the emergence of the "same-sex love" construct from the end of the nineteenth century entailed a new understanding not only of male-male but also of female-female erotic practices and desires, the discursive construction of female-female sexuality in Japan demands a more thoroughgoing treatment than I am able to give it here.[22]

Periodization is at once the bread-and-butter and the bane of historians. All attempts to divide the past into discrete periods imply a discontinuity between one point in time and another that is seldom experienced by living human beings so starkly as historical timelines—which constitute another form of mapmaking—suggest. A number of considerations led me to select

21. Paul Schalow discusses female attitudes toward male-male sexuality in his "Josei no 'nanshokuron,'" *Bungaku* 6.1 (1995): 67–71, but it is telling that the primarily seventeenth-century materials he draws upon were authored exclusively by males.

22. I address changing constructions of female-female sexuality in "'S' Is for Sister: Schoolgirl Intimacy and 'Same-Sex Love' in Early Twentieth-Century Japan," in *Gendering Modern Japanese History*, ed. Barbara Molony and Kathleen S. Uno

the dates 1600 and 1950 as the boundaries of my survey. These reasons are heuristic, however, in the sense that the historical phenomena involved do not lend themselves to strict periodization. It is conceivable that another set of dates would have served the purposes of this inquiry just as well. Explaining my choice of this particular chronological framework may serve therefore to clarify the terms of the analysis, and help to situate my project within a larger historiographic context.

The date 1600 appears often enough in standard textbook accounts of Japanese history. Any high-schooler in Japan will tell you that it is the year in which military forces allied with the regional warlord Tokugawa Ieyasu demonstrated their superiority at the Battle of Sekigahara, thereby bringing to an end a period of ongoing conflict among warrior houses known as the age of Warring States (Sengoku). Generations of historians have explored the political and social changes that this victory ushered in or helped to consolidate: among others, the establishment of the Tokugawa shogunate (in 1603), with its titular unified authority over hundreds of self-governing domains; the maintenance of a carefully delineated status hierarchy that tied a demilitarized peasantry in principle to the land, while settling a bureaucratized samurai elite in burgeoning castle towns; the rapid commercialization of the economy and increasing prosperity of the merchant class; and the emergence of a highly regulated system of foreign relations. The more than two and a half centuries of relative peace and political stability that ensued have thus come to be referred to either by the name of the reigning shogunal dynasty (i.e., "Tokugawa period") or the seat from which it ruled ("Edo period"), or alternatively by invoking a larger narrative scheme of world history (for example, "early modern period") to which their associated developments have been seen to bear some resemblance or relation.[23]

Yet changes in political regimes do not in and of themselves alter the or-

(Cambridge: Harvard University Press, forthcoming). See also Yukiko Hanawa, "Inciting Sites of Political Interventions: Queer 'n' Asian," *Positions* 4 (1996): 459–489; Jennifer Robertson, "Gender-Bending in Paradise: Doing 'Male' and 'Female' in Japan," *Genders* 5 (1989): 50–69; Jennifer Robertson, "The Politics of Androgyny in Japan: Sexuality and Subversion in the Theater and Beyond," *American Ethnologist* 19 (1992): 419–441; Jennifer Robertson, "Theatrical Resistance, Theatres of Restraint: The Takarazuka Revue and the 'State Theatre' Movement in Japan," *Anthropological Quarterly* 64.4 (1991): 165–177.

23. On the issue of periodization, and especially the significance of "early modernity" in a Japanese context, see Kären Wigen, "Mapping Early Modernity: Geographical Meditations on a Comparative Concept," *Early Modern Japan* 5.2 (1995): 1–13. For a convenient survey history of the period, see Conrad Totman, *Early Modern Japan* (Berkeley: University of California Press, 1993).

ganization of sexual knowledge, much less sexual practice. Not surprisingly, it is in the legal realm that the political consolidation of the early seventeenth century had its most direct impact upon the discursive construction of male-male sexuality. In the wake of pacification (and sometimes even shortly preceding it), lawmakers both within the shogunate and in the various domains began issuing a wide variety of pronouncements concerning the appropriate bounds of male-male erotic behavior. Such legislation was an integral, if often overlooked, component in the reconfiguration of the larger sociopolitical landscape, which constituted a realignment of existing covenants between males—what Eve Sedgwick would call a homosocial order.[24] By contrast, in the realm of popular discourse, the year 1600 holds no such immediate significance. Its particular relevance to the popular construction of male-male sexuality lies rather in the fact that it is from around this time that the publishing industry entered a period of rapid expansion, the consequences of which would manifest themselves over the course of decades and centuries and did not necessarily end with the 1868 demise of the Tokugawa shogunate.[25]

Although such factors as pacification, urbanization, and the general commercialization of the economy clearly facilitated the growth of the publishing industry in early seventeenth-century Japan, I do not regard this growth as derivative of, or less important than, political change. Neither would I claim that the new structures of knowledge played a more central role in sustaining the sociopolitical order than the lawmakers who conventionally get top billing. Instead of engaging this chicken-or-egg question, I have relied upon the productive ambiguity of the date 1600, which at once suggests a specific event in history and, because of its numerical roundness (albeit within a Western calendrical system not in common use in Japan at the time), a more general order of historical transformation. The designation "Edo period" that I employ to refer to the years between 1600 and 1868 registers the fact that the city of Edo served during this era not only as a locus of political authority but also as an important—from the eighteenth cen-

---

24. Eve Kosofsky Sedgwick, *Between Men: English Literature and Male Homosocial Desire* (New York: Columbia University Press, 1985).

25. The history of publishing in the Edo period commands an extensive literature. For useful surveys, see Konta Yōzō, *Edo no hon'yasan: Kinsei bunkashi no sokumen* (Nihon hōsō shuppan kyōkai, 1977); Henry D. Smith II, "The History of the Book in Edo and Paris," in *Edo and Paris: Urban Life and the State in the Early Modern Era*, ed. James L. McClain et al. (Ithaca: Cornell University Press, 1994), 332–352; Suzuki Toshio, *Edo no hon'ya*, 2 vols., Chūkō shinsho, nos. 568 and 571 (Chūō kōronsha, 1980).

tury onward the most important—hub of the publishing industry. Still, it must not be assumed that this date has a necessary salience in all realms of discourse. Medical constructions of male-male sexuality, for example, appear to have changed little in the transition from the late sixteenth to the early seventeenth century.

If 1600 is a familiar date in standard narratives of Japanese history, the more recent boundary of this survey, 1950, enjoys no such historiographic distinction. Conventional accounts are more likely to identify the end of the Pacific War in 1945, five years earlier, as a crucial point of rupture. For historians of Japan, the year 1945 has long stood as a kind of border post between the "modern" (*kindai*) and "contemporary" (*gendai*) epochs, separating the realm of history, as it were, from the journalistic present. I have deliberately avoided the temptation of ending my study at this juncture. The orthodox narrative of Japan's military surrender and subsequent "rebirth" as a democratic nation that such a periodization invokes, a legacy of Occupation-period ideology, has the unfortunate effect of obscuring equally significant continuities that link the years before and after, as well as during, the conflict. In none of the three discursive realms to be examined in this study does the construction of male-male sexuality show evidence of such a break. Medical interest in the topic continued unabated throughout the war years, while the spectacularization of the "perverse" so often associated with popular discourse of the late 1920s and early 1930s animated no less vigorously the journalistic and other writings of the late 1940s, after surrender. Even in the realm of law, where one might expect the effects of political transformation to be immediately recognizable, state regulation of male-male sexual behavior even today follows the same basic formulas that it did more than a century ago.

My choice of 1950, again a round number, as a demarcation—though not an end point—is meant to highlight these transwar continuities. It lends itself to this task not because it refers to a particular event in the narrative, but rather precisely because, as Ray Huang wrote ironically of another country and another era, it is, so to speak, a "year of no significance."[26] While I recognize the importance of crossing the 1945 barrier and viewing Japan's "postwar as history," it is as yet too early to assess the century's second half, not quite ended.[27] No doubt changes in the landscape of sexual knowl-

---

26. Ray Huang, *1587, a Year of No Significance: The Ming Dynasty in Decline* (New Haven: Yale University Press, 1981).
27. Andrew Gordon, ed., *Postwar Japan as History* (Berkeley: University of California Press, 1993).

edge of an order comparable to those described in the following chapters are taking place even as I write these words. Historians of the future will map in their own ways the ground we now tread. But, like all cartographers, we can chart only the road traveled; the path ahead remains to be seen.

The three and a half centuries separating 1600 and 1950 witnessed profound changes in the way that male-male sexuality was understood in Japan. Not only did the significance of such practices and desires shift over time in each of the three discursive realms outlined above, but the dynamic interrelation of the different realms and their respective influence within larger cultural constructions of sexuality underwent a remarkable series of transformations. A succession of three paradigms, I argue, characterizes this long-term history of change and interaction. Each of the three paradigms constitutes a mode of understanding male-male sexuality that enjoyed preeminence within a particular chronological era. In all three instances, the influence of the paradigm extended across discursive boundaries—an effect, so to speak, of that paradigm's very preeminence. Yet a special relevance in constructing and authorizing each paradigm fell within a specific realm of discourse: in chronological order, the popular, the legal, and the medical. Naturally, historical phenomena of this order do not allow for precise dating. Just as discourses display mutual intersections and influences at any given moment, so modes of understanding tend to survive and overlap over time. Roughly speaking, I have identified the three paradigms, respectively, with the Edo period (1600–1868), the Meiji period (1868–1912), and the first half of the twentieth century.[28]

It is the realm of popular discourse to which one must turn during the Edo period for the most influential and productive articulation of the first paradigm. This paradigm, which I refer to as disciplinary, framed male-male sexuality as a "way" (*michi* or *dō*) to be pursued and perfected. The rhetoric of Edo-period popular discourse on male-male eroticism was esthetic and ethical, overlaying a fundamental asymmetry of power relations in which the subject and object of pursuit occupied unequal positions within the masculine gender hierarchy. The expression *shudō*, or the "way of youths," aptly expressed this asymmetry, specifying the erotic object as a male of pre-adult status, and figuring the desiring subject implicitly as his senior. Besides the question of age (which was not always literal), the disciplinary paradigm depended upon the articulation of a variety of esthetic and ethical discrimi-

28. Strictly speaking, of course, the early twentieth century begins before the Meiji period ends. I have retained this chronological overlap precisely because it usefully conveys a sense of the gradual and fluid nature of the transitions involved.

nations, which, combined with the profit motive of the publishing industry, provided fuel for the rapid elaboration and multiplication of male-male erotic knowledge on the printed page. During the Edo period, the "way of youths" shaped and was in turn shaped by a diverse range of commercial publications—all serving, through a process of mutual reinforcement and contestation, to delineate proper norms and boundaries for the conduct of male-male erotic relations. Chapter 1 takes these printed texts as its principal source, considering the role of the publishing industry in distributing their knowledge across the social landscape. Its position at the outset of this study is meant to suggest not only the particular salience of popular discourse in shaping the disciplinary paradigm of the era, but also the enduring impact that the Edo-period commodification of male-male erotic knowledge would have upon future conditions of discursive production.

During the Edo period, the boundaries of male-male erotic practice were also a matter of concern to political authorities. But because the chief concern of the ruling samurai class lay with the preservation of social hierarchy and political stability rather than with the expansion of commercial profits, the norms that Edo-period lawmakers encoded in their own textual productions—which is to say written laws—differed fundamentally from those disseminated by the publishing industry. Governing officials put in place a wide range of legislation to police the practice of *shudō*, invoking not the prospect of pleasure but the threat of punishment, often quite painful. Nevertheless, political authorities seldom questioned the framework of the disciplinary paradigm per se, themselves, like the authors of popular texts, understanding male-male eroticism as a complex realm of practice and desire that extended far beyond genital acts, to be evaluated according to a subtle series of discriminations rather than categorical imperatives. Instead of denying the legitimacy of the "way of youths" altogether, Edo-period lawmakers endeavored, albeit with mixed results, to ensure that the various forms of its pursuit would not conflict with larger political goals and with the maintenance of peace and order in the communities they ruled. Chapter 2 surveys a broad spectrum of Edo-period written legislation, whose store of information regarding the construction of male-male sexuality compares in scope and detail (as well as in its relative neglect by historians) to the contemporaneous productions of the publishing industry.

Chapter 3 similarly examines written law, focusing on the Meiji era beginning in the late nineteenth century. In contrast to the patchwork nature of sexual legislation that characterized the fragmented Edo-period polity, an unprecedented degree of uniformity came to inform official discourse on male-male sexuality during the Meiji and subsequent eras. This transformation reflects, on the one hand, the newly centralized political framework within which legal codes were enacted and enforced after the 1868 Restoration, and, on the other, reformulated standards of official morality. During the Meiji period, centrally promulgated law codes came to embody a new paradigm of sexuality whose ultimate authority lay in the power of the state, a paradigm that I refer to with the Meiji catchphrase "civilized." The new mode of understanding cast male-male sexual acts, among other forms of erotic practice outside the bounds of state-sanctioned marriage between males and females, as a "barbarous" vice running contrary to "civilized" norms. In the "civilized" paradigm, evaluation of erotic behavior focused on the nature of the sexual act itself, regardless of the desires that lay behind it or the social context within which it took place. Criminal codes, for the first time publicly promulgated, set explicit limits upon the types of sexual acts in which citizens of the new nation-state might licitly engage. Thus, for example, for a brief period in the 1870s and 1880s, national officials categorically proscribed all acts of male-male anal intercourse. In order to enforce this and other laws, Meiji authorities deployed and integrated on a nationwide scale an extensive apparatus of surveillance and punishment. One cog in this mechanism was the institution of the prison, which required close contact among males (as well as among females) at the same time that it penalized sexual acts between them, thus emblematizing in a sense the "civilizing" project itself. Backed by such coercive institutions, legal discourse came to play a powerful role in defining the terms of "civilized" sexuality.

State regulation of the publishing industry helped to ensure that the "civilized" paradigm came to govern the realm of popular discourse as well. Chapter 4 examines Meiji popular texts ranging from commercially published books, whose audiences continued to grow with expanding education and literacy, to the rising medium of print journalism. Censorship, more stringently enforced than in the Edo period, operated to discourage the commission of sexual acts that authorities considered "obscene," not merely in the sphere of actual practice, but also on the surface of the printed page. As a result, male-male eroticism, a staple of the Edo-period publishing industry, moved steadily during the late nineteenth century toward the margins of what was publicly representable. Yet marginalization did not mean a total silencing: paradoxically, the very act of labeling male-male sexuality "unspeakable" suggests the importance that this form of eroticism continued to hold within a realm of discourse that once allowed it to be quite vocal. Popular writers and journalists of the Meiji period found ways to speak the "unspeakable" even as they cast it as a "barbarous" other that lay outside, hence serving to demarcate, the boundaries of "civilization."

The rapid institutionalization of new forms of medical and scientific knowledge from the late nineteenth century laid the groundwork for the emergence of a third paradigm of male-male sexuality. Chapter 5 briefly surveys earlier medical discourses on male-male sexuality before turning to explore this new mode of erotic understanding, which I term medico-scientific or sexological. The sexological paradigm framed male-male sexuality not as an erotic discipline that must be perfected, or as a breach of propriety requiring punishment or condemnation, but as a sexual pathology that demanded the attention, above all, of medical and scientific professionals. In contrast to the Edo period, when medical authorities were just as likely to facilitate as to discourage the pursuit of erotic pleasure between males, doctors in Meiji and early twentieth-century Japan came to define such behavior in predominantly negative terms. Desire, to which the "civilized" paradigm, with its focus on acts, had paid little attention, played a central role in the new understanding. While sexology elevated sexual desire between male and female to the status of a biological instinct, it labeled erotic desires as experienced or acted upon by one male for another (or, in ostensibly parallel manner, between females) as "unnatural" and "perverse," symptomatic of an aberrant physiology and psychology. Sexologists expounded a scientifically authorized taxonomy in which "same-sex love" (*dōseiai*) served to validate the primacy of male-female sexual interaction, newly conceptualized as "cross-sex love" (*iseiai*), by providing it with a deviant—yet necessary—other. In articulating the new construct of "same-sex love," sexologists were forced to negotiate the contradictory premises of, on the one hand, a native textual legacy that embodied earlier systems of sexual understanding by no means uniformly hostile to male-male erotic relations, and, on the other, a global structure of scientific knowledge that transcended national and cultural boundaries and in which male-male sexuality held a largely negative set of valences.

During the early twentieth century, producers of popular discourse swiftly embraced the new medico-scientific mode of understanding male-male sexuality. The sexological idiom of "same-sex love" offered those who wished to speak the hitherto "unspeakable" in a public forum a language validated by the cultural authority of science. Within the commercialized realm of popular culture, writings on "same-sex love," not only by doctors themselves but also by litterateurs, journalists, and other nonmedical authorities, proliferated. Chapter 6 examines early twentieth-century popular representations of male-male sexuality, exploring the ways in which the realm of "perversion," to which doctors had consigned male-male eroticism, provided a new arena for the elaboration of pleasure and a new matrix for the construction of subjectivities. As the notion of "same-sex love" disseminated through popular writings, it assumed a broader range of nuances, not all of them negative: outside the confines of the clinic, "perversion" might as easily occasion celebration as condemnation. Nor, within this specular economy, was the act of condemnation without pleasures of its own, whether one stood in the position of subject, object, or titillated observer. The resulting alliance of medical science and print capitalism, at once stigmatizing and spectacularizing male-male and other "perverse" sexual relations, is by no means defunct in Japan today.

Thus, this book maps the unfolding of three paradigms of male-male sexuality (disciplinary, "civilized," and sexological) across three realms of knowledge (popular, legal, and medical) over the course of three chronological eras (the Edo period, the Meiji period, and the early twentieth century). If its division of chapters and historical periods suggests a tidy and seamless process, it is necessary to reiterate that the actual interplay of discourses is far more messy and complicated. But it is the work of cartography to make the navigation of complex territory easier, and to indicate useful paths—paths that are nevertheless not quite so smooth and straight when actually traveled. Even if all maps are approximations, we could not set forth on our journeys without them.

In this book, I write primarily as a Japan specialist, encouraging scholars and others engaged with the region to consider some of the ways in which the construction of sexuality has helped to shape its history, and inviting further explorations. At the same time, I have tried to make my study accessible to a broader readership who may know little about Japan, but are interested in issues surrounding the construction of sexuality, gender, and masculinity. If I am able to provide something useful to both audiences, without leading astray either, this preliminary attempt at mapmaking will have been productive. Those who come after may, I hope, find the terrain more hospitable and familiar—if no less challenging.

1 Authorizing Pleasure
Male-Male Sexuality in
Edo-Period Popular Discourse

FINDING THE WAY

For Japanese of the Edo period, "homosexuality" was an unfamiliar and perhaps unimaginable concept. I do not mean to suggest, of course, that people of this era never engaged in sexual practices with nor experienced erotic
desires toward individuals of the same sex. A wealth of contemporary sources
testifies to the fact that they did, often with great relish. Nevertheless, if a
twentieth-century American text on "homosexuality" were to find its way
by some miraculous means to seventeenth-century Japan, a perplexing task
would face the translator who wished to transpose it into the vernacular. To
begin with, how to render the term "homosexuality"? Although the period's
sexual vocabulary offered various expressions that could be used to refer to
erotic activities between males or between females, there was no single word
that signified both, so that even finding an appropriate name for the work
would pose a considerable challenge. Indeed, outside this hypothetical instance, such a term would hardly have been necessary, since male-male and
female-female varieties of sexual behavior were unlikely to appear even in
the course of the same discussion.[1]

How, then, might our imaginary translator have conveyed the subject of

1. One of relatively few Edo-period texts to treat both male-male and female-
female forms of sexual behavior is Yoshida Hanbei's 1686 erotic encyclopedia
Kōshoku kinmō zui (in *Kōshokumono sōshishū*, ed. Yoshida Kōichi, 2 vols., Kinsei
bungei shiryō, no. 10 [Koten bunko, 1968], 1:49–122), which contains illustrated entries for various objects of male-male erotic desire (*wakashu, kaburo, yarō*, etc.) as
well as for the practice of *tomogui*, in which two women obtain mutual pleasure using a double-headed dildo. It is significant, however, that the *tomogui* entry appears
at a considerable distance from the male-male ones in the text, and that no explicit
parallel is drawn between the two.

his text to contemporary readers? I use the masculine pronoun here intentionally, for it is reasonable to assume that the translator would have been male. Literary production in most of its forms (with important exceptions, such as *waka* poetry) was gendered chiefly as a masculine pursuit, requiring an education in Chinese characters that far more seventeenth-century men than women possessed. A substantially larger portion of the female population may have been able to read all or parts of the finished text, particularly if it featured phonetic glosses in the native *kana* syllabary. Nevertheless, given the uneven distribution of reading abilities, readership, too, was likely to be predominantly male. The question of literacy was compounded by that of economic power, which put disposable income, and hence access to the products of a burgeoning publishing industry, disproportionately into the hands of men.

Such factors considered, our translator might even have decided to ignore the female-female content of the work altogether. Such an approach would have offered several advantages. First of all, as a male himself, the translator was more likely to have firsthand knowledge of male-male erotic practices than female-female, and therefore stood on more familiar ground in writing about them. The same would be true of most of his audience, and even female readers would not have been entirely ignorant of the former. More importantly, however, writings on male-male sexuality already possessed an indigenous textual tradition, with its own vocabulary and commercial market. During the seventeenth century, this field of cultural production was in fact undergoing a rapid expansion. By assimilating the twentieth-century treatise to such contemporary works, our translator might even have been able to make himself a pretty penny.

Let us return, though, to the original question: what equivalent would our translator have selected for "homosexuality"? One plausible candidate would be *nanshoku*, a term found, for example, in the title of Ihara Saikaku's best-selling story collection of 1687, *Nanshoku ōkagami*, which Paul Schalow has translated into English as *The Great Mirror of Male Love*.[2] This choice would have been apt in at least one sense, since both *nanshoku* and "homosexuality" derive from classical languages—in the case of the former, Chinese, and in the latter, an awkward mixture of Greek and Latin— and hence carried a certain amount of scholarly cachet.[3] Furthermore, just

2. Ihara Saikaku, *Nanshoku ōkagami*, in *Nihon koten bungaku zenshū*, ed. Akiyama Ken et al., 51 vols. (Shōgakkan, 1970–1976), 39:312–597 (trans. Paul Gordon Schalow under the title *The Great Mirror of Male Love* [Stanford: Stanford University Press, 1990]).

3. According to a standard lexicon (Morohashi Tetsuji, *Dai Kanwa jiten*, rev. ed.,

as "homosexuality" is often conceptually paired with "heterosexuality," *nan-shoku* had a companion term in *joshoku* (also pronounced *nyoshoku*), an expression likewise denoting male-female eroticism.

Here, though, the resemblances ended. *Nanshoku* and *joshoku* could convey only half of what "homosexuality" and "heterosexuality" convey, both these former terms being predicated upon an implicitly male erotic subject. Thus, while *joshoku* was written with ideographs meaning "female" and "love," it referred specifically to a male "love of females," and never the love of one female for another. Similarly, although *nanshoku* contained only one character for "male," it actually signified an erotic interaction between two (or more) males, rather than a "love of males" by women. The *nan-shoku/joshoku* dichotomy, in other words, mapped the universe of sexual possibilities from an exclusively male perspective, and neither female-female eroticism nor female sexual agency vis-à-vis males enjoyed any place within its signifying system.

Nor was the "sexuality" of "homosexuality" quite the same as the "love" of "male love." Such categories as "homosexuality" and "heterosexuality" are deeply embedded in a medico-scientific model of erotic behavior that, in Japan as in the West, gained general currency only in the present century. *Nanshoku* and *joshoku*, on the other hand, were closely linked with Buddhist thought, which passed to Japan by way of China and Korea nearly a millennium and a half earlier. The ideograph that Schalow translates as "love" (Chinese: *se*; Japanese: *iro*) literally meant "color," referring in Buddhist philosophy to the world of visually perceptible forms toward which lower beings, including humans, experienced desire, thus hindering their progress along the path of enlightenment. More specifically, it came to denote the realm of erotic pleasure, which, again from the perspective of the masculine subject, could be divided into *nanshoku* and *joshoku* hemispheres depending upon the nature of the distracting form. The pleasures of this realm sprang neither from purely physiological processes, as the medico-scientific model of "sexuality" suggests, nor from a lofty spiritual source, as the term "love" often implies; instead, more akin to the Greek "eros," they partook equally of physical and emotional elements, both of which were understood to pose a similar degree of threat to the unenlightened soul.

It should not be imagined, however, that *nanshoku* always carried such

---

13 vols. [Taishūkan, 1984–1986], 7:1080), the Chinese term *nanse*, of which *nan-shoku* is the Japanese pronunciation, appears as early as Ban Gu's chronicle of the Han dynasty (*Han shu*), written in the first century C.E. In Japan, its use dates back at least as far as the 1219 story collection *Zoku kojidan*.

overtly religious overtones. During the Edo period, *nanshoku* appears in popular writings as one of the two most widely used expressions for male-male eroticism, featuring prominently in the titles of many works that, far from warning of its dangers, extolled its pursuit. The resident of seventeenth-century Edo (today's Tokyo) was less likely to associate it with religious teachings than with a lively and increasingly commercialized culture that articulated itself not only through such prose texts as Saikaku's, but also in poetry, song, dance, drama, woodblock prints, and, of course, the various pleasures of the flesh. If she or he made a connection with Buddhism, it was probably with the figure of the priest, whom many writers depicted as one of that culture's prime connoisseurs.[4] It is this realm of popular discourse, and within it primarily the media of prose and poetry, that serves as the chief source of materials for this chapter's discussion.[5]

But perhaps our translator would have chosen an alternative expression. Another term for male-male eroticism that frequently appears in popular discourse of the era is *shudō*, which entered into use around the beginning of the Edo period. *Nanshoku* and *shudō* shared certain lexical characteristics, and were used in practice almost interchangeably, yet differences of nuance existed as well.[6] Although *shudō*, like *nanshoku*, could be written in Chinese characters, it would have made little sense to a resident of the continent, since it possessed an entirely indigenous etymology. The fuller form of the word was *wakashudō* or the "way of youths," *wakashu* denoting in vernacular Japanese an adolescent male. More frequently, however, the *wakashu* element was abbreviated into one of its two constituent characters, producing the compounds *nyakudō* (alternately pronounced *jakudō*), whose

4. Although the Shinto religion had its own clergy, the terms "priest" and "monk" will refer in this study, unless otherwise specified (e.g., "Shinto priest" for *kannushi*), to male members of the Buddhist orders, whom popular discourse associated far more closely with male-male eroticism than their Shinto counterparts. I employ the terms "monastery" and "temple," as well as "monk" and "priest," more or less interchangeably, since Buddhism itself made little distinction between these categories. Shinto places of worship will be referred to as "shrines."

5. I have excluded from my analysis several genres of popular discourse, such as kabuki and *jōruri* playbooks, that contributed importantly to the construction of male-male sexuality in the Edo period and with which other, nontheatrical works were often linked in intertextual fashion. Future research will, I hope, help to fill out the picture.

6. Whenever possible, I employ the term *shudō*, rather than *nanshoku*, to signify the prevailing construction of male-male sexuality in the Edo period, since the use of the former was confined largely to that era, whereas the latter's both predated and postdated it. I will continue, however, to use *nanshoku* in certain Edo-period contexts, as, for instance, when the original text employs that word, or in order to provide better symmetry with *joshoku*.

first surviving appearance in a written text dates from 1482, and *shudō*, which became the preferred combination during the seventeenth century.[7]

In *shudō*, too, a masculine erotic subject lurked somewhere beneath the surface of the ideographs. The "way of youths" was not the possession of youths themselves, as the characters might literally suggest, but existed instead from the perspective of their male admirers, specifically those old enough to perceive a contrast with the former's adolescence. *Shudō*, in other words, was not so much the "way of youths" as the "way of *loving* youths," an erotic path that younger males traveled only in their capacity as sexual objects, and females could not tread at all. True, one may find isolated instances in which women are described as pursuing the "way of youths," such as a late eighteenth-century comic verse or *senryū* that pokes fun at a widowed head of household (*goke*) because of her fondness for male prostitutes: "The audacious [literally, obese] widow chiefly travels the path of *shudō*" (*Moppara ni shudō ni kayou futoi goke*).[8] It was the very fact, however, that *shudō* was understood to be a male prerogative that made this verse humorous, while rendering "audacious" (*futoi*)—the word hints, incidentally, that she may also be pregnant—the economically independent female who attempted to usurp the privilege.

Like *nanshoku*, *shudō* had a companion term to signify a male-female, yet nevertheless male-centered, equivalent. *Nyodō* was the "way of women," but in the sense of men's loving women, rather than women's loving men or each other—possibilities that this dichotomy could not articulate. *Nyodō* differed subtly, however, from the more commonly used *joshoku*, as well as from its own counterpart *shudō*, in that it centered the pursuit of erotic pleasure chiefly within a commercial context. The women whom writings on *nyodō* typically depicted as the object of pursuit were courtesans or other types of prostitutes, whereas the *wakashu* of *shudō* might just as easily be amateurs as professionals. In popular discourse of the Edo period, the conjugal and reproductive aspects of male-female sexuality were evidently too pedestrian to deserve the status of a "way," while the intricacy of the "way of youths" was virtually axiomatic.

7. For the 1482 use of the term *nyakudō*, see Ijiri Matakurō Tadasuki, *Nyake kanjinchō*, in *Zoku gunsho ruijū*, ed. Hanawa Hokinoichi and Ōta Tōshirō, 82 vols. (Zoku gunsho ruijū kankōkai, 1957–1969), 33b:19.

8. *Kawazoiyanagi, Nihon meicho zenshū: Edo bungei no bu*, ed. Ishikawa Torakichi et al., 31 vols. (Nihon meicho zenshū kānkōkai, 1926–1929), 26:888. Although such culturally loaded terms as "prostitute" and "prostitution" do not do justice to the complexities of erotic work in Edo-period Japan, I resort to them throughout this study for want of satisfactory substitutes.

To chart the contours of this "way" provides the aim of the present chapter. If *shudō* constituted a "way," in other words, then how did popular discourse of the Edo period configure its boundaries, and what was the nature of its signposts? Like the "color" of *nanshoku*, the character "way" (*michi*, in its native reading) in *shudō* endowed the term with a certain spiritual or ethical nuance, although not one that connected it exclusively with any particular religious tradition. The literary historian Konishi Jin'ichi has argued that *michi* emerged as an esthetic ideal during the medieval period (roughly from the twelfth to the sixteenth century), defining its characteristics as specialization (*senmonsei*), transmissivity (*keishōsei*), normativity (*kihansei*), universality (*fuhensei*), and authoritativeness (*ken'isei*).[9] Thus, while Buddhism (*butsudō* or *shakudō*), Shinto (the "way of the gods"), and Confucianism (*judō*) all constituted "ways," so did such secular pursuits as calligraphy, poetry (*kadō*), the martial arts (*budō*), flower arrangement (*kadō*), and the tea ceremony (*sadō*). Broadly speaking, we may conceive of a "way" as a discipline of mind and body, a set of practices and knowledge expected to bring both spiritual and physical rewards to those who chose to follow its path.

The construction of male-male sexuality as a "way" did not commence with the Edo period, as the appearance of the term *nyakudō*, along with its synonym *mitsudō* or "secret way," in the 1482 text alluded to earlier attests.[10] It was after the Tokugawa pacification, however, and with the help of an expanding publication industry, increasing literacy, and a flourishing market economy, that the "secrets" of this "way" began to be construed not so much as the jealously guarded possession of certain elites, but as a field of knowledge that was available to all who could afford the price. Within a commercialized framework, knowledge surrounding male-male sexuality grew increasingly elaborate and systematized, while disseminating with unprecedented rapidity across social and geographic space. A world of difference lay between the so-called *Chigo no sōshi* (Book of Acolytes) picture scroll of the fourteenth century, which remained sequestered within the walls of a single monastery and even today is inaccessible to public view-

---

9. Konishi Jin'ichi, *Michi: Chūsei no rinen*, Nihon no koten, no. 3 (Kōdansha, 1975), 13–15. In English, see Konishi Jin'ichi, "Michi and Medieval Writing," trans. Aileen Gatten, in *Principles of Classical Japanese Literature*, ed. Earl Miner (Princeton: Princeton University Press, 1985), 181–208.

10. The character "way" appears also in the term *hidō* (Chinese: *feidao*; in Paul Schalow's translation, "mistaken way"), a Chinese-derived expression for male-male sexuality that was already familiar to Ijiri (*Nyake kanjinchō*, 33b:19) in the fifteenth century.

ing, and a work like Saikaku's *Great Mirror*, whose readers ranged from Edo merchants to Kyushu samurai.[11]

Shudō was not the only "way" to be codified and marketed during the Edo period. The formalization and popularization of various fields of knowledge, from flower arrangement to the "way of the warrior" (*bushidō*), stands as one of the cultural hallmarks of the Edo era, which gave birth, in the shape that we know them today, to many of what are all too often regarded as ageless Japanese traditions. Nor was male-male the only form of sexuality to undergo such disciplinization. The construction of *shudō* ran parallel to, and in fact formed an important part of, the articulation of erotic knowledge and pleasure—typically conceived from a masculine perspective—as a "way" on par with all the others, or, as it came to be known, *shikidō*, the "way of colors [or eros]." Indeed, if as the literary historian Noma Kōshin claims, the term *shikidō* dates only from the 1670s, then the emergence of the *shudō* construct provides an important forerunner to its own elaboration.[12] By the time of Saikaku, it was widely acknowledged that the "path of *shikidō*" was twain (*shikidō futatsu*), and that *shudō* and *nyodō* formed its two principal (if principally male-traveled) avenues.[13] No analysis of Edo-period erotic discourse can therefore be complete without taking into account the construction of male-male eros, just as the history of this or any era cannot be understood in isolation from issues of sexuality. In order to survey this landscape, we must follow the path of *shudō*.

YOUTHS, LOVERS, BROTHERS, AND OTHERS

To characterize a relationship as "homosexuality" provides little more information about the individuals involved than that they belong to the same biological sex. To describe a relationship as *shudō*, however, conveyed to an Edo-period audience some additional details. *Shudō* partners, too, belonged as a rule to the same sex, but more specifically to the male one. Only in such comic genres as *senryū* did the patronage of male prostitutes by "audacious" widows and other females qualify as *shudō*—precisely because the stretching of categories beyond their quotidian usage was a key strategy of *sen-*

11. On *Chigo no sōshi*, the most common appellation for what is in fact an untitled work, see Dōmoto Masaki, "*Chigo no sōshi*: Honbun shōkai," *Yasō* 15 (1985): 167–188.

12. Noma Kōshin, "Kaisetsu," in *Nihon shisō taikei*, ed. Ienaga Saburō et al., 67 vols. (Iwanami shoten, 1970–1982), 60:374.

13. Ihara Saikaku, *Kōshoku ichidai otoko*, in *Nihon koten bungaku zenshū*, 38:101.

ryū and other forms of humor. When seen from the perspective of the male prostitute, the same encounter would in fact have constituted *joshoku*. Likewise, although some female prostitutes, such as the *kagema onna* to be introduced in the following chapter, deliberately cultivated a masculine appearance in order to attract devotees of *shudō*, the services that they provided more properly earned the name of *joshoku* than *nanshoku*, or at least lay in a gray area between the two.

In principle, therefore, *shudō* was understood to be an interaction between males. Yet there was nothing inherent in the written characters to indicate that this must be the case. As with *nanshoku*, the masculinity of the erotic subject was assumed rather than explicitly voiced, not dictated by the ideographs but determined by the larger structure of the discourse. To a certain extent, the same was true also of the erotic object, or *wakashu*. Although the characters in this compound literally meant "young people," semantic convention restricted its referent to males, not unlike the English word "youth," which I employ as a rough equivalent. The *shudō* construct, in other words, specified the erotic object in terms not of biological sex, which was implicitly understood to be male, but of age—in this respect differing not only from "homosexuality" but also from the Chinese-derived *nanshoku*.[14]

Youth, however, was a relative matter. When, for instance, did it begin? Few boys under the age of seven appear in *shudō* texts, in part because the status of *wakashu* assumed a degree of personhood that cultural convention did not ascribe to human beings before that age.[15] Prior to becoming youths, males were simply *warabe* or children, a status that was weakly gendered and relatively noneroticized. The borderline between childhood and youth, however, was rather vaguely drawn. Thus the 1643 tract *Shin'yūki* (Record of Heartfelt Friends) suggests that, because youths between twelve

14. In colloquial usage, it should be noted, *nanshoku* conveyed no less an expectation of youthfulness on the part of the erotic object than *shudō*; my point here is simply with regard to etymology.

15. Seven is the lowest age that I have encountered in various descriptions of the *wakashu*. It appears in *Shiratama no sōshi*, a text cited in Baijōken's 1648–1653 *Yodarekake* (in *Edo jidai bungei shiryō*, ed. Hayakawa Junzaburō et al., 5 vols. [Kokusho kankōkai, 1916], 4:53); in the mid-seventeenth-century erotic debate *Iro monogatari* (in *Kanazōshi shūsei*, ed. Asakura Haruhiko and Fukuzawa Akio, 18 vols. to date [Tōkyōdō, 1980–], 4:184); and, much earlier, in Ijiri, *Nyake kanjinchō*, 33b:19. It should be kept in mind that, well into the twentieth century, the system for counting age in Japan differed from that of the contemporary West, so that an individual aged "seven" in Edo-period Japan might be as little as five years and a day but never more than six according to Western reckoning. Since it is in most cases impossible to provide a precise Western equivalent—or in the early twentieth century, some-

and fourteen still displayed considerable immaturity, *shudō* ties with them ought to be written with characters indicating that the beloved was "primarily a child."[16] A youth idolized by some might appear to less appreciative eyes a mere "brat" (*wappa*, a pejorative variant of *warabe*), as one speaker scoffs in the mid-seventeenth-century erotic debate *Denbu monogatari* (Boors' Tale). Yet even here, the critic does not object to adult men's pursuit of the youngster because it constitutes a sexual exploitation of minors—a notion no less recent in Japan than in the West—but instead because it lacks a sufficient degree of esthetic refinement.[17]

For writers on *shudō*, a question of far greater interest than the minimum age of the *wakashu* was determining his prime. *Shin'yūki*, for instance, located the peak of youthful desirability at between fifteen and seventeen, providing alternate ideographs meaning "special way" for *shudō* pursuits with partners of this age.[18] Yet one of the distinguishing characteristics of young male beauty, it was widely opined, was its fleetingness, prompting frequent comparisons with that short-lived blossom, the cherry, as well as with other flowers. Subsequently, according to *Shin'yūki*, *shudō* ties would enter a phase described as the "end of the way" (likewise pronounced *shudō*), corresponding to the years eighteen through twenty. Instead of mere decline, however, *Shin'yūki*'s commentator saw during this period the emergence in the youth of a new maturity and attention to "manly honor" (*otoko no giri*), which did not detract from but served to further refine *shudō*'s pleasures and proprieties.[19]

If the chronological end of youth was no more clearly agreed upon than

times even to determine which system is being used—I retain the ages originally stated in the text throughout this study. Some *shudō* texts place the threshold of youth at eleven (Baijōken, *Yodarekake*, 4:52) or twelve (see sources cited in n. 16 below). On the issue of age, see also Shibayama Hajime, *Edo nanshoku kō: Akusho hen* (Hihyōsha, 1992), 119–128.

16. *Shin'yūki*, in *Nihon shisō taikei*, 60:22 (trans. Paul Gordon Schalow in "Spiritual Dimensions of Male Beauty in Japanese Buddhism," in *Religion, Homosexuality, and Literature*, ed. Michael L. Stemmeler and José Ignacio Cabezón, Gay Men's Issues in Religious Studies Series, no. 3 [Las Colinas, Tex.: Monument, 1992], 90). This orthographic pun appears also in Baijōken, *Yodarekake*, 4:53.

17. *Denbu monogatari*, in *Nihon koten bungaku zenshū*, 37:128–129 (trans. Gary P. Leupp in *Male Colors: The Construction of Homosexuality in Tokugawa Japan* [Berkeley: University of California Press, 1995], 209).

18. *Shin'yūki*, 60:22–23 (Schalow, "Spiritual Dimensions," 90). Similarly, see Baijōken, *Yodarekake*, 4:53.

19. *Shin'yūki*, 60:23 (Schalow, "Spiritual Dimensions," 90–91). Baijōken (*Yodarekake*, 4:53) assigns this phase of *shudō* characters indicating that its focus was "chiefly [polishing] the way."

its beginning, it was unquestionably more debated. As portrayed by the author of *Shin'yūki*, the late stages of youth already betrayed an incipient manhood, much as youth's earliest phase was marked by a residual childishness. At the same time, the passage from youth to manhood constituted a more significant social leap than the earlier one from childhood to youth, and it was from the other side of this crucial divide—that is, from an adult male perspective—that the figure of the *wakashu* assumed his alterity and allure. The age at which this transition took place attracted considerable attention from commentators precisely because it was ultimately arbitrary. Opinions regarding its date varied greatly: from *Shin'yūki's* twenty (or, according to some authorities, earlier), to twenty-two, twenty-three, twenty-five, to as late as thirty and beyond.[20]

The upper boundary of youth managed to retain considerable plasticity because manhood was essentially a social condition, its biological referent far less important than its cultural markings.[21] Various changes in the youth's body—the appearance of body and facial hair, enlarged genitals, taller stature, deeper voice, and so on—were generally recognized as signs of physiological maturation, but did not in themselves confer adult status. In the eyes of some devotees of *shudō*, such secondary sex characteristics (to invoke, anachronistically, a twentieth-century biological conceit) might even serve to enhance a partner's beauty, as with the regional lord or daimyo whom a 1708 story portrays—albeit as "eccentric" (*monozuki*)—as fond of page boys with hair on their shins.[22] Ironically, the physical attribute that most unequivocally signaled manhood, thereby withdrawing the youth from the category of erotic object, consisted not in the appearance of hair but in its removal—namely, the shaved pate that distinguished the coiffure of adult males. Boys and youths, conversely, could be recognized by unshorn forelocks (*maegami*), a feature around which *shudō* esthetics wove a highly fetishistic erotic.

20. These figures, which are by no means exhaustive, derive from Baijōken, *Yodarekake*, 4:52–53; Ejima Kiseki, *Yahaku naishō kagami*, in *Hachimonjiyabon zenshū*, ed. Hasegawa Tsuyoshi et al., 14 vols. to date (Kyūko shoin, 1992–), 2:66; Nishizawa Ippū, *Gozen Gikeiki*, in *Kindai Nihon bungaku taikei*, ed. Nonaka Jirō et al., 25 vols. (Kokumin tosho, 1926–1929), 4:142; *Yarō kinuburui, Kinsei shomin bunka* 13 (1952): 33.

21. Paul Gordon Schalow explores the malleability of the *wakashu* role in his "Male Love in Early Modern Japan: A Literary Depiction of the 'Youth,'" in *Hidden from History: Reclaiming the Gay and Lesbian Past*, ed. Martin Bauml Duberman et al. (New York: NAL, 1989), 118–128.

22. Nishizawa Ippū, *Yakei tomojamisen*, in *Edo jidai bungei shiryō*, 2:326. A late seventeenth-century report on daimyo governance, unpublished during the Edo period, listed at least three (the lords of Hirado [retired], Kōriyama, and Toyama) who prized such mature features as a tall stature or a beard in their male favorites, de-

The transition to manhood was elaborated not only tonsorially but sartorially. A ceremony known as *genbuku* announced the youth's coming of age, at which point he was expected to exchange his wide-sleeved robes (*furisode*) for adult male garb. It was at this time, too, that the forelocks, which a preliminary modification of hairstyle (*sumimaegami*) around the midteens had left untouched, were shaved off completely. Now a man rather than a youth, he ceased to provide a suitable object for the erotic attentions of other males, since his pursuit no longer met the esthetic criteria of *shudō*.[23] This coming-of-age ceremony, however, did not have a fixed date, instead varying widely according to class, locality, and household or individual circumstance—a fact that helps to explain the lack of agreement on youth's upper extremity. Indeed, because the tonsorial and sartorial markings of manhood were relatively easy to manipulate, they offered a convenient tool for regulating the practice of *shudō*. Thus, as we shall see in the next chapter, when lawmakers wished to discourage the erotic pursuit of

---

scribing them as "man-lovers" (*otokozuki*). Of one, the compiler writes with approval that he had recently given up this "aberration" (*higagoto*), and now restricted his attentions to "beautiful boys" (*bishōjin*). See *Dokai kōshūki*, ed. Kanai Madoka (Jinbutsu ōraisha, 1967), 268–269, 270–272, 328–329. On the concept of *otokozuki*, see also Ujiie Mikito, *Bushidō to erosu*, Kōdansha gendai shinsho, no. 1239 (Kōdansha, 1995), 205–218. According to Shōsaiō's mid-eighteenth-century work *Gengenkyō* (in *Sharebon taisei*, ed. Mizuno Minoru et al., 31 vols. [Chūō kōronsha, 1978–1988], 3:311), youths reached the peak of their lovability at the age when pimples (*nikibi*) appeared on their faces—a characteristic commonly associated in Edo-period Japan with the onset of sexual maturity.

23. Erotic relations between men (i.e., males socially recognized as adults) may certainly have occurred in practice, but enjoyed little legitimation from *shudō* textual tradition. The drama scholar Dōmoto Masaki (<*Zōhoban*> *Nanshoku engekishi* [Shuppansha, 1976], 21–26) describes one such encounter as represented in the *kyōgen* play *Rōmusha*, which was written during the medieval period but still performed in Edo times, noting that its effect was farcical and even "grotesque." A similarly comic atmosphere pervades the episode titled "Okashiki koi" (Strange Love) in Nankai no Sanjin's early eighteenth-century story collection *Nanshoku yamaji no tsuyu* (vol. 6 of *Hihon Edo bungakusen*, ed. Yoshida Seiichi et al., 10 vols. [Nichirinkaku, 1988–1989], 105–108), as well as Kitagawa Utamaro's polymorphously perverse 1802 <*Ehon*> *Futahashira* (see Hayashi Yoshikazu, <*Enpon kenkyū*> *Zoku Utamaro*, Enpon kenkyū sōsho, no. 3 [Yūkō shobō, 1963], 136–137), which depicts a cross-dressed male traveler who not only sleeps with the proverbial farmer's daughter but violates her father (and mother) as well. Shibayama (*Edo nanshoku kō: Akusho hen*, 121–123) has asserted that an erotic preference by adult males for other adult males emerged as a subcurrent in *shudō* culture around the mid–eighteenth century, but his evidence is weak and his interpretation of the term *nyakuzokuzuki* (which appears to derive from Dōmoto, *Nanshoku engekishi*, 17–18) something of a stretch.

young male actors or peddlers, they simply ordered them to shear off their voluptuous forelocks, while conversely, the daimyo of the 1708 tale sought to prolong the erotic availability of his hirsute page boys by refusing to allow them to undergo *genbuku* until the age of thirty.[24]

Within the milieu of prostitution, the boundaries of youth came to extend far beyond the "end of the way" as the author of *Shin'yūki* defined it. The logic of the marketplace gave the *kagema* and other types of male prostitute, or more accurately their keepers, the economic incentive to prolong youthful status for as long as possible, thereby maximizing earnings from the adult males who provided their chief clientele. Nevertheless, as he grew older, the *kagema* was likely to find his male patrons replaced increasingly by female, for whom physical maturity was assumed to be a more important consideration than youthfulness. An eighteenth-century *senryū*, for example, satirizes the youth who has "reached the age where his prick sells better than his ass" (*Ketsu yori ka henoko no ureru toshi to nari*).[25] *Senryū* and other forms of popular discourse frequently poked fun at the superannuated male prostitute who, if not dividing his favors—posterior and anterior—between men and women, was, through inadvertent word or deed, giving away the true age that he tried so hard to conceal. Though less frequently, well-seasoned "youths" occasionally crop up in a noncommercial context as well, such as the sixty-three-year-old samurai *wakashu* whom Saikaku depicts in one of the stories of his *Great Mirror*, or among the monks of mounts Kōya and Nachi, whose erotic careers a common adage held to last respectively until the ages of sixty and eighty.[26] Representations of this sort, however, did not so much question the conventional expectation that male erotic objects literally be young as reinforce that ideal by portraying its flouting in a humorous or otherwise remarkable light.

While the issue of age loomed constantly over the figure of the *wakashu*,

24. Similarly, in 1685, the shogunate is reported to have cracked down on *ōwakashu* or "senior youths," who kept their forelocks unshorn until age twenty-five or twenty-six, thereby remaining eligible as erotic objects in *shudō*. See Yoshida Setsuko, ed., *Edo kabuki hōrei shūsei* (Ōfūsha, 1989), 68.

25. <*Yanagidaru yokō*> *Yanaibako*, in *Shodai senryū senkushū*, ed. Chiba Osamu, 2 vols., Senryū shūsei, nos. 5 and 6 (Iwanami shoten, 1986), 2:101.

26. The Saikaku story will be discussed again in chap. 5. While the actual origin of the proverb (*Kōya rokujū Nachi hachijū*) may have had no relation to *shudō* (see, for example, Ōgokudō no Arittake, *Shikidō kinpishō*, ed. Fukuda Kazuhiko, 2 vols., Ukiyoe gurafikku, nos. 2 and 3 [KK besutoserāzu, 1990–1991], 2:52), it was nonetheless widely understood in this sense during the Edo period.

his sex and gender invited a lesser degree of problematization. He was undoubtedly male in terms of anatomy, or else sexual interaction with him would not, by definition, have qualified as *nanshoku*. In a broad sense, he was also masculine, for he acted according to a set of expectations that applied to all males, at least during a certain period of their lives. What he was not was virile (an English word deriving from the Latin *vir*, meaning an adult male), in the sense that he did not yet possess in full the attributes of mature manhood, including the prerogative of phallically penetrating other males. Females, too, lacked virility, but it did not necessarily follow from this fact that the youth was feminine. From the perspective of the adult male, both women and *wakashu* were "other" than himself, but they were also distinct from each other. For one thing, the youth would eventually become a man himself, whereas a woman could not.[27] Impending manhood (as in *Shin'yūki*'s "manly honor") manifested itself even before the youth had attained maturity—a process that *shudō*, far from hindering, was seen as helping bring to fruition.

Shudō texts, which embodied what might be called a "virile gaze," frequently ranged women and youths side by side as comparable objects for esthetic appreciation and erotic consumption.[28] Yet comparability was not the same as homogeneity; indeed, writers on *shudō* took great delight in elaborating the features that set the two erotic objects apart. Saikaku opens his *Great Mirror* with a long list of such contrasts—asking, for instance, which is preferable, "The mouth of a woman as she blackens her teeth [possibly indicating that she is married or a courtesan], or the hand of a youth as he plucks his whiskers?"—although the esthetic sensibilities involved here may be lost on the twentieth-century reader.[29] With a greater economy of language, Saikaku's contemporary, the haiku (or more properly, *haikai*) poet Matsuo Bashō, asked essentially the same question: "Plum and willow,

27. Whether the adult male caught a glimpse of his former self in the youthful object of his desire is not an issue that *shudō* texts addressed, although this silence has not prevented such commentators as the psychologist Watanabe Tsuneo ("'Sekai himitsu' to kannōsei no shisutemu: Bunmei no shinsō ni hisomu 'danseisei no zeijakusa,'" *Dorumen* 3 [1990]: 23–24) from asserting that *shudō* represented a sublimated form of narcissism.

28. The term "virile gaze" is meant to evoke, but at the same time qualify, the notion of the "male gaze" already standard in various fields of esthetic and cultural criticism but in this instance problematic because it obscures crucial differences of age. For a seminal formulation of the latter concept, see Laura Mulvey, "Visual Pleasure and Narrative Cinema," *Screen* 16.3 (1975): 6–18.

29. Ihara, *Nanshoku ōkagami*, 39:317–320 (Schalow, *Great Mirror*, 53–56 [whence the quotation]).

30. Matsuo Bashō, "Hokku hen," in *Nihon koten bungaku taikei*, ed. Takagi Ichinosuke et al., 102 vols. (Iwanami shoten, 1957–1968), 45:39.

wakashu or woman?" (*Ume yanagi sazo wakashu kana onna kana*).³⁰ Neither a woman nor yet a man, the youth shared traits with both, but at the same time significant differences. To classify him as a "third gender" would be misleading, however, since membership in the *wakashu* category was only temporary.³¹

Let us turn now to the youth's lover, or *nenja*. Unlike the term *wakashu*, *nenja* contained no age signifier, meaning simply the "person [implicitly male] who thinks of" a particular youth.³² Though there was a vague expectation that the *nenja* had reached a certain sexual maturity, and that erotic activity waned with advancing age, the chronological bounds of this status were not so clearly defined—or rather, so fervently debated—as in the case of the youth himself. Thus, in one *Great Mirror* story, we find a *wakashu* being courted simultaneously by a nine-year-old schoolmate and a Buddhist ascetic already in his eighties.³³ More important than absolute age was the principle that the *nenja* be older than the *wakashu*, although it was not necessary that he be a full-fledged adult. The malleable nature of youthfulness allowed, nevertheless, for occasional exceptions to the rule. For example, in Saikaku's debut work as a prose author, *Kōshoku ichidai otoko* (Life of an Amorous Man; 1682), the precocious protagonist Yonosuke is taken aback

31. It is in the context of urban prostitution that the *wakashu*, usually referred to by such occupational signifiers as *kagema* or *yarō*, most closely approached the status of a "third gender," his distinctive clothing and coiffure being neither entirely masculine nor feminine, but containing elements of both. We find, for instance, the following 1827 *senryū* (Okada Hajime, ed., <Haifū> Yanagidaru zenshū, 13 vols. [Sanseidō, 1976–1984], 7:158), a play on the folk belief that a whetstone would break if a woman stepped across it: "Straddled by a *kagema*, the whetstone develops a wee crack" (*Kagema ga matagu toishi ni mo chitto hibi*). Like the more general status of *wakashu*, however, that of *kagema* was only temporary. For a cross-cultural perspective on "third gender" categories, see Gilbert Herdt, ed., *Third Sex, Third Gender: Beyond Sexual Dimorphism in Culture and History* (New York: Zone, 1994).

32. The character *nen*, which I have rendered here as "to think of," is difficult to translate precisely, falling somewhere between rational "thinking" and emotive "feeling." Its root connotation is a dwelling or focusing of mental energies upon a particular object, as seen in such compounds as *nenbutsu*, which refers to the practice of "praying to [i.e., focusing one's thoughts upon] the Buddha," and *nengan*, a "deeply felt desire." I thank Henry Smith for drawing my attention to these nuances.

33. Ihara, *Nanshoku ōkagami*, 39:323–325 (Schalow, *Great Mirror*, 60–62). Urushiya Ensai, in his 1702 story collection *Nanshoku kinometsuke* (in *Mikan chinpon shūsei*, ed. Sobu Fukurō and Imaoka Yoshio, 4 vols. [Koten hozon kenkyūkai, 1933–1934], 3:106), introduces a sixty-three-year-old *nenja* with the comment that this is "no age to be polishing *nyakudō*." It is unclear whether *nyodō* pursuits would have been deemed equally inappropriate (which is not to say implausible) in a man of his years.

to discover that the young-looking male prostitute whose favors he has purchased is in fact ten years older than himself—not sufficiently so, however, as to abandon the act. The imagined setting for such unconventional encounters was typically the erotic marketplace, which not only pushed upward the boundaries of youth but also bestowed sexual agency upon all males, the likes of fourteen-year-old Yonosuke included, who could pay the price.[34]

If the *nenja* was not always literally older than the youth, he was nevertheless his senior in terms of linear progression. The role of *nenja* was seen as belonging to a later stage in masculine development than that of *wakashu*, so that while a *wakashu* might eventually become a *nenja*, it was all but inconceivable that a *nenja* should revert to being a *wakashu*. It was the *nenja*'s seniority within his gender category that licensed his virile (which is to say, penetrative) role in sexual intercourse, even if he, like Yonosuke, had purchased the privilege by economic means.[35] This age-based hierarchy of masculine prerogative must not be confused with the class order in a socioeconomic sense, for both fictional and nonfictional sources provide examples of youths paired with lovers humbler in station than themselves; indeed, writers on *shudō* often praised an indifference on the part of the youth to considerations of social status.[36] To be sure, such expressions of romantic egalitarianism required affirmation precisely because the exigencies of class prejudice and socioeconomic inequality were very real: had Saikaku not depicted Yonosuke as enjoying a certain measure of financial independence, his precocious assumption of the *nenja* mantle would have seemed to readers less plausible, while professional youths like his partner often hailed from the lowest of social backgrounds and direst of economic straits. Nevertheless, even the second and third Tokugawa shoguns, who

34. Ihara, *Kōshoku ichidai otoko*, 38:128 (trans. Robert Lyons Danly under the title "Flyboys," in *Partings at Dawn: An Anthology of Japanese Gay Literature*, ed. Stephen D. Miller [San Francisco: Gay Sunshine, 1996], 95; trans. Kengi Hamada under the title *The Life of an Amorous Man* [Rutland, Vt.: Tuttle, 1964], 39). An even wider age discrepancy may be found in Nishizawa Ippū's *Yakei tomojamisen* (2:326), which describes a forty-nine-year-old actor-prostitute who entertained clients "young enough to be his grandsons."

35. Yoshida Hanbei, the putative author of the 1687 *Nanshoku masukagami* (in *Kōshokumono sōshishū*, 1:302–303) warns, therefore, that even if a prostitute's client is younger than the prostitute himself, he must take care not to cede rank (*kurai*) to the latter in such matters of etiquette as seating.

36. The ethnographer Segawa Kiyoko (cited in Richard E. Varner, "The Organized Peasant: The *Wakamonogumi* of the Edo Period," *Monumenta Nipponica* 32 [1977]: 466) has noted in a different context that "in feudal times role differentiation according to age was the only principle of equality."

stood at the pinnacle of the class hierarchy, reputedly took *nenja* lovers in their younger days—a situation that would be unthinkable had roles in *shudō* and social status been strictly isomorphic.[37]

Although the status of *nenja* ostensibly precluded the individual from serving as an insertee to other males, neither the *wakashu* nor *nenja* role was irreconcilable with sexual interaction with females. We have seen an example of this in the case of the *kagema*, who might, particularly if he was older, offer his services alternately to male and female clients—if not, as in the fancy of some woodblock artists, both at the same time.[38] Even more compatible with *joshoku* pursuits was the role of *nenja*, which involved a similarly virile status and penetrative stance. Yet, though *nanshoku* and *joshoku* were not mutually exclusive, Edo-period authors frequently portrayed the former as preceding the latter in the male life cycle, with male-female interactions tending to eclipse male-male over time.[39] When Bashō wrote, at the age of twenty-nine, that he was "once fond of *shudō*" (*mukashi wa shudōzuki*), he implied that sexual habits, including the gender of one's partners, might change over the years.[40] Upon marriage, if not sooner, a man was expected to fully embark upon a career of *joshoku*, although *nanshoku* liaisons in the role of *nenja* were still permissible, and the sanctioned range of female partners included not only wives but concubines and prostitutes.

37. Mitamura Engyo, "Tsukiyo no sandai shōgun," in *Mitamura Engyo zenshū*, ed. Mori Senzō et al., 28 vols. (Chūō kōronsha, 1975–1983), 1:54–55.

38. The compatibility of both roles with *joshoku* allowed for the creation of male-male-female love triangles, perhaps the most notorious of which involved the early nineteenth-century kabuki actor Bandō Mitsugorō III, whose wife, Oden, eloped with his *wakashu* and fellow actor, Segawa Kikunojō V. On this incident and its representations, see Hayashi Yoshikazu, *Edo ehon besutoserā* (Shinchōsha, 1991), 168–216; Ozaki Kyūya, "Oden Mitsu Segawa no sankaku kankei," *Edo nanpa kenkyū* 2 (1925): 49–63; Ozaki Kyūya, "Oden Mitsu Segawa no sankaku kankei ni okeru seikaku naru bunken," *Hentai shiryō*, December 1927, 65–78. On the combination of two males and a female in woodblock prints, see the comments of Paul Schalow in "Josei no 'nanshokuron,'" *Bungaku* 6.1 (1995): 71.

39. Although Edo-period authors far more commonly depicted the transition from an exclusively male-male pattern of erotic behavior to a predominantly male-female one, they could also imagine the process taking place in reverse, as occurs, for example, in: Azuma no Kamiko, *Fūryū hiyokudori*, in *Edo jidai bungei shiryō*, 5:86–87, 110–112; Ihara, *Nanshoku ōkagami*, 39:467–472 (Schalow, *Great Mirror*, 189–193); and Nankai no Sanjin, *Nanshoku yamaji no tsuyu*, 182–183. A character in Ejima Kiseki's 1706 work *Fūryū kyokujamisen* (in *Hachimonjiyabon zenshū*, 1:356) notes punningly, however, that the latter order is "ass-backward from most people" (*seken no hito wa urahara*).

40. For a discussion of male-male eroticism in Bashō's life and work, see Iwata Jun'ichi, "Haijin Bashō no dōseiai," in *Honchō nanshoku kō* (Toba: Iwata Sadao, 1974), 253–267 (the above quotation appears on p. 256).

By this time, *shudō* ties might have evolved into less erotic forms of masculine friendship, as their youthful objects matured, all too inevitably, into fellow men. An eighteenth-century *senryū* depicts this situation with a bittersweet irony, describing the peculiar emotion that "introducing one's wife to one's former *wakashu*" (*Nyōbō ni mukashi no wakashu hikiawase*) might elicit on the part of the *nenja*.[41]

If the gender of the *wakashu* received little comment, the masculinity of the *nenja* was hardly subject to question. All men might at some time or other fall into the category of *nenja*, a status that was not generalized but existed only in relation to a particular youth. The term did little more than to indicate that a certain *wakashu* had struck one's fancy—literally, provoked "thoughts" or "feelings" (*nen*); one was, in other words, his "lover." The capacity for thinking such thoughts, however, did not distinguish the *nenja* from the rest of the male population, since the virile gaze construed the erotic attraction of youths as comparable, albeit not identical, to that of females. Some men, of course, had never experienced a relationship with a youth, nor were all affected by the erotic charms of the *wakashu* to the same degree. Certain individuals might express an active distaste for *shudō* pursuits, earning themselves the name of *wakashugirai* or "youth-haters." At the other end of the spectrum stood the *wakashuzuki* or "youth-lover," whose indulgence in such pleasures was copious or conspicuous enough to warrant special comment. Yet the label of *wakashuzuki* did not automatically imply that its recipient was uninterested in erotic ties with women, just as the fictional Yonosuke's notoriety as a "woman-lover" did not prevent him from allegedly forming liaisons over the course of a lifetime with no fewer than 725 youths.[42] "Loving youths" or "loving women" was something that one did rather than what one was, as the not infrequent appearance of these terms in verb form (that is, with the verb *su[ru]* or "to do") attests. Thus Bashō's admission that he was once a *shudōzuki* (literally, a "lover of *shudō*") meant little more than that he now indulged in such pursuits less than before, not that he could never imagine doing so again. Some biographers maintain, indeed, that male-male erotic relationships would occupy the later years of Bashō's life as well.[43]

Male erotic behavior could be described in terms not only of what the individual engaged in but also of what he eschewed. A close relative of the "youth-lover" was the *onnagirai* or "woman-hater," who disdained the com-

41. *Mutamagawa*, in *Nihon meicho zenshū*, 26:89.
42. Ihara, *Kōshoku ichidai otoko*, 38:103. (Hamada excises this passage.)
43. Iwata Jun'ichi, "Haijin Bashō," 265–266.

pany of females, whether as sexual partners or as social consorts. Erotic ties
with youths were not essential to a reputation as a "woman-hater," yet as
an alternative to *joshoku*—indeed, the only sanctioned one for adult males—
the two often went hand in hand. Thus Ejima Kiseki, a contemporary of
Saikaku, wrote matter-of-factly of one of his characters, a townsman: "A
died-in-the-wool *onnagirai*, Jūgorō in all his days never took a wife, but
loved to keep attractive youths with forelocks by his side." By rejecting one
of his erotic options and preferring an "all-male household" (*otokozetai*) to
matrimony, Jūgorō emerges from Ejima's brush a somewhat eccentric
figure. Significantly, however, Ejima chooses to present Jūgorō's bias less as
reprehensible in kind than as extreme in degree. Indeed, compared to that
of his elder brother, the woman-loving priest, Jūgorō's conduct appears by
the end of the story as virtually commendable: how remarkable his behavior, comments the narrator, in a "fickle world [*ukiyo*] where even ordained
monks display a fondness for women."[44]

Together, the *wakashu* and *nenja* formed the two asymmetric halves of
the *shudō* couple, each role complementing and predicated upon the existence of the other. The bond between them did not need to be exclusive: numerous literary examples are to be found of *wakashu* with multiple admirers
or of *nenja* who exchange vows simultaneously with more than one youth—
not to mention the tangled web of prostitution. Nevertheless, what we might
be tempted to call "monogamy" served as an important, if not universally
observed, principle in *shudō* ethics—even more so, arguably, than in the
sphere of male-female relations, where the institution of concubinage enjoyed long-standing recognition.[45] In fiction, as no doubt often in real life,
the much-sought-after *wakashu* tended to spark rivalry and even violence
among his suitors, while resentment and jealousy were apt to reward the
fickle *nenja*.[46] As with women in the pleasure quarters, male prostitutes often acquired regular patrons, whose visits were construed as a sign of devotion rather than a purely commercial transaction, and who might, if the
youth were lucky, purchase his freedom from a life of forced promiscuity.

Yet "monogamy," with its conjugal connotations, is an inappropriate term

44. Ejima Kiseki, *Seken musuko katagi*, in *Hachimonjiyabon zenshū*, 6:23–28.
45. In the opening story of Urushiya Ensai's *Nanshoku kinometsuke* (3:70), a
divine messenger describes the principle of "one *chigo* [i.e., *wakashu*], one *nenja*"
as a "basic sanction" (*konpon no inka*) of *shudō*. Such a principle would mean, in
effect, that a single male could have two *shudō* partners over the course of a lifetime: a *nenja* during his youth, and a *wakashu* after he grew older.
46. It should be noted, however, that, in the genre of the erotic debate, the propo-
nents of *shudō* sometimes cited youths' supposed lack of jealousy as one of the advantages of their path. See, for example, Azuma no Kamiko, *Fūryū hiyokudori*, 5:91, 98.

to describe the bond between *wakashu* and *nenja*, who were more likely to compare theirs to another form of relationship. It was brotherhood, not marriage, that served as the central kinship metaphor in *shudō*, casting *nenja* and *wakashu* in the role of elder and younger siblings respectively, rather than husband and wife. Fictive bonds of brotherhood (*kyōdaibun, gikyōdai*) had long furnished a device for cementing ties between males unrelated by blood, and were by no means confined to erotic alliances.[47] *Shudō* couples often chose to formalize their fraternal devotion through oral and written vows (*keitei keiyaku*), if not through more dramatic tokens of loyalty (*shinjū*) such as self-mutilation, whether by piercing the flesh of the thigh or arm, removing a fingernail, or even cutting off a finger.[48] The brotherhood metaphor suited itself ideally to the context of *shudō* because it conveyed both the permanence of the bond to which the couple aspired—*shudō* oaths spoke commonly of "sharing life and death together"—and the asymmetric hierarchy that ordered this tie.[49] As the senior sibling, the *nenja* offered the youth physical and social protection, a role model, and material aid (it was this last factor upon which the prostitution industry capitalized), which the latter reciprocated through obedience, respect, and intimate access to his person.

The asymmetric and hierarchical nature of the *shudō* tie manifested itself also in the couple's sexual practices. In the same way that vaginal coitus was regarded as the quintessential practice of male-female eroticism, anal intercourse functioned as the central act of the *shudō* sexual repertoire, the *nenja* assuming the part of inserter and the *wakashu* that of insertee.[50] In contrast to vaginal coitus, however, popular discourse construed only the inserter role in anal intercourse as intrinsically pleasurable, while taking it

47. For an ethnographic perspective on fictive brotherhood bonds, see Takeda Akira, *Kyōdaibun no minzoku* (Kyoto: Jinbun shoin, 1989).

48. On *shudō* vows and demonstrations of loyalty, see also Shibayama, *Edo nanshoku kō: Akusho hen*, 154–161.

49. The permanence of the *shudō* bond was likely more of an ideal than a reality, for according to Konoe Nobuhiro's *Inu tsurezure* (in *Kanazōshi shūsei*, 4:23), dated 1619 but published only in 1653, it was "rare" for such oaths to withstand the test of time—although the same was undoubtedly true of male-female vows as well.

50. Apart from kissing, which was usually referred to as "sucking mouth" (*kuchi o suu*), *shudō* writings seldom mention oral forms of copulation. A notable exception may be found in Baijōken's *Yodarekake* (4:47), which describes fellatio, as well as insertion of the penis between a bent knee or elbow, albeit as obsolete and disreputable practices. An Edo-period anecdote (cited in Hiratsuka Yoshinobu, *Nihon ni okeru nanshoku no kenkyū* [Ningen no kagakusha, 1983], 105–106) portrays fellatio and anilingus in a humorous light, each representing a mismatch of the conventional mouth-mouth and penis-anus combinations. Besides anal coitus, the only sexual acts to surface with any frequency in *shudō* texts are interfemoral intercourse

for granted that the anal insertee allowed himself to be penetrated only out of duty, affection, coercion, or the prospect of material reward.[51] Seldom was the latter role seen as bringing any physical enjoyment or erotic gratification; on the contrary, writers typically emphasized the pain that accompanied it.[52]

(*sumata*, literally "bare thighs"), which is typically represented as a somewhat un-satisfactory substitute for anal penetration, and manual stimulation of the penis, which served among other things to allow the youth to gauge the size of the soon-to-be-inserted organ, and which Yoshida Hanbei (*Nanshoku masukagami*, 1:335) pronounces "uncouth" (*yabo*). (See also n. 52 below.)

The division between anal inserter and insertee in *shudō* texts is remarkably inflexible. In the works I have examined (though these certainly do not constitute the entire corpus), I have not encountered a single example of reciprocal penetra-tion, nor of a *nenja* being penetrated by a youth. Rather than concluding that such practices were rare or nonexistent, however, we can at most assume only that they lay outside the conceptual boundaries of *shudō* as codified in popular texts. It is quite possible, moreover, that they appear in other genres of writing: a 1601 entry in the journal of a Zen priest (cited by Iwata Jun'ichi in Hasegawa Kōzō and Tsukikawa Kazuo, eds., *Minakata Kumagusu nanshoku dangi: Iwata Jun'ichi ōfuku shokan* [Yasaka shobō, 1991], 297–298), for example, seems to allude to reciprocal anal pen-etration. The same is true of mutual masturbation and reciprocal interfemoral in-tercourse, neither of which play a conspicuous role in *shudō* texts but which occa-sionally surface in other types of discourse. A Catholic work published in Europe in 1632 (cited in Shibayama, *Edo nanshoku kō: Akusho hen*, 208) records a Japanese convert's confession to the former practice, while the existence of the latter may be conjectured from the fact that an early Meiji sexological work (Seki Yuidō, *Danjo kōgō tokushitsu mondō* [Takebe Takisaburō and Kimura Inosuke, 1886], 145–149) describes it as a well-entrenched habit among young rural males.

51. The early nineteenth-century nativist Motoori Uchitō (*Wakanoura tsuru shō*, in <Zōho> *Motoori Norinaga zenshū*, ed. Motoori Seizō, 13 vols. [Yoshikawa kō-bunkan, 1926–1928], 12:393) characterized males who desired to be sexually pen-etrated, as opposed to penetrating, as an "anomaly" (*kishu*), although he acknowl-edged that a few such "incomprehensible" (*fushigi*) types could be found even in his own domain of Wakayama. Motoori's description of these "males who should have been born female" (*onna no umarezokonai*) bears a greater resemblance, however, to the *otoko-onna*, a chiefly adult figure whom we shall encounter again in chap. 3, than to the youths whom *shudō* texts typically depicted in the role of insertee. Among the latter type, Nishizawa Ippū (*Yakei tomojamisen*, 2:334) introduces one *kagema* who "liked it [i.e., anal intercourse]" (*sorezuki*) with the telling comment that such a trait was "unexpected in a youth" (*wakashu ni nai hazu no koto*).

52. According to an oral tradition reported by Minakata Kumagusu (letter to Nakamatsu Morio, n.d., *Minakata Kumagusu zenshū*, ed. Iwamura Shinobu et al., 12 vols. [Heibonsha, 1971–1975], 7:126; letter to Iwata Jun'ichi, 19 January 1934, *Minakata Kumagusu zenshū*, 9:232), monks on Mount Kōya around the end of the Edo period believed that a secretion took place inside the rectum of youths who had come by habit to enjoy being anally penetrated, referring to it as *uchimore* or "in-ternal ejaculation," as opposed to *sotomore* or "external ejaculation," which desig-nated seminal emission on the part of the insertee. The latter might occur as a result of manual stimulation of the penis by the inserter, which one early nineteenth-century erotic manual (Keisai Eisen, <Keichū kibun> *Makura bunko hoi*, in *Nihon*

Thus, quipped an 1825 *senryū,* "All too obvious a lie are the pleasurable moans of the *kagema*" (*Anmari no uso wa kagema no yogariyō*).[53] Similarly, when Tokugawa Mitsukuni, a seventeenth-century lord of Mito domain, wished to describe the evils of harsh governance, it was anal intercourse with page boys that he chose as the most apt metaphor, since in both cases the party on top (inserter or ruling class) derived satisfaction while the other (page boy or populace) suffered.[54]

Yet the *wakashu* and *nenja* roles comprised more than merely sexual positions. Sexual intercourse was not even a sine qua non element of the *wakashu-nenja* relationship. One of the speakers in a seventeenth-century work maintains, for example, that in the course of one or two years, it might take place only once or twice, and sometimes not at all.[55] The "way of youths" governed the behavior of each party outside the bedroom as well as within it, offering a discipline that, while highly specialized in Konishi's sense of the term, also provided order and meaning to a broad spectrum of human (or at any rate, masculine) activities. The normativity that served as a distinguishing characteristic of the "way" manifested itself not only in the conventions of sex and age discussed above, but also in a larger system of ethical and esthetic standards that framed and even dwarfed the sexual act. When pursued within this normative framework, *shudō* was seen as having positive value, while outside of it, male-male sexuality might exist, but constituted something less than a "way." The eighteenth-century author Shōsaiō wrote, for example, of men who violate young shop boys (*kodetchi*) and other preadolescents that they "do not love *shudō,*" but "only like to fornicate [*okasu*]"—a distinction that would be moot within the present-day conceptual framework of "homosexuality."[56]

---

seiten taikan, ed. Takahashi Tetsu, 2 vols. [Nihon seikatsu shinri gakkai, 1954], 1:101) recommends as a means of making the youth more receptive to penetration. In *Kōshoku kinmō zui* (1:91), Yoshida Hanbei writes that actor-prostitutes might experience erection when they sensed their partner approaching orgasm (lit., "when the breathing behind them gets rough" [*ushiro no hanaiki no arai toki*]), but describes this phenomenon as "annoying" (*urusashi*) for the insertee rather than pleasurable. According to the early eighteenth-century *Yarō kinuburui* (35), it was unseemly for male prostititutes engaging in sexual intercourse with a male client to display an erection.

53. Okada Hajime, *Yanagidaru zenshū,* 7:61.
54. Cited in Minakata Kumagusu to Iwata Jun'ichi, 20 August 1931, *Minakata Kumagusu zenshū,* 9:30 (trans. William F. Sibley in "Morning Fog (Correspondence on Gay Lifestyles)," in Miller, *Partings at Dawn,* 158).
55. Konoe, *Inu tsurezure,* 4:23.
56. Shōsaiō, *Gengenkyō,* 3:306.

How, though, were these norms arbitrated, and what was the mode of their transmission? Beginning in the seventeenth century, I will argue, these processes took place increasingly through commercial mechanisms, and particularly through the medium of what I call the *shudō* text. The latter spanned a number of genres, both fictional and nonfictional, their common characteristic lying in the fact that they dispensed a knowledge of male-male sexuality to the literate public—a somewhat loose constituency that centered upon, but was by no means limited to, urban males of the townsman (*chōnin*) and samurai classes.[57] Although the sheer number of such texts (Iwata Jun'ichi has counted close to six hundred Edo-period works dealing with *nanshoku*) does not permit an exhaustive description, the following section will provide some sense of the general terrain.[58]

CONTEXTUALIZED PLEASURES

The early eighteenth-century story collection *Nanshoku yamaji no tsuyu* (*Nanshoku* Dew on a Mountain Path), by Nankai no Sanjin, introduces a youth named Kamematsu, who is the younger brother of a restaurant owner. Between his duties waiting upon tables, the lad finds a moment to retire to the establishment's second floor, where he leafs through the pages of an illustrated book (*ehon*) on *nanshoku*—perhaps not unlike the one in which he is himself represented. One of the clients at the restaurant, a townsman by the name of Chūji, has observed him stealing off, and, leaving behind the other youth with whom he has hitherto been carousing, follows him stealthily upstairs. Upon spying the work in Kamematsu's hands, Chūji

---

57. A note on terminology is in order here. "Townsman" has become the standard English translation for the urban-commoner stratum, composed chiefly of merchant and artisan households, legally designated in Edo times as *chōnin*. Although this segment of the population included roughly equal numbers of women and men, I have felt justified in using the term "townsman" in spite of its inherently sexist connotations because my discussion centers primarily upon males, whether as sexual actors or as producers and consumers of discourse, and because such alternatives as "bourgeoisie" and "townspeople" have seemed, respectively, too Eurocentric and overly generic. Occasionally I will use the term "townswomen" to refer specifically to females of this stratum. A similar problem arises with respect to "samurai" and its idiomatic equivalent "warrior," which are sometimes used to signify an entire social class (*bushi* in Japanese), women as well as men, and sometimes only its male constituents. In this study, I adhere to the former usage, specifying gender when significant and not obvious from context. It is useful to remember that the legal unit of class in the Edo period was not the individual but the household.

58. Iwata Jun'ichi, *Nanshoku bunken shoshi* (Toba: Iwata Sadao, 1973), 35–166. While not all the works that Iwata lists would qualify as *shudō* texts as I have defined them—that is to say, commercially published texts devoting substantial attention to

makes the following remark: "Your friends will laugh at you if you don't know the intricacies described in that book; let me teach you directly." What ensues is a near-rape, cut short only by the appearance of the jealous drinking companion, but for the purposes of the present discussion I would like to focus upon Chūji's words.[59]

The "intricacies" (*showake*) to which Chūji referred signified not only the various physical embraces that featured in the book's illustrations—or so it seems at least in the accompanying picture—but also an elaborate code of conduct and etiquette surrounding male-male sexuality, the production and distribution of which served as one of the chief functions of the *shudō* text. Familiarity with this code had by the eighteenth century become a form of marketable knowledge, an expertise the possession of which justified a certain outlay of money, and ignorance of which might diminish one's stature in the eyes of peers. The secrets of the "way" took the form of a tangible commodity, no longer confined to a closed circle of initiates but available on the open market, where they might come into the hands even of a humble son of the merchant class like Kamematsu. Naturally, such intricacies could still be communicated from person to person (as Chūji attempts to do, albeit not necessarily for pedagogical reasons), and *shudō* was no doubt practiced by many who had never read a book in their lives. Yet just as the rise of new forms of urban prostitution significantly altered the landscape of male-male erotic culture, the proliferation of *shudō* texts brought about far-reaching changes in the organization of erotic knowledge.

What emerged during the seventeenth century was a vigorous, integrated, and broadly based discourse on male-male sexuality—one for the first time truly deserving of the name "popular"—its contours molded chiefly through the medium of the printed text, and its diffusion facilitated by a rapidly growing publishing industry. Texts dealing with male-male sexuality had existed prior to this period, largely in the form of hand-copied manuscripts, but such writings had circulated within a highly restricted milieu, due not only to their scarcity but to considerations of education and literacy as well. *Nyake kanjinchō* (Subscription Book on Behalf of *Nyake*), the 1482 work mentioned earlier in this chapter, was written, for example, entirely in Chinese charac-

---

male-male eroticism—I cite this figure, which does not even include the hundred or so actor evaluation books (*yarō hyōbanki*) that Iwata lists in a separate part of the bibliography (241–254), as a means of suggesting the vastness of the Edo-period archive, which represents one of the richest caches of written material on male-male sexuality to survive from any part of the world before the twentieth century.

59. Nankai no Sanjin, *Nanshoku yamaji no tsuyu*, 148–152.

ters, and would have been comprehensible to only a tiny segment of the population.[60] Its chief readership was likely the Buddhist clergy, for whom literacy served as an occupational skill and within whose monasteries male-male erotic relations evidently flourished.[61] The prominence of acolytes (*chigo*) and other young temple dwellers among the erotic objects listed in the text provides further indication of such an audience, as do its title and format, which mimic those of documents drafted to solicit donations for the construction and repair of religious images and buildings. Also unlikely to travel far beyond temple confines or the libraries of the aristocracy were hand-illustrated picture scrolls (*emaki*), such as the medieval priest-acolyte romances known as *chigo monogatari* or the frankly sexual *Chigo no sōshi*.[62]

By Nankai no Sanjin's time, however, male-male erotic texts circulated in a much broader geographic and social orbit. The rapid growth of the publishing industry in the seventeenth century had facilitated the virtually simultaneous production of multiple copies of a single text, supplementing (though never entirely supplanting) the laborious process of transcribing manuscripts by hand. Well-received works might go through multiple editions, such as the 1643 *Shin'yūki*, which was reissued in 1661 under the title *Shudō monogatari* (Tales of *Shudō*), or Saikaku's 1687 *Great Mirror*, a newly abridged version of which appeared as late as 1757. As a result of mass production, it became economically feasible for nonelites to own a book, or alternatively to borrow one at substantially less than the purchase price from the growing number of book lenders (*kashihon'ya*). At the same time, increasing literacy, not only among the pacified warrior class but also among commoners, served to expand the reading public, albeit, as earlier noted, a gender gap persisted. For the less scholarly members of this audience—such types as the young Kamematsu no doubt included—publishers offered texts

60. *Nyake* was a synonym for *nyakudō*, or what during the Edo period would come to be called *shudō*. The author's name (Ijiri Matakurō Tadasuki), which incorporates several bawdy puns, is evidently a pseudonym.

61. On the acolyte-focused erotic culture of medieval monasteries, see Tsuchiya Megumi, "Chūsei jiin no chigo to warawamai," *Bungaku* 6.1 (1995): 40–49.

62. For a discussion of the *chigo monogatari* genre, along with a translation of one such work (*Aki no yo no nagamonogatari*), see Margaret H. Childs, "*Chigo Monogatari*: Love Stories or Buddhist Sermons?" *Monumenta Nipponica* 35 (1980): 127–151. Another tale (*Genmu monogatari*) appears in Margaret Helen Childs, *Rethinking Sorrow: Revelatory Tales of Late Medieval Japan*, Michigan Monograph Series in Japanese Studies, no. 6 (Ann Arbor: Center for Japanese Studies, 1991), 31–52. Childs (*Rethinking Sorrow*, 26) notes, significantly, that a manuscript of the latter text characterized it as having been handed down for generations on "this mountain" (i.e., within a monastic complex), and that it was during the Edo period that a printed edition first appeared.

that furnished a generous proportion of phonetic characters or glosses, an early example of which may be found in the seventeenth-century genre known as *kana* books (*kanazōshi*), which featured numerous titles with *shudō* themes, among them the earlier-mentioned *Shin'yūki* and *Denbu monogatari*.[63] In such works, not unlike the book Kamematsu is depicted perusing, illustrations typically accompanied the written word, providing yet another level of entry into the text.

It is important to note that the publishing industry was based in the cities, and in particular the three great metropolises of Edo, Kyoto, and Osaka.[64] Here among the townsmen and samurai who composed the bulk of the urban population, publishing houses also found their chief clientele. Scholars have tended to identify the popular literature of the era with an increasingly prosperous townsman class—that is to say, merchants (a constituency that would presumably have included the fictional Kamematsu's brother-guardian, for example) and artisans—yet it is clear that the boundaries of the discourse were not tightly confined to any single social stratum. While commercial publishers were by definition merchants, authors hailed from various backgrounds, including not only townsmen but also samurai and members of other social groups such as the court nobility and the Buddhist clergy. Samurai, with their relatively high rates of literacy and largely urban residence, also provided a significant portion of the audience for commercial texts, just as they patronized the kabuki theater even in the face of legal proscriptions. Even a high-ranking samurai official like Yamamoto Tsunetomo, the author of *Hagakure* (In the Shadow of Leaves), was familiar enough with Saikaku's work in the early eighteenth century to be able to quote with reasonable accuracy a line from the *Great Mirror*.[65]

<hr />

63. Paul Gordon Schalow ("The Invention of a Literary Tradition of Male Love: Kitamura Kigin's *Iwatsutsuji*," *Monumenta Nipponica* 48 [1993]: 3) estimates that some 10 to 15 percent of surviving *kanazōshi* "treat exclusively or in large part the topic of male love."

64. To my knowledge, the only *shudō* text of significance to have been produced outside the three metropolises is *Akaeboshi* (in *Tokugawa bungei ruijū*, ed. Hayakawa Junzaburō, 12 vols. [Kokusho kankōkai, 1914–1916], 12:420–426), a 1663 guide to actor-prostitutes published in the provincial town of Furuichi (present-day Ise), an entertainment center that flourished because of its proximity to the Ise shrine.

65. Yamamoto Tsunetomo, *Hagakure*, in *Nihon shisō taikei*, 26:263 (trans. William Scott Wilson under the title *Hagakure: The Book of the Samurai* [Kodansha International, 1979], 58). The quote appears in a passage of Yamamoto's work purporting to represent the views of his father, Jin'emon, but since the latter had passed away before Saikaku's book appeared, I have taken it to be Tsunetomo's own interpolation.

The geographic setting of Yamamoto's remark is no less revealing than its content. Between 1710 and 1716, during which time a scribe recorded his now-famous sayings on samurai ethics, the retired warrior-bureaucrat Yamamoto was living in seclusion in his native domain of Saga, which lay on the southwestern island of Kyushu. He thus cited the words of Saikaku even while residing some four hundred miles (a journey of several weeks) from Kyoto and Osaka, where the *Great Mirror* had first appeared on bookshelves in 1687, and twice that distance from Edo, where a second edition followed shortly thereafter. In the span of a few decades, Saikaku's text had not only traveled half the length of the Japanese archipelago, but gained sufficient respectability for Yamamoto to refer to one of its lines as an "illustrious passage" (*meibun*). Whether the Kyushu warrior actually owned a copy of the *Great Mirror*, and if so, whether he had obtained it in Edo during the course of official duties, or in Saga, or somewhere in between, is of little consequence to our argument. Rather, what this exchange suggests is that, as the result of its commercialization, knowledge about male-male sexuality was able to traverse significant class and regional barriers, and to bring individuals as different as Saikaku and Yamamoto together within a single discursive space.

The extent to which the other inhabitants of Yamamoto's Saga domain, and particularly the peasantry that made up over 80 percent of the Japanese population, may have participated in this discourse is a matter about which we can only speculate. It is likely, however, that the commercialization of the agrarian economy, increasing literacy among the rural populace, and improvements in the transportation and communications infrastructure brought *shudō* texts into the hands of at least some peasant readers, especially those of the wealthy *gōnō* stratum, some of whom amassed impressive libraries. Future research may indeed uncover many works such as Saikaku's moldering in provincial storehouses, whether they arrived there as souvenirs of a trip to the city or on the back of an itinerant bookseller. Nevertheless, the chiefly urban producers of such works seldom went out of their way to cater to a rural audience, and the image of the peasantry that emerges in their pages, as will be discussed later, was by no means a flattering one.

Such, then, was the broad, if by no means homogeneous, social field within which the *shudō* text operated. *Shudō* texts did not, however, simply circulate a common knowledge already shared by this readership, or by the various social constituencies that it comprised; had this been the case, there would have been little reason for anyone to buy them. It may be useful at this point to recall the distinguishing characteristics of a "way" or discipline. As a "way," *shudō* represented not merely an objective category of practices, but also a specialized body of knowledge that enabled the practitioner to perform these in a manner that conformed to authorized norms and that held out the promise of reward. What the *shudō* text did was to provide a new mode for the transmission of this knowledge, the printed word coming to supplant the authority of the personal master who had stood at the center of the medieval paradigm. Published texts offered a means of communicating the intricacies of the "way" that was instantly available and physically durable (that is, readable many times over), that was highly uniform across time and space, and that was accessible to all who possessed a certain amount of literacy and economic power. This textual mode of transmission may have been particularly well suited to such erotic disciplines as *shudō*, which, unlike the tea ceremony or the flower arrangement of more recent times, did not boast accredited teachers or licensed schools of instruction.

Yet *shudō* texts did more than distribute a preexisting body of knowledge; they also served as a site for its creation. The market mechanism provided a powerful stimulus for the elaboration and multiplication of erotic knowledges, as is reflected in the remarkable outpouring of texts, both on *shudō* and on *shikidō* more generally, that helped to fuel the rapid expansion of the publication industry in the seventeenth century. As a wider market for erotic texts emerged, authors and publishers developed new narrative and merchandising strategies to secure the patronage of audiences. This marketplace formed a highly integrated network, so that producers of discourse, whether they were based in Edo or Kyoto or Osaka, had to compete with as well as emulate one another in order to gain the attention of readers. A successful work might spawn imitators almost overnight, and authors often cited and borrowed liberally—by present-day standards even plagiaristically—from the work of their colleagues. Yet innovation, too, was a prized commodity, and the publication industry was always on the lookout for new niches in the market. It was precisely the competitiveness of this environment that led Urushiya Ensai, the author of the 1702 story collection *Nanshoku kinometsuke* (*Nanshoku* Pickled in Young Pepperleaf Brine), to boast that his material was "entirely novel" (*minamina shintō o erabitareba*) and that "you won't find anything [else] like it in the bookstores."[66]

Novelty alone, however, was not enough to sell a *shudō* text. As an encoded discipline, it was necessary that the text claim some sort of authoritativeness for the knowledge it dispensed, and that therefore made its acquisition valuable. This goal could be achieved in several ways, two of which stand out as paradigmatic. The first was to ground its legitimacy in an out-

66. Urushiya, *Nanshoku kinometsuke*, 3:70.

side source, often some form of religious authorization. Although Urushiya, for instance, emphasized the originality of his work, he at the same time turned to a more conventional narrative device in framing it as a manuscript that had been conveyed to an earthly plane by the guardian deity Bishamonten (Sanskrit: Vaiśravaṇa) of Kyoto's Kurama shrine, a site whose association with male-male eroticism dated back to medieval legend.[67] This invocation echoed pre-Edo tradition in more ways than one, for medieval writers, too, had frequently portrayed male-male erotic knowledge as a form of religious teaching. A work known as *Kō chigo shōgyō hiden* (earliest dated manuscript: 1450), for example, purported to be "Expounding the Sacred Doctrine of Acolytes Secretly Transmitted" in a direct line from the Buddhist guardian deity Konpira (Sanskrit: Kumbhira).[68] What was peculiarly Edoesque about Urushiya's conceit, therefore, was not its assertion of a sacred and esoteric wisdom, but the way in which the author combined this with an exoteric and decidedly secular appreciation of market needs.

As Paul Schalow has detailed, a favorite legitimating figure in *shudō* iconography was the Buddhist monk Kūkai or Kōbō Daishi, whom medieval tradition had identified as responsible for introducing male-male sexual practices to Japan at the beginning of the ninth century.[69] An early use of this authorizing strategy may be found in *Kōbō Daishi ikkan no sho* (Book of Kōbō Daishi), dated 1598, which bears the signature of one Mitsuo Sadatomo, who professed to be a Kyushu samurai entrusted with the manuscript by an apparition of the Great Teacher himself.[70] Although this work claimed to be for the eyes of Mitsuo's "intimate friends" only and seems to have remained unpublished during the Edo period, Mitsuo's successors would not hesitate to invoke the saint's name in order to boost their sales. One example is Kishōken Kōyūshi, who modeled his 1697 *Yarō jitsugokyō* (True Word Teaching on Actor-Prostitutes) after a primer (*Jitsugokyō*) that was widely used in elementary education and became one of the most reprinted books of the Edo period. Since tradition ascribed the older work to Kūkai, a more auspicious title for a didactic work on *shudō* can hardly be imagined, par-

67. The legend in question concerned an encounter between the youthful Minamoto Yoshitsune (Ushiwaka) and a goblin (*tengu*), and is the subject of the nō play *Kurama tengu*, for a discussion of which see Dōmoto, *Nanshoku engekishi*, 51–55.

68. For an introduction to this manuscript, which remains unpublished, see Kon Tōkō, *Chigo* (Ōtori shobō, 1947).

69. Paul Gordon Schalow, "Kūkai and the Tradition of Male Love in Japanese Buddhism," in *Buddhism, Sexuality, and Gender*, ed. José Ignacio Cabezón (Albany: State University of New York Press, 1992), 215–230.

70. Mitsuo Sadatomo, *Kōbō Daishi ikkan no sho*, *Kinsei shomin bunka* 13 (1952):

ticularly if its author aspired to similar commercial success.[71] The contents of "Kūkai's" teaching, however, consisted no longer of the pithy moral platitudes of the original primer, nor even the priest-acolyte relations described in Mitsuo's manuscript, but rather the intricacies of the contemporary demimonde of the actor-prostitute (*yarō*).[72]

As the above example illustrates, the modeling of *shudō* texts after canonical works and authoritative literary genres offered a convenient means of external legitimation. Similarly, *Shin'yūki* (whose narrator identifies himself as a monk) takes the form of a catechism (*mondō*), in which an adept master answers the questions of the unenlightened, whereas erotic debates, as we shall see later, were often patterned after Buddhist polemical tracts. Religious works did not provide the only model, however, for *shudō* texts, which might evoke an equivalent aura of legitimacy by emulating, and sometimes echoing in their titles, the classics of a secular literary canon that the publishing explosion of the seventeenth century had recently helped popularize. Over the course of the Edo period, there appeared *shudō* variations on Japanese classics ranging from literary miscellanies (*Inu tsurezure*) to medieval war tales (*Nanshoku taiheiki*) to the celebrated preface of an imperial poetry anthology ("Kokin wakashu no jo").[73] Even Saikaku sought to confer a venerable pedigree upon his *Great Mirror* by invoking the name of a much older secular work, the eleventh- or twelfth-century historical tale *Ōkagami*.

While the above strategies relied on external sources of legitimacy to establish their authoritativeness, a second, often complementary, approach was internal to the text itself. In the medieval disciplinary paradigm, one of the prerogatives of the master had been to evaluate the performance of disciples according to a certain set of critical norms; by in effect exercising this function, *shudō* texts were able to appropriate some of the former's authority. The text spoke, as it were, from a position of consummate mastery, the terminal point in a linear trajectory (the "way" itself) that had total ig-

13–24. This text is discussed and partially translated in Schalow, "Kūkai." Some scholars (e.g., Saitō Shōzō, *Edo kōshoku bungakushi* [Seikō shoin, 1949], 73) express doubts as to the work's date and authorship.

71. Similarly, a portion of Baishōken's 1648–1653 work *Yodarekake* was reissued in 1700 as *Nanshoku jitsugokyō* (True Word Teaching on *Nanshoku*).

72. The text of *Yarō jitsugokyō* may be found in Ishizuka Hōkaishi, *Okaba yūkaku kō*, in *Mikan zuihitsu hyakushu*, ed. Mitamura Engyo, 12 vols. (Chūō kōronsha, 1976–1978), 1:73–80.

73. Strictly speaking, Hosokawa Yūsai's "Kokin wakashu no jo" (in *Misonoya*, ed. Ōta Nanpo; ed. Hayakawa Junzaburō et al., 4 vols. [Kokusho kankōkai, 1917], 4:479–482) predates the Edo period, having been composed in 1589; it was during

norance at one end and perfect wisdom (the text's own position) at the other. Such a narrative stance cast the reader in the role of the uninitiated, or at least not yet completely enlightened, who stood to benefit from the expertise that the work had to offer. What, precisely, were these benefits? Depending upon the text, they included positive rewards, such as sexual gratification, as well as negative ones, such as the ability to avoid various misfortunes that attended its improper pursuit. Often, however, knowledge served as its own reward, since to remain ignorant of matters that others knew betokened social disgrace; recall here Chūji's warning that "Your friends will laugh at you if you don't know the intricacies described in that book." In this sense, the production of knowledge generated its own demand, so that the intricacies of the "way" tended to grow ever more intricate.

Among *shudō* genres, the most overtly magisterial was the didactic text, which focused on spiritual and practical cultivation (*kokoroe, tashinami*). This form did not originate in the Edo period, but had antecedents in such medieval works as *Kō chigo shōgyō hiden*, mentioned previously, and *Chigo kyōkun* (Precepts for Acolytes), attributed to the fifteenth-century Zen priest and linked-verse poet Sōgi, which describes the behavior of the "bad youths of this world" as a counterexample for the young acolyte.[74] By the seventeenth century, the audience for didactic texts on male-male eroticism had come to embrace a broader segment of the general population. Yoshida Hanbei, the presumed author of the 1687 *Nanshoku masukagami* (Lucid Mirror of *Nanshoku*), recognized the diversity of his readership by tailoring his advice to fit the various classes from which it hailed, including warriors, townsmen, peasants, physicians, and members of both the Buddhist and Shinto clergies, as well as the different contexts, both commercial and noncommercial, within which such groups might pursue male-male erotic relations. Yoshida made little claim of religious significance for his work, but relied chiefly on the appeal of its pragmatic focus and encyclopedic scope, offering readers tips on matters ranging from how to compose a love letter, including stock phrases, to how to avoid foul breath by chewing iris root in the morning, to how to mutilate one's flesh as a token of loyalty without bleeding too profusely or becoming permanently crippled. Yoshida's work

---

the seventeenth century, however, that it first received publication. For the other works cited, see Konoe, *Inu tsurezure*, 4:5–26; <*Yunootōge magojakushi*> *Nanshoku taiheiki*, in *Edo no ehon: Shoki kusazōshi shūsei*, ed. Koike Masatake et al., 4 vols. (Kokusho kankōkai, 1987–1989), 4:35–52.

74. Sōgi, *Chigo kyōkun*, in <*Shinkō*> *Gunsho ruijū*, ed. Hanawa Hokinoichi et al., 24 vols. (Naigai shoseki, 1928–1937), 14:161–165.

also deals explicitly with the mechanics of the bedroom, yet judging from the space that this section occupies within the text as a whole, sexual intercourse formed only a small part of the "way" as Yoshida conceived it.[75]

The magisterial functions of the *shudō* text were by no means confined to works of nonfiction. While Yoshida titled his book of practical advice a "mirror," so did Saikaku, whose *Great Mirror* of the same year (for which Yoshida executed the illustrations) consisted of a series of fictional narratives, albeit many of them were based on actual events and personages. By offering contextualized examples of the "way," both as it ought and ought not to be practiced, story collections by such authors as Saikaku, Ejima, Urushiya, and Nankai no Sanjin, along with other types of fiction, provided edification no less than entertainment. Authors explicitly acknowledged the didactic function of such works, as when Saikaku had his narrator declare that he had "attempted to reflect in this 'great mirror' all of the varied manifestations of male love," or Urushiya that his manuscript was meant to "light the path" of *shudō*.[76] To carry this image a step further, one might say that the logic of the mirror was a triangular one, in which the text not only offered up external objects, in condensed and illuminated form, to the gaze of the viewer, but allowed the reader, through the contemplation of its lens, to see his or her own figure reflected, and be tempted to mold appearance and behavior accordingly.

But who was this figure in the mirror? It is safe to assume that the majority of readers of the *shudō* text were male, not only for the reasons of literacy and socioeconomic power alluded to earlier, but because its subject matter, the pursuit of male-male erotic relations, allowed them to partake more fully of its rewards. This is not to say that women never read *shudō* works, or did not have their own means of enjoying or profiting from their contents; yet whatever such female reading strategies may have been, the magisterial voice of the *shudō* text did little to acknowledge them, instead

75. Yoshida Hanbei, *Nanshoku masukagami*, 1:285–291, 313, 333–337. For similar didactic works, see *Akaeboshi, Edo shunjū* 1 (1976) 38–43 (not to be confused with the identically named work of n. 64 above); Baijōken, *Yodarekake*, 4:45–64; Konoe, *Inu tsurezure*; Saiseiki, in *Nihon shomin bunka shiryō shūsei*, ed. Geinōshi kenkyūkai, 16 vols. (San'ichi shobō, 1973–1978), 9:113–130. Guidelines to the practice of *shudō* also appear in more general erotic manuals (i.e., those dealing also with male-female sexuality), for examples of which see Keisai, *Makura bunko hoi*, 1:100–102; Kōshokken Ariwara no Narihira, *Kōshoku tabimakura*, in *Nihon seiten taikan*, 1:55–58; Ōgokudō, *Shikidō kinpishō*, 2:48, 52; Tsukioka Settei, *Onna dairaku takarabako, Kinsei shomin bunka* 19 (1953):18–20.

76. Ihara, *Nanshoku ōkagami*, 39:320 (Schalow, *Great Mirror*, 56 [whence the quotation]); Urushiya, *Nanshoku kinometsuke*, 3:70.

addressing itself to the males who constituted its potential disciples. Insofar as the *shudō* tie consisted of a dyad, male readers, like male characters, may be seen as falling into two basic groups, corresponding to the *wakashu* and *nenja* halves of the erotic couple. That both were among the intended readership of the *shudō* text is illustrated by Yoshida's *Lucid Mirror*, which divided its advice for *wakashu* and *nenja* (or as Yoshida called the latter, *anibun* or older brother) into two separate sections. The text spoke to these parties in different ways; or more precisely, their distinct subject positions emerged as an effect of the text itself.

Since the *shudō* tie was asymmetric and hierarchical—that is to say, a relationship of power—it becomes necessary to ask which of the two parties' interests *shudō* texts served. Inasmuch as the *nenja*, as the senior male, was more likely to enjoy the economic and educational qualifications necessary to own or consume them, they are more appropriately described as a literature of the *nenja* than of the *wakashu*, just as *shudō* connoted the "way of loving youths" rather than the possession of youths themselves. Nor did they comprise a literature by the youth, since authors, too, generally fell into an age category that exceeded all but the most generous definitions of youthfulness: Saikaku, for instance, was some forty-two years old when he wrote his *Great Mirror*. The question remaining, then, is whether they represented a literature for the youth. In the sense that youths numbered (along with *nenja* and potential *nenja*) among their intended readers, the answer is, at least in part, yes. At the same time, it should be recognized that these intentions were hardly innocent, nor was the chief aim of such texts to promote the subjective interests of the youth himself.

Shudō texts configured the *wakashu* primarily from the viewpoint of his senior male admirers—that is to say, from the perspective of the *nenja*. More often than not, the youths portrayed in their pages were paragons of physical beauty and grace, their attributes conforming to a set of conventional tropes, some of which could be similarly employed to refer to feminine beauty, others used more or less exclusively of the *wakashu*. Such idealized depictions not only provided erotic stimulation for the adult male reader, but also furnished a benchmark against which to evaluate the charms of youths in real life. Because such a textual tradition existed, comparison to a legendary youth or famous actor might serve as a compliment whether or not the person who paid or received it had actually seen the individual in question. A manual such as Yoshida's supplied the *wakashu* with practical advice on how to attain these standards, offering him pointers on matters such as clothing, coiffure, cosmetics, and personal hygiene. The object in doing so, of course, was less to bring satisfaction to the youth himself—who naturally could not see himself without the aid of a mirror, whether literal or textual—than to the man who beheld him. It is telling, for instance, that Yoshida dispensed tips for enhancing youthful beauty not only in that portion of his work that addressed the *wakashu* directly, but also in a separate section that taught the *nenja* how to "groom" (*shitate*) a youth for his personal pleasure.[77]

Shudō texts provided models not only for the youth's appearance but also for his conduct. In doing so, they appropriated the *nenja's* function as role model and pedagogue while preserving the senior male's position of advantage within the relationship. Yoshida, for example, gave as one of the main reasons for educating the *wakashu* the fact that any faux pas that he committed would bring disgrace upon his lover.[78] Disgrace might even have mortal consequences, as when a tactless response by a youth already involved in a *shudō* relationship to a love letter from a third-party male led to enmity and dueling between the older rivals. The youth "well versed in the intricacies" (*wakeshiri*) of *shudō*, wrote Yoshida, knew how to dissuade the interloper with reason and compassion, even if his lover had instructed him to send a cold reply.[79] As the above example illustrates, the ethics of *shudō* called upon the youth to act at times in pursuance of a *nenja's* long-term welfare rather than the latter's immediate wishes. An analogous situation might arise when a lord's affection for one of his male favorites led him to neglect visiting his wife's quarters, and, by implication, his patriarchal as well as political duty to secure an heir. In a scenario echoing Confucian notions of the proper relationship between loyal minister and errant ruler, the *Lucid Mirror* advised the youth in such an instance to remonstrate with his sovereign even at the risk of losing his own life.[80] In *shudō* texts, the ideal *wakashu* always placed the interests of the *nenja* above his own.

How the *wakashu* might go about fulfilling his own desires, however, and what the nature of these desires might be, were questions that *shudō* texts seldom addressed.[81] Indeed, it was the very lack of desire on the part of the youth, except perhaps of a mercenary sort, that writers often portrayed as one of the distinguishing characteristics of *shudō*. Yoshida denied that "amorous desire" (*aiyoku*) arose on the part of the youth, regarding this asymmetry as one of *shudō's* greatest blessings—for the *nenja*, that is to say—since the powerful love that females conceived for males had led

77. Yoshida Hanbei, *Nanshoku masukagami*, 1:295–297, 311–313.
78. Yoshida Hanbei, *Nanshoku masukagami*, 1:291, 311.
79. Yoshida Hanbei, *Nanshoku masukagami*, 1:329.
80. Yoshida Hanbei, *Nanshoku masukagami*, 1:318–319.
81. *Saiseiki* is somewhat of an exception in that it devotes considerable attention

many a man to his ruin.[82] Similarly Nankai no Sanjin asked: "Who ever heard of [a man] being pined after [*kogaruru*] by a youth?"[83] It was the *nenja*, the "one who thought of," rather than the *wakashu*, who was defined by his subjective state of longing.

If the youth did not experience desire for the *nenja*, what was it, then, that led him to respond to the latter's affections? According to Yoshida, it was compassion (*nasake*), or what Paul Schalow has translated as "responsive love," along with a sense of obligation (*giri*).[84] In order to facilitate the pursuit of youths, it was necessary for the *shudō* text to instill these qualities in the young male. This function is nowhere more evident than in the earlier-mentioned *Shin'yūki*, which comprises an ethical tract on the value of compassion, heavily laced with both Buddhist and Confucian concepts.[85] The hermit-master depicted in the text chides "cold-hearted youths" who spurn their male suitors, predicting dire misfortune for them in this lifetime and karmic retribution in the next. "No youth," he asserts, "even one who is happy without a lover, should refuse a man who expresses a sincere interest in him."[86] Such a doctrine worked all too obviously in the interests of the *nenja*, even as it blithely negated the subjective wishes of the youth himself. The hermit seeks not only to expand the pool of youths available as erotic objects, but also to ensure its more egalitarian distribution among men of different social ranks: to reject a lover on the basis of wealth or status, he argues, runs contrary to the Confucian virtue of humanity (*jin*).[87] Through sophistry and barely disguised intimidation, the masterly voice of the text would deprive the youth of his greatest power over his senior: the power to refuse.

If the ideal youth of the *shudō* text was marked by his selfless compassion, it was connoisseurship that characterized the ideal *nenja*.[88] Although youths provided the object of his appreciation—like tea and its utensils in

---

(9:121–122) to the various stratagems that a youth might use to "hook" (*tsuru*) a *nenja*. It is possible, however, that the intent of the author was less to encourage such desires on the part of the *wakashu* than to equip the *nenja* with the knowledge necessary to recognize them.

82. Yoshida Hanbei, *Nanshoku masukagami*, 1:273–274.

83. Nankai no Sanjin, *Nanshoku yamaji no tsuyu*, 166.

84. Yoshida Hanbei, *Nanshoku masukagami*, 1:282.

85. On *Shin'yūki*, see also Schalow, "Spiritual Dimensions," which includes a complete translation.

86. *Shin'yūki*, 60:19–20 (Schalow, "Spiritual Dimensions," 88 [whence the quotation]).

87. *Shin'yūki*, 60:9 (Schalow, "Spiritual Dimensions," 80).

88. Schalow discusses the notion of sexual connoisseurship in his introduction to *Great Mirror*, passim.

the "way of tea" or incense in the "way of scent" (*kōdō*)—the connoisseurial ideal also implicated the *nenja* in a set of relationships with other adult males and with the erotic culture of *shudō* as a whole. In this sense, the *nenja* himself became an object of esthetic scrutiny, the *shudō* text functioning as a mirror of his appearance and conduct. Significantly, Yoshida urged the *nenja* to pay attention to oral hygiene not only because youths disliked men whose breath was not fresh (and would ostensibly be less responsive to their advances), but because "even a crude man [*kiotoko*] observing from the side might wonder, 'How can such an uncouth [*butashinami*] fellow expect to follow the path of *shudō* [literally, grasp this hilt]?' finding him laughable."[89] The author thereby insinuated into the picture the lateral gaze of the adult male peer group, with its power to admire or to ridicule.

No one wished to appear crude or uncouth, much less laughable. Yet though the imagined laughter came from the mouths of peers, it was the masterly voice of the text that claimed an authoritative knowledge of what was admirable and what was ridiculous. By imparting these criteria to the adult male reader, *shudō* texts derived a marketable value, enabling him to incorporate them into his personal style and to avoid potential embarrassment. "Elegance" (*kyasha*) and "stylishness" (*fūryū*), as Yoshida pointed out, characterized *shikidō* in both its forms, although there were subtle differences between the esthetic standards that prevailed in the "way of youths" and in the "way of women." Although there was room for debate—indeed, an entire literature devoted to it—as to which discipline was esthetically superior, the principle of value judgment in both was the same: at the positive end of the scale lay sophistication (designated by such terms as *sui* and *tōrimono*) and at the negative end boorishness (*yabo*).[90] The path of *shudō* could be seen as a gradual progress, guided by increasing knowledge and cultivation, from one end of the scale to the other; for this reason, it was not something that one mastered instantaneously, much less understood innately, but that one needed to "polish" (*migaku*).

When Yoshida spoke of the "way of women" (*nyodō*), what he had in mind was not male-female sexuality of a conjugal or reproductive variety—which was not generally conceived as a "way" that needed to be polished, and had little to do with stylishness or sophistication—but rather the professional services of female courtesans. The latter type of pleasure was mar-

89. Yoshida Hanbei, *Nanshoku masukagami*, 1:278.
90. On the ideal of sophistication in a male-female erotic context, see Cecilia Segawa Seigle, *Yoshiwara: The Glittering World of the Japanese Courtesan* (Honolulu: University of Hawaii Press, 1993), 131–133 and passim.

keted through an elaborate commercial infrastructure that centered on such urban licensed quarters as Edo's Yoshiwara and that gave rise to a distinctive erotic culture, surrounded by its own disciplinary texts.[91] Although the *shudō* construct, as noted earlier, embraced both amateur and mercantile forms of male-male eroticism, popular writings, particularly from the second half of the seventeenth century, devoted increasing attention to the latter, thereby reflecting as well as contributing to the rapid growth of commercialized urban *shudō* culture and its institutions. The intricacies of the "way" came to be more and more commonly, though still by no means exclusively, identified with the customs and fashions of this professional milieu, and especially the world of the actor-prostitute, whose "etiquette" (*sahō*), Yoshida commented in 1687, had come in recent times to rival that of the female courtesan in its elaborateness.[92] The difference between sophistication and boorishness depended to a large extent upon one's familiarity with this environment, and the circle of peers one sought to impress was often that of fellow clients, the favor of the demimonde serving as a barometer of one's success.

Within a commercialized framework, the *nenja* took on the guise of an erotic consumer. *Shudō* texts supplied him with the information necessary to partake of its pleasures in a knowledgeable and rewarding manner, thereby enhancing the value of the money he disbursed upon their procurement, or allowing him to relish them vicariously. In this sense, the publication and prostitution industries enjoyed a kind of symbiotic relationship, although their institutions were not for the most part directly linked. A prominent example may be found in the so-called actor evaluation book (*yakusha hyōbanki*), which assessed the merits of contemporary kabuki players, critiquing not only their histrionic talents but also their physical looks and proficiency in lovemaking.[93] Other works, belonging to the genre of the *saiken* or "detailed inspection," contained lists (*nayose*) of the more or less full-time male prostitutes whose services could be enjoyed at teahouses known as *kagemajaya*, and provided maps of the districts where such establishments were located. Real-life actors and prostitutes appeared as well in the pages of fiction, a narrative practice that profited from even as it amplified their professional reputations.

Shudō texts thus aided the male erotic connoisseur in selecting among a

91. On the history and culture of the Yoshiwara, see Seigle, *Yoshiwara*.
92. Yoshida Hanbei, *Nanshoku masukagami*, 1:300–301.
93. On the *yakusha hyōbanki* genre, see Shibayama, *Edo nanshoku kō: Akusho hen*, 129–138.

wide variety of objects and services, including both "amateur youths" (*ji-wakashu*) and their mercenary brethren. Since the path of *shikidō* was twain (to use Saikaku's phrase), however, he also enjoyed a choice of erotic disciplines. *Shudō* and *nyodō* were not mutually exclusive; it was possible and evidently quite common to partake of both types of pleasure, although not, as a rule, at one place and time.[94] The separate infrastructures of the two disciplines, at least in their commercialized form, as well as the different esthetic and ethical codes that prevailed in their milieux, made selection between them an often unavoidable, if always ongoing and reversible, process. Rather than constituting a permanent and inflexible choice, an erotic path could be traveled and retraced even in the course of a single day—as occurs, for instance, in a Saikaku story about a group of townsman revelers who purchase the favors of male prostitutes in the afternoon and move on to female entertainment in the evening, the title of which may be loosely translated as "Courtesans are better; no, actors are better" (*Jorō ga yoi to iu yarō ga yoi to iu*).[95] Saikaku's title captures the spirit of an entire genre of writing known to latter-day literary historians as the erotic debate (*danjo yūretsuron* or *yakeiron*), which provides a useful tool for understanding the complementary rather than antithetical nature of the two "ways."

Debates on the relative merits of male-male and male-female erotic pursuits may be found in the literary traditions of many cultures, including not only Japan, but also ancient Greece, medieval Europe, the Middle East, and China.[96] The classicist David Halperin has drawn our attention to the interpretive pitfalls that such texts pose for twentieth-century Western readers, who are apt to view them simply as arguments for or against "homo-

94. Pleasure-quarter etiquette deemed it problematic to mix male-male and male-female erotic entertainment. A mid-eighteenth-century *senryū* (*Haifū yanagidaru shūi*, in *Nihon meicho zenshū*, 26:840) compares the esthetic clash that such a combination was felt to engender to *mamakodate*, a game using black and white pieces, although the writer may be hinting here that the contrast also provoked a certain amount of charm. According to one of the characters in Anayoshi's *Hōshin kōwa* (in *Sharebon taisei*, 9:300), a 1780 *sharebon* that depicts just such an outing, another concern was that female prostitutes might feel a greater attraction to their male counterparts than toward their patrons—certainly a common enough theme in woodblock prints. Iwata Jun'ichi ("Edo kagema no matsuro," in *Honchō nanshoku kō*, 215) maintains that in the teahouses of Edo's Yushima district it became fashionable for female geisha and *kagema* to entertain together only in the first decades of the nineteenth century.

95. Ihara Saikaku, *Saikaku okimiyage*, in *Nihon koten bungaku zenshū*, 40: 609–615.

96. See David M. Halperin, "Historicizing the Subject of Desire: Sexual Preferences and Erotic Identities in the Pseudo-Lucianic *Erôtes*," in *Foucault and the*

sexuality." As the earlier exercise in translation showed, "homosexuality" was not a concept that Edo-period Japanese would immediately have understood, in part because male-male and female-female erotic behaviors were not seen as having anything to do with each other.[97] Yet even if we overlook this fact, it is still all too easy to read such works as reflecting a rigid dichotomy in masculine sexual identities, especially since their authors place arguments for *nanshoku* and *joshoku* in the mouths of two separate and indeed antagonistic factions. To adopt such an interpretation, however, is to misapprehend entirely their nature.

The pleasure that erotic debates held for the reader, it seems clear, lay less in the championing of one or the other erotic option than in the pleasure of debate itself. Although narrative convention sometimes demanded that one side prevail in the end, the arguments presented by both are often equally convincing; after all, if the victory of either had been a foregone conclusion, what would be the point of debating in the first place? As Hiraga Gennai pointed out in the eighteenth century, the debate in question had gone on for ages without resolution, nor was a victory likely to emerge in the future.[98] There was room in such texts to accommodate a number of readings and subjectivities, and their contents might easily leave a more lasting impression than their conclusions. For example, while *Denbu monogatari*, the mid-seventeenth-century work that is commonly cited as the progenitor of the genre, awards its laurels in the end to the *nyodō* faction, the title's characterization of them as "boors" (*denbu*), in contrast to the "elegant" (*kyasha*) aficionados of *shudō*, conveys a much greater sense of ambiguity.[99] Similarly, the earlier-cited litany of contrasts between mouth-blackening women

Writing of History, ed. Jan Goldstein (Oxford: Blackwell, 1994), 19–34, which provides a list of sources. Depending upon how they are defined, erotic debates from the Edo period number at least a dozen; additional examples are known by name, but no longer survive.

97. Unlike the late antique (possibly fourth-century C.E.) Greek text analyzed by Halperin, none of the Edo-period debates that I have examined draws a parallel between male-male and female-female eroticism, suggesting that the conceptual association between the two has considerably older roots in Western than in Japanese discourse.

98. Hiraga Gennai, <*Nanshoku saiken*> *Mitsu no asa*, in *Nihon shomin bunka shiryō shūsei*, 9:103.

99. Even more ambiguous is Shōsaiō's *Gengenkyō*, in which the *nanshoku* faction loses the formal part of the debate, but whose narrator closes with an exhortation to "leave behind the lesser vehicle [*shōjō*] of courtesan pleasures and attain greater enlightenment in this path [i.e., *shudō*]" (3:311). For an earlier polemical work on male-male sexuality, see the fifteenth-century *Nyake chōrō monogatari*

and whisker-plucking youths in Saikaku's *Great Mirror* does not give the latter party nearly so indisputable an advantage as the narrative voice of the text, which is doubtless intended to be ironic, pretends.[100]

Nor did such debates always declare a formal winner. In *Iro monogatari* (Tales of Eros; mid–seventeenth century), an elderly arbiter, after hearing the impassioned arguments of the two sides, counsels that the wisest course is to follow both paths in moderation, thereby helping to prevent overindulgence in either. Similarly, in Nishizawa Ippū's 1708 *Yakei tomojamisen* (Friendly Shamisen of Actors and Courtesans), a moderator ends the dispute by affirming the equal validity of both "ways," encouraging each party merely to be devout in his chosen discipline.[101] Even in those debates that do assign a formal victor, the conclusions reached do not always apply equally to all strata of society. In *Denbu monogatari,* for instance, the victorious *joshoku* faction concedes that male-male erotic pursuits are well suited to the higher circles of the warrior aristocracy, while their counterparts in Azuma no Kamiko's 1707 *Fūryū hiyokudori* (Stylish Pair of Wing-Sharing Birds) deem them perfectly appropriate for the members of the Buddhist clergy.[102]

It is important not to lose sight of the fundamentally rhetorical nature of the genre. The speakers of the erotic debate do not so much personify a dichotomy in social identities as provide a device for the articulation of various esthetic judgments that the male erotic subject might be called upon to make in his pursuit of ultimate connoisseurship. The arguments that they enunciate might be combined in different ways by different individuals, or even by the same individual at different moments in time; it is possible, for instance, to read the two points of view expressed in the title of Saikaku's story ("Courtesans Are Better; No, Actors Are Better") as issuing from the mouth of one and the same person. The two sides in such debates merely defined the poles of the erotic field, without requiring that readers align themselves exclusively with one or the other. At times, the very extremity of both positions seems intended for humorous effect, and it is precisely because of the rhetorical excesses preceding it, one cannot help but feel, that

(Imanishi Makoto, "<Shiryō honkoku> Matsudaira bunko *Nyake chōrō monogatari," Yamanobe no michi* 9 [1962]: 73–78), which constitutes less of a debate than a one-sided (anti-*nyake*) diatribe.

100. Christopher Drake makes this point cogently in "Mirroring Saikaku," *Monumenta Nipponica* 46 (1991): 518.

101. *Iro monogatari,* 4:188–197; Nishizawa, *Yakei tomojamisen,* 2:320–321.

102. Azuma no Kamiko, *Fūryū hiyokudori,* 5:116; *Denbu monogatari,* 37:128 (Leupp, *Male Colors,* 208–209).

the moderate voice of the arbiter in *Iro monogatari* and *Yakei tomojamisen* is able to persuade.

One would likewise be amiss to construe the heated rhetoric of the erotic debate as mirroring a widespread hostility in social relations between those who engaged in different forms of pleasure. The arbiter in *Yakei tomojamisen* notes that, although the denizens of Yoshiwara might sometimes curse men who chose to patronize actors, just as actors consigned to hell those who frequented their female counterparts, such expressions were merely a reflection of "professional rivalry" (*shokugataki*) and should not be paid serious heed.[103] Erotic debates also recall another form of institutional rivalry—namely, that among religious denominations. Many of them liken the two erotic paths to competing religious disciplines, such as Shōsaiō's mid-eighteenth-century *Gengenkyō* (Sutra of Opaque Wisdom), which pits a Cult of Female Prostitutes (*jorō shūmon*) against a Cult of Male Prostitutes (*nanshō shūmon*). A famous seventeenth-century exchange of broadsides among spokesmen for the Nichiren, Tendai, and Jōdo sects of Buddhism provides inspiration for several works in this genre, beginning with Nishizawa's 1708 *Fūryū sangokushi* (Stylish Romance of the Three Kingdoms), while Ejima's 1711 *Keisei kintanki* (Courtesans Must Not Have Short Tempers) makes reference to an earlier religious contest held in Azuchi castle in 1579 under the auspices of the hegemon Oda Nobunaga.[104]

The sectarian metaphor is suggestive, however, not only because of the sense of rivalry that it conveys but also because it does not preclude the possibility of peaceful coexistence and even commingling. Syncretism constituted a far more respectable tradition in Japanese than in Judeo-Christian theology, and the perennial religious strife of medieval times had dwindled by the Edo period chiefly to the level of textual polemics. Thus, after hearing the representatives of *shudō* and *nyodō* compare their disciplines respectively to Buddhism and Shinto, the arbiter in *Yakei tomojamisen* points out that the latter faiths are "no further apart than waves and water" (*suiha no hedate*) and calls for a prompt end to the debaters' wrangling.[105] Just as Shinto shrines and Buddhist temples often stood in the same compound, authors such as Ejima and Nishizawa were content to place stories about actors and about courtesans side by side in the same collection, as were readers, presumably, to read about them. While religious zealots,

103. Nishizawa, *Yakei tomojamisen*, 2:321.

104. On the influence of the religious debate, see Noma Kōshin, "Kaisetsu," in *Nihon koten bungaku taikei*, 91:22–25.

105. Nishizawa, *Yakei tomojamisen*, 2:321.

to whom the authors of the debates often likened their speakers, might choose to focus their devotion upon a single creed, there was nothing to prevent the ordinary practitioner from professing more than one faith, as many Japanese in fact did. Likewise in the temporal realm, an individual might acquire proficiency in several disciplines, becoming, say, an adept server of tea as well as a skilled poet. It was only because *shudō* and *nyodō* existed in close proximity, in other words, that their mutual borders required negotiation.

THE BOUNDARIES OF *SHUDŌ*

Of Konishi's five criteria of "wayness," only that of universality remains to be addressed. Because a "way" was immanent and transcendent, it was in theory present in all times and places. Let us take another of Nankai no Sanjin's stories by way of illustration. In it, a Kyoto man named Tagasuke, having already mastered the "profoundest secrets of Japanese *shudō*," conceives a desire to experience the "taste of Chinese youths." He befriends some Chinese merchants in Nagasaki and succeeds in making his way to the continent, where he is presented at the court of the Chinese emperor. Wearing a Chinese-style headdress (*tōkan*) over his unmistakably Japanese shaved pate, Tagasuke disports himself night and day with the youths of the emperor's harem, coming to the conclusion that, "Whether it's China or Japan, the gist [*shukō*] of this way never changes."[106] Beneath external differences of place, culture (symbolized here by the headdress), and time (ironically, even the character used for "China" is that of the long-extinct Tang dynasty), the substance of *shudō*, implies the story, is constant and universal.

Tagasuke's specific desire to visit China may be understood at several levels. Though Korea, for example, lay geographically closer, Edo-period writers displayed relatively little interest in its male-male erotic culture, although, conversely, the conspicuous prevalence of male prostitution in Japan made a strong impression upon at least one eighteenth-century Korean visitor.[107] Despite its relative distance, China loomed larger in the Edo-period

---

106. Nankai no Sanjin, *Nanshoku yamaji no tsuyu*, 182–186.
107. Choi Park-Kwang, "Japanese Sexual Customs and Cultures Seen from the Perspective of the Korean Delegation to Japan," in *Imaging/Reading Eros: Proceedings for the Conference, Sexuality and Edo Culture, 1750–1850*, ed. Sumie Jones (Bloomington: East Asian Studies Center, Indiana University, 1996), 76–78; Eiko Ikegami, *The Taming of the Samurai* (Cambridge: Harvard University Press, 1995), 306.

imagination, figuring not only as an exotic other but also as a venerable point of origin for numerous cultural practices that later made their way to Japan. Although restrictions imposed by the Tokugawa shogunate made most travel outside the country practically impossible—Nankai no Sanjin, we may note, ultimately reveals Tagasuke's trip to be a dream—Japanese familiarity with Chinese texts offered ample proof that male-male erotic practices enjoyed a long tradition in that civilization's history. Such knowledge provided writers on *shudō* with a useful strategy for establishing the authority of their "way," since the citing of Chinese precedents had long functioned as a conventional means of legitimating native phenomena. The association of male-male eroticism with China was further reinforced by the folk belief that Kūkai had originally introduced *shudō* from the continent, and in a sense Tagasuke's imaginary voyage duplicates that earlier journey.[108]

Edo-period knowledge of male-male sexual practices outside Japan was not limited, however, to the Chinese cultural sphere. Buddhist texts revealed the historical existence of such practices in India as well; indeed, narratives of *shudō*'s origins often place that holy land at the beginning of their chronicle. There was a recognition among Edo-period authors that, in what were often called the "three countries" (*sangoku*; in their conventional order, India, China, and Japan), designations for and attitudes toward male-male eroticism differed, so that what some Buddhist sutras characterized as a "mistaken way" (*hidō*), Ming-dynasty Chinese might jocularly refer to as "familiarity with bricks" (Japanese: *asen*; Chinese: *xia zhuan*), or Fujianese locals as "planting tail" (*saibi*; Chinese [Mandarin]: *zaiwei*).[109] Even in Japan, noted Baijōken in 1653, the most common term for male-male eroticism had changed in recent years from *nyakudō* to *shudō*.[110] Nonetheless, in the words of an earlier writer, although designations for the "way" might vary, its "uses" were everywhere the same.[111]

Although Western observers sometimes regarded Japan as pursuing a policy of national seclusion, isolationism was never so literal as to prevent Edo-period Japanese from gaining a familiarity with European male-male sex-

108. Chinese of the same era sometimes associated male-male sexual practices with a barbarous Japan. In the mid-eighteenth-century novel *Yesou puyan* (cited in Setagaya Uboku, "Shina no ryūyōheki," *Kōgai*, June 1926, 22), for example, a male Chinese envoy barely escapes being raped by a figure who is apparently modeled after the sixteenth-century hegemon and would-be ruler of China Toyotomi Hideyoshi.

109. Some authors assigned *asen* alternate characters that gave it the meaning "pushing bricks."

110. Baijōken, *Yodarekake*, 4:48.

111. Ijiri, *Nyake kanjinchō*, 33b:19.

ual culture. "Sodomy" had in fact been one of the central preoccupations of the first Western visitors to the archipelago, the Christian missionaries who began arriving in the mid–sixteenth century. In the eyes of these visitors, the prevalence of male-male erotic practices, particularly among the Buddhist clergy, furnished proof of the diabolical character of the local religion and of the heathen's need for conversion.[112] The term *nyakudō* is attested in one of the oldest European dictionaries of the Japanese language, the 1603–1604 *Vocabvlario da lingoa de Iapam,* which was compiled primarily for the benefit of Portuguese Jesuit missionaries. Catholic confessors asked their Japanese converts whether they had engaged in its pursuit, which, together with masturbation, went against God's commandment.[113] Nevertheless, the imposition of harsh strictures against Christianity, which became increasingly systematized after the dynastic founder Tokugawa Ieyasu's expulsion order of 1614, put a halt to the open dissemination of such doctrines for most of the Edo period. Rather, it was chiefly through the avenue of trade, and specifically the Dutch and Chinese merchant settlements at Nagasaki— not coincidentally, the city that serves as a key stepping-stone for Tagasuke's imaginary journey—that knowledge of the West and of its erotic culture continued to reach Japanese ears.

Through their reading as well as personal contact with Europeans, eighteenth- and nineteenth-century scholars of "Dutch learning" (*rangaku*) were well aware that male-male erotic practices existed among the "red-haired barbarians" of the West, and through them this knowledge sometimes permeated into the realm of popular discourse. Hiraga Gennai, who was a keen enthusiast of "Dutch learning," noted in his 1768 "detailed inspection" *Mitsu no asa* (Three Courts) that *nanshoku* was to be found not only in Japan, India, and China, but also in Holland and Jakarta—the last, of course, being a Dutch colony.[114] At least one European term for male-male eroticism, transliterated into Japanese as *besu,* seems to have gained a bit of currency in mid-eighteenth-century Edo, despite the fact that, as the au-

---

112. For examples of these perceptions, see Michael Cooper, ed., *They Came to Japan: An Anthology of European Reports on Japan, 1543–1640* (Berkeley: University of California Press, 1965), 46, 47, 315, 318, 319, 322.

113. Shibayama, *Edo nanshoku kō: Akusho hen,* 207–209.

114. Hiraga Gennai, *Mitsu no asa,* 9:111. Similarly, Morishima Nakayoshi (*Bankoku shinwa,* 5 vols. [Edo: Suwaraya Ichibei], 4:4), a prominent scholar of "Dutch learning," noted in 1789 that *nanshoku* was prohibited by the Spanish overlords of Luzon (the Philippines). For the observations of Daikokuya Kōdayū, a late eighteenth-century castaway, concerning *nanshoku* in the Russian empire, see Timon Screech [Taimon Sukurīchi], *Ō-Edo ijin ōrai,* trans. Takayama Hiroshi, Maruzen bukkusu, no. 36 (Maruzen, 1995), 119.

thor of *Gengenkyō* put it, the expression had originated in a "vulgar country at the ends of the earth" (*iyashiki hashi no kuni*).[115] By the close of the
Edo period, some Japanese possessed a surprisingly detailed, though not always factually correct, knowledge of "sodomy" and its persecution in Europe. A notable example may be found in the writings of Yamamura Saisuke,
whose 1848 *Seiyō zakki* (Miscellaneous Jottings on the West) includes a
lengthy account of the biblical cities of Sodom and Gomorrah, a description
of the Dutch fruit known as the "Sodom's apple," and the claim that in Italy
(by which Yamamura may have had in mind the circuses of ancient Rome)
the punishment for individuals who engaged in *nanshoku* was mutilation
by wild animals.[116]

The realm of *shudō* in fact extended far beyond the geographic boundaries of the world as twentieth-century cartographers would come to define
them. Maps of the Edo period commonly featured such legendary places as
the "Isle of Women" (Nyōgogashima) or "Woman Land" (Nyoninkoku),
whose natives were believed to be exclusively female. The reader of the 1820
Zatto ichiran (General Overview), a work belonging to a genre of fiction
known as the *sharebon*—quaintly rendered by James Araki as "books for
men of mode"—would thus not have been surprised to learn of the existence of an equivalent "Isle of Men" (Onokojima).[117] Well over a century
earlier, the misogynistic narrator of Saikaku's *Great Mirror* had voiced a
wish that Japan itself might become just such an all-male realm, in which
the "way of youths" would reign supreme.[118] For some authors of the *sharebon*, the milieu of urban male prostitution already presented such a world

115. Shōsaiō, *Gengenkyō*, 3:312. The exact European term and its language of
origin are unclear. Screech (*Ō-Edo ijin ōrai*, 118–119) notes that scholars of "Dutch
learning" were familiar with a Russian word (transliterated as *zoppaebyōto*) for *nanshoku*, as well as with a Dutch expression for *oyama* (transliterated as *yari*), which
referred in Japan to male kabuki actors who specialized in female parts and were
sometimes also available for prostitution. In both cases, the original European expression is unclear.
116. Yamamura Saisuke, *Seiyō zakki*, 4 vols. (Edo: Suzuki bun'enkaku, 1848),
1:27–30.
117. James T. Araki, "*Sharebon*: Books for Men of Mode," *Monumenta Nipponica*
24 (1969): 31–45; Suisaishi, *Zatto ichiran*, in *Sharebon taisei*, 26:248. In a similar
vein, Hayashi Yoshikazu (*Enpon Edo bungakushi* [Kawade shobō, 1991], 134) cites
a circa-1775 work (<*Ikai kikei*> *Oshō bobo*) featuring an all-male "Country of Rear-
Lovers" (Kōkokuku). Ejima Kiseki (*Ukiyo oyaji katagi*, in *Hachimonjiyabon zenshū*, 7:458) likens a diminutive male prostitute to a *yarō* from the "Isle of Dwarves"
(Kobitojima), another land commonly appearing on Edo-period maps.
118. Ihara, *Nanshoku ōkagami*, 39:596 (Schalow, *Great Mirror*, 310).

in microcosm (notwithstanding the fact that it received the patronage of female clients as well). Santō Kyōden's revision of Angyūsai's 1754 *Kari tsūshō kō* (Treatise on Trade with the Flowery Quarters), which in turn parodied a geography text by the early scholar of "Dutch learning" Nishikawa Joken, thus described Kyoto's chief district for male prostitution, Miyagawachō, as a distant kingdom that had been founded by the monk Kūkai, paid allegiance in the present day to the celebrated kabuki actor Sanogawa Ichimatsu, and was haunted by a ferocious creature known as the *kongō*—an attendant to the male prostitute whom popular writings stereotypically vilified for his greed.[119]

Writers on *shudō* envisioned its existence even beyond the terrestrial plane. The Buddhist notion of *rokudō* identified six realms of being, ranging from the deities of heaven to the demons of hell, with the various worlds of humans, asuras (a race of titans), animals, and hungry ghosts (*gaki*) occupying the intermediate tiers.[120] The "way of youths" manifested itself not only in the human realm, but also at other levels of this ontology. At the highest, folk belief linked male-male erotic pursuits with various Buddhist deities, in particular Monju (Sanskrit: Mañjuśrī), a patron bodhisattva of wisdom, whom legend held to have given Kūkai personal instruction in the "way" during the latter's sojourn in China, and an alternate form of whose name (Monjushiri) fortuitously incorporated the Japanese word for "buttocks" (*shiri*). Urushiya attributed male-male erotic ties also to such divinities as Bishamonten, Fudō (Sanskrit: Acala), and Yakushi (Sanskrit: Bhaiṣajya-guru), writing that, among the principal figures (*honzon*) of the Buddhist pantheon (whom he implicitly conceived as male), there was not a single one without his favorite "boy" (*dōji*).[121]

At the opposite end of the scale, the path of *shudō* descended into the farthest reaches of hell. This conceptual association can be traced as far back as the tenth century, when the monk Genshin, drawing upon a Theravada text known as the Sutra of the Remembrance of the True Law (*Saddharma-smṛty-upasthāna*), described a subdivision of hell—or, more precisely, of Shugō Jigoku (Sanskrit: Saṃghāta), one of eight Buddhist hells—where

119. Ishizuka, *Okaba yūkaku kō*, 1:55. For a similar portrayal of Miyagawachō as a "Land of *Nanshoku*" (Nanshokkoku), see Kōman Sensei, *Rokuchō ichiri*, in *Sharebon taisei*, 12:64–65.

120. On the concept of *rokudō*, see William R. LaFleur, *The Karma of Words: Buddhism and the Literary Arts in Medieval Japan* (Berkeley: University of California Press, 1983), 26–59.

121. Urushiya, *Nanshoku kinometsuke*, 3:73. See also chap. 2, n. 7, with respect to Shinto deities.

males who had fornicated with other males would burn in each other's embraces or, if they tried to escape from this spot, would plummet from a cliff, to be devoured by fire-breathing birds and foxes.[122] Edo-period authors, too, attempted to chart this infernal landscape, but with intentions that were clearly more titillating than pious. Perhaps the most detailed account is to be found in the 1715 tale *Shin sayoarashi* (New Storm at Night), which depicts the myriad agonies that awaited patrons who failed to observe proper etiquette when frequenting houses of male prostitution, such as those who borrowed but did not return umbrellas, who would be subject to incessant rain, or clients who poked holes in the establishment's sliding partitions (*shōji*), who were fated to be pilloried in them after their demise.[123] The torments of hell served in this case less to discourage the reader from engaging in male-male sexual practices than to encourage their pursuit according to certain professional norms.[124] The afterworld also provides a setting for Hiraga's best-selling satire *Nenashigusa* (Rootless Grass; 1763), in which Enma (Sanskrit: Yama), a guardian king of hell, dispatches a *kappa* or water goblin to kidnap a kabuki actor with whom he has fallen in love, and whose sequel of 1769 features an erotic debate pitting the spirit of Kūkai against other infernal deities.[125]

On a more quotidian plane, how did Edo-period writers map *shudō* onto the geography of their own archipelago? Here again, Nankai no Sanjin's story is suggestive. The author describes Tagasuke, who had exhausted the pleasures of "Japanese *shudō*" (*Nihon shudō*), as being familiar not only with the "stage boys" (*butaiko*) of the three metropolises, but also with the non-professional youths of "warrior houses, temple precincts, towns, and rural

122. Genshin, *Ōjō yōshū*, vol. 6 of *Nihon shisō taikei*, 17 (trans. A. K. Reischauer under the title "Genshin's Ojo Yoshu: Collected Essays on Birth into Paradise," *Transactions of the Asiatic Society of Japan*, 2d ser., 7 [1930]: 33). For another translation of this passage, see Childs, *Rethinking Sorrow*, 47. On Buddhist notions of hell, see Daigan Matsunaga and Alicia Matsunaga, *The Buddhist Concept of Hell* (New York: Philosophical Library, 1972).

123. *Shin sayoarashi*, in *Nihon meicho zenshū*, 9:719–756.

124. Similarly, *Yarō jitsugokyō* (in Ishizuka, *Okaba yūkaku kō*, 1:80) promised infernal punishment for readers who did not heed its lessons, while Shōsaiō's *Gengenkyō* (3:305) asserted that a place in hell awaited those who hated male prostitutes.

125. Hiraga Gennai, *Nenashigusa*, in *Nihon koten bungaku taikei*, 55:33–94; Hiraga Gennai, *Nenashigusa kōhen*, in *Nihon koten bungaku taikei*, 55:95–151. Enma appears in the role of a love-smitten *nenja* as early as the medieval *kyōgen* play *Yao*, on which see Dōmoto, *Nanshoku engekishi*, 27–34. Taigasha Kihō again portrays him as a devotee of *shudō* in his 1772 *Sanzen sekai iro shugyō* (in *Tokugawa bungei ruijū*, 3:278–281).

districts"—in other words, the inhabitants of every social sphere. For Nankai no Sanjin, the most conspicuous regional distinction divides metropolis from hinterland—that is to say, the "three ports" (*sanganotsu*) of Edo, Kyoto, and Osaka on the one hand, and the rest of the country on the other. Because the publication industry was based in these metropolitan centers, the gaze of the *shudō* text tended to extend outward from the former to the latter. Although urban authors portrayed the "way of youths" as penetrating into the farthest reaches of the country—the kabuki actor Segawa Kikunojō II possessed ardent admirers even in the distant castle-town of Matsumae (on today's island of Hokkaido, then on the very fringes of Tokugawa hegemony), notes Hiraga—their works generally implied that its most elaborate and sophisticated forms, personified in Nankai no Sanjin's story by the figure of the "stage boy" or actor-prostitute, were to be found in a metropolitan setting.[126] Fujimoto Kizan writes, for instance, of a young man he met during a 1674 visit to Kumamoto that the provincial lad was pitifully ignorant of the "ways of eros" (*shikidō*), in contrast to his peers fortunate enough to be born in Kamigata, the highly urbanized region around Kyoto and Osaka, who were without exception versed in the intricacies of both *joshoku* and *nanshoku*.[127]

What is especially striking about Fujimoto's observation is the fact that the very area in which he traveled—namely, the southwestern island of Kyushu—was one that in the Meiji period (see chapter 4) would gain a notoriety not for the poverty of its male-male erotic culture, but rather for an unseemly abundance. Edo-period writers, by contrast, did not conventionally associate male-male sexual practices with any particular region of the archipelago. For them, the most significant boundaries on the erotic landscape were social rather than geographic, as Nankai no Sanjin's litany of "warrior houses, temple precincts, towns, and rural districts" illustrates. Each of these spaces was the preserve of a distinct social class—warrior, priest, townsman, and peasant—and Nankai no Sanjin's enumeration of them as archetypal sites of *shudō* suggests that he regarded the "way" not only as broadly distributed throughout Japanese society, but as differing subtly in character among the various groups. As a way of exploring the class dimensions of *shudō* discourse, let us examine Nankai no Sanjin's four constituencies in order.

The prominent position that Nankai no Sanjin accords "warrior houses"

126. Hiraga Gennai, *Nenashigusa kōhen*, 55:108.
127. Fujimoto Kizan, *<Kanpon> Shikidō ōkagami*, ed. Noma Kōshin (Kyoto: Yūzan shobō, 1973), 500–501.

is by no means accidental. Samurai, who made up somewhere between 5 and 10 percent of the population of the archipelago, formed the dominant social elite of the Edo period, and held a tight grip on the reins of government. Their place in Nankai no Sanjin's list mirrors the official ideology of "four estates," a similarly quadripartite division of society, which asserted the precedence of samurai over, in descending order, peasants, artisans, and merchants. Nankai no Sanjin's privileging of warriors was a reflection not only of their elite status, but of a link that popular discourse commonly made between the "way of youths" and the ways of this particular class. Samurai are a conspicuous presence in the pages of the *shudō* text (Saikaku devotes nearly the entire first half of his *Great Mirror* to them), while conversely, accounts of warrior life make frequent reference to male-male eroticism. One of Nankai no Sanjin's characters, the townsman Takujūrō, goes so far as to describe *nanshoku* as the "flower of the military estate" (*bumon no hana*).[128]

Yet just as Takujūrō's remark falls from the lips of a townsman, the image of warrior culture that *shudō* texts helped to disseminate was to a large extent a product of the commoner's brush. Some authors, including Hiraga, the poet Bashō, and the dramatist Chikamatsu Monzaemon, sprang from samurai roots, yet the majority wrote about a class to which they did not themselves belong, and toward which many in their audience felt a certain amount of awe. *Shudō* texts therefore tell us more about the perceptions and expectations of nonelites than about the lifestyles and values of samurai themselves, which varied greatly with individual circumstance and underwent significant changes over the course of the Edo period. For a more nuanced picture of samurai society, and of the place that male-male sexuality held within it, it is necessary to compare popular writings with other types of documentary evidence, including diaries, letters, and other texts produced outside the framework of the publishing industry; such an undertaking, however, lies outside the scope of the present study.[129] Samurai ideology also received expression in legal discourse, which the following chapter will examine in detail. Here, the discussion will focus on the world of the warrior as it was constructed in popular texts, keeping in mind that representation did not always correspond to lived reality.

Popular representations of samurai *shudō* implicated its practice in a class-

---

128. Nankai no Sanjin, *Nanshoku yamaji no tsuyu*, 46.
129. For a broader survey of male-male eroticism in samurai culture, see Ujiie, *Bushidō to erosu*.

specific code of masculine honor. The central ideal of this code was the notion of *giri*, which Caryl Callahan has defined as the "complex of obligations which the individual samurai was honor-bound to fulfill," even at the cost of his own life.[130] Although townsmen and other social classes had their own versions of *giri*, the demands of honor were seen to fall most heavily upon male members of the warrior estate. As portrayed in popular texts, the *giri* ideal informed *shudō* practices among samurai in several ways. First of all, *shudō* ties provided a means of transmitting the values and skills essential to the pursuit of *giri* from the senior to the junior party, thereby serving a pedagogical function. According to Yoshida, it was the *nenja*'s task to instruct the samurai youth in the military arts (*budō*), which included not only such practical accomplishments as fencing, lancemanship, archery, and horseback riding, but, most importantly, the mental attitude (*kokorogake*) and etiquette befitting of a warrior.[131] At the same time, the *shudō* bond was supposed to stimulate the cultivation of honor on the part of the *nenja* by encouraging him to strive in order to prove himself worthy of his partner; in this sense, *shudō* was believed to have a mutually ennobling effect. The *wakashu* and *nenja* were expected, furthermore, to assist each other in fulfilling the various obligations that made up the social fabric of *giri*, ranging from their primary responsibility as retainers to a lord to such private matters as duels and vendettas (*katakiuchi*), all of which furnished favorite themes of popular fiction. Finally, the *shudō* tie was itself construed as a form of personal obligation subject to the codes of *giri*, demanding a loyalty no less exacting than that of the lord-vassal bond itself.

Popular discourse often linked warrior *shudō* with violence and death. A mid-eighteenth-century verse thus warns: "*Nanshoku* leads to dangerous obligations" (*Abunai giri no dekiru nanshoku*).[132] Certainly this is the impression one would get from reading popular accounts of samurai *shudō*, in which swordplay is frequently a key element of the drama, and death, whether at the hands of another or through ritual disembowelment (*seppuku*), an all too familiar denouement. Although the reaction of contemporary audiences is a difficult matter to judge, it is likely that such representations appealed to samurai and townsman readers in different ways. For townsmen, who were prohibited as a class from wearing the long sword that

130. Caryl Ann Callahan, introduction to *Tales of Samurai Honor*, by Ihara Saikaku, trans. Callahan, Monumenta Nipponica Monograph no. 57 (Sophia University, 1981), 10.

131. Yoshida Hanbei, *Nanshoku masukagami*, 1:291–292, 315.

132. *Mutamagawa*, 26:49.

was the most prized possession of the samurai male, they no doubt underscored the "otherness" of warrior culture, offering a comfortable glimpse
into a world where the pursuit of *shudō* involved greater (or at least different) risks than in their own. But even for the samurai among their readers, the world portrayed in such works stood at a considerable remove from
daily experience, not least because the setting for such narratives lay often
in the historical past. For all their blood and gore, the days in which their
ancestors had routinely braved death for the sake of honor (the historical
accuracy of this portrait is, of course, open to question) may have evoked a
sense of nostalgia among urbanized warriors living in an era of peace where
the sword was found more often in the pawnshop than on the battlefield,
giri was a largely formulaic notion, and male-male eroticism was increasingly a commodity for sale.

In this masculine world of honor and violence, women enjoyed only a marginal place. The social obligations that constituted *giri* were directed primarily
toward other samurai males, while the sense of pride or *ikiji* that fueled the
pursuit of honor, and which Yoshida defined as the very essence of *shudō*,
was understood to be a fundamentally masculine trait.[133] Such legendary warrior women as Tomoe Gozen notwithstanding, females not only were excluded as a rule from direct participation in warfare, but were perceived as a
threat to the martial valor of their menfolk. The samurai male who formed
ties with women, wrote Yoshida, would be less inclined to risk death on the
battlefield.[134] (Never mind that such an argument testified more to the power
of men's attraction to women than to the latter's unworthiness, or that by
the time that Yoshida wrote these words, Japan's battlefields had been silent
for many decades.) The obverse of warrior homosociality and androcentrism
was thus a profound misogyny. It is no coincidence that many of the
"woman-haters" portrayed in *shudō* texts are warriors, their abhorrence for
the female sex at times assuming hyperbolic proportions. Urushiya, for example, describes one samurai male who would not eat a certain type of rice
dumpling (*kusamochi*) because it was associated with the annual Girls' Fes-
tival, while in *Fūryū hiyokudori*, a masterless swordsman (*rōnin*) proclaims
that, had he known then what he knows now of women, he would never have
suckled at his mother's breast.[135] Among his rationales for avoiding women,

133. Yoshida Hanbei, *Nanshoku masukagami*, 1:276.
134. Yoshida Hanbei, *Nanshoku masukagami*, 1:269.
135. Azuma no Kamiko, *Fūryū hiyokudori*, 5:90; Urushiya, *Nanshoku kinometsuke*, 3:95–96. Azuma no Kamiko borrows practically verbatim a similar passage in
Saikaku (Ihara, *Nanshoku ōkagami*, 39:316 [Schalow, *Great Mirror*, 52–53]).

the latter also cites the danger of menstrual pollution (*tsuki no sawari*), a Shinto-related belief that was by no means limited to the warrior class.[136]

The stalwart warrior-misogynist represents only one of several samurai types to appear in the pages of the *shudō* text. Within the samurai class, there existed a wide range of status groups, the hierarchy among them more minutely graded and their socioeconomic circumstances no less varied than the "four estates" themselves. At the top of the pyramid stood the warrior aristocracy, including the shogun, his higher-ranking vassals, and the several hundred daimyo. Among this elitest of elites, popular discourse held male-male erotic ties not only to be widespread, but to assume a highly conspicuous and even ostentatious form. The object of affection here was usually represented as a page boy or *koshō*, as in the case of the hairy-shinned attendants we saw favored by the "eccentric" daimyo of the 1708 story. The figure of the page, bedecked in finery and accompanying his lord on flower-viewing expeditions and other refined pursuits, holds an attraction even for the "boorish" proponent of the "way of women" in *Denbu monogatari,* who concedes that he, too, would take pleasure in surrounding himself with such elegant minions had he been born of a station that permitted it.[137] Not all samurai could afford to maintain a private retinue of youths, however, nor did all live in such a rarefied atmosphere. Among the characters depicted as clients at houses of male prostitution, for instance, was the stock figure of the rustic samurai (*inakazamurai*), whose shabby dress and crude manners make him an object of derision even among those who are theoretically his social inferiors.

Unlike samurai, the second constituency in Nankai no Sanjin's list, the Buddhist clergy, fell outside the Confucian-based taxonomy of "four estates." The same was true also of various other groups populating the *shudō* text, including the court nobility, Shinto priests, Confucian scholars, physicians, the blind (*zatō*), and outcasts (*eta, hinin,* and so forth). What distinguished the Buddhist clergy from these other outsiders, guaranteeing it such a prominent place in Nankai no Sanjin's social topography, was not official ideology but textual tradition, for popular discourse had long associated Buddhist monasteries and temples with male-male eroticism. Some of the earliest male-male erotic texts, we have seen, emerged from this environment, and even with the advent of commercial publishing, clerical settings remained commonplace in *shudō* literature. Just as *nanshoku* represents for Nankai no Sanjin's Takujūrō the "flower of the military estate," a charac-

136. Azuma no Kamiko, *Fūryū hiyokudori,* 5:90.
137. *Denbu monogatari,* 37:127–128 (Leupp, *Male Colors,* 208–209).

ter in *Fūryū hiyokudori* describes it as the "delight of the Buddhist clergy" (*shukke no kōbutsu*).[138]

As in the case of samurai, priestly *shudō* was popularly associated with an ideological hostility toward women. An episode from *Taihei hyaku monogatari* (Hundred Tales from an Age of Great Peace), a collection of ghost stories dating from 1732, helps to illustrate this point. In the course of a pilgrimage, a priest named Gūzen encounters a beautiful young widow—in actuality an evil spirit—who wishes to give him not only lodging, but her own hand in marriage as well. Gūzen's response summarizes some of the religious considerations that discouraged him and his colleagues from pursuing erotic relations with women, while drawing them conversely toward youths. The priest reminds his temptress that the Buddha has forbidden those who joined the religious orders from engaging even in the briefest of flirtations, much less entering into marriage; indeed, the very word for monk (*shukke*) literally signifies one who has "left the household." "Priests love beautiful boys [*bidō*]," the widow retorts, "so why should women present any more of a problem?" Much like the speaker in an erotic debate, Gūzen lists three aspects of *shudō* that make it a lesser obstacle to Buddhist discipline than the "way of women" (*onna no michi*). First, the affection (*aichaku*) one feels for a youth gradually fades as he grows older, so that desire for him is only a temporary distraction. Second, an affair with a youth does not result in offspring and the karmic attachments that this entails. Finally, to associate with women is to consort with morally inferior creatures fated to suffer in this life from the "five obstacles" (*goshō*) and the "three obediences" (*sanjū*), the former a Buddhist doctrine holding females to be incapable of attaining enlightenment and the latter a no less misogynistic Confucian notion. Evidently persuaded by his logic, the widow transforms herself obligingly into a comely youth, upon which the priest realizes her true identity and rescues himself from being cannibalized.[139]

The "beautiful boys" of whom the widow so matter-of-factly assumes priests to be fond appear in popular writings in one of two guises. The first is that of the acolyte or *chigo* (alternatively, *terakoshō* or "temple page"), an adolescent male, technically a layperson, often sent to serve in a temple or monastery in order to receive an education. The figure of the acolyte had played a central role in medieval writings on male-male eroticism, ranging from the *Book of Acolytes* picture scroll, to such didactic treatises as *Chigo kyōkun*, to the genre of the *chigo monogatari*, in which a priest's infatua-

138. Azuma no Kamiko, *Fūryū hiyokudori*, 5:116.
139. Keichū Koji, *Taihei hyaku monogatari*, in *Tokugawa bungei ruijū*, 4:324–325.

tion with a youth, in many cases the incarnation of a Buddhist deity, leads him to attain enlightenment. In popular discourse of the Edo period, however, priest-acolyte relations were less likely to occasion spiritual salvation than earthy humor, whether in such forms of comic verse as *senryū* or in the pages of the anecdote book (*hanashibon*). Acolytes feature prominently in *Seisuishō* (Rousing Laughter; completed in 1623), one of the progenitors of the latter genre, whose humorous stories the author Anrakuan Sakuden had gathered over many decades of monastic life. Anrakuan typically depicts the acolyte as a less than willing sexual partner to the senior inhabitants of the temple: one youth curses the "hateful" (*niku ya*) Kūkai for bringing such a "bothersome" (*nangi*) thing as *shudō* to Japan.[140] The monastic culture of male-male eroticism in which the acolyte found himself the object of such unwanted attentions possessed a set of conventions and specialized vocabulary that were not always familiar to those who lived beyond its walls, so that the youths in several of Anrakuan's stories are hard-pressed to explain to their parents the meaning of such terms as *nyake* (referring to an anus) or *subari* (signifying a particularly constricted orifice).[141]

A second object of the priest's affections was the male prostitute. Just as the lay youth, upon becoming an acolyte, entered—if only temporarily and often unwillingly—into a centuries-old intramural culture of male-male eroticism, so did the clergy venture out into the arena of commercialized *shudō* that had arisen more recently outside the cloister. In the *Great Mirror*, Saikaku portrays the supply-demand imbalance that resulted when clerics from around the country gathered in Kyoto in 1659 for religious services in commemoration of a famous Zen master. Visiting the entertainment district of Shijōgawara, they "fell in love with the handsome youths there, the likes of which they had never seen in the countryside, and began buying them up indiscriminately without a thought for their priestly duties." As a result, reports the market-savvy townsman Saikaku, the fee for actor-prostitutes rose overnight, so that "their extravagance continues to cause untold hardship for the pleasure-seekers of our day."[142] While Saikaku's account can hardly be taken as historical fact, it serves as literary testament to the entry of the Buddhist clergy into the burgeoning *shudō* market of the seventeenth century. Saikaku's tone of coy resentment should be read less as malicious

---

140. Anrakuan Sakuden, *Seisuishō*, in *Hanashibon taikei*, ed. Mutō Sadao and Oka Masahiko, 20 vols. (Tōkyōdō, 1975–1979), 2:133.

141. Anrakuan, *Seisuishō*, 2:142–144.

142. Ihara, *Nanshoku ōkagami*, 39:467–468 (Schalow, *Great Mirror*, 190 [whence the quotation]).

anticlericalism than as good-natured irony: beneath the ascetic façade of the clergy, he and his fellow authors imply, lie some very human desires.

Nankai no Sanjin's third constituency, that of townsmen, comprised two separate groups in the "four estates" schema—namely, artisan and merchant households. Popular usage, however, made little distinction between the two. Many of the authors of the *shudō* text, including Saikaku, belonged to this social stratum, along with a substantial portion of their readership. Because a distinctly townsman culture of male-male eroticism had received little articulation prior to the Edo period, the ideals of *shudō* that popular texts enunciate—honor, pride, sincerity, compassion, and so forth—borrowed heavily from those of other classes. With the exception of compassion, however, these ideals drew less upon the conceptual vocabulary of the Buddhist clergy than upon that of the samurai elite. Saikaku himself suggests something of this indebtedness by devoting the first half of his *Great Mirror* to stories of warrior *shudō* before proceeding in the second to describe the world of the townsman. It was by measuring itself against the standards of the samurai, as it were, that the townsman culture of *shudō* maintained a sense of its own distinctiveness.

We see a metaphorical representation of this relationship in the figure of Takujūrō, whom Nankai no Sanjin, it will be remembered, had made to praise the "flower of the warrior estate." Despite his townsman lineage, the wealthy merchant Takujūrō is described as cultivating a "warriorlike spirit" (*bushi no katagi*). Honor, violence, and misogyny are all part of his adopted persona: he lectures his *wakashu* on the need to "polish manliness" (*otoko o migaku*), he practices the martial arts, and bans all females—canine as well as human—from his household. Nevertheless, when a visit from some robbers puts his mettle to the test, Takujūrō proves himself a helpless coward. Challenged by his *wakashu* to redeem his masculine honor by disemboweling himself, as a samurai would do, Takujūrō can only exclaim: "It's times like this that one is grateful to be a townsman, for life itself is the source [literally, the seed] of all things" (*Soko ga chōnin no katajikenasa. Inochi ga monodane*).[143]

Takujūrō's remark would surely have chagrined Yamamoto Tsunetomo, who held that "The Way of the Samurai is found in death," or at least confirmed his sense of class superiority.[144] Although Nankai no Sanjin's account, too, conveyed the message that townsmen, no matter how wealthy,

143. Nankai no Sanjin, *Nanshoku yamaji no tsuyu*, 43–48.
144. Yamamoto Tsunetomo, *Hagakure*, 26:220 (Wilson, *Hagakure*, 17 [whence the quotation]).

must not presume to imitate their social betters, it implied that the "way of the townsman" (although Nankai no Sanjin does not use this term) had rewards of its own—an opinion unlikely to issue from the Kyushu warrior. Whereas Yamamoto valorized death, Takujūrō's experience causes him to take stock in the value of life: although death, in Yamamoto's paradigm, might lead to honor, it is life—the "seed of all things"—that makes possible the generation of wealth and opportunities so essential to merchant activity. Popular representations of townsman *shudō* often echo this affirmation of life and focus on the material, presenting an implicit contrast to the culture of death and preoccupation with honor seen as characteristic of its samurai counterpart.

The role of money was a key factor distinguishing townsman and samurai versions of *shudō* culture. Warrior ideology held commercial dealings to be base—a prejudice confirmed by the merchant's lowly status in the official class hierarchy. For townsmen, on the other hand, monetary exchange was the essence of their livelihood—the catalyst, as it were, that served to transform "life" into "things." In the commercialized milieu of the townsman, even sexual pleasure and erotic knowledge commanded a price, as the entrepreneurs of the prostitution and publishing trades were well aware. Although samurai numbered among the consumers of both these industries, the commodification of male-male sexuality troubled many warrior ideologues, who viewed erotic ties between males as in principle a matter of loyalty and honor. Even Yamamoto, who professed his admiration for Saikaku's prose, could scoff in the same breath that a samurai youth who pledged himself to more than one male lover in the course of a lifetime was no better than a *yarō* or *kagema*—two types of male prostitute that Saikaku glorifies in the very work that Yamamoto praised.[145] It was one thing, evidently, for a warrior to sample the products of townsman *shudō* culture, and another to endorse, much less embody in his own person, its mercenary ethic.

For samurai observers like Yamamoto, the commodification of male-male sexuality was most concretely personified in the figure of the prostitute. The *yarō*, or kabuki actor, and his colleague the *kagema*, with his more tenuous theatrical credentials, stood at the heart of an urban culture of male prostitution that Yamamoto had seen expand phenomenally in the course of his lifetime, and that provides the thematic focus for the second half of Saikaku's

145. Yamamoto Tsunetomo, *Hagakure*, 26:263 (Wilson, *Hagakure*, 58). As I have indicated in n. 65 above, it is not entirely clear if the remarks in this passage represent the opinion of Yamamoto, his father, or someone else. In any event, Yamamoto evidently found them worthy of repetition.

Great Mirror. Although townsmen (and townswomen) were not the only clients for its services, the male prostitution industry was a quintessentially townsman phenomenon in that both entrepreneurs and prostitutes were, legally speaking, members of this class, and because the kabuki theater that served to advertise their wares formed one of the central institutions of urban culture. It was in this milieu, and in the popular texts that represented it, that sexuality and cash came to be most blatantly equated. "Both boys," writes Saikaku, for example, of two *yarō*, are "easily worth 1,000 pieces of gold"; or elsewhere, with respect to their clients, "merchants are well aware that you get what you pay for."[146]

The outlay of cash served to measure not only the worth of the prostitute, but also the quality of the buyer. The well-heeled townsman patron and the elaborate entertainments that he provided for fellow revelers form a favorite subject of popular fiction, whose readers might thereby partake vicariously of pleasures that their economic circumstances did not otherwise afford. The epitome of townsman extravagance is to be found in Nishiki Bunryū's 1705 tale *Karanashi daimon yashiki* (Mansion of the Great Quince Gate), which describes a "rivalry in love" (*iroarasoi*) between two fabulously rich Osaka merchants over the favors of a kabuki actor: when one bribes the city's night watchmen to prevent the other from freely passing through its gates, the latter retaliates by hiring up its entire fleet of palanquins so as to immobilize his rival.[147] Such extreme examples of conspicuous consumption, however, did not necessarily provide an ideal for emulation, whether from the standpoint of the shogunate, which had earlier in the same year confiscated the riches of a prosperous merchant house that served as the inspiration for Nishiki's work, or from that of *shudō* esthetics, which dictated that the display of wealth be accompanied by a commensurate degree of taste. From the perspective of shogunal officials, the ostentation of affluent merchants like those described by Nishiki represented a challenge to the class hierarchy; from the latter, it was a "boorish" breach of etiquette. Yet paradoxically, even taste was something that was difficult to acquire without a certain expenditure of money, whether in order to imbibe the consummate refinement of the pleasure quarters or to peruse the texts that served to codify its canons. The courtier Konoe Nobuhiro had recognized as much in 1619 when he wrote in his didactic work *Inu tsurezure*

146. Ihara, *Nanshoku ōkagami*, 39:503, 587 (Schalow, *Great Mirror*, 221, 300 [whence the quotations]).
147. Nishiki Bunryū, <*Naniwa chōja*> *Karanashi daimon yashiki*, in *Kindai Nihon bungaku taikei*, 4:381–387.

(Mongrel Essays in Idleness; published in 1653) that poverty, far from being "stylish" (*fūryū*), as some claimed, was in fact a "hindrance to all ways" (*shodō no samatage*), and that the indigent were best advised not to pursue the "way of youths."[148]

Not all forms of townsman *shudō*, of course, involved an exchange of cash. Nankai no Sanjin himself distinguishes between "stage boys," whose services were available for a nominally fixed price, and amateur *wakashu* of the town, who, apart from an occasional gift perhaps, did not ordinarily require remuneration. According to Yoshida's *Lucid Mirror*, it was uncouth for a youth of the latter variety to speak of such monetary matters as commodity prices, market conditions, or the laying-in of stock, even if his townsman upbringing had made him clever with the abacus.[149] Male-male erotic ties also took place between fellow employees of merchant houses, as in the *senryū* stereotype of the adult store clerk (*bantō, tedai*) who is loath to scold by day the shop boy (*detchi*) whose favors he enjoys at night. Clerks at clothing stores (*gofukuya*), often predominantly male establishments, seem to have been especially notorious in this respect: it is to a clothing store, suggestively, that the subject of a 1789 verse chooses to pass on a used copy of a guidebook on actor-prostitutes (*Yarō no saiken o gofuku-dana e sage*).[150] *Senryū* and other forms of popular discourse also associated male-male sexual practices with the figure of the delivery boy (*goyō, taruhiroi*) at the sake shop, whose peripatetic rounds taking orders and collecting empty containers exposed him on a regular basis to the advances of lecherous customers, and sometimes to outright rape. From the perspective of the author of *Gengenkyō*, however, such forcible assaults upon shop boys and other preadolescents were the work not of a true lover of *shudō*, but of undiscriminating brutes whose need for a "hole" (*ikketsu*) might be just as easily satisfied by a wolf in forelocks.[151]

Townsman ideology displayed far less hostility toward erotic ties between men and women than that of samurai or of the Buddhist clergy. This is not to say that there were no townsman "woman-haters": indeed, we have already encountered literary representations of two such figures, Ejima's Jūgorō and Nankai no Sanjin's Takujūrō. It is significant, however, that in both cases the authors imply that the character's misogyny is more typical of other social classes. Ejima presents Jūgorō as a foil to the hypocritical wom-

---

148. Konoe, *Inu tsurezure*, 4:11. Konoe evidently quoted from a now-lost work.
149. Yoshida Hanbei, *Nanshoku masukagami*, 1:228.
150. Okada Hajime, *Yanagidaru zenshū*, 2:233.
151. Shōsaiō, *Gengenkyō*, 3:306.

anizing of his priestly brother, while Nankai no Sanjin connects Takujū-rō's disdain for women with his warriorlike pretensions. In a townsman setting, the "way of youths" and the "way of women" were more apt to be portrayed as equivalent options for male pleasure, as with the townsman revelers who debate, in Saikaku's story, whether "courtesans are better" or "actors are better." The erotic-debate genre itself primarily addressed a townsman and lower-ranked samurai audience, as reflected in the fact that its speakers sometimes bracket the erotic practices of the higher warrior aristocracy (in *Denbu monogatari*) and of Buddhist priests (in *Fūryū hiyoku-dori*) as belonging to a world with different standards than their own. The pursuit of one or the other erotic path rested, in this townsman-centered construction, largely on esthetic rather than ideological considerations, and occasionally on little more than a whim: "Waking from a drunken stupor," a late eighteenth-century *senryū* reads, "I find myself embracing a *kagema*" (*Yoi samete mireba kagema o daite iru*).[152]

Let us turn last to the final constituency in Nankai no Sanjin's list, the peasantry who made up the overwhelming majority of the Japanese population. In the official class hierarchy, peasants ranked second only to the ruling elite, who deemed agricultural labor a more noble activity than artisanship or commerce. What Nankai no Sanjin did in effect, then, was to reverse the positions of peasants and townsmen in the status order, relegating peasants to the last, and implicitly lowest, rung on the social ladder. Whether this reshuffling is a mark of the author's own class pride is unclear, for we know little of Nankai no Sanjin's identity or social status. What is certain, however, is that in according the peasantry so undistinguished a place in his topography, Nankai no Sanjin shared a common bias of the *shudō* text, which, when it paid attention to peasants at all, was apt to portray them in a rather uncomplimentary light.

The peasantry constitutes a far less conspicuous presence in the *shudō* text than its absolute numbers might lead one to expect. Saikaku, for example, sets none of the stories in his *Great Mirror* in a specifically peasant milieu, instead focusing upon the two main components of the urban population, samurai and townsmen. Peasants emerge occasionally on the sidelines of the narrative, yet with little elaboration of character or suggestion of individuality. For the most part, they are a faceless mass, evoked primarily to demonstrate the extent of *shudō*'s cultural sway: "Even . . . farm boys slaving in the fields," writes Saikaku in one story, "yearned to sacrifice their lives for

152. *Kawazoiyanagi*, 26:914.

the sake of male love." The "even" is, of course, significant, suggesting an essential disharmony between the drudgery of peasant life and the refinement proper to the "way"; similarly, the "sons of merchants sweating over their scales" and "salt makers' sons burnt black on the beaches" who appear together with the toiling farm boy in this passage provide an implicit contrast with such *shudō* ideals as lack of greed and fairness of complexion.[153] (Yoshida, we may note, recommended that youths lightly powder their faces.)[154] The *Lucid Mirror*, too, is largely silent on the subject of the peasantry, except to say that peasant *wakashu*, along with their townsman counterparts and youths loved by priests, must be taught the virtue of filial piety.[155]

It should not be imagined, however, that the peasant's low profile in the *shudō* text necessarily reflects a lower incidence of male-male erotic relations among that segment of the population—a matter about which we have little knowledge, and, given the paucity of reliable data, perhaps never shall. Instead, it is an understandable consequence of the *shudō* text's fundamentally urban perspective. In the eyes of city dwellers, peasants were an unsophisticated and culturally impoverished lot: it is no coincidence that several terms for "boor," including *yabo* and *denbu*, incorporate characters literally meaning "field." Because peasants lived outside the metropolitan centers of *shudō* culture, they were imagined to have little appreciation for its intricacies, like the country bumpkin whom Nankai no Sanjin portrays as becoming involved in an argument at a kabuki theater because he refuses to believe that a skilled actor of feminine roles (*onnagata*) is in fact male.[156] Together with the rustic samurai, the figure of the peasant yokel commonly appears in *shudō* texts as an object of condescension and humor, providing a conventional foil to the presumed urbanity of townsmen and their city-dwelling samurai neighbors. Yet, just as there were surely peasants who gained a more than rudimentary understanding of urban *shudō* culture, it is not difficult to imagine that rural communities may have harbored their own forms of male-male erotic culture, the nature of which the metropolitan producers of the *shudō* text had little interest in and therefore never recorded.

As Nankai no Sanjin's reordering of classes illustrates, the medium of the *shudō* text permitted authors to fashion a vision of the world different

153. Ihara, *Nanshoku ōkagami*, 39:340 (Schalow, *Great Mirror*, 76 [whence the quotation]).
154. Yoshida Hanbei, *Nanshoku masukagami*, 1:311.
155. Yoshida Hanbei, *Nanshoku masukagami*, 1:292–293.
156. Nankai no Sanjin, *Nanshoku yamaji no tsuyu*, 48–49.

from that prescribed by ruling authorities. While few writers questioned the assumption that society was and should be divided into different status groups, some, including Nankai no Sanjin, sought to relativize the rigidity of the class structure by juxtaposing it against the transcendent and universal qualities of male-male erotic desire. "Even if [the object be] the frail son of a daimyo or other lordly house," asks a townsman character in another of Nankai no Sanjin's stories, "can any love lie beyond reach?"[157] In a society as status-conscious as that of Edo-period Japan, the answer was obviously yes: the humble shop clerk who spoke these words stood little chance of courting, much less winning the hand of, a young aristocrat. Nevertheless, since readers, as well as authors, were more likely to number among the peers of the former than the latter, it was only natural that they should desire to believe that the power of love could overcome class privilege, and would prize a literature that made such liaisons possible. It is this sentiment that I have earlier referred to (following an observation made by Shibayama Hajime) as a sort of romantic egalitarianism.[158] Yet before we laud it too highly, we should note that the egalitarianism involved was a fundamentally skewed one, operating for the benefit of the *nenja* rather than the *wakashu*. Its ideal was not so much a world of equal erotic actors, but one in which youths, and particularly those of good rank (here symbolized by the son of the daimyo, whose "frail" [*ki no yowai*] temperament is presumably a sign of his sheltered upbringing), were no less available to men of lower than of higher status. Few would have argued that the street urchin should enjoy equal access to the favors of the daimyo.

THE END OF THE WAY

The discussion in the preceding section has focused on the spatial and social coordinates of *shudō*; let us turn our attention last to its chronological dimensions. It may seem a contradiction of sorts to claim that the "way of youths," if conceived as universal, could have a beginning and an ending. The example of Buddhism (in its Edo-period construction, the "way of Buddha" or "way of Śākyamuni") demonstrates, however, that this is not nec-

---

157. Nankai no Sanjin, *Nanshoku yamaji no tsuyu*, 173. Contrary to the editor's punctuation of this passage, I read these words as issuing from the character Kihei rather than from the narrator.

158. Shibayama, *Edo nanshoku kō: Akusho hen*, 142–144. Shibayama maintains that the *shudō* notion of love as an ideal that transcended the established social order had much in common with Western romanticism as it was introduced in the Meiji period.

essarily the case. Whereas the principles of Buddhist philosophy were perceived, at least by the faithful, as embodying an everlasting and unchanging truth, human awareness of these principles, and practice in accordance
with them, were recognized as having arisen in a specific time and place—
namely, the ancient India where the historical Buddha (Śākyamuni) had first
attained enlightenment and passed his doctrine on to others. Furthermore,
it was part of Śākyamuni's teaching itself, according to Buddhist scripture,
that the fortunes of Buddhism—the "law" (*nori/hō*; Sanskrit: *dharma*), to
use a Buddhist formulation—would eventually undergo a period of degeneration, to be revived at the commencement of a new cosmic cycle or kalpa
by the appearance of another Buddha. Long before the beginning of the Edo
era, many Japanese had come to believe that the Buddhist "way" had already entered the last phase of the current cycle, and that the world was
now witnessing the "end of the law" (*mappō*).[159]

Like Buddhism, the "way of youths," too, was understood to have a concrete and knowable history, and likewise, the trajectory of this "way" was
often perceived in terms of origination, efflorescence, and decline. The construction of a historical discourse on male-male eroticism forms one of the
period's lasting legacies, one to which my own narrative is greatly indebted
even as I seek to place that discourse in historical perspective. Writers not
only wove an elaborate timeline of male-male eroticism, but continued
throughout the period to debate its contours and validity, modifying its contents in light of their needs and of the historical conditions surrounding
them. The concluding section of this chapter will reflect historically upon
these historical reflections.

When medieval Japanese attributed the introduction of male-male sexual practices to the monk Kūkai, they had already begun the process of constructing a historical narrative. In order to establish the authority of a discipline, it was important to demonstrate the legitimacy of its origins, since
the notion of a "way" implied a sense of linear transmission from an authoritative source. Kūkai fit this bill admirably not only because his supposed patronage of *shudō* helped account for the prevalence of male-male
erotic practices among the monastic population (including the inhabitants
of the Shingon sect's headquarters on Mount Kōya, founded by Kūkai himself), but because legend already associated Kūkai with such cultural inno-

159. On the concept of *mappō*, see Michele Marra, "The Development of Mappō
Thought in Japan," *Japanese Journal of Religious Studies* 15 (1988): 25–54, 287–305;
Jan Nattier, *Once upon a Future Time: Studies in a Buddhist Prophecy of Decline*,
Nanzan Studies in Asian Religions, no. 1 (Berkeley: Asian Humanities, 1991).

vations as the invention of the phonetic *kana* script. The credibility of the Kūkai connection, however, would not emerge from the Edo period unscathed, as writers brought to bear upon it a textual scrutiny and logical rigor that were characteristic of Edo-period scholarship as a whole. The townsman scholar Hayashi Jiken, for example, wrote in 1764 that references to male-male eroticism predating the monk's lifetime showed the "vulgar adage" (*sezoku no kotowaza*) that *nanshoku* originated with Kūkai to be patently false.[160]

By way of example, Hayashi pointed to the founding emperor of Han-dynasty China, who reigned from the third to second century B.C.E., and whose infatuation for one of his male minions, Jiru, the official histories of that period chronicle in detail.[161] In his study *Passions of the Cut Sleeve*, the historian Bret Hinsch has traced the development of a textually centered tradition of male-male sexuality in China, whereby male-male eroticism "came to be described through reference to famous individuals of ancient times," with "successive authors taking references from previous works and making them relevant to the collective experience of a writer's own time."[162] Many of the texts upon which this tradition was based had long been available in Japan as well, and Japanese authors no less than Chinese drew upon its resources for their own narrative purposes—as we saw, for example, in the case of Hayashi, who used it to debunk native legend. The foreignness of the tradition did not detract from its relevance, but instead served to enhance its authority, for Japanese had long regarded China as a font of literate culture; indeed, one of the functions of the Kūkai myth had been to legitimate male-male erotic practices by linking them with the ostensibly higher civilization of the continent. Writers of the Edo period were not the first to cite "famous [Chinese] individuals of ancient times" in connection with male-male sexuality, for references to youths who reputedly won the affection of emperors and other males under various Chinese dynasties, such as the aforementioned Jiru, appear in Japanese literature as early as the medieval *Saga monogatari* (Tale of Saga).[163] During the Edo period, however, Japanese authors greatly expanded the imagined roster of conti-

160. Hayashi Jiken, *Zassetsu nōwa*, in *Nihon zuihitsu taisei*, ed. Hayakawa Junzaburō et al., 81 vols. (Yoshikawa kōbunkan, 1973–1979), 2d ser., 8:383.

161. On male-male erotic culture in Han-dynasty China, see Bret Hinsch, *Passions of the Cut Sleeve: The Male Homosexual Tradition in China* (Berkeley: University of California Press, 1990), 34–54.

162. Hinsch, *Passions of the Cut Sleeve*, 3.

163. *Saga monogatari*, in *Muromachi jidai monogatari shūsei*, ed. Yokoyama Shigeru and Matsumoto Ryūshin, 15 vols. (Kadokawa shoten, 1973–1988), 5:337. Mar-

nental practitioners of the "way," occasionally making connections where their Chinese counterparts had seen none: Jie, for example, the last sovereign of the archaic Hsia dynasty, came to number among the putative ancestors of *shudō* because the Japanized pronunciation of his name (Ketsu-ō) sounded like the "king of anus," while Guo Ju, celebrated in Chinese legend for having dug up a golden pot, achieved a similar notoriety because the image of the pot (*kama*) served in Japanese, although not in Chinese, discourse as an emblem of male-male eroticism.[164]

The historical exploration of *shudō* extended also into the Indian past, although the Buddhist canon, apart from numerous warnings against clerical lasciviousness, did not furnish the same sort of self-conscious tradition of male-male eroticism that classical Chinese writings did. Nevertheless, as the home of Buddhism and nominally the first among the "three countries," India offered a source of legitimacy that defenders of the "way" hastened to exploit. The Kūkai legend, by positing the deity Mañjuśrī as Kūkai's teacher, had already hinted at an Indian origin for the received knowledge, so that the route of its transmission in effect reproduced the historical passage of the Buddhist faith from India to China to Japan (thus neatly bypassing Korea, a more immediate source for some of the earliest strains of Buddhism); an alternate version of the story had Kūkai traveling as far as India himself. A speaker in *Iro monogatari* states categorically that *shudō* began not in China or Japan, but rather on the Indian subcontinent, with Śākyamuni as its progenitor.[165] For some authors, Śākyamuni's supposed woman-hating proclivities found confirmation in the legend that the Enlightened One had been born not from his mother's vagina but from her flank.[166] Just as certain writers alleged that Confucius had been erotically involved with some of his male

---

garet Childs ("*Chigo Monogatari*," 131) points out that this work, although conventionally classed as a *chigo monogatari*, has in fact little to do with priest-acolyte relations.

164. A 1786 *senryū* (Okada Hajime, *Yanagidaru zenshū*, 2:169) reads: "It seems fitting that *shudō* should have begun with King Jie" (*Ketsu-ō ni hajimarisō na shudō nari*). For other *senryū* on Jie and Guo Ju, see Okada Hajime, *Yanagidaru zenshū*, 3:312; 4:130; *Yanagigori*, in *Shodai senryū senkushū*, 2:177. Similarly, Citong, male minion of one Zhou-dynasty emperor, was associated even more strongly with male-male eroticism in Japan than in China because the chrysanthemum flower with which Chinese legend had linked him served in Japan as a symbol for the anus. For *senryū* examples, see *Haifū yanagidaru shūi*, 26:805; Okada Hajime, *Yanagidaru zenshū*, 7:60; 11:75, 76; Satō Kōka, *Senryū hentai seiyokushi* (Onko shobō, 1927), 163.

165. *Iro monogatari*, 4:184.

166. Nishizawa, *Yakei tomojamisen*, 2:319; Urushiya, *Nanshoku kinometsuke*, 3:63.

pupils, some maintained that Śākyamuni himself engaged in male-male erotic practices, either with his disciples Ānanda—the youngest of the group, depicted in the scriptures as the Buddha's favorite—and Mahāmaudgalyāyana, or in the role of *wakashu* to his own spiritual mentor Ārāḍa Kālāma.[167] At the same time, the presence of numerous admonitions against male-male sexual behavior (a "mistaken way") in the Buddhist canon provided useful ammunition for opponents of *shudō*, both among the fictional characters of the erotic debate and among living ideologues.

In turning to China and India as historical sources of the "way," authors echoed a long-standing veneration for the cultural authority of these ancient civilizations. But the Edo period was also an era in which Japanese vigorously explored the indigenous past, elevated native tradition, and canonized a "national" literature, thereby allowing for the emergence of a historical narrative of male-male eroticism that centered on Japan itself. Hayashi, for example, in order to refute the Kūkai legend, relied not only upon the testimony of Chinese dynastic historians, but also upon an episode from the eighth-century Japanese work *Shoku Nihongi* (Chronicles of Japan, Continued), which had been cited earlier by the Confucian scholar Kaibara Yoshifuru in his 1683 compendium *Yamato kotohajime* (Origins of Things Japanese).[168] The passage referred to, relating the 757 exile of an imperial prince for dallying with a young attendant (or attendants) during a period of mourning, was in fact the subject of some controversy among Edo-period writers: while Kaibara and Hayashi assumed the attendant(s) to be male, the Shinto scholar Izawa Banryō noted that the term in question (*shidō*) might in classical usage just as easily designate a female.[169] Edo-period authorities also debated such historical and philological matters as a possible reference to male-male eroticism in another of the ancient annals, *Nihongi* (Chronicles of Japan)—more on this debate in the next chapter—and the meaning of the archaic word *kawatsurumi*, which some took to refer to anal intercourse and others to male masturbation.[170]

---

167. Azuma no Kamiko, *Fūryū hiyokudori*, 5:88; *Denbu monogatari*, 37:131 (Leupp, *Male Colors*, 210); Ishizuka, *Okaba yūkaku kō*, 1:83; Okada Hajime, *Yanagidaru zenshū*, 2:127; Shōsaiō, *Gengenkyō*, 3:306–307; Urushiya, *Nanshoku kinometsuke*, 3:76.

168. Kaibara Yoshifuru, *Yamato kotohajime*, in *Ekiken zenshū*, ed. Ekiken kai, 8 vols. (Ekiken zenshū kankōbu, 1910–1911), 1:707. For the episode in question, see *Shoku Nihongi*, vols. 12–15 of *Shin Nihon koten bungaku taikei*, ed. Satake Akihiro et al., 68 vols. to date (Iwanami shoten, 1989–), 14:178.

169. Ise Sadaharu, *Yamato kotohajime seigo*, in *Ekiken zenshū*, 1:823.

170. For the *Nihongi* episode, see chap. 2. On the *kawatsurumi* debate, see Kimoto Itaru, *Onanī to Nihonjin* (Intanaru shuppan, 1976), 47–58.

The sharpened interest in native origins that is reflected in the title of Kaibara's work was shared also by the emerging school of nativism (*koku-gaku*).[171] While nativists, particularly in the latter part of the Edo period, sometimes wrote critically of *shudō*, their research into ancient texts and fore-grounding of native tradition echoed an earlier search for indigenous sources of *nanshoku* in the pages of the *shudō* text. Baijōken, the author of the 1648–1653 work *Yodarekake* (Bib), for example, located the genesis of *shudō* in the mists of Japanese antiquity as represented in *Nihongi* and *Kojiki* (Record of Ancient Matters), two imperially commissioned accounts of Japanese history compiled in the eighth century but incorporating much older oral traditions that later nativists would come to regard as repositories of a Japanese spirit as yet unsullied by continental influence. Baijōken noted that, according to these mythological narratives, the first three generations of gods were male, deducing from this fact that *nanshoku* had reigned supreme in the archipelago "for several thousand years" before the appearance of the female creator deity Izanami and her male counterpart Izanagi.[172] Baijōken's argument thus implied that *nanshoku* enjoyed a more venerable pedigree than *joshoku* itself. Saikaku borrowed and built upon this historical conceit in his *Great Mirror*, casting the fictional narrator of the work not only as an expert on *Nihongi* but as a lecturer on a parallel text of Saikaku's own imagining titled "Record of the Origins of Boy Love" (*Nyakudō kongenki*).[173] Urushiya elaborates this theory further in his *Nanshoku kinometsuke*, reintroducing Kūkai into the narrative not as the progenitor of *shudō* but rather as a repopularizer after a long period of decline.[174] In this way, Urushiya was able to retain the legitimizing potential of the Kūkai legend while at the same time asserting the priority of indigenous phenomena.

The evocation and creative manipulation of existing texts, including one another's, by Baijōken, Saikaku, and Urushiya is but one example of the construction of what, in a Chinese context, Bret Hinsch has referred to as

---

171. On the emergence of nativism, see H. D. Harootunian, *Things Seen and Unseen: Discourse and Ideology in Tokugawa Nativism* (Chicago: University of Chicago Press, 1988); Peter Nosco, *Remembering Paradise: Nativism and Nostalgia in Eighteenth-Century Japan*, Harvard-Yenching Institute Monograph Series, no. 31 (Cambridge: Harvard University PressPress, 1990).

172. Baijōken, *Yodarekake*, 4:46–47.

173. Ihara, *Nanshoku ōkagami*, 39:312, 315–320 (Schalow, *Great Mirror*, 49, 51–56 [whence the translation]).

174. Urushiya, *Nanshoku kinometsuke*, 3:59. For further elaborations of Baijōken's creation myth, see Azuma no Kamiko, *Fūryū hiyokudori*, 5:88–89; Hiraga Gennai, *Fūryū Shidōken den*, in *Nihon koten bungaku taikei*, 55:183; Nishizawa, *Yakei tomojamisen*, 2:319.

"tradition." Also common to Chinese and Japanese inventors of tradition was a narrative convention by which male-male eroticism could be designated "through reference to famous individuals of ancient times." In much the same way that continental writers had invoked various imperial minions and other youths as canonical embodiments of male-male erotic attraction, Japanese authors plumbed their own historical and literary record to create an indigenous iconography of *shudō* that extended from such figures as Shōtoku Taishi, an imperial prince of the sixth and seventh centuries; to Ariwara Narihira and Hikaru Genji, celebrated protagonists of Heian court literature; to such famed medieval warriors as Minamoto Yoshitsune and Taira Atsumori and priestly favorites as the acolyte Shiragiku; to, in more recent times, Mori Ranmaru and Fuwa Bansaku, beloved pages of the sixteenth-century hegemon Oda Nobunaga and regent Toyotomi Hidetsugu respectively. Such associations did not always rest on unshakable textual ground, but writers felt few qualms in supplementing historical "fact" with creative embellishments that, over time, tended to reinforce one another.[175]

Like the "cut sleeve" in China, to which the title of Hinsch's volume refers, the image of the "rock azalea" (*iwatsutsuji*) accrued rich associations of male-male eroticism for Japanese readers during the Edo period. The familiarity of this emblem was ensured by the publication, in 1713, of a work that Paul Schalow and Noguchi Takenori have dubbed the world's first anthology of male-male erotic literature, which bore the name of that flower for its title.[176] Compiled by Kitamura Kigin originally in 1676, *Iwatsutsuji* consisted of a selection of excerpts and summaries of literary references to the love of youths culled from Japanese poetry and prose—a task for which Kitamura, as a *haikai* master and scholar of classical literature, was superlatively qualified. The work's title derives from the earliest item in the collection, a verse from a tenth-century imperial anthology, whose anonymous author (alleged by Kitamura to be Shinga Sōzu, one of Kūkai's disciples) compares his secret love to the "stony silence" of the rock azalea—no less ardent for

175. In "The Divine Boy in Japanese Art" (*Monumenta Nipponica* 42 [1987]: 9–13), Christine M. E. Guth traces the development of a medieval iconographic tradition in which Shōtoku Taishi (like Kūkai) came to be represented as a beautiful boy.
176. Noguchi Takenori and Paul Schalow, "Homosexuality," in *Kodansha Encyclopedia of Japan*, 9 vols. (Kōdansha, 1983), 3:217–218. Schalow discusses and translates Kitamura's work in "Invention." For the original text, see Kitamura Kigin, *Iwatsutsuji*, in *Kanazōshi shūsei*, 5:349–369. Ōta Nanpo appends a selection of verses omitted from Kitamura's collection in his 1804 compendium *Misonoya* (1:383–386). For a contemporary anthology of Japanese male-male erotic literature, see Miller, *Partings at Dawn*.

its muteness—and whose addressee Kitamura identifies as none other than the youthful Ariwara Narihira. In addition to securing the place of the rock azalea as an enduring symbol of *nanshoku*, Kitamura's anthology did much to solidify a literary tradition of male-male eroticism whose elements reached deep into the Japanese past but had never before been brought together in such a systematic fashion. Subsequent authors of the *shudō* text were conscious that their writings formed part of a continuous tradition, as when Hiraga described his *Nenashigusa* sequel of 1769 as belonging to a textual lineage that extended from the "Iwatsutsuji" poem through the *chigo monogatari* genre to works that had still to be published in the future, all sharing a similar function as "vessels" (*utsuwamono*) of—that is to say, media for transmitting—the "way."[177] Even the early nineteenth-century nativist Hirata Atsutane, who was by no means favorably disposed toward *shudō*, was familiar with Kitamura's work, citing the clerical authorship of much of its content as evidence that, despite their pious preaching, there were few Buddhist priests (Hirata was a vociferous champion of the indigenous Shinto faith) who could escape a "pernicious fate" (*maen*).[178]

Where did the present day and age fit into this imagined timeline of male-male erotic history? It is useful here to distinguish between earlier and later writings, since the more than two and a half centuries of the Edo period witnessed significant changes in *shudō* culture and in the discourses within which it was represented. During the seventeenth century and much of the eighteenth, popular authors typically envisioned *shudō* as a vital and even ascendant discipline, although the implications that they drew from this fact sometimes differed. In the mid-seventeenth-century debate *Iro monogatari*, for example, an advocate of *joshoku* charges that, whereas male-male erotic practices had not enjoyed much favor in antiquity (*jōdai*), their prevalence among the contemporary warrior aristocracy testified to the excessive pomp and prosperity (*eiga*) of the current age.[179] Others presented *shudō*'s vitality in a more positive light, as when Saikaku wrote in his *Great Mirror* that there was no day like the present for "excitement and titillation."[180] What both sides could agree upon, at least in the seventeenth century, was that the society around them offered no lack of opportunities for pursuing the "way of youths."

177. Hiraga Gennai, *Nenashigusa kōhen*, 55:150.
178. Hirata Atsutane, *Kokon yōmi kō*, in <*Shinshū*> *Hirata Atsutane zenshū*, ed. Hirata Atsutane zenshū kankōkai, 21 vols. (Meicho shuppan, 1976–1981), 9:162.
179. *Iro monogatari*, 4:180.
180. Ihara, *Nanshoku ōkagami*, 39:474 (Schalow, *Great Mirror*, 197 [whence the quotation]).

Contributing to this imagined efflorescence was a perceived spread of *shudō* among the lay population. It is significant, for instance, that the speaker in *Iro monogatari* points to the warrior class, rather than to the Buddhist clergy, in referring to present-day male-male erotic culture. Konoe Nobuhiro, too, seems to have had a samurai milieu in mind when he described, in 1619, how, during the last decades of the sixteenth century, as "people's hearts grew fierce," *nenja* began to cut off their fingers, remove fingernails, and pierce their flesh as a token of affection.[181] Although warriors had certainly engaged in male-male erotic practices before this time, they had not so often committed such experiences to paper as their clerical counterparts, and it was not until Konoe's day that the samurai class came to be portrayed in a wide range of written sources as trendsetters in the realm of *shudō* culture. (Similarly, the codification of *bushidō*, the "way of the warrior," postdates by many centuries the appearance of the samurai on the social landscape.) It appeared to Konoe, therefore, that the present-day laity had "stolen" (*ubaeri*) *shudō* from its original practitioners, the Buddhist clergy.[182]

Konoe was only one of the first in a long line of Edo-period writers to comment upon recent changes in *shudō* culture. In the latter part of the seventeenth century, for example, as the kabuki theater and the various forms of male prostitution that it spawned became a conspicuous feature of metropolitan life, a growing awareness of the "way's" commercialization began to inflect the earlier theme of laicization. The "sale of *nanshoku*" (*nanshoku o urihanberu*), noted Yoshida in 1687, was a phenomenon that had arisen only in the recent past (*nakagoro*), and had undergone significant changes even in his own lifetime. Some thirty-odd years ago, Yoshida claimed, the actors of the kabuki theater had placed foremost value upon masculine pride (*ikiji*) and had demonstrated sincerity (*makoto*) toward their patrons, while their keepers and attendants had barely given a thought to making money. Nowadays, he alleged, the milieu of the actor differed little from that of the female prostitute, with varying professional ranks, fixed prices, and an elaborate code of etiquette, a command of whose intricacies distinguished the "sophisticated" (*sui*) from the "boorish" (*yabo*) client. The consumer of such pleasures, warned Yoshida, must keep in mind that the

181. Konoe, *Inu tsurezure*, 4:17–18. The author contrasts the period in question (extending from the Tenshō [1573–1592] to the beginning of the Keichō [1596–1615] era) with an earlier one, lasting from Kyōroku (1528–1532) through Genki (1570–1573), in which the "way" had still been "shallow" (*asakarishi*), and with the present age, in which people had grown more familiar with its intricacies.

182. Konoe, *Inu tsurezure*, 4:9. Kōshokken Ariwara no Narihira uses a similar turn of phrase in his 1695 work *Kōshoku tabimakura* (1:57).

expectations that prevailed in the "ordinary" (*tsune no*) pursuit of youths did not always apply within this specialized demimonde: it was quite common, for instance, for the actor-prostitute to be older in years than his buyer.[183] Yoshida's nostalgic account thus contrasted an older, implicitly more authentic, version of *shudō* culture, based upon such samurai values as pride and sincerity, with a more recently arisen commercialized one centering upon the ideal of refinement, in which the profit motive of the townsman had modified, indeed literally prostituted, the former's norms.[184] Although both versions of *shudō* coexisted and intermingled throughout the Edo period, Yoshida perceived the latter as a historically newer, if not entirely laudable, development, much as Saikaku's organization of his *Great Mirror* into samurai and townsman halves implied not only a sense of class difference, but also one of chronological progression.

Just as the fortunes of a discipline could flourish, however, so could they fade. Already in Yoshida's narrative there is a sense that the "way" was experiencing a qualitative, if not necessarily quantitative, degeneration. The theme of degeneration reveals itself as well in the widespread Edo-period trope of *shudō* as symptomatic of the "end of the law" according to Buddhist cosmology. Konoe, for example, saw as a sign of *masse*—the "end of the world" (equivalent to *mappō*)—the practice of expressing devotion to a youth by mutilating the limbs of one's body (*gotai*), commonly regarded as a gift from one's parents, a custom that seems to have originated among late sixteenth-century warriors.[185] Yoshida, meanwhile, linked the notion of *masse* with the Buddhist clergy, to whom Kūkai, in an age of deteriorating moral standards, had granted *shudō* as a special dispensation from the rigors of priestly celibacy. Azuma no Kamiko, on the other hand, identified *masse* with a commercialized, secular realm, in which *shudō* was "free so long as you have money," as did the author of a late eighteenth-century *senryū* who observed, "It's the end of the world when the laity [as opposed to the Buddhist clergy] go to Yoshichō" (*Yoshichō e zoku no yuku no ga masse nari*).[186] For Hiraga Gennai, finally, it was not the commodification of male-male but rather of male-female sexuality—its "selling by the piece" (*kiriuri*)—that characterized the present era of *masse*, a corruption of the original princi-

---

183. Yoshida Hanbei, *Nanshoku masukagami*, 1:299–302.

184. For similarly nostalgizing passages in Saikaku, see Ihara, *Nanshoku ōkagami*, 39:467–468, 473–474, 593 (Schalow, *Great Mirror*, 189–190, 196–197, 307).

185. Konoe, *Inu tsurezure*, 4:17

186. Azuma no Kamiko, *Fūryū hiyokudori*, 5:112; Okada Hajime, *Yanagidaru zenshū*, 1:268. Koikawa Harumachi further develops the latter theme in his 1778 work *Mudaiki* (in *Edo no parojī ehon*, ed. Koike Masatane et al., 4 vols., Gendai kyōyō

ples of the "way of men and women" (*nannyo no michi*) to which *nanshoku* served less as a contributing factor than as a palliative antidote.[187]

Although the "way of youths" figured in the above examples as part of a larger eschatology, it became increasingly common in the latter half of the Edo period to view *shudō* as a discipline itself on the decline. Already in Takaratsu Shusō's (according to other sources, Niimi Masatomo's) memoir *Mukashi mukashi monogatari* (Tales of Long Long Ago), dating from 1732 or 1733, *shudō* numbers among a host of cultural practices that the author witnessed diminish or disappear in the city of Edo over the course of the previous seventy or eighty years. The specifics of the account make clear that what the author had in mind was not so much the commercialized culture of *shudō* prevalent in townsman society—he reserves his remarks on kabuki actors, for example, for a separate section—as its older manifestations among the samurai class (to which the author may himself have belonged), whose forefathers, the text asserts, had once taken pride in maintaining attractive young pages and sandal bearers (*kozōritori*) among their retinues, and among whom even the most ordinary-looking youth had in former times allegedly possessed a *nenja*. Whereas parents of previous decades had been afraid to let their attractive young sons go out unaccompanied, and the charms of page boys and sandal bearers had prompted frequent incidents of fighting, such unsettling phenomena, the author maintains, had in recent times "ceased" (*taete*) and the streets of Edo grown "quiet."[188] While narrative as well as political considerations may have encouraged the author, whose memoir dates from around the time of the Kyōhō reforms of the shogun Yoshimune (publication would not come until more than a century later), to exaggerate the contrast between a not too distant "long ago" and a more peaceful and orderly present, his work clearly implies that social conditions and cultural tastes had changed considerably since the early years of the Edo period, and that the popularity of male-male erotic practices, at least in some forms and among certain segments of the population, had suffered in the process.

The commercialized culture of *shudō*, too, was often perceived in the lat-

bunko, nos. 1037–1040 [Shakai shisōsha, 1980–1983], 1:124, 135), which depicts a topsy-turvy Edo tens of thousands of years in the future where priests freely patronize female prostitutes while laymen turn to *kagema*.

187. Hiraga Gennai, *Nenashigusa kōhen*, 55:132.

188. Takaratsu Shusō [or Niimi Masatomo], *Mukashi mukashi monogatari*, in *Zoku Nihon zuihitsu taisei*, ed. Mori Senzō and Kitagawa Hirokuni, 24 vols. (Yoshikawa kōbunkan, 1979–1983), supp. vol. 1, 57–58.

ter half of the Edo period as having shed some of its earlier vitality. Relying on evidence from the *saiken* genre, the historian Shibayama Hajime has shown that the number of *kagemajaya*, teahouses where customers could summon male prostitutes, declined steadily in the city of Edo during the late eighteenth and early nineteenth centuries, as did the number of districts where they were located and the number of youths there available.[189] After introducing one such work, Hiraga's 1768 *Mitsu no asa*, to his latter-day readership in the 1840s, the scholar and bibliophile Ishizuka Hōkaishi concluded that the "way" had dissipated by two-thirds in strength since Hiraga's time.[190] Yet even in Hiraga's own day and age (that is to say, the 1760s), Hiraga had detected an ebb in the demand for "love boys" (*iroko*)—in other words, male prostitutes—among his fellow Edoites. Hiraga linked this phenomenon, in a sort of vicious circle, with the simultaneously diminishing profile of *wakashu* actors on the kabuki stage: because fewer youths trod the boards, he explained, they lost a chance to build up their public reputations, and because celebrated *wakashu* thus ceased to emerge, it had become more difficult to obtain parts. Though Hiraga anticipated an imminent "resurgence" (*saikō*) of *nanshoku* both onstage and off, *shudō* institutions would not in fact experience a conspicuous reinvigoration during the late eighteenth or early nineteenth century.[191] Legal regulation was one factor contributing to the deterioration of *shudō*'s commercial infrastructure, as chapters 2 and 3 will examine in greater detail.

The perceived decline of *shudō* must also be seen in the context of male-female gender relations. Although the latter topic undoubtedly deserves a separate study, there is ample reason to believe, for example, that the misogynistic ethos of the samurai male may have attenuated gradually over the course of the Edo period as warrior and townsman cultures became increasingly integrated in the metropolises. The author of *Mukashi mukashi monogatari* notes, for instance, that, whereas etiquette in well-to-do households once required that page boys or other male attendants wait upon one's guests, by his own time it had become the custom for female servants to attend to such needs, reflecting a sort of feminization of domestic labor.[192] Ujiie

189. For a useful chart, see Shibayama Hajime, *Edo nanshoku kō: Shikidō hen* (Hihyōsha, 1993), 27.

190. Ishizuka, *Okaba yūkaku kō*, 1:72–73. Yamazaki Yoshishige (*Gimonroku*, in *Zoku enseki jisshu*, ed. Ichijima Kenkichi et al., 2 vols. [Kokusho kankōkai, 1908–1909], 2:372) used similar guidebooks (*hyōbanki*) to estimate in the early 1830s that *nanshoku* had shrunk to a tenth of its Hōreki-era (1751–1764) popularity.

191. Hiraga Gennai, *Mitsu no asa*, 9:103–104.

192. Takaratsu, *Mukashi mukashi monogatari*, supp. vol. 1, 56.

Mikito points out also that samurai males of the Edo period married at a younger age than their forefathers.[193] Among the Buddhist clergy, another bastion of misogyny, patterns of gender interaction may also have changed over time: a *senryū* of 1784, for example, alleges that it had become "old-fashioned" (*kofū*) for priests to indulge in male-male anal intercourse, the implication being not that the clergy now abided by stricter standards of celibacy, but, on the contrary, that they pursued female sexual objects with greater license.[194]

The flow of fashions between the male and female demimondes, as well as between these two milieux and the townsman public, also suggests a gradual shift in tastes between the early and late Edo periods. The characters in Ejima's erotic debate of 1711, *Keisei kintanki*, may bear witness to one phase of this process when they observe that, whereas until now townswomen had copied the fashions of male kabuki actors, it was a new breed of unlicensed female prostitute, known in Kyoto and Osaka as the *hakujin* or "amateur," who had most recently come to occupy the cultural spotlight, numbering even actors among her devoted admirers.[195] While, for the arbiter of the debate, it is this last argument that clinches the victory of the *nyodō* faction, we should nevertheless be cautious in assuming, as was often the convention in this genre, that the rivalry between the two "ways" constituted a zero-sum game, and that an increase in the popularity of one signified an inevitable decrease in that of the other. It is important, for instance, to distinguish among different varieties and providers of erotic services and pleasures—as Ejima does between licensed and unlicensed female prostitutes, and between both of these and "ordinary women" (*jionna*)—the availability of and demand for which must have been in a constant state of flux. Cecilia Seigle writes, for instance, of the "decline of the Yoshiwara" as an institution during the latter part of the Edo period, yet we would be hasty to conclude from this fact that the "way of women" in Edo, much less the

---

193. Ujiie, *Bushidō to erosu*, 193–194; Ujiie Mikito, "From Young Lions to Rats in a Ditch," in *Imaging/Reading Eros*, 117.

194. *Yanaibako*, 2:101.

195. Ejima Kiseki, <*Shikidō taizen*> *Keisei kintanki*, in *Nihon koten bungaku taikei*, 91:225–227. Long-term shifts in the cultural influence of the male and female demimondes are a favorite theme in the writings of the twentieth-century Edologist Mitamura Engyo. See, for example, the following essays in *Mitamura Engyo zenshū*: "Choichoi no honzon" (12:178–189); "Dōseiai no iseika" (14:366–379); "Edo ni sukunai onnagata" (12:212–233); "Ningenbi no kyōsō" (12:167–178); "Onnagata seijuku no jōken" (12:199–211); "Ryūyō no kenkyū" (12:344–354); "Ryūyō no mochinushi" (12:354–359).

overall incidence of male-female sexual activity in Japan, necessarily declined along with it.[196]

It is evident, nevertheless, that by the last decades of the Edo period, many authorities had come to view male-male sexual practices as more typical of an earlier era in their country's history than their own. The nineteenth-century nativist Motoori Uchitō, for example, located the temporal zenith of *nanshoku* in the medieval past, and especially the age of Warring States (Sengoku) that began with the Ōnin disturbance of 1467–1477, when more or less constant warfare had allegedly prevented samurai from taking women with them into the field of battle. Even after the Tokugawa pacification, Motoori wrote, this "vulgar custom" (*zokushū*) had continued to flourish down until the Genroku (1688–1704) and Kyōhō (1716–1736) eras, after which time it had diminished among the general populace, persisting only among such groups as the clergy, warriors, and professional entertainers.[197] By 1840, the infrastructure of male prostitution in Edo had withered to the point that Motoori's contemporary, the townsman scholar Yamazaki Yoshishige, could claim that *kagema* existed there "until quite recently"—that is to say, no longer—although he admitted the possibility of their survival in Kyoto and Osaka.[198] For the student of manners Kitagawa Morisada, writing more than a decade later, even the term *shudō* itself belonged to a "dialect of old" (*mukashi no hōgen*).[199]

Clearly, much had changed during the course of the Edo period. I have chosen, nonetheless, to treat the two and a half–plus centuries of this era as a single unit because, although the term *shudō* may have grown increasingly obsolete by its end, no equally powerful paradigm of male-male sexuality would inherit its place in the field of representation until the emergence of a new discursive regime during the latter part of the nineteenth century. Moreover, although the publication of *shudō* texts—Hiraga's "vessels" of the "way"—may have grown fewer and farther between from around the time of Hiraga's revivificatory efforts in the mid–eighteenth century, male-male erotic themes continued to surface regularly in popular writings for many more decades, including such best-selling works of fiction as Taki-

196. Seigle, *Yoshiwara*, 204–224.

197. Motoori Uchitō, *Senja kō*, in *Motoori Norinaga zenshū*, 12:174. Yamazaki Yoshishige (*Gimonroku*, 2:369) similarly pinpointed the historical peak of *nanshoku* as falling between the Eiroku (1558–1570) and Genroku eras.

198. Yamazaki Yoshishige, *San'yō zakki*, in *Nihon zuihitsu taisei*, 2d ser., 6:85.

199. Kitagawa Morisada, *Morisada mankō*, ed. Asakura Haruhiko and Kashikawa Shūichi, 5 vols. (Tōkyōdō, 1992), 3:35.

zawa Bakin's *Kinsesetsu bishōnenroku* (Modern Narrative of Beautiful Boys; 1829–1848) and Tamenaga Shunsui's *Iroha bunko* (Library of ABCs; 1836–1872).[200] Even the commercial infrastructure of male prostitution in Edo, as chapter 3 will show, did not meet so absolute an end as Yamazaki's account implies.

There is another reason, though, for emphasizing the lasting importance of Edo-period popular constructions of male-male sexuality. It was during the Edo period, I have argued, that a broad, textually rooted discourse on male-male sexuality first came into being in Japan. The very prominence of this discourse meant that later claimants to discursive authority would be forced to reckon with this inheritance, often in ways that reveal much about the nature of their own paradigms. Later chapters will explore some of these transformations. Yet even more than the specific content of that discourse, the notion that male-male sexual behavior was a matter for negotiation and representation in the medium of the printed text would have enduring consequences for later generations of Japanese. Although latter-day authorities sometimes attempted to silence this textual legacy, they were never completely successful, in part because they themselves were so heavily reliant upon the written word. The notion that there was something to be silenced or forgotten—the positing of an unspeakable or an unprintable—was itself a recognition of that legacy's importance.

200. Takizawa Bakin, *Kinsesetsu bishōnenroku,* ed. Miura Osamu, 2 vols. (Yūhōdō shoten, 1913–1917); Tamenaga Shunsui, <*Seishi jitsuden*> *Iroha bunko,* ed. Miura Osamu (Yūhōdō shoten, 1913).

2 Policing the Perisexual
Male-Male Sexuality in Edo-Period Legal Discourse

> Their Priests, as well as many of the Gentry, are much given
> to Sodomy, that unnatural passion, being esteemed no sin, nor
> shameful thing amongst them.
>
> François Caron, 1636

> I cannot forbear taking notice, before I proceed any further, that
> on the chief street of this town [Okitsu], thro' which we pass'd,
> were built nine or ten neat houses, or booths, before each of which
> sate one, two, or three young boys, of ten to twelve years of age,
> well dress'd, with their faces painted, and feminine gestures, kept
> by their lew'd and cruel masters for the secret pleasure and
> entertainment of rich travellers, the Japanese being very much
> addicted to this vice. However, to save the outward appearances,
> and lest the virtuous should be scandaliz'd, or the ignorant and
> poor presume to engage with them, they sit there, as it were, to
> sell the abovesaid plaister to travellers. Our Bugio, or Commander
> in chief of our train, whose affected gravity never permitted him
> to quit his Norimon [palanquin], till we came to our Inns, could
> not forbear to step out at this place, and to spend half an hour in
> company with these boys. . . .
>
> Engelbert Kaempfer, 1691

DIVINE PLEASURES/DEVILISH PURSUITS

The path of *shudō* wound its way across a complex and shifting discursive
terrain. The preceding chapter examined how Edo-period popular discourse
mapped the "way of youths." Beginning in the seventeenth century, we saw,
a proliferation of *shudō* texts, disseminated through the commercial mechanisms of the publishing industry, constructed male-male sexuality as a discipline leading to various pleasures and rewards, and negotiated the appropriate boundaries of its practice along such multiple axes as sex, age, esthetic

---

The epigraphs are from, respectively, François Caron and Joost Schouten, *A True
Description of the Mighty Kingdoms of Japan and Siam*, trans. Roger Manley, ed.
C. R. Boxer (London: Argonaut, 1935), 43; and Engelbert Kaempfer, *The History
of Japan, Together with a Description of the Kingdom of Siam, 1690–92*, trans.
J. G. Scheuchzer, 3 vols. (Glasgow: MacLehose, 1906), 3:53.

and ethical propriety, geographic space, social class, and historical time. When *shudō*'s path traversed other realms of discourse, further contestations of meaning took place. The present chapter explores the realm of legal discourse—that is to say, the framework of pronouncements and silences by means of which political authorities of the Edo period sought to establish and maintain control over the significance of male-male sexuality. Through the codification and enforcement of various types of legislation, the era's warriors-turned-bureaucrats attempted to circumscribe *shudō* within parameters that would serve their own interests and secure the orderly functioning of the communities in their charge. In contrast to the profit motive of the publishing industry, the concerns of legislators centered around hierarchy and stability. As with popular discourse, however, the legal construction of male-male sexuality was by no means uniform, varying significantly with geographic locale and chronological era, as the subsequent discussion should amply illustrate.[1]

An examination of legal discourse serves as a useful counterweight to the all too frequently encountered idealization of the Edo period as a "golden age" for the pursuit of male-male sexual pleasures, which tends to emerge from an uncritical perusal of popular texts alone. For, in addition to a profusion of popular discourse on *shudō*, the Edo period witnessed—not coincidentally—an unprecedented proliferation of legislative efforts to regulate male-male erotic behavior, albeit not always so effectively as lawmakers hoped. Rather than viewing the period as one in which male-male sexual relations remained blissfully free from official intervention, it would be more accurate to say that legal regulation assumed a different form from that which prevailed in Western societies at the time or in later eras of Japanese history. In the West, the Judeo-Christian stigmatization of nonprocreative sexual acts, and particularly the sin of "sodomy," made a profound mark on legal discourse, resulting in centuries of persecution by both church and state agencies lasting even to this day.[2] Yet, as Europeans who visited in the Edo period found to their dismay, political authorities in Japan

1. Chap. 3 will again take up the theme of chronological change in Edo-period legal discourse.

2. Christian views of male-male sexuality and their impact upon European legislation are examined in John Boswell, *Christianity, Social Tolerance, and Homosexuality: Gay People in Western Europe from the Beginning of the Christian Era to the Fourteenth Century* (Chicago: University of Chicago Press, 1980); James A. Brundage, *Law, Sex, and Christian Society in Medieval Europe* (Chicago: University of Chicago Press, 1987); Michael Goodich, *The Unmentionable Vice: Homosexuality in the Later Medieval Period* (Santa Barbara, Calif.: Ross, 1979).

did not criminalize male-male sexual practices per se. On the contrary, Caron's "Gentry" (in other words, the ruling samurai class, and in particular its upper echelons) and even the high-ranking official who escorted the German physician Kaempfer on his journey to the shogunal capital demonstrated their taste for such pleasures more or less openly. What appeared to Western observers as legislative unconcern resulted in large part from differences in religious discourse, so that a brief excursion into the latter realm is necessary here.[3]

As many scholars have noted, the religious system known as Shinto traditionally placed greater emphasis on the notion of pollution than on sin in a Judeo-Christian ethical sense. While male-female coitus was seen as inherently defiling, obliging those (and in particular males) who had engaged in it to undergo purification before entering into the presence of the gods, Shinto authorities did not so characterize male-male sexual practices, showing far less preoccupation with the theological implications of such behavior than their European counterparts. No explicit condemnation of male-male sexuality appears in the Shinto canon, which in fact remains silent on the topic altogether. The sole episode in ancient Shinto lore that might be construed in such a sense may be found in the eighth-century chronicle *Nihongi*, which tells of a male ritualist (*hafuri*) who killed himself so as to be buried with his "intimate friend" (*uruwashiki tomo*), a fellow ritualist—an event that displeased the gods and resulted in three days of continuous darkness.[4] However, the actual significance of the "stain of *azunai*" (*azunai no tsumi*), as the transgression is described, is far from clear. The reference might as easily have been to the unconventional manner of burial, suicide, or dereliction of sacral duties as to the pair's intimacy itself, the sexual aspects of which the text does not specify. In any case, despite intriguing parallels, later exegetes did not expatiate upon this account with the same relish with which Christians reiterated—and reinterpreted—the biblical story of Sodom and Gomorrah.[5] One exception is the early nineteenth-century na-

---

3. The construction of male-male sexuality in Japanese religious discourse is discussed also in Sandra A. Wawrytko, "Homosexuality and Chinese and Japanese Religions," in *Homosexuality and World Religions*, ed. Arlene Swidler (Valley Forge, Pa.: Trinity International, 1993), 199–230.

4. *Nihon shoki*, vol. 1 of <*Shintei zōho*> *Kokushi taikei*, ed. Kuroita Katsumi et al., 66 vols. (Yoshikawa kōbunkan, 1964–1967), 1a:252; W. G. Aston, trans., *Nihongi: Chronicles of Japan from the Earliest Times to A.D. 697* (London: Allen, 1956), 238.

5. On the reworking of the Sodom myth, see Boswell, *Christianity*, 92–98; Mark D. Jordan, *The Invention of Sodomy in Christian Theology* (Chicago: University of Chicago Press, 1997), 30–37.

tivist Okabe Tōhei, who asserted that the couple's tie was an erotic one, although he admitted that some readers might question why, if *nanshoku* so
angered the deities, the current age, in which it flourished, did not experience "perpetual nightfall" (*tokoyami*). The failure of the "Ōharae no norito," a similarly ancient purificatory ritual, to include male-male sexual
practices in a list of "earthly transgressions" (*kuni-tsu-tsumi*), while at the
same time censuring incest and bestiality, Okabe explained on the other
hand, was not a sign of indifference, but rather proof that *nanshoku* was a
"polluted act" (*waikō*) unknown to Japanese of antiquity and imported only
in later times from a corrupt continent.[6]

Popular discourse of the Edo period, meanwhile, implicated the divinities of Shinto as intimately in the workings of *shudō* as in all human affairs. In popular texts, men prayed to the gods to grant them a night with
the youth whom they desired, or conversely to speed the demise of one
who had spurned their advances; male couples invoked their name in swear-
ing oaths of brotherhood; and brothel keepers besought their aid so that
their charges would not physically mature too quickly and hence lose business.[7] Saikaku extracted canonical legitimation for *shudō* from the very

6. Okabe Tōhei, "Azunai kō," in *Ōō hitsugo*, ed. Nonoguchi Takamasa, in *Nihon
zuihitsu taisei*, ed. Hayakawa Junzaburō et al., 81 vols. (Yoshikawa kōbunkan,
1973–1979), 1st ser., 9:160–164. The text of the "Ōharae no norito" may be found
in *Engishiki*, in *Kokushi taikei*, 26:169–170 (trans. Felicia Gressitt Bock under the
title *Engi-shiki: Procedures of the Engi Era*, 2 vols. [Sophia University, 1970–1972],
2:85–87). For the comments of another nativist thinker on the "stain of *azunai*,"
see Motoori Uchitō, *Wakanoura tsuru shō*, in <*Zōho*> *Motoori Norinaga zenshū*,
ed. Motoori Seizō, 13 vols. (Yoshikawa kōbunkan, 1926–1928), 12:261, 392–395.

7. For representative examples, see Ihara Saikaku, *Nanshoku ōkagami*, in *Nihon
koten bungaku zenshū*, ed. Akiyama Ken et al., 51 vols. (Shōgakkan, 1970–1976),
39:457, 560 (trans. Paul Gordon Schalow under the title *The Great Mirror of Male
Love* [Stanford: Stanford University Press, 1990], 184, 274–275); *Yarō kinuburui*,
Kinsei shomin bunka 13 (1952): 30. Saikaku speaks of the "gods of *shudō*" (*shudō
no kami*) in his 1686 work *Kōshoku gonin onna* (in *Nihon koten bungaku zenshū*,
38:401 [trans. Wm. Theodore de Bary under the title *Five Women Who Loved Love*
(Rutland, Vt.: Tuttle, 1956), 193]), but does not seem to have identified them with
any Shinto deities in particular. In the early eighteenth-century story collection *Nanshoku yamaji no tsuyu* (vol. 6 of *Hihon Edo bungakusen*, ed. Yoshida Seiichi et al.,
10 vols. [Nichirinkaku, 1988–1989], 147, 158), Nankai no Sanjin portrays a "Great
Deity of *Shudō*" (Shudō Daimyōjin) as governing the affairs of male-male couples,
although such a divinity does not figure in the standard (if such a thing exists) Shinto
pantheon. Ejima Kiseki, in his 1710 tale *Keisei denjugamiko* (in *Shin Nihon koten
bungaku taikei*, ed. Satake Akihiro et al., 68 vols. to date [Iwanami shoten, 1989–],
78:286), describes the Shinto gods as capable of appreciating young male beauty,
though not of joining together male-male, as they are male-female, pairs. Saikaku
depicts them as capable of both in Ihara, *Nanshoku ōkagami*, 39:332 (Schalow, *Great
Mirror*, 69).

work where Okabe saw it condemned, opening his *Great Mirror* with a narrative of divine origins that he ascribed to *Nihongi*.[8] Though Saikaku's attribution was fanciful, his playfulness at the very least suggests that male-male eroticism was not perceived as being so antithetical to heavenly wishes as to invite charges of blasphemy. Male-male erotic culture also found a lucrative niche within Shinto's institutional infrastructure, since many *kagemajaya*—including those in the Edo neighborhoods of Yushima, Shiba, Kōjimachi, and Ichigaya—were located in or near the grounds of shrines, which, in addition to drawing visitors, enjoyed a certain measure of immunity from the ordinary channels of taxation and administration.

In the case of Buddhism, institutional links with male-male sexuality were even more conspicuous, and it is no doubt partly for this reason that Okabe and other nativists, who championed the indigenous faith of Shinto over its exogenous rival, also numbered among the Edo period's most outspoken critics of *shudō*. As we have seen, popular discourse represented Buddhist monasteries and temples as teeming sites of male-male eroticism, and the Buddhist clergy as greedy consumers of its commercialized culture. From the perspective of Buddhist philosophy, *nanshoku* and *joshoku* constituted analogous forms of worldly temptation, both of which could distract males from the path of enlightenment.[9] Yet although specific warnings against male-male (as well as female-female) sexual behavior surface occasionally in Buddhist scripture, the greater emphasis by far fell upon the dangers of male-female sexual involvement, particularly in the case of the clergy, upon whom most sects imposed a vow of celibacy. Because Japanese Buddhism interpreted this vow chiefly in terms of *joshoku*, erotic relations between males came to be perceived, both within the clergy and among the lay population, as a significantly lesser evil. Thus, in an eighteenth-century *senryū*, a parishioner remarks of an errant priest that "at least it was only a matter of *nanshoku*" (*madashimo no koto nanshoku*), implying that, if the compromising situation had involved a woman, the priest's breach would have been less forgivable.[10]

8. Ihara, *Nanshoku ōkagami*, 39:312 (Schalow, *Great Mirror*, 49).

9. On Buddhist views of male-male sexuality, see José Ignacio Cabezón, "Homosexuality and Buddhism," in *Homosexuality and World Religions*, 81–101; Bernard Faure, *The Rhetoric of Immediacy: A Cultural Critique of Chan/Zen Buddhism* (Princeton: Princeton University Press, 1991), 248–257; Leonard Zwilling, "Homosexuality As Seen in Indian Buddhist Texts," in *Buddhism, Sexuality, and Gender*, ed. José Ignacio Cabezón (Albany: State University of New York Press, 1992), 203–214.

10. Okada Hajime, ed., *<Haifū> Yanagidaru zenshū*, 13 vols. (Sanseidō, 1976–1984), 1:134.

The cleric in question had more to worry about, however, than the opinion of his parish, for secular authorities backed up sectarian regulations concerning priestly chastity with the force of criminal law. Penal provisions both in shogunal territory and in many of the domains prescribed harsh, in some cases even capital, punishment for "priests who fornicate with women" (*nyobon no sō*).[11] No equivalent legislation restricted the clergy's pursuit of male-male sexual relations, however, so that its members could indulge in the latter with relatively little fear of interference from either church or state. Thus, as another *senryū* noted, "The priest goes to Yoshichō in his everyday garb" (*Yoshichō e yuku ni wa oshō tachi no mama*), whereas a visit to the Yoshiwara might compel him to disguise his class identity by donning the robes of a physician—a similarly shaven-headed social status.[12] Alternatively, the priest who wished to engage in illicit (that is, male-female) sexual practices might disguise the gender identity of his partner—hence the familiar literary conceit of the woman ensconced in the temple as an acolyte, her ostensibly male sex allowing the cleric to bestow his attentions upon her with impunity.[13] Like European "sodomy" statutes, the legal regulation of priestly sexuality in Japan furnishes an example of the replication of canon law in civil legislation, the difference in the latter case being that the proscribed form of sexuality was male-female, and that its effect was to encourage rather than to discourage male-male practices.

While some might debate whether Confucianism, with its secular focus, is properly regarded as a religion, the place of male-male sexuality within its ethical system is nonetheless significant to our inquiry. Confucianism had entered Japan from the continent many centuries earlier, but it was not until the Edo period that it gained a degree of official patronage bordering on orthodoxy, as well as disseminating broadly within the realm of popu-

---

11. For examples from various regions, see Hanpō kenkyūkai, ed., *Hanpōshū*, 14 vols. (Sōbunkan, 1959–1975), 2:518 (Tottori), 5:171 (Matsushiro); Harafuji Hiroshi, *Keijihō to minjihō*, Bakuhan taisei kokka no hō to kenryoku, no. 4 (Sōbunsha, 1983), 523–524, 526 (Kanazawa); Kyōto daigaku Nihon hōshi kenkyūkai, ed., *Hanpō shiryō shūsei* (Sōbunkan, 1980), 62 (Morioka), 329 ([Tanba] Kameyama); Naikaku kirokukyoku, ed., *Hōki bunrui taizen*, 88 vols. (Hara shobō, 1980), 54:35 (shogunal territory).

12. Okada Hajime, *Yanagidaru zenshū*, 2:110. For more *senryū* on this theme, see Hanasaki Kazuo, *Edo no kagemajaya* (Miki shobō, 1980), 62.

13. For an examination of this motif in Edo-period literature, see Shibayama Hajime, *Edo nanshoku kō: Akusho hen* (Hihyōsha, 1992), 114–118. A famous depiction of such a menage appears in Ihara Saikaku, *Kōshoku ichidai onna*, in *Nihon koten bungaku zenshū*, 38:473–477 (trans. Ivan Morris under the title *The Life of an Amorous Woman*, in *The Life of an Amorous Woman and Other Writings*, by Ihara Saikaku [New York: New Directions, 1969], 148–153).

lar discourse. According to Confucian teachings, a moral society was based upon five quintessential human relationships: those uniting lord and vassal, parent and child, husband and wife, elder and younger sibling, and friends. Though this ethical schema gave no explicit sanction to male-male sexual relationships, the conceptual vocabulary of *shudō* nonetheless drew heavily upon its archetypes. The bond between lord and vassal provided an analogue, for instance, for the absolute loyalty that *shudō*, particularly in its samurai elaborations, called for in erotic partners, although as we shall see, there was potential for conflict between the two. Similarly, the hierarchical relationship of elder and younger brother furnished a convenient metaphor for the age stratification characteristic of male-male erotic ties, and was echoed in *shudō* terminology. Finally, *shudō* was often portrayed as an intense form of masculine friendship, as reflected, for example, in the term *chiin*, which derived from a Chinese legend concerning two proverbially close friends but had come in Edo times to connote a distinctly erotic form of male-male (and only by extension male-female) intimacy.[14]

The fact that Edo-period commentators seldom likened male-male erotic ties to parental or conjugal bonds is equally suggestive.[15] The last two relationships made up the principal axes of the household (*ie*), the importance of which Confucianism, which placed great emphasis upon the continuity of the ancestral lineage, served to reinforce. Few in the Edo period would have asserted that male-male sexual relations, which offered no direct means of generating progeny, could provide a full-fledged substitute for marriage and parenthood. By the same token, however, so long as male-male sexual behavior did not directly challenge these or other Confucian principles, a certain amount of room remained for it within the pale of ethical legitimacy.

14. The legend in question told how Bo Ya gave up the lute after the death of his friend Zhong Ziqi, lamenting that only the deceased Zhong had truly "understood the sound"—the literal meaning of *chiin*—of his instrument (or heart). For one version of this story, see A. C. Graham, trans., *The Book of Lieh-Tzŭ: A Classic of the Tao* (New York: Columbia University Press, 1990), 109–110.

15. As always, exceptions may be found. For example, the hermit-master in the 1643 *Shin'yūki* (in *Nihon shisō taikei*, ed. Ienaga Saburō et al., 67 vols. [Iwanami shoten, 1970–1982], 60:20–21 [trans. Paul Gordon Schalow in "Spiritual Dimensions of Male Beauty in Japanese Buddhism," in *Religion, Homosexuality, and Literature*, ed. Michael L. Stemmeler and José Ignacio Cabezón, Gay Men's Issues in Religious Studies Series, no. 3 (Las Colinas, Tex.: Monument, 1992), 8]), a work rich in Confucian motifs, compares the relationship between a youth and his lover to that of child and parent by noting (with a certain amount of rhetorical disingenuousness) that, in erotic sign language, a youth could indicate his consent to a lover by touching his thumb (in Japanese, "parent finger") to his little finger ("child finger"). Similarly, with respect to marriage, one finds an early seventeenth-century anec-

Since male-male erotic practices were regarded more often as complementary than as antithetical to male-female, they did not automatically conjure up the specter of household demise.[16] And when an individual's indulgence in the former threatened family fortunes, the affected household might take appropriate action without the need for outside intervention.

At the same time, Confucianism emphasized that the responsibility for promoting ethical conduct, including proper sexual behavior, fell not only upon individuals and households, but also upon a sage and virtuous rulership. The legal regulation of sexuality, while by no means a new phenomenon, thus received a new degree of attention from political authorities during the Edo period, reflecting the ruling class's perception of itself as guardians of a pacified and stabilized social order. Conspicuous throughout the Edo period's sexual legislation was a concern on the part of warrior-bureaucrats for preserving the status quo in class and gender relations and harmony within the community at large, regardless of whether the object of legislation was male-male or male-female sexuality. (Edo-period lawmakers, it should be noted from the outset, paid scant notice to erotic activity between females.) In addressing such concerns, officials drew heavily on Confucian ideals and vocabulary, as may be seen, for example, in the emphasis they placed on such ideologically privileged values as moderation and decorum.

In contrast to "sodomy" legislation in Europe, however, Japanese laws dealing with *shudō* expressed little concern with the illicit nature of sexual acts in and of themselves. Since prevailing religious discourses in Japan had

---

dote (Anrakuan Sakuden, *Seisuishō*, in *Hanashibon taikei*, ed. Mutō Sadao and Oka Masahiko, 20 vols. [Tōkyōdō, 1975–1979], 2:147) depicting a samurai wife who, jealous over her husband's relationship with a *wakashu*, threatens to hand her rice ladle (a symbol of her position as housewife) over to the youth permanently. It should be noted, however, that the humor of the latter story rests on the very incongruity of the *wakashu* and housewifely roles, which the wife, in her ignorance of *shudō*, fails to comprehend but the implicitly male listener/reader is supposed to appreciate.

16. Again, there are exceptions to this generalization. In a 1707 erotic debate (Azuma no Kamiko, *Fūryū hiyokudori*, in *Edo jidai bungei shiryō*, ed. Hayakawa Junzaburō et al., 5 vols. [Kokusho kankōkai, 1916], 5:109), for example, an opponent of *shudō* asserts that infatuation with a youth might lead a man to forgo marriage, resulting in a lack of progeny and the forfeit of his birthright. As I have suggested in chap. 1, however, such rhetorical extremes were one of the distinguishing characteristics of the genre. In *Denbu monogatari* (in *Nihon koten bungaku zenshū*, 37:135 [trans. Gary P. Leupp in *Male Colors: The Construction of Homosexuality in Tokugawa Japan* (Berkeley: University of California Press, 1995), 213]), the *shudō* faction had made use of the same argument, charging that household demise was the outcome of male-female rather than male-male lust.

not stigmatized male-male sexual practices as particularly sinful, such in-difference was only to be expected, much as it may have disturbed the sen-sibilities of early Western visitors. Edo-period lawmakers chose instead to scrutinize what I shall call the "perisexual" aspects of *shudō*—that is to say, the social context in which male-male sexual acts took place and the cul-tural infrastructure through which they were articulated. *Shudō* legislation thus spoke not of genital positions, much less of such minutiae as proof of ejaculation or degree of intromission, as contemporary European legal au-thorities were wont to do, but rather of such peripheral—which is not to say insignificant—factors as social statuses, ethical proprieties, and exter-nal appearances. In short, the legal regulation of male-male sexuality en-compassed as broad a conceptual realm as the path of *shudō* itself.

OUTRAGEOUS SPECTACLES

Any survey of Edo-period legal discourse concerning male-male sexuality must take into account not only many different objects of regulation, but also a wide range of regulatory authorities. Edo-period Japan, though unified as compared to the preceding Sengoku (Warring States) period, was by no means a homogeneous polity, instead comprising a plethora of legal jurisdictions un-der the hegemony of the Tokugawa shogunate or bakufu. While approxi-mately one-seventh of the country's land fell under the direct control of the Tokugawa house, the remainder was divided into between 250 and 300 semi-autonomous domains or han, each headed by its own daimyo ruler. Although all domains paid formal allegiance to the shogunate, the extent of Edo's influence over their internal affairs varied, and in some cases antagonism to-ward shogunal authority was only thinly veiled. Even the han, however, did not represent the smallest unit of jurisdiction, for each of the period's tens of thousands of peasant villages, too, held its inhabitants accountable to spe-cial forms of local law.[17] And in the period's thriving cities, particularly the bakufu-administered metropolises of Edo, Kyoto, and Osaka, a distinct set of urban problems gave rise to a vast corpus of municipal legislation.

While it would be a mistake to view shogunal legislation as "national" law in a present-day sense, there is good reason to begin our discussion here. First of all, as already mentioned, the bakufu governed a sizable though scat-tered parcel of territories, so that shogunal law directly prevailed over a greater geographical expanse than that of any other political authority. In

17. A useful discussion of village law may be found in Herman Ooms, *Tokugawa Village Practice: Class, Status, Power, Law* (Berkeley: University of California Press, 1996), esp. 192–242.

addition, issuing from the most powerful administrative organ in the land, bakufu legislation provided an influential model for lawmakers elsewhere, albeit with significant local variation. Finally, in their role as overseers of the three metropolises, it was shogunal officials who most persistently confronted the problems of a commercialized *shudō* culture that centered on these urban areas.

During the same centuries in Europe, legal pronouncements on male-male sexuality typically found their place in penal law. By contrast, the bakufu penal code, formalized by the 1742 compilation of the *Kujikata osadamegaki*, made no specific mention of male-male (or female-female) sexual practices.[18] Instead the authors of the code, which prescribed standard punishments in a Chinese-derived *ritsu* format, associated criminal sexuality chiefly with male-female acts outside the bounds of marriage and concubinage (*mittsū* or *fugi*) and with unlicensed female prostitution (*kakushibaijo*). Harsh penalties for adultery served several purposes: to confirm the bond between husband and wife, one of the foundations of Confucian ethics; to enforce men's unilateral right of possession over women's bodies, given that adultery by the husband generally went unpunished; and, insofar as punishment reflected the relative status of the male parties, to bind men to a stable social hierarchy.[19] Official regulation of female prostitution, meanwhile, mediated two subtly conflicting perceptions of male sexuality: on the one hand, that it constituted a legitimate desire that could not be contained by marriage and concubinage alone; and on the other that, if left entirely unchecked, it threatened social stability. Bakufu lawmakers did not perceive in male-male sexual relations the same order of social threat as they did in illicit coupling between male and female, and consequently instituted no categorical punishments. In this respect, they differed not only from their European counterparts, but also from their contemporaries in Qing China, whose penal code from 1740 mandated severe penalties for male-male anal intercourse.

Although the *Kujikata osadamegaki* did not criminalize male-male sex-

18. The *Kujikata osadamegaki* provided a set of standard guidelines for bakufu administrators and was not disseminated among the general populace—a fact that distinguishes it and other Edo-period penal codes from Western and later Japanese criminal legislation. In the form that it had assumed by the end of the Edo period, it appears in Naikaku kirokukyoku, *Hōki bunrui taizen*, 54:14–55. For an English translation, see John Carey Hall, *Japanese Feudal Law* (Washington: University Publications of America, 1979), 149–266.

19. For an in-depth study of male-female adultery in Edo-period Japan, see Ujiie Mikito, *Fugi mittsū: Kinjirareta koi no Edo*, Kōdansha sensho mechie, no. 88 (Kōdansha, 1996).

ual acts per se, the pursuit of *shudō* was not unaffected by its provisions. Male-male sexual relations, like their male-female equivalents, might be implicated, for instance, in the commission of other crimes, such as murder or kidnapping (*kadokawashi*). Let us begin with an example of the latter. In the year 1688, according to bakufu legal records, an itinerant actor (*tabi-yakusha*) by the name of Shinroku abducted a certain Shichinosuke, son of the caretaker (*yamori*) at a commercial establishment in one of Edo's theater districts, while the lad was on a pilgrimage to the Ise shrine (or such, at least, was the pretext of the journey) in the company of a servant. Spiriting Shichinosuke away to Osaka, Shinroku "kept" (*kakoiokisōrō*) him there—a locution typically used in connection with female concubines or prostitutes—for a period as long as a year before word of their whereabouts reached authorities. The death sentence that Shinroku received upon apprehension, however, was not for participation in illicit sexual practices, but rather for the perisexual offense of kidnapping. The exact sort of sexual activity that had taken place was not even a question that the record of this case addresses, although the theatrical milieu of the incident and Shichinosuke's youth strongly suggest that erotic considerations were involved.[20] Nowhere is there explicit mention, for instance, of *shudō*, although an Edo-period adjudicator examining the record would presumably have had little trouble reading between the lines.

Erotic ties might also give rise to incidents of love suicide, referred to in popular discourse as *shinjū* (because they revealed "what is in the heart") or *jōshi* ("death out of passion"). Bakufu lawmakers, who were far less enthusiastic about the practice in question, pointedly avoided these terms.[21] The *Kujikata osadamegaki* stipulated that the bodies of "illicit" (*fugi*) male-female couples who committed joint suicide (*aitaijini*; literally, "mutual death") by compact be disposed of without funeral rites, and that individuals who survived must undergo beheading. Incidents of love suicide took place not only between men and women, however, but also between males.[22] In the year 1782, one such case occurred near Sunpu (today's Shizuoka), ancestral seat of the ruling Tokugawa house. A Zen temple servant (*genan*)

---

20. Ishii Ryōsuke, ed., *Kinsei hōsei shiryō sōsho*, rev. ed., 3 vols. (Sōbunsha, 1959), 1:224. Another manuscript gives the abductor's name as Shinpei.

21. Since the category of *shinjū* included murder-suicides as well as multiple and sometimes single (as in the case described in n. 24 below) suicides, I have eschewed the term "double suicide," a standard English translation for *shinjū*, in favor of "love suicide," although it should be kept in mind that the "love" in question need not be mutual.

22. For a representation of male-male love suicide in popular discourse, see

named Kinji, who was in his thirties, attempted suicide together with one Sojun, an eighteen-year-old novice (*shoke*) at another temple, with whom he had been involved in a *shudō* relationship.[23] After cutting his partner's veins with a razor (with Sojun's full consent, the record implies), Kinji turned the blade upon himself but, before he had a chance to expire, was discovered clinging to Sojun's lifeless body by a villager passing through the shogunally administered forest where the incident took place. Uncertain whether the provisions regarding male-female love suicide applied also to male-male couples, and not finding the pair to have been involved in any other "suspicious" (*ayashiki*) activities, the Sunpu town magistrate (*machibugyō*) referred the case to his superiors at the Hyōjōsho in Edo, which functioned as the bakufu's supreme judiciary organ. In response, the council handed down a judgment stating that, although no legal precedent existed regarding such matters, "no distinction should be made between male and female in cases of joint suicide [*aitaijini*]."

In reaching their verdict, shogunal officials paid close attention to the fact that the couple had conspired together in planning the act and the ritualized form that it had taken—both parties dressing in white robes and seating themselves upon a throw rug (*mōsen*) that they had brought along for this purpose—concluding that there was "no question at all" that the incident constituted the equivalent of a male-female love suicide. This scrutiny of external details was significant because, besides the possibility of murder, ritual suicide involving two or more males was known to take place in other, less explicitly eroticized contexts (as in the case of *junshi*, the practice of vassals following their deceased lord into death, which the bakufu had outlawed in 1663), and because it was precisely the esthetic and performative aspect of these pacts that captured the imagination of the populace, whom bakufu administrators attempted to screen from such influences by banning the portrayal of love suicides in kabuki and other popular media.[24] Yet the element in the relationship that was unethical from

---

Shohōken's 1704 work *Shinjū ōkagami* (in *Kinsei bungei sōsho*, ed. Hayakawa Junzaburō et al., 12 vols. [Kokusho kankōkai, 1910–1912], 4:223–225), which depicts an episode that allegedly took place in Okayama domain. In Shohōken's rendering of the incident, the *wakashu* of a slain country-dwelling samurai (*gōshi*) takes his own life after killing the man who murdered the samurai in order to obtain the youth's favors.

23. I have pieced together this narrative from two sources: Kikuchi Shunsuke, ed., *Tokugawa kinrei kō kōshū*, 6 vols. (Yoshikawa kōbunkan, 1931–1932), 4:147–148; and Ōta Nanpo, *Ichiwa ichigen*, supp. vols. 1–5 of *Nihon zuihitsu taisei*, 1:71–72. The latter gives the year of the incident as 1781.

24. Legal documents surrounding a 1733 *shinjū* between a samurai male and a

the perspective of shogunal bureaucrats was not the fact that two males had possibly engaged in sexual intercourse—after all, both were denizens of temples, where such practices were known to be common—but that they had taken their lives for the sake of a bond that was entirely private in nature, thereby denying their obligations to external authority. The tie between them may also have held unsavory implications of status indecorum, since Kinji, an adult and presumably the *nenja* of the pair, was of humbler rank within the temple hierarchy than his partner, a budding priest, and was officially a townsman rather than a cleric, compounded by the fact that the two belonged to different religious institutions; perhaps these complicated circumstances even prompted the suicide in the first place. It was such perisexual considerations as these, rather than a particular sexual act, that facilitated higher authorities' conceptual connection with male-female adultery or *fugi*, whose component characters literally signified a deviation from one's rightful obligations.[25]

Penal law, however, comprised only a small fraction of bakufu legislation concerning male-male sexuality. The legal instrument that dealt most explicitly with *shudō* was the *ofuregaki* (*machibure*) or municipal decree. This form of legislation differed from *ritsu*-type penal law in a number of ways. First of all, it did not prescribe specific punishment, at most demanding that violators be reported to authorities. Second, it was intended for the consumption of the general populace within a particular locality—neighborhood leaders might read such pronouncements aloud, for instance, to assembled local residents—whereas penal provisions circulated only in judicial circles. Third, it addressed concerns that were mainly urban in character, usually targeting the townsman classes. Finally, its intent was more hortatory than punitive, as is evident from the fact that officials reissued similar decrees repeatedly. The legal historian Dan Henderson writes that *ofuregaki* were "used to scold or jog the memories of the populace and were often not intended to be justiciable on their face."[26]

---

thirteen-year-old *kagema* in Edo similarly concluded that the incident was a love suicide on the basis of clothing and attendant paraphernalia. In the latter case, bakufu officials decided to expose (*sarashi*) the corpse of the samurai for public viewing in the grounds of the Yushima shrine, but turned the body of the *kagema* over to his employers, whether out of consideration for the lad's youth, or perhaps because they feared that it might provide too erotic a spectacle. See Yoshida Setsuko, ed., *Edo kabuki hōrei shūsei* (Ōfūsha, 1989), 178.

25. Similarly, Azuma no Kamiko's *Fūryū hiyokudori* (5:88) characterizes a clandestine tie between a retainer and one of his lord's page boys as an act of *fugi*.

26. Dan Fenno Henderson, "The Evolution of Tokugawa Law," in *Studies in the*

Bakufu decrees relating to male-male sexuality become conspicuous around the middle of the seventeenth century. The majority of them deal with commercialized, urban *shudō*, reflecting the rapid growth of cities and accompanying integration of male-male erotic culture into the cash nexus, processes accelerated by the Tokugawa pacification. Particularly in the newly established shogunal capital at Edo, lawmakers faced the daunting task of preserving social harmony in a city whose population would before the end of the century become the largest in the world; where sword-wielding samurai males rubbed shoulders daily with members of the merchant, artisan, and other social classes; and where representatives of rival domains gathered in attendance upon a shogun who was expected to provide a guarantee of stability and order. It is no coincidence, therefore, that *shudō* both found its most elaborate institutional articulation within this metropolitan environment and elicited greater bureaucratic solicitude here than in any other urban center. The regulation of a vibrant yet volatile *shudō* culture also occupied urban administrators in Kyoto and Osaka, likewise under bakufu jurisdiction, but it was Edo, the main focus of the following discussion, that set the pattern for much of the legislation elsewhere implemented.

In the minds of shogunal officials, the growth of a commercialized *shudō* culture presented the same visions of unbridled male sexual desire and the consequent disruption of social order as did unlicensed female prostitution, although, judging from the larger volume of legislation targeting the latter, on a somewhat lesser scale. Sexual moderation was a key tenet of bakufu ideology, which construed "lasciviousness" (*kōshoku*), so often lauded in popular discourse, as an undesirable and even dangerous trait, particularly among samurai males. At the highest level of the social and political hierarchy, overindulgence in erotic pleasures held the potential for leading men astray from their official duties, and for introducing private desires into an arena where, at least in theory, conduct was supposed to be based on public good. The 1615 *Buke shohatto*, a bakufu-issued code governing the affairs of daimyo, thus cited addiction to "lasciviousness" as a cause of "state ruin" (*bōkoku*), without specifying whether the object of lust was male or female.[27] Nevertheless, official ideology did not identify sexual desire as pernicious

---

Institutional History of Early Modern Japan, ed. John W. Hall and Marius B. Jansen (Princeton: Princeton University Press, 1968), 220.

27. Ishii, *Kinsei hōsei shiryō sōsho,* 2:1. For English translations of the code, see John Carey Hall, *Japanese Feudal Law,* 100–104; David John Lu, ed., *Japan: A Documentary History* (Armonk, N.Y.: Sharpe, 1997), 206–208; Ryusaku Tsunoda et al., eds., *Sources of Japanese Tradition* (New York: Columbia University Press, 1958), 335–338.

in itself, as was the case, for instance, in Buddhist thought. What was problematic, rather, was the failure to partake of its pleasures with a proper sense of moderation and decorum—ideals more closely associated with Confucian thinking.

Samurai bureaucrats applied these ideals to other classes as well, but in diluted form and with less conviction that the lower orders, whom they regarded as possessing a lesser sense of virtue, could or would adhere to them. Whereas samurai continence was in a sense axiomatic, the sexual excesses of townsmen called for more explicit restraints. This was the role of the *ofuregaki*, and one of the reasons that its admonitions underwent constant repetition. Bakufu officials in the metropolises typically promulgated such decrees in response to specific incidents or conditions that had come to their attention, and reiterated them when further violations all too blatantly demonstrated that the original warnings had gone unheeded. One source alleges that the appearance of the first Edo edict dealing with *shudō* was triggered by an acrimonious dispute over the favors of a young sandal bearer (*kozōritori*) named Shikazō, although in this case the parties involved were not townsmen but samurai.[28] Whether as a result of this particular incident or not, an *ofuregaki* issued in Edo in 1648 clearly departs from similar decrees of the past by incorporating in the midst of more familiar provisions concerning such matters as unlicensed female prostitution and proper procedures in the event of fire the following clause: "One must not importune [youths] regarding *shudō*, or lose one's head over *wakashu*."[29]

The fact that samurai administrators used the term *shudō* to refer to male-male eroticism suggests the degree of currency that the disciplinary paradigm enjoyed even outside the realm of popular discourse. It would be a mistake, however, to view the decree as outlawing *shudō* in and of itself. Rather, bakufu authorities focused their attention on two specific forms of its pursuit, both of which contravened official ideals of moderation and decorum. The first, which I have translated as "importuning" (*mutai naru koto o mōshikake*), denoted unsolicited sexual advances, such as might occur, for example, on the streets of Edo, with the senior male, the implied subject of the decree, in the role of initiator. The key word here is *mutai*, which carries a sense of exceeding proper bounds or using force, not unlike the Eng-

28. This interpretation appears in the late Edo-period chronicle *Bukō nenpyō* (see Yoshida Setsuko, *Edo kabuki*, 33), which cites an ambiguous passage in the early eighteenth-century memoir *Mukashi mukashi monogatari* (in *Zoku Nihon zuihitsu taisei*, ed. Mori Senzō and Kitagawa Hirokuni, 24 vols. [Yoshikawa kōbunkan, 1979–1983], supp. vol. 1, 57–58), by Takaratsu Shusō or Niimi Masatomo.

29. Yoshida Setsuko, *Edo kabuki*, 33.

lish term "outrage." It encompassed within its semantic field incidents that would now be described as rape. The second object of proscription was *wakashugurui*, which literally meant "going crazy over youths."[30] Once again the keynote was excess, but the context here was more likely to be a commercialized one, such as flourished around the institution of *wakashu kabuki* at the time. Patronage of actors and other youths had become a fashionable urban pastime that, if overzealously pursued, had consequences that shogunal authorities found alarming, including overheated passions, unseemly mingling of classes, conspicuous consumption, and neglect of other social responsibilities. Yet, by using the term *wakashugurui*, bakufu officials implicitly recognized that *shudō* had its legitimate place as long as it remained within certain limits, and did not spell out precisely at what point one began to "lose one's head."

A renewed Edo decree of 1652 was more specific about the object and means of *shudō* importuning, stating that it was forbidden (*hatto*) to send "outrageous" letters to the children of townsmen or to pages (*koshō*).[31] Senior males conventionally used such missives to communicate their unspoken interest in a youth, particularly when the two were not formally acquainted, as must often have been the case in an urban environment. If the youth already possessed a lover or other admirers, however, such advances could spark resentment and jealousy, leading to incidents of violence. Indeed, when officials in Edo issued another ban on importuning in 1653, they cited as their reason the fact that disputes (*deiri*) over *shudō* had been taking place of late in various parts of the city. Bakufu lawmakers characterized persons who engaged in such activities as "ill-mannered" (*busahō*), enjoining their neighbors to point out the error of their ways and, if all else failed, to report them to the offices of Edo's town magistrates.[32]

Whereas the object of reproof in the above decrees was the *nenja* or would-be *nenja* (in a commercial context, the erotic consumer), shogunal officials more typically attempted to regulate the supply side of urban *shudō* culture. The most familiar example is the kabuki theater, one of the latter's central institutions, and it is this aspect of *shudō* culture to which we will turn our attention next.[33] With respect to sexuality, bakufu policy toward

---

30. The bakufu had already prohibited *wakashugurui* among its guardsmen (*go-banshū*) in 1624, but this provision would not have affected the townsman populace of Edo, nor bakufu retainers at large. See Kikuchi, *Tokugawa kinrei kō kōshū*, 3:1–2.

31. Yoshida Setsuko, *Edo kabuki*, 38.

32. Yoshida Setsuko, *Edo kabuki*, 42.

33. For another discussion of theater policy, see Donald H. Shively, "*Bakufu*

kabuki involved two main elements: an effort to strip the stage of blatant eroticism; and an attempt to sever the connection between the theater and prostitution. In the eyes of samurai administrators, the theater and its attendant institutions represented a celebration of eroticism in a setting that, given its commercial nature, encouraged the most wanton forms of indecorum and immoderation. The present discussion will center on Edo, but developments in Kyoto and Osaka seem to have unfolded along similar, if not necessarily identical, lines.

Bakufu concern with sexuality on the kabuki stage centered chiefly upon the representation of *joshoku* and especially on the display of female or feminine eroticism. Conventional accounts attribute kabuki's origins to a woman named Okuni, whose troupe of male and female players performed in Kyoto as early as 1603, the year of the Tokugawa bakufu's founding.[34] Though the genre has become in later times associated with the "impersonation" of women by male actors, in these early days it was just as common to find female performers acting the part of men, complete with topknot, sword, and other virile accoutrements. Story lines—if they may be called that, since narrative was originally far less important than song and dance—frequently revolved around visits to female prostitutes (sometimes played by males), and many artists were themselves professional courtesans. Distressed by this theatrical glorification of lasciviousness and by the violence that often broke out among overenthusiastic patrons, bakufu officials banned female and mixed companies from the stage in 1629.[35]

While *onna* (women's) kabuki thus met an early demise, shogunal officials were not overly concerned yet with the social impact of another form of kabuki, whose principal players were adolescent males with unshorn forelocks. *Wakashu* kabuki, as it was called, was at least as old as its female counterpart, and relied similarly upon the erotic charms of its performers. The genre drew its subject matter not only from the world of *joshoku*, but also from *shudō*, so that male-male eroticism developed into a staple theme for

---

versus *Kabuki*," in *Studies in the Institutional History of Early Modern Japan*, 231–261.

34. The most detailed Western-language account of early kabuki history may be found in Benito Ortolani, *Das Kabukitheater: Kulturgeschichte der Anfänge*, Monumenta Nipponica Monograph no. 19 (Sophia University Press, 1964).

35. Yoshida Setsuko, *Edo kabuki*, 24–25. Reiterations of the ban as late as 1646 (Yoshida Setsuko, *Edo kabuki*, 25–26, 28, 31) indicate that it was not entirely effective at first.

kabuki drama, as it had long been in the nō theater.[36] Bakufu administrators worried less about the dramatic representation of male-male sexuality, however, than about the interaction of masculine and feminine genders that even an all-male cast could enact onstage. In 1642, therefore, lawmakers in Edo proscribed skits in which male actors, bedecked in feminine apparel, imitated women in a "provocative" (*namamekishi*) manner. Earlier in the year, bakufu authorities had cut short just such a performance by the actor Murayama Sakon, whose beguiling poses reportedly caused a great stir among Edo audiences.[37]

That the concern of bakufu officials lay with the unregulated interplay of masculine and feminine genders, rather than with *shudō* per se, is evident from the conditions under which authorities allowed such performances to resume in the following year. A clear legal distinction arose at this time between the players of masculine (*otokogata*) and feminine (*onnagata*) roles, or as they came to be called in theatrical argot, *tachiyaku* and *oyama*. Companies were required to identify explicitly the gender specialty of each performer, and actors could not switch from one to the other during the course of a single season.[38] Such administrative measures did little, however, to dampen the passions that kabuki actors instilled in their audiences, and it was amid just such an atmosphere that the aforementioned Edo decree about "going crazy over *wakashu*" appeared. Of particular worry to shogunal authorities was patronage of the theater and its demimonde by members of the samurai class, who were expected to embody exemplary moral standards and decorum, yet whose hotheaded tempers led to frequent incidents of violence. In 1652, Edo was abuzz, for instance, with news of a closely averted duel between two high samurai officials in Osaka, its alleged cause a drunken argument over "kabuki boys" (*kabukiko*). Another source reports an attempted love suicide by the wife of a daimyo and an actor, so it is possible that shogunal administrators were as much alarmed by stage-related *joshoku* as by *shudō* violence. Much as they had earlier proscribed women's kabuki, bakufu authorities moved to reaffirm social order by banning *wakashu* kabuki in all three metropolises.[39]

36. On *shudō* themes in nō and kabuki, see Dōmoto Masaki, <*Zōhoban*> *Nanshoku engekishi* (Shuppansha, 1976).
37. Yoshida Setsuko, *Edo kabuki*, 29.
38. Yoshida Setsuko, *Edo kabuki*, 29–30. By the end of the Edo period, the distinction between *otokogata* and *onnagata* had grown somewhat blurred, with actors sometimes appearing in both masculine and feminine guise during the course of a single play.
39. Yoshida Setsuko, *Edo kabuki*, 37–42. Ogasawara Kyōko (cited in Jurgis Elisonas,

By the following year, however, kabuki had returned to the stage in each of these cities. The conditions under which bakufu officials agreed to relicensing suggest again that the most ideologically troubling aspect of kabuki was not its association with male-male sexuality, but instead the lascivious interaction of genders that it was able to conjure up onstage even in the absence of female players.[40] In response, samurai bureaucrats attempted to moderate young thespians' ability to represent femininity by regulating certain aspects of their physical appearance—particularly coiffure, which functioned in the Edo period as a crucial marker of social identity.[41] In order to make kabuki not only all-male but more nearly all-masculine, bakufu officials stipulated that players of all ages shave their forelocks in the manner of adult males (*yarō*); hence, theater historians refer to the genre as it was reconstituted after 1653 as *yarō* (men's) kabuki in order to distinguish it from the earlier *wakashu* kabuki. Players of feminine roles and *joshoku* themes continued to appear onstage, but bakufu authorities evidently hoped that the performers' bald pates would provide a continual reminder that the actors were in fact male, while the tonsorial initiation of these youths into the ranks of adulthood removed them from the category of erotic objects in *shudō*.[42]

By a peculiar semantic logic, the term *yarō*, which originally carried the connotation of an adult male, thus came to refer in common parlance to kabuki actors and other youthful purveyors of *shudō* whose business depended precisely upon their erotic "otherness" from men. Actors, whether they specialized in youths' or women's roles, soon found a way to mitigate the jarring dissonance imposed by the bakufu between their gendered personae and their physical appearance by concealing their shaven foreheads—that unmistakable sign of manhood—with purple caps known as *yarō bōshi*, and later with wigs, although the use of both articles was originally

---

"Notorious Places: A Brief Excursion into the Narrative Topography of Early Edo," in *Edo and Paris: Urban Life and the State in the Early Modern Era*, ed. James L. McClain et al. [Ithaca: Cornell University Press, 1994], 267–268) connects the 1652 ban on *wakashu* kabuki with the death in the previous year of the shogun Tokugawa Iemitsu, whose partiality for this genre, Ogasawara argues, had earlier afforded it some legal protection.

40. For the same reason, Edo officials in 1658 and again in 1664 banned skits revolving around the procurement of female courtesans, known colloquially as Shimabara (after the courtesan quarter in Kyoto). See Yoshida Setsuko, *Edo kabuki*, 47, 51–52.

41. Actors' clothing, which served as a marker not only of gender but of class, was also the target of repeated sumptuary legislation.

42. Yoshida Setsuko, *Edo kabuki*, 42–43.

proscribed.[43] The former item of apparel became so intimately associated with the erotic allure of kabuki that it served, by metonymy, as a virtual synonym for the actor-prostitute, and, conveniently for modern-day viewers, provides a clue as to his sex in pictorial representations of that milieu. Bakufu efforts to regulate gender onstage thus succeeded less in the suppression of eroticism than in its stylization.[44]

The theater and prostitution—or, one might say, artistic and sexual performance—were closely aligned in Edo-period popular culture. In dealing with kabuki, shogunal authorities sought, again with limited success, to drive a wedge between the two. As early as 1648, Edo officials explicitly prohibited the "outrageous" (*mutai*) pursuit of *shudō* with actors or dancers, following closely upon the heels of their more general interdiction of importuning and "going crazy over youths."[45] Once again, we note that this decree outlaws not the entire realm of *shudō*, but only vaguely defined "outrages" taking place among specific status groups. It is unclear, for instance, whether a sexual relationship between two performers, by all accounts a common occurrence within the theatrical demimonde, would have fallen under the scope of the ordinance.[46] In spite of such warnings, however, the pool of youthful talent that furnished the kabuki stage with actors continued to provide a major source of male-male as well as male-female prostitution in Edo and other cities well into the nineteenth century.

Bakufu bureaucrats attempted to discourage prostitution by actors by segregating them from the populace at large and by confining their professional activities to the stage. Segregation involved both ideological and physical aspects. In official class ideology, actors and other entertainers occupied one of the lowest rungs of the social hierarchy, not far removed from such out-

43. Yoshida Setsuko, *Edo kabuki*, 51–52, 55–58.
44. Indeed, as Saikaku alleges (Ihara, *Nanshoku ōkagami*, 39:491–492 [Schalow, *Great Mirror*, 214–215]), tonsorial legislation may ironically have expanded opportunities for actors to engage in prostitution (I quote from Schalow's translation): "Theater proprietors and the boys' managers alike were upset at the effect [that the regulations of 1653] might have on business, but looking back on it now the law was probably the best thing that ever happened to them. It used to be that no matter how splendid the boy, it was impossible for him to keep his forelocks and take on patrons beyond the age of twenty. Now, since everyone wore the hairstyle of adult men, it was still possible at age 34 or 35 for youthful-looking actors to get under a man's robe. How strange are the ways of love!"
45. Yoshida Setsuko, *Edo kabuki*, 33–34.
46. By the eighteenth century, customary norms in the theater world barred erotic liaisons between members of the same troupe, yet such rules remained uncodified and were often infringed. See Kawatake Shigetoshi, *Kabukishi no kenkyū* (Tōkyōdō, 1943), 332–333.

cast groups as leather artisans and beggars, who did not even rank among the "four estates." Nevertheless, unlike the latter groups, kabuki actors did not fall under the administrative jurisdiction of Edo's *etagashira* or pariah chief.[47] Legally speaking, they constituted a species of townsman, albeit one to whom special restrictions applied. Nor was social prejudice against them nearly so strong as against outcasts proper; indeed, stage performers were among the idols of the age. Because of the fascination that actors held for urban audiences, bakufu lawmakers struggled to keep the official stigma against them visible to the public, requiring, for instance, that they wear deep-brimmed wicker hats (*amigasa*) on their forays outside the theater, in the manner of convicted criminals.[48] In addition to concealing their erotic attractions from the passing gaze, this measure underscored their quasi-pariah status, conveying a sense of shamefulness and marginality. A similar implication lay behind such derogatory legal designations as *kawaramono*—literally, "riverbank person"—which harked back to the riverside flatlands (such as Shijōgawara in Kyoto) that had escaped municipal taxation in the medieval period and thus come to serve as home to indigent entertainers.[49]

During the Edo period, this riparian association was more figurative than literal, but the physical isolation of actors from the rest of the populace remained a key principle of urban policy. Bakufu administrators strove to contain the two "evil places" (*akusho*)—that is, the licensed brothel quarter and the theater district—within clearly defined geographical boundaries, where ethically suspect activities, while tolerated, might be carefully watched and regulated.[50] In Edo, kabuki theaters were confined for most of the period to the three wards of Sakaichō, Fukiyachō, and Kobikichō. A 1662 edict ordered

47. For legal decisions affirming kabuki actors' independence from the pariah administration, see Yoshida Setsuko, *Edo kabuki*, 108–109, 227–229.

48. Yoshida Setsuko, *Edo kabuki*, 225–226, 420–433. Interestingly, a 1652 decree (Yoshida Setsuko, *Edo kabuki*, 42–43) prohibited actors from wearing these very same hats (along with hoods or other concealing headgear), presumably because they facilitated illicit trysts.

49. *Kawaramono* was a term also favored by Confucian moralists such as Ogyū Sorai, who complained in the early eighteenth century of the powerful cultural influence that actors exerted over their social superiors, and opposed their involvement in mercantile activities or intermarriage with other classes. See Ogyū Sorai, *Seidan*, in *Nihon shisō taikei*, 36:283–284 (trans. J. R. McEwan in *The Political Writings of Ogyū Sorai* [Cambridge: Cambridge University Press, 1962], 54–55).

50. On the significance of the "evil place," see Hirosue Tamotsu, *Henkai no akusho*, Heibonsha sensho, no. 27 (Heibonsha, 1973); Hirosue Tamotsu, <*Shinpen*> *Akubasho no hassō* (Chikuma shobō, 1988), esp. 170–206.

actors to live within these areas, and to refrain from venturing elsewhere—although many in fact did.[51] Conversely, the notion of the "evil place" marked ingress into these districts, though not necessarily illegal, as unbecoming of worthy citizens, and particularly for members of the moral elite. Although occasional visits might be excused among the vulgar classes, the kabuki theater and its environs were in theory no place for samurai, for whom the only form of dramatic entertainment deemed respectable was the centuries-old nō theater. Such official disapproval notwithstanding, urban warriors, including daimyo and even an occasional shogun, along with the women of their households, numbered among kabuki's most enthusiastic patrons, exhibiting a disregard for class decorum that social critics constantly bewailed.

While tolerating a certain amount of contact between actors and other social strata within the confines of the theater district, bakufu administrators devised various measures to restrict that contact to a spectatorial level. A 1668 decree, for instance, prohibited Edo's *yarō* from paying unnecessary calls upon patrons of the townsman or peasant classes, much less from meeting with samurai retainers, further stipulating that theater boxes (*sajiki*), where such meetings sometimes took place, must not be outfitted with hanging blinds so as to screen out the regulatory gaze.[52] Edo authorities also forbade private entertaining at the homes of actors or troupe managers (*zamoto*), as well as in the teahouses of the theater districts.[53] In view of these restrictions and the general opprobrium adhering to the "evil places," a tempting alternative, particularly for members of the samurai elite, was to summon performers to their own residences, but this practice, too, faced numerous legal strictures. An Edo decree of 1655, for example, warned kabuki actors not to visit daimyo mansions "even if invited," while a similar one of 1678 commented on their propensity to spend the night there, creating a "disorderly [or lewd] atmosphere" (*midarigamashiki fuzei*).[54] Typically, such legislation addressed not so much the actor himself as the entrepreneur responsible for his activities, enjoining the latter not to "send out" performers or to "allow them to walk about" on the town.

In the urban market for male-male erotic services, the kabuki actor occupied only the highest niche in a broad range of occupational types. It did

51. Yoshida Setsuko, *Edo kabuki*, 50–51. When the residential order was repeated in 1678 (Yoshida Setsuko, *Edo kabuki*, 63), it further stipulated that actors could not live in the same premises with members of other social groups.

52. Hanpō kenkyūkai, *Hanpōshū*, 8a:351; Yoshida Setsuko, *Edo kabuki*, 55–58.

53. Yoshida Setsuko, *Edo kabuki*, 60, 120–137, 220–221, 308–309, 510–511.

54. Yoshida Setsuko, *Edo kabuki*, 43–44, 63.

not take long for imitators to appear, who emulated various aspects of his esthetic style but did not necessarily command the same connoisseurial esteem or equally high fees. A bakufu edict of 1666, for example, decried the recent popularity among Edo townsmen of "fake" (*nise*) *yarō*, who carried their props along with them, including false locks (*tsukegami*) and rented stage apparel, in order to entertain at private venues.[55] "Ordinary townsmen" (*tsune no chōnin*), who were not bound by the confines of the theater district, also met some of the demand for male-male entertainment at samurai homes.[56] Even female prostitutes appropriated some of the erotic allure that emanated from the all-male stage. A 1694 Edo decree, for instance, listed among the various types of performer-prostitutes whom it was forbidden to hire out an intriguing figure called the *kagema onna* ("*kagema* woman"), who draped her biological femaleness with the erotic trappings of a professional youth. Though all too few details are known about her calling, she appears to have attracted clients not merely by her provision of *joshoku* services but by her stylistic evocation of *shudō*.[57]

It was this last figure's male equivalent and namesake, the *kagema*, who came to serve as a virtual synonym for male prostitution, at least in the city of Edo. In the extant legal record, the *kagema* makes one of his earliest appearances in a 1689 prohibitory decree, the language of which implies that the term was a colloquial one and somewhat beneath the dignity of bakufu lawmakers.[58] Samurai legislators preferred instead such designations as "masterless" (*rōnin*) *yarō*—drawing a parallel between the *kagema* and the warrior who was not in service to a particular lord, and therefore somewhat suspect—or simply a youth "with forelocks who does not appear onstage." The key distinction here was between bona fide kabuki actors, who were affiliated with accredited troupes, and the denizens of a broader demimonde

55. Yoshida Setsuko, *Edo kabuki*, 53–54.

56. Yoshida Setsuko, *Edo kabuki*, 82–83, 84–85, 90–91, 101–103, 112.

57. Hanpō kenkyūkai, *Hanpōshū*, 8a:32; Yoshida Setsuko, *Edo kabuki*, 78–79. A decree (Yoshida Setsuko, *Edo kabuki*, 81–82) of the following year contained a similar list, and further forbade the procurement of such entertainers for boat excursions. An Osaka counterpart to the *kagema onna* may be found in the *wakashu jorō*, a type of female prostitute whom a 1678 erotic guidebook (Fujimoto Kizan, <Kanpon> *Shikidō ōkagami* [Kyoto: Yūzan shobō, 1973], 103) describes as shaving her pate and wearing youths' clothing so as to "win the patronage of those fond of *shudō*." For a Kyoto equivalent—the ancestor of today's *maiko*—see Ihara, *Kōshoku ichidai onna*, 38:435–439 (Morris, *Amorous Woman*, 126–129); Ihara Saikaku, *Kōshoku ichidai otoko*, in *Nihon koten bungaku zenshū*, 38:191 (trans. Kengi Hamada under the title *The Life of an Amorous Man* [Rutland, Vt.: Tuttle, 1964], 112).

58. Yoshida Setsuko, *Edo kabuki*, 72–73.

surrounding the theater, which drew upon its cachet but, since it was not officially supposed to exist, was not subject to the same system of controls. The ranks of the latter were filled in part by apprentice actors, still young in years and immature in terms of artistic talent, but whom troupes required to ensure their continuity or to populate a sparse stage; one plausible etymology for the term *kagema* thus has him waiting "in the shadows" (*kage no ma*) of the theater. Many *kagema*, however, had little hope of ever treading the boards, the arena of their performance centering instead upon on the institution of the teahouse.

The *kagemajaya* or "*kagema* teahouse" has appeared in the context of popular discourse in the previous chapter. Let us take a moment now to consider its legal status. Contrary to the impression that popular discourse all too easily conveys, this institution was never entirely legal, at least in the city of Edo. While female prostitution enjoyed official recognition, and was even taxed, under the condition that it remained within the licensed quarter, bakufu lawmakers defined the theater district, that other "evil place," as a site for esthetic, not carnal, pleasure. Nevertheless, by the eighteenth century male prostitution in Edo had assumed a highly institutionalized form, not only within the latter's precincts but also in the teahouses of such neighborhoods as Yoshichō, which lay near the major playhouses, or of Yushima and Shiba, whose shrine grounds were home to the periodic stage performances known as *miyashibai*. The lack of bureaucratic sanction under which these establishments operated and their geographic dispersion gave them more in common with the various sites of unlicensed female prostitution collectively referred to as *okabasho* (literally, "places on a hill") than with the established courtesan quarter in Yoshiwara; it is significant, for instance, that the early nineteenth-century bibliophile Ishizuka Hōkaishi appends a lengthy section on *kagemajaya* to his study of these (not always literally) hilly places.[59] At the same time, unauthorized male prostitution did not earn the same categorical punishments in bakufu penal law as did its female equivalent, resting in a legal gray area that permitted a variety of official attitudes ranging from benign tolerance to fitful repression.

Before the nineteenth century, bakufu attempts to regulate the erotic culture of the *kagemajaya* focused less upon the teahouse itself than upon the establishment that supplied it with youthful prostitutes. The latter, known colloquially as a *kodomoya* or "boy [literally, child] house," was in most

---

59. Ishizuka Hōkaishi, *Okaba yūkaku kō*, in *Mikan zuihitsu hyakushu*, ed. Mitamura Engyo, 12 vols. (Chūō kōronsha, 1976–1978), 1:55–84.

cases physically and financially distinct from the teahouse proper, which merely provided a venue for the assignation. In the three metropolises, it was forbidden throughout much of the Edo period not only to send out actors for private liaisons, but also to keep any other youth on call for such purposes, so that the *kodomoya*'s line of business was in principle illegal. Edo officials made this perfectly clear in 1689 when they ordered all *yarō* who did not perform onstage to be returned, with forelocks shorn, to their parents or guarantors (*ukenin*), forcing employers to write off their contracts at a loss.[60] While bakufu authorities "graciously exempted" bona fide kabuki actors from this provision, they required their employers to submit a written pledge (*tegata*) that they would not provide the actors' company to offstage patrons or retain the services of nontheatrical youths.[61] In order to maintain a semblance of legality, *kodomoya* had thus to resort to various subterfuges, such as billing themselves as studios for kabuki choreography, lodgings for itinerant performers, or even hair-oil (*binzukeabura*) dealers. Judging from the degree of notoriety that such establishments enjoyed in popular writings, it seems unlikely that samurai officials were utterly unaware of the true nature of their business, yet so long as external appearances were maintained, a certain amount of bureaucratic leniency prevailed throughout much of the period.[62] When bakufu authorities took action against them, it was not necessarily to shut them down, but sometimes only to curb their most conspicuous excesses. We find, for instance, a 1750 document pledging a lodging house in Edo's Shiba district not to allow its wards to wear garments of a color or fabric reserved for girls and the elite, or to chatter too loudly while hanging their clothes out to dry or otherwise in view of the general public.[63]

It would be a mistake, however, to interpret bakufu regulation of commercialized male eroticism, whether in the context of the theater or the

60. Yoshida Setsuko, *Edo kabuki*, 70–76.

61. For examples of such documents, see Dokushō Koji, "Danshō," *Edo kaishi*, November 1889, 60–62; Yoshida Setsuko, *Edo kabuki*, 74–75. A 1694 Edo decree (Yoshida Setsuko, *Edo kabuki*, 79–80) limited the number of *yarō* actors and apprentices that a troupe manager might employ to twenty and ten respectively.

62. Bribery may have had something to do with it as well, since *kagemajaya* in Edo customarily furnished neighborhood elders (*nanushi*) with tips called *bōshikin* or "cap money" during the year-end count of actors and apprentices. See Yoshida Setsuko, *Edo kabuki*, 214. According to the Meiji author Jōno Denpei (Saigiku Sanjin, <Sannin kyōkaku> *Kagema no adauchi* [Junseidō, 1899], 29), the going rate in early nineteenth-century Yoshichō was two *shu* of gold per *kagema*, paid twice yearly.

63. Dokushō Koji, "Danshō," 61–62.

teahouse, solely in terms of *shudō*. We have seen, for example, that the banning of *wakashu* kabuki may have resulted in part from an intrigue between an actor and the wife of a high-ranking warrior. Similarly, one of the most notorious legal incidents in kabuki history arose from the discovery in 1714 of an illicit liaison between Ikushima Shingorō, an actor, and Ejima, a lady-in-waiting to the shogun's mother. The latter episode led to punishments ranging from loss of post to banishment and execution for dozens of parties implicated in the affair, as well as to the closing of a major Edo playhouse, tightened restrictions upon the architecture of theaters and teahouses as far away as Kyoto, and renewed warnings about actors socializing with patrons.[64] By all accounts, however, *kagemajaya* in Edo continued for more than a century to count females among their steady customers, conspicuous among them the occupants of the women's quarters of shogunal or daimyo residences (like Ejima and her companions) as well as the widowed heads (*goke*) of townsman households. A legal document from 1842 specifically mentions female moneylenders—no doubt some of them widows—among their clientele, a situation that helped prompt a large-scale bakufu crackdown on *kagemajaya* in that year (see chapter 3).[65]

Other forms of erotic work by males were not directly related to the kabuki theater. Among the warrior class, as well as wealthy townsmen who tried to emulate them, young male attendants called *kozōritori*, for example, were sometimes expected to provide services beyond their nominal duty as sandal bearers. Legislation surrounding the *kozōritori* reveals two central concerns on the part of shogunal authorities: an anxiety over conspicuous consumption linked to the enforcement of status decorum; and an attempt to restrict the supply side of urban male prostitution. As early as 1629, the bakufu forbade its retainers to bring *kozōritori* with unshorn forelocks into the shogunal castle, either fearing the distraction that they might cause there, or because to strut about with them in tow, unless one were the shogun himself, was regarded as excessively ostentatious, much like the wearing of crimson scabbards proscribed by the same directive.[66] The 1652 decree cited

---

64. For legal documents relating to the so-called Ejima incident, see Kyōto machibure kenkyūkai, ed., *Kyōto machibure shūsei*, 15 vols. (Iwanami shoten, 1983–1989), 1:213–214; Yoshida Setsuko, *Edo kabuki*, 120–137. In 1706, the bakufu had already punished Ikushima's younger brother Daikichi, an *onnagata*, for his affair with the widow of the lord of Nagoya. See Yoshida Setsuko, *Edo kabuki*, 98.

65. Yoshida Setsuko, *Edo kabuki*, 433–434.

66. Naimushō keihokyoku, ed., *Tokugawa jidai keisatsu enkakushi*, 2 vols., Keisatsu kenkyū shiryō, nos. 6 and 7 (Naimushō keihokyoku, 1927), 1:534.

earlier in connection with *shudō* letter writing suggests, moreover, that the favors of sandal bearers were sometimes available to third parties for a fee. A separate section of the edict commanded the lowly retainers known as *rokushaku* and *komono*, who were often classed as townsmen, to stop hiring out sandal bearers with whom they shared an "intimate friendship" (*chiin*) or "bond of brotherhood or blood relation" (*kyōdai shinrui no keiyaku*). If a contract existed between them, the youth was to be set free, and his master investigated and punished.[67] Similarly, Minakata Kumagusu quotes an Edo decree of the previous year denying lodging to "clandestine" (*kakushi*) sandal bearers.[68]

Another target of bureaucratic vigilance was the *kōguuri* or incense peddler, whose trade sometimes served as a screen for the door-to-door purveyance of sexual services.[69] As in the case of the kabuki actor, bakufu officials turned to tonsorial policy in an attempt to limit the erogenous potential of his calling. A pair of Edo decrees from 1670 ordered that *kōguuri* and other young male peddlers with unshorn forelocks be registered with authorities and henceforth go about their business with shaven pates.[70] When officials in Edo carried out a crackdown against "kabuki boys and similar types" (*kabukikodomo no rui*) in 1689, they were careful to state that such provisions applied equally to those who "use other forms of commerce as a pretext" (*hoka no shōbai ni kakotsukesōrōte*) for erotic dealings.[71] Ironically, by assimilating such nontheatrical occupations as that of the *kōguuri* to the milieu of kabuki, bakufu bureaucrats tacitly admitted that the profession of actor, with whom he was seen to share something in common, and to whom his coiffure was made to conform, was itself deeply implicated in the marketing of *shudō*.

The commercial culture of male-male eroticism that developed in Edo had equivalents in the westerly metropolises of Kyoto and Osaka; indeed, many of its fashions, as well as much of its personnel, sprang originally from the latter area. Bakufu legislation, however, flowed mainly in the opposite

67. Yoshida Setsuko, *Edo kabuki*, 38.

68. Minakata Kumagusu to Iwata Jun'ichi, 16 September 1931, *Minakata Kumagusu zenshū*, ed. Iwamura Shinobu et al., 12 vols. (Heibonsha, 1971–1975), 9:67.

69. Popular sources link other types of peddlers with male prostitution, including vendors of sundry goods (*komamonouri*) and fan paper (*jigamiuri*). For a literary portrait of the incense seller, see Ihara, *Kōshoku ichidai otoko*, 38:142–144 (Hamada, *Amorous Man*, 55–57).

70. Yoshida Setsuko, *Edo kabuki*, 59–60.

71. Yoshida Setsuko, *Edo kabuki*, 72–72. For a 1689 Osaka decree equating incense peddling with clandestine male prostitution, see Ōsaka-shi sanjikai, ed., *Ōsaka shishi*, 7 vols. (Osaka: Ōsaka-shi sanjikai, 1911–1915), 3:107–108.

direction. A number of Edo decrees explicitly included Kyoto and Osaka within their provisions; in other cases, officials in the latter cities applied Edo laws by analogy. Nevertheless, legal restrictions surrounding *shudō* and its institutions varied to some extent from city to city, just as the dramatic style of Kamigata kabuki differed from its Edo counterpart. To tease out these local peculiarities remains an important task for future research, along with the intricacies of bakufu law in other regions.[72]

DANGEROUS LIAISONS

If regional variation cannot be ignored when considering the legal construction of male-male sexuality within bakufu territory, it is of even greater importance when we extend our gaze to the domains. The *Buke shohatto*, as revised in 1635, declared that all daimyo must obey the laws of Edo, yet with respect to the affairs of his own han, the daimyo was also a lawgiver in his own right.[73] The volume of legislation issuing from castle chambers in the more than five hundred domains that existed for all or part of the Edo period is immense. Of the fraction that survives, only a limited portion has been published, yet even this quantity is more than any one scholar can navigate with ease. The present section of this inquiry therefore does not claim to offer an exhaustive survey; instead, through a necessarily restricted sampling, it will identify three general features of han legislation concerning male-male sexuality, exceptions to any of which may exist in the individual instance.[74] The first of these features is the simple fact of diversity; more research is necessary before regional patterns can be charted. The second is a focus on perisexual elements, as opposed to sexual acts, as previously observed in the

72. While lying somewhat outside the chronological scope of this inquiry, an intriguing question arises in connection with Nagasaki, another bakufu-controlled city. Shortly before the Edo period, Nagasaki had been ceded for a brief time (1580–1587) to the Society of Jesus, which assumed sole responsibility there for the administration of justice. Is it possible therefore that European-style "sodomy" punishments once had a legal basis on Japanese soil?

73. For the revised code, see Ishii, *Kinsei hōsei shiryō sōsho,* 2:3–4; John Carey Hall, *Japanese Feudal Law,* 105–109. On domain laws in general, see Harafuji Hiroshi, "*Han* Laws in the Edo Period with Particular Emphasis on Those of Kanazawa *Han,*" *Acta Asiatica* 35 (1978): 46–71.

74. Hanpō kenkyūkai, *Hanpōshū,* and Kyōto daigaku Nihon hōshi kenkyūkai, *Hanpō shiryō shūsei,* have served as my chief sources of han legislation, supplemented by a variety of collections for individual domains. Apart from ease of access to materials, no strict organizing principle has guided my choice of domains. Since domains were often known by more than one name, I have employed the designations found in Kimura Motoi et al., eds., *Hanshi daijiten,* 8 vols. (Yūzankaku, 1988–1990).

case of bakufu law. A final characteristic is that han lawmakers tended to devote a greater degree of attention to noncommercialized forms of *shudō* than their Edo counterparts, a situation reflecting not only differing socioeconomic conditions but also the underlying nature of domain power itself.

Domain governments, just like the bakufu, compiled their own penal codes, which typically included a section on sexual offenses. As with the *Kujikata osadamegaki* that guided bakufu adjudicators, this type of legislation was largely silent or at least neutral on the subject of male-male sexuality.[75] For example, authorities in Kanazawa, roughly coterminous with today's Ishikawa prefecture and one of the largest and most economically productive of Edo-period domains, incorporated no specific penalties for male-male sexual relations in the domain penal code despite the fact that *shudō* had clearly come to official attention in connection with other crimes. Among the judicial precedents that make up the bulk of the code, for instance, is the summary of a 1688 murder case that mentions a *shudō* tie as part of the background of the slaying, yet without attaching any particular censure to the relationship itself. The entry in question relates that Katsumi Sōsuke, a samurai male of the lowly *wakatō* rank, had exchanged *shudō* vows with one Kakusuke, a *komono* serving in the same household. Nevertheless, during an official procession from Edo, Katsumi, having become "intimate" (*nengoro*) with a third male, secretly slew Kakusuke on the outskirts of the town of Uozu, where their entourage was lodging. It is unclear from the rather terse account whether his act was premeditated or resulted from a quarrel. Although domain authorities beheaded (*zanzai*) Katsumi for the crime of murder, the third male, whose identity is not given and who apparently did not participate in the killing, seems to have gone unpunished. Neither Katsumi's *shudō* tie with a fellow retainer nor his "intimacy" with the unnamed third party, it would appear, merited legal action in and of itself. Rather, the compilers of the code record these details chiefly in order to attach a plausible motive to the slaying—a motive that future officials consulting the record in search of precedents might, if not necessarily condone, at least easily comprehend.[76]

---

75. Explicit provisions on male-male sexuality are absent from penal codes issued by the following domains (all except that of Tottori to be found in Kyōto daigaku Nihon hōshi kenkyūkai, *Hanpō shiryō shūsei*): Hirosaki (1797–1848; 5–50); (Tanba) Kameyama (1789; 291–356); Kumamoto (1754–1839; 359–511); Morioka (1809; 53–111); Nagoya (1745–1854; 185–239); Shibata (c. 1783; 160–180); Tottori (?–1868; Hanpō kenkyūkai, *Hanpōshū*, 2:501–531); Wakayama (c. Kyōwa era [1801–1804]; 243–288).

76. Harafuji, *Keijihō*, 482.

A 1708 case from the same domain provides another glimpse of *shudō* ties among provincial warriors, as well as their sometimes violent consequences. Here again, the situation is a triangular one, involving one Katsuki Genzō, a direct vassal (*kerai*) to the Sasahara house; his colleague Nakanishi Gen'emon; and a page boy (*kogoshō*) by the name of Nakajima Kanjūrō. Katsuki had incurred the enmity of Nakanishi by helping the young Nakajima dress his unshorn locks (a moderately intimate act by Edo-period standards), not knowing that the youth had already sworn a "bond of brotherhood" with Nakanishi. When Nakanishi's subsequent animosity threatened to hinder his career, Katsuki took advantage of a chance meeting after nightfall to cut down his fellow retainer by the roadside. Katsuki's confessed motive apparently failed at first to satisfy domain officials, since they attempted to torture him into admitting further misdeeds, albeit with no success. As in the previous instance, the judicial record passes no judgment on the relationship between Nakanishi and Nakajima, but only on Katsuki's act of murder, for which the sentence was beheading.[77]

A recognition of *shudō* ties as a legitimate, if potentially trouble-causing, part of the social fabric was not limited to domain authorities in Kanazawa, nor to cases involving the warrior class—as is illustrated by a 1724 incident from Sendai domain (Miyagi prefecture). Tanakaya Kiemon, whose name suggests that he was a merchant or artisan, had been "diverting himself in *nanshoku*" with his servant (*genin*) Gonpachi. This situation aroused the envy of Kiemon's wife, who requested that she, too, be allowed to share in Gonpachi's favors. Kiemon agreed to send Gonpachi to her bed, but, after the relationship was consummated, had a change of heart—out of jealousy for whom? one wonders—and locked her up on the pretext that she was mentally deranged (*ranshin*). Authorities investigating the situation found the wife to be sane, but guilty of adultery (*fugi*), an act they deemed inexcusable "even if the husband had permitted it." The adulterers, both wife and servant, were thus banished to the isle of Aji. Kiemon, on the other hand, received the nominally lighter sentence of exile north of the Kitakami River despite the fact that he was deemed responsible for abetting his wife's infidelity and had misrepresented the situation to authorities. While officials

77. Harafuji, *Keijihō*, 482–483. For another Kanazawa murder arising from "*shudō*-related matters" (*shudōgoto*), see Kōshaku Maeda-ke henshūbu, ed., *Kagahan shiryō*, 18 vols. (Ishiguro Bunkichi, 1929–1958), 4:521–522. In this 1677 case, han officials not only decapitated the killer, who was the son of a high-ranking retainer, but ordered his disgraced father, in whose home the incident had taken place, to commit *seppuku*, thereby bringing an end to his line of succession (*zekke*).

in Sendai domain thus saw in male-female sexual intercourse outside a legally sanctioned framework such as marriage or the licensed quarter a fundamental breach of morality demanding strict punishment regardless of the circumstances, male-male sexual practices, at least in a master-servant context, appeared to them merely as a form of "diversion" (*asobi*), posing no ethical problem so long as they did not lead to other criminal deeds.[78]

The diversity of han legislation prevents us from concluding, however, that penal law in the domains invariably left male-male sexual practices uncriminalized. In the domain of Kumamoto, for example, a penal code originally compiled in 1754 lists no specifically male-male sexual acts, but gave han officials the latitude to invoke provisions on male-female rape by analogy in cases where the victim was a male. The *Keihō sōsho*, which drew heavily upon Ming-dynasty Chinese precedent, mandated one hundred lashes and a punitive tattoo for men found guilty of raping a woman, or decapitation and exposure of the severed head (*zankyōshu*) if death or severe bodily harm resulted. Consensual intercourse with girls twelve years or under constituted statutory rape, except that the offender received no tattoo. In cases of light injury, the code granted magistrates discretion in determining the proper sentence. In 1797, Kumamoto authorities applied the above provisions to a case in which a peasant male named Naoemon had performed anal intercourse upon a six-year-old boy, causing damage to the latter's rectum, and inscribed this judgment in the penal code itself for the benefit of later adjudicators. Since the extent of injury is unclear, we do not know whether Naoemon was subjected to whipping, execution, or some intermediate penalty.[79] The implementation of a statute dealing with male-female sexuality to punish a male-male equivalent parallels the treatment of love suicide by the bakufu, and raises the possibility that administrators elsewhere resorted to similar analogies when penal law was silent about forms of male-male sexual behavior that they felt threatening to peace and order.

Finally, at least one case may be found in which han law prescribed a specific penalty—indeed, one of the harshest sort—for male-male sexual relations. The *Hatto no jōmoku*, a thirty-article code promulgated in 1625 by Kōchi domain on the island of Shikoku, mandated capital punishment not only for direct pages of the daimyo (*jikijiki koshō*) who formed ties in *shudō* (*nyakudō no chiin*), which "went without saying," but also for sec-

---

78. Shitō Masataka, *Sendai rukeishi* (Sendai: Hōbundō, 1980), 199–200. As a condition of exile, Kiemon lost his possessions, while his wife forfeited her dowry.
79. Kyōto daigaku Nihon hōshi kenkyūkai, *Hanpō shiryō shūsei*, 471–472.

ondary pages (*matakoshō*) who engaged in such relations.[80] It is revealing that the law targets a particular status group, and not male-male sexual practices as a whole. To begin with, pages were likely to be young, and thus a frequent target of sexual advances. Second, as attendants to those who filled the highest ranks of the samurai hierarchy, enjoying close access to their ears, thoughts, and persons, pages represented a weak link in domain security, most critical in the vicinity of the daimyo himself—hence the phrase "needless to say" in connection with the ruler's immediate entourage. Finally, since pages often served their masters as erotic partners, such prohibitions helped to reinforce the latter's exclusive claim to their sexual favors. One detects here an echo of the ditty reportedly sung by the hegemon Oda Nobunaga in the late sixteenth century, which intimated that he would lop off the head of any man who stole another's *wakashu* (including, presumably, his own), thus sending terror through the hearts of his retainers.[81]

In a sense, however, the relationship between page and daimyo represented only a highly eroticized form of the vertical link between males upon which the larger structure of domain power, its fundamental unit the bond of loyalty between vassal and lord, was based. *Shudō* ties among warriors could serve either to bolster this structure by encouraging the cultivation of *giri*, or, conversely, to undermine it, inasmuch as they established private and horizontal loyalties outside the official hierarchy of power. This was the dilemma expressed by Edayoshi Saburōzaemon, a retainer of Saga domain, as reported in *Hagakure*.

> To lay down one's life for another is the basic principle of *shudō*. If it is not so, it becomes a matter of shame. However, then you have nothing

---

80. Yamauchi Toyoaki et al., eds., *Yamauchi-ke shiryō: Dainidai Tadayoshi-kō ki*, 4 vols. (Kōchi: Yamauchi jinja hōmotsu shiryōkan, 1980–1981), 2:52. I am indebted to Luke Roberts for helping me to locate this reference. Yoshinaga Toyomi (*Tosa-han hōseishi* [Izumi shuppan, 1974], 52) interprets the phrase *matakoshō* to mean pages in general, although the wording is peculiar. Domain officials in Okayama (Ōsawa Koresada, *Kibi onko hiroku*, vols. 6–10 of *Kibi gunsho shūsei*, ed. Tanaka Seiichi and Morita Keitarō, 10 vols. [Kibi gunsho shūsei kankōkai, 1921–1932], 9:140) and Tokushima (Hanpō kenkyūkai, *Hanpōshū*, 3:1021) required page boys to subscribe to a written oath (*seishi*) that they would not engage in *shudō*. For a 1671 Aizu incident in which a page who had broken a similar pledge (*shinmon*) managed to escape the death penalty because of his youth, unlike his unlucky partner, see Toyoda Takeshi et al., eds., <*Aizu-han*> *Kasei jikki*, 16 vols. (Yoshikawa kōbunkan, 1975–1990), 2:572–573. Aizu is also the setting of a fictionalized account in Ihara, *Nanshoku ōkagami*, 39:326–332 (Schalow, *Great Mirror*, 63–68).

81. Konoe Nobuhiro, *Inu tsurezure*, in *Kanazōshi shūsei*, ed. Asakura Haruhiko and Fukuzawa Akio, 18 vols. to date (Tōkyōdō, 1980–), 4:17.

left to lay down for your master [in this case, the daimyo]. It is therefore understood to be something both pleasant and unpleasant.[82]

Viewed from the perspective of the daimyo, the *shudō* ideal of mutual loyalty unto death presented a potential challenge to his authority over the lives
of his vassals, and threatened to divert the technology of violence, which
was concentrated in the hands of the samurai class, away from his exclusive
command.[83]

Domain efforts to control horizontal links among samurai males are especially conspicuous around the beginning of the Edo period, as han governments sought to consolidate their domestic polities and bring an end to
a long era of *gekokujō*, or "those below overturning those above." Two terms
appear repeatedly in such legislation. The first of these is *chiin*, which, as
previously mentioned, signified an intimate bond of male friendship, often
encompassing an erotic element. The second is *totō* or conspiracy, denoting
any combination of forces that was not officially sanctioned. Just as peasant uprisings frequently earned this label, so might han administrators perceive erotic bonds between samurai males as cells of potential insurrection
against the domain order.

The Mōri house of Hagi domain (today's Yamaguchi prefecture) attempted to dissuade its retainers from forming *chiin* ties with one another
as early as 1596, even before the Tokugawa pacification. If a pair of vassals
insisted on pursuing such a relationship, warned a set of regulations issued
in that year, they must take care to maintain their loyalty (*chūsetsu*) to their
lord, reprimand each other's conduct when necessary, and understand that
they would be held equally responsible for any offense that their partner

82. Yamamoto Tsunetomo, *Hagakure*, in *Nihon shisō taikei*, 26:264 (trans.
William Scott Wilson under the title *Hagakure: The Book of the Samurai* [Kodan-
sha International, 1979], 59). I have used Wilson's translation, but substituted the
original *shudō* for the translator's "homosexuality."
83. The subversive potential of this double loyalty played itself out in many works
of popular fiction. In Urushiya Ensai's 1702 story collection *Nanshoku kinometsuke*
(in *Mikan chinpon shūsei*, ed. Sobu Fukurō and Imaoka Yoshio, 4 vols. [Koten hozon kenkyūkai, 1933–1934], 3:167), for example, a page boy, warned to cut short his
relationship with another retainer as a "disloyal" (*fuchū*) breach of domain law,
boldly declares: "Even if it results in death at the hands of one's lord, a *shudō* bond
is not a thing to be lightly abandoned." In a similar vein, Saikaku (Ihara, *Nanshoku
ōkagami*, 39:426–427 [Schalow, *Great Mirror*, 156]) has a page boy utter the following words to his lord (I quote from Schalow's translation): "A certain man has
fallen in love with me. . . . If I refuse him, I betray my honor as a follower of the
way of boy love [*jakudō*]. If I act freely, it means breaking my lord's laws and is tan-
tamount to rejecting your long-standing benevolence toward me. Please kill me so
that I may escape this quandary."

committed. Their bond thus constituted in a sense a legal union. If, on the other hand, a retainer turned to a *chiin* comrade for aid in settling a quarrel or some other "useless"—which is to say, private—matter by violent means, it was the equivalent of drawing a bow against the sovereign.[84] These regulations were amended in 1608 to prohibit retainers entirely from seeking *chiin* relationships with youths, call for the termination of previously existing bonds, and promise punishment for both parties if such relations continued in secret. Interestingly, the document's preceding clause addresses the problem of the *kabukimono*, suggesting that Hagi officials linked *shudō* practices with this flamboyant and ruffianly breed of early seventeenth-century warrior, whose violence and ganglike tendencies caused headaches for administrators all over the country.[85] Following a similar chain of association, a lengthy house code (*Tōke seihō jōjō*) of 1660 forbade retainers' "overindulgence in sex with males or females"—the antecedence of the male element is intriguing—then immediately went on to condemn all forms of conspiracy, citing the "exchange of written oaths pledging to share life and death," a conventional practice among *shudō* partners, as a prime example.[86]

Apprehensions over horizontal integration among samurai males surface around the same time in Yonezawa domain (in present-day Yamagata prefecture), at the opposite end of Honshu. A 1603 code issued by the ruling house of Uesugi banned conspiracy in the form of "intimate ties" (*konsetsu o musubi*) or "compacts of mutual aid" (*tanomoshidō no mōshiawase*) with youthful fellow retainers, not to mention with those of other military houses.[87] A stricter set of guidelines in 1612 prohibited all pledges of *chiin*, particularly in the case of youths, and, somewhat contradictorily, forbade excessive visiting "even among intimate [*chiin*] friends." Despite its privileged position in Confucian ethics, masculine friendship emerges in such legislation as a double-edged sword. As the 1612 document put it: "There

---

84. Yamaguchi-ken monjokan, ed., *Yamaguchi-ken shiryō*, 4 vols. to date (Yamaguchi: Yamaguchi-ken monjokan, 1973–), 5:3–4.

85. Yamaguchi-ken monjokan, *Yamaguchi-ken shiryō*, 5:6–7. On the *kabukimono* (whose name was related only indirectly to the kabuki theater), see Eiko Ikegami, *The Taming of the Samurai* (Cambridge: Harvard University Press, 1995), 203–211; Yamamoto Hirofumi, *Junshi no kōzō*, Sōsho shi no bunka, no. 19 (Kōbundō, 1994), 146–166.

86. Yamaguchi-ken monjokan, *Yamaguchi-ken shiryō*, 5:48.

87. *Godaidai goshikimoku*, 6 vols., *Yonezawa shishi hensan shiryō* 7, 10, 13, 16, 17, 19 (1981–1987), 7:40–41.

are both profitable and unprofitable friends, and one must take care with whom one consorts."[88]

In Yonezawa, the bureaucratic association of male-male erotic ties with samurai conspiracy long outlasted the early era of domain consolidation. A 1751 directive denounced the persistence of "immoderate [or illegal] forms" (*hōgai no shikata*) of *shudō* among retainers, laying blame not only upon the parties directly involved but also upon those who acted as go-betweens, as well as persons in a position of authority who overlooked such conduct among their underlings.[89] The pattern of behavior distressing to Yonezawa officials assumes somewhat clearer shape in a directive of 1775, which deserves quotation in full.

> Despite the fact that successive orders have been issued in the eighth month of 1612, the fifth month of 1723, and the third month of 1749 concerning persons who, calling *nanshoku* by the name of *shudō*, form cliques and enter into feuds, *shudō* incidents have been taking place of late in various neighborhoods. In the course of visiting one another, the parties' initial aspirations of loyalty turn to disagreement, and trivial admonitions, knowing no end, lead to matters of life and death. Such behavior results in a loss of trust among friends, and is contrary to the correct and harmonious path. Parents are inconvenienced on account of their children, and neighborhood disturbances, discord, and estrangement ensue. It is a profitless situation. Therefore, let it be ordered that previous restrictions be once and for all upheld, and that parents and heads of households firmly put an end to such practices. Not only group leaders, but also children of similar rank and post, should be instructed to control such behavior.[90]

We catch a glimpse here of a local male-male erotic culture far removed from the milieu of metropolitan kabuki, its ultimate currency not cash but violence. While youthful participants in this culture referred to their own activities as *shudō*, domain elders preferred to characterize them as *nanshoku*, implying that their true substance was not so elevated as the former

---

88. *Godaidai goshikimoku*, 7:43–44.

89. *Godaidai goshikimoku*, 13:22. A similar emphasis on moderation characterizes a 1656 han directive (*Godaidai goshikimoku*, 7:89–90) ordering retainers not to "go crazy over *shudō*" (*nyakudōgurui*) in an "excessive/lawless" (*muhō*) fashion. Would a more "moderate" degree of indulgence, one wonders, have met with domain approval?

90. *Godaidai goshikimoku*, 13:172. The 1612 ban has been mentioned above, but those of 1723 and 1749 are apparently no longer extant. For a 1788 reiteration, see *Godaidai goshikimoku*, 16:80.

term suggested, and thus illustrating that these two widely used signifiers for male-male eroticism could be employed in subtly different senses. The "way" that Yonezawa officials aimed to promote instead was that of "correctness and harmony" (*junro kaiwa*), which was based on such Confucian values as trustworthy friendship, filial piety, and loyalty to the ruler—the last of which entailed adherence to his pronouncements and abstinence from private alliances or the unauthorized use of force. Like much Yonezawa legislation of the 1770s, this directive bears the imprint of the reformist daimyo Uesugi Harunori, whose "politics of virtue," as the historian Mark Ravina characterizes it, drew inspiration from the moralistic Confucianism of the philosopher Hosoi Heishū.[91] From the point of view of Yonezawa authorities, *shudō*, at least in some of its forms, represented a departure from the proper "way," beckoning young males down a "profitless" (*kainaki*) path marked by soured friendships, distressed parents, and strained community relations.

In castle towns, where the bulk of the warrior population of the domains resided, violent manifestations of *shudō* continued to vex administrators long after officials in the metropolises had come to focus their attention upon its commercialized forms. In 1793, for instance, we find authorities in the Shikoku castle town of Matsuyama voicing displeasure over young samurai males who engaged in constant fighting over "matters of *nanshoku*." A favorite hangout for such rowdies was training places (*keikoba*) for martial and other arts, which, by drawing adolescents away from the safety of their homes, provided an ideal hunting grounds for would-be *nenja*. Matsuyama officials complained that this situation created a "nuisance" (*meiwaku*) for younger students and kept them from their studies. Adopting a rhetorical tack similar to that found in the earlier Yonezawa decree, Matsuyama authorities chided the troublemakers for forgetting such Confucian values as "loyalty and filial piety" (*chūkō*) and "courtesy" (*reijō*) toward their teachers, and for acting with an "imprudence" (*fushin*) unworthy of their station. Nevertheless, Matsuyama administrators were less sweeping in their condemnation of *nanshoku* than their Yonezawa counterparts, censuring the violence and disorder that it occasioned rather than the subject of contention, and attributing the offenders' misbehavior somewhat leniently to youthful "high spirits" (*kekki*).[92]

---

91. On Uesugi and his "politics of virtue," see Mark Ravina, *Land and Lordship in Early Modern Japan* (Stanford: Stanford University Press, forthcoming).

92. Kageura Tsutomu, ed., *Matsuyama-han hōreishū* (Kondō shuppansha, 1978), 305.

Elsewhere, the pursuit of *shudō* by "high-spirited" young samurai might have far more serious legal consequences. Drawing upon the official chronicle (*Kasei jikki*) of Aizu domain (in present-day Fukushima prefecture), the historian Ujiie Mikito has sketched the outlines of a youth culture in which *shudō* at times assumed an extremely ruthless form, prompting authorities in the castle town of Wakamatsu to carry out extensive prosecutions at least six different times during the late eighteenth and early nineteenth centuries.[93] Bureaucratic concern centered on male-male sexual assaults by young warriors, including the sons of high-ranking retainers, who felt little compunction in plucking victims of both samurai and townsman classes from the street as the unfortunate targets made their way to and from lessons (*keiko*), or else showing up en masse at a desired youth's doorstep so as to intimidate his parents into compliance. Such incidents, a 1777 entry notes, took place "both day and night," with the result that some young males in the castle town, like their contemporaries in Matsuyama, had become afraid to attend their lessons. Assailants often operated in groups, in some cases neighborhood based (and hence to some extent status linked), so that a sexual assault upon a victim from one part of town might draw retaliation against a resident of the offending district. Fearing the consequences of involving the domain bureaucracy, parents apparently preferred to settle such conflicts through private mediation. Nevertheless, a string of particularly brazen incidents between 1777 and 1805 proved too much for Aizu officials to overlook, resulting in sentences ranging from partial domiciliary confinement (*enryo*) for two of the victims, who had merely lied about being already involved with other *nenja* in an attempt to deter their assailants, to full house arrest (*kinsoku* or *chikkyo*), removal from the line of succession (*taichaku*), expulsion from the castle town (*jōka oiharai*), banishment from the fief (*ryōnai taikyo*), and incarceration (*agarizashiki*) for various perpetrators, as well as for members of their families.[94] This pattern of gang violence appears to have had something in common with the "immoderate" and "illegal" forms of *shudō* plaguing authorities in nearby Yonezawa, and would be echoed more than a century later by the "roughneck" students of Tokyo and other Meiji cities (to be discussed in chapter 4).

93. For a fuller narrative of events, see Ujiie Mikito, *Edo no shōnen* (Heibonsha, 1989), 122–128. For the original sources, see Toyoda, *Kasei jikki*, 12:46–47, 258–261; 13:370–372. Further incidents, not cited by Ujiie, appear in Toyoda, *Kasei jikki*, 10:558; 14:50–51, 228–229; 15:452–453.

94. While the sources do not provide a precise legal basis for these penalties, we may note that one samurai father rebuffed his son's pursuers on the grounds that the domain had previously issued decrees against *nanshoku*, and that the family's

The examples of domain law so far examined have dealt mostly with un-commercialized forms of *shudō,* and especially its more violent manifestations among the samurai class. Such concerns were not absent from the minds of bakufu lawmakers, who were in a sense domain administrators writ large, but from the latter part of the seventeenth century these issues were increasingly overshadowed by an anxiety over the commercial culture of male-male sexuality that had developed in the great metropolitan centers. In the same way, castle towns in the domains may be seen as Edos in miniature, sometimes harboring their own types of *shudō* enterprise. In 1777, for example, the poet Tomita Koreyuki, passing through the castle town of Shirakawa (in present-day Fukushima prefecture), was surprised to come across a teahouse there named Hoteiya, whose shop curtain (*noren*) boldly proclaimed that its business was "sending out *yarō*" (*deyarō*).[95] Such candid advertising is particularly striking in view of the fact that, just a few years later, Shirakawa's ruler was to be none other than Matsudaira Sadanobu, whose moralistic style of governance would earn him a nationwide reputation. The establishment in question may have continued in operation even during the reign of this Confucian-inspired reformer, since it appears in a local gazetteer compiled under Sadanobu's patronage.[96] As Iwata

---

position of responsibility in the han administration made it even more difficult to consent to such a relationship (Toyoda, *Kasei jikki,* 12:259). In Aizu, legal strictures on *shudō* seem to have extended across a broad range of classes: a 1621 law (*Shinpen Aizu fūdoki,* vols. 30–34 of *Dainihon chishi taikei,* ed. Ashida Ijin et al., 40 vols. [Yūzankaku, 1929–1933], 30:226–227) prohibited not only "outrageous advances" (*rifujin ni mōshikakeru*) on the part of *wakatō* and *komono,* but also the forming of *shudō* ties (*wakashudō ni tsukisorōte no chiindate*) by the children of townsmen. For incidents of *shudō*-related murder, suicide, and assault in Aizu, see Ogawa Wataru, *Shigure sōshi* (Iinuma Sekiya, 1935), 3–4, 217–218; Toyoda, *Kasei jikki,* 2:203–206; 5:227–228; 7:166–167.

95. Tomita Koreyuki, *Okushū kikō,* in *Nanbu sōsho,* ed. Ōta Kōtarō et al., 11 vols. (Morioka: Nanbu sōsho kankōkai, 1927–1931), 6:489. Minakata Kumagusu (postcard to Iwata Jun'ichi, 25 April 1933, *Minakata Kumagusu zenshū,* 9:181) suggests that the teahouse's name made playful reference to the potbellied god of fortune Hotei (Chinese: Budai), who was originally a monk and became known in folklore for his love of children. For a *kagemajaya* by the same name in early eighteenth-century Nagoya, see Nagoya shiyakusho, *Nagoya shishi: Fūzoku hen* (Nagoya: Nagoya shiyakusho, 1915), 424. Note also the following 1752 *senryū* (cited in Hanasaki, *Edo no kagemajaya,* 124): "The inn with Hotei on its sign turns out to be a *kagemajaya*" (*Kanban no Hotei o toeba kagemayado*).

96. The Hoteiya or a similar establishment dates back at least as far as 1693, when a conflagration that originated there earned the local nickname of the "*yarō* teahouse fire" (*yarōgajaya kaji*). See Shirakawa-shi, ed., *Shirakawa shishi,* 6 vols. to date (Shirakawa: Shirakawa-shi, 1989–), 10:240.

Jun'ichi has pointed out, Shirakawa was a favorite stop for daimyo processions and other travelers on the chief route to northeastern Honshu, so that provincial *kagemajaya* such as this one likely catered to a clientele similar to the one Kaempfer witnessed in the shogunally administered post town of Okitsu (today's Shimizu) on the Tōkaidō highway, whose balm-vending prostitutes the official accompanying him to Edo found so diverting.[97]

We do not know the legal basis under which establishments such as the Hoteiya operated. The activities that went on inside may well have looked quite respectable on paper, just as Okitsu's salesboys maintained a front of professional legitimacy "lest the virtuous should be scandaliz'd." Yet the smaller scale of most provincial towns seems to have allowed local officials, if so inclined, to keep a tighter (though never fully hermetic) lid on *shudō* enterprise than was possible for their metropolitan counterparts. Thus, in a popular text of the early eighteenth century, a male prostitute complains that in castle towns where scrutiny (*ginmi*) over such matters was particularly strict, revelers had to keep their voices down and forgo such pleasures as music and sake, while the hired youth might find himself being secreted to his place of assignation inside a wicker box (*tsuzura*).[98] Domain authorities sometimes cracked down on *kagemajaya* with a boldness that their Edo colleagues would not attempt until the nineteenth century. In the domain of Nagoya, for example, *kagemajaya* that had openly prospered for a number of years met a sudden demise when han officials decided to close the booming pleasure district of Maezu near the foot of Nagoya castle in 1738.[99] Elsewhere, such establishments survived considerably longer, as in the post town of Mikkaichi (present-day Kawachi Nagano), which lay along the route used by the monks of Mount Kōya in journeying to and from Kyoto and Osaka. According to Minakata Kumagusu, one *kagemajaya*, by then con-

---

97. Iwata Jun'ichi, "Yadoba no kagemajaya," in *Honchō nanshoku kō* (Toba: Iwata Sadao, 1974), 211–212. The castle town of Odawara, another station on the Tōkaidō post road, was also famous for its salesboy-prostitutes, who sold the locally made pills known as *uirō*. For literary representations, see Ejima Kiseki, *Yahaku naishō kagami*, in *Hachimonjiyabon zenshū*, ed. Hasegawa Tsuyoshi et al., 14 vols. to date (Kyūko shoin, 1992–), 2:107; Nishizawa Ippū, *Onna daimyō Tanzen nō*, in *Kindai Nihon bungaku taikei*, ed. Nonaka Jirō et al., 25 vols. (Kokumin tosho, 1926–1929), 4:312–313.

98. *Yarō kinuburui*, 30.

99. Fujisawa Akie, *Maezu kyūjishi* (Nagoya: Sohotsunoya, 1935), 116–117; Nagoya shiyakusho, *Nagoya shishi*, 424–425. This is not to say that male prostitution came to an end in the domain after 1738; indeed, Nagoya features prominently in a 1768 listing (Hiraga Gennai, <*Nanshoku saiken*> *Mitsu no asa*, in *Nihon shomin bunka shiryō shūsei*, ed. Geinōshi kenkyūkai, 16 vols. [San'ichi shobō, 1973–1978], 9:111) of provincial centers of *nanshoku*.

verted into a female brothel, remained standing there in the 1880s, an exotic waterworks (*karakuri*) still decorating its garden.[100]

As the above examples suggest, the network of post roads that connected the metropolises with the hinterland provided an important artery for the propagation of urban *shudō* culture. Domain lawmakers sought to counteract this influence at both poles: by attempting to insulate their fiefs from the penetration of its institutions and demimonde, and by regulating the behavior of their own subjects at Edo. The latter was necessary as a result of the *sankin kōtai* or alternate attendance system, which the bakufu had formalized in 1635 as a means of maintaining hegemony and which served as a major impetus behind the development of the transportation and communications infrastructure. The system required most daimyo to spend alternate years in the shogunal capital, as well as to maintain permanent establishments in that city for their wives and children, who functioned as virtual hostages. Consequently, a small portion of each domain's population, consisting chiefly of samurai males, was resident at any time in Edo. In the shogunal seat, of course, han officials exercised no legal control over the institutions and purveyors of *shudō* culture. Instead, they sought to minimize the contact of their retainers with its tempting erotic milieu. The norm of sexual moderation that applied to the samurai class as a whole provided an ideological foundation for these efforts, augmented by a desire to avoid incidents of friction in their host city and to prevent the importation of metropolitan values back into the domain.

Examples may be cited from various parts of the country. Domain authorities in Okayama prohibited *kachi koshō*, attendants who accompanied lordly processions, from "going crazy over youths" in Edo as early as 1611.[101] Their counterparts in Hirosaki (in present-day Aomori prefecture) banned the pursuit of *wakashudō* (that is, *shudō*) among retainers attached to the domain's Edo establishment in 1662, adding that it was likewise forbidden for them to act as go-betweens for such liaisons.[102] And in 1665, when administrators in Shikoku's Tokushima domain issued a long list of regulations regarding retainers' conduct en route to and in the city of Edo, they

100. Minakata Kumagusu to Iwata Jun'ichi, 5 May 1932, postcard, *Minakata Kumagusu zenshū*, 9:127. Administration of Mikkaichi was divided between the bakufu and Zeze domain.

101. Hanpō kenkyūkai, *Hanpōshū*, 1b:941–942.

102. Kokuritsu shiryōkan, ed., *Tsugaru-ke osadamegaki*, Shiryōkan sōsho, no. 3 (Tōkyō daigaku shuppankai, 1981), 141–142. A 1671 house code (267–268) extended the same provision to all the domain's retainers.

made a point of reminding page boys (*kogoshō*) that they had pledged not to engage in *shudō* upon entering their lord's service, and must refrain from making private excursions. If unavoidable business called a page away from his duties, he was required to explain the circumstances to one of the watchdog officials known as *metsuke*, who would send one of his underlings along to keep an eye on him.[103] Such legislation targeted not only commercialized forms of pleasure (it is significant that Hirosaki lawmakers grouped *shudō* together with such urban enterprises as brothels and bathhouses), but also the much broader range of erotic contacts that might occur in this vast and predominantly male city, including the sort of horizontal alliances among retainers that worried officials back home.[104]

The kabuki theater was an especially notorious feature of metropolitan culture, tempting many a provincial visitor into its precincts. While bakufu authorities regarded theater attendance by their townsman subjects with some tolerance, their counterparts in the domains, whose Edo legations consisted largely of samurai, tended to adopt a harsher stance toward this particular form of indulgence. The penal code of Wakayama domain listed various punishments for retainers and menials who attended theater performances in Edo, including the loss of post and stipend and domiciliary confinement. Private liaisons with prostitutes—legally euphemized as frequenting an "evil place"—met with similar penalties, regardless of whether the entertainment provided was that of males or females. In 1769, for example, Wakayama officials imposed a heavy fine upon a manservant (*genan*) who had engaged the services of "theater boys" (*shibaiko*), his transgression compounded by the fact that he had been sporting clothing inappropriate to his station.[105] By all accounts, however, samurai, whether they served the bakufu or the domains, formed a conspicuous segment of kabuki's audience, as well as providing a significant portion of the *kagemajaya*'s clientele.[106]

---

103. Hanpō kenkyūkai, *Hanpōshū*, 3:1019–1022.

104. On the sex ratio in Edo, see Gary Leupp, "Male Homosexuality in Edo During the Late Tokugawa Period, 1750–1850: Decline of a Tradition?" in *Imaging/Reading Eros: Proceedings for the Conference, Sexuality and Edo Culture, 1750–1850*, ed. Sumie Jones (Bloomington: East Asian Studies Center, Indiana University, 1996), 108. I reject, however, the demographic determinism implicit in Leupp's analysis.

105. Kyōto daigaku Nihon hōshi kenkyūkai, *Hanpō shiryō shūsei*, 277, 281–282.

106. For an account in English of a Hirosaki retainer who went so far as to appear onstage himself, see Edwin McClellan, *Woman in the Crested Kimono: The Life of Shibue Io and Her Family Drawn from Mori Ōgai's "Shibue Chūsai"* (New Haven: Yale University Press, 1985), 36–38.

If kabuki was strictly regulated in the metropolises, it faced a more hostile reception in some of the domains. In the domain of Kanazawa, for instance, kabuki, which had enjoyed great popularity and even official patronage during the 1610s and 1620s, thereafter entered a long period of hibernation as castle-town authorities sought to tame what the historian James McClain describes as a "free-wheeling social life" into a "more placid urban culture."[107] The freewheeling life of the local theater district was marked by some of the same forms of social disorder that troubled samurai officials in Edo, including outbreaks of violence among patrons and indiscriminate mingling of social classes. Yet domain authorities themselves did not hesitate to use violence in order to ensure the castle town's placidity. A townsman met with death by burning in the late 1620s for opening an unlicensed theater in spite of an earlier ban, while another suffered beheading in 1673 after summoning a troupe of *yarō* from outside the domain.[108] Even in Kanazawa, however, licensed theaters began to reappear by the early nineteenth century, conveniently equipped with holding tanks (*rō*) to confine brawling patrons until the show had ended.[109] Local kabuki theaters could also be found in such domains as Shikoku's Tokushima and Kyushu's Funai, whose players toured nearby provinces as well.[110]

In regions where no established theaters existed, the demand for male-male erotic services was often filled by traveling actor-prostitutes. Known colloquially as *tobiko* or "fly boys," these itinerants hailed frequently from the Kamigata area, although their peregrinations took them all up and down the archipelago.[111] In 1768, the polymath Hiraga Gennai listed more than a dozen spots where their services were available, from the northerly domains of Aizu and Sendai to a number of sites along the well-traveled Inland Sea coast.[112] Among the latter was the isle of Miyajima, adjacent to Hi-

107. See James L. McClain, *Kanazawa: A Seventeenth-Century Japanese Castle Town* (New Haven: Yale University Press, 1982), esp. 63–64, 112–113, 144–145.

108. Kōshaku Maeda-ke henshūbu, *Kaga-han shiryō*, 2:670–672; Yoshida Setsuko, *Edo kabuki*, 62.

109. Moriya Takeshi, *Murashibai: Kinsei bunkashi no susono kara* (Heibonsha, 1988), 253.

110. Hiraga Gennai, *Mitsu no asa*, 9:911. For 1825 and 1840 lists of provincial theaters, see Moriya, *Murashibai*, 250–257.

111. For literary representations of the *tobiko*, see Ejima Kiseki, *Yakei tabitsuzura*, in *Hachimonjiyabon zenshū*, 2:478–494; Nishizawa Ippū, *Yakei tomojamisen*, in *Edo jidai bungei shiryō*, 2:340–342; Ihara, *Kōshoku ichidai otoko*, 38:125–128 (trans. Robert Lyons Danly under the title "Flyboys," in *Partings at Dawn: An Anthology of Japanese Gay Literature*, ed. Stephen D. Miller [San Francisco: Gay Sunshine, 1996], 94–95; Hamada, *Amorous Man*, 36–39).

112. Hiraga Gennai, *Mitsu no asa*, 9:911.

roshima domain, whose Itsukushima shrine, numbered among the so-called Three Scenic Wonders of Japan, and seasonal fairs attracted legions of visitors, as did the dramatic performances that han authorities licensed there as a stimulus to local commerce. Saikaku had already described the revelry that took place at these fairs in 1682, including the spectacle, no doubt comic from a metropolitan point of view, of country dwellers swooning at the sight of "theater boys."[113] Also mentioned by both Saikaku in the seventeenth century and Hiraga in the eighteenth were the Okayama town of Miyauchi (in today's city of Okayama), which grew up in front of the renowned Kibitsu shrine and to which the bakufu's commissioner for religious affairs (*jisha bugyō*) had given special permission to stage theatrical performances early in the Edo period, and Konpira (present-day Kotohira) on the island of Shikoku, another favorite destination of pilgrims.[114] As in such Edo haunts as Yushima and Shiba, shrine drama and male prostitution in the provinces evolved in close proximity.

Such accounts as Saikaku's are noteworthy because they bring face-to-face two elements of the population about whose interaction Edo-period popular discourse, with its metropolitan and class biases, is more often silent: the *shudō* demimonde and the provincial peasantry. Although neither can legal discourse reveal the actual extent of contact between the two, it certainly bespeaks the desire of domain authorities to ward off its occurrence. From the point of view of domain rulers, urban *shudō* culture embodied an ethos of consumption and leisure that threatened to sap peasant productivity, upon which the han economy, and hence their own extractive livelihoods, were based. Toward this end, domain governments (as well as the bakufu) issued countless bans upon kabuki and other types of theatrical performance in the village, whether staged by peasants themselves or by itinerant outsiders.[115] In the latter case, the economic rationale was accompanied by a sort of political xenophobia, since han officials viewed the subjects of any other fief or region as potentially subversive foreigners.

Officials in many domains set up legal barriers in order to keep the demimonde of urban *shudō* off their territory, or at the very least to restrict their

---

113. Ihara, *Kōshoku ichidai otoko*, 38:220 (Hamada, *Amorous Man*, 150). In the same work (Ihara, *Kōshoku ichidai otoko*, 38:127 [Danly, "Flyboys," 95; Hamada, *Amorous Man*, 38]), a *tobiko* names Miyajima among the places he once plied his trade.

114. Ihara, *Kōshoku ichidai otoko*, 38:127 (Danly, "Flyboys," 95; Hamada, *Amorous Man*, 38). Miyajima, Miyauchi, and Konpira also appear on a fictional *tobiko* itinerary in Ejima Kiseki's 1715 work *Yakei tabitsuzura* (2:491–492).

115. For a representative example of such legislation, see Hanpō kenkyūkai, *Hanpōshū*, 2:430.

movements upon it. Bureaucratic vigilance focused first upon the point of ingress: the border station (*bansho* or *sekisho*), where main arteries such as post roads entered the boundaries of the domain. Here, inspectors questioned travelers about the nature of their business, turning back those whose presence was unwelcome. Performers and prostitutes of both male and female varieties ranked high on the list of undesirables. Domain authorities in Akita, for example, instructed border guards to deny entry to all kabuki players and incense peddlers unless they carried a seal of approval (*goshuin*) from the shogunate itself.[116] If such persons had to pass through Tottori domain, han officials there warned in 1741, it was the duty of peasants to speed them on their way to the opposite border.[117]

Such legislation betrayed han administrators' fear that these rootless "idlers" (*yūmin*), far from hastening to leave, would ensconce themselves within the agricultural community, distracting inhabitants from their productive labors and encouraging forms of consumption that were incompatible with peasant status. Other restrictions targeted their potential hosts and patrons within the rural districts (*kōri* or *zai*). Tottori authorities, for example, forbade rural dwellers to furnish "even a single night's lodging" to kabuki performers and other types of entertainers, while their counterparts in Okayama banned from their rural districts all *yūjo* (female prostitutes) and *yarō*.[118] In the case of the latter domain, we possess a recorded instance of the law's enforcement. In 1682, the town magistrate in Okayama received a tip that there was a *yarō* staying in a nearby village, where young men of the town had been visiting him daily. The *yarō* turned out to be one Yoshida Rokunosuke, a "fly boy" from Osaka who had been drawn to the area by the Miyauchi shrine festivities, and his hosteler a peasant by the name of Hisaya. Domain officials had Yoshida marched to the border of the neighboring province under armed escort, while casting Hisaya and other locals into jail for investigation. Although several of the parties involved ultimately received pardon, han authorities sentenced Hisaya, along with his grandson, to death and extinction of his family line (*danzetsu*) for ignoring the law of the realm and "corrupting the mores of youth" (*wakaki mono no*

---

116. Imamura Yoshitaka and Takahashi Hideo, eds., *Akita-han machibureshū*, 3 vols. (Miraisha, 1971–1973), 1:68–69, 134–135.

117. Hanpō kenkyūkai, *Hanpōshū*, 2:250–251.

118. Hanpō kenkyūkai, *Hanpōshū*, 1a:4, 638–639, 710; 2:220–223, 233–234. Likewise, officials in Hachiman domain (straddling present-day Gifu and Fukui prefectures) prohibited *yarō* or *yūjo* from being "kept" in any of its villages. See Hanpō kenkyūkai, *Hanpōshū*, 5:53–58.

fūzoku o midashisōrō), and cut off the noses of two townsmen who had been either Yoshida's pimps or his clients.[119]

Were it not for the informer or informers (who apparently were residents of the town), these gruesome punishments might never have come to pass. Since samurai bureaucrats rarely set foot inside rural villages, violations of the law might easily escape detection unless reported by inhabitants themselves. As often noted, law enforcement in the Edo period depended much less upon direct surveillance by higher officials than on a system of mutual legal responsibility and vigilance among peers. Although this principle applied to all social classes, it was especially relevant in the case of the peasantry. So long as they produced their annual tax rice and did not openly revolt against their rulers, Edo-period villagers enjoyed a considerable measure of autonomy in governing their internal affairs.[120] The compact between peasants and their overlords took concrete form in a document known as the *goningumichō* or "five-person group register," in which villagers pledged to observe a barrage of restrictions on their everyday lives, with the understanding that infractions would bring punishment not only upon the offending individual but also upon his or her neighbors (grouped, in principle though not necessarily in practice, in units of five households). Designed to encourage local residents to keep an eye on one another's conduct, the system also provided a powerful incentive to screen offenses from the view of higher authorities.

The depth to which the regulation of male-male sexuality penetrated Edo-period legal discourse may be gauged from these registers. Such documents, examples of which survive both from bakufu territory and from the domains, typically include an article banning kabuki performances, along or combined with one that prohibited the lodging or "keeping" of prostitutes both male and female. Indeed, the variety of signifiers for male prostitute that appear in village registers—*kagema, kagerō, yarō, kabukiko, wakashu, uriwakashu, kōdō, kōguuri,* and so forth—nearly rivals that found in urban decrees.[121] In itself, of course, this fact does not necessarily reflect the preva-

---

119. Ōsawa, *Kibi onko hiroku*, 9:253. For a fictional account of a *tobiko* who eludes an investigation by the local magistrate (*mokudai*) by taking refuge in the home of an outcast (*hinin*), see Ejima, *Yakei tabitsuzura*, 2:479–484.

120. See Harumi Befu, "Village Autonomy and Articulation with the State," in *Studies in the Institutional History of Early Modern Japan*, 301–314; Ooms, *Tokugawa Village Practice*, 192–242.

121. Hozumi Nobushige, ed., *Goningumi hōkishū* (Yūhikaku, 1930), 113, 178, 226, 243, 519, 675, 694, 699; Hozumi Shigetō, ed., *Goningumi hōkishū zokuhen*, 2

lence of commercialized *shudō* in the countryside, especially since the text of such registers was often drafted by urban-based or at least urban-born bureaucrats. Nevertheless, since village elders customarily read the registers aloud at New Year's and other local gatherings, the lexicon of metropolitan *shudō* culture may have become familiar over the course of the Edo period to a broad spectrum of rural inhabitants—surely a consequence that lawmakers had not intended.[122] Ironically, village registers in some parts of the country would continue to spread such knowledge even after the Meiji Restoration, long after the *kagema* and his brethren had passed their heyday and as the legal regulation of male-male sexuality stood on the brink of a profound transformation.[123]

THE VIEW FROM ABOVE

The foregoing survey of Edo-period legal discourse has traversed a variety of regions, jurisdictions, classes, and statuses. Diversity itself formed one of the chief characteristics of the discourse, rendering problematic any notion of a uniform "Edo-period" legal attitude toward male-male sexuality. Certainly we find no equivalent of the European preoccupation with "sodomy," which branded certain male-male sexual acts as illicit regardless of the identity of the persons involved and the circumstances under which they took place. While in Edo-period Japan, too, male-male sexual practices could lead to harsh and sometimes even capital punishment, it was the context and consequences of these practices—what I have called the realm of the perisexual—that was of crucial importance, rather than the fact of genital contact itself. Thus, by the same token that *shudō* was not categorically proscribed, neither was it in all instances legal.

Legality depended, to begin with, upon geographical and jurisdictional considerations. Acts and institutions that faced penalties in one place might not do so in another, and even within a single jurisdiction there existed pockets of relatively greater license. The theater districts served as one such site

---

vols. (Yūhikaku, 1944), 1:213, 237, 245, 259, 366, 401, 466, 550, 556, 567, 620, 627, 691, 724, 809–810, 847, 858, 879; 2:25, 952, 1014, 1046, 1132, 1249, 1271, 1308, 1360, 1442, 1450, 1464, 1517, 1638; Hozumi Nobushige, *Goningumi seidoron* (Yūhikaku, 1921), 193–194; Nomura Kanetarō, *Goningumichō no kenkyū* (Yūhikaku, 1943), 22, 53, 104, 118, 135, 185, 191, 209, 259, 297, 308, 381, 497, 513.

122. For a description of an annual reading (as witnessed in 1857 by the American consul Townsend Harris), see Oliver Statler, *Shimoda Story* (New York: Random House, 1969), 248–250.

123. See chap. 3, n. 33.

of recognized "evil" in the metropolises, while in the provinces such plea-sure centers as Nagoya's Maezu and Hiroshima's Miyajima played a simi-lar role. Yet even within these openly licentious precincts, male-male erotic behavior faced many restrictions, and physical segregation itself provided a means of regulation. The stringency of law enforcement varied also from locality to locality (not to mention period to period), a situation of which the "fly boy," cramped inside his wicker box, must have been painfully aware.

It would be difficult, if not downright impossible, to produce a definitive map of the myriad regional variations pertaining to the legal regulation of male-male sexuality during the Edo period. Nevertheless, it is clear that the issues occupying the minds of bakufu lawmakers in the metropolis of Edo were not identical to those of their domain counterparts in such provincial castle towns as Aizu, and that rural legislation addressed still another set of concerns. In part, such disparities reflected differing rates in the commer-cialization of male-male erotic culture. This process commenced earliest and advanced most rapidly in the metropolises, where, by the end of the seven-teenth century, the center of bakufu attention had shifted as a consequence from *shudō*-related "importuning" and other noncommercial transgressions to the regulation of a flourishing apparatus for the marketing of male-male eros. The same process unfolded more slowly and unevenly in the castle towns, where domain administrators continued to be preoccupied with older, noncommercialized forms of male-male sexuality well into the nineteenth century. Both bakufu and domain officials, however, strove consistently throughout the period to prevent commercialized *shudō* culture from tak-ing root in the countryside, while turning a largely blind eye to any other male-male erotic practices that may have existed there.

Legislative differences between metropolis, castle town, and countryside were also a function of class dynamics. Virtually all of Edo-period legisla-tion was class specific, whether the status group or groups involved were explicitly named or implicit in the form of document or issuing authority. In Edo, for example, laws dealing with male-male sexuality most frequently took the form of *ofuregaki* or decrees, targeting a townsman population that would over the course of the period surpass their samurai neighbors in num-ber and, despite the lowly status of merchants and artisans within the official class hierarchy, often in terms of economic prosperity. From the perspective of bakufu bureaucrats, the integration of male-male eroticism into a thriv-ing market economy threatened to link sexual desire to a commercial mech-anism driven not by considerations of official morality, with its governing ideals of moderation and decorum, but rather by the supposedly unbridled avarice and lesser virtue of the townsman estate. Nor did the emergence of this erotic marketplace affect townsmen alone, for samurai, too, as inhabitants of the same urban space, could not help being tempted by its pleasures. The metropolitan environment, with its teeming and diverse population, created multiple possibilities for the transgression of social boundaries and status norms, especially when such volatile passions as erotic pleasure and monetary gain were involved. Metropolitan administrators chose to focus their efforts on the regulation of *shudō's* commercial infrastructure, chiefly a townsman enterprise, hoping thereby to contain its most explosive energies and conspicuous excesses.

In castle towns, by contrast, legislation dealing with male-male sexuality typically addressed the samurai class that was gathered there in permanent attendance upon their lord. The maintenance of a stable domain polity depended upon the regimentation of this warrior band, particularly since its male constituents wielded that ultimate instrument of violence, the sword. Domain governments sought to achieve this goal by enforcing a vertical chain of authority and inculcating the principle of absolute loyalty to the daimyo. Male-male erotic ties, although deeply embedded within warrior culture, posed a significant challenge to this hierarchical structure by creating alliances along horizontal lines, thus embodying a conspiratorial potential against which administrators remained perpetually vigilant. In castle towns, therefore, legal pronouncements on *shudō* typically appeared in the context of retainer regulations and directives, while the archetypal mode of excess was not indecorous consumption (with the notable exception of metropolitan legations) so much as violence.

Finally, in the countryside, legislative scrutiny fell upon the peasantry, who made up the bulk of the rural populace and, indeed, over 80 percent of the population of the archipelago. The official duty of this class was the production of rice, which the ruling warrior class exacted in the form of tribute and which provided a foundation for the economy as a whole. In the eyes of rural administrators, male-male sexuality was threatening insofar as it diverted the energies of the peasantry away from their appointed labors, and its most worrisome manifestation was to be found in the infiltration of pleasure-centered *shudō* institutions—specifically, kabuki and prostitution—from the cities. The "mores" (*fūzoku*) that Okayama officials wished to preserve signified not so much a particular pattern of sexual behavior as an ethic of diligence and frugality that stood in contrast to the frivolity and luxury personified by such nonproductive "idlers" as the "fly boy," and that was equally subverted by male-female and male-male varieties of erotic commerce. The prospect of two peasant males copulating in the fields, on the other hand, was a matter of small concern to urban-based bureaucrats, who were content to leave the day-to-day policing of sexual activity to villagers themselves and to the self-regulating operation of what twentieth-century legalists would come to call "social morality." Only in instances involving the use of force (a monopoly of the samurai class) and bodily injury, as in Naoemon's assault upon a six-year-old boy, did administrators feel the need to take legal action against noncommercial male-male sexual practices within the confines of the village.

As chapter 3 will show, the diversity that characterized Edo-period legal discourse on male-male sexuality would give way during the ensuing Meiji period to a more uniform regime of sexual regulation. As a centralized nation-state unified the veritable maze of jurisdictions that had constituted the Tokugawa polity, regional factors ceased to play a significant role in determining the legality of sexual behavior, while the official repudiation of the notion of "four estates" leveled earlier distinctions of class and status. Reflecting a larger shift from what Dan Henderson has called "rule of status" to "rule by law," sexual legislation grew more systematized and more precisely formulated, while new disciplinary technologies enhanced authorities' capacity to directly enforce those statutes on their books.[124] Finally, the perisexual concerns that were of supreme importance to Edo-period legislators were subsumed by an intensified scrutiny of genital acts.

124. Henderson, "Evolution of Tokugawa Law," 209.

3 The Forbidden Chrysanthemum

Male-Male Sexuality in Meiji Legal Discourse

Historians of Japan commonly use the phrase "civilization and enlighten-ment" (*bunmei kaika*) to designate a cultural era extending from shortly af-ter the Meiji Restoration of 1868 until the late 1870s or early 1880s. For many intellectuals of the era, this pair of terms served to define the changes re-cently taking place in Japanese society and, echoing the nineteenth-century European belief that social progress was unilinear and inevitable, to indi-cate the trajectory of its future transformation. "Civilization" represented for such thinkers and their audiences the ultimate destination on an evolu-tionary path upward from "barbarism" (*yaban*), a goal understood as hav-ing been achieved most fully at the time by the societies of Europe and North America. Along this imaginary axis, Japan's current stage of development lay somewhere in the middle—"half-enlightened" (*hankai*); the emulation of contemporary Western practices and values thus seemed indispensable in order for Japan swiftly to join the comity of "civilized" nations. This convic-tion, together with the pragmatic aim of winning more equitable treaty terms from imperialist powers, was also strongly embraced by Meiji lead-ers, helping to generate policies ranging from the adoption of Western-style governmental and civic structures to the prohibition of social practices that might diminish Japan's cultural status in the eyes of foreigners.

My use of the term "civilization" echoes this historiographic convention, but also departs from it in at least two ways. First, whereas most scholars have associated the era of "civilization" with the years immediately follow-ing the Restoration, I have expanded its boundaries to embrace the full length of the Meiji period (1868–1912). Critics, particularly from the late 1880s, of-ten questioned the means by which "civilization" might be achieved, yet few denied its validity as a goal toward which Meiji society must strive. Indeed, as social conditions changed and Japan's prestige on the international stage grew, many Japanese came to feel that it had well nigh been accomplished.

Second, rather than equating "civilization" with the mere aping of Western manners, as early nationalist critics were fond of doing and many historians have subsequently implied, I have sought to ground its meaning within a native context. This involves recognizing, on the one hand, that "civilized" discourse had both Western and indigenous roots, and, on the other, that Meiji "civilization," while combining the two, remained a distinctly Japanese phenomenon. Take for example the 1872 proscription of mixed bathhouses (*danjo irigomi no yu*) so often cited as an illustration of *bunmei kaika* policy.[1] It is seldom noted that, far from marking an abrupt departure from previous legal attitudes, this measure simply reinforced a ban that had existed in the city of Edo since at least 1790.[2] The crucial difference lay in the fact that, while earlier legislation was typical of Edo-period moral reform efforts in its hortatory character (hence the need for periodic repetition), inconsistent enforcement, and ingenious contravention, the Meiji state, with the aid of a centralized police force, was more effective in bringing actual practice in line with official morality. Clearly, the desire to avoid offending Western, or what are sometimes loosely referred to as "Victorian," sensibilities provided additional incentive, yet it is not the only factor that deserves consideration. It was at the point of intersection between Confucian propriety and "Victorian" prudery, rather, that such measures were born.

In fact, much of the "civilized" legislation usually ascribed to the Westernizing zeal of the late 1860s and early 1870s rested solidly on Edo-period precedent, including prohibitions against public nudity and seminudity, the sale of erotic images (*shunga*) and phallic objects, and public urination. These, however, were only the most superficial features of a more profound refor-

1. This ban was promulgated by the Tokyo metropolitan government in March 1872 and incorporated into its code of misdemeanors (*ishikizai*) later that year; in 1873, a similar code was issued for "the provinces" (*chihō*). See Naikaku kirokukyoku, ed., *Hōki bunrui taizen*, 88 vols. (Hara shobō, 1980), 54:538; 55:5, 51. For equivalent ordinances pertaining to Osaka and various territorial jurisdictions in Hokkaido, see Naikaku kirokukyoku, *Hōki bunrui taizen*, 55:94, 100, 102, 104, 115, 121, 128; Osaka-shi, ed., *Meiji Taishō Ōsaka shishi*, 8 vols. (Nihon hyōronsha, 1933–1935), 6:45, 317, 361, 528.

2. For the 1790 and subsequent Edo edicts, see Kikuchi Shunsuke, ed., *Tokugawa kinrei kō*, 6 vols. (Yoshikawa kōbunkan, 1931–1932), 5:670–672, 674. Similar laws for Kyoto, Osaka, and Kumamoto domain may be found in Hanpō kenkyūkai, ed., *Hanpōshū*, 14 vols. (Sōbunkan, 1959–1975), 7:949; Kikuchi, *Tokugawa kinrei kō*, 6:30; Kyōto machibure kenkyūkai, ed., *Kyōto machibure shūsei*, 15 vols. (Iwanami shoten, 1983–1989), 11:211–212, 225, 343–344; Ōsaka-shi sanjikai, ed., *Ōsaka shishi*, 7 vols. (Osaka: Ōsaka-shi sanjikai, 1911–1915), 4b:1553, 1599, 1720, 1824, 2006.

mulation of official discourse surrounding sexuality that occurred during the Meiji period and shall be referred to here as a discourse of "civilized morality." The consolidation of the fragmented Tokugawa political system into a centralized nation-state, the accompanying breakdown of regional and status barriers, and a heightened consciousness of Japan's international stature each played an important role in shaping this discourse—a process whose complexity such monolithic notions as "Westernization" and "modernization" do not adequately express.[3]

One significantly changed aspect of Meiji sexual legislation was its newly national scope. With the abolition of the domains in 1871, Japan became a highly centralized political entity, its basic laws emanating from a Tokyo-based bureaucracy and, after the opening of the Imperial Diet in 1890, elected national legislature.[4] Codes of law established by central authorities bound all Japanese, regardless of region, to a uniform set of legal standards, replacing the patchwork of bakufu, domain, and village legislation that had characterized the Edo period. Furthermore, with the repudiation of the system of "four estates," distinctions of class—though not, as we shall see, of gender and age—came to lose their relevance in determining the legality of sexual behavior. In adjudicating sexual offenses, the nature of the crime, so to speak, became more important than the social status of the person. Finally, Meiji penal codes, unlike those of the Edo period, were intended for public as well as professional perusal, clearly stipulating the penalty for each offense, as was customary in nineteenth-century Western jurisprudence. In part, this systematization was due to the Meiji government's desire to persuade the treaty powers to relinquish extraterritorial privileges, whereby Westerners could be tried in their own courts rather than submit to the vagaries of "barbarian" justice.[5]

In codifying "civilized" standards of sexual behavior, Meiji officials had to

3. For an example of a "modernization" approach to changing sexual morality, see Watanabe Tsuneo, "Kindai, dansei, dōseiai tabū," pt. 1 of "Bunmei oyobi tōsaku no gainen," *Kōchi daigaku gakujutsu kenkyū hōkoku: Jinbun kagaku* 29 (1980): 27–45; Tsuneo Watanabe and Jun'ichi Iwata, *The Love of the Samurai: A Thousand Years of Japanese Homosexuality*, trans. D. R. Roberts (London: GMP, 1989), 121–133.

4. Under the Meiji political system as it took shape during the 1880s, prefectures and municipalities possessed severely circumscribed legislative powers, yet exercised a certain measure of administrative authority over such sexually related matters as the licensing of female prostitution.

5. Even before the end of the Edo period, lawmakers began to make greater efforts to familiarize the populace with existing legal provisions—as, for example, in

choose among laws and customs that varied widely with class and locality. With regard to marriage and the family, for instance, it was the samurai-based model of strong patriarchal authority over household (*ie*) members and succession by a single heir, usually the firstborn male, that prevailed over nonelite patterns to form the cornerstone of the 1898 Civil Code (*Minpō*).[6] As has often been pointed out, this model had theretofore held far less relevance for ordinary peasants, who formed the majority of the population and enjoyed greater latitude than their elite counterparts in such matters as individual choice of spouse and premarital sexuality (as seen, for example, in the widespread practice of "night crawling" or *yobai*).[7] Western precedents, too, influenced the framing of Meiji family law, but were rejected, as in the case of the aborted 1890 Civil Code, when it was felt that they departed too much from native tradition.

At the center of "civilized morality" lay male-female sexuality within the framework of state-sanctioned marriage. Officially, marriage was monogamous, an arrangement promoted by such spokesmen of Japanese "enlightenment" as Mori Arinori and Fukuzawa Yukichi.[8] The 1880 Penal Code (*Keihō*) thus nullified a long-standing legal recognition of female concubines (*mekake*) as kin, nor was such a familial relationship mentioned in the 1898 Civil Code, although concubinage certainly continued to exist in practice. Even within this nominally monogamous system, however, legal expectations of marital fidelity continued to fall more heavily on wives than on husbands. Divorce on grounds of adultery (*kantsū*), for example, was granted to men without restriction, but to women only if their husband had engaged in intercourse with a married woman and been prosecuted in a court of law

the early 1840s, when Edo officials sanctioned the commercial publication of a compendium of municipal edicts (<Gomen> *Ofuregaki shūran: Shūshin kōgi no kagami*), complete with glosses for the less literate, as a means of promoting Tenpō reforms—an example of the way that the profit motive of publishers and the political objectives of lawmakers occasionally converged. See Arakawa Hidetoshi, ed., *Tenpō kaikaku machibure shiryō* (Yūzankaku, 1974); Kumakura Isao, "Bunmei kaika to fūzoku," in *Bunmei kaika no kenkyū*, ed. Hayashiya Tatsusaburō (Iwanami shoten, 1979), 573–574.

6. Takamure Itsue, *Josei no rekishi*, vols. 4 and 5 of *Takamure Itsue zenshū*, ed. Hashimoto Kenzō, 10 vols. (Rironsha, 1965–1967), 5:575–578.

7. On the practice of "night crawling," see the following works by Akamatsu Keisuke: *Sonraku kyōdōtai to seiteki kihan: Yobai gairon* (Gensōsha, 1993); *Yobai no minzokugaku* (Akashi shoten, 1994); *Yobai no seiairon* (Akashi shoten, 1994).

8. Key articles in the early Meiji debate on monogamy may be found in English in William Reynolds Braisted, trans., *Meiroku Zasshi: Journal of the Japanese Enlightenment* (Cambridge: Harvard University Press, 1976).

by the aggrieved husband. A man's illegitimate male offspring, furthermore, enjoyed rights of inheritance ahead of female children born from wedlock. Finally, despite an 1872 proclamation liberating female prostitutes (*shōgi*) from indentured servitude, state-licensed female prostitution survived— indeed, spread to all corners of the nation—under the legal euphemism of the "room lending" (*kashizashiki*) trade.[9]

Under the magnified regulatory powers of the Meiji state, matters of reproduction and population underwent close scrutiny. Abortion and infanticide, both of which were widely proscribed but commonly practiced in the Edo period, became issues of amplified concern to Meiji authorities aiming to secure the human resources necessary to build a "wealthy nation and strong military" (*fukoku kyōhei*).[10] Likewise, government officials placed severe restrictions on the dissemination of contraceptive technologies, as they continue to do in the twentieth century.[11] To facilitate state surveillance over the population, every Japanese citizen, once born, entered the household registry (*koseki*) system, which established and tracked the individual's legal identity throughout his or her lifetime.[12]

Although class distinctions faded in importance, gender remained a key component of official identity. Thus, for instance, it became an issue of keen interest for medical jurisprudence whether an intersexed (*han'in'yō*) infant should be classed as male or female, since this fact would determine his or

9. The propriety of licensed female prostitution in a "civilized" society was sorely contested, and a movement for its abolition arose early in the Meiji period. For useful overviews, see Fujime Yuki, "The Licensed Prostitution System and the Prostitution Abolition Movement in Modern Japan," *Positions* 5 (1997): 135–170; Fujime Yuki, *Sei no rekishigaku: Kōsho seido dataizai taisei kara baishun bōshihō yūsei hogohō taisei e* (Fuji shuppan, 1997); Sheldon Garon, *Molding Japanese Minds: The State in Everyday Life* (Princeton: Princeton University Press, 1997), 88–114; Takemura Tamio, *Haishō undō: Kuruwa no josei wa dō kaihō sareta ka*, Chūkō shinsho, no. 663 (Chūō kōronsha, 1982).

10. On historical as well as contemporary attitudes toward abortion in Japan, see William R. LaFleur, *Liquid Life: Abortion and Buddhism in Japan* (Princeton: Princeton University Press, 1992); Helen Hardacre, *Marketing the Menacing Fetus in Japan* (Berkeley: University of California Press, 1997).

11. For the life of a prominent twentieth-century birth-control activist, see Helen M. Hopper, *A New Woman of Japan: A Political Biography of Katō Shidzue* (Boulder, Colo.: Westview, 1996); Shidzué Ishimoto, *Facing Both Ways: The Story of My Life* (Stanford: Stanford University Press, 1984).

12. Edo-period administrators, too, had maintained population registers in connection with the system of temple affiliation (*shūmon aratame*), although this system varied according to region and social class. For an example, see Torao Haraguchi et al., trans., *The Status System and Social Organization of Satsuma: A Translation of the "Shūmon Tefuda Aratame Jōmoku"* (Honolulu: University Press of Hawaii, 1975).

her rights and duties within the family (such as marriage and inheritance) and within the state (military service, voting privileges, educational and professional opportunities, and so forth).[13] Legal regulation of gender extended, too, to such matters as hairstyle, as when Tokyo officials in 1872 proscribed the recent fashion among women of cutting their hair short (*danpatsu*) like their male contemporaries, who, with government encouragement, were abandoning the traditional topknot in increasing numbers. Women who had been cited for this offense but whose hair had yet to grow back were required to carry a special certificate in order to avoid further trouble with authorities.[14]

The wearing of clothing conventionally ascribed to the other sex was similarly perceived as a matter of concern for the state because it blurred gender distinctions and made it more difficult to regulate the identities and movements of its citizens. In the context of communal celebrations and entertainments—such as the *ējanaika* dance frenzy, a burst of millenarian revelry on the eve of the Restoration—the frequent incidence of crossdressing, across boundaries not only of gender but also of age and class, contributed to the atmosphere of the carnivalesque that Meiji officials were bent on containing within the bounds of "civilized" order.[15] In 1873, the Ministry of Doctrine (Kyōbushō) pronounced the "corrupt custom" (*heifū*) of "men and women exchanging their appearance" (*danjo shishō o kae*) at Bud-

---

13. For Meiji medico-legal discussions of hermaphrodism, see Hiraga Seijirō, *Kanmei hōigaku* (Kinbara iseki shoten, 1899), 249–253 Ishikawa Kiyotada, *Jitsuyō hōigaku* (Nankōdō, 1900), 380–383; Katayama Kuniyoshi and Eguchi Jō, *Saiban igaku teikō*, 2 vols. (Shimamura Risuke, 1888), 1:26–28; Katayama Kuniyoshi et al., <Zōho kaitei> *Hōigaku teikō*, 4 vols. (Shimamura Risuke, 1891–1897), 1:141ff; Shimizu Sadao, *Jitsuyō saiban igaku* (N.p.: Eimeikan, 1890), 290–295; Yamamoto Yoshio, *Saiban igaku* (Shimamura Risuke, 1886), 121–125; Yoshii Bantarō, <Jitchi ōyō> *Saiban igakuron* (Taihōkan, 1887), 23–29.

14. On *danpatsu*, see Murakami Nobuhiko, *Meiji joseishi*, 4 vols. (Rironsha, 1969–1972), 2:287–293. Misdemeanor codes prohibited women from cutting their hair short "without reason" (*iware naku*) not only in Tokyo (1872), but also in "the provinces" (1873) and Hokkaido (1873, 1876). See Naikaku kirokukyoku, *Hōki bunrui taizen*, 55:6, 52, 95, 117. One reason deemed legitimate for shearing one's locks was the death of a husband. See Edamatsu Shigeyuki et al., eds., *Meiji nyūsu jiten*, 9 vols. (Mainichi komyunikēshonzu, 1983), 1:27.

15. For a discussion of the "carnivalesque" in the context of early Meiji Japan, see James Edward Ketelaar, *Of Heretics and Martyrs in Meiji Japan: Buddhism and Its Persecution* (Princeton: Princeton University Press, 1990), 50–52. For references to cross-dressing among *ējanaika* participants, see Itō Tadashi, "*Ējanaika*" *to kinsei shakai* (Kōsō shobō, 1995), 48–51; Takagi Shunsuke, *Ējanaika*, Kyōikusha rekishi shinsho Nihonshi, no. 93 (Kyōikusha, 1979), 35, 38, 43, 45, 106, 120, 121, 124, 126, 129, 138, 139, 145, 156, 157, 181, 190.

dhist and Shinto festivals to be "disgraceful" (*shūtai*) and "blasphemous to
the gods and bodhisattvas" (*shinbutsu o waitoku*).[16] This precept was formalized shortly thereafter by amending the Tokyo code of misdemeanors
to prohibit men from attiring themselves as women (*josō*) and women as
men (*dansō*). In the process, the scope of the original decree, which had been
limited to religious occasions, expanded into a general provision. Still, lawmakers saw fit to exempt theatrical cross-dressing, with its centuries-old tradition, and the wearing of *hakama*, a type of skirt-trousers conventionally
gendered as masculine but which had lately been adopted by female students.[17] The 1880 *Keihō*, which superseded this and other local misdemeanor
codes, made no specific mention of cross-dressing. Nevertheless, Meiji police continued in their attempts to suppress such "disgraceful," though still
relatively common, practices as cross-gendered masquerading at cherry-
viewing (*hanami*) time, and routinely stopped for questioning individuals
whose clothing violated gender conventions.[18]

The regulation of gendered appearance was not, however, without Edo-
period precedent. As we saw in the previous chapter, such a concern had long
attended bakufu dealings with the kabuki demimonde. Nor was the object
of such regulation exclusively male. Jennifer Robertson, for example, discusses one early nineteenth-century figure, the masculine-identified but biologically female Take/Takejirō, a petty thief and extortionist, whom bakufu
officials ordered several times to wear clothing and hairstyle more appropriate to her sex.[19] Similarly, at the height of the Tenpō reform period in

16. Naikaku kanpōkyoku, ed., *Hōrei zensho*, annual publ. (Naikaku kanpōkyoku,
1887–), 1876 vol.: 1635.
17. Naikaku kirokukyoku, *Hōki bunrui taizen*, 55:12–13. For an example of the
implementation of this law, see Umehara Hokumei, ed., *Meiji seiteki chinbunshi*, 3
(?) vols. (Bungei shiryō kenkyūkai, 1926–?), 1:12. In 1879, a similar ordinance
(Naikaku kirokukyoku, *Hōki bunrui taizen*, 55:142) was issued for the Japanese concession at Pusan, Korea.
18. For *hanami* regulations, see "Hanami ni tsuite no fūzoku torishimari," *Yorozu
chōhō*, 2 April 1899, 3; "Hanami zuii," *Yorozu chōhō*, 9 April 1899, 2; "Hanamiren
iyoiyo anshin subeshi," *Yorozu chōhō*, 11 April 1899, 2. As newspaper accounts of
the late Meiji period attest, police surveillance over gendered appearance sometimes resulted in the apprehension of criminals or indentured prostitutes who had
cross-dressed as a means of escape, disguise, or making off with stolen goods. On
cross-dressing in the context of male criminality, see Shimokawa Kōshi et al., *Josō
no minzokugaku* (Hihyōsha, 1994), 81–128; Koishikawa Zenji et al., *Hanzai no minzokugaku: Meiji Taishō hanzaishi kara* (Hihyōsha, 1993), 38–55.
19. Jennifer Robertson, "The Shingaku Woman: Straight from the Heart," in
Recreating Japanese Women, 1600–1945, ed. Gail Lee Bernstein (Berkeley: University of California Press, 1991), 92. It should be noted that Robertson's account
of the incident contains a number of factual errors. For the original sources, see Ishii

1843, Osaka authorities had explicitly proscribed parents' custom of dressing female children as boys so as to spare the expense of feminine apparel and hair ornaments, claiming that this practice adversely affected a girl's future ability to perform "womanly duties" (*onna no shogyō*) and "public mores" (*fūzoku*) in general.[20]

Folk wisdom, somewhat contradictorily, had long advised parents who lacked the wherewithal or divine favor necessary to raise healthy male offspring to bring them up as girls.[21] Such was the case with one Ooto—the personal name, it is significant to note, is a feminine one, its characters possibly indicating that the parents wanted this to be their "last" child—who was born in a Shikoku village in 1850, and whose early training in needlework allowed him to find employment as a maidservant (*hashitame*). In 1874, the Meiji legal system caught up with Ooto. After living for three years as the wife of a lacquerware artisan (who, not surprisingly, was fully aware of his partner's sex), Ooto was discovered to be male by local authorities routinely investigating the household registers in order to enter the couple's marriage. As a consequence, Ooto was compelled to cut his flowing locks, a "clarification" of gender that one journalist praised as a "blessing of the glorious imperial reign" (*akiraka na ōmiyo no goontaku*).[22]

Ooto's run-in with authorities, at least in its journalistic representation, focused on his "mistaken" gender identity rather than his sexual behavior per se. Indeed, the above-quoted newspaper account reports of Ooto's sexual behavior only that his earlier position as a maidservant had allowed him to indulge in illicit relations with females. "Civilized morality" did, however, have important consequences for the legal construction of male-male sexuality. The year prior to the above incident, 1873, saw the promulgation of a new national penal code that categorically proscribed, for the first time in Japanese history, the practice of anal intercourse (*keikan*), which had figured as a central act of the *shudō* sexual repertoire. Later sections of this chapter will examine at greater length the evolution of the 1873 statute and subsequent Meiji legislation on male-male sexuality. Foreign precedents, we shall see,

---

Ryōsuke, ed., *Oshiokirei ruishū*, 16 vols. (Meicho shuppan, 1971–1974), 16:12–13, 142–143, 166–167.

20. Ōsaka-shi sanjikai, *Ōsaka shishi*, 4b:1688–1689.

21. For a folk adage to this effect, see Saigiku Sanjin [Jōno Denpei], <*Sannin kyōkaku*> *Kagema no adauchi* (Junseidō, 1899), 28.

22. Umehara, *Meiji seiteki chinbunshi*, 1:85. For a color reproduction of an Ochiai Yoshichika print (*shinbun nishikie*) based on this newspaper article, see Takahashi Katsuhiko, *Shinbun nishikie no sekai: Takahashi Katsuhiko korekushon yori* (PHP kenkyūjo, 1986), 83.

played a significant part in the legislative process, yet were neither uniform nor exclusively Western. Furthermore, although the shape and scope of Meiji laws differed in many respects from that of their Edo-period precursors, the regulation of male-male sexuality, as chapter 2 has already shown, had occupied the minds of Japanese lawmakers for more than two and a half centuries.

Indeed, even before the end of the Edo period, bakufu legal strictures surrounding male-male sexuality had undergone fortification.[23] This was true in particular of prostitution, long an object of bureaucratic concern and regulation. In urban areas such as Edo, the legal instrument typically used to control male prostitution was the *ofuregaki* or decree, which pronounced certain practices unseemly and commanded the townsman populace or specific segments thereof to desist from them, although without stipulating any specific penalties for infringement. The ideals set forth by samurai administrators were offset to some degree, however, by a lack of faith in the common classes' ability to abide by the highest standards of moral behavior, and laws were widely circumvented through lax enforcement or benign neglect. Thus, although various Edo edicts banned prostitution by kabuki actors and their *kagema* brethren, commercial establishments specializing in this very activity existed throughout much of the period.

During periods of moral reform, however, bakufu authorities tended to perceive the gap between official ideals and actual practice as a symptom of weakness and decline, and to renew their efforts to bring the two in line. Under the reformist shogun Yoshimune in 1723, for instance, officials reportedly "punished," by means presumably including execution, "several tens" of individuals for violating theretofore widely flouted strictures against *kagema*, and forced theater companies to remove "love boys" (*iroko*) from their rosters. While this was not the first time that Edo authorities had carried out their threat of punishment for male prostitution, it may well represent the most extensive prosecution of its kind in the Edo period, comparable in scale to, though clearly different in ideological valence from, the wave of "sodomy" trials, resulting in many death sentences, that took place in Holland during the following decade.[24] An interval of relative lenience ensued after Yoshimune's death in 1744, allowing Edo's *kagema-*

23. The following discussion pertains chiefly to the city of Edo, and does not necessarily reflect legal trends in all of bakufu-administered territory or in the domains, which bear further investigation.

24. Yoshida Setsuko, ed., *Edo kabuki hōrei shūsei* (Ōfūsha, 1989), 154. For earlier examples of bakufu prosecution, see Yoshida Setsuko, *Edo kabuki*, 43 (1653), 112 (1709). On the situation in 1730s Holland, see Arend H. Huussen, Jr., "Sodomy in the Dutch Republic during the Eighteenth Century," in *Hidden from History: Reclaiming*

jaya to experience a midcentury boom. Institutionalized male prostitution continued to enjoy a measure of bureaucratic toleration even under the late eighteenth-century Kansei reforms of the shogunal regent Matsudaira Sadanobu, who was renowned for his stern Confucian principles, yet whose own domain of Shirakawa, as we saw in the previous chapter, had known at least one "*yarō* teahouse." Still, a hint of the Kansei era's heightened concern for moral rectitude may be detected in a 1789 Edo decree making it legally binding for "love boys" to wear wicker hats (*amigasa*) on their way to and from the theater or teahouse, publicly signaling their status as quasi outcasts within the official social order.[25]

A more thoroughgoing attempt to eradicate male prostitution came with the Tenpō reforms launched by the early nineteenth-century bakufu administrator Mizuno Tadakuni, which have often been cited as a prelude to the Meiji Restoration. As part of these reforms, shogunal authorities, concerned with the deterioration of "public mores" in Edo, embarked in the early 1840s upon a two-pronged campaign to contain the baneful influences of commercialized eroticism: on the one hand, by clamping down on female prostitution outside the licensed quarter of Yoshiwara; and, on the other, by moving the theater district farther away from the city's center. Edo's *kagemajaya* were affected by both parts of this plan. In 1842, bakufu officials, having already ordered the closing of teahouses that served as a site for unregulated female prostitution, decided to extend the scope of the crackdown to their male counterparts. Documents of the time reveal less of a concern, however, with sexual relations between *kagema* and their male clientele (mainly, it appears, Buddhist priests) than with the male-female sexual relations that transpired in such premises: between *kagema* and female patrons, between priestly customers and the establishments' female staff, and among illicit (*mittsū*) couples for whom they furnished a convenient trysting place.[26] As was so often the case in the Edo period, unsanctioned forms

the *Gay and Lesbian Past*, ed. Martin Bauml Duberman et al. (New York: NAL, 1989), 141–149; Theo van der Meer, "The Persecutions of Sodomites in Eighteenth-Century Amsterdam: Changing Perceptions of Sodomy," in *The Pursuit of Sodomy: Male Homosexuality in Renaissance and Enlightenment Europe*, ed. Kent Gerard and Gert Hekma (New York: Harrington Park, 1989), esp. 273–274.

25. Yoshida Setsuko, *Edo kabuki*, 225–226. In Osaka, Kansei-period administrators seem to have adopted a firmer stance against male prostitution than in Edo. Regulations issued in 1794 (Yoshida Setsuko, *Edo kabuki*, 256–258), for instance, explicitly prohibited Osaka's theatrical entrepreneurs from forcing a "living similar to that of a female prostitute" (*yūjo dōzen no misugi*) upon their young charges.

26. Yoshida Setsuko, *Edo kabuki*, 432–434, 475–476. A similar crackdown on male

of male-female sexuality provoked greater anxiety among shogunal officials than male-male, although the regulation of the former inevitably had an impact upon the latter, inasmuch as *kagema* teahouses played host to both. Several months later, Edo authorities dealt another blow to the infrastructure of male prostitution by ordering itinerant actors (*tabiyakusha*) to change their occupation or move to the new theater district to apprentice in legitimate kabuki, but specifically forbade *kagema*, who were often registered under this guise, from signing up with the reformed troupes.[27]

It is indicative, however, of the limited potency of the era's legislation that even this unprecedentedly far-reaching attempt to enforce high standards of "public morality" was not fully implemented. Although *kagema-jaya* and *kodomoya* in Yoshichō, Shiba, and Hatchōbori closed shop, at least ostensibly, in 1842 and 1843, those near the Yushima shrine managed to stay in business for the remainder of the Edo period, their licenses renewed as restaurants for priestly cuisine (*shōjin ryōri*). Bakufu authorities evidently made this concession as a favor to the shogunally patronized Kan'eiji temple, which administered the nearby shrine and provided its *kagemajaya* with much of their clientele.[28] Still, even at Yushima, the Tenpō reforms resulted in new austerities. Subsequently, it is reported, the district's *kagema* no longer decked themselves in feminine robes and coiffure, but in a style more appropriate to their legal status as adolescent males.[29] Four such establishments, employing ten or so *kagema*, remained in operation during the 1860s, although some switched around this time to the more lucrative business of

---

prostitution took place in Kyoto and Osaka around this time. See Kitagawa Morisada, *Morisada mankō*, ed. Asakura Haruhiko and Kashikawa Shūichi, 5 vols. (Tōkyōdō, 1992), 3:236; Ōsaka-shi sanjikai, *Ōsaka shishi*, 4b:1678–1679; Yoshida Setsuko, *Edo kabuki*, 475–476.

27. Yoshida Setsuko, *Edo kabuki*, 444–445, 447–448.

28. Enomoto Haryū, "Shitaya no konjaku," *Bungei kurabu*, August 1900, 180; Iwata Jun'ichi, "Edo kagema no matsuro," in *Honchō nanshoku kō* (Toba: Iwata Sadao, 1974), 213–214; Yoshida Setsuko, *Edo kabuki*, 494–495, 525–528, 529–535. Legal documents of 1843 (Yoshida Setsuko, *Edo kabuki*, 475–476, 478–482) indicate that clandestine male prostitution persisted in Yoshichō and Shiba for some time after the initial crackdown. By the 1840s, the eight establishments in Hatchōbori no longer specialized in male-male prostitution, but in male-female prostitution (available to clients of either sex) and illicit trysting.

29. Enomoto, "Shitaya no konjaku," 180; Kitagawa Morisada, *Morisada mankō*, 3:236. According to Enomoto's informant, a retired chief maid (*jochūgashira*) at one of the area's restaurants, entrepreneurs considered a revival of feminine dress in the early 1860s in order to boost their flagging trade, but this proposal, along with a plan to open a teahouse nearer to Kan'eiji, never materialized.

providing the entertainment of female geisha.[30] A further blow to Yushima's *kagemajaya* came with the 1868 Meiji Restoration, one of whose key battles was fought in nearby Ueno, laying waste to Kan'eiji and scattering its priestly population.[31]

The demise of Edo's *kagemajaya* was hastened not only by bakufu policies, but also, as touched upon in chapter 1, by their dwindling popularity. As a consequence of both these factors, commercialized *shudō*, which occupied so prominent a place in earlier legal discourse, was by Meiji times barely perceived as a threat to public order. Indeed, national legislation since the Restoration, including the 1956 Prostitution Prevention Law, has in principle defined prostitution as a female activity, with the ironic result that, so long as minors or coercion are not involved, its male forms are technically legal in contemporary Japan.[32] Rather than policing perisexual behaviors and institutions, official regulation of male-male sexuality came during the Meiji period to focus upon genital acts, while relying on increasingly direct means

30. Enomoto, "Shitaya no konjaku," 180; Iwata Jun'ichi, "Edo kagema," 215. Note also the following entry, dated 5 May 1860, from the journal of Francis Hall (*Japan through American Eyes: The Journal of Francis Hall, Kanagawa and Yokohama, 1859–1866*, ed. F. G. Notehelfer [Princeton: Princeton University Press, 1992], 165), an American journalist and businessman living in nearby Yokohama: "Until within eight years houses of catamites were quite common, patronized mainly by the priests. Thay have fallen into disrepute of late years under the royal [i.e., imperial] favor. There are said to be still at Yedo [Edo] these houses for the nefarious prostitution. The boys are dressed like girls and faces are powdered in like manner." I thank Robert Eskildsen for calling my attention to this reference.

31. Iwata Jun'ichi, "Edo kagema," 215–216. Some sources claim that Yushima's *kagemajaya* survived as late as 1871. See, for example, "Iroko to iu otoko," *Kono hana* 10 (1910): 18; Miyatake Gaikotsu, *Kitai ryūkōshi*, in *Miyatake Gaikotsu chosakushū*, ed. Tanizawa Eiichi and Yoshino Takao, 8 vols. (Kawade shobō, 1985–1992), 4:355. At least two former *kagema* are known to have pursued Meiji careers as ostensibly legitimate teahouse or restaurant operators, for references to which see "Haiyū to fujin," pt. 17, *Yorozu chōhō*, 13 May 1900, 3; Enomoto, "Shitaya no konjaku," 181.

32. While the 1880 *Keihō* (Naikaku kirokukyoku, *Hōki bunrui taizen*, 54:431) punished persons who "solicited [*kan'yū*] or acted as go-between [*baigō*] for lewd activities by males or females under the age of sixteen," the phrase "lewd activities" (*inkō*) referred primarily to male-female sexual interaction, as is clear from Waseda daigaku Tsuruta monjo kenkyūkai, ed., *Nihon keihō sōan kaigi hikki*, Waseda daigaku toshokan shiryō sōkan, no. 1, 6 vols. (Waseda daigaku shuppanbu, 1976–1977), 3:2062. The equivalent clause of the 1907 *Keihō* (Naikaku kanpōkyoku, *Hōrei zensho*, 1907 vol., [hōritsu] 99) proscribed only the procurement of females "not habituated to" (*jōshū naki*) such activities—that is to say, women with respectable reputations. In present-day Japan, prostitution by minors is regulated also by the 1947 Child Welfare Law (*Jidō fukushihō*).

of surveillance and enforcement. The emergence of this new legal regime took place in two successive phases. In the first, which the following section explores in some detail, lawmakers centered their efforts to regulate male-male sexuality on the practice of anal intercourse—a central element of *shudō* that now came to exemplify sexuality outside the bounds of "civilized" order.

ANAL VIOLATIONS

At the dawn of the Meiji period, Edo-period legal attitudes toward male-male sexuality remained largely intact. In rural villages, compacts pledging inhabitants not to consort with various types of male prostitute remained in force, or in some cases were even newly issued, for several years after the Restoration.[33] Before their abolition in 1871, domains also maintained their own systems of criminal law, which as a rule did not prescribe categorical punishments for male-male sexual acts.[34] And in the former bakufu territories, now administered by the imperial government in Tokyo, the 1742 *Kujikata osadamegaki* initially retained its status as the basic penal code, male-male (and female-female) relations still absent from its sexual provisions.

The noncriminalization of male-male sexual acts that had typified Edo-period law also survived in two new penal codes promulgated by the imperial government: the 1868 *Kari keiritsu* and the 1871 *Shinritsu kōryō*, the latter being the first such code to be implemented nationwide.[35] This situ-

33. Hozumi Nobushige, ed., *Goningumi hōkishū* (Yuhikaku, 1930), 658; Hozumi Shigetō, ed., *Goningumi hōkishū zokuhen*, 2 vols. (Yuhikaku, 1944), 1:666; 2:1335. Peasant regulations issued by the newly established Meiji government for Kai province in 1868 (Hozumi Shigetō, *Goningumi hōkishū zokuhen*, 2:1674) and for the rural districts of Kyoto in 1869 (Nomura Kanetarō, *Goningumichō no kenkyū* [Yūhikaku, 1943], 627) contain similar clauses.

34. No mention of male-male sexuality appears in post-Restoration penal codes compiled by Okayama (1869), Sendai (c. 1869), or Wakayama (1870) domains, for which see Kyōto daigaku Nihon hōshi kenkyūkai, ed., *Hanpō shiryō shūsei* (Sōbunkan, 1980), 515–533 (Sendai), 529–533 (Okayama); Tezuka Yutaka, *Meiji keihōshi no kenkyū*, vols. 4–6 of *Tezuka Yutaka zenshū*, ed. Fujita Hiromichi and Terasaki Osamu, 10 vols. (Keiō tsūshin, 1982–1994), 5:142–146 (Wakayama).

35. Naikaku kirokukyoku, *Hōki bunrui taizen*, 54:55–84, 129–194. For a detailed discussion of these and other early Meiji penal codes, as well as an English translation of the *Shinritsu kōryō*, see Paul Heng-chao Ch'en, *The Formation of the Early Meiji Legal Order: The Japanese Code of 1871 and Its Chinese Foundation* (Oxford: Oxford University Press, 1981). In the absence of specific provisions on male-male sexuality, one wonders how officials dealt with such incidents as the 1872 rape of a twelve- or thirteen-year-old male shop apprentice (*detchi*) by a man in his fifties, a newspaper account of which appears in Edamatsu, *Meiji nyūsu jiten*, 1:462. One pos-

ation was to change dramatically, however, with their successor, the 1873 *Kaitei ritsuryō*, whose Article 266 reads as follows:

> Those engaging in anal intercourse [*keikan*] shall each be sentenced to ninety days of penal servitude [*chōeki*]. In the case of the peerage [*kazoku*] and ex-samurai [*shizoku*], this shall be treated as a dishonorable offense. Violated youngsters fifteen years and under shall not be held criminally liable. Those committing [anal] rape [*gōkan*] shall be sentenced to ten years of penal servitude. For attempted [rape], the penalty shall be reduced by one degree.[36]

Although the term *keikan* was occasionally used to refer to male-female anal intercourse, the phrase "violated youngsters" (*kanseraruru no yōdō*), whose lack of a gender marker by default implied a male referent, indicates that the framers of this provision had foremost in their mind sexual relations between males, and, furthermore, assumed an age asymmetry in which older males acted as inserters and younger as insertees.[37]

One feature of the *Kaitei ritsuryō* that distinguished it from later Meiji penal codes was its differentiation of penalties by class, a legacy of Edo-period juridical practice. While samurai lost many of their privileges after the Restoration, they continued to receive official stipends until 1876, and retained the hereditary designation of *shizoku* until 1914. Rank, but not stipend, was forfeited (*jozoku*), however, when a member of the ex-samurai class or of the newly created peerage committed a "dishonorable" (*harenchi*) offense, reflecting the lingering legal dictum that the social elite must embody a higher standard of virtue than the general populace. This category included not only *keikan*, but also various types of male-female "fornication" (*kan*) and some nonsexual crimes such as theft.[38] *Shizoku* and peers also enjoyed privileged treatment in the manner of their punishment, again

---

sibility is that male-male rape was prosecutable under the *Shinritsu kōryō* upon analogy with male-female rape, as had been the case in Kumamoto domain, upon whose laws the code was partially based. Another is that authorities invoked a generic provision, inherited from Chinese jurisprudence, on "doing what ought not to be done" (*fuōi*) even if not explicitly forbidden by law, for which see Ch'en, *Early Meiji Legal Order*, 174–175; Naikaku kirokukyoku, *Hōki bunrui taizen*, 54:189–190.

36. Naikaku kirokukyoku, *Hōki bunrui taizen*, 54:303.

37. An 1873 court document (cited in Kasumi Nobuhiko, *Meiji shoki keijihō no kisoteki kenkyū*, Keiō gijuku daigaku kenkyūkai sōsho, no. 50 [Keiō tsūshin, 1990], 110) mentions a case of forcible *keikan* against a girl victim, but is ambiguous as to its disposition.

38. A proposed revision of the *Kaitei ritsuryō*, drafted in 1874 and known as the *Kōsei ritsuryō kō*, would have removed *keikan* from the list of "dishonorable offenses," but was abandoned as the compilation of the *Keihō* got under way. See Oka

a carryover from Edo-period practice. In cases where the ordinary sentence was penal servitude for less than one hundred days, as with consensual *keikan*, lawmakers waived the need for incarceration, perhaps in the belief that loss of status was punishment enough. If the prescribed term for a "dishonorable offense" was longer, as in the case of anal rape, peers and *shizoku* received the same penalty as commoners (*heimin*). Equal treatment, however, in effect doubled their disgrace, since members of these elites could serve out the sentence for other crimes in the relatively comfortable confinement of their own homes (*kinko*), or, between the years 1874 and 1881, in a privileged form of state incarceration (*kingoku*).[39]

It is tempting to conclude that the *Kaitei ritsuryō*'s Article 266 was modeled after European "sodomy" statutes, which had been known to Japanese for at least a century and which it resembles in some respects.[40] In fact, however, the influences at work behind its drafting were more complex. To begin with, the initiative for creating such a law came from Japanese officials themselves, in response to specific local conditions. The legislative process was set in motion by an inquiry (*ukagai*) submitted to the Justice Ministry (Shihōshō) by authorities in Kumamoto (then known as Shirakawa) prefecture in September 1872, requesting instructions for dealing with cases of *keikan* in the growing number of schools, both public and private, that had been established in the prefecture since the Restoration.[41] One document refers to existing "offenders" (*hanzaisha*), suggesting that local officials perceived their "offense" as criminal even before

---

Takurō, ed., *Nihon kindai keiji hōreishū*, 3 vols., Shihō shiryō bessatsu, no. 17 (Shihōshō hishoka, 1945), 2:366.

39. Naikaku kirokukyoku, *Hōki bunrui taizen*, 54:273–275, 325–326. Under the provisions of the *Kaitei ritsuryō*, offenders could also redeem (*shokuzai* or *shūshoku*) their sentences by paying a fine, provided there were attenuating circumstances. Commutation schedules varied according to such factors as class, sex, age, infirmity, and government service. See Naikaku kirokukyoku, *Hōki bunrui taizen*, 54:258–267.

40. For Edo-period accounts of European "sodomy" legislation, see Morishima Nakayoshi, *Bankoku shinwa*, 5 vols. (Edo: Suwaraya Ichibei, 1789), 4:4; Morishima Nakayoshi, *Kōmō zatsuwa*, in *Bunmei genryū sōshō*, ed. Kokusho kankōkai, 3 vols. (Taizansha, 1940), 1:467; Umehara, *Meiji seiteki chinbunshi*, 1:4–7; Yamamura Saisuke, *Seiyō zakki*, 4 vols. (Edo: Suzuki bun'enkaku, 1848), 1:30. Regarding Japanese knowledge of European "sodomy," see also Timon Screech [Taimon Sukurīchi], *Ō-Edo ijin ōrai*, trans. Takayama Hiroshi, Maruzen bukkusu, no. 36 (Maruzen, 1995), 117–120.

41. The full text of the inquiry may be found in Kasumi, *Meiji shoki keijihō*, 92. Kumamoto was known as Shirakawa prefecture from 1873 to 1876.

it was formally criminalized.[42] Significantly, as we saw in chapter 2, the penal code of Kumamoto domain had since 1797 incorporated an explicit precedent for dealing with male-male sexual violence, at least in cases where it resulted in death or injury. The fear of prefectural officials that the "lingering evil custom" (*korai yori no akushū*) of *nanshoku* was getting in the way of younger students' studies also echoed periodic complaints by domain bureaucrats in other regions such as Matsuyama and Aizu. Kumamoto authorities had presumably been able to handle such incidents satisfactorily under domain law during the Edo period, but no longer possessed the legal means to do so once Kumamoto domain was abolished in 1868 and such national codes as the 1871 *Shinritsu kōryō*, which was silent on the subject, were implemented.

Justice Ministry officials in Tokyo agreed that such behavior deserved punishment, and by October 1872 had drafted a pair of articles for incorporation into the *Kaitei ritsuryō*, then in the last stages of preparation.[43] It was only at this point that foreign legislation was consulted. The foreign examples that lawmakers specifically examined were the penal codes of contemporary (Qing dynasty) China and of France. All in all, the resulting Article 266 bears the imprint of Chinese law much more strongly than that of French, as is true of the *Kaitei ritsuryō* as a whole. Qing lawmakers had proscribed male-male anal intercourse (*jijian*; written with the same characters as the Japanese *keikan*) as early as 1679, formally incorporating these provisions into their criminal code (*Da Qing luli*) in 1740.[44] While the *Kaitei ritsuryō*'s Article

---

42. Naikaku kirokukyoku, *Hōki bunrui taizen*, 54:313.
43. Naikaku kirokukyoku, *Hōki bunrui taizen*, 54:313. The draft version reads as follows:

Keikan Regulations

Those engaging in anal intercourse by seduction [*kan'yū*] shall be sentenced to ninety strokes with a heavy bamboo stick [*jō*]. In the case of the peerage and ex-samurai, this shall be treated as a dishonorable offense. Violated youngsters fifteen years and under shall not be held criminally liable. Those sixteen years and over shall be charged with the same offense.

Those committing rape shall be sentenced to banishment [*ru*] of the third degree. For attempted offenses, the penalty shall be reduced by one degree. If [the violated youngster is] twelve years of age or under, the act shall be treated as rape even in cases of seduction.

The term *kan'yū* implied that seducers needed to overcome the disinclination of insertees through "sweet" (one of the characters in *kan'yū*) words or other favors. It should be noted that, since 1871, "banishment" involved not actual exile but instead a harsher form of penal servitude. See Ch'en, *Early Meiji Legal Order*, 41–42.
44. Qing legal discourse on male-male sexuality is discussed in Bret Hinsch, *Pas-*

266 was neither so detailed nor so harsh as its Chinese equivalent, which prescribed various styles of execution for different categories of rape, it resembled the latter in several key respects, including the name of the crime; the consequent impunity of male-male sexual practices other than anal intercourse; the placement of the article among the code's "fornication" (*hankan*; Chinese: *fanjian*) provisions; the penalization, but at the same time relatively mild punishment, of consensual acts; and the explicit expectation that insertees would be young in age. This resemblance is even more striking in the draft version, which, like Qing law, established an age of consent at thirteen, and whose penalty for consensual intercourse (ninety strokes with a heavy bamboo stick) was not far removed from the Chinese (one hundred strokes plus a month in the cangue). Ironically, therefore, the criminalization of "uncivilized" sexual behavior owed much to the example of a nation many Japanese would before long come to regard as a bastion of "barbarism."

The compilation of the *Kaitei ritsuryō* marked the first time that Western legislation exerted a direct influence upon the content of Japanese penal law. At this stage, however, lawmakers' familiarity with various systems of Western jurisprudence was still relatively limited. Thus, while the *Kaitei ritsuryō's* framers examined the French *Code pénal*, they were either unaware of or chose to ignore other European statutes regarding male-male sexuality. The latter were often far less tolerant, as in Victorian Britain, where "buggery" warranted ten years to life in prison and in Scotland even capital punishment.[45] Nevertheless, French influence on Article 266 was significantly less pronounced than Chinese. Although the French example may have helped tone down the severity of Qing punishments and, in the case of the draft version, confirmed the establishment of an age of consent at thirteen, the code's authors flatly rejected the immunity of consensual male-male relations between adults that set Napoleonic legislation apart from its European contemporaries. Nor did they feel a need to punish male-male sexual practices other than anal intercourse, as French law did when such acts involved minors or the use of force. It is thus another of Article 266's ironies that its focus on anal penetration and intolerance even of consensual acts,

---

sions of the Cut Sleeve: The Male Homosexual Tradition in China (Berkeley: University of California Press, 1990), 142–145; M. J. Meijer, "Homosexual Offenses in Ch'ing Law," *T'oung Pao* 71 (1985): 109–133; Vivien W. Ng, "Ideology and Sexuality: Rape Laws in Qing China," *Journal of Asian Studies* 46 (1987): 67–69. On the origins of the term *jijian/keikan*, see Hinsch, *Passions of the Cut Sleeve*, 88–89.

45. Matsui Junji, trans., *Eibei hankanritsu* (Tsuchiya, 1879), 16; Jeffrey Weeks, *Coming Out: Homosexual Politics in Britain, from the Nineteenth Century to the Present* (London: Quartet, 1977), 14.

superficially similar to much of European "sodomy" legislation, did not derive from the sole Western code that was actually consulted.

The Sain, a bureaucratically selected legislative body, gave its "careful consideration" and consent to the Justice Ministry's draft regulations in October 1872, and a directive for their incorporation into the *Kaitei ritsuryō* was issued in the following month.[46] For reasons that remain unclear, however, the draft provisions underwent further revision between this time and the code's promulgation in June 1873.[47] The most significant change was the removal of the statutory-rape clause, which was a feature of both Qing and French legislation and remained in effect in the case of male-female coitus. Japanese lawmakers seem to have felt that absolving male insertees under the age of sixteen from criminal liability for their actions provided sufficient consideration for their status as minors.[48] The initially prescribed sentences of flogging for consensual acts and banishment for rape were also amended in the final version, physical confinement at hard labor having replaced the Chinese system of "five punishments" (*gokei*; Chinese: *wuxing*) as the code's standard penalty for noncapital offenses.

The criminalization of *keikan* enjoyed a favorable reception in Meiji Japan's fledgling press, which was quick in embracing the goal and rhetoric of "civilization." In an 1874 newspaper article, one journalist praised the statute as the mark of an "enlightened age" (*meisei*) and a "blessing for young boys" (*yōnen danji no saiwai*), noting that *kagema* had by now entirely disappeared from Yushima and Yoshichō. From the writer's "civilized" perspective, the "immoral practice" (*hairin no shogyō*) of *nanshoku* befitted the world of Sengoku warriors and decadent priests, not the present era of "imperial influence" (*kōka*).[49] In other, more traditional genres of popular discourse, however, the *keikan* statute elicited a less moralistic response. A

---

46. Naikaku kirokukyoku, *Hōki bunrui taizen*, 54:313. As Kasumi (*Meiji shoki keijihō*, 93–96) has persuasively argued, the *Kaitei ritsuryō*'s *keikan* provisions appear to have gone into effect prior to the full implementation of the code in July 1873.

47. One factor awaiting clarification in this context is the relevance of a petition (Irokawa Daikichi and Gabe Masao, eds., *Meiji kenpakusho shūsei*, 5 vols. to date [Chikuma shobō, 1986–], 2:431–432) submitted in February 1873 by Kō Eiichi, an official of the Sain, to the Shūgiin, another bureaucratic body, demanding the speedy criminalization of *keikan* (glossed in this case as *danshoku* [= *nanshoku*]).

48. In an 1876 court case, however, prosecutors invoked the female age of consent in order to sentence a man to ten years for engaging in ostensibly consensual *keikan* with a four-year-old boy. See Kasumi, *Meiji shoki keijihō*, 102–103.

49. Umehara Hokumei, ed., <*Meiji Taishō*> *Kidan chinbun daishūsei*, 3 vols. (Bungei shijōsha, 1929–1931), 1:136–137.

verse in an 1878 *senryū* anthology, for instance, poked fun at the law's arbitrary distinction between two receptacles for the male organ: "The grappling ginger is allowed and the chrysanthemum forbidden" (*Dakimyōga yurushite kiku o kinjirare*).[50] "Grappling ginger" and chrysanthemum were two well-known heraldic crests, but here represented the female genitalia and male anus respectively. The humor of the verse took on additional pungency from the fact that, contrary to Restoration history, the imperial house (symbolized by the chrysanthemum) had in this metaphorical instance met with ignoble defeat.

Three *keikan* cases from the 1870s and 1880s provide a glimpse into the actual implementation of Article 266.[51] The first involves one Matsui Masakata, a male resident of Shirakawa (Kumamoto) prefecture, of uncertain age—though possibly a student, in light of the 1872 complaint by prefectural authorities that prompted the drafting of the article in the first place—and *shizoku* rank. In June of 1875, Matsui, together with two male accomplices, lured a certain Katō Eijirō to a secluded mulberry orchard, where he raped him anally (*gōkeikan*). A patrolman (*junsa*) happened upon the scene, and Matsui was arrested. Invoking the *Kaitei ritsuryō*, a court one year later sentenced Matsui to ten years of penal servitude; the fate of his accomplices is not entirely clear. In the days of Kumamoto domain, local officials had enjoyed the authority to adjudicate such cases upon analogy with male-female rape if death or injury resulted, so that Matsui's prosecution was not a complete departure from earlier practice. Nevertheless, the Tokyo journalist reporting the incident praised as an example of Meiji "enlightenment" (*kaimei*) the fact that such "evil deeds" (*akuji*) now met their just punishment.[52]

The means by which Matsui's crime was discovered suggests the growing importance of the police as an agency of law enforcement. Whereas Edo-period officials had relied heavily on networks of mutual responsibility such as *goningumi* for ensuring compliance with the law, the establishment of a professional constabulary allowed the Meiji state to keep a more direct watch over its citizens.[53] Police stations and police boxes (*kōban*) sprang up

50. Yamamoto Seinosuke, ed., *Senryū Meiji sesōshi* (Makino shuppan, 1983), 49–50.

51. Actual *keikan* prosecutions under Article 266 appear to have been relatively rare. Kasumi (*Meiji shoki keijihō*, 100) lists twenty convictions (two for rape) between 1876 and 1881, but this figure evidently does not include incidents of prison *keikan*, convictions under appeal, or (for reasons that are unclear) the Inaba case described below.

52. Umehara, *Meiji seiteki chinbunshi*, 2:12–14.

53. On the evolution of the Meiji police force, see James B. Leavell, "The Polic-

throughout city and countryside, their functions coordinated after 1873 by the Home Ministry (Naimushō) in Tokyo. Another new feature on the Meiji landscape was the uniformed police officer, whose peripatetic duties provided the state with a highly effective means of surveillance over the daily activities of the populace. Thus, even a secluded mulberry orchard did not always provide sufficient protection from the eyes of the law.

A second incident illustrates the fact that prosecution of *keikan* took the form of a public action (*kōso*), in which it was the state's role to press charges rather than that of the aggrieved party. In January 1880, the Daishin'in, the nation's highest court, requested informal instructions (*naikun*) from the Justice Ministry in connection with a case then receiving its attention. Unnamed parties A and B had engaged in consensual anal intercourse while both were serving ten-year terms at a Tokyo penitentiary. B subsequently imagined that a third prisoner, C, had reported their "fornication" (*kanji*) to authorities, and, in the heat of an argument, bashed C with a railroad tie. Ironically, authorities learned of A and B's relationship only while investigating the fighting incident. The justices wished to know whether they should uphold a December 1879 lower-court verdict sentencing B alone for inflicting injury in a fight (*tōō seishō*), an offense that involved a forty-day term, and merely "reprimanding" (*shikarioku*) A, or whether they should simultaneously prosecute the crime of *keikan*, in which event a longer term of ninety days would take precedence and A would also face charges. Officials in the criminal-law section of the Justice Ministry advised the latter course, providing that police could offer "certain evidence" (*kakushō*) of anal intercourse, and the Daishin'in issued a ruling to this effect in February.[54] B's fears demonstrate that any individual could lodge an accusation of *keikan*—a person directly involved, a third party, or law-enforcement authorities—which the state, given sufficient evidence, might then prosecute. *Keikan* differed in this respect from the crime of adultery, where a third-party accusation did not constitute sufficient grounds for prosecution.[55] Although it remains unclear what constituted "certain evidence" of *keikan*, the proof of seminal emission that European "sodomy" law sometimes re-

ing of Society," in *Japan in Transition: Thought and Action in the Meiji Era, 1868–1912*, ed. Hilary Conroy et al. (Rutherford, N.J.: Fairleigh Dickinson University Press, 1984), 22–49.

54. Kasumi, *Meiji shoki keijihō*, 103–105; Naikaku kirokukyoku, *Hōki bunrui taizen*, 54:365–366.

55. Kasumi, *Meiji shoki keijihō*, 105–106; Naikaku kanpōkyoku, *Hōrei zensho*, 1874 vol., 1346.

quired, in part for doctrinally rooted reasons, does not appear to have been necessary in Meiji Japan.[56]

The third incident, taking place in 1881, is interesting because it reveals a pattern of male-male sexual behavior clearly at odds with the age-stratified and inserter-initiated contacts that the *Kaitei ritsuryō's* authors had envisioned. The case revolved around one Inaba Kotoji, a twenty-six-year-old *shizoku* male employed at a restaurant in Tsuchiura, Ibaragi prefecture. Inaba had reportedly enjoyed being anally penetrated since childhood, and thereafter, according to the court, "forfeited the normal condition of males" (*danshi no jōtai o ushinaitaru*). Dressing in feminine clothing and adopting the name Okoto, he passed as a woman, although rumors sometimes circulated that he might be a "hermaphrodite" (*henjō danshi, futanari*). One night in February 1881, Inaba crept into the bed of a rickshaw puller also sleeping at the restaurant, and, "using the same methods as a woman," prevailed upon him to act as the inserter in anal intercourse. In April, he was stripped of his *shizoku* rank and sentenced to ninety days of penal servitude.[57]

Whereas the law framed *keikan* as an act taking place between an initiative-taking older inserter and an often unwilling young insertee, Inaba's story demonstrates that male-male sexual behavior did not always conform to this pattern. Inaba's critics, and likely Inaba himself, viewed his role as insertee not as a function of male age hierarchy (by most reckonings, he was already an adult) but of his feminine gender identity, which extended beyond the sexual realm into other aspects of daily life. Because of the convention that gender should match sex, males who assimilated feminine gender, as well as masculine-identified females, faced considerable ridicule and curiosity as to their anatomical makeup—hence the speculation about Inaba's "hermaphrodism." In Tokyo, such gender-anomalous males were re-

56. Some of the legal intricacies of "sodomy" prosecution in Europe (esp. Britain) were familiar to Japanese at the time, as is reflected in Torigoe Miyoshi, trans., *Gōkan kensatsuhō* (Matsui Chūbei, 1879), 112–115; Umehara, *Meiji seiteki chinbunshi*, 1:4–7. Seminal emission was not necessary for an act of *keikan* to be considered "completed," as confirmed by a Daishin'in ruling of 1886 (see Kasumi, *Meiji shoki keijihō*, 103).

57. *Yūbin hōchi shinbun*, 30 April 1881, 2. According to the original provisions of the *Kaitei ritsuryō*, Inaba would only have forfeited his rank; an 1877 amendment (Naikaku kirokukyoku, *Hōki bunrui taizen*, 54:326–327), however, mandated that *shizoku* who committed "dishonorable offenses" be incarcerated even if the ordinary sentence for their crime was less than one hundred days, as in the case of consensual *keikan*.

ferred to as "men-women" (*otoko-onna* or *onna-otoko*).[58] A feminine gender identity, however, did not necessarily involve sexual relations with other males, nor did it preclude the possibility of liaisons with females. In early nineteenth-century Edo, for example, a biologically male acupuncturist nicknamed Okatsu is reported to have gone about his job in feminine dress but had a wife and several children, while Shikoku's Ooto, during his days as a maidservant, is said to have "fornicated" with a young female in his employer's household as well as dallying with several neighborhood women.[59]

Although twentieth-century commentators would increasingly equate the two, the association of male-male sexuality with feminine gender identity remained at best a subcurrent in Meiji discourse. The *Kaitei ritsuryō's* framers had taken for granted that age hierarchy would structure male-male sexual practices rather than gender identity, and insertees acquiesce to anal intercourse only through seduction ("sweet enticing" [*kan'yū*], in the language of the draft version) or the use of force. The possibility, for instance, of a junior male penetrating his senior, much less seeking the insertee role for his own pleasure, does not seem to have entered their minds. The code's construction of male-male sexuality was no doubt reinforced by the class and geographical origins of its authors: Etō Shinpei, for example, who presided over the Justice Ministry at the time, was a former samurai of Saga domain in Kyushu (home of Yamamoto Tsunetomo, the author of *Hagakure*), where the age-structured model of *shudō* was deeply ingrained in local warrior culture.

Such expectations suited Article 266 ideally for cases like Matsui's, but less so in instances where male-male sexual relations did not fit this mold, as was clearly true of Inaba, and perhaps as well of Ooto, whom authorities evidently chose not to prosecute for his sexual behavior at all. In the case of Inaba, the sexual advances had been made by the insertee, who, as an adult and a *shizoku*, should, in the eyes of his judges, have known better than to thus disgrace himself. Inaba's flagrant violation of gender (not to mention

58. Miyatake Gaikotsu, *Futanari kō*, in *Miyatake Gaikotsu chosakushū*, 5:362; Umehara, *Kidan chinbun daishūsei*, 1:192. Note also Motoori Uchitō's late Edo-period description of the "male who should have been born a female" (*onna no umare-zokonai*), cited in chap. 1, n. 51. *Otoko-onna* could also refer to a gender-anomalous female, for an example of which usage see Miyatake, *Futanari kō*, 5:361.

59. Miyatake, *Futanari kō*, 5:362. For an 1876 episode in which a seventeen-year-old Tokyo male with a reputation as an *otoko-onna* surprised neighbors by becoming romantically involved with a female, see Umehara, *Kidan chinbun daishūsei*, 1:192.

class) norms clearly disturbed the court, which dwelt on it at some length in its verdict, but did not in itself constitute an offense against the penal code; at best, Inaba might have been slapped with a fine for cross-dressing. Similarly, while the court placed the blame for the incident squarely on Inaba, it could not prosecute him for rape, since he had been the insertee. The lowly rickshaw puller, meanwhile, though at twenty-six far from being one of the "violated youngsters" that lawmakers had envisioned, is portrayed in the verdict as a hapless victim and barely mentioned in newspaper coverage of the case, although he presumably received the same ninety-day prison term as Inaba. At times, the very inflexibility of the law made it an unwieldy instrument for punishing "uncivilized" behavior.

ENACTING THE OBSCENE (OR, NAPOLEON IN JAPAN)

Ironically, Inaba might have escaped punishment had he committed his indiscretion eleven months later. A new penal code, the *Keihō* (sometimes referred to as the *Kyūkeihō* or "Former Penal Code" in order to distinguish it from its identically named 1907 successor), came into force in January 1882, in effect legalizing consensual anal intercourse between adult males. Promulgated in 1880, the *Keihō* introduced significant changes not only in the legal status but also in the legalistic construction of male-male sexual activity. The term *keikan*, and the preoccupation with anal penetration that it bespoke, dropped out of the penal code entirely. Male-male (and male-female) anal intercourse now fell under the broader category of "obscene acts" (*waisetsu no shogyō*), which lawmakers patterned after such European terms as the French *attentats à la pudeur* and the German *unzüchtige Handlungen*.[60] While never precisely defined, "obscene acts," in theory, included all forms of male-male and female-female sexual activity, as well as all male-female sexual acts besides penile penetration of the vagina.

"Obscene acts" under the 1880 *Keihō* were illegal, however, only under a limited set of circumstances. Only in cases involving minors or coercion did the state undertake to punish them, while "obscene acts" between consenting adults were in theory immune from official interference. Articles 346 and 347 of the new code prescribed punishment for those who performed an "obscene act" with a boy or girl not yet twelve years old, or using "violence or threat" (*bōkō kyōhaku*) with an individual of any age. Uncoerced

---

60. While the compound *waisetsu* rarely appears in legal discourse before the Meiji period, the first of its characters could also be read as *midari*, a term that Edo-period legislators frequently used to signify the lewd and/or disorderly.

sexual relations with minors warranted imprisonment at hard labor (*jū-kinko*) for a period of one month to a year, plus a fine of two to twenty yen. Coerced acts with persons twelve or over met with the same penalty. When violence or threat accompanied an "obscene act" with a minor, the prescribed range of penalties doubled.[61] Although the 1880 *Keihō* granted judges a certain amount of discretion in determining the proper sentence for each particular offense, the two-year limit in cases of anal rape was nevertheless considerably shorter than the ten years meted out by the *Kaitei ritsuryō*.

The implementation of the *Keihō* also brought to an end the differentiation of penalties by class, along with the option, hitherto available under certain circumstances, of redeeming offenses through the payment of cash. Apart from the imperial family, all Japanese were now equal, at least in principle, in the eyes of criminal law. In addition, the responsibility for prosecuting "obscene acts" no longer fell to the state, as had previously been the case with *keikan*, but to the victim and his or her household. Article 350 of the 1880 *Keihō* stipulated that only the violated party or immediate relatives (*shinzoku*) had the right to press such charges.[62] Later commentators explained that the public knowledge of "obscene acts" that resulted from prosecution might blemish the victim's "honor" (*meiyo*), and thus add to, rather than alleviate, the injury.[63] As this provision illustrates, sexual honor

61. Naikaku kirokukyoku, *Hōki bunrui taizen*, 54:431. The full text of the provisions ran as follows:

Article 346: Those who commit an obscene act with a male or female who has not yet reached the age of twelve, or with a male or female twelve years of age or over using violence or threat, shall be sentenced to imprisonment at hard labor for a period of between one month and one year, in addition to which a fine of between two and twenty yen shall be imposed.

Article 347: Those who, using violence or threat, commit an obscene act with a male or female who has not reached the age of twelve shall be sentenced to imprisonment at hard labor for a period of between two months and two years, in addition to which a fine of between four and forty yen shall be imposed.

A draft proposal by the French legalist Gustave Boissonade ("Daiichian"; Waseda daigaku Tsuruta monjo kenkyūkai, *Nihon keihō*, 3:2032–2033) differed from the final version in several key respects: (1) it called for severer punishment when victims of coercion were under the age of fifteen, rather than twelve; (2) it prescribed heavier penalties across the board, demanding one to five years' imprisonment and a fine of ten to one hundred yen in the case of Article 346, and a more rigorous form of incarceration (*keichōeki*) in the case of Article 347; (3) it explicitly defined "obscene acts" as involving contact with the genitals (*in'yō no gu ni fure*); (4) it augmented the penalty for "obscene acts" committed by persons in a position of authority over the victim.

62. Naikaku kirokukyoku, *Hōki bunrui taizen*, 54:431.

63. Dandō Shigemitsu, *Keihō kōyō kakuron* (Sōbunsha, 1964), 399; Kōke Yoshio,

extended beyond the level of the individual to the entire household, and to the patriarch whose duty it was to defend it. "Obscene acts" also brought dishonor upon the family of the offender, since criminal convictions were entered permanently into the household register.

In the *Keihō*, the influence of French law, only dimly visible in its predecessor, assumed a central importance. In 1876, the Justice Ministry commissioned Gustave Boissonade, a French jurist, to supervise the compilation of a new penal code. Boissonade's participation in this project, including authorship of the draft proposal, gave the legislation a strongly French cast, clearly evident in its stance on male-male sexuality. Scholars of Western sexual history have often commented on the spread of "sodomy" law reform, a product of the Enlightenment, across Europe in the wake of the Napoleonic campaigns; few have noted, however, that this tide of decriminalization reached as far as Japan. In contrast to the earlier regime of "sodomy" prosecution, in which the state took it upon itself to punish a sin originally defined by the church, Napoleonic law (building on Revolutionary precedent) deemed sexual acts, so long as they did not involve minors or coercion, as belonging to a private sphere outside the realm of state intervention.[64] In explaining this principle to his colleagues, Boissonade drew a parallel between "sodomy" and such acts as incest and bestiality, which, although constituting "disgraceful sins" (*shūtai no tsumi*) from the perspective of Christian morality, had long since vanished from the French penal code. While individuals who engaged in such acts no longer faced criminal prosecution, Boissonade pointed out, they were nevertheless subject to "disdain and loathing" (*iyashimi nikumaruru*) in civil society, which provided an equally effective means of punishment.[65] Through Boissonade, the tolerance (which is not to say approval) of male-male sexual acts between consenting adults that distinguished Napoleonic law left its imprint on the Japanese criminal

<Shinpan> Keihō kōwa (Chikura shobō, 1949), 199; <Kokkei shinbun furoku> Nihon shinkeihō (N.p., n.d.), 28. A turn-of-the-century journalist noted that since the "victims [of male-male sexual assaults by student gangs] are mostly sons of well-to-do families, the parents for obvious reasons do not like to make their grievances public and refrain from appealing to the police." See "Degeneration of Students," *Yorozu chōhō*, 18 May 1899, 2.

64. Regarding the origins of Napoleonic legislation on male-male sexuality, see Michael David Sibalis, "The Regulation of Male Homosexuality in Revolutionary and Napoleonic France, 1789–1815," in *Homosexuality in Modern France*, ed. Jeffrey Merrick and Bryant T. Ragan, Jr. (New York: Oxford University Press, 1996), 80–101.

65. Waseda daigaku Tsuruta monjo kenkyūkai, *Nihon keihō*, 3:2044.

code, and the categorical prohibition of *keikan* lapsed after less than a decade of enforcement.

Boissonade and his Japanese associates clearly patterned the *Keihō*'s "obscene act" provisions after similar articles in the French *Code pénal*.[66] Nevertheless, in the course of its transposition to Japan, the Napoleonic model underwent several modifications. On the whole, these changes diminished rather than augmented contemporary French penalties for "obscene acts" (*attentats à la pudeur*). In cases involving the use of violence, for instance, French law regarded the offense as more serious if the victim had not yet reached the age of fifteen, whereas the final version of the 1880 *Keihō* set the equivalent age at only twelve. In assenting to this change, Boissonade commented, drawing upon nineteenth-century European racial theory, that the age of sexual maturity arrived at different times in different countries depending on their geographical latitude and climate.[67] In addition, Japanese lawmakers fixed the maximum sentence for "obscene acts" at only two years plus fine, thereby rejecting the penalty of lifetime servitude that the *Code pénal* called for in certain instances. Even the one-to-five-year sentence that Boissonade had originally proposed struck his Japanese associates as exceedingly harsh.[68] Finally, the adopted version of the *Keihō* failed to incorporate a clause corresponding to Article 333 of the *Code pénal*, which mandated harsher penalties for *attentats à la pudeur* committed by persons in a position of authority over the other party, including parents and other senior relatives, educators, servants, and civil or religious functionaries, or with the aid of one or more accomplices. Boissonade's draft proposal had in fact contained such a provision, but his Japanese colleagues felt that it contradicted the code's silence on the topic of incest.[69] Lawmakers may have feared that such a clause would undercut patriarchal authority and foster disharmony within the household and in other social relations, just as their Edo-period predecessors had once discouraged suits between parents and children.

The *Keihō*'s decriminalization of anal intercourse between consenting

66. For the relevant sections of the *Code pénal* (as amended in 1863), see Adrien Charpentier, ed., *Codes et lois pour la France, l'Algérie, et les Colonies*, 7th ed. (Paris: Marchal, 1903), 58–59.

67. Waseda daigaku Tsuruta monjo kenkyūkai, *Nihon keihō*, 3:2036.

68. Waseda daigaku Tsuruta monjo kenkyūkai, *Nihon keihō*, 3:2035, 2073–2074.

69. Waseda daigaku Tsuruta monjo kenkyūkai, *Nihon keihō*, 3:2040–2048, 2075–2077. Similarly, the drafters of the 1880 *Keihō* failed to adopt a section of the *Code pénal*'s Article 331 dealing with "obscene acts" committed by senior relatives with unmarried minors of any age.

adults seems to have provoked little comment or criticism from the Japanese public or among lawmakers themselves, unlike the same code's removal of legal protections for concubines, which sparked a furor.[70] Several factors help to account for this relative indifference. First, the categorical proscription of *keikan* possessed no firm basis in Japanese juridical tradition, but derived instead from foreign precedent, which was easier set aside. Moreover, by the early 1880s the Chinese ancestry of this provision was, if anything, a liability. At the same time, the French credentials of the new code likely served to allay fears that Western observers would perceive official leniency toward male-male sexual relations as "uncivilized." Since acts involving minors and/or coercion played a significant role within the larger spectrum of male-male sexual practice, legal sanctions against these particular forms of behavior appear to have satisfied both the public and lawmakers. Boissonade himself noted that, even in France, "persons who have reached the legal age of majority do not ordinarily practice sodomy with one another," so that most incidents could be prosecuted as "obscene acts" against minors.[71]

In one instance where criticism of the *Keihō*'s treatment of male-male sexuality arose, it originated, not surprisingly, from the local foreign community. In 1899, the *Eastern World*, an English-language weekly based in Yokohama, responded to a recent report in the Japanese press about the prevalence of "unnatural crimes" among Tokyo students. The newspaper called upon authorities to deal with the situation by rectifying a "serious defect" in the criminal code: its failure to prescribe penalties for male-male sexual acts, which, along with bestiality and incest, were "condemned and punished as crimes in all civilized countries." Like the *Kaitei ritsuryō*'s ban on anal intercourse, legal strictures against incest had disappeared with the 1880 *Keihō*, while Japanese legislators had seldom regarded bestiality as a matter of significant concern. The journalist also recommended the inclusion of provisions similar to Paragraph 174 of the German *Strafgesetzbuch*, which, like Article 333 of the *Code pénal*, magnified the punishment for persons in a position of authority who committed "obscene acts" with their wards.[72] This proposal was seconded by an English-language columnist in

70. On the contemporary debate over the legal status of concubines, see Sotozaki Mitsuhiro, *Nihon fujinron shi*, 2 vols. (Domesu shuppan, 1986–1989), 1:78–82.
71. Waseda daigaku Tsuruta monjo kenkyūkai, *Nihon keihō*, 3:2044. Although the Japanese transcript gives the word *keikan*, I assume that Boissonade himself used the French term *sodomie*.
72. "Prevalence of Unnatural Crimes amongst Tokyo Students," *Eastern World*, 20 May 1899, 6.

the *Yorozu chōhō* (possibly the Christian journalist Uchimura Kanzō), who hoped that the "sensible remarks of the *Eastern World* will find echoes in the Government and judicial circles."[73]

Not all foreigners shared the *Eastern World*'s indignation, however. In an essay submitted to the German sexologist and social reformer Magnus Hirschfeld, Doriphorus, evidently a European resident of Tokyo, justified the Meiji government's unwillingness to act on the newspaper's proposals.[74] He maintained that acceptance of male-male sexual practices was too deeply rooted in Japanese society to afford such measures widespread support or sympathy. The Buddhist clergy's open indulgence in male-male sexual relations, he argued, was particularly influential in reinforcing public tolerance. According to Doriphorus, Meiji officials were also aware of the fact that Paragraph 175 of the German penal code, whose emulation the *Eastern World* had recommended, was the target of a contemporary repeal campaign led by Hirschfeld and others.[75] In the midst of domestic indifference and foreign controversy, such isolated calls for the criminalization of male-male sexual acts as the *Eastern World*'s, which would in effect have resurrected the *Kaitei ritsuryō*'s ban on *keikan*, went unheeded.

It would be a mistake, however, to view the transition from *Kaitei ritsuryō* to *Keihō* simply in terms of decriminalization, for even as the latter code eased legal restrictions against one type of sexual act, it imposed them upon others for the first time. Although anal intercourse was often regarded as the "pinnacle" (*kyokuten*) of "obscene acts," it is unclear if it was the most prevalent, or even whether male-male or male-female "obscene acts" were the more frequently prosecuted.[76] As the Meiji period progressed, medico-legal authorities made increasing reference to such practices as the

73. "Prevalence of Unnatural Crimes amongst Tokyo Students," *Yorozu chōhō*, 23 May 1899, 2.

74. Friedrich S. Krauss, *Das Geschlechtleben in Glauben, Sitte, und Brauch der Japaner*, Beiwerke zum Studium der Anthropophyteia, no. 2 (Leipzig: Deutsche, 1907), 81–89. Although Krauss (78) identifies Doriphorus as a "Japanese statesman" (*japanischer Staatsmann*), certain features of the essay—for example, the distinction that the writer makes between Japanese soldiery and "our own" (*bei uns*; 84)— suggest a European, most likely German, author. Since Doriphorus claimed to have contact with high Meiji officials and army officers, it is possible that he served the Japanese government or was a foreign diplomat.

75. On German law-reform efforts, see John Lauritsen and David Thorstad, *The Early Homosexual Rights Movement (1864–1935)* (New York: Times Change, 1974); James D. Steakley, *The Homosexual Emancipation Movement in Germany* (New York: Arno, 1975).

76. "Yaban gakusei no torishimari," *Yorozu chōhō*, 16 February 1898, 2. While one forensic-pathology text (Shimizu, *Jitsuyō saiban igaku*, 312) claimed that anal

masturbation (*shuin*) of one male by another as "obscene acts" demanding punishment if carried out by force or with minors.[77] Interestingly, fellatio continued to receive little attention in published accounts of male-
male sexual behavior, just as it had seldom appeared in *shudō* texts of the
Edo period.[78] Nevertheless, unlike *keikan*, the ill-defined notion of "obscenity" allowed for an expanding interpretation: even kissing or lifting
someone's skirts constituted potential "obscene acts," according to one
commentator.[79]

It was the duty of forensic pathologists not only to catalogue the different varieties of "obscene act," but also to establish scientific means of proving their commission. In order to do so, they delved heavily into the contemporary European literature on the subject. While it was generally agreed
that semen in the insertee's anus provided the surest proof of anal intercourse, authorities cited other telltale signs that ranged from the obvious to
the preposterous. Fecal matter or friction marks on the penis could reveal
an inserter, or a glans with a pointed, "doglike" shape or annular depression if he engaged in such activity frequently. The young or first-time insertee might exhibit lesions of the anus and rectum, venereal infection, or
semen residue on his buttocks and clothing (in which case it was necessary
to determine whether the individual himself was capable of ejaculation). The

intercourse between males accounted for the largest number of "obscene act" suits,
another (Yoshii, *Saiban igakuron*, 53) maintained that most "obscene acts" were
committed by males against females.

77. Hiraga Seijirō, *Kanmei hōigaku*, 272; Ishikawa Kiyotada, *Jitsuyō hōigaku*,
417–424; Katayama Kuniyoshi and Eguchi Jō, *Saiban igaku teikō*, 1:52–53; Katayama
Kuniyoshi et al., *Hōigaku teikō*, 1:188–190; Shimizu, *Jitsuyō saiban igaku*, 312, 314;
Yoshii, *Saiban igakuron*, 53–55. Lawmakers deliberating the proposed "obscene acts"
provisions in 1876 repeatedly refer to the act of "playing" (*ganrō*) with another person's genitals. See Waseda daigaku Tsuruta monjo kenkyūkai, *Nihon keihō*, 3:2028,
2035–2038.

78. Published references to male-male fellatio become common only in the 1920s,
and even then were subject to heavy censorship. See, for instance, Nakamura Kokyō,
Hentai seikakusha zakkō, Hentai bunken sōsho, no. 3 (Bungei shiryō kenkyūkai,
1928), 80; Satō Kōka, "Seiyokugaku goi," pt. 1, *Hentai shiryō*, November 1926,
64–66; Satō Kōka, *Senryū hentai seiyokushi* (Onko shobō, 1927), 12.

79. <*Kokkei shinbun furoku*> *Nihon shinkeihō*, 27. As mentioned above in n. 61,
the initial draft of the *Keihō* had clearly defined "obscene acts" as involving genital
contact, but lawmakers chose to delete this clause in the belief that its explicit language would tarnish the "dignity of the written law" (*shohō no teisai*). See Waseda
daigaku Tsuruta monjo kenkyūkai, *Nihon keihō*, 3:2037. In a 1918 decision, the
Daishin'in ruled that the "obscene" was characterized by a capacity to stimulate or
satisfy sexual desire and to elicit "shame" (*shūchi*) or "revulsion" (*ken'o*) in others. See Hioki Norio et al., eds., *Nihon hanrei taisei*, 26 vols. (Hibonkaku, 1936),
14:470.

habitual insertee reputedly bore such distinguishing marks as a weakened sphincter, a funnel-shaped or prolapsed anus, a diminution of anal wrinkles, chronic inflammation or catarrhal ulcer of the rectum, and hemorrhoids.[80] Experts could offer no definitive means of proving the masturbation of one male by another, although they noted that engorgement with blood, a loosened foreskin, or miscellaneous injury sometimes resulted in the manipulated organ.[81] Though forensic medicine had been practiced in Japan during the Edo period, typically in the form of postmortem examination, it had paid little attention to male-male sexual practices until its Meiji reinvigoration as a discipline for regulating the living body.

Forensic pathologists' exposure to Western medico-legal texts also brought them in contact with the recently formulated construct of "homosexuality" (or, in its original German form, *Homosexualität*).[82] As early as 1890, Shimizu Sadao coined the term "same-sex intercourse" (*dōsei no kōsetsu*) to translate this concept, which he explained to his readers as synonymous with *keikan* or anal intercourse between males.[83] By 1900, Ishikawa Kiyotada had distinguished both male and female forms of "same-sex intercourse" (*dōsei sōkan* or *dōseikan*), although he still equated the former with anal coitus.[84] By virtue of their profession, forensic pathologists of the Meiji era tended to understand "homosexuality" as a category of sexual acts, anal intercourse central among them, that were potentially criminal, rather than as a category of individuals or a distinct psychological type. Shimizu, for instance, regarded "mental and neurological disorders" in the male insertee not as the underlying cause of his behavior, but as a danger resulting

---

80. I have distilled this catalogue of symptoms from Hiraga Seijirō, *Kanmei hōigaku*, 273; Ishikawa Kiyotada, *Jitsuyō hōigaku*, 425–426; Katayama Kuniyoshi and Eguchi Jō, *Saiban igaku teikō*, 1:54–57; Katayama Kuniyoshi et al., *Hōigaku teikō*, 1:191–194; Shimizu, *Jitsuyō saiban igaku*, 312–314; Yoshii, *Saiban igakuron*, 55–56.

81. Hiraga Seijirō, *Kanmei hōigaku*, 272; Katayama Kuniyoshi and Eguchi Jō, *Saiban igaku teikō*, 1:53; Katayama Kuniyoshi et al., *Hōigaku teikō*, 1:190; Shimizu, *Jitsuyō saiban igaku*, 314; Yoshii, *Saiban igakuron*, 54–55.

82. On the emergence of the "homosexuality" construct in Europe and America, see George Chauncey, Jr., "From Sexual Inversion to Homosexuality: The Changing Medical Conceptualization of Female Deviance," in *Passion and Power: Sexuality in History*, ed. Kathy Peiss and Christina Simmons (Philadelphia: Temple University Press, 1989), 87–117; David M. Halperin, "One Hundred Years of Homosexuality," in *One Hundred Years of Homosexuality and Other Essays on Greek Love* (New York: Routledge, 1990), 15–40; Gert Hekma, "'A Female Soul in a Male Body': Sexual Inversion as Gender Inversion in Nineteenth-Century Sexology," in *Third Sex, Third Gender: Beyond Sexual Dimorphism in Culture and History*, ed. Gilbert Herdt (New York: Zone, 1994), 213–239.

83. Shimizu, *Jitsuyō saiban igaku*, 312.

84. Ishikawa Kiyotada, *Jitsuyō hōigaku*, 417, 425–427.

from the awakening of his erotic feelings (*shunjō*) before their proper time.[85] Here again, he followed *shudō* convention in assuming the insertee's youth. Furthermore, although Meiji forensics experts were among the first Japanese to encounter the medical model of "homosexuality" rising in prominence at the time in the West, this knowledge remained limited to a relatively small circle of professionals and seldom entered into the realm of popular discourse.

The gender-blind "obscene acts" formula employed by the *Keihō* also brought female-female sexual relations for the first time within the purview of criminal law. Female-female sexual practices had fallen outside Edo-period legal definitions of "fornication," nor had they been affected by the *keikan* provisions of the *Kaitei ritsuryō*. The possibility of "obscene acts" between females, however, was noted in the forensic-medicine literature as early as 1887.[86] Medico-legal authorities' familiarity with such practices derived partly from the work of their Western colleagues, as reflected in their frequent use of the German term *Tribadie*, often naturalized into the native syllabary.[87] Nevertheless, Japanese experts tended to appropriate those aspects of foreign medico-legal knowledge that fit most closely with indigenous constructions of female-female sexual behavior. Thus, when an 1891 forensic-pathology text claimed that "intercourse between females" (*josei sōkan*) occurred most frequently when large numbers of nubile young women lived together with limited access to males, as in prisons or well-to-do households (*ryōke*), it echoed not only the European literature, but also native stereotypes regarding the depravity of female criminals, erotic practices within the segregated women's quarters of the elite, and the assumed preference of women for a male-attached phallus.[88]

The emergence of female-female sexuality in medico-legal discourse also reflected the growing attention that this topic was beginning to receive in the courtroom. One such scandal, dating from 1888, centered around the daughter of an elite Tokyo family named Fukuda and her former maid,

---

85. Shimizu, *Jitsuyō saiban igaku*, 314. Yoshii Bantarō (*Saiban igakuron*, 55) foresaw psychological damage to the insertee only when *keikan* had been carried out by force.

86. Yoshii, *Saiban igakuron*, 54.

87. Ishikawa Kiyotada, *Jitsuyō hōigaku*, 425, 427; Katayama Kuniyoshi et al., *Hōigaku teikō*, 1:194.

88. Katayama Kuniyoshi et al., *Hōigaku teikō*, 1:194. Edo-period and Meiji discourses on female-female eroticism have yet to receive detailed study, but for a brief introduction see my "'S' Is for Sister: Schoolgirl Intimacy and 'Same-Sex Love' in Early Twentieth-Century Japan," in *Gendering Modern Japanese History*, ed. Barbara Molony and Kathleen S. Uno (Cambridge: Harvard University Press, forthcoming).

Maeda Otoki. Twenty-eight and thirty-four respectively, the couple had been romantically involved over a period of thirteen years, at one point exchanging "marriage vows" (*fūfu no yakusoku*). Legal proceedings arose not from their intimacy in and of itself, however, but from the fact that Maeda had attempted to murder Fukuda, whom she perceived as having grown cold toward her, and then kill herself. Prosecutors dwelt at some length on the couple's sexual practices, revealing their phallocentric expectations by asking which of the two was the "husband" (*teishu*), whether either of them possessed an unusual anatomy (presumably a large clitoris), or whether they used some "instrument" (*dōgu*). Yet, although the pair had engaged in the "obscene act" of mutual masturbation (*tagai ni shujutsu o mochiyuru*), they could not be punished for this act, since neither party had been underage or participated unwillingly. The forensic pathologist Eguchi Jō offered the court his expert opinion that Maeda suffered from "sexual inversion" (*shikijō tentōshō*)—like "homosexuality," a concept of recent origin even in the West—and it is likely no coincidence that the 1891 edition of a textbook he coauthored included a section on female-female "obscene acts" where there had previously been none.[89] Nevertheless, forensic pathologists generally agreed that sexual acts between females seldom involved violence, threats, or the very young, and—a matter of obvious professional interest to them— left behind few telltale signs.[90]

In 1907, the existing *Keihō* was replaced by a thoroughly revised measure of the same name. With respect to male-male, as well as female-female, sexuality, however, the new penal code followed largely along the lines of its French-influenced predecessor. Although legislators strengthened "obscene acts" provisions to some degree, these changes would hardly have satisfied critics at the *Eastern World*. Some of the revisions were merely cosmetic: Articles 346 and 347 of the existing code, for example, were combined into a single clause (Article 176), and the term for "obscene acts," *waisetsu no shogyō*, replaced with the virtually identical *waisetsu no kōi*.[91] More substantively, the new article raised the sentence for criminal "obscene acts"—

89. Katayama Kuniyoshi et al., *Hōigaku teikō*, 1:194; Tanaka Kōgai, *Ai to zankoku* (Osaka: Fukuinsha shoten, 1925), 168–174; Tanaka Kōgai, *Ningen no seiteki ankoku-men* (Ōsaka yagō shoten, 1922), 74, 77–90.

90. Hiraga Seijirō, *Kanmei hōigaku*, 274; Ishikawa Kiyotada, *Jitsuyō hōigaku*, 427; Katayama Kuniyoshi et al., *Hōigaku teikō*, 1:194. Mori Ōgai commented tellingly in 1889 that it was "Päderastie" and not "Saphismus" (sic) that was of "value" to forensic pathologists. See "Gaijō no koto o rokusu," in *Ōgai zenshū*, ed. Kinoshita Mokutarō et al., 38 vols. (Iwanami shoten, 1971–1975), 29:155.

91. The 1907 provisions may be found in Naikaku kanpōkyoku, *Hōrei zensho*, 1907 vol., (hōritsu) 98.

still defined only as those performed by coercion or with minors—to penal servitude (*chōeki*) for six months to seven years (previous penalties had ranged from one month to two years), and revoked the supplementary monetary fines. Lawmakers also lifted the age of consent by one year to thirteen.[92] While the minority of the victim in a coerced "obscene act" no longer mandated a higher range of penalties, in practice, of course, age might influence the sentence imposed.

Changes also appeared in the accompanying provisions. Article 178 specified that "obscene acts" committed against a person who was unconscious or otherwise incapable of resisting, whether the offender had caused this state or was merely taking advantage of it, were subject to the same penalties as if he or she had exercised violence or threat. Under the 1880 code, such a provision had existed only in the case of male-female coitus.[93] A contemporary commentator explained that this clause applied in cases where the victim was mentally deranged, drunk, or under the influence of narcotics or hypnosis.[94] Furthermore, the new code's Article 179 explicitly subjected attempted "obscene acts," like completed ones, to punishment, whereas the framers of the 1880 *Keihō* had not regarded the former as serious enough to warrant prosecution.[95] Finally, Article 181 of the new code prescribed a sentence of three years to life imprisonment when criminal "obscene acts," either completed or attempted, resulted in the other party's death or injury.[96]

These various modifications were not targeted specifically against male-male sexual practices, however, since they applied equally to male-female and to female-female relations. Rather, they formed part of a general tight-

---

92. According to a 1925 Daishin'in decision regarding male-female coitus (*kan'in*), a conviction for statutory rape (under Article 177) required that the male party had known that his partner was under the age of thirteen. See Hioki et al., *Nihon hanrei taisei*, 14:476. Presumably, the same was true of "obscene acts," whatever the sex of the individuals involved.

93. Naikaku kirokukyoku, *Hōki bunrui taizen*, 54:430.

94. <*Kokkei shinbun furoku*> *Nihon shinkeihō*, 27. Subsequent court decisions held that sleep, misrecognition, and consent to medical treatment constituted potentially incapacitating conditions. See Dandō, *Keihō kōyō kakuron*, 396; Hioki et al., *Nihon hanrei taisei*, 14:479–480.

95. In Boissonade's opinion, the criminalization of attempted "obscene acts" would have such undesirable consequences as the potential prosecution of a person (presumably male) who had merely lifted a girl's skirts in jest. See Waseda daigaku Tsuruta monjo kenkyūkai, *Nihon keihō*, 3:2036–2037.

96. Prosecution in such cases did not require a suit by the victim or his or her family, as Article 180 demanded for other types of "obscene act." See Hioki et al., *Nihon hanrei taisei*, 14:486–487. The 1880 *Keihō* (Naikaku kirokukyoku, *Hōki bun-*

ening of sexual-offense provisions that included a similar raising of the age of consent in the case of male-female coitus. At the same time, the changes were symptomatic of the broader characteristics of the new code. Monetary fines disappeared for many crimes, and the greater leeway given to judges in imposing sentence was likewise typical of the 1907 judicial reforms as a whole. Overall, the 1907 *Keihō* was more succinct than its 1880 predecessor (containing 264 instead of the earlier 430 articles), but also covered areas of behavior that the latter's framers had not seen fit to address—how to deal, for instance, with new technologies for altering an individual's consciousness or sense of responsibility, whether by chemical means, hypnosis, or exploiting the prestige attached to the medical profession.

The Napoleonic formula proved so enduring that, with only two exceptions, the "obscene acts" provisions of the 1907 *Keihō* have remained intact until the present day. First, a temporary measure of 1941 augmented the penalties for "obscene acts" and other crimes committed under unsettling wartime conditions, such as blackouts or fear of enemy attack.[97] Otherwise, the legal status of male-male sexual activity changed little during the war years. We find no Japanese equivalent for German fascists' tightening of the infamous Paragraph 175 of the *Strafgesetzbuch,* much less the concentration camps where untold numbers of European sexual "criminals" met their demise.[98] And while Japanese officials were familiar with the eugenics laws of Nazi Germany, which provided for the castration of "homosexuals," they showed no particular concern for male-male sexuality in drawing up their own eugenics legislation in 1940.[99] The first permanent modification of Japanese "obscene acts" provisions came long after the war, in 1958, when law-

---

rui taizen, 54:426–427, 431) had deferred to a separate section on wounding through assault and battery (*ōda sōshō*), which tailored the penalty according to the type and extent of physical damage.

97. Shigematsu Kazuyoshi, *Nihon keibatsushi nenpyō* (Yūzankaku, 1972), 225–226.

98. On Nazi policies toward male-male sexuality, see Günter Grau, ed., *Hidden Holocaust? Gay and Lesbian Persecution in Germany 1933–45,* trans. Patrick Camiller (London: Cassell, 1993); Erwin J. Haeberle, "Swastika, Pink Triangle, and Yellow Star: The Destruction of Sexology and the Persecution of Homosexuals in Nazi Germany," in *Hidden from History,* 365–379; George L. Mosse, *Nationalism and Sexuality: Middle-Class Morality and Sexual Norms in Modern Europe* (Madison: University of Wisconsin Press, 1988); Richard Plant, *The Pink Triangle: The Nazi War against Homosexuals* (New York: New Republic, 1986); Frank Rector, *The Nazi Extermination of Homosexuals* (New York: Stein, 1981); Steakley, *Homosexual Emancipation Movement,* 103–121.

99. Article 3 of the 1940 National Eugenics Law listed individuals with a "hereditarily pathological personality of a strong and pernicious nature" (*kyōdo katsu aku-*

makers, aiming to curb gang violence, added a clause to Article 180 (the equivalent of the 1880 *Keihō*'s Article 350) exempting cases involving two or more offenders from the ordinary requirement that the victim or his or her family must themselves press charges.[100] Despite isolated calls by postwar ultrarightists, legislative attempts to specifically criminalize male-male or female-female sexual acts have been absent from the Japanese political scene for well over a century.[101] In the words of one 1930s legalist, "It is not that Japanese society is indifferent to [male-male sexual practices], but rather that it does not regard the punishment of such things in the penal code as appropriate."[102]

If "civilized" society was not indifferent to such practices, what, then, were the "appropriate" means of regulation? The twentieth-century legal scholar Kōke Yoshio, echoing the perspective of Boissonade, answered that these matters were best left to "social morality" (*shakai no dōtoku*).[103] Yet Kōke's "social morality" was not identical in all respects to Boissonade's *morale*, particularly since the latter took for granted centuries of Judeo-Christian ethical teaching. Kōke, like Boissonade, regarded male-male sexual acts as contrary to "good mores" (*zenryō no fūzoku*), yet the phrase that he invoked was associated more with the workings of the family system and with communal standards than with religious authority. When the sexual behavior of the individual threatened the honor or continuity of the household, family pressures were often more effective than the threat of criminal punishment in enforcing "civilized" norms, especially since civil law underwrote the authority of the patriarch.[104] This was true not only in

shitsu naru idensei byōteki seikaku) as candidates for state-sponsored sterilization (in principle voluntary), but it is unclear if this provision was ever applied in cases involving male-male sexuality. See Kōseishō yobōkyoku, *Kokumin yūseihō gaisetsu* (Kōseishō yobōkyoku, 1940). One eugenics expert wrote that, in comparison with foreign countries, "sexual inversion" (*seiteki tōsaku*) was not a conspicuous problem in Japan. See Aoki Nobuharu, *Yūsei kekkon to yūsei danshu* (Ryūkinsha, 1941), 229.

100. For the currently standing "obscene acts" provisions, see *Iwanami dairoppō*, 1992 ed. (Iwanami shoten, 1992), 1828.

101. For an example of ultrarightist propaganda, see Sugawara Michinari, *Dōseiai* (San'aku tsuihō kyōkai, n.d.).

102. Ono Seiichirō, *Keihō kōwa* (Yūhikaku, 1932), 450.

103. Kōke, *Keihō kōwa*, 196–197.

104. At the same time, family law recognized the importance of household continuity by establishing relatively liberal conditions for adoption, with the ironic result that same-sex couples, such as the twentieth-century author Yoshiya Nobuko and her partner Monma Chiyo, sometimes turned to this form of legal union as an alternative to marriage. On Yoshiya and Monma, see Yoshitake Teruko, *Nyonin Yoshiya Nobuko* (Bungei shunjū, 1982).

the case of men, but also for women, whose lives were if anything more tightly circumscribed by family structures. "Social morality" was also constituted and policed through popular discourse, the Meiji transformations of which shall be explored in the following chapter.

If the *Keihō*, in either version, relied more heavily than had the *Kaitei ritsuryō* on noncriminalizing means of discouraging "uncivilized" sexual behavior, all three codes nevertheless shared important characteristics. Each fixed the legal gaze on the sexual act, construing it as a discrete physical event, a specific conjuncture of bodies, that could be precisely identified and, if necessary, punished. In the *Kaitei ritsuryō*, male-male sexuality was equated with the act of *keikan* or anal intercourse, while the two versions of the *Keihō* subsumed it under the larger category of "obscene acts." The social context of these practices was no longer the primary consideration, as it had been in the perisexual legislation of the Edo period, which had stigmatized not so much genital acts as the ethical impropriety that was involved, for example, when townsmen "went crazy over youths," retainers fraternized with pages, or peasants expended their productive energies on male prostitutes. Distinctions of social status were now reduced to a simple dichotomy between adults, who must be responsible for their own sexual behavior, and minors, who were permitted none (Boissonade stated categorically that persons under the age of twelve were incapable of feeling genuine desire for sexual intercourse), and in the case of the *Kaitei ritsuryō*, to a vestigial differentiation in the means of punishment for the elite and commoners.[105] As the individual, unmarked by status, came to the fore as the juridical subject of his or her actions, the notion of sexual coercion or consent also assumed a prominence and clarity that it had not possessed in Edo-period legal discourse.

It was this focus on physical acts, capable of observation and precise definition, that facilitated the rapid development of new technologies for policing the erotic body. A centralized constabulary was one element in this mechanism of surveillance, distributing the gaze of the law across the physical landscape in order to prevent and detect the commission of sexual offenses. If detected, these acts were exposed under the stern light of the courtroom, where centrally appointed judges matched them with the written provisions of penal law and handed down the prescribed punishment. Here, witnesses provided detailed testimony, as did medico-legal authorities, before whose

105. Waseda daigaku Tsuruta monjo kenkyūkai, *Nihon keihō*, 3:2035, 2037–2038.

probing eyes and professional expertise even hidden truths were supposed to reveal themselves. Finally, the acts received atonement in prisons, where the behavior of offenders was even more closely scrutinized, disciplined, and "civilized."

PENILE SERVITUDE

In 1856, Toyokichi, a twenty-nine-year-old drifter (*mushuku*), was convicted by bakufu authorities of a crime no longer recorded, and banished to Niijima, a volcanic island some one hundred miles southwest of Edo. There, he met and was courted by his fellow exile Takijirō, a male of outcast (*nohinin*) status ten years his elder, and soon the couple were living together "like husband and wife." By 1864, however, Takijirō had become involved with a female denizen of the island, thus breaking his vow of fidelity to Toyokichi. Although Takijirō offered him three gold pieces by way of consolation (*tegirekin*), Toyokichi was not appeased and, in the early hours of one winter morning, set fire to Takijirō's hut. On the following day, authorities punished Toyokichi's "unprecedented" (*zendai mimon*) act by putting him to death.[106]

It is important to note that the "unprecedentedness" of the affair lay not in the fact of Toyokichi's sexual relationship with another male, but rather in the ruthlessness with which he clung to it—that is to say, its perisexual consequences. Authorities must have been aware of the two men's intimacy, which was said to have lasted for six years, but evidently did nothing to stop it. Official indifference to sexual relations between prisoners seems also to have prevailed in Edo-period jails (*rō*).[107] For the most part, jailors let inmates regulate their own social interaction, much in the same way that the bakufu and domain bureaucracies granted a broad measure of administrative autonomy to villagers, giving rise to a quasi-official hierarchy of power and unwritten code of conduct among the incarcerated. In some cases, this code was verbally articulated in the form of a "rap" (*oshaberi*), which was

106. Maeda Chōhachi, ed., *Niijima ryūninchō* (Niijima Honson: Niijima kyō-dokan, 1941), 95, 101.

107. For some examples of Edo-period jail regulations (*rōnai hatto*), none of which specifically mentions male-male (or female-female) sexuality, see Ōhara Torao, *Nihon kinsei gyōkeishi kō*, 2 vols. (Keimu kyōkai, 1943), 1:207–209. Edo-period jails, it should be noted, were officially conceived less as a form of punishment per se than as a place for holding criminals, often for prolonged periods of time, before sentencing—although, because of the severe conditions that prevailed in them, a sizeable portion of suspects did not survive such detention. For a detailed description of an Edo-period jail, see Dani V. Botsman, "Punishment and Power in the Tokugawa Period," *East Asian History* 3 (1992): 9–16.

sung to the new inmate as other prisoners beat him on the naked buttocks or otherwise subjected him to ritualized humiliation.[108]

As in the case of villages, however, Meiji prison reforms brought with them more direct forms of state surveillance. Meiji officials admired and adopted many of the disciplinary technologies that Foucault describes as having re-molded the prisons of nineteenth-century Europe and North America, aimed at forging docile bodies and repentant souls.[109] The panoptic model that so fascinated Foucault made its appearance in Japan as early as 1872, when the first national prison code, the *Kangokusoku*, prescribed it as the ideal form of penitentiary, even providing detailed blueprints.[110] The configuration of the cell blocks in a radiating pattern around a central watchtower allowed guards to maintain a constant vigil over the prisoners' activities, including their sexual conduct. In a similar regimentation of space, the *Kangokusoku* recommended that each cell house an odd number of prisoners (preferably five) in order to prevent "obscene" coupling.[111] The ambition of early Meiji officials, however, often exceeded their financial means, so that only a limited number of these panoptically designed prisons were actually constructed.

Like the penal code, early Meiji prison regulations specifically targeted anal intercourse between males, or *keikan*. For example, Tokyo's Keishichō, the metropolitan police authority, included *keikan*, along with gambling and jailbreaks, in an 1874 list of "improper" (*hibun*) acts to be posted in prisons under its jurisdiction, promising "severe" punishment for violators.[112] Interestingly, an equivalent list for female prisoners issued in the same year made no mention of female-female sexual acts, although it proscribed the exchange of letters and gifts with male inmates.[113] In 1878, Tokyo authorities again warned against prison *keikan*, characterizing it as an "evil deed" (*akuji*) and providing an alternate gloss of *nanshoku* in the phonetic syl-

108. Ōhara, *Nihon kinsei gyōkeishi kō*, 1:209–211; 2:364–367, 406–407; Ōmori Kaiin, "Rōgokunai no shūjin seikatsu," *Hanzai kōron*, July 1932, 172–173.

109. Michel Foucault, *Discipline and Punish: The Birth of the Prison*, trans. Alan Sheridan (New York: Vintage, 1979). On the "birth of the prison" in Japan, see Yasumaru Yoshio, "'Kangoku' no tanjō," in *Bakumatsu Meijiki no kokumin kokka keisei to bunka hen'yō*, ed. Nishikawa Nagao and Matsumiya Hideharu (Shin'yōsha, 1995), 279–312.

110. Foucault, *Discipline and Punish*, 200–209; Naikaku kirokukyoku, *Hōki bunrui taizen*, 57:78–80.

111. Naikaku kirokukyoku, *Hōki bunrui taizen*, 57:63. Likewise, a former warden wrote in 1889 that *keikan* could be significantly reduced by assigning each prisoner his own spot within the cell. See Ōhara, *Nihon kinsei gyōkeishi kō*, 2:574.

112. Naikaku kirokukyoku, *Hōki bunrui taizen*, 57:139.

113. Naikaku kirokukyoku, *Hōki bunrui taizen*, 57:140.

labary. Apparently, the term *keikan*, having been adopted from Chinese law, was still not common in colloquial parlance, while *nanshoku*, with its long pedigree, would have been familiar to the most illiterate child of Edo.[114]

Between 1873 and 1881, as we have seen, *keikan* was simultaneously an offense against the penal code. Thus, male prisoners who engaged in anal intercourse, like the earlier-mentioned convicts A and B, might face new charges and receive additional sentencing in court. Records survive from a number of such cases. In one incident, dating from May 1873, the inserter was a thirty-seven-year-old man named Kojima Jinzaburō, in jail awaiting conviction for armed robbery. According to his deposition, Kojima chose out of "idleness" (*kotonaki*) to taunt a newly arrived cellmate named Okada Zenkichi, claiming it was the "rule of the joint" (*kenchū kisoku*) that if Okada would not sing a ballad (*hayariuta*)—a variant of the Edo-period prisoner rap—he must allow Kojima to penetrate him anally. That night, Kojima carried out his threat, and on the following morning Okada complained to authorities. By the time a court reached a decision in June (the *Kaitei ritsuryō*, we may note, had at this point not yet been officially promulgated), Kojima had already been sentenced to death on the earlier count of armed robbery, so that officials could do little more than append the *keikan* offense to his verdict. The fate of Okada, the unwilling insertee, is unknown, but it is likely that he escaped punishment.[115]

A second incident dates from 1875. The inserter here was Inoue Kenkichi, a thirty-one-year-old male serving time for three counts of robbery, and now in his fourth year of imprisonment. On June 25, a court found Inoue guilty of consensual *keikan*, adding ninety days to his ten-year sentence. The story does not end here, however. On July 13, the desire for anal

---

114. Shigematsu Kazuyoshi, *Zukan Nihon no kangokushi* (Yūzankaku, 1985), 42. It should be noted that, from the Meiji period on, the characters for *nanshoku* came increasingly to be read as *danshoku*, a reflection not only of broader phonetic and orthographic changes but also of the growing obsolescence of Edo-period erotic culture. Although both pronunciations are today considered correct, I have retained the older form throughout this study for the sake of consistency.

115. Kasumi, *Meiji shoki keijihō*, 95–96; Umehara, *Meiji seiteki chinbunshi*, 1:25. While the *Kaitei ritsuryō* made no specific provisions regarding the legal status of the insertee in cases of male rape, the same may be said of male-female rape, where the victim was clearly not regarded as culpable. Okada's ordeal bears resemblance to a fictional episode in Ihara Saikaku's *Kōshoku ichidai otoko* (in *Nihon koten bungaku zenshū*, ed. Akiyama Ken et al., 51 vols. [Shōgakkan, 1970–1976], 38:178–179 [trans. Kengi Hamada under the title *The Life of an Amorous Man* (Rutland, Vt.: Tuttle, 1964), 95–96]), a work written nearly two centuries earlier, in which the newly incarcerated protagonist Yonosuke is likewise forced to sing a ballad before his cellmates in order to win their favor.

intercourse arose again in the "unrepentant" (*kaishin fushō*) Inoue. Inoue communicated this fact to the twenty-year-old Matsumoto Tasaburō, a fellow prisoner, who complied with the older man's wishes. Thereafter, the pair developed an "intimate relationship" (*tagai ni fukaku majiwari*), engaging in "clandestine intercourse" (*mikkai*) on a number of occasions. Prison authorities became aware of their activities after an incident on September 15, in which Inoue assaulted a cell boss (*yakuzuki*) with a kettle and bit the arm of a guard who attempted to restrain him. Inoue's anger evidently stemmed from his protective attitude toward Matsumoto, whose stomachache the previous night had, he felt, been treated with unacceptable callousness. As a result, both Inoue and Matsumoto received an additional ninety-day sentence.[116]

Unlike the incident between Kojima and Okada, Inoue and Matsumoto's sexual relationship was, at least legally speaking, consensual. This is not to say that such ties did not involve considerations of power. Inoue's status as a seasoned convict and the protection a liaison with him might afford may have influenced the younger Matsumoto's decision to comply with his sexual demands, which Inoue's deposition hints took some persuasion. Furthermore, in male prisoner subculture as on the outside, inserter/insertee roles conventionally followed an age hierarchy. At Kabato penitentiary in Hokkaido, a maximum-security prison operating from 1881 to 1919, convicts reportedly preferred young inmates with feminine features as insertees, making them wear "smart" (*kozappari*) articles of clothing to enhance their attractiveness, and currying their favor with gifts of food.[117] Accounts of prison life tell of "lovers' quarrels" (*chiwagenka*) among such couples, as well as rivalries and contests over particular favorites, occasionally resulting in murder.[118] "Intimate relationships" like Inoue and Matsumoto's challenged prison discipline in at least two ways: by creating horizontal links between prisoners that undermined the institutional goal of vertical control (not unlike the *shudō* bonds among samurai that domain bureaucrats had equated with conspiracy); and by generating powerful emotions that could lead to incidents of discord and violence.

At the same time, Inoue's willingness to engage in "unrepentant" be-

116. Umehara, *Kidan chinbun daishūsei*, 1:183–184.
117. Teramoto Kaiyū, *Kabato kangoku shiwa* (Tsukigata, Hokkaido: Tsukigatamura nanajūshūnen kinen sonshi hensan iinkai, 1950), 40–41.
118. Habuto Eiji and Sawada Junjirō, *Hentai seiyokuron* (Shun'yōdō, 1915), 191–192; Ōmori, "Rōgokunai," 174; "Shūto shūto o korosu," *Yorozu chōhō*, 7 October 1900, 3; Teramoto, *Kabato*, 41; Tsuchiya Terumi, "Keimushonai no sei no nayami," *Seiron*, December 1928, 63; Umehara, *Kidan chinbun daishūsei*, 1:183.

havior so soon after his earlier sentencing for *keikan* suggests that sexual activity in prison stood a good chance of going undiscovered, or at least that punishment was not so effective as officials would have liked. The eyes of the institution were never truly panoptic, nor did its regimentation of space rule out all possibility of "clandestine intercourse." This was even more true of the coal mines of Hokkaido, whose dark recesses provided a "paradise" (*tōgen senkyō*) for "obscene acts" among convicts sent to work there, according to an observer who visited the area in 1893.[119] The same legal authority that forbade sexual activity among prisoners also forced them to live in close quarters with those of their own sex, so that both the proscriptions and their violation functioned as interrelated aspects of a single disciplinary mechanism. Perhaps for the same reason, the link in discourse and practice between male-male sexuality and the prison has long outlasted the Meiji period.

Under the *Kaitei ritsuryō*, the penalty for acts of *keikan* committed by prisoners depended to some extent upon the length of their original sentences. We see an example of this in an 1881 incident involving three male convicts.[120] While the insertee, Kikuchi Ryūkichi, was due for eventual release, the inserter, Tomita Eikichi, was serving a life sentence, as was a third inmate, Kobayashi Kenkichi. Kikuchi not only was willing to be penetrated by Tomita, but apparently solicited the act (*keikan itasasuru*), although he repented and subsequently confessed the deed to prison authorities. The court, ruling that in such a case voluntary confession did not merit a reduced penalty, as was true of some offenses, added ninety days to Kikuchi's original term.[121] It could obviously not do the same in the case of Tomita, a life-term convict, and therefore ordered him to stand in "rod chains" (*bōsa*) for three days.[122] This device prevented the wearer from sitting or bending at the knees by means of two stiff metal rods, held fast at one end by a belt around the waist and at the other by cuffs around the ankles. In 1882, it was replaced by the somewhat less excruciating ball and chain, which, by re-

119. Okada Chōtarō, *Nihon keihōron* (Yūhikaku, 1894), 765, 768.

120. Miyatake Gaikotsu, ed., *Meiji kibun*, in *Miyatake Gaikotsu chosakushū*, 1:117.

121. For the *Kaitei ritsuryō's* provisions on voluntary confession, see Naikaku kirokukyoku, *Hōki bunrui taizen*, 54:280–281.

122. The source for this punishment was an 1876 supplement to the prisoner-offense (*chōekinin matahanzai*) section of the *Kaitei ritsuryō*, as amended the following year, for which see Naikaku kirokukyoku, *Hōki bunrui taizen*, 54:278, 334–335. A sketch of the device appears in Naikaku kirokukyoku, *Hōki bunrui taizen*, 57:92.

stricting the movements of the insubordinate, provided a sort of prison within a prison, and remained in use as late as 1908.[123]

Kobayashi's part in the sexual transaction was as a "go-between" (*na-kōdo*). Yet since the *Kaitei ritsuryō* named such an offense only in the case of male-female sexual interactions such as adultery or unlicensed prostitution, the court decided to pronounce Kobayashi guilty of an unspecified generic (*fuōi*) offense and to commute the thirty-day sentence he would receive were he not a life-term convict to one day in rod chains.[124] Like the *Kaitei ritsuryō*'s differentiation of penalties by class, the notion that a "crime" might be prosecuted even if it did not explicitly appear in the penal code was a carryover from older juridical practice that would disappear with the 1880 *Keihō*, already promulgated though not yet in force at the time of this incident. Judges could also apply the generic-offense clause in cases where consensual *keikan* had been attempted but not actually carried out, since the *Kaitei ritsuryō* had made specific provisions only for attempted rape. Such was the outcome, for example, of an 1874 case involving two prisoners, the would-be inserter receiving a thirty-day sentence in addition to his existing three-year term, and his willing (*tokushin no ue*) partner apparently escaping punishment.[125]

With the enforcement of the *Keihō* in 1882, consensual anal intercourse between adult males became legal in civil society. Within the confines of the prison, however, such acts continued to face penalties, although punishment was usually administered by prison authorities without the involvement of the courts. At the same time, the language of regulations dealing with male-male sexuality in prison reflected a shift in conceptualization similar to that found in the penal code itself. The early Meiji preoccupation with *keikan* disappeared, while the notion of "obscene acts" broadened the scope of proscribed sexual practices. All sexual acts between prisoners, whether consensual or coerced, were deemed an infraction of institutional discipline, since they represented an articulation of power relations independent of vertical control and undermined the deprivation of sensory pleasures that was meant to hasten the repenting experience.

123. Naikaku kirokukyoku, *Hōki bunrui taizen*, 57:179, 194–195; Naikaku kan-pōkyoku, *Hōrei zensho*, 1889 vol., (chokurei) 221.

124. In another *keikan* case involving prisoners (see Kasumi, *Meiji shoki keijihō*, 105–107), Daishin'in justices chose to apply the male-female go-between provision by analogy. For the generic-offense clause (Article 99), see Naikaku kirokukyoku, *Hōki bunrui taizen*, 54:284; for the go-between provisions (Articles 260 and 267), see Naikaku kirokukyoku, *Hōki bunrui taizen*, 54:303.

125. Edamatsu, *Meiji nyūsu jiten*, 1:298.

This shift is visible in the 1881 revision of the *Kangokusoku*, which was enforced together with the *Keihō* from the following year. The new version of the code required prison officials to post a list of "easily understood" rules governing prisoner conduct in each cell, and to read this list aloud to illiterate convicts within twenty-four hours of their incarceration.[126] Among the various regulations was one prohibiting "acts that bring disgrace upon a cellmate or are obscene" (*dōbō no mono ni ojoku o kōmurashime waisetsu ni wataru ga gotoki shoi*).[127] As in the *Keihō*, "obscene acts" might refer not only to *keikan*, but also to other male-male, as well as female-female, sexual practices. The simultaneous reference to "disgrace," on the other hand, reflected a concern with private power relationships more peculiar to prison authorities, as well as a recognition that sexual interaction among prisoners not infrequently involved intentional humiliation. The prisoner rap of Edo times would no doubt, by these standards, no longer have been tolerated.

Bylaws (*saisoku*) accompanying a second overhaul of the *Kangokusoku* in 1889 retained essentially the same wording, but substituted "cellmate" with "another person."[128] Officials had possibly realized that acts of humiliation and "obscenity" took place not only within the relative privacy of the cell, but in other parts of the penitentiary as well. Indeed, sexual acts might even occur before a convict ever entered the prison walls. In 1903, the celebrated robber and fratricide Watanabe Chiyomatsu, about twenty years old at the time, reportedly engaged in *nanshoku* while under "guarded escort" to Kabato prison.[129]

Prison authorities scrutinized not only genital contact, but even the holding of hands by inmates. This common expression of same-sex intimacy reinforced private bonds of the type that challenged prison discipline, and may

126. Naikaku kirokukyoku, *Hōki bunrui taizen*, 57:176. After 1899, rules for prisoner conduct were distributed in the form of booklets. See Naikaku kanpōkyoku, *Hōrei zensho*, 1899 vol., (shōrei) 526; 1908 vol., (shōrei) 198.

127. Naikaku kirokukyoku, *Hōki bunrui taizen*, 57:177. In 1886 (Ōhara, *Nihon kinsei gyōkeishi kō*, 2:521), cell leaders (*denkokusha*) were especially warned against "obscene acts" (*waisetsu no kōi*; also glossed as *midarigamashiki furumai*), perhaps in the fear that they would abuse their position of power to obtain sexual favors, as did some of their Edo-period predecessors (see, for example, Ōmori, "Rōgokunai," 174).

128. Naikaku kanpōkyoku, *Hōrei zensho*, 1889 vol., (shōrei) 123. Rule booklets issued following an 1899 revision of the *Kangokusoku* (Ōhara, *Nihon kinsei gyōkeishi kō*, 2:652, 660; Shigematsu, *Zukan Nihon no kangokushi*, 164) replaced the earlier reference to bringing "disgrace" on other inmates with the phrase "making an unseemly spectacle" (*shūtai o arawashi*; glossed idiomatically as *minikuki sugata*).

129. Teramoto, *Kabato*, 173.

also have provided an opportunity for the exchange of proscribed objects. The revised *Kangokusoku* of 1881 prohibited convicts from "conversing or holding hands with their fellows" on work forays into the outside world or from calling out to passersby.[130] The 1889 bylaws expanded the scope of this provision, forbidding all hand-holding and "unruly" conversation outside one's cell.[131] Apparently, however, hand-holding did not in itself constitute an "obscene act," nor did prison regulations specifically discourage it within the confines of the cell.

Since jails were gender-segregated and the post-1882 rules applied to prisoners of either sex, female-female sexual practices became the subject of correctional legislation simultaneously with their emergence in penal law. Popular discourse, too, drew attention to the prison subculture of female-female sexuality, generally in connection with celebrated criminals. Perhaps the best-known Meiji account is to be found in the 1904 autobiography of Fukuda (née Kageyama) Hideko, a radical activist who was arrested in 1885 for her part in a plot to overthrow the Korean government.[132] Awaiting trial in Osaka's Nakanoshima jail, Fukuda formed a close tie with a "beautiful" cellmate, an intimacy that she compared to the love between a parent (herself) and child. Prison officials, however, apparently saw in their relationship a threat to the institutional order, and decided to separate the pair. Using a familial metaphor with more blatantly sexual connotations than the parent-child one Fukuda chose for herself, a male prison guard afterward taunted Fukuda by saying she must be lonely now without her "wife" (*saikun*). Perhaps authorities had mistaken the pair's habit of sleeping together head to foot for warmth as an "obscene act."

Although Fukuda maintained that theirs was a "pure devotion" (*junketsu naru itsukushimi*) and was able to win the return of her companion, she acknowledged that "immoral love" (*furin no ai*) was rampant among her fellow inmates, and often took a form "similar to the relation of husband and wife." Among such couples, according to Fukuda, the "gentler" (*yasashiki*) party would take on a wifely role, while the more "manly-hearted" (*kokoro ooshiki*) of the two assumed the airs of a husband. As among male convicts,

130. Naikaku kirokukyoku, *Hōki bunrui taizen*, 57:177.
131. Naikaku kanpōkyoku, *Hōrei zensho*, 1889 vol., (shōrei) 122. For an 1899 version, see Shigematsu, *Zukan Nihon no kangokushi*, 164.
132. On the life of Fukuda, see Fukuda Hideko, *Warawa no hanseigai*, Iwanami bunko, no. 33–121–1 (Iwanami shoten, 1983); Mikiso Hane, ed., *Reflections on the Way to the Gallows: Rebel Women in Prewar Japan* (Berkeley: University of California Press, 1988), 29–50. Fukuda's jail experiences appear in Fukuda, *Warawa no hanseigai*, 60–88.

these relationships sometimes gave rise to jealous passions, along with in-cidents of suicide—one of which Fukuda herself witnessed—and other forms of violence. To Fukuda, therefore, her jailors' vigilance was "understand-able" (*muri naranedo*), although it both angered and amused her that they had thought that she, a person of "character" (*hinsei*), would be capable of such an "indecent and immoral crime" (*harin hidō no zaiaku*), about which she found it "loathsome" (*kegarawashiki*) even to write.

Fukuda, a highly educated political prisoner, thus attempted to distance herself from the common lot of female criminals with whom the state had classed her, and whose erotic appetites popular discourse depicted as vora-cious and depraved. One such figure was Shimazu Masa, who had been sen-tenced to life imprisonment for theft and other crimes in 1881 and briefly shared a cell with Fukuda.[133] In addition to her various sexual involvements with men, Shimazu had lavished much of the money she stole on female geisha, attracting the attention of the police during an especially extrava-gant moon-viewing expedition to Kyoto, for which occasion she attired her-self in virile clothing and hairstyle and adopted the masculine name of Shi-mazu Harusaburō. By the time that Fukuda came to know her, she had "repented" and become a model prisoner, and the two women reportedly swore "sisterly vows" (*kyōdai no gi*)—a kinship metaphor that, had it been invoked in a *shudō* context, might have hinted at sexual relations. Never-theless, Fukuda writes that she could not help wondering what "karma" (*in-nen*) it was that had led Shimazu, a woman, to "go crazy over geisha" (*geisha-gurui*). After a special pardon in 1888, Shimazu took the tonsure and became an imperially appointed religious lecturer (*gon no chūkōgi*), while her story furnished a subject for popular writings and a stage play in which Shimazu herself appeared in the title role.[134]

The forced separation that Fukuda experienced was an informal measure for dealing with inmate couples, and does not appear in written legislation. After 1882, as we have seen, "obscene acts" could be prosecuted under the

---

133. On Shimazu, see Kawamura Taichi, *Shimazu Masa-jo kaishinroku* (Yokohama: Kinrindō, 1891); Suzuki Kura, <*Meiji gonin dokufu no hitori*> *Shimazu Masa kaishin jitsuroku* (Yōmanrō, 1895); Yoshida Kōu, <*Akuji kaishun*> *Shimazu Omasa no rireki* (Osaka: Taikadō, 1888). I thank Valerie Durham for providing me with these sources.

134. For a prison episode linking two other celebrated "poisonous ladies" (*dokufu*) of the Meiji period, the murderer Hanai Ume and the thief-arsonist "Mamushi no Omasa" ("Omasa the Viper"), see Itō Shigure, "Keibatsu to seiyoku," *Ningen tankyū*, May 1951 (zōkan), 102. On the "poisonous lady" genre in Meiji literature, see Valerie Durham, "Meiji shoki no dokufumono ni okeru akujo zōkei no retorikku," pts. 1 and 2, *Tōkyō keizai daigaku jinbun shizen kagaku ronshū* 86 (1990): 220–242; 88 (1991): 90–108; Christine Marran, "'Poison Woman' Takahashi Oden and the

penal code if they involved coercion or minors, in which case a prisoner or family members might, in theory, press charges in court and the offender receive additional sentencing. However, it is unlikely that this situation often arose, partly because of the increasingly strict segregation of adult and juvenile prisoners, partly because reporting transgressions to officials violated the inmate code of honor and could lead to retaliation, and partly because the line between coercion and consent was less distinct in prison than in civil society. From the point of view of prison authorities, all sexual acts represented a challenge to the vertical power structure, and therefore deserved punishment. The task of determining the appropriate penalty, however, fell not upon the courts but upon correctional officials.

Rather than constituting criminal offenses, "obscene acts" in jail were treated as an infraction of prison regulations (*gokusoku*), and hence as a denial of the authority of the institution itself. Punishment was designed to impress this authority upon the mind and body of the prisoner, as well as upon other inmates. Apart from the ball and chain reserved for life-term convicts, the revised *Kangokusoku* of 1881 listed five types of punishment for disobedient inmates: loss of correspondence and visiting privileges (*zesshin*); solitary confinement with labor (*heikin*) or without (*dokushin*); reduced rations (*genshoku*); and confinement in a dark cell (*anshitsu*).[135] It was up to jailors to decide the proper disciplinary action for each infraction, although some attempts were made to standardize penalties. An 1883 conference of Kyushu prison wardens, for example, recommended that inmates who committed "obscene acts" have their meals cut by two-thirds for a period of one to seven days.[136] For at least one observer in the 1930s, even the legally prescribed range of penalties appeared insufficient: hearing of a fellow inmate who had been placed in solitary for engaging in *nanshoku* in the prison factory, the ultranationalist and postwar politician Kodama Yoshio wrote in his diary that such men should be castrated and sent to one of the more grueling penitentiaries in Hokkaido.[137]

Spectacle of Female Deviance in Early Meiji," *U.S.-Japan Women's Journal, English Supplement* 9 (1995): 93–110.

135. Naikaku kirokukyoku, *Hōki bunrui taizen*, 57:178–179. Revisions of the *Kangokusoku* in 1889 and 1899 retained these categories, while modifying their content. See Naikaku kanpōkyoku, *Hōrei zensho*, 1889 vol., (chokurei) 220–221; 1899 vol., (chokurei) 538. Under the 1908 *Kangokuhō* (Naikaku kanpōkyoku, *Hōrei zensho*, 1908 vol., [hōritsu] 42–43), the range of penalties for disciplinary infractions expanded to twelve.

136. Ōhara, *Nihon kinsei gyōkeishi kō*, 2:559.

137. Kodama Yoshio, <*Zuihitsushū*> *Gokuchū gokugai* (Ajia seinensha, 1942), 96.

While correctional officials did not (at least to my knowledge) go to such lengths as castration to discipline inmates, various irregular punishments seem to have occurred within prison walls. Popular accounts of prison life from the early twentieth century mention such unauthorized punishments for "obscene acts" as suspending offenders from the ceiling, although it is unclear to what extent they represent actual practice and to what extent a form of sadomasochistic fantasy designed to titillate readers.[138] Just as they lost the right to engage in sexual activity with other consenting adults, convicts lost their civic rights (*kōken*) upon entering the penitentiary, and had limited recourse to ordinary judicial mechanisms. Jailors, on the other hand, exercised broad powers over their wards while being themselves subject to relatively little regulatory scrutiny. The lack of explicit rules of procedure for investigating inmate infractions, for example, gave authorities a wide berth for arbitrary judgment. It is hardly surprising, therefore, that a "people's rights" (*minken*) activist like Fukuda, keenly aware of the arbitrary powers of the state, should have found this situation unfair.

The enforcement of "civilized morality" thus took different forms in different periods and at various levels of society. Between 1873 and 1881, criminal law banned the act of male-male anal intercourse among private individuals, whether consensual or coerced, while the job of detecting and punishing "uncivilized" behavior fell directly upon such state agencies as the police and courts. From 1882 on, however, although such acts continued to be regarded as "uncivilized" and "obscene," state officials allowed their regulation, along with that of other male-male as well as female-female sexual practices, to take place through the family system and other organs of "social morality," so long as minors or coercion were not involved. Nevertheless, outside the bounds of civil society, as in the case of the jail, authorities could not rely upon such self-regulating mechanisms to maintain the "civilized" order necessary for their smooth institutional functioning. Here, where the notion of the consenting adult was meaningless, "civilization" was forced to turn to more direct methods of disciplining the erotic body.

138. Katō Yoshikazu, "Tessō yawa," *Hanzai kagaku*, February 1932, 48.

4 Toward the Margins

Male-Male Sexuality
in Meiji Popular Discourse

Meiji lawmakers were not the sole propagators of "civilized morality." Indeed, in a cultural environment where knowledge spread more swiftly and authoritatively than ever through the medium of print, the effectiveness of a "civilized" regime of sexuality depended in no small measure upon its tenets becoming as much a part of popular as of official discourse. During the Edo period, as we have seen, these two modes of discourse had stood in relative opposition, popular writings frequently contradicting the dictates of warrior morality as codified in law. In the Meiji period, however, a different situation would prevail. Within the newly established framework of a centralized nation-state, "civilized" norms came to imbue public discourse on sexuality (which is not to say, of course, all forms of erotic discourse, much less sexual behavior itself) with an astonishing thoroughness and rapidity, disseminating not only through legal pronouncements but also through popular writings ranging from journalism to fiction to poetry. As part of this process, male-male sexuality, which had enjoyed a prominent and respectable place in Edo-period popular texts, came during Meiji times to be routinely represented as "barbarous," "immoral," or simply "unspeakable."

The present chapter traces this process of marginalization. Its starting point is the changing representation of male-male sexuality in the genre of *senryū* verse, where the tempo of marginalization reveals itself perhaps most clearly. Next to be considered are the ways in which popular discourse helped to marginalize the cultural status of male-male sexuality by associating it with certain of "civilization's" fringes—in particular, the Japanese past, the southwestern periphery, and the world of adolescence. The last is explored at greater length in a third section, which draws heavily upon turn-of-the-century newspaper accounts of male-male sexual assaults by student "roughnecks."

While moral panic over the "roughneck" allows us to plot the shifting significance of the male-male inserter role in Meiji constructions of gender and sexuality, changes and continuities surrounding the insertee role provide the topic of the final section. The "civilization" of morality, we shall see, brought both the "beautiful boy" and his pursuer into increasing disrepute, albeit in differing ways, disarticulating them once and for all from the cognitive context of *shudō* within which the disciplinary paradigm had framed them, and setting the stage for the popularization of pathological models of male-male sexuality in the early twentieth century.

FORGETTING EDO

One way of gauging change in the popular representation of male-male sexuality is by examining the *senryū* genre. *Senryū* remained a widely practiced form of comic and satiric expression in Meiji Japan, finding a new home in the periodical press that arose during this period. For the purposes of this inquiry, *senryū* are useful in two respects. First, as we have seen earlier, male-male sexuality had been a common theme in *senryū* from the genre's inception. Second, because of the continuous production of *senryū* from the mid–eighteenth century, it is possible to trace the evolution of representational strategies over time. The question here to be explored, then, is to what extent and in what forms did male-male sexuality manifest itself in the discourse of Meiji *senryū*. The present survey will focus on the widely read humor magazine *Marumaru chinbun* (nicknamed "Maruchin"), which was launched in 1877 along the lines of such European forebears as the British *Punch,* and over the next three decades provided a nationwide forum for largely amateur versifiers.

Judging from the *senryū* columns of "Maruchin," some stock characters associated with male-male sexuality fared better after the Restoration than others. The most typical of these figures in the latter part of the Edo period had been the *kagema* or male prostitute, whose clientele included both men and women. To conjure up his image, the *senryū* writer had needed only invoke the name Yoshichō, since this was one of the districts of Edo where organized male prostitution flourished. However, the declining popularity of the *kagema* teahouse from the latter part of the eighteenth century, capped by Edo authorities' shutdown of most remaining establishments in the early 1840s and the final demise of Yushima around the time of the Restoration, was paralleled by a gradual diminishing of the *kagema's* profile in *senryū* collections.[1] By the Meiji period, Yoshichō served no longer as a topos for male prostitution, but for the female geisha who now monopolized the quarter.[2]

The virtual disappearance of the *kagema* from *senryū* and other forms of popular discourse, together with a similar silence on the part of lawmakers, suggests that male-male prostitution remained largely out of public view in Meiji Japan. This is not to say that such commerce did not go on clandestinely. One may find, for instance, accounts of young male "masseurs" who plied their trade in the foreign settlement at Yokohama, or a Tokyo milk bar (*mirukuhōru*) that provided the sexual services of penurious students.[3] However, open traffic in male-male sexuality, which had been a conspicuous feature of Edo culture, was unthinkable in the "civilized" environment of Meiji. One author wrote in 1889 that if "children of today" were told about the existence of *kagema* earlier in the century, they "would think it the tale of a foreign country and not our own."[4] Those of an older generation might still recall the pre-Restoration culture of male prostitution, such as one writer whose aunt had recounted to him as a young boy how she annually witnessed groups of *kagema* in feminine garb playing the traditional girls' New Year's game of shuttlecock (*oihanetsuki*) on the grounds of the

1. This observation is based on a survey of various *senryū* anthologies published during the latter half of the Edo period, prominent among them Okada Hajime, ed., <*Haifū*> *Yanagidaru zenshū*, 13 vols. (Sanseidō, 1976–1984), whose original 167 volumes appeared between 1765 and 1840.

2. An exception may lie in the following verse ("Kyōku," *Marumaru chinbun* 169 [1880]: 2703): "The priest's wife won't let him do it in the Yoshichō manner" (*Yoshichō no mane daikoku ni kotowarare*). If the reference here is to male-male sexual practices (specifically anal intercourse), textual tradition would seem to have played a greater role in its conception than contemporary experience. A plausible reading of the verse is that the priest, precisely because he no longer has recourse to male prostitutes, must seek similar satisfaction from his wife, albeit unsuccessfully.

3. "Bidō no heifū," *Yomiuri shinbun*, 13 July 1889, 4; Kawaoka Chōfū, "Gakusei no anmen ni wadakamareru nanshoku no ichidai akufū o tsūba su," *Bōken sekai*, August 1909, 78. Another milieu in which male-male prostitution appears to have survived, if in attenuated form, is the world of the theater. The above-cited *Yomiuri* article, for example, mentions rendezvous between young male actors and male patrons at teahouses—the descendants, as it were, of Edo's *kagemajaya*—in Tokyo's Asakusa theatrical district. Minakata Kumagusu has alleged that the early Meiji *onnagata* Arashi Daishi contracted a fatal case of syphilis while selling his sexual favors to an exclusively Western clientele. See his letter to Iwata Jun'ichi of 16 September 1931 in *Minakata Kumagusu zenshū*, ed. Iwamura Shinobu et al., 12 vols. (Heibonsha, 1971–1975), 9:67.

4. Dokushō Koji, "Danshō," *Edo kaishi*, November 1889, 58.

Yushima shrine.[5] Yet the tone of such accounts is that of a world long past and increasingly forgotten.

The popular imagery of male-male eroticism that had developed over the course of the Edo period did not vanish immediately with the Restoration. In the pages of "Maruchin," such motifs appear in *senryū* well into the 1880s (I have counted over a dozen such verses in the magazine between 1879 and 1888). Two figures, for example, who continued to be associated with male-male sexuality were the *bantō* and *detchi*—clerk and apprentice, respectively, in a commercial house. The *bantō* wielded considerable authority over other employees, and had been portrayed in *senryū* since the Edo period indulging his lechery with young male coworkers. The *detchi*, on the other hand, may be seen as the merchant version of the priestly *chigo* or samurai page boy: male adolescents for whom the favor or disfavor of senior males might have significant consequences for their professional advancement. Thus the 1882 verse: "The shop boy who flaunts his ass [alternative meaning: is diligent] is beloved by the clerk" (*Shirigaru na detchi bantō ni aiserare*).[6]

One factor contributing to the survival of *bantō* and *detchi* in early Meiji *senryū* was the continued economic vigor of the commercial sector and its traditional system of apprenticeship, which contrasted with the *kagema*'s professional demise. Further reinforcement of the former figures' association with male-male sexuality came from an 1844 incident in which the *bantō* of Shimaya, an Edo clothing store, brutally raped a young shop boy. This event, along with the clerk's death in a fire the next year, provided a subject for *senryū*, woodblock prints, songs, riddles, and a children's ditty that was sung as late as the twentieth century, as well as lending its name to a contemporary flu epidemic.[7] So great was the notoriety of this affair

---

5. Sasanoya, "Nanshoku," pt. 5, *Fūzoku gahō*, February 1894, 18–19. Similar reminiscences may be found in Aikikusei, "Ōsaka no kagema," *Kono hana* 11 (1910): 19; Enomoto Haryū, "Shitaya no konjaku," *Bungei kurabu*, August 1900, 177–181; Tanaka Kōgai, "Danseikan ni okeru dōseiai," *Nihon oyobi Nihonjin* 792 (1920): 112–113.

6. "Kyōku," *Marumaru chinbun* 294 (1882): 4416.

7. Contemporary accounts of the Shimaya incident and its popular representations appear in Murata Seiichi, "<Tokui nanshoku kō> Shimaya no bantō," *Kitan kurabu*, February 1954, 166–169; Satō Kōka, *Jinrui hiji kō* (Bungei shiryō kenkyūkai, 1929), 91–93; Shunroan Shujin, *Edo no shikidō: Seiai bunka o himotoku kindan no ezu to kosenryū*, 2 vols. (Yōbunkan shuppan, 1996), 1:80–87. A personal informant, Koizumi Masami, claims to have heard the children's ditty from a female relative who grew up in Tokyo during the first years of the twentieth century. Another Edo-period children's song (*temariuta*) that survived into the Meiji era asked: "Isn't that a *kagema* going by over there?" (*Mukō tōru wa kagema ja*

that, for decades thereafter, "the clerk at Shimaya" (*Shimaya no bantō*) served in colloquial parlance as a euphemism for anal intercourse.[8]

In passing, it may be interesting to note that a multicolored woodblock print (*nishikie*) sold shortly after the Shimaya incident is said to have depicted the notorious clerk disconcerted by the sudden visit to his store of a *kappa* or water goblin—the same creature that, in Hiraga Gennai's eighteenth-century work *Nenashigusa*, Enma, love-smitten king of the underworld, had sent to abduct a renowned kabuki actor. The significance of the 1840s print thus rested on a shared association with anal penetration: the clerk, for obvious reasons; and the *kappa*, not simply because of Hiraga's story, but because folk belief held this creature to covet a jewel (*shirikodama*) found in the human rectum, the removal of which was thought to cause imbecility or death.[9] The implication of the picture, then, is that the Shimaya clerk may be about to receive his just deserts. Decades later, writers still made a conceptual link between the *kappa* and male-male eroticism, as in this 1883 verse from "Maruchin": "In the Palace of the Dragon King [a mythic underwater realm] the *kappa* has a run-in with the *keikan* statute" (*Ryūgū de keikan-ritsu ni kappa ai*).[10] In the *senryū* genre, the enforcement of "civilized morality" thus affected not only living humans, but also the otherworldly beings who had populated the realm of *shudō* in the Edo period.[11]

Another personification of male-male sexuality in *senryū*'s traditional cast of characters was the Buddhist priest, for whom *nanshoku* had commonly been deemed a lesser transgression than fornication with women. The priest's erotic interaction with other males continued to furnish a mo-

---

nai ka). See Sasakawa Tanerō, *Genroku jiseishō* (Hakubunkan, 1901), 134. As with Western nursery rhymes, however, one doubts that children always understood the verses' original significance.

8. For an example of such a usage (in this case within a male-female context), see "Daiyonjūgō rairai mondō tsukiyo no kama o nuku no kotae," *Marumaru chinbun* 45 (1878): 712.

9. I thank Adam Kabat, author of a forthcoming study on the subject, for enlightening me on various aspects of *kappa* lore. In prison slang as recently as the 1970s, *kappa* signified the penetrating party in male-male sexual relations. See, for example, K. O., <*Jitsuroku shikeishūtachi no sei*> *Zoku saraba waga tomo* (Tokuma shoten, 1981), 187 and passim.

10. "Kyōku," *Marumaru chinbun* 381 (1883): 5794.

11. Other *senryū* pondered whether or not the anti-*keikan* statute would have affected Guo Ju, a filial son of Chinese legend who saved his starving parents by digging up a golden pot (*kama*, also used as a metaphor for anal intercourse). See "Kyōku," *Marumaru chinbun* 217 (1881): 3186; "Kyōku," *Marumaru chinbun* 343 (1883): 5166.

tif for early Meiji *senryū*, but the humor of such verses now revolved less around the contradiction between the priest's personal indulgence and the ascetic ideals of his religion, as had been the case previously, than around the incongruity between his particular form of pleasure and the secular standards of "civilized" sexuality. Such lampoons formed one flank of a broader attack on Buddhist institutions during the early Meiji period, in which the priest figured as an emblem of "ancient evils" (*kyūhei*) in dire need of reform.[12] Moreover, what was once a peccadillo had, under the provisions of the 1873 *Kaitei ritsuryō*, become a criminal offense. A pair of "Maruchin" *senryū* from the late 1870s thus contrasted the "old-fashioned" (*kyūhei*) priest still fond of male-male intercourse with the "refined" (*ga*) one who had recently abandoned the practice.[13] In a similar vein, a verse in an 1880 anthology poked fun at the "enlightened" cleric who went so far as to avoid using chrysanthemums (a common metaphor for the anus) in his flower arrangements (*Ikebana ni kiku o tsutsushimu kaikasō*).[14]

Early Meiji attempts to "civilize" the Buddhist clergy involved not only discouragement of male-male erotic practices but also a relaxation of strictures on male-female sexuality. A key component of the latter was the central government's 1872 rescinding of a ban on priestly marriage (traditionally condoned only within the Jōdo Shinshū sect) that had long been underwritten by bakufu and domain legislation.[15] The following year's *Kaitei ritsuryō* further stipulated that sexual offenses by priests and nuns be prosecuted according to the same provisions of criminal law as applied to the general public, rather than mandating stricter penalties for them as had the 1871 *Shinritsu kōryō*.[16] Such measures formed part of a broader move by the Meiji state to divest itself of special ties with Buddhist institutions, but also reflected a vision of "civilized" sexuality, centered around

12. On the refiguration of Meiji Buddhism, see James Edward Ketelaar, *Of Heretics and Martyrs in Meiji Japan: Buddhism and Its Persecution* (Princeton: Princeton University Press, 1990).

13. "Senryū," *Marumaru chinbun* 88 (1878): 1405; "Senryū," *Marumaru chinbun* 98 (1879): 1566. A verse similar to the first appears also in the early Meiji *senryū* collection *Kaika yanagidaru*, vol. 1 (Ikeda Tamotsu, ed. [n.p., n.d.]), n.p.

14. Hamano Senzō, ed., *Kaika shinsen yanagidaru* (Hamano Senzō, 1880), 18.

15. This decree, issued by the Council of State (Dajōkan), may be found in Naikaku kanpōkyoku, ed., *Hōrei zensho*, annual publ. (Naikaku kanpōkyoku, 1887–), 1872 vol.: 93.

16. Naikaku kirokukyoku, ed., *Hōki bunrui taizen*, 88 vols. (Hara shobō, 1980), 54:187–188, 304. The 1880 and 1907 penal codes made no specific mention of sexual offenses by Buddhist clerics.

male-female marriage, whose standards pertained to clergy and laity alike. A "Maruchin" editorialist voiced a similar perspective when he claimed that, while clerical marriage might contravene sectarian regulations, it clearly conformed to "universal reason and humanity" (*tenri jindō*), and would lead to fewer violations of the *keikan* statute.[17]

Despite such prognostications, male-male sexual practices among the priesthood would by no means disappear overnight. The monastic culture of male-male eroticism survived long after the Restoration, as attested by the ethnographer Minakata Kumagusu.[18] And since much of the Buddhist clergy still did not marry, critics continued to call for an end to priestly celibacy and the "evil habits" that it supposedly encouraged.[19] The common association of priests with male-male sexuality persisted well into the twentieth century, when sexologists came to identify Buddhist temples and monasteries as an archetypal site of "same-sex love" (*dōseiai*). Writing for a German audience, the early twentieth-century observer Doriphorus even claimed that familiarity with such practices by the clergy accounted for what seemed to him a relative tolerance for the "love of boys" among the Japanese population.[20]

It is suggestive that the term used by Doriphorus to express the notion of tolerance was *Stillschweigen*, which has a sense of intentional overlooking or silence. For although male-male sexual practices undoubtedly continued to take place among various social groups, *senryū* on such themes are, with very few exceptions, noticeably absent from "Maruchin's" pages between the late 1880s and the magazine's folding in 1907.[21] At least two factors, I would argue, interacted to produce this silence. One was state regulation of the representation of sexuality in printed media. The second was

17. Kusai Koenosuke, "Dainiketsu no setsu," *Marumaru chinbun* 213 (1881): 3110.

18. See, for example, the following letters from Minakata Kumagusu to Iwata Jun'ichi in *Minakata Kumagusu zenshū*: 29 October 1932 (9:131, 133); 7 October 1936 (9:261–262); 14 June 1938 (9:288–289). A *senryū* associating temple servants (*teraotoko*) with male-male sexuality may be found in "Kyōku," *Marumaru chinbun* 223 (1881): 3282.

19. See, for instance, "Shinsho ryakuhyō," *Yorozu chōhō*, 30 October 1901, 1, citing an article in the religious journal *Bukkyō*.

20. Friedrich S. Krauss, *Das Geschlechtleben in Glauben, Sitte, und Brauch der Japaner*, Beiwerke zum Studium der Anthropophyteia, no. 2 (Leipzig: Deutsche, 1907), 89. The question of Doriphorus's nationality has already been discussed in chap. 3, n. 74.

21. I have located only two exceptions: a verse featuring a *wakashu* in a series that draws its themes from the Edo-period folk paintings known as *Ōtsue* ("Kyōku,"

an emerging discursive framework in which male-male sexuality had either to be passed over unspoken or articulated from the higher moral perspective of "civilization."

The erasure of male-male erotic themes from "Maruchin" *senryū* coincides roughly with the ascendance of the notion of the "obscene" (*waisetsu*) in legal discourse. "Obscenity" encompassed not only sexual behaviors, but also their public display and representation. Censorship of erotic material had been practiced with varying degrees of severity and success during the Edo period, but the Meiji state put in place a nationally integrated, and arguably far more effective, set of mechanisms for regulating such forms of expression.[22] Much of the necessary bureaucratic apparatus took shape during the late 1870s and early 1880s, culminating in the issuance of two parallel codes of publication law, the *Shinbunshi jōrei* (governing periodicals) and the *Shuppan jōrei* (for book publishing) in 1887. Although these documents were superseded by later legislation, their basic provisions remained intact until the end of the Pacific War.[23]

Two basic categories defined the type of material whose appearance in print warranted suppression by the Home Ministry: that which disturbed "peace and order" (*chian*); and that which was injurious to "public morals" (*fūzoku*). The explicit depiction of sexuality generally fell under the latter heading, whose interpretation varied with time and with the whim of regulatory officials. Although Meiji publication law nowhere singled out the portrayal of male-male sexuality for special scrutiny, its provisions clearly affected the form that such representations could take. Increasingly, Edo-period texts featuring male-male eroticism appeared in expurgated editions or, like a complete set of Saikaku's works in 1894, were banned outright. In later decades, even writings that had passed the relatively lax standards of early Meiji censors might require some bowdlerizing—such as the practice of replacing salacious phrases and passages with circles or X's known as *fuseji*—in order to be republished.[24]

Marumaru chinbun 1201 [1899]: 22), and another crediting Kagoshima men with a special fondness for chrysanthemums (= anal eroticism; "Kadai," *Marumaru chinbun* 1502 [1904]: 30).

22. Bakufu censorship of erotic publications tended to intensify during periods of moral reform, with peaks in the Kyōhō (1716–1736), Kansei (1789–1801), and Tenpō (1830–1844) eras. On Edo-period censorship, see Konta Yōzō, *Edo no kinsho*, Edo sensho, no. 6 (Yoshikawa kōbunkan, 1981).

23. A more detailed examination of Meiji censorship may be found in Jay Rubin, *Injurious to Public Morals: Writers and the Meiji State* (Seattle: University of Washington Press, 1984).

24. For example, one of the characters in the term *ryūyō* (referring to a male-

State censorship of male-male erotic themes was not limited to publications, but occurred in other media as well. The repertoire of the kabuki theater, which once abounded in *shudō* motifs, emerged from the Meiji period largely stripped of this heritage, due at least in part to official intervention. In 1899, for example, police authorities in Tokyo demanded that changes be made to the script of *Chidaruma* (Bloodstained Bodhidharma), a play that had been performed on the kabuki stage since at least 1712, on the grounds that its depiction of *nanshoku* threatened "public morality."[25] Similar constraints affected the pictorial representation of male-male sexuality, which had once been a staple of Edo-period erotic prints. Such illustrations could now be considered "obscene material" (*waisetsu no buppin*), the public display or sale of which merited criminal punishment.[26] As early as 1870, the artist Kawanabe Kyōsai was jailed for drawing a caricature of the Meiji oligarch Sanjō Sanetomi engaged in sexual relations with a male foreigner, although in this case the charge was not public obscenity but the even graver offense of insulting a government official.[27]

Within the boundaries set by such legal notions as "obscenity" and "public morality," producers of popular discourse generally approached the representation of male-male sexuality in one of two ways. The first was to place male-male sexual practices firmly beyond the pale of what could legitimately be spoken. Even when mentioning such practices, Meiji commentators often labeled them "unmentionable" (*iu ni shinobizaru*), a formula echoing in part Christian rhetorical precedents. By the latter part of the Meiji period, the unspeakability of male-male sexuality had come to form one of the protocols of respectable discourse, its effects felt even in such playful genres as *senryū*. Thus, while some early "Maruchin" *senryū* had taken the marginalization of male-male sexual behaviors in "civilized" society as their

male sexual favorite) is replaced by a circle in a 1926 edition of Tsubouchi Shōyō's 1885–1886 novel <*Ichidoku santan*> *Tōsei shosei katagi* (vol. 1 of *Meiji bungaku meicho zenshū*, ed. Yamaguchi Tsuyoshi et al., 12 vols. [Tōkyōdō, 1926–1927], 136, 142, 165). Naturally, astute readers might still make out what was being signified.

25. Shōsei, "Meijiza," *Yorozu chōhō*, 13 March 1899, 1. This play (or rather set of plays) is discussed in Dōmoto Masaki, <*Zōhoban*> *Nanshoku engekishi* (Shuppansha, 1976), 236–253. According to Morita Yūshū (*Hentai seiyoku hiwa* [Heibonsha, 1930], 176), some early twentieth-century productions went so far as to recast the page boy Ōkawa Kazuma as a female character.

26. The relevant articles of the 1880 (whence the phrase *waisetsu no buppin*) and 1907 penal codes may be found in Naikaku kanpōkyoku, *Hōrei zensho*, 1907 vol., (hōritsu) 98.

27. Itō Sei, *Nihon bundanshi*, 18 vols. (Kōdansha, 1953–1973), 1:125; Oikawa Shigeru and Yamaguchi Seiichi, *Kyōsai no giga* (Tōkyō shoseki, 1992), 166.

explicit theme, later examples marginalized these forms of sexuality implicitly by rendering them invisible.

Alternatively, Meiji writers found license to speak the unspeakable by representing male-male sexuality in the pejorative idiom of "civilized morality." This strategy made it possible for male-male sexual practices to be articulated in discourse even as their ethical validity was expressly denied. In the "civilized" lexicon of sexual (mis)behavior, male-male sexual acts were signified by a wide variety of euphemisms, all incorporating some term or character to convey their impropriety: "barbarous practices" (*bankō*), "wicked deeds" (*akuji*), "immoral conduct" (*hairin no shogyō*), and so forth. The precise nature of the acts involved had to be inferred largely from context, yet this deductive process, too, might figure among the secret pleasures of reading.

While the "civilized" idiom did not lend itself easily to the terse format and humorous tone of *senryū* verse, it was to prove a valuable tool for Meiji journalists. Turn-of-the-century newspapers, as we will see shortly, routinely deployed such language in order to maintain respectability while exposing male-male sexual behavior to public view. By contrast, reporters earlier in the Meiji period had seen fit to cast stories involving male-male eroticism in an unabashedly comic vein. In 1876, for example, a newspaperman introduced his account of a Chinese in Yokohama who had a narrow brush with police after hiring an acupuncturist-masseur to penetrate him anally with the comment that the whole episode was a "big laugh" (*ōwarai*).[28] (The xenophobic overtones of this laughter must, of course, be taken into account as well.) As the Meiji period progressed, however, male-male sexuality became less likely to elicit a humorous response from journalists than one of moralistic outrage—a shift in sensibilities to which the disappearance of male-male erotic themes from "Maruchin" *senryū* is surely not unrelated.

Explaining silence is, of course, a tricky business, and it is difficult to pinpoint which of many factors—state censorship, editorial discretion, authorial inclination, public taste—was most relevant to the "Maruchin" case. Rather, all of these elements interacted to make male-male sexuality problematic material for the journal's *senryū* columns. In prose, too, the rather earthy treatment of male-male sexuality characteristic of the magazine's earlier years seems to have given way to a growing reticence.[29] Nor was this

28. Umehara Hokumei, ed., *Meiji seiteki chinbunshi*, 3 (?) vols. (Bungei shiryō kenkyūkai, 1926–?), 2:16.

29. Compare, for example, the bawdy humor of "Daiyonjūgō" with the more

process limited to male-male eroticism: "Maruchin" *senryū* on male-female sexual themes also became less ribald over the course of the Meiji period, although they remained a staple feature.

While there is much room for further research, the "Maruchin" example suggests that the representation of male-male sexuality in Meiji *senryū* may be divided roughly into two phases. *Shudō* themes and tropes continued to circulate with relative frequency in this medium until at least the mid-1880s, although their distribution and form were affected by the shifting social landscape and the new demands of "civilized morality." By the latter part of the Meiji period, however, male-male eroticism had become less acceptable as a subject for *senryū* humor as a consequence of such factors as state regulation of "obscene" expression and a discursive regime that consigned male-male sexual practices either to unspeakability or to condemnation. In *senryū*, as in other forms of popular writing, male-male eroticism thus moved gradually but unmistakably toward the margins of discourse.

ENCOMPASSING THE MARGINS

If "civilization" stood at the center of Meiji mappings of sexuality, then what were the margins toward which male-male sexuality was displaced? One, of course, was the realm of silence, in which male-male sexual practices were altogether ignored—which is not to say erased from consciousness. Yet even when popular discourse of the Meiji period explicitly acknowledged the existence of such practices, it tended to relegate them to certain peripheral areas of experience. My use of the term "encompassing" has thus a double sense: to indicate that male-male sexuality remained inside the larger field of discourse, and to suggest that there were particular directionalities to its marginalization. Specifically, this section will identify three cardinal points toward which representations of male-male sexuality in Meiji popular discourse gravitated: the Japanese past, the southwestern periphery, and the world of adolescence. Just as these sites were set off from and served to define more mainstream subjectivities—the new Japanese, the national citizen, the responsible adult—the assignment of male-male sexual practices to these marginal spaces helped to demarcate the limits of "civilized" behavior.

By the latter part of the Edo period, as we saw in chapter 1, commentators typically described the trajectory of *shudō* over recent centuries as one

---

guarded tone of Fūryūjin, "Mazu jinsukeshin o haisubeshi," *Marumaru chinbun* 738 (1890): 6.

of decline. Whether they located it in the Sengoku period or the Genroku era (the age of Saikaku), observers agreed that the heyday of male-male erotic practices lay in the past, and that later manifestations of such behavior represented mere historical vestiges. This association of male-male sexuality with a receding past was decisively reinforced by the Meiji Restoration. The preceding centuries of Tokugawa hegemony were now cast as a backward and "feudal" age, whose institutions and customs Japan must abandon in order to achieve "civilization." Within this narrative schema, male-male sexual practices figured as a "barbarism" or "ancient evil," the repudiation of which served to distinguish the new Japan from the old.

Changing social formations contributed to the Meiji perception of male-male sexual behavior as a phenomenon whose day had passed. Some of the groups most closely associated with male-male erotic culture in the Edo period were faced with obsolescence or forced to radically renegotiate their identities in post-Restoration society. One such group was the Buddhist priesthood, which, as has already been noted, met with widespread persecution during the early years of the Meiji regime. Another was the samurai class, known after 1870 as *shizoku*, which forfeited its status as an entrenched elite as well as its monopoly on the military and bureaucratic professions. The warrior culture of honor, violence, and misogyny, in which samurai versions of *shudō* were deeply enmeshed, now appeared increasingly outdated or suspect in the light of "civilized morality." In 1876, for instance, a newspaper article reported an incident of male-male rape involving a *shizoku* perpetrator (the previously introduced Matsui) with the warning that readers should not dismiss such "evil deeds" (*akuji*) as a mark of "heroic behavior" (*gōketsu-fū*) as would have been the case in earlier days.[30] Nevertheless, an awareness of *shudō* traditions may have lasted longer among heritage-conscious *shizoku* than in other segments of Meiji society.[31]

Although contemporary settings were not unheard of, Meiji litterateurs usually depicted male-male sexuality in a milieu that was safely historical.

30. Umehara, *Meiji seiteki chinbunshi*, 2:12–14.
31. Minakata Kumagusu ("*Ichidai otoko o yomu*," in *Minakata Kumagusu zenshū*, 4:15) recalls, for instance, that when he entered middle school in Wakayama in 1879, sons of *shizoku* families generally knew the story of Fuwa Bansaku, a page who followed his lord and lover, the sixteenth-century regent Toyotomi Hidetsugu, into death. On Fuwa, see Iwata Jun'ichi, "Bishōnen Fuwa Bansaku no koi," in *Honchō nanshoku kō* (Toba: Iwata Sadao, 1974), 240–252 (trans. D. R. Roberts in *The Love of the Samurai: A Thousand Years of Japanese Homosexuality*, by Tsuneo Watanabe and Jun'ichi Iwata [London: GMP, 1989], 52–65). Taoka Reiun describes male-male erotic culture among *shizoku* youths in Kōchi prefecture during the 1880s in

The most common backdrop was samurai society of the Sengoku and Edo eras, for the assumed prevalence of male-male erotic relations in that environment licensed authors to represent them in the interest of historical accuracy or simply ambiance. Even in such a context, however, there were limits to permissible candor, sexual acts being more often hinted at obliquely than explicitly portrayed. The novelist Kōda Rohan, for instance, wove his fictionalized account of the 1575 battle of Nagashino, titled *Higeotoko* (Man with a Beard; 1890–1896), around a passionate bond of brotherhood between a "beautiful boy" (*bishōnen*) and an older samurai, yet did not venture to describe any physical involvement beyond the level of hand-holding.[32] Alternatively, by intentionally leaving certain passages blank (*fuseji*), authors could suggest the occurrence of sexual activity.[33]

Other Meiji literary works portrayed *shudō* in a townsman, rather than a samurai, environment. One example is Jōno Denpei's *Kagema no adauchi* (*Kagema's* Vendetta), which is set in Yoshichō during the late 1820s, and has as its protagonist a professional "love boy" of the kind that the author, who was born in 1832, had personally encountered during his childhood.[34] By the time Jōno's novel appeared in 1899, however, the author had to introduce this milieu to a largely unfamiliar audience, and to add the disclaimer that "from today's perspective" the hero's occupation was "disgraceful"

his autobiography *Sūkiden*, in *Taoka Reiun zenshū*, ed. Nishida Masaru, 3 vols. to date (Hōsei daigaku shuppankyoku, 1969–), 5:551–553. For similar practices among their eighteenth- and early nineteenth-century forebears, see Moriguchi Kōji, "Tosa hansei kōki ni okeru 'chiin' kō: Wakazamurai no 'koi' no shūzoku," *Tosa shidan* 200 (1997): 45–52, for which reference I thank Luke Roberts.

32. Kōda Rohan, *Higeotoko*, in *Rohan zenshū*, ed. Kagyūkai, 44 vols. (Iwanami shoten, 1978–1980), 5:273–393. On this work's representation of male-male sexuality, see Komori Yōichi, "Nihon kindai bungaku ni okeru nanshoku no haikei," *Bungaku* 6.1 (1995): 78–83. Other works of Meiji fiction that situated male-male sexuality in the samurai past include Inaoka Masafumi, *Bishōnen* (Osaka: Shinshindō, 1900); Otowaan Shujin [Ōhashi Matatarō], "Otoko no ude," *Bungei kurabu*, April 1896, 91–161; Tenshū Koji [Nishimura Tenshū], "Satsuma shinjū," *Miyako no hana*, 15 February 1891, 1–22.

33. See, for instance, Inaoka, *Bishōnen*.

34. Saigiku Sanjin [Jōno Denpei], <Sannin kyōkaku> *Kagema no adauchi* (Junseidō, 1899), 1. Other Meiji literary works that portray commercialized urban *shudō* include Emi Suiin, "Chizomezakura," in <Tanpen shōsetsu> *Meiji bunko*, ed. Ōhashi Shintarō, 18 vols. (Hakubunkan, 1893–1894), 17:1–42; Okamoto Kisen, *Sawamura Tanosuke akebono sōshi*, vol. 11 of *Meiji bungaku meicho zenshū*. For a Meiji kabuki play featuring a pair of *kagema*—interestingly, in a scene that has been excised from the current repertory—see Takeshiba Kisui, *Kami no megumi wagō no torikumi*, in *Nihon gikyoku zenshū*, ed. Ihara Seiseien et al., 50 vols. (Shun'yōdō, 1929), 32:356–417. I thank Mark Oshima for this information.

(*keshikaru*).[35] By presenting male-male erotic practices as part of the cultural fabric of a bygone era, Jōno was able to treat them with relative openness, and to create a character toward whom readers might feel some admiration despite his unsavory profession and ambiguous gender identity. In other words, so long as Jōno identified his morally suspect subject matter as safely removed from the present day and age, he was free to explore it with a certain amount of candor.

The general oblivion into which the Edo-period culture of male-male eroticism had fallen by the latter part of the Meiji period gave rise, in addition to Jōno's historical fiction, to a complementary genre of historical ethnography. In such writings, *shudō* practices figured as folkways, curious and even immoral by contemporary standards, yet nonetheless worthy of remembrance because they formed part of Japan's cultural heritage. In 1893, for instance, the pseudonymous Sasanoya prefaced a magazine article on pre-Restoration *nanshoku* with the adage that "we can understand the present only by knowing the past" (*onko chishin*).[36] Such accounts as Sasanoya's represent one aspect of a late-Meiji revival of interest in Edo-period popular culture, among whose other manifestations were a renewed appreciation for woodblock prints, which Japanese collectors earlier in the Meiji period had disparaged, and the establishment of societies and publications to preserve Edo-period artifacts and lore. At the same time, one of their effects was to "museumify" male-male erotic traditions by ensconcing them in the recesses of history, where they could be studied but no longer lived.[37]

A second compass point in the marginalization of male-male sexuality was Japan's southwestern periphery. This region could be defined to include various parts of Kyushu, Shikoku, and Honshu, but its epicenter was invariably seen to lie in Kagoshima prefecture (the former domain of Satsuma).[38] During the Meiji period, common knowledge came to hold that male-male erotic practices were more prevalent here than in the rest of the

35. Saigiku Sanjin, *Kagema no adauchi*, 11.

36. Sasanoya, "Nanshoku," pt. 1, *Fūzoku gahō*, September 1893, 12. For other examples of this genre of historical ethnography, see Dokushō Koji, "Danshō"; Enomoto, "Shitaya no konjaku"; Noguchi Takejirō, <*Onko chishin*> *Edo no hana* (Hakubunkan, 1890), 250–253; Saitō Ryūzō, *Genroku sesōshi* (Hakubunkan, 1905), 226–231; Sasakawa, *Genroku jiseishō*. From 1910, such accounts also appear in Miyatake Gaikotsu's antiquarian journal *Kono hana*.

37. I borrow the notion of "museumification" from Joseph R. Levenson, *Confucian China and Its Modern Fate*, vol. 3, *The Problem of Historical Significance* (Berkeley: University of California Press, 1965).

38. Occasionally, the "north country" (*hokkoku*), encompassing such present-

country. While this distinction was primarily geographic, it also involved a chronological dimension, for the southwest was perceived as a stronghold of social customs that had once been more widespread. Distinctions of class came into play as well, since the mores of the samurai class were seen to have made a lasting imprint on its regional character. During the Edo period, the concentration of warrior families within the general population had been somewhat denser here than the national average, in Satsuma perhaps exceeding a third. In addition, the political geography of the time led a number of southwestern domains, many of them former enemies of the Tokugawa, to enforce a high level of martial discipline—a factor that contributed to their prominent role in the Meiji Restoration.

Although *shudō* texts, with their metropolitan focus, had not especially linked male-male sexual practices with this particular region of the country, various Edo-period sources testify to the presence of such practices among southwestern warriors.[39] The scholar-daimyo Matsuura (also known as Matsura) Seizan, for instance, writing in the first decades of the nineteenth century, describes a Satsuma institution called the *hekogumi*, in which young samurai males banded together to study and to polish their martial skills. Members were required to avoid contact with females, and violations or criticisms of this rule—even so simple an act as staring at a passing woman—could be punished with death. Male-male erotic interaction, on the other hand, was reportedly common within such groups, where "beautiful boys," Matsuura asserts, held their admirers in thrall like feudal masters (a status the daimyo author himself ironically shared).[40] Although Matsuura writes that the *hekogumi* were banned during the latter part of the eigh-

---

day prefectures as Fukushima and Yamagata, was cited together with the southwest as a region where male-male sexual practices had survived from the Edo period. See, for instance, Sasanoya, "Nanshoku," pt. 1, 12. I find no such references after the 1890s, a timing that suggests the decisive influence of turn-of-century journalism in labeling such practices as southwestern.

39. Satsuma natives occasionally appear in a *shudō* context in Edo-period works of fiction (see, for example, Ihara Saikaku, *Kōshoku gonin onna*, in *Nihon koten bungaku zenshū*, ed. Akiyama Ken et al., 51 vols. [Shōgakkan, 1970–1976], 38:403–423 [trans. Wm. Theodore de Bary under the title *Five Women Who Loved Love* (Rutland, Vt.: Tuttle, 1956), 195–229; trans. Ivan Morris under the title *Five Women Who Chose Love*, in *The Life of an Amorous Woman and Other Writings* (New York: New Directions, 1969), 100–118]), as well as in *senryū* (e.g., Okada Hajime, *Yanagidaru zenshū*, 1:101], but they do not stand out in this respect from their counterparts in other parts of the archipelago.

40. Matsuura Seizan, *Kasshi yawa*, ed. Yoshikawa Hanshichi (Kokusho kankōkai, 1910), 249–250.

teenth century, similar local institutions, such as the youth associations known as *gojū*, continued to socialize young samurai males up until the Restoration in a single-sex environment where male-female contact was discouraged and male-male erotic attachments flourished.[41]

Following the Restoration, a centralized school system began to supplant these local institutions, while the martial ethos of the samurai class slowly dissolved under the pressure of social change and "civilized morality."[42] Contemporary observers correlated the deterioration of *shiki* or "warrior morale" with a decline in male-male erotic practices. As early as 1872, a visitor to Kagoshima reported that *nanshoku* had lost some of its popularity there, and that entrepreneurs planned to establish female brothels, which the Satsuma domain had previously banned.[43] Nevertheless, a student traveler in 1886 found that there was remarkably little erotic banter on the subject of women among young Kagoshima males—a fact that he attributed, following a familiar chain of association, to the strength of *shiki*.[44]

Despite some indications that, even in the southwest, male-male erotic practices were becoming less prevalent than before, they remained by all accounts more firmly entrenched here than in the rest of the country. When the Niigata-born educator Honpu Yasushirō took up a teaching post in Kagoshima in 1889, he was surprised at the extent to which local society countenanced erotic ties between young males. Far from being unspeakable, they were considered a fit topic to be brought up in front of parents.[45] Using the idiom of "civilized morality," Honpu explained to readers that, while

41. On the *gojū* institution, see Ivan Parker Hall, *Mori Arinori* (Cambridge: Harvard University Press, 1973), 32–46; Kagoshima-ken kyōiku iinkai, ed., *Kagoshima-ken kyōikushi* (Maruyama gakugei tosho, 1976), 83–126. *Gojū* (as opposed to Hall's *gōjū*) is the local pronunciation. The most comprehensive ethnographic treatment may be found in Mishina Shōei, *Chōsen kodai kenkyū, daiichibu: Shiragi karō no kenkyū* (Sanseidō, 1943), (sankōhen) 3–39.

42. In Kagoshima, the functions of the earlier *gojū* devolved not only on schools, but also on the extracurricular *gakusha*, which continued to promote spartan values and to provide a nexus for male-male erotic interaction well into the twentieth century. On *gakusha*, see Kagoshima-ken kyōiku iinkai, *Kagoshima-ken kyōikushi*, 532–559.

43. Edamatsu Shigeyuki et al., eds., *Meiji nyūsu jiten*, 9 vols. (Mainichi komyunikēshonzu, 1983), 1:462. Licensed female prostitution commenced in Kagoshima only in 1888, on which see Kanbashi Norimasa, *Kagoshima kuruwa monogatari: Urakaidō onna no rekishi* (Maruyama gakugei tosho, 1989).

44. Honpu Yasushirō, *Satsuma kenbunki*, in *Nihon shomin seikatsu shiryō shūsei*, ed. Miyamoto Tsuneichi et al., 32 vols. (San'ichi shobō, 1968–1984), 12:406.

45. Similarly, when Kawade Masumi, another nonnative of the region, entered Kagoshima's Seventh Higher School in 1903, he was surprised to find that athletic day featured a race called *nise-chigo kyōsō*, in which older and younger male stu-

the courting of "beautiful boys" was a "barbaric custom" (*banpū*), domain authorities during the Edo period had tacitly encouraged it as a means of preventing young men from going "soft" (*nyūjaku*) through erotic involvement with women (*joshoku*). He welcomed the apparent decline of such practices in recent years, but worried that local educators were unprepared to deal with the indulgence in male-female eroticism and general moral laxness that had begun to arise in their place.[46]

Various localisms inflected the culture of male-male eroticism that Honpu observed in Kagoshima schools. A number of dialect terms existed, for example, to describe male-male erotic relations, including *yokachigo* for a "beautiful boy," *senpe(-don)* or *kasette* for his suitor, and *chigokasegi* for the pursuit of the former by the latter.[47] Another distinctive feature was the singing of *chigouta*, ballads extolling the charms of young male favorites, at youthful gatherings of males.[48] The central text of this local erotic culture, however, was an Edo-period work known as *Shizu no odamaki* (Humble Bobbin), which recounted the martial exploits and romantic involvement of a pair of sixteenth-century Satsuma warriors, one a youth, the other an adult male.[49] Private schools in Kagoshima are said to have prescribed the reading of this tale on the first day of the new year. The area's famed lute

---

dents, holding hands, ran as couples before a cheering faculty. See Kawade Masumi, "Kagoshima-shi to Shichikō," in *Kinenshi* (Kagoshima: Daishichi kōtō gakkō kinen shukugakai, 1926), 324–325. I am grateful to Kanbashi Norimasa for helping me locate this reference.

46. Honpu, *Satsuma kenbunki*, 12:406–407.

47. Hashiguchi Mitsuru, *Kagoshima-ken hōgen jiten* (Ōfūsha, 1987), 847; Honpu, *Satsuma kenbunki*, 12:420, 422; Shōgaku tosho, *Nihon hōgen jiten*, 3 vols. (Shōgakkan, 1989), 1:544.

48. Honpu, *Satsuma kenbunki*, 12:383. For examples of *chigouta*, some of which remained in circulation as late as the Pacific War period, see Kagoshima-shi gakusha rengōkai, ed., *<Satsuma hekouta> Shikon* (Kagoshima: Shun'endō, 1970), 12–49. Satsuma troops reportedly sang a variant of the *chigouta* as they escorted the sixteen-year-old Meiji emperor to his new capital in 1868. In it, the young sovereign was referred to as the "august chrysanthemum" (*okikusama*), a designation that played on that flower's association with both the imperial house and male-male eroticism. See Minakata Kumagusu to Iwata Jun'ichi, 7 September 1931, *Minakata Kumagusu zenshū*, 9:53.

49. *Shizu no odamaki* (Ichikawa Teishiro, 1885). There are various theories concerning the origins of this work, one of them (see Kawaoka, "Gakusei no anmen," 74) reporting that a Satsuma daimyo ordered its redaction from an earlier male-female romance, another (see Maeda Ai, "*Shizu no odamaki kō*," *Ōgai* 18 [1966]: 24) alleging a female author. On the significance of the work within a Meiji context, see Komori, "Nihon kindai bungaku," 73–78; Maeda Ai, "*Shizu no odamaki kō*," 21–27.

(*biwa*) musicians, too, sang of the story's *wakashu* hero, Hirata Sangorō, whose name alone reportedly provoked appreciative outbursts from male members of the audience.[50]

Familiarity with such cultural practices helped establish the southwest's, and particularly Kagoshima's, reputation in the Meiji period as a hotbed of male-male sexual activity. Thus, a doctor addressing a medical society in Tokyo in 1899 suggested that, in order to ascertain the physiological consequences of male-male anal intercourse, it might be expedient to ask a Kyushuite.[51] In the same year, we find a Tokyo newspaper reporter describing male-male erotic practices as a "Satsuma habit" (*Satsujin tsūyū no seiheki*; literally, "common quirk of Satsumaites").[52] Such locutions figured male-male sexuality as a regional peculiarity lying outside the mainstream of an increasingly centralized (which is to say, Tokyo-centered) national culture. Since the southwestern periphery appeared from this central perspective as a backwater of "feudal" traits, the identification of male-male erotic practices with this particular area of the country served to underscore their "uncivilized" nature. Far from a universal "way," like *shudō*, male-male erotic practices assumed the status of "folkways" (*fūzoku*), surviving on the cultural margins of a newly "civilized" nation-state. Later on in the twentieth century, this spatial containment of male-male sexuality would be given a medical tinge by sexologists, who diagnosed such areas as Kagoshima with a hereditary condition they called "regional same-sex love" (*chihōteki dōseiai*).[53]

In the case of such southwestern prefectures as Kagoshima, Kōchi, and Kumamoto, cultural geography was also closely linked with political geography. Their predecessor domains had played a significant role in the Restoration, and as a consequence these areas produced a disproportionately large

50. Honpu, *Satsuma kenbunki*, 12:407; Kawaoka, "Gakusei no anmen," 74; Mori Ōgai, *Wita sekusuarisu*, in *Ōgai zenshū*, ed. Kinoshita Mokutarō et al., 38 vols. (Iwanami shoten, 1971–1975), 5:114 (trans. Kazuji Ninomiya and Sanford Goldstein under the title *Vita Sexualis* [Rutland, Vt.: Tuttle, 1972], 63). The lyrics of the lute ballad ("Katami no sakura") may be found in Hagiwara Akihiko, ed., <Chūkai> Satsuma biwa kashū (Kagoshima: Ryūyōkai, 1965), 184–206.

51. Funaoka Einosuke, "Nanshoku ni tsuite," *Kokka igakkai zasshi*, May 1899, 4–5.

52. "Teikoku kaigun to Yamamoto Gonnohyōe," pt. 4, *Yorozu chōhō*, 6 July 1899, 1.

53. For references to "regional same-sex love," see Habuto Eiji and Sawada Junjirō, *Hentai seiyokuron* (Shun'yōdō, 1915), 107; Komine Shigeyuki, *Dōseiai to dōsei shinjū no igakuteki kōsatsu*, in *Dōseiai to dōsei shinjū no kenkyū*, by Komine Shigeyuki and Minami Takao (Komine kenkyūjo, 1985), 59; Sawada Junjirō, *Shinpi naru dōseiai*, 2 vols. (Tenkadō shobō, 1920), 1:130–131.

number of Meiji officials. To many contemporary observers, the Meiji regime appeared as little more than an oligarchic clique dominated by natives of the southwest (and in particular the former domains of Satsuma and Hagi [also known as Chōshū]). It is somewhat ironic, therefore, that the "Satsuma habit" was proscribed by a government that included many Satsuma-born leaders. Anecdotal accounts even link some of them personally with such practices: it has been claimed, for instance, that the rivalry between the oligarchs Ōkubo Toshimichi and Saigō Takamori stemmed from a dispute over the favors of a "beautiful boy" in the days when both were members of the same *gojū*.[54]

Within the Meiji government, Kagoshima men enjoyed a particularly high profile in the imperial navy. Satsuma had been especially active among pre-Restoration domains in importing Western naval technology and hardware, thus setting the stage for a Kagoshima dominion over the national fleet that lasted well into the twentieth century. While Europeans had for many centuries associated seafaring with male-male eroticism, such a connection was not generally made in Japan until the Meiji period. Yet interestingly, the growing perception of the imperial navy as a training grounds for male-male sexual behavior appears originally to have had as much to do with the regional—which is to say land-based—origins of its personnel as with the conditions of shipboard life. In 1899, for instance, a journalist asserted that the navy had earned the nickname of the "buggery fleet" (*keikan kaigun*) because its Satsuma-born minister, Yamamoto Gonnohyōe, had favored his *bishōnen* schoolmates at the naval academy with top posts.[55]

A third margin toward which popular representations of male-male sexuality drifted during the Meiji period was the world of adolescence. This, again, was not an entirely new association, since the sexual object in *shudō* had always been defined as a young male; indeed, this sense was embedded in the term itself. In Meiji popular discourse, as in that of the Edo period, it was generally understood that youthfulness formed one of the conditions of male-male erotic desirability. More and more commonly, however, the desiring party too was presumed to be an adolescent, older than his partner as a rule, but neither of them yet an adult. It was not simply that their chronological ages had changed—although there was undoubtedly an element of this as well, such adult figures as the samurai and the Buddhist priest having become a less conspicuous presence on the erotic landscape. Rather,

54. Minakata Kumagusu to Iwata Jun'ichi, postcard, 1 February 1933, *Minakata Kumagusu zenshū*, 9:174.

55. "Teikoku kaigun to Yamamoto Gonnohyōe," pt. 2, *Yorozu chōhō*, 3 July 1899, 1.

both parties (the youth and *nenja*, in Edo-period terms) were becoming implicated in a newly evolving conception of adolescence (*seishun*) as an "institutionalized moratorium between childhood and adulthood."[56] In the
process, male-male sexuality was confined to a social space where adult standards did not fully apply, and where "uncivilized" behavior could be dis-
missed as youthful folly.

During the Meiji period, the world of the adolescent male, particularly
among the more privileged classes, revolved increasingly around the school.
The Meiji regime early recognized the utility of a centralized educational
system in molding the citizens of a "civilized" nation-state. It therefore
proclaimed the goal of universal primary education in 1872, supplemented
in ensuing decades by an expanding network of middle and higher schools,
open, at least in theory, to all qualified male students. These and other public schools, along with numerous private institutions, accommodated a
growing segment of the adolescent male population. In 1901, for instance,
some 12,024 males reportedly attended middle schools in Tokyo alone.[57] It
was here, too, in the turn-of-the-century capital that male-male sexual practices among students first sparked a journalistic uproar. Since this phenomenon helps to illuminate the link in Meiji popular discourse between
male-male sexuality and adolescence, the following section will examine its
dimensions and implications in detail.

ROUGHNECKS AND SMOOTHIES

Institutions of formal education were by no means new to Meiji Japan, but
had flourished during the Edo period as well. Typically, these had been restricted to particular status groups and, in keeping with the Confucian dictum that males and females should not sit together after reaching the age
of seven, segregated by sex. While the notion that male-male erotic practices were endemic to the school and its environs was not so persistent a
motif in popular discourse as it would become in the Meiji and later periods, such practices appear to have been relatively common among Edo-period
students.[58] A graduate of the shogunal academy, Shōheikō, described them
as an "everyday occurrence" (*jōtai*) at that institution in the 1850s, and one

56. Donald Roden, *Schooldays in Imperial Japan: A Study in the Culture of a
Student Elite* (Berkeley: University of California Press, 1980), 72.
57. "Gakusei no daraku," pt. 1, *Yorozu chōhō*, 24 April 1901, 3.
58. Though by no means frequent, school settings were not entirely unknown
in *shudō* literature. For one example, see Ihara Saikaku, *Nanshoku ōkagami*, in *Nihon koten bungaku zenshū*, 39:323–324 (trans. Paul Gordon Schalow under the

that led in some cases to violence between rivals in love.[59] Educational authorities, too, were well acquainted with their disruptive potential. When Confucian scholars (*jusha*) at the Aizu domain school in Edo complained of *nanshoku* ties among their students in 1790, han officials, then in the midst of a program of moral reform, issued a stiff warning against such "misguided" (*kokoroechigai*) behavior.[60] Likewise, authorities at the domain school in Mori (located in today's Shimane prefecture) cautioned pupils not to engage in idle discussion about *nanshoku*, nor to broach such topics as male-female eroticism (*joshoku*) or money.[61] Such prohibitions were distinctly informed by the ideology of the samurai class, whose sons the domain academies were primarily meant to educate, and which deemed excessive interest in sexual or mercenary matters unbefitting of warriors.

Male-male erotic practices also took place in other pedagogical settings. Young samurai males in the castle towns of Wakamatsu and Matsuyama, we saw, sometimes preyed upon their juniors as they commuted to and from various types of lessons or practice (*keiko*). And in the *hekogumi* and *gojū* of Satsuma, which were largely self-governing bodies, male-male erotic ties apparently thrived. The above examples, it should be noted, all involve the samurai class; whether equivalent practices were widespread among nonelite groups deserves further research.[62]

Following the Restoration, schools proliferated throughout the nation as a result of the centralization of the educational system and a widespread

---

title *The Great Mirror of Male Love* [Stanford: Stanford University Press, 1990], 59–61).

59. Oka Rokumon, *Zaioku waki*, in *Zuihitsu hyakkaen*, ed. Mori Senzō et al., 15 vols. (Chūō kōronsha, 1980–1981), 2:216. For another discussion of male-male eroticism among Edo-period and Meiji students, see Ujiie Mikito, *Edo no shōnen* (Heibonsha, 1989), 121–140.

60. Toyoda Takeshi et al., eds., <Aizu-han> *Kasei jikki*, 16 vols. (Yoshikawa kōbunkan, 1975–1990), 13:430–431.

61. Monbushō sōmukyoku, ed., *Nihon kyōikushi shiryō*, 9 vols. (Monbushō sōmukyoku, 1890–1892), 1:110. R. P. Dore (*Education in Tokugawa Japan* [London: Routledge, 1965], 76) has suggested that a regulation barring senior students at Yonezawa's Kōjōkan from receiving younger schoolmates in their dormitories, even during an illness, was designed to prevent "seduction."

62. A set of precepts surviving from an Okayama village school (possibly one of those that the domain established for the education of peasants in the seventeenth century) warns against the "evil practices" (*jakō*) of *nanshoku* and *joshoku*, particularly among the young. Such prohibitions, however, say more about elite ideology than about the prevalence of the proscribed behaviors in peasant society. See Ōsawa Koresada, *Kibi onko hiroku*, vols. 6–10 of *Kibi gunsho shūsei*, ed. Tanaka Seiichi and Morita Keitarō, 10 vols. (Kibi gunsho shūsei kankōkai, 1921–1932), 9:563–564.

emphasis on "success" through study.[63] To be sure, gender and class differences continued to affect the type of education that individuals received; as an ideal social type, however, the student loomed large in the Meiji imagination. The male student (*shosei* or *gakusei*) and his female counterpart (*jo-gakusei*), particularly that select group attending postprimary institutions, drew much attention in public discourse as symbols of a new age and future inheritors of the Meiji task of nation building. As such, their conduct underwent constant scrutiny from adult critics, in whose eyes school days were a time for diligent study and not for sexual diversion.

Male-male sexuality served as a key site in the competition of discourses over student behavior, most conspicuously around the turn of the century. (For the sake of convenience, "student" will henceforth refer primarily to males.) Perceptions of student sexuality reflected not only broader anxieties about contemporary youth, but also shifting definitions of masculinity, regional and political rivalries, and the ongoing "civilization" of morality. A central feature in this discursive terrain may be found in a pair of terms from Mori Ōgai's 1909 autobiographical novel *Wita sekusuarisu* (Vita Sexualis) that I have chosen to translate as "roughnecks" (*kōha*) and "smoothies" (*nanpa*).[64] Since the distinction they articulate runs through many Meiji discussions of student culture and sexuality, let us first attempt to clarify their meaning.

When Mori looked back upon his experiences at the Tokyo English Academy during the 1870s, he recalled student behavior at this prestigious middle school as falling into two basic patterns. On the one hand, there were the "smoothies," who displayed a keen interest in male-female eroticism; on the other, there were the "roughnecks," who eschewed it, preferring instead to engage in male-male sexual relations.[65] On the surface, Mori's classification may seem to reproduce the "homosexual"/"heterosexual" di-

63. On the Meiji ideal of "success," see Earl H. Kinmonth, *The Self-Made Man in Meiji Japanese Thought: From Samurai to Salary Man* (Berkeley: University of California Press, 1981).

64. I have borrowed the term "roughneck" from Roden, but replaced his "softie" with the more symmetrical "smoothie." The discussion below is based on Mori, *Wita sekusuarisu*, 5:110–143. For an English translation, in which *kōha* and *nanpa* are rendered as "queer" and "masher" respectively, see Ninomiya and Goldstein, *Vita Sexualis*, 57–101. Mori's novel was banned shortly after its initial publication, although it had already circulated widely. See Rubin, *Injurious to Public Morals*, 130–135.

65. It is uncertain whether *kōha* and *nanpa* (literally, "hard faction" and "soft faction," used often in a political context) were terms that students at Mori's school would themselves have employed.

chotomy then on the rise in Western medical circles and with which Mori, a German-trained physician, was no doubt familiar.[66] A closer examination, however, reveals crucial differences.

First of all, it is important to note that both categories in Mori's taxonomy ranged students primarily along the axis of male-female relations. "Roughnecks" were "rough" (literally, "hard" or "obdurate") not because they engaged in male-male sexual practices, but because they steadfastly rejected erotic involvement with females. Male-male sexual practices fit into this schema as the less tabooed alternative to which "roughnecks" turned, as it were, by default. For Mori, it was not the nature of students' "sexual desire" (*seiyoku*) that was bifurcated, but rather the means by which they chose to enact it. Both "roughnecks" and "smoothies," after all, sought a penetrative role. Apparently, Mori did not regard the former's junior male sexual partners as "roughnecks" themselves, but instead as their "victims" (*gisei*) and "love objects" (*koi no taishōbutsu*)—or in student argot, simply "boys" (*shōnen*). Nor did Mori's labels designate a permanent status: the character Henmi, for instance, makes a swift transition from "roughneck" to "smoothie" at one point in the novel.

Mori's "roughneck"/"smoothie" classification can be understood as signifying two contending styles of masculinity. These styles encoded male-male and male-female sexual practices respectively, but also other aspects of student behavior, including apparel, mannerisms, pastimes, and speech. "Smoothies" at Mori's school, for example, did not tuck up their sleeves or swagger about with menacing shoulders like their "roughneck" peers, but instead dandified themselves in silk kimonos and white socks (*tabi*) in order to win the favor of women. The two styles also correlated with regional differences: Mori reports that his "roughneck" schoolmates hailed mostly from Kyushu, with some admixture from the southwest Honshu prefecture of Yamaguchi (the former Hagi domain), while "smoothies" sprang from regions farther to the northeast.

Tsubouchi Shōyō's 1885–1886 novel *Tōsei shosei katagi* (Spirit of Present-

66. For Mori's understanding of Western medical notions of male-male sexuality, see his 1889 article "Gaijō no koto o rokusu" (*Ōgai zenshū*, 29:154–156), which appeared originally in a forensic-pathology journal. In *Wita sekusuarisu* (5:111), Mori on one occasion uses the German term *Urning* to refer to the insertee partner in male-male sexual relations. On the representation of male-male eroticism in another one of Mori's novels (*Seinen*), see Dennis Washburn, "Manly Virtue and the Quest for Self: The *Bildungsroman* of Mori Ōgai," *Journal of Japanese Studies* 21 (1995): 24.

Day Students) provides further illustration of this dichotomy.[67] While Tsubouchi does not use the term itself, the quintessentially "roughneck" character here is Kiriyama Benroku, a male Kyushu native of twenty-three or twenty-four studying at a Tokyo school.[68] Like Mori's "roughnecks," he is described as wearing coarse garb and avidly reading *Shizu no odamaki*. A devotee of the martial arts, Kiriyama rejects any suggestion that the exercise of "brute strength" (*wanryoku*) might be "barbaric." In contrast to the manly vigor of Sengoku warriors, he regards his womanizing peers (Mori would have called them "smoothies") as weak—both the cause and effect of their consorting with females. Instead, Kiriyama, using the Chinese-derived term *ryūyō*, espouses erotic ties between males, maintaining that, unlike their male-female counterpart, they provide for an exchange of knowledge and foster ambition, neither of which qualities women in his view apparently possess.[69] Kiriyama is careful to insist, however, that such male-male intimacies must remain platonic (literally, "theoretical" [*rironjō*]), a stance that his fellow students, suspecting him of a less than purely philosophical interest in his young companion Miyaga, find somewhat disingenuous.

As exemplified in the figure of Kiriyama, the "roughneck" style drew heavily upon samurai ideals of masculinity. The notion, for instance, that males' proper company was with other males and that dalliances with women were undignified and emasculating echoed warrior traditions of homosociality and misogyny. Like Kiriyama, samurai critics would no doubt have described "smoothies" as *bunjaku*—weak through neglect of martial pursuits. This voluptuous, primarily urban *bunjaku* style had served during the Edo period as an alternate code of masculinity, "effeminate" from the point of view of samurai orthodoxy, yet much celebrated in popular writings and drama, especially among townsmen (and townswomen). Seen over the long term, it waxed in prominence as warrior culture declined. At Mori's school in the 1870s, however, the *bunjaku*/"smoothie" style had not yet eclipsed its "roughneck" rival: despite their numerical superiority, even "smoothies" recognized that the student's proper manner (*honshoku*) was "roughneck." In Tsubouchi's novel, too, which is set in the early 1880s, the two styles of masculinity are portrayed as locked in bitter contest, although

67. See Tsubouchi, *Tōsei shosei katagi*, 127–170.
68. Tsubouchi's equivalent for "roughnecks" is the "diehard party" (*gankotō*) or "brute-strength party" (*wanryokutō*); "smoothies" are referred to as the "profligate crowd" (*hōtōren*).
69. On the origin of the term *ryūyō* (Chinese: Long Yang), see Bret Hinsch, *Passions of the Cut Sleeve: The Male Homosexual Tradition in China* (Berkeley: University of California Press, 1990), 32. See also n. 24 above.

the rather lonely figure that Kiriyama cuts suggests that "roughnecks" were steadily losing ground.

Violence was another element of the "roughneck" style that harked back to the samurai past. The "brute strength" equated by Kiriyama with masculine prowess often held sway as well in "roughneck" erotic dealings. "Roughneck" sexual relations were not always coercive, of course. Mori describes, for instance, a set of crude hand signals whereby a "boy" could consent to or refuse a senior male's overtures; subtler forms of seduction involved treats, favors, and the prospect of "special protection" (*tokubetsu na hogo*) by the older party.[70] Resisting such advances, however, might in some cases lead to more forcible ones, as Mori's alter ego Kanai Shizuka discovers at the hands of a "roughneck" suitor. Indeed, the strict age hierarchy that prevailed in student society constrained the very notion of consent, since junior males were in principle supposed to obey the dictates of senior schoolmates. In such an environment, male-male sexual practices often took a predatory form, with younger students providing fodder for older ones.

One locus that emerges repeatedly in accounts of "roughneck" sexual aggression is the dormitory or student boardinghouse. Kanai in Mori's novel experiences two close calls in such a setting, in one of which multiple attackers attempt to gain his compliance by pinning him down under some bedding (*futonmushi*). The same type of assault appears in an anecdote related by Minakata Kumagusu about a schoolmate in the 1880s who, upon visiting some Kyushu students, was offered his choice of a sweet potato or a "boy."[71] Such victimization was occasionally ritualized, as in the custom of the "storm" (*sutōmu*) at the elite higher schools, which the historian Donald Roden describes as having "degenerated by the early 1900s into a nightly ordeal of violence and sometimes homosexual predation."[72] Similarly, Miura Gorō arrived at his post as principal of the army officers' academy in 1882 to find that students there were carrying out nocturnal "raids" (*shūgeki*) on the adjoining preparatory school, a practice he claims to have

70. Erotic hand signals had been used among priests and acolytes since at least the fifteenth century, on which see Kon Tōkō, *Chigo* (Ōtori shobō, 1947), 103–107. For a later example, see Mitsuo Sadatomo, *Kōbō Daishi ikkan no sho*, Kinsei shomin bunka 13 (1952): 15–16; Paul Gordon Schalow, "Kukai and the Tradition of Male Love in Japanese Buddhism," in *Buddhism, Sexuality, and Gender*, ed. José Ignacio Cabezón (Albany: State University of New York Press, 1992), 217–218.

71. Minakata Kumagusu to Iwata Jun'ichi, 20 September 1931, *Minakata Kumagusu zenshū*, 9:77. Inagaki Taruho ("Nanshoku kō yodan," in *Minakata Kumagusu zenshū*, 9:618–619) comments that middle-school students told similar stories for many more decades, although he regards them as by and large apocryphal.

72. Roden, *Schooldays in Imperial Japan*, 141.

put an end to by permitting younger cadets to defend themselves from their seniors by any means. Those who did not resist such "humiliation" (*ryōjoku*) faced expulsion as unsuited for military office.[73]

"Roughneck" violence drew most attention, however, when it emerged into the public spaces of the urban landscape. Like the Aizu rowdies who had vexed the authorities of their castle town during the late eighteenth and early nineteenth centuries, "roughneck" students at times did not hesitate to pursue their quarry on the streets of Tokyo and other Meiji cities. The scandal-laden "third pages" of turn-of-the-century newspapers provide abundant examples. The typical scenario in such accounts featured older adolescents, singly or in groups, stalking urban neighborhoods in search of a "beautiful boy," whom they would lure to a secluded place and exploit sexually through the use of force and intimidation. At times, such incidents were cut short by the intervention of police or passersby, and it was under these circumstances that they were most likely to reach the ears of the press. A second type of "roughneck" disturbance took the form of a fight or "showdown" (*kettō*), occasionally involving dozens of students, and was routinely attributed by newspapermen to rivalries over a "beautiful boy."

In reporting such incidents, the press was by no means a disinterested party. The wide publicity they gained around the turn of the century must be seen in part as the result of deliberate commercial strategy. By exposing such practices to public view and presenting them in ways calculated to stir alarm and outrage, newspaper companies sought to gain readers, and hence profits, as well as to demonstrate their social utility. Stories concerning students possessed a special relevance for newspapers' largely middle- and upper-class readership, since this was the stratum most likely to provide its offspring with an extended education. "Roughnecks" were also said to favor as victims "beautiful boys" from well-to-do families. Sensationalistic accounts of student (mis)behavior served to confirm existing anxieties over youth culture, but also to amplify them, following a pattern that the sociologist Stanley Cohen has labeled "moral panic."[74] The Tokyo-based daily *Yorozu chōhō* played a particularly vocal role in this process, and provides much of the material for the following discussion.[75]

The norm-breaking "folk devil" (to use Cohen's terminology) around whom moral panic erupted was in this case the "decadent student" (*daraku*

73. Miura Gorō, *Kanju shōgun kaikoroku* (Seikyōsha, 1925), 139–141.

74. Stanley Cohen, *Folk Devils and Moral Panics: The Creation of the Mods and Rockers*, 2d ed. (Oxford: Robertson, 1980).

75. I have examined *Yorozu chōhō* from the end of the Sino-Japanese (April 1895) to the beginning of the Russo-Japanese War (February 1904), a period that such

shosei). "Roughneck" behavior, particularly in its more violent and visible forms, figured as one of his traits; however, the category also embraced students who precociously indulged in male-female erotic relations (that is to say, "smoothies") or whose transgressions, such as skipping out of a restaurant without paying the bill, were of a nonsexual nature. The "decadent students" who appeared in newspaper accounts generally attended middle schools, although many of them were already in their twenties. Sometimes they were not even students, or at least not currently enrolled as such, but merely assimilated into this group by virtue of their adolescence.

In referring to male-male sexual practices among "decadent students," journalists availed themselves of, thereby reinforcing, the prevailing idiom of "civilized morality." A *Yorozu* editorialist, for example, excoriated present-day students for being either "weak" (*nanjaku*) or "bestial" (*yajū no gotoki*)—another variant of the "smoothie"/"roughneck" dichotomy—and asserted that the latter group, with their "barbarous activities" (*yaban no kōi*), would have felt right at home in the *nanshoku*-ridden days of ancient Rome.[76] The author of a Chinese-style poem (*kanshi*), on the other hand, reached back into the Japanese past for an analogy, suggesting that the prevalence of *nanshoku* among middle-school students portended a return to the decadence of the Genroku era.[77] Publicization of such contemporary practices thus raised the alarming possibility that male-male sexuality was not receding into the past, its usual trajectory in Meiji discourse, but threatened to break out of the "museum" of history into the living present.

Moral panic over "roughneck" practices was further fueled by the rhetoric of contagion and cabalism.[78] In the spring of 1899, *Yorozu* alerted readers to the existence of a shadowy organization of "decadent students" known as Byakkotai, after the white skirt-trousers (*hakama*) its adherents were said to wear.[79] Members reportedly coerced "beautiful boys" into sexual submission by threatening to call out their comrades in force; victims

authors as Takada Giichirō (*Tōseijutsu* [Hakubunkan, 1928], 100), Tanizaki Jun'ichirō (*Yōshō jidai*, in *Tanizaki Jun'ichirō zenshū*, 28 vols. [Chūō kōronsha, 1966–1971], 17:119), and Ubukata Toshirō (*Meiji Taishō kenbunshi* [Chūō kōronsha, 1978], 100–101) have described as the heyday of the "roughneck."

76. "Gakusei no daraku," pt. 2, *Yorozu chōhō*, 9 April 1899, 1.

77. "Ryūyō-kun," *Yorozu chōhō*, 6 February 1897, 1.

78. On the role of contagion and cabalism in the rhetorical inventory of moral panic, see Cohen, *Folk Devils*, 62–64.

79. The group's name is homophonous, perhaps not fortuitously, with that of a band of young Aizu samurai who fought valiantly but perished on the bakufu side at the time of the Restoration.

were then initiated into the organization, and would eventually use similar means to ensnare their own prey.[80] In this way, journalists evoked the image of a growing conspiracy that was menacing the student body and endangering the well-being of the nation at large. And indeed, subsequent coverage portrayed Byakkotai activities as expanding into new areas (among them male-female erotic pursuits), while also revealing the operation of similar groups throughout Tokyo.

Such reportage surely had its factual basis, although it is difficult to separate this out from the embellishments and misperceptions of journalists themselves. Newspapers appear, however, to have presented a distorted picture of these groups through such techniques as inflating their numbers (it was claimed, for example, that Byakkotai had as many as eighteen hundred members), focusing on their most nefarious activities, and suggesting a greater degree of intra- and interorganizational cohesion than actually prevailed.[81] As depicted in the press, the structure of some was suspiciously elaborate: a group known as Sōryū gidan ("Righteous Band of the Blue Dragon"), for instance, was alleged to have separate divisions devoted to raping females, dueling, eating and drinking, firing pistols, and, of course, ravishing boys.[82] Journalists also tended to attribute incidents to previously known groups without a proven connection, thus augmenting the sense of conspiracy.

If *Yorozu* and other newspapers sought to promote fear and panic, their efforts appear to have been successful. Readers wrote to express their alarm at this new menace, while young students, particularly those with attractive features, were said to be afraid to go out alone or even attend school.[83] The author Tanizaki Seiji later recollected of his boyhood in turn-of-the-century Tokyo that whenever he and his brother Jun'ichirō, the later novelist, heard a whistle (rumored to signal a "roughneck" attack) on the street at night, they would start running immediately.[84] The public knowledge of "roughneck" predation that press accounts helped spread even prompted one fifteen-year-old to invent a story about being assaulted by an older adoles-

80. "Byakkotai no ōkō," *Yorozu chōhō*, 6 March 1899, 3.

81. "Mitabi Sōryū gidan no koto," *Yorozu chōhō*, 11 March 1900, 3.

82. "Sōryū gidan no koto," *Yorozu chōhō*, 7 March 1900, 3; "Mitabi Sōryū gidan no koto."

83. "Gakusei no fūki mondai," *Nihon*, 28 February 1898, 2, citing the educational journal *Kyōiku jiron*; "Yorozu kogoto," *Yorozu chōhō*, 8 March 1900, 3.

84. Quoted in Inagaki Taruho, "Miyatake Gaikotsu no *Bishōnenron*," in *Inagaki Taruho taizen*, ed. Hagiwara Sachiko and Kawahito Hiroshi, 6 vols. (Gendai shichōsha, 1969–1970), 2:345. Tanizaki Jun'ichirō recalls similar brushes with "roughnecks," and in one case an army officer, in *Yōshō jidai*, 17:94–96, 118–119.

cent, complete with the requisite *hakama* and Kagoshima accent, in order to escape punishment for returning tardily to his parental home.[85]

Newspapers called for, and no doubt encouraged, increased vigilance on the part of what Cohen refers to as the "control culture." Police and educational authorities around the turn of the century devoted much attention to the "roughneck" problem, which journalists, particularly those at *Yorozu*, were quick to credit to their own expository efforts. Measures devised to deal with it included guarding youngsters on their way to and from school, keeping tabs on known troublemakers, and stricter enforcement of "obscenity" provisions.[86] Campaigns to discourage "roughneck" behavior were also launched in such institutions as Tokyo's First Higher School, where the accession of the Christian educator Nitobe Inazō as headmaster in 1906 is said to have marked a critical turning point.[87] One journalist recommended the time-honored method of serving culprits with a ritual beating (*tekken seisai*), while a foreign observer suggested that students form councils of honor along the lines of the German *Ehrenrat* to monitor the activities of their peers.[88] Newspapers also urged greater watchfulness in the home, chastising parents who let their sons go about in white *hakama*.[89]

The journalistic crusade against "roughnecks" must also be seen in a political context. It was no accident that press attacks on the "Satsuma habit" surfaced at a time when domination of the national government by the so-called "Satsuma clique" (*Satsubatsu*) faced mounting criticism, especially in such liberal organs as *Yorozu*. "The greatest influence that the leaders of domain-clique government have bestowed on the youth of Tokyo," charged the newspaper sardonically, "is [to encourage] *nanshoku* and fighting."[90] Those who chased "beautiful boys," one writer suggested, were either the progeny of such officials or were imitating what they had done in their younger days.[91] The journalist and social critic Ubukata Toshirō has claimed

85. "Kokuso no torikeshi," *Yorozu chōhō*, 21 October 1898, 3.

86. "Gakusei no hogo kantoku," *Yorozu chōhō*, 19 November 1899, 2; "Yaban gakusei no torishimari," *Yorozu chōhō*, 16 February 1898, 2; "Yotabi Sōryū gidan no koto," *Yorozu chōhō*, 12 March 1900, 3.

87. Roden, *Schooldays in Imperial Japan*, 206, citing a student essay by Watsuji Tetsurō.

88. "The Defect in the Criminal Code," *Eastern World*, 27 May 1899, 7; Kawaoka, "Gakusei no anmen," 78. For a description of *tekken seisai*, see Roden, *Schooldays in Imperial Japan*, 147–150.

89. "Daraku shōnen Byakkotai no shūkō," *Yorozu chōhō*, 25 March 1899, 3.

90. "Sōryū gidan no koto."

91. Matsui Shōyō, "Bōkokuron," pt. 4, *Yorozu chōhō*, 18 April 1899, 1.

that police often overlooked "roughneck" offenses because both patrolmen and perpetrators tended to be fellow Satsumaites.[92] Yet while there may have been an element of truth to this perception, it is also clear from newspaper accounts that offenders were by no means limited to natives of Satsuma or even of the general southwest region.

Yorozu's implication that a "Satsuma wind [or flu] was sweeping east-ward" toward the capital, carrying male-male sexual practices with it, was a frightening reversal of conventional trajectories.[93] All three vectors of mar-ginalization, in fact, converged in press coverage of the "roughneck." He was an adolescent, standing at a critical juncture in masculine development and in that of the nation. He embodied practices that harked back to Japan's "barbarous" past. And he embraced a style strongly associated with regional particularism. This was not a social type, journalists fulminated, that an "en-lightened age" (*kaimei no yo*) should countenance, especially in the impe-rial capital of Tokyo, which, as one *Yorozu* editorialist put it, ought to be the "most civilized place in the country."[94] The fact that Westerners were from 1899 allowed to dwell freely among the Japanese populace, where they could witness firsthand any "uncivilized" behavior, lent further resonance to such exposés and, by *Yorozu's* own admission, provided a tool for shaming au-thorities into action.[95]

The turn-of-the-century panic over the "roughneck" reveals a crucial moment in the discursive contestation of masculinity and of male sexual-ity. From the point of view of the control culture, any form of student sex-ual activity was improper; what was being contested in the main was whether male-male or male-female eroticism represented the greater dan-ger. Journalistic exposés presented both as equivalent forms of "decadence," but in the process raised male-male sexual practices to a new level of vis-ibility, highlighting their most violent and socially disruptive manifesta-tions. It was becoming increasingly difficult to maintain that male-male eroticism was a permissible alternative to male-female—at least publicly. When education minister Komatsubara Eitarō allegedly remarked in 1909 that *nanshoku* was "at any rate masculine" (*tomokakumo otokorashii*), and thus preferable to "chasing the skirts of schoolgirls," his words provoked a

92. Ubukata, *Meiji Taishō kenbunshi*, 71.
93. "Byakkotai no ōkō."
94. "Byakkotai no ōkō"; "Gakusei no daraku," pt. 1, *Yorozu chōhō*, 26 April 1901, 1.
95. Matsui Shōyō, "Bōkokuron"; "Degenerated Tokyo Students," *Yorozu chōhō*, 26 May 1899, 2. See also the (possibly concocted) letter from a foreigner in "Yorozu kogoto."

furor.[96] Nevertheless, for all the attention that "roughnecks" received, their skirt-chasing schoolmates continued to elicit a greater degree of public anxiety. In a 1909 magazine poll, for example, while *nanshoku* ranked high among the "most heinous temptations corrupting young students," it was *joshoku* that qualified as the number-one response.[97]

By placing "roughnecks" in the public spotlight, journalists contributed to a growing discursive association of male-male sexuality with the world of adolescence. Henceforth, discussions of male-male sexuality in post-Restoration Japan would inevitably mention student society, and dormitories in particular, as a typical—perhaps the most typical—site of its occurrence. Conversely, accounts of school life frequently portray the culture of male-male eroticism as one of its distinctive features, including memoirs by such figures as Ōsugi Sakae (himself a former "roughneck"), Iwaya Sazanami, and Ubukata Toshirō, and novels and stories by Dazai Osamu, Hori Tatsuo, Kawabata Yasunari, Mushanokōji Saneatsu, Origuchi Shinobu, Satomi Ton, Tanizaki Jun'ichirō, and Uno Kōji, to name just a few.[98]

One function of the discursive link between male-male sexuality and adolescence was to maintain a respectable distance between the former and the world of "civilized" adulthood. When adults railed against "roughnecks," it was with the hope that they could still be reformed into mature and responsible citizens like themselves; that, given time, they would come to regard their adolescent misdeeds as part of a youth now past, of a subjectivity they no longer embraced or even understood. It is this mood of recollection in tranquillity, of lost youth, that pervades many of the memoirs and fictional writings already mentioned. In some cases, the perception of male-male sexuality as an adolescent aberration served to soften adult responses to it. Even in journalistic treatments of the "roughneck," one may

96. Iwaya Sazanami, "Nanshoku no benkai," *Chūō kōron*, March 1909, 75. Komatsubara was evidently misquoted.

97. "<Kingindōhai kenshō mondai> Seinen gakusei o fuhai daraku seshimuru mottomo nikumubeki yūwaku no jibutsu goko o tōhyō no kekka," *Bōken sekai*, September 1909, 7. Exact rankings appear only for the five most popular answers (the other four are "obscene" novels, dandyism, "evil places," and leisure), but *nanshoku* is listed at the top of the "other" category.

98. Dazai Osamu, "Omoide," in *Dazai Osamu zenshū*, 13 vols. (Chikuma shobō, 1957–1972), 1:22–60; Hori Tatsuo, "Kao," in *Hori Tatsuo zenshū*, ed. Nakamura Shin'ichirō et al., 11 vols. (Chikuma shobō, 1977–1980), 1:267–288; Hori Tatsuo, "Moyuru hō," in *Hori Tatsuo zenshū*, 1:207–222 (trans. Jack Rucinski under the title "Les joues en feu," in *The Shōwa Anthology: Modern Japanese Short Stories*, ed. Van Gessel and Tomone Matsumoto, 2 vols. [Tokyo: Kodansha International, 1985], 1:28–37); Iwaya Sazanami, *Watakushi no konjaku monogatari* (Waseda

detect two strains of criticism—one branding him as "wicked" and "immoral," the other as merely "foolish" (*bakabakashii*). It should be remembered, too, that since "roughneck" sexual assaults constituted criminal "obscene acts," due both to the use of coercion and to the fact that many victims were minors, they were subject to severe punishment under penal law (up to two years plus a fine under the 1880 code); yet a surprising number of offenders seem to have been let off with no more than a reprimand (*setsuyu*) from police.

Before leaving the "roughneck," let us trace his footsteps a bit further into the twentieth century. The student culture of male-male eroticism long outlasted turn-of-the-century attempts to extirpate it. When Kagoshima authorities launched such a campaign around 1909, it even met with some pedagogical opposition.[99] *Chigo-nise* ties (that is, erotic relationships between junior and senior youths) were reportedly common here as late as the 1940s, while student memoirs and other accounts describe similar attachments in schools outside the region.[100] With the twentieth-century rise of the notion of "same-sex love," however, popular representations of such relationships would come increasingly to focus on their psychological features, rather than on physical predation of the Meiji type. By midcentury, the nuance of male-male sexual activity that was once embedded in the term "roughneck" (*kōha*) had largely dropped out, although *nanpa* is still used by present-day students to signify "picking up" girls.

The "roughneck"/"smoothie" dichotomy emerges also in early twentieth-century discussions of the "juvenile delinquent" (*furyō shōnen*). This figure was less specifically linked with the school environment than the turn-of-the-century "decadent student," but shared with him a notoriety for banding together with fellow "no-goods" (this is the literal meaning of

daigaku shuppanbu, 1928), 52–55; Kawabata Yasunari, *Shōnen*, in *Kawabata Yasunari zenshū*, ed. Yamamoto Kenkichi et al., 37 vols. (Shinchōsha, 1980–1984), 10:141–255; Mushanokōji Saneatsu, "Kare," in *Mushanokōji Saneatsu zenshū*, ed. Inagaki Tatsurō et al., 18 vols. (Shōgakkan, 1988–1991), 1:3–17; Origuchi Shinobu, "Kuchibue," in *Origuchi Shinobu zenshū*, ed. Origuchi hakase kinen kodai kenkyūjo, 32 vols. (Chūō kōronsha, 1965–1968), 24:1–78; Ōsugi Sakae, *Jijoden* (Kaizōsha, 1948; trans. Byron K. Marshall under the title *The Autobiography of Ōsugi Sakae* [Berkeley: University of California Press, 1992]); Satomi Ton, *Kimi to watashi*, in *Satomi Ton zenshū*, 10 vols. (Chikuma shobō, 1977–1979), 1:85–201; Tanizaki Jun'ichirō, "Akubi," in *Tanizaki Jun'ichirō zenshū*, 1:299–329; Tanizaki Jun'ichirō, "Itansha no kanashimi," in *Tanizaki Jun'ichirō zenshū*, 4:377–452; Ubukata, *Meiji Taishō kenbunshi*; Uno Kōji, "Futari no Aoki Aizaburō," in *Uno Kōji zenshū*, ed. Hirotsu Kazuo et al., 12 vols. (Chūō kōronsha, 1978–1979), 3:196–241.

99. Kawaoka, "Gakusei no anmen," 78.
100. Kagoshima-shi gakusha rengōkai, *Shikon*, 15.

furyō) to disturb the urban peace. Observers commonly divided youth gangs into *kōha* and *nanpa* varieties, these labels again connoting a wide array of masculine behaviors in addition to distinct sexual codes. Echoing Mori, one commentator wrote in 1914 that "juvenile delinquents" of the "rough-neck" stripe saw themselves as "toughs" (*sōshi*) and "swashbucklers" (*kyō-kaku*), while "smoothies" fancied themselves "high-collar dandies" (*haikara danji*).[101] Among their various depredations, "roughneck" gangs followed the Byakkotai pattern of roaming the streets in search of "beautiful boys," and by the early 1910s had been spotted not only in Tokyo, but in such cities as Nagoya, Osaka, Kobe, and Nagasaki.[102] With the close of the Meiji period, however, such reports began gradually to diminish, until, by the end of the 1920s, most "juvenile delinquents" had become, according to one authority on the subject, confirmed *nanpa*.[103] In the popular imagination, "rough" was no match for "smooth."

BEAUTIFUL BOYS

In examining the "roughneck," we have thus far focused our attention on one half of the asymmetric dyad that made up a male-male erotic relationship as it was conceived in the Edo period—namely, the senior, sexually penetrative partner. To round out the discussion, let us now turn to its other half, who in Meiji times was often designated the *bishōnen* or "beautiful boy." By fixing our gaze on the *bishōnen*, we are in effect assuming the characteristic stance of Edo-period popular discourse on male-male sexuality. The *wakashu* had stood at the center of this discourse, but primarily as the target of masculine consumption, an erotic object more than a desiring subject. This ambiguity was contained in the word *shudō*, whose characters literally meant the "way of youths," yet whose actual sense was the "way of loving youths," its unspoken yet implicit subject a senior male. The emblematic usage of the boy or youth to signify male-male sexuality as a whole remained common throughout the Meiji period. Thus, when Kōmurō

101. Yamamoto Seikichi, *Gendai no furyō seinen, tsuketari furyō joshi* (Shun'yōdō, 1914), 46.
102. Hanabusa Shirō [Nakano Masato], *Nanshoku kō* (Hassōdō shoin, 1928), 76; Hino Mitsuo, ed., "<Gojūnenkan no vēru o nuida kisho> Kōmurō Shujin-cho *Bishō-nenron, ichimei dōsei shikijōshi*," pt. 1, *Erochika*, October 1970, 221. For the activities of Tokyo-based "roughneck" and "smoothie" gangs in and around the seaside resort of Misaki, see "Furyō shōnen hishochi o nerau," *Tōkyō nichinichi shinbun*, 25 July 1913, 7.
103. Nakahara Keizō, "Saikin furyō shōnen shōjo monogatari," *Chūō kōron*, December 1929, 152.

Shujin—literally, the "master of the red dream mansion"—penned in 1911 what seems to be the period's only book-length treatise on male-male eroticism, it was the "beautiful boy" that he chose for his title.[104]

Kōmurō Shujin's *Bishōnenron* (On the Beautiful Boy) presents an intriguing mixture of inherited Japanese, classical Chinese, and contemporary medico-scientific knowledge concerning male-male sexuality. By the second decade of the twentieth century, the medical model of "same-sex love" had begun to move outside such specialized realms as forensic pathology and into the broader arena of public discourse, as the following two chapters will examine in detail. In Kōmurō Shujin's work, the primary effect of this paradigm was to bring to the fore the psychology and physiology of the "beautiful boy" in a manner that would become increasingly common as the century progressed. Kōmurō Shujin cited an impressive array of Western authorities on "same-sex love," most of them doctors or scientists who believed that the "passive" partner in male-male intercourse differed from others of his sex on the basis of certain mental and physical peculiarities, both inborn and acquired. At the same time, the author's understanding of Western sexology was filtered through a set of native assumptions, emerging in a form that often differed in telling ways from the intentions of the original theorists.

Thus, for instance, when Kōmurō Shujin spoke of the "congenital" (*sententeki*) factors that marked a "passive" (*judōteki*) partner, what he had in mind was not so much the biological issue of heredity, as was typically the case in the Western literature he quoted, but simply "attractive features" (*bibō*) and a "gentle disposition" (*yūjū no saga*).[105] In citing the first characteristic, Kōmurō Shujin shared the perspective of many of his Edo-period and Meiji predecessors, who viewed beauty as existing not in the eye of the beholder but as an intrinsic quality of the youthful male form. Beauty could be expected to stimulate erotic desire in men whether it was embodied in a

104. The original work was withdrawn from publication at the last minute because the author would not agree to revise its more explicit passages (some of which are reproduced in Kimoto Itaru, <Hyōden> *Miyatake Gaikotsu* [Shakai shisōsha, 1984], 641–642) so as to avoid censorship. A truncated version nevertheless circulated under various titles during the 1910s, making a strong impression upon the young Inagaki Taruho. One of these surreptitious editions is reprinted in Hino, "Kōmurō Shujin-cho *Bishōnenron*," although Hino's claim (pt. 1, 216–217) that Kōmurō Shujin was none other than Minakata Kumagusu I find difficult to swallow. See also Inagaki Taruho, "Miyatake Gaikotsu no *Bishōnenron*," 2:340–398, which contains a modernized version of the text, and Kimoto, *Miyatake Gaikotsu*, 357–360, which mentions a contemporary rumor that the author was a former newspaper reporter.
105. Hino, "Kōmurō Shujin-cho *Bishōnenron*," pt. 1, 220, 225.

woman or a youth, and those who appreciated it were not regarded as in any way physiologically distinct or pathological. Thus, in dealing with the "roughneck," some commentators reacted by in effect blaming the victim, as when a Nagasaki physician claimed, toward the end of the Meiji period, that "roughneck" assaults were prompted by schoolboys' habit of rolling up their hems, thus exposing bare legs, on rainy days, or when a contemporary journalist attributed the prevalence of *nanshoku* among students to the proximity of "beautiful boy" schoolmates.[106]

Meiji literature, like that of the Edo period, often paid homage to young male beauty, although changes could be observed in both form and content. Yamada Bimyō, a member of the Ken'yūsha circle, for example, chose a traditional array of "beautiful boys"—Hirata Sangorō, Oda Nobunaga's cherished page Mori Ranmaru, *Chidaruma*'s Ōkawa Kazuma, among others—for the subject matter of his 1886 *Wakashu sugata* (Youthful Figures), but selected as his medium the *shintaishi*, a new genre of freestyle verse that had emerged under the influence of Western poetry.[107] Similarly, beneath its more contemporary diction and format, Inaoka Masafumi's 1900 novel *Bishōnen* echoed many aspects of Takizawa Bakin's *Kinsesetsu bishōnen-roku*, published over a half a century earlier—chief among them the authors' contrast between one youth who uses his charm to serve his lord and country and another who employs it against them.[108]

While Yamada and Inaoka linked the "beautiful boy" with the Japanese past, featuring him as page boy, youthful warrior, or acolyte, others presented him in a more up-to-date guise. By the end of the Meiji period, the term *bishōnen* itself was perhaps most likely to evoke the figure of a young student, decked out in a stylish (*haikara*) Western-style school uniform. This was the image that a magazine illustrator chose in 1909 to characterize the "beautiful boy of today" (see cover illustration); with him in the drawing stood his Edo-period counterpart, evidently a *kagema*, described in an accompanying caption as "emasculated" (*otoko no kusatta*).[109] The Meiji period also saw the rise of "boys' literature" (*shōnen bungaku*), whose *bishō-*

106. Hino, "Kōmurō Shujin-cho *Bishōnenron*," pt. 1, 224; Kawaoka, "Gakusei no anmen," 73.

107. Yamada Bimyō, <*Shintai shika*> *Wakashu sugata* (Kōun shooku, 1886).

108. Inaoka, *Bishōnen*. On representations of the "beautiful boy" in Bakin's works, see Matsuda Osamu, *Hanamoji no shisō: Nihon ni okeru shōnen'ai no seishinshi* (Peyotoru kōbō, 1988), 80–145; Takada Mamoru, *Edo gensō bungakushi* (Heibonsha, 1987), 226–253.

109. Kawaoka, "Gakusei no anmen," 74. Alternatively, the essayist Yokoyama Kendō (Kurozukin, "Gashu no bishonen," *Chūō kōron*, January 1912, 137) recommended that Westerners who wished to gain a sense of the ideal Japanese *bishōnen*

nen heroes were typically schoolboys, but might also be called upon to sail the seven seas in search of adventure or take part in other stirring exploits. Unlike the equally well-beloved Meiji genre of "boys' theater" (*shōnen shibai*), whose audience consisted largely of adults, "boys' literature" was consumed primarily by boys themselves, its characters intended to provoke not only admiration but emulation.

In portraying the *bishōnen*, Meiji authors continued to employ conventional literary tropes of youthful male beauty: snowy white skin, lustrous black hair, flowery red cheeks, and so forth. While these figures were also used to describe female beauty, there remained alive in Meiji popular discourse a sense of the young male as esthetically distinct from both women and men.[110] This perception was rooted in the virile gaze, which in the Edo period had imagined the *wakashu* not so much as a co-member of the masculine gender, except in the broadest sense, but rather as belonging to a special status, albeit only a temporary one. The "beautiful boy" of Meiji times, too, represented both the antithesis and the antecedent of adult masculinity. Although he might share certain qualities of form and temperament with women—Kōmurō Shujin's "attractive features" and "gentle disposition," for example—he was set apart from them because of his potential manhood,

---

should observe young cadets aboard a naval training ship. Inagaki Taruho ("Minakata Kumagusu chigo dangi," in *Inagaki Taruho taizen*, 2:403) has suggested that the *bishōnen* esthetic of the Meiji period favored the more rough-and-ready *hankara* type over the somewhat androgynous delicacy of the *kagema*. Class and regional dynamics may have been involved here, since the former echoed the ideal of provincial warriors, while the latter was associated with metropolitan *shudō* culture.

110. I do not share Watanabe Tsuneo's view that post-Restoration Japan saw a "de-eroticisation of the male body," since the *adult* male was not eroticized (from the perspective, at least, of other adult males) either before or after the Restoration, while the de-eroticization of the *wakashu/bishōnen* belongs more properly to the early twentieth century than to the "first years" of the Meiji era. See Watanabe Tsuneo, "Kindai, dansei, dōseiai tabū," pt. 1 of "Bunmei oyobi tōsaku no gainen," *Kōchi daigaku gakujutsu kenkyū hōkoku: Jinbun kagaku* 29 (1980): 27–45; Tsuneo Watanabe and Jun'ichi Iwata, *Love of the Samurai*, 129–133. Interestingly, in contemporary Japanese popular culture, the figure of the *bishōnen* serves as an object of erotic longing or identification primarily for adolescent girls, on which see Tomoko Aoyama, "Male Homosexuality As Treated by Japanese Women Writers," in *The Japanese Trajectory: Modernization and Beyond*, ed. Gavan McCormack and Yoshio Sugimoto (Cambridge: Cambridge University Press, 1988), 186–204; Midori Matsui, "Little Girls Were Little Boys: Displaced Femininity in the Representation of Homosexuality in Japanese Girls' Comics," in *Feminism and the Politics of Difference*, ed. Sneja Gunew and Anna Yeatman (Boulder, Colo.: Westview, 1993), 177–196.

the incipient manifestations of which only underscored the fleetingness of his beauty.

There were signs, however, particularly from around the turn of the century, of a growing concern over the "beautiful boy's" place in the scheme of gender and sexuality. During the Edo period, the transition from youth to adult manhood had rarely been problematized, appearing instead as a natural part of masculine development. Indeed, folklore furnished many examples of male favorites who had gone on to achieve adult greatness, including the twelfth-century warrior-hero Minamoto Yoshitsune and the powerful sixteenth-century daimyo Ishida Mitsunari. Meiji commentators, on the other hand, began to suggest that a less enviable future awaited "beautiful boys" who submitted to the erotic attentions of older males.

The author and journalist Kawaoka Chōfū, for example, incensed by Mori's casual portrayal of male-male sexuality in *Vita Sexualis*, responded with a magazine exposé titled "Denouncing the Great Evil of *Nanshoku* That Lurks beneath the Surface of Student Society." In it, Kawaoka warned not only that the pursuit of "beautiful boys" would impede the accumulation of phosphorus in a "roughneck's" brain, thus stunting intellectual and moral growth, but that "beautiful boys" involved in *nanshoku* would themselves never attain the full flower of manhood. Once corrupted, even the most promising *bishōnen* was doomed to spend his adult days as, at best, a "humble office worker" (*koshiben*) or an "impertinent prig" (*chokozaishi*), since serving as sexual partner to another male bred such unmanly qualities as suspicion, jealousy, and a desire to curry the favor of others. Furthermore, this "evil" was self-perpetuating, for those males who had experienced a position of sexual subservience were bound to take their revenge upon the next generation of "beautiful boys."[111]

While Kawaoka saw the effects of male insertee status as dangerous and long lasting, he nevertheless envisioned an eventual transition from this role to that of inserter, and did not exclude the possibility of subsequent male-female relations. Others, however, began to view the *bishōnen* as the youthful phase of a more permanent sexual psychology, whose ultimate trajectory was exclusively male-male sexual interaction and feminine rather than masculine gender identity. Kōmurō Shujin, for instance, devoted much of his essay to the phenomenon of "effemination" (*joseiteki keikō*), originally elaborated by such Western sexologists as Richard von Krafft-Ebing. By engaging in male-male sexual practices as the "passive" partner, Kōmurō Shujin maintained, the *bishōnen* ran the risk not only of acquiring the psy-

111. Kawaoka, "Gakusei no anmen," 75–78.

chological characteristics of a woman, but of actually manifesting physiological changes that would bring his body in closer alignment with female anatomy.[112]

This medicalization of male-male sexuality will be discussed at greater length in the following chapters; here, we need only note that its initial impact fell more heavily upon the "beautiful boy" than on his pursuer. In the Meiji period, the "roughneck" appeared a problem more of morality than of medicine, Kawaoka's warnings about phosphorus depletion constituting in this respect the exception rather than the rule. Kōmurō Shujin noted, for instance, that while the "passive" partner in *nanshoku* was inherently suited for this role by virtue of his looks and temperament, any male might take the "active" (*shudōteki*) role as a result of environment, customs, lack of education, or a "diminished moral sense" (*tokugishin no teigen*). By the same token, not even the sternest of upbringings or disciplined education could prevent a "beautiful boy" from falling victim to "roughnecks."[113] Desire for a "beautiful boy," in other words, existed potentially in the heart of every man; the important issue was whether or not he acted upon it.

This separation of desire and practice was, in a sense, the very essence of "civilized morality." It was only through a constant moral effort that "civilization" could be prevented from reverting to "barbarism"; or, as Kōmurō Shujin put it, "Strip away the mask of civilization, and we see the beast."[114] No such schism had existed in the *shudō* construct: its disciplinary norms served, rather, to regulate the translation of male-male sexual desire into practice in a manner that was both pleasurable and proper. By contrast, under the regime of "civilized morality," while pleasure remained polymorphous, propriety belonged only to those sexual acts that took place between married males and females.

Thus, positive affirmations of male-male eroticism in popular discourse (examples of which are comparatively few in number) inevitably stopped short of its physical consummation. We have already seen how the character Kiriyama in *Tōsei shosei katagi* was careful to preach his doctrine of "*ryūyō*ism" (*ryūyōshugi*) at a "theoretical" rather than "practical" (*jissai*) level. Similarly, when the Meiji literary critic Taoka Reiun waxed nostalgic over male-male erotic ties during his youth in 1880s Kōchi prefecture, he

---

112. Hino, "Kōmurō Shujin-cho *Bishōnenron*," pt. 1, 229–245; Hino, "Kōmurō Shujin-cho *Bishōnenron*," pt. 2, *Erochika*, November 1970, 209–212.

113. Hino, "Kōmurō Shujin-cho *Bishōnenron*," pt. 1, 225.

114. Hino, "Kōmurō Shujin-cho *Bishōnenron*," pt. 2, 214.

felt obliged to differentiate between their "emotional" (*seishinteki*) component, in no way inferior to male-female love, and physical "acts" (*kōdō*), which ran contrary to law and "nature" (*shizen*).[115] At the base of such distinctions lay a dichotomy between the body and spirit akin to the earlier-mentioned separation of desire and practice, and reflected also in the emergence during the Meiji period of a Western-influenced notion of spiritual "love" (*rabu*) between men and women that stood in contrast to the older and more physically grounded *iro*.[116]

Meiji discourse likewise constructed a barrier between male-male sexuality and masculine friendship, which in *shudō* had formed part of the same continuum. In a 1907 essay titled "Dōsei no koi" (Love for the Same Sex), the future playwright Akita Ujaku described at length the deep emotional bond that had existed between himself and a male friend, recently deceased, noting that "in olden times" such attachments as theirs "might even have involved physical relations."[117] The implication, of course, was that "civilized" society would not tolerate such a mixture. Now, even the suspicion of sexual involvement might taint the purity of friendship, prompting Kawaoka to wonder if the day would not soon come when older and younger males could not associate intimately for fear of gossip, nor migrants from the same locality (*dōkyō*) set up housekeeping together without raising eyebrows—both distinct possibilities, it might be added, in Japan today.[118]

The decoupling of desire and practice, body and spirit, sexuality and sociality all helped to undermine the cognitive foundations of *shudō*. Cut loose from the broader ethical and esthetic context in which the *shudō* construct had framed them, male-male sexual practices came to be perceived as no more than physical events—"obscene acts," in legal parlance. *Shudō*, which as a word was growing obsolete by the end of the Edo period, had by the end of Meiji become all but incomprehensible.[119] As a consequence, writers would find it necessary to expend increasing amounts of ink in order to explain its significance.

115. Taoka, *Sūkiden*, 5:553.

116. On shifting conceptions of male-female love, see Saeki Junko, "'Ren'ai' no zenkindai, kindai, datsukindai," in *Sekushuariti no shakaigaku*, ed. Inoue Suguru et al., Iwanami kōza gendai shakaigaku, no. 10 (Iwanami shoten, 1996), 167–184.

117. Akita Ujaku, "Dōsei no koi," *Waseda bungaku*, June 1907, 32.

118. Kawaoka, "Gakusei no anmen," 75.

119. Thus, one 1904 erotic manual for women, its author female, used the term *shudō* to signify male-female anal intercourse—a meaning it had not carried, except

Some of the most painstaking efforts to preserve *shudō*'s lost resonances issued from the brush of the ethnographer and biologist Minakata Kumagusu. Minakata's own life span encompassed an era of rapidly changing sexual cartographies. Born in 1867 in Wakayama domain, he was able to hear firsthand accounts of monastic sexual practices on nearby Mount Kōya from those who had served as acolytes there in the waning years of the Edo period. Likewise, as a student in early Meiji Japan, Minakata was no stranger to "roughneck" eroticism. In addition, through his prolonged residence and travel abroad, Minakata became one of the first Japanese to acquire an extensive knowledge of Western literature on male-male sexuality. In his largely epistolary writings on the subject, dating from the 1890s until shortly before his death in 1941, Minakata could thus combine a command of native (and classical Chinese) sources that few educated after the Meiji period could claim with a cosmopolitan erudition that encouraged him to regard them in a broader cross-cultural and transhistorical perspective.[120]

In 1931, Minakata approached fellow ethnographer Iwata Jun'ichi, thirty-three years his junior, with some words of advice concerning the latter's recently published research into the history of male-male sexuality in Japan, thereby launching a correspondence that would last a decade and fill several hundred pages of Minakata's collected works.[121] In addition to providing a wealth of factual information, Minakata's letters bear witness to the profound shift in perceptions of male-male eroticism that had occurred over the course of his lifetime. According to Minakata, Japanese of Iwata's generation had lost sight of the spiritual and ethical dimensions of *nanshoku* (a term he preferred to the by then more popular *dōseiai* or "same-sex love"), mistakenly regarding the love of "beautiful boys" in earlier times as simply a matter of "getting ass" (*kōtei o nerōte*; literally, "aiming for the

---

perhaps in a jocular sense, during the Edo period. See Kinkin Joshi, *Jokeikun*, in *Nihon seiten taikan*, ed. Takahashi Tetsu, 2 vols. (Nihon seikatsu shinri gakkai, 1954), 2:122–123.

120. For a more detailed discussion of Minakata's views on male-male sexuality, see Nakazawa Shin'ichi, "Kaidai: Jō no sekusorojī," in *Minakata Kumagusu korekushon*, ed. Nakazawa Shin'ichi, 5 vols. (Kawade shobō, 1991–1992), 3:7–57.

121. *Minakata Kumagusu zenshū*, 9:5–329. Iwata's side of the correspondence may be partially found in Hasegawa Kōzō and Tsukikawa Kazuo, eds., *Minakata Kumagusu nanshoku dangi: Iwata Jun'ichi ōfuku shokan* (Yasaka shobō, 1991). William F. Sibley ("Morning Fog [Correspondence on Gay Lifestyles]," in *Partings at Dawn: An Anthology of Japanese Gay Literature*, ed. Stephen D. Miller [San Francisco: Gay Sunshine, 1996], 135–171) provides abridged translations of five of the two men's letters.

rear garden").[122] What they failed to understand, he maintained, was that *nanshoku* contained both "pure" (*jō*) and "impure" (*fujō*) elements, as had also been the case among the ancient Greeks described by the Victorian intellectual John Addington Symonds, an original edition of whose 1883 work *A Problem in Greek Ethics* Minakata proudly owned.[123] In Japan, Minakata wrote, *nanshoku* in its "pure" form had represented the epitome of the Confucian virtue of friendship (*yūdō*), or what he called the "masculine way" (*nandō*). As a latter-day example of this "way," he described to his young colleague the depth of devotion and (evidently platonic) intimacy that had existed between himself and two "beautiful boys" during the 1880s—a far cry from what seemed to him the casual and self-serving character of contemporary male friendships.[124]

In his "civilized" distinction between "pure" and "impure," between "love" (*aijō*) and "lust" (*innen*), as well as in the freer scope he allowed male-male erotic desire than practice, Minakata's Meiji upbringing was clearly reflected.[125] At the same time, Minakata invoked "civilized" principles for the purpose of validating a construct that they were more commonly used to vilify, *nanshoku* playing a role here similar to the ancient Greek *paiderastia* that Symonds had sought to redeem for his nineteenth-century European audience. Idealized though it may have been, Minakata's vision of *nandō* was intended to suggest that male-male sexuality, instead of merely constituting an "obscene act," had once formed, and might perhaps still form, part of a larger "way" or discipline interlaced with such positive social values as friendship, education, and spirituality. To dismiss such traditions as

122. Minakata Kumagusu to Iwata Jun'ichi, 20 August 1931, *Minakata Kumagusu zenshū*, 9:17 (Sibley, "Morning Fog," 148).

123. Minakata Kumagusu to Nakayama Tarō, 8 August 1931, *Minakata Kumagusu zenshū*, 9:5–6. For more on Symonds, see John Addington Symonds, *The Memoirs of John Addington Symonds*, ed. Phyllis Grosskurth (New York: Random House, 1984); John Addington Symonds, *Male Love: A Problem in Greek Ethics and Other Writings*, ed. John Lauritsen (New York: Pagan, 1983); Jeffrey Weeks, *Coming Out: Homosexual Politics in Britain, from the Nineteenth Century to the Present* (London: Quartet, 1977), 45–56.

124. Minakata to Iwata, 20 August 1931, 9:15, 22–45 (Sibley, "Morning Fog," 147, 151–163).

125. Minakata Kumagusu to Iwata Jun'ichi, 7 November 1932, *Minakata Kumagusu zenshū*, 9:135. Although Minakata allegedly abstained from sexual relations until his marriage at age forty (Minakata to Iwata, 7 September 1931, 9:55), he was nevertheless capable of considerable ribaldry on the subject of "beautiful boys," as may be seen in his youthful correspondence, which is discussed in Matsueda Itaru, "Jō no nandō: Minakata Kumagusu 'zaibei shokan' bekken," *Yasō* 15 (1985): 108–125.

"filthy" or "immoral," he insisted, was to misunderstand the meaning they had carried for their participants in the context of their time.[126] In this way, Minakata, like few among his contemporaries, not only relativized the moral absolutes of Meiji "civilization," but was able to resist the totalizing impulses of the medical model of male-male sexuality that had become so influential during the second half of his lifetime. It is to the development of the latter paradigm that we must turn next.

126. Minakata to Iwata, 20 August 1931, 9:36, 38 (Sibley, "Morning Fog," 161, 162); Minakata to Iwata, 7 September 1931, 9:52–55.

5   Doctoring Love

*Male-Male Sexuality in Medical
Discourse from the Edo Period through
the Early Twentieth Century*

That sexuality had significant implications for the health of the human body
was a widely accepted premise in the Edo period. Chinese medical discourse
assigned an important place to "matters of the bedchamber" (*fangshi*; Japanese: *bōji*), situating the sexual, as the historian Charlotte Furth has written, "at the fulcrum of body experiences implicating human longevity and
even spiritual regeneration on one side, and generativity and reproduction
on the other."[1] This aspect of Chinese learning had disseminated to Japan
at least as early as the tenth century, when the court physician Tanba Yasuyori included a chapter on the subject in his medical compendium *Ishinpō* (Essential Medical Prescriptions), thereby preserving for posterity several classics of Chinese erotic knowledge that later became lost on the
continent. By the Edo period, "bedchamber" medicine was familiar not only
to Sinophiles but to a broad segment of the general population, its terminology invoked even in such popular genres as *senryū*.

As conceived in Sino-Japanese medicine, however, the "bedchamber" was
exclusively the site of male-female sexuality. Regulation of this realm was

---

1. Charlotte Furth, "Rethinking Van Gulik: Sexuality and Reproduction in Traditional Chinese Medicine," in *Engendering China: Women, Culture, and the State*,
ed. Christina K. Gilmartin et al., Harvard Contemporary China Series, no. 10 (Cambridge: Harvard University Press, 1994), 145. On medical constructions of sexuality in China, see also Joseph Needham et al., *Science and Civilisation in China*, 14
vols. to date (Cambridge: Cambridge University Press, 1954–), 2:146–152; 5.5:
184–218; R. H. Van Gulik, *Sexual Life in Ancient China: A Preliminary Survey of
Chinese Sex and Society from ca. 1500 B.C. till 1644 A.D.* (Leiden: Brill, 1974); Douglas Wile, *Art of the Bedchamber: The Chinese Sexual Yoga Classics, Including
Women's Solo Meditation Texts* (Albany: State University of New York Press, 1992).

seen as necessary precisely because it brought masculine and feminine essences into potentially volatile contact, acting, to borrow the language of Foucault, as an "especially dense transfer point" for the cosmic forces of yin and yang. Chinese erotic alchemy was concerned with managing this interaction in such a way as to benefit the male party, preserving his own sexual energy (*jing*; Japanese: *sei*) through such techniques as withholding ejaculation, while absorbing that of his female partner. Men were advised to engage in coitus with moderation, lest it lead to exhaustion of what was imagined as a kidney-centered urogenital system—a condition referred to in Edo-period Japan as *jinkyo* (Chinese: *shenxu*). If properly and prudently performed, however, intercourse with females was believed to enhance male longevity.

Although sexual relations between males might theoretically be understood as violating the yin-yang order, Chinese medical discourse was by and large unconcerned with their physiological implications, much less those of female-female sexual behavior.[2] This indifference was, if anything, more pronounced in its Japanese offshoot. References to male-male sexuality from the perspective of Sino-Japanese medicine are few and poorly elaborated, if not positively contradictory. To give an example, in one Edo-period erotic debate, an opponent of *shudō* asserted that it led to a shortened life span, because, unlike in vaginal coitus, the inserter in anal intercourse lost large quantities of semen (*jinsui* or "kidney water"; Chinese: *shenshui*), presumably without gaining any vital essence in return.[3] At least one historical personage, the early seventeenth-century daimyo Asano Yoshinaga, is reported to have expired as a result of overindulging in this pleasure.[4] Yet at other times, male-male sexual relations were seen as a physiologically less dangerous alternative to male-female intercourse. Thus, in the early 1860s, the Confucian scholar Yasui Sokken advised his

2. Giovanni Vitiello, "Taoist Themes in Chinese Homoerotic Tales," in *Religion, Homosexuality, and Literature*, ed. Michael L. Stemmeler and José Ignacio Cabezón, Gay Men's Issues in Religious Studies Series, no. 3 (Las Colinas, Tex.: Monument, 1992), 95–96.

3. Azuma no Kamiko, *Fūryū hiyokudori*, in *Edo jidai bungei shiryō*, ed. Hayakawa Junzaburō et al., 5 vols. (Kokusho kankōkai, 1916), 5:109. His opponent in the debate associated the dangers of *jinkyo*, on the other hand, with *joshoku* (5:89, 90).

4. Naitō Chisō, *Tokugawa jūgodaishi*, 12 vols. (Hakubunkan, 1892–1893), 1:183. For *senryū* depictions of priests who die from excessive anal intercourse, see Hanasaki Kazuo, *Edo no kagemajaya* (Miki shobō, 1980), 151; <*Yanagidaru yokō*> *Hakoyanagi*, in *Shodai senryū senkushū*, ed. Chiba Osamu, 2 vols., Senryū shūsei, nos. 5 and 6 (Iwanami shoten, 1986), 1:291.

young student, the shogunal loyalist Kumoi Tatsuo, to turn to *nanshoku* as a means of sloughing off his budding sexual energies, since engaging in *joshoku* would harm both his physical and intellectual development.[5]

In folk medicine, *shudō* was even thought to possess healing properties. Anal intercourse was said to be particularly efficacious in curing beriberi on the part of the inserter. Hence, in an early nineteenth-century *senryū*, a Buddhist priest chases an acolyte around the monastery in search of "beriberi medicine" (*kakke no kusuri*), his very perseverance giving the lie to the seriousness of his ailment.[6] References to this belief usually have a monastic setting, reflecting, on the one hand, the popular association of male-male sexual practices with the Buddhist clergy, and on the other, perhaps also the relatively high incidence of this disease among the priesthood, whose consumption of polished rice, present-day medical science tells us, was apt to induce a thiamin deficiency.[7]

Not all anuses, evidently, were as salubrious as others. As early as 1598, *Kōbō Daishi ikkan no sho* had warned of the "poisonous ass" (*dokketsu*), the telltale signs of which were a lump near the acolyte's coccyx and coldness about the groin. Penetration of such an orifice exposed the inserter to "fecal poison" (*fundoku*), in which case he must wash his member after the act with urine. If, on the other hand, he detected the aroma of boiled prawns and chrysanthemum leaves during intercourse, he would know that he was dealing with a "superior ass" (*jōketsu*), which served as "medicine" (*kusuri*) to the penis; in this case, the member should not be washed for several days.[8] "Poisonous asses" were held by some to be more common among amateur insertees than professionals, presumably because the latter had mastered certain tricks of the trade.[9] Erotic manuals such as the 1834 *Shikidō kinpishō*

5. Omi Aya and Sakurai Yoshinari, "Kumoi Tatsuo den," in <*Tōhoku ijin*> *Kumoi Tatsuo zenshū*, ed. Omi Aya and Sakurai Yoshinari (Tōyōdō, 1894), (furoku) 4–5.

6. Okada Hajime, *Senryū suetsumuhana shōshaku*, 2 vols. (Yūkō shobō, 1955), 2:624–625.

7. For *kakke no kusuri* references, see Hayashi Yoshikazu, *Enpon Edo bungakushi* (Kawade shobō, 1991), 45; Ishikawa Ichirō, *Edo bungaku zokushin jiten* (Tōyōdō, 1989), 78–79; Shunroan Shujin, *Edo no shikidō: Seiai bunka o himotoku kindan no ezu to kosenryū*, 2 vols. (Yōbunkan shuppan, 1996), 1:66–70. On the history of beriberi in Japan, see Yamashita Seizō, *Kakke no rekishi: Bitamin hakken izen* (Tōkyō daigaku shuppankai, 1983).

8. Mitsuo Sadatomo, *Kōbō Daishi ikkan no sho*, *Kinsei shomin bunka* 13 (1952): 21–22.

9. Kimuro Bōun, *Kanokomochi*, in *Nihon koten bungaku taikei*, ed. Takagi Ichinosuke et al., 102 vols. (Iwanami shoten, 1957–1968), 100:359–360. In this source,

(Court Record of *Shikidō* Secrets) taught inserters how to prevent fecal matter from adhering to the glans, a condition colloquially likened to a *hachimaki* or headband, by pinching their partner's buttocks before withdrawing, although the motivation here was as much esthetic as health-related.[10]

As for the health of the insertee himself, the chief danger perceived in anal intercourse was physical injury to the anus, generally subsumed under the term "hemorrhoids" (*ji*). According to one Edo-period adage, hemorrhoids were a professional hazard among *kagema*, just as "hysteria" (*shaku*), a type of convulsion, spelled bad business for female prostitutes.[11] An opponent of *shudō* in the seventeenth-century work *Denbu monogatari* claimed that youths who developed this condition would become bowlegged and have to walk with a cane for the rest of their lives.[12] For the most part, however, hemorrhoids were regarded as a temporary inconvenience, for which such remedies as ointments, boiled onions, and hot springs, as well as prayers to a so-called god of hemorrhoids (*ji no kami*), existed.[13] The waters of Sokokura near the town of Hakone were thought to be particularly beneficial in this respect; many a *senryū* depicted Edo's *kagema* recuperating here, along with similarly plagued shop boys.[14] And if overly vigorous

---

an anecdote collection dating from 1772, a concerned father asks a doctor of Sino-Japanese medicine whether male-male erotic pursuits might provide a means of lifting the spirits of and thereby help cure his ailing son. The physician warns of the "poisonous nature" (*dokki*) of amateur anuses, but also of the dangers of surfeit (*motareru*) from intercourse with a skilled professional. After consulting a ponderous medical tome, he recommends instead intercourse with a *yakko*, a type of footman whose role in samurai processions left his posterior exposed to the cold (*samuzarashi*), ostensibly ridding it of poisons.

10. Ōgokudō no Arittake, *Shikidō kinpishō*, ed. Fukuda Kazuhiko, 2 vols., Ukiyoe gurafikku, nos. 2 and 3 (KK besutoserāzu, 1990–1991), 2:48.

11. Watanabe Shin'ichirō, "Kagemajaya hanjōki," *Kokubungaku: Kaishaku to kanshō*, February 1975 (zōkan), 106.

12. *Denbu monogatari*, in *Nihon koten bungaku zenshū*, ed. Akiyama Ken et al., 51 vols. (Shōgakkan, 1970–1976), 37:129 (trans. Gary P. Leupp in *Male Colors: The Construction of Homosexuality in Tokugawa Japan* [Berkeley: University of California Press, 1995], 209). Yoshida Hanbei repeats this assertion in his 1686 *Kōshoku kinmō zui* (in *Kōshokumono sōshishū*, ed. Yoshida Kōichi, 2 vols., Kinsei bungei shiryō, no. 10 [Koten bunko, 1968], 1:91).

13. On *ji no kami*, see Ishikawa Ichirō, *Edo bungaku zokushin jiten*, 165–166. The reference to boiled onions may be found in an untitled Edo-period source cited by Minakata Kumagusu (Minakata to Iwata Jun'ichi, 27 September 1931, *Minakata Kumagusu zenshū*, ed. Iwamura Shinobu et al., 12 vols. [Heibonsha, 1971–1975], 9:82). The same source (9:81) recommends that, in order to avoid hemorrhoids, the insertee should take care to evacuate semen from his anus immediately after intercourse, thereby preventing it from turning into "poison" (*doku*).

14. Hanasaki, *Edo no kagemajaya*, 130–132; Watanabe Shin'ichirō, "Kagemajaya

anal intercourse resulted in a torn perineum, a popular work recommended mixing the charred head of a snapping turtle (*suppon*) in oil and applying it to the affected area.[15]

The pharmacopoeia of the Edo period offered solutions not only for dealing with the potential aftereffects of anal intercourse, but also for making its accomplishment easier in the first place. While the use of clove oil as a lubricant is recorded as early as the fourteenth-century picture scroll *Chigo no sōshi*, the most commonly mentioned recipes of Edo times contained such ingredients as a form of hibiscus (*nerigi*) root, seaweed, and egg whites. One such preparation was marketed in dried form as Tsūwasan, which could be reconstituted as needed with saliva.[16] At a pharmacy near Edo's Kan'eiji temple, it was sold in packages bearing the motto Rebirth in Paradise (*gokuraku ōjō*), and reportedly circulated as a well-appreciated gift within the religious complex.[17] Besides lubricants, there were "stick medicines" (*bōgusuri* or *bōyaku*), coated with such agents as copper sulfate and inserted into the anus of male prostitutes-in-training (*shinbeko*) for the purpose of dilation.[18] Drug merchants also employed the erotic charms of young males as a means of selling their products, such as the balm (*kōyaku*) makers of Okitsu, whose attractive salesboys, as we saw in chapter 2, found an appreciative clientele for themselves as well as for their wares among the daimyo retinues that passed through this post town, much to the astonishment of Kaempfer, a physician hailing from a very different medical tradition.[19]

In sum, male-male sexuality was viewed in the Edo period not so much as pathological in itself as an aspect of bodily experience that required proper management in order to preserve, or in some cases even enhance, health. Thus, while in Saikaku's 1696 work *Yorozu no fumihōgu* (Myriad Letter

---

hanjōki," 106. Kansai equivalents included the spas of Arima, Kinosaki, and Totsugawa, for references to which see *Denbu monogatari*, 37:129 (Leupp, *Male Colors*, 209); Hiraga Gennai, *Nenashigusa*, in *Nihon koten bungaku taikei*, 55:44; Yoshida Hanbei, *Kōshoku kunmō zui*, 1:91.

15. Tsukioka Settei, *Onna dairaku takarabako*, *Kinsei shomin bunka* 19 (1953): 19.

16. Botai Michian, *Senryū Yotsumeya kō* (Taihei shooku, 1983), 113–121; Hanasaki, *Edo no kagemajaya*, 133–137; Minakata Kumagusu to Iwata Jun'ichi, 20 September 1931, *Minakata Kumagusu zenshū*, 9:72–73; Shunroan Shujin, *Edo no shikidō*, 1:21–33.

17. Mitamura Engyo, "Kan'eiji no Ueno," in *Mitamura Engyo zenshū*, ed. Mori Senzō et al., 28 vols. (Chūō kōronsha, 1975–1983), 8:320.

18. Shunroan Shujin, *Edo no shikidō*, 1:16–17.

19. For a similar pharmaceutical marketing strategy in eighteenth-century Edo, see Hanasaki Kazuo, *Fūryū tebako no soko* (Taihei shooku, 1980), 130–134.

Scraps) a priest jokes that his "chronic ailment" (*jibyō*) is a liking for "beautiful boys" (*bidō*), his admission would not have been humorous had such a predilection been regarded as truly diseased.[20] To maintain the harmony of health and pleasure, medical intervention was occasionally seen as necessary, but the two principles were not perceived as fundamentally opposed. Balancing out every warning about sexual exhaustion, fecal infection, or hemorrhoids, there may be found an acknowledgment of the positive benefits to be derived from male-male sexual practices, with a vast area of indifference in between. Medical knowledge thus served not only to discourage but also to facilitate *shudō*. Similarly, sickness was sometimes conceived as the result of male-male sexual practices, sometimes the consequence of such pleasures being withheld. Thus, the 1643 *Shin'yūki* portrayed unrequited lovers as prone to a "hundred diseases" (*hyakubyō*), the only preventive medicine being a more responsive attitude on the part of the beloved *wakashu*.[21] Such a prescription would no longer be imaginable in the Meiji period, when a more unequivocally negative stance on male-male sexuality came to dominate the medical field.

THE NATURE OF THE UNNATURAL

Medical discourses often claim a privileged insight into the workings of the physical world, or what Westerners are fond of calling "nature." Thus, Sino-Japanese doctors explained the erotic capacities of the body in terms of the cosmic interplay of yin and yang, a theoretical understanding of which formed one of the bases of their professional expertise. Likewise, the author of *Shin'yūki* wrote from a Buddhist perspective that viewed all events, including illness, as implicated in a vast grid of karmic retribution, so that the responsive *wakashu* not only rescued his suitor from fatal lovesickness, but saved himself from ailments brought on by others' resentment, as well as from being afflicted with ugliness or physical deformity in the next lifetime.[22] Neither would have thought to argue against male-male

20. Ihara Saikaku, *Yorozu no fumihōgu*, in *Nihon koten bungaku zenshū*, 40:313.

21. *Shin'yūki*, in *Nihon shisō taikei*, ed. Ienaga Saburō et al., 67 vols. (Iwanami shoten, 1970–1982), 60:9; Paul Gordon Schalow, "Spiritual Dimensions of Male Beauty in Japanese Buddhism," in *Religion, Homosexuality, and Literature*, 80. For a depiction of *nanshoku*-related lovesickness, see also Ihara Saikaku, *Nanshoku ōkagami*, in *Nihon koten bungaku zenshū*, 39:413–415 (trans. Paul Gordon Schalow under the title *The Great Mirror of Male Love* [Stanford: Stanford University Press, 1990], 143–145).

22. *Shin'yūki*, 60:11–12 (Schalow, "Spiritual Dimensions," 82).

sexual practices from a purely zoological standpoint, as did Watanuki Yosa-burō, the vice-director of the Japanese Philanthropic Hospital in Shanghai, writing in 1905:

> Look at all the animals on earth. Not a bird or beast, not an insect or fish practices masturbation, much less [male-male] interfemoral inter-course [*kosaiin*]. When sexual passion [*shunjō*] arises, the male seeks out the female to copulate and thereby propagate the species, does he not? How, then, can it be proper for humans, the most lofty of all crea-tures [*banbutsu no rei*], to engage in practices that are beneath any beast?[23]

Several centuries earlier, Saikaku had indeed found male-male sexual practices among the birds and insects, claiming that Japan had earned the sobriquet Land of Dragonflies for precisely this reason.[24] Among four-footed creatures, too, foxes and badgers were occasionally known to change into human form in order to win a "beautiful boy," or conversely to become "beautiful boys" themselves so as to trick admirers.[25] *Shudō*'s universality as a "way" put it within the reach of sentient beings other than humans—recall that in Buddhist cosmology the animal world represented one of the "six paths" (*rokudō*) of existence—allowing the author of *Kōbō Daishi ikkan no sho* to assert that even "monkeys living in the mountains and fields" understood the love of youths.[26] Thus, in pre-Meiji times, the realms of *nan-*

23. Watanuki Yosaburō, <*Enju tokushi*> *Fujin to danshi no eisei* (Shanhai shin-chisha Tōkyō bunkyoku, 1905), 106.

24. Ihara, *Nanshoku ōkagami*, 39:315 (Schalow, *Great Mirror*, 51). Similarly, the seventeenth-century scholar Kumazawa Banzan (*Shūgi washo*, in *Nihon shisō taikei*, 30:363–364) found an insect equivalent for the *onnagirai* in the digger wasp (*jiga-bachi*), which was commonly believed to kidnap other insects' offspring instead of engaging in reproduction. Hiraga Gennai (*Nenashigusa kōhen*, in *Nihon koten bun-gaku taikei*, 55:150–151) denied the existence of ornithological *shudō*, but rather than using this fact as an argument against the human practice, asked, "Why should people be no better than birds?"

25. Iijima Hosaku, *Kagetsu zuihitsu* (Toyamabō, 1933), 621–624; Mutō Sadao, *Edo kobanashi jiten* (Tōkyōdō, 1965), 159; Seikanbō Seiwa, *Kaidan toshiotoko*, in *Tokugawa bungei ruijū*, ed. Hayakawa Junzaburō, 12 vols. (Kokusho kankōkai, 1914–1916), 4:457–458.

26. Mitsuo, *Kōbō Daishi ikkan no sho*, 15. Similarly, Konoe Nobuhiro (*Inu tsurezure*, in *Kanazōshi shūsei*, ed. Asakura Haruhiko and Fukuzawa Akio, 18 vols. to date [Tōkyōdō, 1980–], 4:9) reported in the early seventeenth century that on Mount Kōya, which was off-limits to women, even dogs "go crazy over youths" (*wakashugu-rui o suru*). Hiraga Gennai (*Nenashigusa kōhen*, 55:150), however, denied that "dogs and like creatures" (*inujimono*) were capable of male-male erotic desire.

shoku and "nature" had often overlapped.[27] The persuasiveness of Wata-nuki's biological argument depended, therefore, upon a new understanding of the natural order and of the "nature" of human sexuality.

To be sure, even before the Meiji period, the attraction of male and female had been regarded as intrinsic to the larger scheme of things. In representing male-female coitus as an encounter of yin and yang, for instance, Sino-Japanese medicine related it to an elemental dyad whose interaction served as the moving force behind the entire universe. While nativist writers such as Hirata Atsutane and Miyahiro (also known as Miyaoi) Sadao rejected such continental notions, they likewise found a primordial basis for male-female sexuality, viewing it as a reenactment of the coupling of the native creator deities Izanami and Izanagi.[28] Yet even in claiming a "natural" foundation for male-female sexuality, such discourses did not necessarily attempt to discredit male-male (much less female-female) sexual practices, or at least not so vociferously as would become the case in the Meiji period. Miyahiro condemned the sexual habits of Buddhist monks, but less because the cleric made a nightly "plaything" (*nagusamimono*) of the "poor" (*aware*) young acolyte than because his vow of celibacy negated divinely bestowed capacities for male-female erotic pleasure and reproduction.[29] Hirata also dealt with clerical *nanshoku*, but its place in his argument was to prove that sexual passion (*yogokoro*) was rife even among those who claimed to have rooted it out, forming an inescapable part of "human nature" (*honshō*).[30]

27. The arbiter in Nishizawa Ippū's 1708 erotic debate *Yakei tomojamisen* (in *Edo jidai bungei shiryō*, 2:321) went so far as to claim that, just as the human body had two eyes and two ears, the existence of two modes of sexuality (i.e., *nanshoku* and *joshoku*) formed one of "heaven and earth's natural principles" (*tenchi shizen no dōri*).

28. Hirata Atsutane, *Kokon yōmi kō*, in <Shinshū> *Hirata Atsutane zenshū*, ed. Hirata Atsutane zenshū kankokai, 21 vols. (Meicho shuppan, 1976–1981), 9:154–155; *Miyahiro Sadao, Minka yōjutsu*, in *Kinsei chihō keizai shiryō*, ed. Ono Takeo, 10 vols. (Yoshikawa kōbunkan, 1931–1932), 5:267. On nativist views of sexuality, see also H. D. Harootunian, *Things Seen and Unseen: Discourse and Ideology in Tokugawa Nativism* (Chicago: University of Chicago Press, 1988), 156, 240, 256–257, 297–301; William R. LaFleur, *Liquid Life: Abortion and Buddhism in Japan* (Princeton: Princeton University Press, 1992), 107–113.

29. Miyahiro Sadao, *Kokueki honron*, in *Nihon shisō taikei*, 51:294–296.

30. Hirata, *Kokon yōmi kō*, 9:154–162. Similarly, the nineteenth-century nativist Motoori Uchitō (*Senja kō*, in <Zōho> *Motoori Norinaga zenshū*, ed. Motoori Seizō, 13 vols. [Yoshikawa kōbunkan, 1926–1928], 12:174) wrote that *nanshoku* was the "natural outcome" (*onozukara no ikioi*) of priestly celibacy.

Likewise, while a conceptual link between male-female sexuality and re-production existed in Edo-period discourse, it did not automatically dis-qualify nonprocreative sexual practices, which received alternate legitima-tion from what Harry Harootunian has called the "culture of play."[31] Even Miyahiro, who wrote of conjugal intercourse as "planting the seed of hu-man life" (*ningen no tanemaki*), did not deny husbands the privilege of vis-iting female prostitutes: evidently, there was enough semen to go round.[32] In the Edo period, procreation was seen more as a matter of begetting de-scendants for the household, and thus a moral responsibility toward one's ancestors, than as a biological imperative essential to the survival of the species. In the eighteenth-century erotic debate *Keisei kintanki*, a patron of female courtesans charges—with only a tinge of irony—that *shudō* put to "useless" (*muyaku*) ends semen that could be better spent on "producing heirs" (*shison sōzoku*).[33] Yet even in this genre, advocates of *nyodō* turn to procreative arguments only as a means of defending themselves against their opponents, who denied the validity of male-female intercourse altogether. Outside of the polarized rhetoric of such debates, *shudō* and *nyodō* were seldom seen as mutually exclusive, so that male-male erotic practices and household continuity were not, in principle, incompatible.

For a Meiji doctor like Watanuki, on the other hand, an exclusively male-female pattern of sexual interaction appeared as part of an evolutionary de-sign that could be observed among all animal species, and that humankind, as the most highly developed product thereof, ought therefore to heed. De-spite his liberal use of literary Chinese phraseology (it should be noted that the book was first published in Shanghai for a continental audience), Watanuki's understanding of "nature" drew heavily on contemporary sci-

31. Conversely, it was sometimes asserted that male-male sexual practices could lead to conception, a condition that acolytes on Mount Kōya referred to as *sebarami* or "spinal pregnancy." See Minakata Kumagusu, "Onna o wakashu ni daiyō seshi koto," in *Minakata Kumagusu zenshū*, 2:443. A proponent of *shudō* in Nishizawa Ippū's *Yakei tomojamisen* (2:319) claimed that the Han-dynasty Chinese emperor Wen had impregnated his male favorite Deng Tong, while Arai Hakuseki (*Kijinron*, in *Nihon shisō taikei*, 35:167) cited examples of male childbirth during the Song and Ming dynasties. For the term "culture of play," see H. D. Harootunian, "Late Toku-gawa Culture and Thought," in *The Cambridge History of Japan*, ed. John W. Hall et al., 5 vols. to date (Cambridge: Cambridge University Press, 1988–), 5:168–182. On the ludic aspects of *shudō*, and of *shikidō* more generally, see also Saeki Junko, *Bishōnenzukushi* (Heibonsha, 1992), esp. 145–156.
32. Miyahiro, *Minka yōjutsu*, 5:267, 269.
33. Ejima Kiseki, <*Shikidō taizen*> *Keisei kintanki*, in *Nihon koten bungaku taikei*, 91:198.

entific knowledge, and in particular the rising disciplines of reproductive and evolutionary biology. The first of these disciplines claimed an authoritative understanding of the sexual and reproductive capacities of the human body and the functions for which they were supposedly intended. The second placed emphasis on male-female sexual activity as a means of propagating not simply households but entire species, and raised the possibility that other forms of sexual behavior could endanger the well-being of nations, races, and even the future of humanity itself. Thus, in addition to being "uncivilized," male-male sexual practices came in the Meiji period to be increasingly stigmatized as "unnatural."

By the end of the Edo period, knowledge of "Dutch" science and medicine already extended to various aspects of sexuality, ranging from the fallacy of the belief that the kidneys were responsible for producing semen and could be depleted, to the internal arrangement of the female reproductive anatomy (which even inspired a new perspective in erotic prints), to the contraceptive efficacy of the *rūdesakku* (from the Dutch *roed-zak*) or condom.[34] Yet it was largely silent on the topic of male-male sexuality—in part a reflection of the indifference or neutrality that characterized Edo-period medical discourse as a whole, and in part because Western medical authorities themselves devoted relatively little attention to this subject before the mid–nineteenth century.[35] The rapid influx of medical knowledge from Europe and North America during the Meiji period, however, coincided with a wave of vigorous theorizing about sexuality by Western doctors, who espoused the belief that sexual phenomena were based on biological laws that, if yet imperfectly understood, could be determined through scientific study, and that the regulation of sexual behavior was chiefly a task for the medical profession. Male-male and female-female practices occupied a prominent, if dishonorable, place within this medico-scientific model of sexuality, which shall be referred to here as sexology.[36] As Meiji doctors domesticated the

34. Keisai Eisen, *<Keichū kibun> Makura bunko hoi*, in *Nihon seiten taikan*, ed. Takahashi Tetsu, 2 vols. (Nihon seikatsu shinri gakkai, 1954), 1:97–100; Satō Kōka, "Seiyokugaku goi," pt. 1, *Hentai shiryō*, November 1926, 42; Sugimoto, *Shimeshigoto amayo no takegari*, in *Edo no bidō o tanoshimu: Seiai bunka no tankyū*, ed. Shunroan Shujin (Miki shobō, 1995), 74; Masayoshi Sugimoto and David L. Swain, *Science and Culture in Traditional Japan*, A.D. 600–1854, M.I.T. East Asian Science Series, no. 6 (Cambridge: MIT Press, 1978), 391.

35. As early as 1684, the surgical compendium *Geka ryōjishū* described a Dutch theory imputing hemorrhoids to diet, but at the same time implied an entirely native etiology by attaching an illustration of a hemorrhoid-afflicted *wakashu*. See "Wakashu no jishitsu," *Kono hana* 18 (1911): 19.

36. Strictly speaking, the term "sexology" (or in German, *Sexualwissenschaft*)

new medical knowledge, they came to embrace many of its premises regarding sexuality, and were quick to take note of the emerging sexological interest in male-male sexual behavior.

Some of the earliest Meiji expositions of sexology were, to say the least, highly imaginative.[37] One widely disseminated theory, which drew on the ideas of the American Edward Hood (his exact name and identity are unclear), claimed that sexual intercourse involved "three types of electricity" (*san ereki*).[38] These forces were brought fully into play only in the case of vaginal coitus, preferably between the most positively charged of males and the most negatively charged females. The appeal of this notion lay partly in its creative interweaving of the recently introduced disciplines of reproductive biology and electrodynamics, but also in its subtle echoing of more familiar yin-yang polarities. Within the newly electrified field of sexology, however, male-male eros presented a more disruptive force than in the "bedchamber" of old.

The author of one widely read 1886 work, for example, launched into an explanation of sexual dynamics in response to a letter from Tochigi prefecture.[39] His provincial correspondent had wished to know whether there was any harm in interfemoral intercourse (*sumata*), which the writer described as a means by which "ordinary young males" (*seken no toshiwakaki danshi*), by mutual arrangement, derived erotic pleasure (*yoki kokochi*) in lieu of vaginal coitus. The author's answer was that such practices could never substitute for the latter act, since, as with masturbation, they depended on "frictional electricity" (*masatsu denki*) alone, and not the negative-positive interaction of "body electricity" (*jinshin denki*) or the "chemical electricity" (*seimi denki*) that resulted from contact between the acidic penis and the alkaline vagina. Rather than relieving fatigue and nourishing the spirit, as did "natural passion" (*shizen no jōai*), they weakened the body and dulled mental vigor. Edo-period writers, by contrast, had seen no particular dan-

was not born until the early twentieth century, when it was coined by Iwan Bloch. Japanese equivalents included *seiyokugaku*, *seigaku*, and *sei kagaku*.

37. On early Meiji sexology, see also Kawamura Kunimitsu, *Sekushuariti no kindai*, Kōdansha sensho mechie, no. 86 (Kōdansha, 1996), 39–80; Kimoto Itaru, *Onanī to Nihonjin* (Intanaru shuppan, 1976), 68–93; Ueno Chizuko, "Kaisetsu," in *Nihon kindai shisō taikei*, ed. Katō Shūichi et al., 24 vols. (Iwanami shoten, 1988–1992), 23:518–535.

38. This theory surfaces in various Meiji sexological works, the earliest of them, according to Kimoto (*Onanī*, 76), the 1877 *Zōkakiron nihen*.

39. Seki Yuidō, *Danjo kōgō tokushitsu mondō* (Takebe Takisaburō and Kimura Inosuke, 1886), 145–149.

ger in interfemoral intercourse, at worst portraying it as a fraudulent imitation not of male-female sexual relations, but of the more genuine male-male practice of anal coitus.[40]

What was peculiarly Meijiesque about the 1886 argument was the perfect congruence in which it aligned "civilized morality," the laws of "creation" (*zōka*), and bodily hygiene (*eisei*). While the author drew on such Confucian and Shinto language as "celestial order" (*tenri*) and the "will of the gods" (*kami no mikokoro*) to articulate his vision of "nature," its authority derived ultimately from the apparatus of contemporary science rather than religious canon. Nineteenth-century biological notions regarding the workings of "creation" thus permeated deeply into Japanese discourse even while the Judeo-Christian image of an all-powerful Creator made a far less lasting impression. "Creation" appeared as an ongoing process, echoed, for instance, in the Meiji term "creative organs" (*zōkaki*)—an early sexological designation for the reproductive system.

Since "nature" had supposedly designed these organs for the purpose of procreation, it stood to reason that other uses should have a deleterious impact on human health. Following in the footsteps of their Western colleagues, Meiji doctors identified a wide variety of physiological and psychological disorders that might result from such "unnatural" practices as anal and interfemoral intercourse or masturbation. (Indeed, the conceptual link between male-male sexuality and autoeroticism was itself largely a product of the new sexological discourse.) We have encountered, for instance, the assertions of forensic pathologists concerning the canine phallus and the funnel-shaped anus, by which the body cried out the fact of its abuse to the trained examiner. Here, the emphasis was on detecting the telltale signs of "unnatural" behavior after it had transpired. Popular-sexology tracts, on the other hand, aimed to prevent its occurrence in the first place, in which case the threat of physical and psychic ailment, often immediate and irreversible, served as a powerful disincentive.

Although Meiji authorities no longer spoke of the dangers of the "poisonous ass," the anal inserter now faced the more formidable prospect of becoming "permanent human refuse" (*shūsei haibutsu*) or even losing his life. Such practices led, it was claimed, to physical and mental debilitation, depression, and insanity.[41] Moreover, as one newspaper columnist, billed as

---

40. See, for example, Ejima, *Keisei kintanki*, 91:208. As noted in chap. 1 (n. 50), *shudō* texts typically represent *sumata*, like anal intercourse, as a unilateral and hierarchical practice rather than a reciprocal one.

41. Habuto Eiji, *Seishoku eiseihen* (Kateisha, 1907), 74; Murata Tenrai and Saitō

"The Woman Physician," warned, young males who resorted to *keikan* as a substitute for "natural intercourse" (*shizenteki kōsetsu*) might find, upon reaching adulthood, that they could not achieve erection with females—a condition that nineteenth-century Western doctors referred to as sexual neurasthenia.[42] While this dulling of male sexual response was reminiscent of the Sino-Japanese notion of *jinkyo*, Meiji authorities associated it with the nervous system rather than the urogenital tract, linked it specifically with autoerotic and male-male sexual practices, and pronounced it more likely to strike at a young age.

The panoply of ailments threatening the anal insertee, meanwhile, far outshadowed Edo-period warnings about "hemorrhoids." Needless to say, an excursion to the hot springs would hardly cure such complaints as the funnel-shaped anus or rectal gonorrhea. Nor were the ravages of anal intercourse limited to the posterior region. Watanuki, for instance, related the story of a North American male who had taken pleasure in being anally penetrated since the age of ten, and was therefore afflicted in adulthood not only with incontinence, but also with a weak constitution, an overexcitable nervous system, and headaches.[43] Being drawn from Western medical writings, such case histories rarely involved Japanese subjects, yet this fact did not necessarily diminish their dissuasive power. Rather, in an age that presumed the superiority of foreign medical knowledge, Western credentials could only bolster their claim to scientific truth.

The negative impact of "unnatural" sexual practices extended beyond the level of the individual to affect broader collectivities. Sexual neurasthenia prevented males from fulfilling the "goal of procreation" (*seishoku no mokuteki*) and, from an evolutionary viewpoint, endangered the survival of that new creature, the "human species" (*ningen shuzoku*).[44] Matsumoto Yasuko, a president of the Central Nursing Guild and an accredited midwife, thus found fault with Schopenhauer's suggestion that older men's erotic attraction to young males was a stratagem of "nature" for preventing the birth of weak offspring, charging that the German philosopher had failed to take into account the damage that male-male sexual practices wrought upon the reproductive abilities of the youthful partner. She also scoffed at the claim

Masaichi, *Seiyoku to jinsei* (Bunkodō shoten, 1912), 112; Sōma Hiroyoshi, <Eisei> *Danjo hōten* (Keibunkan, 1908), 90.

42. Shūkin Joshi, *Onna isha* (Seikōkan, 1902), 238. Little is known concerning the actual identity of the author.

43. Watanuki Yosaburō, *Fujin to danshi*, 107–109.

44. Shūkin Joshi, *Onna isha*, 238; Sōma, *Danjo hōten*, 90.

of some Satsumaites that their "bonds of brotherhood" (*keitei no yaku*), far
from being motivated by "base passions" (*retsujō*), were intended to serve
the nation (*kokka*), asking why, in that case, they invariably sought ties with
"beautiful boys" and not the plain.[45] By implication, it was an act of greater
patriotism to enter into "civilized" marriage and beget the next generation
of citizens. Kōmurō Shujin, meanwhile, speculated chauvinistically that the
"dull and slovenly national character" (*rodon chikan no kokuminsei*) of the
Korean people—whose nation had in the year prior to his writing been swal-
lowed into the Japanese empire—was due in part to widespread male-male
sexual practices among its young.[46]

Even as Meiji medical authorities emphasized the physical and social dangers resulting from male-male sexual behavior, they sought a basis for such
behavior in the laws of biology, in the somewhat paradoxical belief that even
the "unnatural" possessed a scientifically intelligible nature. Here, Meiji sexologists relied heavily on the research of their Western colleagues, who were
busily refining the construct of "homosexuality." As we have seen earlier,
forensic pathologists began coining Japanese equivalents for this term as
early as the 1890s, which by the 1920s would become standardized as *dōseiai* or "same-sex love."[47] Embedded in this concept was the implicit assumption that erotic practices and desires between members of the same
sex constituted a discrete category of sexual behavior whose essence transcended ages and cultures, and whose phenomenology could be explained
according to the laws of science. While medical authorities recognized that
"same-sex love" had occurred throughout human history, they nevertheless characterized it as abnormal or pathological, although various opinions
existed regarding its etiology and cure. The notion of "same-sex love" also
drew an explicit parallel, for the first time in the record of Japanese erotic
discourses, between male-male and female-female sexualities.[48]

45. Matsumoto Yasuko, *Danjo seishoku kenzenhō* (Chūō kangofukai, 1900),
101–103. The emergence of such female authors as Matsumoto, Kinkin Joshi (see
chap. 4, n. 119), and the aforementioned Shūkin Joshi (assuming that this writer was
indeed a woman) marks a significant turning point in the gendering of public discourse on male-male sexuality, although I would argue that the discourse as a whole
remained overwhelmingly male-dominated throughout the period under study.

46. Hino Mitsuo, ed., "<Gojūnenkan no vēru o nuida kisho> Kōmurō Shujin-
cho *Bishōnenron, ichimei dōsei shikijōshi*," pt. 2, *Erochika*, November 1970, 221.

47. I will use the terms "same-sex love" and *dōseiai* as broad designations for a
distinctly Japanese sexual category that developed in interaction with, yet was more
than simply a mirror image of, the Western construct of "homosexuality," although
the vocabulary employed by individual authors was by no means uniform.

48. On the construction of female "same-sex love," which, despite the model's

Like a great deal of medical information that entered Meiji Japan, much of the new knowledge about "same-sex love" was of Germanic origin. The earliest work to devote sustained attention to the phenomenon was an 1894 translation of *Psychopathia Sexualis* by the German-Austrian doctor Richard von Krafft-Ebing, which was published under the auspices of the Japanese Forensic Medicine Association only eight years after its initial appearance in Europe. Although this volume, despite its respectable credentials, was promptly banned as "obscene," Krafft-Ebing's classification of "contrary sexual instinct" (*ijō jōyoku kandō*) as a form of "erotomania" (*shikijōkyō*) had a profound impact on subsequent writers.[49] Through the influence of this and other works of sexology, male-male sexuality would increasingly be viewed not as an erotic discipline like *shudō*, or even a moral failing as in the "civilized" paradigm, but as a sexual pathology demanding medical and psychiatric attention.

Through sexology, knowledge about male-male erotic culture in contemporary Europe also found its way into Meiji Japan, including efforts to win greater legal and social rights for that category of individuals coming to be designated in the West as "homosexuals." Mori Ōgai noted the German lawyer and journalist Karl Ulrichs's call for state recognition of male-male unions as early as 1889, although he characterized it incredulously as an attempt to "pass off the false for the true" (*ka o rōshi shin o nashinu*).[50] Likewise, the Berlin-based Scientific-Humanitarian Committee, founded by Magnus Hirschfeld in 1897, makes an appearance in Kōmurō Shujin's 1911 *Bishōnenron*, where it receives the genteel moniker of the "Club for Research on *Nanshoku*" (Nanshoku kenkyū kurabu).[51] Japan played an im-

implications, was not entirely symmetric with its male counterpart, see my "'S' Is for Sister: Schoolgirl Intimacy and 'Same-Sex Love' in Early Twentieth-Century Japan," in *Gendering Modern Japanese History*, ed. Barbara Molony and Kathleen S. Uno (Cambridge: Harvard University Press, forthcoming).

49. Nihon hōigakkai, trans., *Shikijōkyō hen* (Hōigakkai, 1894). Authorities did not ban *Psychopathia Sexualis* when it was translated again in 1913 as *Hentai seiyoku shinri* (trans. Dainihon bunmei kyōkai [Dainihon bunmei kyōkai]).

50. Mori Ōgai, "Gaijō no koto o rokusu," in *Ōgai zenshū*, ed. Kinoshita Mokutarō et al., 38 vols. (Iwanami shoten, 1971–1975), 29:155. On Ulrichs, see Hubert Kennedy, *Ulrichs: The Life and Works of Karl Heinrich Ulrichs, Pioneer of the Modern Gay Movement* (Boston: Alyson, 1988); Karl Heinrich Ulrichs, *The Riddle of "Man-Manly" Love: The Pioneering Work on Male Homosexuality*, trans. Michael A. Lombardi-Nash, 2 vols. (Buffalo, N.Y.: Prometheus, 1994).

51. Hino, "Kōmurō Shujin-cho *Bishōnenron*," pt. 2, 213. On Hirschfeld and the Scientific-Humanitarian Committee (Wissenschaftlich-humanitäre Komitee), see Charlotte Wolff, *Magnus Hirschfeld: A Portrait of a Pioneer in Sexology* (London: Quartet, 1986).

portant role, in fact, for researchers in the latter organization, as in German sexology more broadly. In the eyes of one Committee member, Benedict Friedländer, Japan stood together with ancient Greece as an example of a "civilized" yet non-Christian nation where male-male eros reinforced masculine solidarity and values—in contrast to an increasingly feminine-influenced and hence culturally imperiled Europe. Friedländer found living proof for his thesis that male-male sexuality and military prowess were closely linked in the outcome of the 1904–1905 Russo-Japanese War, in which the victorious Japanese side had been led by generals hailing from the southwestern periphery, where "pederasty" supposedly enjoyed the greatest social acceptance.[52]

German sexologists derived their information regarding Japan in part from Western observers who had traveled or lived there (including perhaps Doriphorus), or conversely from Japanese sojourning abroad. During a teaching stint in Berlin, for example, Iwaya Sazanami, a writer of "boys' literature," was asked to contribute an article, "Nan-šo-k' (die Päderastie in Japan)," to the 1902 *Jahrbuch für sexuelle Zwischenstufen*, the annual publication of the Scientific-Humanitarian Committee.[53] In this essay, Iwaya briefly outlined the history of *nanshoku* in previous eras before turning to such contemporary phenomena as the "roughneck" problem, the kabuki *onnagata*, and the "Satsuma habit." Subsequent writers, including Friedländer, Hirschfeld, Friedrich Karsch-Haack, and Friedrich Krauss, were deeply indebted to Iwata for their knowledge of Japanese "pederasty." For his own part, Iwaya, in his memoirs, portrayed the Committee as an exotic gathering of European sexual fauna, complete with males who did not look like men and females who did not look like women, and related how he and another Japanese scholar (a professor at the Peers' School, no less) had beaten a hasty retreat from an annual function after provoking curious glances and whispers among the other dinner guests, who had evidently taken Iwaya and his companion for a visiting pair of *warme Brüder*.[54]

52. Benedict Friedländer, "Dōseiteki jōkō ni tsuite," *Jinsei*, April 1906, 183–186. This source is an abridged translation of an essay that originally appeared in the 1905 *Jahrbuch für sexuelle Zwischenstufen*. On Friedländer, who split from the Committee in 1907 because of theoretical and personal differences with Hirschfeld, see Harry Oosterhuis and Hubert Kennedy, eds., *Homosexuality and Male Bonding in Pre-Nazi Germany: The Youth Movement, the Gay Movement, and Male Bonding before Hitler's Rise: Original Transcripts from "Der Eigene," the First Gay Journal in the World* (New York: Harrington Park, 1991).

53. Suweyo-Iwaya [Iwaya Sazanami], "Nan-šo-k' (die Päderastie in Japan)," *Jahrbuch für sexuelle Zwischenstufen* 4 (1902): 265–271.

54. Iwaya Sazanami, "Hi-hakase to watashi," *Hanzai kagaku*, January 1932,

As this brief encounter of orientalism and occidentalism suggests, cultural exchange was a highly selective process of perception and interpretation. Westerners like Friedländer employed Japan for their own ideological ends, while Japanese likewise modified Western constructs to fit native needs and expectations. Thus, the notion of "same-sex love" as it emerged in Japan was not identical on all points with Western "homosexuality." Nevertheless, in Japan as in the West, the ascendance of the medico-scientific model had a profound impact upon the understanding of male-male sexuality in the twentieth century, its effects remaining powerful even today.

DICHOTOMIES OF LOVE

Intrinsic to the notion of "same-sex love" were two binary oppositions that provided it with meaning and enhanced its aura of scientific objectivity. The first and most basic was a distinction between "same" and "other," expressed in European languages by the Greek prefixes "homo-" and "hetero-" and in Japan by the Chinese characters *dō* and *i*. The criterion of sameness/difference rested solely on biological sex, conceived as another binary. Thus, so long as no intersexed individuals were involved, any erotic interaction between two humans could be classed either as "same-sex love" (*dōseiai*) or "cross-sex love" (*iseiai*).

During the first decades of the twentieth century, these categories came largely to replace the older division of sexual topography into *nanshoku* and *joshoku* hemispheres. While the two mappings overlapped to a certain degree, they were not coextensive. The *nanshoku/joshoku* dyad was patently phallocentric, representing the sexual alternatives available only to the male erotic subject; female-female sexuality, therefore, had no place within its signifying system. The early twentieth-century sexologist Takada Giichirō characterized it for this reason as "irrational" (*fugōri*) and "unscientific" (*hikagakuteki*), a lexical embodiment of "male supremacy" (*danson johi*).[55] The *dōseiai/iseai* distinction, on the other hand, weighed the sexes of the

---

215–219; Iwaya Sazanami, *Watakushi no konjaku monogatari* (Waseda daigaku shuppanbu, 1928), 51–52; Iwaya Sazanami, *Yōkō miyage*, 2 vols. (Hakubunkan, 1903), 2:66–70.

55. Takada Giichirō, *Hentai iwa* (Chiyoda shoin, 1936), 164; Takada Giichirō, *Hentai seiyoku kō*, Sei kagaku zenshū, no. 12 (Bukyōsha, 1931), 211–212; Takada Giichirō, *Tōseijutsu* (Hakubunkan, 1928), 73–74. Similarly, Morita Yūshū (*Dōseiai no kenkyū* [Chiba: Jinsei sōzōsha, 1931], 2, 17; *Hentai seiyoku hiwa* [Heibonsha, 1930], 7, 30) complained that native Japanese words for *dōseiai* were "folkloric" (*dozokuteki*) rather than "academic" (*gakujutsuteki*), typically designating the sexual object rather than the larger phenomenon involved.

parties in relation to each other, as if from the ungendered stance of an objective observer, and had the advantage of embracing male-female, male-male, and female-female forms of sexual behavior within a single taxonomy.

In bringing the last two together under the rubric of "same-sex love," the new taxonomy implied that the resemblance between male-male and female-female sexualities outweighed their differences. The key trait they held in common, of course, was that neither involved the pairing of male with female—that is to say, that neither constituted "cross-sex love." In this way, the notion of "same-sex love" was built upon the expectation that male-female interaction represented the sexual norm. At the same time, it was precisely the existence of "same-sex love" as a deviant other that furnished the concept of "cross-sex love" with definition and clarity. As with Western "heterosexuality," the term *iseiai* arose, in fact, somewhat later than *dōseiai,* not passing into common usage until the 1920s.[56] Furthermore, both "cross-sex love" and "same-sex love" carried a sense of exclusivity that had not characterized their *joshoku* and *nanshoku* predecessors. While a notion of "bisexuality" (*ryōseiai* or "two-sex love") also existed, it figured less as an autonomous category of sexual behavior than as an "impure" mixture of two antithetical elements, or, following Krafft-Ebing's formulation, a sort of "psychic hermaphrodism" (*seishinteki han'in'yō*).

The distinction between "sameness" and "otherness" was grounded, in turn, upon a perceived polarity of the sexes. In the scientific scheme of sex there was no third term, except perhaps for the hermaphrodite, but even here, doctors and sexologists went to great lengths to determine if the intersexed individual was "properly" male or female. This rigid dichotomy of the sexes became the sole basis for determining the likeness or dissimilarity of erotic partners, and hence whether their interaction constituted "same-sex love" or "cross-sex love." Age was no longer a factor, as it had been in the *shudō* construct. By definition, one of the parties in *shudō* had to be a youth or *wakashu,* not only male in sex, but also preadult in social status. A *shudō* relationship had therefore been construed not so much as a pairing of likes, but as an asymmetric exchange between individuals with distinct physical attributes and differing ranks within the masculine gender hierarchy. Sexual contact between two adult males of equivalent age and

---

56. On the emergence of the "heterosexuality" construct in the West, see Jonathan Ned Katz, *The Invention of Heterosexuality* (New York: Dutton, 1995). In its variant form *isei jōyoku,* "cross-sex love" appears as early as the 1894 translation of Krafft-Ebing's *Psychopathia Sexualis* (Nihon hōigakkai, *Shikijōkyō hen,* 150).

status thus fell outside the boundaries of *shudō*, although it qualified unproblematically as "same-sex love."

Furthermore, insofar as the category of *wakashu* was a social construction, it had exhibited a considerable amount of plasticity. The upper age limit for the *wakashu*, for example, was never clearly defined, but could be manipulated with relative ease through the management of external appearances such as hairstyle and clothing. The cultural markings of *wakashu* status even allowed females a place at the outskirts of the *shudō* demimonde, as with the *kagema onna*, who appropriated adolescent male trappings in order to attract a youth-loving clientele, and whom bakufu lawmakers saw fit to class alongside the "genuine" article. By contrast, the criterion of sex that separated *dōseiai* from *iseiai* was in principle inflexible. Although Japanese, influenced by continental traditions, had for many centuries recognized the possibility of males turning into females or vice versa, biological science taught that sex was a permanent condition, inscribed not only in the genitals but in such mysterious depths of the anatomy as cell structure and hormones.[57] Under the scalpel and the microscope, the "truth" of sex could always be determined.

It is important to note that, in early twentieth-century biology, the designations "male" (*dansei*) and "female" (*josei*) involved, in addition to the physical attributes of sex, numerous aspects of behavior and personality, or what would today be called gender.[58] Although few authorities could explain the precise mechanisms involved, most agreed that such qualities as "passivity" in women and "aggressiveness" in men were physiologically rooted, thereby reducing social inequalities to anatomic destiny. Biological sex was also thought to dictate the orientation of "sexual desire" (*seiyoku*), a force that evolutionary science had elevated to the status of an instinct. In males, the sexual drive was seen as aimed inherently toward females, and in females toward males, following the principle that likes repelled while opposites attracted.[59] Male-male and female-female sexuality thus contradicted not only erotic norms, but the integrity of the sex/gender system as

---

57. Older visions of intersexuality did not disappear immediately. As late as 1901, a newspaper carried a report of a tailor in Nagano prefecture who spent half the month as a male and the other half as a female (reflecting the Chinese-influenced notion of the *haniwari*), and advised physiologists to look into the matter. See "Kii no henshōsha," *Yorozu chōhō*, 18 February 1901, 3.

58. For a useful discussion of the word *sei*, which might refer variously to "sex," "gender," or "sexuality," see Oda Makoto, *Ichigo no jiten: Sei* (Sanseidō, 1996).

59. Habuto Eiji and Sawada Junjirō, *Hentai seiyokuron* (Shun'yōdō, 1915), 11. On the rise of the *seiyoku* construct, see Kawamura Kunimitsu, *Sekushuariti no kindai*, 81–115.

a whole. As the title of a 1920 work suggested, "same-sex love" was, by its very nature, a "mystery" (*shinpi*).[60]

The task of unraveling this mystery fell to sexologists, a group that during the 1910s and 1920s gained a mass audience. Sexologists, the vast majority of whom were males, found a forum for their views not only in medical journals, but also in general-circulation periodicals and commercially published monographs. Some, like Habuto Eiji and Sawada Junjirō, were remarkably prolific, turning out as many as ten books in a single year.[61] A significant portion possessed professional credentials as doctors, including Habuto, who opened a clinic in Tokyo for the treatment of venereal diseases in 1914 after obtaining an advanced medical degree in Germany.[62] Takada Giichirō, like Habuto, held a doctorate in medicine, his specialty lying in forensic pathology—a field that had claimed privileged knowledge of male-male (as well as female-female) sexual practices since the Meiji period. Tanaka Kōgai, meanwhile, sprang from a long line of Sino-Japanese physicians, yet candidly admitted that he "dislike[d] examining sick people," abandoning a post as professor of medicine in 1914 in order to pursue a life of independent research and writing.[63]

60. Sawada Junjirō, *Shinpi naru dōseiai*, 2 vols., (Tenkadō shobō, 1920). Similarly, Morita was wont to describe "same-sex love" as a "puzzle" (*nazo*) or "sphinx" (*sufinkusu*).

61. Habuto and Sawada's very prolificacy makes full citation of their works cumbersome. Subsequent references will be primarily to their collaborative effort *Hentai seiyokuron*, which went through repeated printings, and to Sawada's *Shinpi naru dōseiai*, which contains the author's most exhaustive treatment of "same-sex love." Other of Habuto and Sawada's writings dealing with "same-sex love" (of both male and female varieties) include the following. Habuto: *Fujin sei no kenkyū* (Jitsugyō no Nihonsha, 1921); *Fujin seiyoku no kenkyū* (Shichōsha, 1928); *Gendai fujin to seiyoku seikatsu* (Hakubunkan, 1922); *Hentai seiyoku no kenkyū* (Gakugei shoin, 1921); *Koi oyobi sei no shinkenkyū* (Hakubunkan, 1921); <*Nanpito mo koko-roubeki*> *Seiyoku no chishiki* (Hōkōdō, 1924); *Onna to sono seiteki genshō* (Gakugei shoin, 1921); *Ryōsei no seiyoku oyobi sono sai* (Gakugei shoin, 1921); *Seikan* (Meishōsha, 1927); *Seishokki oyobi seiyoku zensho* (Seihōdō, 1926); *Seiyoku to ren'ai* (Nihon hyōronsha, 1921); *Tsūzoku seiyokugaku* (Nihon hyōronsha, 1920); <*Wakaki danjo no kokoroubeki*> *Seiyoku no chishiki* (Seikōdō shoten, 1921). Sawada: *Hentaisei to kyōraku*, Sekai ryōki zenshū, no. 9 (Heibonsha, 1932); *Ren'ai to seiyoku* (Kōbundō, 1922); *Seiai jinsei* (Isseidō shoten, 1936); "Seikan ijō no byōri oyobi shinri," pt. 1, *Sei*, February 1921, 31–36. For an examination of the two men's work within the larger context of 1920s sexology, see Furukawa Makoto, "Ren'ai to seiyoku no daisan teikoku: Tsūzokuteki seiyokugaku no jidai," *Gendai shisō*, July 1993, 110–127.

62. Tametō Gorō, *Taishō shin risshiden* (Dainihon yūbenkai, 1921), 171.

63. Tanaka Kōgai, *Ki chin kai* (Hōmeidō shoten, 1953), 220; Tanaka Kōgai, "Shippitsu o oete," *Hentai seiyoku*, December 1924, 284.

Other sexologists could boast no formal medical training, but simply a familiarity with Western writings on the subject. Sawada, for instance, had in his younger days worked in a pedagogical institute as an instructor of natural history, turning only later to a career as a professional writer.[64] His journal *Sei* (Sex) was one of the longest-lived of a host of popular magazines devoted to sexology to appear during the 1920s. Morita Yūshū, too, was an author and journalist, and had resided for many years in Europe. An ardent socialist, Morita was among the most iconoclastic of his peers, characterizing his perspective on "same-sex love" as that of a social scientist rather than a doctor, and confessing that, unlike many of his medical colleagues, he felt no desire to lead those who practiced it back onto the "path of normality."[65] The analysis below considers these five men and their peers in the medical and sexological communities as a single group, regardless of the extent or nature of the particular individual's medical training, for all shared a common vision of sexuality as a realm of behavior properly understood only through scientific study by professional experts like themselves.

Most sexologists dealt with the issue of "same-sex love" somewhere in their writings, precisely because its anomaly within the sex/gender system begged for explanation. In doing so, they relied on several basic interpretive strategies, or tropes, all of which attempted to solve the "mystery" of "same-sex love" without compromising the system's larger premises. These tropes derived largely from Western literature, although the mode of their deployment was tailored to fit native expectations. The first may be called the "inversion" (*tōsaku* or *tentō*) trope, and reflects the ideas of such German authorities as Ulrichs, Karl Westphal, and Krafft-Ebing. In this interpretation, the male who experienced erotic desire toward other members of his sex was perceived, by virtue of this fact, as "feminine," and emphasis was placed on identifying various features of his physiology and psychology that were analogous to those of women. It was as if his "contrary" sexual orientation could be made intelligible only by rendering other aspects of his being female.

In *shudō*, the charms of youths had sometimes been compared to those of women, but their gender identities had remained for the most part distinct. The qualities that the *wakashu* shared with females were seen largely as a function of age, and coexisted with an incipient virility. It was expected

64. Furukawa, "Ren'ai to seiyoku no daisan teikoku," 121.
65. Morita, *Dōseiai no kenkyū*, (jo) 1; Morita, *Hentai seiyoku hiwa*, (jo) 2–3, 5; Morita Yūshū, *Jiyū ren'ai hiwa* (Heibonsha, 1930), 272–274.

that youths would eventually grow into men, except in some exceptional cases, such as the one depicted in the Great Mirror chapter titled "Two Cherry Trees Still in Bloom."[66] Here, Saikaku had portrayed a sixty-three-year-old samurai male named Tamashima Mondo who continued to serve as a love object for his even older nenja Toyoda Han'emon—a relationship whose disregard for age conventions surely struck seventeenth-century readers as outlandish and amusing. Yet although Saikaku describes the characters as "eccentric" (monozuki), nowhere does he liken Tamashima to a woman. In order to retain his erotic desirability, Tamashima models himself not after females, but after the youth that he has long outgrown in chronological terms, plucking his whiskers and keeping his temples unshaven. Toyoda thus thinks of him "as a boy of sixteen." Much less does Toyoda's sexual desire for a male render him feminine; instead, he is pictured as a "woman-hater" (onnagirai), hypermasculine rather than emasculated.

Had Saikaku been writing in the early twentieth century, these characters would no doubt have emerged quite differently. Given his presumably lengthy experience as a sexual insertee, Tamashima would have been a prime candidate for "effemination" (joseika, joka) or, as it was alternatively called, "eviration" (dansei dakka). According to this theory, most fully elaborated by Krafft-Ebing, males involved in "same-sex love" typically adopted feminine behavioral characteristics and came to assume the psychic persona of a woman. At the most advanced level of this progressive (or rather, degenerative) scale, called "androgyny," the very body of the individual came to resemble the female anatomy with regard to such features as voice timbre, growth of body hair, hair and skin texture, muscular and skeletal structure, distribution of fatty tissue, body odor, and breast development.[67] Some "androgynes" were even said to experience a periodic bleeding akin to menses. Morita maintained, for instance, that this had been the case with one early twentieth-century shinpa ("new school" of theater) actor—a claim that drew inspiration not only from Western sex-

66. Ihara, Nanshoku ōkagami, 39:432, 452–456 (Schalow, Great Mirror, 180–183 [whence the title]).

67. Habuto and Sawada, Hentai seiyokuron, 219–220; Kure Shūzō, "Dōsei no ai," Fujin gahō, October 1920, 25–26; Morita, Dōseiai no kenkyū, 122–124, 139–154; Morita Yūshū, "Sakutōkyōsha to shite no shijin Hoittoman," Seiron, July 1928, 59–60; Nakamura Kokyō, "Dōseiai no kaibō," Fujin kōron, June 1932, 437; Sawada, Shinpi naru dōseiai, 1:85–86; Sugie Kaoru, "Hidōteki sodomiya no ichirei," Sei, September 1920 (zōkan), 432–433; Sugita Naoki, "Hentai seiyoku no shujusō," Kenkō no tomo, January 1932, 5; Tanaka Kōgai, Ai to zankoku (Osaka: Fukuinsha shoten, 1925), 206–207; Tanaka Kōgai, "Danseikan ni okeru dōseiai," Nihon oyobi

ological writings but from an older kabuki tradition that had portrayed the consummate *onnagata* as subject to the same bouts of *chi no michi*, a form of hysteria associated with menstruation, as "real" women.[68]

More commonly, however, sexologists detected the marks of "effemination" in the individual's manner and tastes—that is to say, at the level of gender. Here, society's gender prejudices revealed themselves quite blatantly. Thus, according to Habuto and Sawada, "feminine males" (*onnarashiki otoko*) were "indolent" (*fukappatsu*), lacked "ability" (*rikiryō*), and possessed "weak" (*nyūjaku*) characters. Since these qualities rendered them unfit for such manly professions as manual labor, the authors recommended that they seek work in the fields of handicrafts, literature, and, above all, the theater.[69] "Inverted" gender was also reflected in their pastimes: "effeminates" did not smoke or drink, nor did they enjoy the up-and-coming sport of baseball.[70] In putatively congenital cases, feminine proclivities were often traced backed to childhood, when the individual in question was likely to have preferred girls' games to boys' and the companionship of females to that of his male peers. Naturally, the gendering of specific activities might differ from that of the contemporary West: thus, playing with a ball (*mari-tsuki*) was considered a sign of girlishness in boys, while among girls only the "virago"—the "effeminate's" female counterpart—would feel a desire to skip rope.[71]

Cross-dressing played an important part within the trope of "inversion." According to Habuto and Sawada, one of the defining characteristics of "same-sex love" in males was a tendency to enjoy dressing in women's

Nihonjin, 20 September 1920, 115; Tanaka Kōgai, "Dōseiai ni kansuru gakusetsu ni tsuite," pt. 1, *Hentai seiyoku*, March 1924, 121; Tanaka Kōgai, "Joseiteki danshi," *Hentai seiyoku*, February 1923, 51–52; Tanaka Kōgai, "Joseiteki danshi (andoroginī, Androgynie) no hanashi," in *Ki chin kai*, 205–206.

68. Morita, *Dōseiai no kenkyū*, 136–139; Hiraga Gennai, *Nenashigusa*, 55:62.

69. Habuto and Sawada, *Hentai seiyokuron*, 113–114.

70. Habuto and Sawada, *Hentai seiyokuron*, 215; Sawada, *Shinpi naru dōseiai*, 2:77; Tanaka, "Joseiteki danshi," 54; Tanaka, "Joseiteki danshi (andoroginī, Androgynie)," 206. Conversely, Morita (*Dōseiai no kenkyū*, 180) maintained that "evirated" males possessed a strong liking for tobacco and alcohol. Baseball had not repelled but attracted the older figure of the "roughneck," who was reputed to hang around stadiums in search of "beautiful boys." See, for example, Yamamoto Seikichi, *Gendai no furyō seinen, tsuketari furyō joshi* (Shun'yōdō, 1914), 50. On the emergence of baseball as a signifier of masculinity as well as of national pride, see Donald Roden, "Baseball and the Quest for National Dignity in Meiji Japan," *American Historical Review* 85 (1980): 511–534.

71. Habuto and Sawada, *Hentai seiyokuron*, 214; Sawada, *Shinpi naru dōseiai*, 2:69, 77.

clothing.[72] Thus, if the law were to permit cross-dressing—never mind that, in point of fact, it did—many more, they claimed, would take up the practice.[73] This was not simply in order to approach other members of their own sex (who, it was presumed, would be drawn to their feminine appearance), but also because they felt that such apparel and hairstyle best suited their psychically female bodies.[74] Sexological accounts of "same-sex love" commonly featured anecdotes, for example, about men who had shown up at their compulsory army physical in women's undergarments and Takashimada hairdo, had been sighted on the streets of Tokyo flaunting a "nauseatingly" pink waist cloth (*koshimaki*), or powdered their faces well into their fifties.[75] According to Takada, the appearance of the "flapper"-like *moga* in the 1920s was a boon to male cross-dressers, since long hair no longer served as a prerequisite of femininity.[76] Meanwhile, sexologists denounced the folk custom of dressing boys, particularly those with weak constitutions, in girls' clothing—the case of Ooto in chapter 3 represents an extreme example of this practice—as based on "superstition" (*meishin*), although not necessarily an indication of "same-sex love" unless the child himself possessed an inborn predilection for it.[77]

A second strategy for situating *dōseiai* within the sex/gender system,

72. Habuto and Sawada, *Hentai seiyokuron*, 163.

73. Sexologists often displayed a faulty grasp of Japanese law, in part because the Western authorities they drew upon were writing within a different legal context. Habuto and Sawada (*Hentai seiyokuron*, 330–333) railed, for instance, against the supposed noncriminalization of female-female (as opposed to male-male) "obscene acts," a situation that was true of such countries as Germany and England but not of Japan.

74. Habuto and Sawada, *Hentai seiyokuron*, 156–158; Komine Shigeyuki, *Dōseiai to dōsei shinjū no igakuteki kōsatsu*, in *Dōseiai to dōsei shinjū no kenkyū*, by Komine Shigeyuki and Minami Takao (Komine kenkyūjo, 1985), 99–100; Sawada, *Shinpi naru dōseiai*, 2:2, 6–7, 70; Tanaka Kōgai, "Josō suru hentai otoko to dansō suru hentai onna no hanashi," *Kenkō jidai*, December 1931, 108–112.

75. Komine, *Dōseiai to dōsei shinjū*, 100; Sawada, *Shinpi naru dōseiai*, 2:3, 6; Tanaka, "Joseiteki danshi," 58.

76. Takada Giichirō, *Hentai iwa*, 153–154; Takada Giichirō, *Hentai seiyoku kō*, 198–199; Takada Giichirō, *Hentai seiyoku to hanzai, hanzai to jinsei*, Kindai hanzai kagaku zenshū, no. 1 (Bukyōsha, 1929), 298. On the figure of the *moga*, see Barbara Hamill Sato, "The *Moga* Sensation: Perceptions of the *Modan Gāru* in Japanese Intellectual Circles during the 1920s," *Gender and History* 5 (1993): 363–381; Miriam Silverberg, "The Modern Girl as Militant," in *Recreating Japanese Women, 1600–1945*, ed. Gail Lee Bernstein (Berkeley: University of California Press, 1991), 239–266.

77. Komine, *Dōseiai to dōsei shinjū*, 93, 100; Morita, *Dōseiai no kenkyū*, 111; Sawada, *Shinpi naru dōseiai*, 2:4–5.

complementary rather than contradictory to the first, involved the notion of an "intermediate sex" (*chūsei*). In this trope, sexologists relegated individuals who engaged in "same-sex love" to a category that was neither entirely male nor entirely female, but lay somewhere in between. This mode of interpretation stressed the dissimilarities between this class of persons and the rest of the population, as if they formed a distinct gender unto themselves. As Morita remarked, there was always "something different" about them.[78] On the other hand, by positioning this group somewhere midway along the male-female axis, sexologists were able to preserve the fundamental polarity of the system as a whole.[79]

One of the first European authors to posit the existence of an intermediate sex was Ulrichs, who dubbed its (more or less) male and female representatives the *Urning* and *Urningin* respectively. By the early twentieth century, this terminology had come to be widely used in the German-speaking world, and to enjoy some currency in Japan as well. Mori Ōgai, for example, employs the former term in the Latin alphabet at one point in his 1909 *Vita Sexualis*, perhaps not surprisingly in view of his German medical training.[80] Also influential in carving out a niche for "same-sex love" in the gray area between male and female was the British socialist thinker Edward Carpenter, a Japanese version of whose 1908 work *The Intermediate Sex* appeared in 1914.[81] Japanese sexologists were also familiar with the "sexual interstage" theories of Magnus Hirschfeld, founder of the Scientific-

78. Morita, *Dōseiai no kenkyū*, 187.

79. Something akin to the "intermediate sex" paradigm may be discerned in an early nineteenth-century anecdote that has a man speculating that a drowned body is that of a *kagema* because it is floating sideways—a reference to the folk belief that female corpses faced upward and male downward. It should be noted, however, that this anecdote, along with others like it (see also the *senryū* quoted in chap. 1, n. 31), assigned "intersexed" status not to all individuals who engaged in *shudō* but specifically to the occupation of *kagema*, which constituted an elective (which is not to deny that many individuals were forced into it through poverty) and temporary status. See Matsuura Seizan, *Kasshi yawa zokuhen*, ed. Yoshikawa Hanshichi, 3 vols. (Kokusho kankōkai, 1911), 1:584.

80. Mori Ōgai, *Wita sekusuarisu*, in *Ōgai zenshū*, 5:111 (trans. Kazuji Ninomiya and Sanford Goldstein under the title *Vita Sexualis* [Rutland, Vt.: Tuttle, 1972], 58).

81. Aoyama Kikue, trans., *Chūseiron*, pts. 1–3, *Safuran*, May 1914, 1–22; June 1914, 130–153; July 1914, 55–76. For Carpenter's views on male-male (and female-female) sexuality, see Edward Carpenter, *Selected Writings*, ed. David Fernbach and Noël Greig, vol. 1, *Sex* (London: GMP, 1984); Jeffrey Weeks, *Coming Out: Homosexual Politics in Britain, from the Nineteenth Century to the Present* (London: Quartet, 1977), 68–83.

Humanitarian Committee, who visited Japan in 1931 as part of a worldwide lecture and research tour.[82]

Hirschfeld served as an important source of inspiration for Morita, whose *Dōseiai no kenkyū* (Study of Same-Sex Love) appeared in the same year as the German doctor's visit. Morita compared that segment of the human population that engaged in "same-sex love" to worker bees—a particularly apt metaphor coming from a socialist—who were not involved in the task of reproduction yet nevertheless necessary to the survival of their species, more crucially, in fact, than many a "meaningless" drone living off the labor of others. He appealed for greater understanding of this "intermediate sex," and an end to its social, legal, and religious persecution, praising Hirschfeld as a great "humanitarian fighter" (*jindō no senshi*). As an example of a "sexual intermediate" who had contributed to the "political freedom of the human race," he was fond of citing the nineteenth-century French revolutionary Louise Michel, a participant in the Paris Commune. Morita differed from many sexologists in calling openly not only for recognition of the "intermediate sex's" existence and value to society, but also for its right to follow its erotic inclinations without outside interference.[83]

A third strategy, which may be described as the "compound sex" (*fukusei*) trope, emphasized that all living creatures were in fact a mixture of male and female, and that "same-sex love" and "cross-sex love" were therefore not so radically distinct as they might first appear. A key influence here was the misogynistic and antisemitic Austrian thinker Otto Weininger, whose 1903 work *Geschlecht und Charakter* drew heavily upon turn-of-the-century biological theories and was twice translated into Japanese (in 1906 and 1925).[84] Explanations of this variety commonly turned for illustration to the animal kingdom, in the same manner as the previously quoted Watanuki. In asserting, however, that the capacity for "same-sex love," and even masturbatory practices, existed among lower organisms, whence humankind had inherited them, they were ironically in closer agreement with Saikaku than with the latter authority. Likewise, the notion that maleness or femaleness represented a preponderance, rather than the exclusive presence, of one or

82. For Hirschfeld's account of his visit, see *Men and Women: The World Journey of a Sexologist*, trans. O. P. Green (New York: Putnam's, 1935), 7–39. A summary of his speech before the Thirty-First Congress of Japanese Dermatologists may be found in "Gendai ni okeru seibyōrigaku no chiho," *Hanzai kagaku*, June 1931, 236–241.

83. Morita, *Dōseiai no kenkyū*, 293–301.

84. Katayama Masao, trans., *Danjo to tensai* (Dainihon tosho, 1906); Murakami Akio, trans., *Sei to seikaku* (Arusu, 1925).

the other element echoed an important tenet of yin-yang theory. Sawada went so far as to suggest that Chinese wisdom about the sexes prefigured Darwin's, as exemplified in an old adage about trouble being afoot when a hen manifested her latent masculinity and began crowing like a rooster.[85]

According to Weininger and his followers, human separation into male and female, itself the recapitulation of a longer evolutionary process, was not complete until puberty. Even then, however, a secondary sex continued to lie hidden beneath the main one, and might emerge to the surface (as in the aforementioned case of the crowing hen) if the latter suffered damage or "degeneration" (*taika*).[86] "Same-sex love" was the erotic manifestation of this imperfect separation of the sexes, existing potentially in all individuals. As Sawada put it, the "disposition" (*soshitsu*) for "same-sex love" was distributed generally within the human population, although only those in whom it was "particularly developed" actually experienced erotic "feelings" (*kanjō*).[87] Given the composite nature of the sexes, *dōseiai* could be explained not so much as a pairing of likes, but as an interaction between the feminine and masculine parts embedded in any two individuals, regardless of genitalia. In this sense, wrote Sawada, "same-sex love" and "cross-sex love" were "essentially one and the same."[88]

What these three sexological tropes—"inversion," "intermediate sex," and "compound sex"—shared was an attempt to make "same-sex love" intelligible in terms of male-female dichotomy, which contemporary science defined as the basis of human sexuality. In the process, each rooted "same-sex love" deep within the psychology and physiology of the individual. Thus, at the same time that sexology created the notion of *dōseiai*, it gave birth to the *dōseiaisha* or "same-sex love person." In this figure, too, the polarity of gender was unmistakably revealed. Sexologists insisted, for instance, that in any given couple, one party played the "masculine" role and one the "feminine," under the assumption that erotic attraction could be based only in gender difference. This dichotomy was often expressed in terms of "active" (*nōdō*) and "passive" (*judō*)—qualities deemed synonymous with masculinity and femininity and specifically associated with inserter and insertee roles in sexual intercourse. Within this paradigm, the primary kinship metaphor used in speaking of male-male sexuality was less

85. Sawada, *Shinpi naru dōseiai*, 1:133–135.
86. Habuto and Sawada, *Hentai seiyokuron*, 153–155; Katayama Masao, *Danjo to tensai*, 51–52; Murakami Akio, *Sei to seikaku*, 76–78; Sawada, *Shinpi naru dōseiai*, 1:134–135, 178–180.
87. Sawada, *Shinpi naru dōseiai*, 1:53.
88. Sawada, *Shinpi naru dōseiai*, 1:8.

likely to be that of elder and younger brother (that is to say, a pair of masculine elements), as had been the case in the earlier *shudō* paradigm, than that of husband and wife, a masculine-feminine coupling. This newly gendered dichotomy also manifested itself in the insider parlance of an emerging male-male erotic subculture (on which the next chapter will further elaborate), where the respective equivalents of "active"/masculine and "passive"/feminine were *tachi* (one meaning of which is "standing") and *uke* ("receiving"). According to Minakata Kumagusu, such terms were a "direct translation" of Western concepts and, by implication, foreign to an Edo-period mentality.[89]

In *shudō*, it will be remembered, the "passive" party had typically been designated by age, rather than by sexual position or proclivity. Every adolescent male was, in theory, a youth, the only qualification being preadult status. The category of *wakashu*, in other words, represented a vast pool of erotic objects available to the adult male, the desires of the potential objects themselves remaining unspecified. Apart from age, therefore, the *wakashu* did not differ essentially from others of his sex. In the same way, while such occupational categories as *kagema* might imply that the individual was available to perform an insertee role in male-male sexual relations, they conveyed little about that person's erotic subjectivity. If anything, the youth, and even the *kagema*, was assumed to possess an inherent disinclination toward being anally penetrated, which inserters overcame only through seduction, force, or remuneration. Thus, according to Konoe Nobuhiro's *Inu tsurezure*, written in 1619, the *wakashu* "yielded easily" (*nabikiyasui*)—not quite the same as actually desiring—to such materially rewarding types as the daimyo and the generous gift giver, but it was the list of his "dislikes" (*kiraimono*), including men who were penniless and those with "large tools" (*daidōgu*), that contained the greater number of items.[90]

The rise of the "same-sex love" model brought the erotic subjectivity of the male insertee into the foreground. The so-called "passive" was, ironically, quite active in his desire for men, in the same way that women were assumed to be inherently drawn to the opposite sex. Indeed, while the youth in *shudō* had to be enticed into sexual compliance, the "passive" male fre-

89. Minakata Kumagusu to Iwata Jun'ichi, 20 August 1931, *Minakata Kumagusu zenshū*, 9:15 (trans. William F. Sibley in "Morning Fog [Correspondence on Gay Lifestyles]," in *Partings at Dawn: An Anthology of Japanese Gay Literature*, ed. Stephen D. Miller [San Francisco: Gay Sunshine, 1996], 147–148).

90. Konoe, *Inu tsurezure*, 4:13.

quently took the initiative in luring susceptible inserters. The "temptation" that he represented was not simply the unintended consequence of his "attractive features" and "gentle disposition," as in the case of Kōmurō Shujin's "beautiful boy"; it was a conscious act stemming from his psychic identification with women. Like the *wakashu* of the seventeenth-century text, the "passive" male exhibited various preferences regarding partners, but his criteria for selection rested more on gender attributes than on material gain. What he sought was a "masculine man" (*otokorashiki otoko*), an adult male who could serve as the virile counterpart to his own femininity.[91] The men who appealed to him, according to Sawada, were such rugged types as laborers, soldiers, farmers, and sumo wrestlers, or, for the more sophisticated, "gentlemen" (*shinshi*) and students. He did not, however, share his Western counterpart's taste for monks, pugilists, waiters and other male service staff (*bōi*), and occasionally classical statues, nor was he, like the "active" *dōseiaisha*, attracted to boyish *chigo*.[92]

The "passive" male might himself be of any age, from the child in whom this "disposition" was inherited to men who turned to such practices in old age as a result of "degeneration." It was the adult "passive," however, who occupied center stage in early twentieth-century sexologists' vision of male-male sexuality, rather than the adolescent youth upon whom *shudō* texts had focused their gaze. This is not to say that *dōseiai* was judged more prevalent among adult males than adolescents—indeed, the reverse was true—but rather that its manifestation in grown men, particularly in a "passive" form, presented a more flagrant challenge to the sex/gender system and therefore provoked a greater measure of anxiety and speculation. Although sexologists in the early twentieth century wrote at length about adolescent *dōseiai*, they were motivated to a large extent by the perception that it could set a pattern for the individual in adulthood. The most unsettling prospect, not just for sexologists but for parents and other readers, was that a male who assumed a "passive" sexual role in his youth might adopt a permanent and exclusive preference for this and other aspects of feminine gender behavior. This prognosis was not so life-threatening as the physical ailments of which Meiji authorities more typically warned, but in a patriarchal and conformist society it was equally alarming.[93]

In the case of *shudō*, by contrast, the erotic future of the youth had

---

91. Sawada, *Shinpi naru dōseiai*, 2:71.
92. Sawada, *Shinpi naru dōseiai*, 2:37–38. A variant list appears in Habuto and Sawada, *Hentai seiyokuron*, 204–205.
93. This is not to say that early twentieth-century sexologists perceived no phys-

roused little apprehension. There was no suggestion that taking an inser-tee role as an adolescent would preclude subsequent, or even concurrent, inserter relations with women, largely because the former was conceived more as an expression of the inserter's desires than of his partner's. The *kagema*, particularly as he grew older, might be called upon to play both parts, and temple acolytes accustomed to the sexual advances of their mas-ters were known to scurry off to the local whorehouse when they had an opportunity.[94] Passage to adulthood, however, signaled an end to the role of youth and a time for marriage and the begetting of progeny, although it was permissible to continue sexual relations with other males in the role of inserter. Such characters as Saikaku's Tamashima were exceptional in this respect, their stories entertaining precisely because of their uncon-ventionality. Nevertheless, as we have seen, a superannuated youth like Tamashima was not perceived as following a feminine gender trajectory, as was apt to be the case with the twentieth-century "passive." Some *ka-gema*, it is true, pursued adult careers as *onnagata*, whether in legitimate kabuki or in traveling theater companies, but this choice was construed more as the outcome of artistic skill and economic necessity than of erotic inclination.[95]

A somewhat closer equivalent in earlier times to the ideal type of the

---

iological harm in "same-sex love." While admitting that precise research on the sub-ject was not available, Habuto and Sawada (*Hentai seiyokuron*, 297–301) asserted, for example, that *dōseiai* led, particularly in acquired cases, to depleted vigor; a short-ened life span; impaired nutrition; nerve damage; neurasthenia; stunted physical growth; brain disease; dementia; the spread of venereal infection, tuberculosis, and trachoma; and, of course, the perennial hemorrhoids.

94. For the acolyte reference, see Minakata Kumagusu to Iwata Jun'ichi, 16 Sep-tember 1931, *Minakata Kumagusu zenshū*, 9:68–69.

95. The adult *onnagata* enjoyed a higher profile in twentieth-century sexologi-cal accounts of "same-sex love" than he had in *shudō* texts, where adolescent play-ers of youths' (*wakashugata*) and young female roles (*wakaonnagata*) outshone him in prominence. Significantly, the author of a 1714 actor evaluation book (cited in Mette Laderrière, "Yoshizawa Ayame [1673–1729] and the Art of Female Imper-sonation in Genroku Japan," in *Europe Interprets Japan*, ed. Gordon Daniels [Ten-terden, Kent: Norbury, 1984], 235) writes of the celebrated *onnagata* Yoshizawa Ayame, about forty-one at the time: "If he were young and had *iro* [erotic appeal], a lot of people would die of love for him." Western observers were especially fasci-nated with the *onnagata*, to whose purportedly femalelike anatomy Iwaya ("Nan-šo-k' [die Päderastie in Japan]," 270) had drawn attention as early as 1902. Before its destruction by the Nazis in 1933, Magnus Hirschfeld's Institute for Sexual Sci-ence had on exhibit several portraits of *onnagata*, whom it described as "homosex-ual actors." See Koizumi Eiichi, *Berurin yawa* (Waseda daigaku shuppanbu, 1925), 207; Maruki Sado [Hata Toyokichi], "Chūkansei Hirushuferudo," *Hanzai kagaku*, June 1931, 220.

"passive" male *dōseiaisha* as sexologists pictured him was the *otoko-onna*: the "man-woman" who had permanently adopted aspects of a feminine gender role. We have already encountered this figure in the person of Inaba Kotoji/Okoto, whose 1881 prosecution (see chapter 3) for the crime of *keikan* stood in contrast to the age-stratified and inserter-initiated patterns of male-male sexual practice more familiar to Meiji lawmakers. Representations of the *otoko-onna* date as far back as the late Edo period, yet emphasize his transgression of gender conventions rather than his sexual behavior per se; indeed, in some instances he might even engage in male-female relations.[96] The *otoko-onna* was at best a marginal figure in the world of *shudō*, his age and other factors sometimes violating its basic disciplinary norms. In sexological accounts of *dōseiai*, on the other hand, individuals like him assumed a conspicuous profile, providing the ultimate embodiment of the gender "inversion" believed to accompany sexual "passivity." Stories of males who took on women's names and dress, earning their living in such feminine occupations as geisha, prostitute, concubine, waitress, maid, hairdresser, and female factory hand (*jokō*), appear repeatedly in such writings, borrowed largely from the pages of early twentieth-century journalism.[97] While some authorities pointed out that such persons were not necessarily *dōseiaisha*, their presence in the narrative nevertheless implied that their anomalous gender identity was intimately linked with "passive" sexual desire.[98]

At the same time, the rise of the *dōseiai* model involved changing perceptions of the male-male inserter. In many ways, the "active" male *dōseiaisha* was a murkier and more convoluted figure than his "passive" counterpart. The latter, despite his flamboyance, was at least consistent: he

96. For Edo-period and Meiji accounts of the *otoko-onna*, see, respectively, Miyatake Gaikotsu, *Futanari kō*, in *Miyatake Gaikotsu chosakushū*, ed. Tanizawa Eiichi and Yoshino Takao, 8 vols. (Kawade shobō, 1985–1992), 5:362; Umehara Hokumei, ed., <*Meiji Taishō*> *Kidan chinbun daishūsei*, 3 vols. (Bungei shijōsha, 1929–1931), 1:192. See also chap. 1, n. 51.

97. Hanabusa Shirō [Nakano Masato] ("Petchi ruiza sono ta," *Hanzai kagaku*, December 1930, 78) wrote that newspaper readers typically encountered articles about such cross-dressers, both male and female, once or twice yearly. One of the most celebrated among the male variety was Yagizawa Kiyokichi ("Kiyo-chan"), a hairdresser in the hot-springs resort of Shiobara, who was occasionally described as one of that town's "local attractions" (*meibutsu*). For an interview with Yagizawa, see Sakuragi Menzō, "Josō no hentai otoko o tōte sono sei shinri o kiku," *Kenkō jidai*, January 1932, 96–99.

98. Habuto and Sawada, *Hentai seiyokuron*, 160–163, 276–277, 283; Komine, *Dōseiai to dōsei shinjū*, 101–103; Morita, *Dōseiai no kenkyū*, 85; Nakamura Kokyō, *Hentai seikakusha zakkō*, Hentai bunken sōsho, no. 3 (Bungei shiryō kenkyūkai,

thought of himself as a woman, and therefore took on a "feminine" role in sexual relations. The former, on the other hand, while preferring the "masculine" role appropriate to his sex, enacted it with a male partner—a seemingly incongruous choice of sexual object. If, as sexology suggested, what attracted him was his partner's femininity, why did he not simply consort with women? As one writer put it in 1920, he could understand why present-day prisoners, isolated as they were from the opposite sex, would turn to one another for erotic release, but it was "unfathomable" (*fushigi de naranai*) why shoguns and daimyo, who had their pick of beautiful women, had chosen to lavish their attention on youths.[99]

Such behavior was, of course, quite comprehensible to Edo-period observers. In the erotic debate *Denbu monogatari*, even the habitué of female prostitutes deemed it perfectly natural for the daimyo to surround himself with attractive page boys, as he himself would do if his station in life allowed it.[100] In *shudō*, a capacity for loving youths was regarded as inherent in all men, although not everyone might yet have discovered its pleasures or mastered its proprieties. Rather than being a generalized status, like the "active" *dōseiaisha*, the *nenja* existed only in relationship to a particular youth: he was the "person who thought of" him—in other words, his lover. The disciplinary texts of *shudō* constructed an elaborate etiquette around the role of male-male inserter, or more precisely, sexual penetration constituted one aspect, and not even a necessary one, of a more comprehensive social role. It was partly for this reason that Minakata objected to designating the *nenja* by his "standing" genitals alone. By the same token that no male was born into this role, neither was any male deemed constitutionally incapable of performing it. In the *dōseiai* model, on the other hand, the "active" partner, inasmuch as he was a *dōseiaisha*, belonged to a class distinct from the rest of the male population, embodying a psychology that had mastered him instead of his mastering it.

Japanese of the Edo period, it is true, had noted that some persons,

1928), 75–77, 79–81; Sawada, *Shinpi naru dōseiai*, 2:17–20; Takada Giichirō, *Hentai iwa*, 153–154; Takada Giichirō, *Hentai seiyoku kō*, 198–199; Takada Giichirō, *Hentai seiyoku to hanzai*, 298–299; Tanaka Kōgai, "Onna ni narisumashita otoko: Seiyoku tentōshō no ichirei," *Hentai seiyoku*, June 1925, 303–309.

99. Chidarumasei, "Nanshoku ni yoru fukakai no shinri," *Sei*, April 1920 (zōkan), 136. Similarly, Katō Tokijirō, a socialist physician, wrote in 1926 that indulgence in *nanshoku* by polygamous daimyo was the "most perverse of perversions" (*hentaichū no hentai*). See "Seiyoku no jiyū to seigen," in *Katō Tokijirō senshū*, ed. Narita Ryūichi (Kōryūsha, 1981), 435.

100. *Denbu monogatari*, 37:128 (Leupp, *Male Colors*, 208–209).

whether by taste or circumstance, indulged in male-male sexual pleasure more often than others. One who did so to a conspicuous degree might, for instance, earn a reputation as a *wakashuzuki* or "youth-lover." Such a label, however, said little about that person's sexual behavior with or erotic feelings toward women, which might be equally prodigious, whereas the "active" *dōseiaisha* was, unless a "psychic hermaphrodite," presumed exclusively attracted toward members of his own sex. Moreover, the term *wakashuzuki* explicitly defined the sexual object as a youth—that is to say, a preadult male who was ideally younger in years than the inserter— whereas the "active" *dōseiaisha* was not constrained by considerations of age. This is not to say that, in the realm of social practice, the relative age of partners ceased to be an influential factor in determining sexual roles; age hierarchy continued, and to some extent continues today, to function as an important, if not exclusive and inflexible, principle in organizing male-male erotic relationships. Nevertheless, pairings between adult male insertees and younger inserters—a combination seldom, if ever, encountered in *shudō* texts—surface with newfound frequency in early twentieth-century accounts of "same-sex love." "Active" men whose erotic interest lay specifically in prepubescent males (together with those who desired sexually immature females) received, on the other hand, the sexological diagnosis of "pedophilia" (*shōni shikōshō*), thereby distinguishing them from "ordinary" *dōseiaisha*.[101]

In the Edo period, an inserter role in male-male sexual practices had also been associated with the *onnagirai* or "woman-hater." This figure was defined by his aversion to erotic and other forms of contact with females— a taste for which, unless otherwise stated, all adult males were presumed to share. Male-male sexual relations were not a necessary component of his identity but, insofar as a capacity for loving youths was taken equally for granted, provided the alternative to which he commonly turned. During the early twentieth century, the system of religious beliefs and code of samurai ethics that had once served to justify this figure's misogyny came under fire from sexologists. Since male-female sexuality appeared to sexologists as biological destiny, they chose to characterize such ideas as "superstition," "misunderstanding," and "willful distortion."[102] Although sexologists accepted unquestioningly many of society's gender prejudices, and were in

101. Habuto and Sawada, *Hentai seiyokuron*, 205; Sawada, *Shinpi naru dōseiai*, 2:39

102. Habuto and Sawada, *Hentai seiyokuron*, 206–208; Sawada, *Shinpi naru dōseiai*, 2:39–43.

many cases opponents of the women's rights movement, they at times found themselves in the ironic position of having to defend women before their more virulent detractors. In 1928, for instance, the physician Fukushima Masanori described a visit he had received from a thirty-three-year-old male who claimed to have turned to "same-sex love" because his *shizoku* father had taught him since childhood that women were "base" (*iyashiku*) and "unclean" (*kitanai*). The doctor assured him that they were none of these things, but in fact "just as noble [*tōtoi*] as men," and that he should therefore proceed with his planned marriage, father children, and discover "true happiness in life."[103] In this way, what had once been an honorable misogyny came to be characterized by sexologists as a pathological "fear of the opposite sex" (*isei kyōfushō*).[104]

The above patient's account of the origins of his *dōseiai*, as well as Fukushima's rather facile prescription for its cure, betray a belief that "same-sex love" was in many cases a product of environment. The emergence of the *dōseiai* model also raised the possibility, however, that, in some persons, a predisposition to male-male sexual practices was present from birth, if not before.[105] Sexologists referred to the former type of "same-sex love" as "acquired" (*kōtensei*), and the latter as "congenital" (*sentensei*), setting up another dichotomy within a construct already riddled with binary oppositions. *Shudō* texts, of course, had made no such distinction, assuming the capacity to love youths to be an inherent feature of the masculine psyche, and hence devoting little attention to the question of etiology. Minakata Kumagusu notes the existence of a Sino-Buddhist tract identifying four karmic causes for the desire of some men to be sexually penetrated by other males, such as having committed slander or incest in a previous life, but it is doubtful that this theory gained much currency in Edo-period Japan, where the role of male-male insertee was seldom perceived as a mat-

103. Fukushima Masanori, *Sei no kunō to ankoku no seiwa* (Osaka: Ibundō, 1928), 33–37.

104. For clinical diagnoses of the *onnagirai*, see Morooka Son, "'Otokogirai' to 'onnagirai' to sono chiryōhō," *Kenkō no tomo*, April 1932, 14–19; Tanaka Kōgai, "Onnagirai," in *Ki chin kai*, 144–148.

105. Edo-period authors occasionally described fictional characters as "born" (*umaretsuki*) *onnagirai* or *wakashugirai*, but chiefly as a form of hyperbole, and without implying a physical basis for such traits. In much the same way, Ejima Kiseki (*Yahaku naishō kagami*, in *Hachimonjiyabon zenshū*, ed. Hasegawa Tsuyoshi et al., 14 vols. to date [Kyūko shoin, 1992–], 2:58) wrote early in the eighteenth century that one of his characters was "by nature deeply versed in *shudō*" (*tennen to jakudō no tashinami fukaku*), thereby rhetorically positing a "natural" facility for *shudō* even as he retained its conventional construction as a "versed" (i.e., learnt) behavior.

ter of preference.[106] Likewise, in the early nineteenth century, the retired daimyo scholar Matsuura Seizan speculated that extreme *onnagirai*—like a certain whaler in his own domain of Hirado who, apart from a few scullery maids, refused to allow any women under his roof—had been born under the influence of an "eccentric whim of heaven and earth" (*tenchi no henki*), but here, the perceived eccentricity (literally "bias") was not that of desiring other males but of so utterly spurning females.[107]

So vague a formulation as Matsuura's "eccentric whim" would hardly have satisfied early twentieth-century sexologists, for whom etiology was central to their hermeneutic enterprise. In their search for causative mechanisms, they relied heavily on the new science of biology, which taught that the origins of human behavior lay within the physical body, rather than in such external powers as "heaven and earth" or karma. Congenital explanations of *dōseiai* were deeply influenced by Krafft-Ebing, who himself maintained that "contrary sexual instinct" revealed a "degeneration" of the organism—specifically, an anomaly of cerebral organization—that could be passed on through heredity. Thus, some sexologists suggested that Kyushuites' proclivity for male-male sexual practices, notorious since the Meiji period, had become inbred in Lamarckian fashion through several centuries of *nanshoku* among their ancestors.[108] On the whole, however, Japanese authorities showed noticeably less concern than Krafft-Ebing had with determining whether an individual's *dōseiai* represented a "hereditary taint" running in a particular family.[109]

Another strain of congenital explanation held that "same-sex love" resulted from a physiological insufficiency of male and overabundance of female elements in the male *dōseiaisha*, and the converse in the case of females. The exact nature of these elements and their location within the body, however, was a matter of divided opinion. One of the earliest versions of this theory, found in a 1904 work that Sawada coauthored with the educa-

106. Minakata Kumagusu, "Gekka hyōjin: Keizu funran no hanashi," in *Minakata Kumagusu zenshū*, 3:283; Minakata Kumagusu, "Ichidai otoko o yomu," in *Minakata Kumagusu zenshū*, 4:19.

107. Matsuura Seizan, *Kasshi yawa*, ed. Yoshikawa Hanshichi (Kokusho kankōkai, 1910), 408.

108. Habuto and Sawada, *Hentai seiyokuron*, 107, 342; Komine, *Dōseiai to dōsei shinjū*, 59; Sawada, *Shinpi naru dōseiai*, 1:130–131.

109. Among medical authorities, an exceptionally staunch proponent of the theory of hereditary causation was the psychiatrist Kure Shūzō, a former student of Krafft-Ebing. Kure claimed ("Dōsei no ai," 26) that heredity was responsible for some 70 to 80 percent of all cases of *dōseiai*, the predisposition for which often skipped a generation.

tor and anthropologist Ōtorii Sutezō, attributed maleness and femaleness
to the operation of loosely defined "reproductive organs" (*seishokki*). The
authors illustrated their point by describing a case in which an intersexed
individual, previously thought male, had been enabled to lead an "ordinary"
life as wife and mother through surgery to open up the vagina and cut the
clitoris down to "proper" size, and another in which a thirteen-year-old boy
who had injured his testicles upon falling from a tree had subsequently developed womanly features and frame, a liking for feminine dress, and shy-
ness in the company of other males. In a brief aside, they conjectured that
similar genital deformity or injury might account for many of "those persons who, while themselves male, love [*shitai*] males, or, while female, love
[*koisuru*] females."[110] By drawing so simplistic an equation between sexual
orientation and genitalia, such reasoning ran the risk of conflating "same-
sex love" with hermaphrodism, and indeed, in many sexological accounts
the two may be found in close proximity.

A more subtle means of accounting for imperfect maleness and femaleness, and by extension "same-sex love," was linked with the rapid growth
of endocrinology in the first decades of the twentieth century, and particularly to the discovery of sex hormones. Tanaka Kōgai followed European en-
docrinological research closely, positing that the *dōseiaisha* suffered from a
hormonal imbalance resulting from the weak functioning of the testicles or
ovaries (sometimes influenced by adrenal secretions), along with vestigial
traces of gonads proper to the opposite sex. Faced with the objection that
the latter could not always be detected, he speculated that such "microtis-
sue," though ostensibly producing hormones, might simply be too minute
to see.[111] Morita, on the other hand, admitted that no one could yet explain
the precise mechanism that gave birth to the *dōseiaisha*, but favored
Hirschfeld's theory that the "sexual interstages" arose from arrested fetal
development.[112]

For Morita, once again following Hirschfeld's lead, the supposedly con-

110. Ōtorii Sutezō and Sawada Junjirō, *Danjo no kenkyū* (Kōfūkan shoten, 1904),
96–97.

111. Tanaka, *Ai to zankoku*, 203–215, 232–235; Tanaka Kōgai, "Danseiteki joshi
(ginandorīru)," *Hentai seiyoku*, March 1924, 109–110; Tanaka, "Joseiteki danshi,"
50–51; Tanaka Kōgai, "Joshi no danseika no byōriteki gen'in ni kansuru chiken hoi,"
Hentai seiyoku, December 1924, 255–257; Tanaka Kōgai, "Joshi no danseika no gen'in
ni kansuru shinchiken," *Hentai seiyoku*, July 1924, 1–7; Tanaka Kōgai, "Tasei henshin no gen'in ni kansuru gakusetsu ni tsuite," *Hentai seiyoku*. March 1925,
105–113.

112. Morita, *Dōseiai no kenkyū*, 202–203.

genital origins of "same-sex love" provided a rationale for defending persons so born from social prejudice and persecution. On the whole, however, sexological research on "same-sex love" took place in a less emancipatory context than in the West, if only because of the relative weakness of corresponding strictures. Thus, when Morita condemned religious and legal oppression of the "intermediate sex," it was primarily to their situation in Western countries that he referred. Nor did the emergence of sexology in early twentieth-century Japan give rise to concerted organizing efforts by those whom it labeled *dōseiaisha*, due in part to the conformist pressures of "social morality." In describing the existence of "clubs" for such individuals in Europe, Habuto and Sawada asked rhetorically whether anyone in Japan would have the "courage" to set up such a group, and speculated that the reaction of most Japanese would be that "even eccentricity has its limits" (*monozuki ni mo hodo ari*).[113]

Further militating against such a possibility was the fact that the *dōseiaisha* as a social identity did not, in the early twentieth century, take root so firmly as the notion of *dōseiai* itself. Most Japanese sexologists admitted that much of "same-sex love" was etiologically acquired and phenomenologically temporary, something one might "fall" (*ochiiru*) into and in many cases out of. Even in congenital cases, they claimed, the "latent" (*senpuku*) factors might never surface unless triggered by external events and circumstances, while conversely, individuals without an inborn predisposition toward "same-sex love" might come to practice it under the influence of environment.[114] The latter phenomenon was often designated "pseudo" (*kasei*) *dōseiai*, after a term coined by Iwan Bloch, in contrast with "true" (*shinsei*) *dōseiai*, which was conceived as permanent, exclusive, and chiefly congenital.[115] Sexologists did not need to search far in the native literature for examples of behavior fitting Bloch's description. They were therefore able to illustrate their accounts of acquired "same-sex love" with settings and characters that both Edo-period audiences and newspaper readers of a later era would easily have recognized, whereas depictions of the congenital variety were more likely to draw upon Western sources.

113. Habuto and Sawada, *Hentai seiyokuron*, 315.
114. For a list of triggering factors, including "disappointment in [male-female] love" (*shitsuren*) and "temptation" by a member of the same sex, see Habuto and Sawada, *Hentai seiyokuron*, 336–337; Sawada, *Shinpi naru dōseiai*, 2:182.
115. This distinction is most succinctly stated in Nakamura, *Hentai seikakusha zakkō*, 69–70.

Sawada, for instance, described the causes of acquired *dōseiai* as follows:

1. Prohibition of normal sexual relations. [The specific examples subsequently given are monks and nuns (of both Buddhist and Christian orders), servants in the women's quarters of daimyo households, with "vestiges" (*ifū*) of the last among the contemporary peerage and the wealthy.]
2. Prolonged interruption of [male-female] sexual relations. [The examples chosen are soldiers at war, sailors on long voyages, prisoners, and those living in strict dormitories.]
3. An obsessive belief that the opposite sex is unclean. [Here, the *onnagirai* and his female counterpart, the *otokogirai* or "man-hater," make their appearance.]
4. Curiosity. [Sawada detects this motive among daimyo and nobles grown tired of "normal" sexual relations.]
5. A reaction to the unpleasantness of forced intercourse [with males]. [The representatives of this exclusively female category are prostitutes, both licensed and unlicensed.]
6. Suggestion [*anji*] or geographical custom. [Such was the case, Sawada maintains, among the ancient warriors of Satsuma and Sparta.]
7. Mental disease, etc.[116]

The contents of this list implied that much of the *dōseiai* that took place in historical and contemporary Japan did not belong to the "true" variety as identified by Western sexologists, here represented only by the last category—"mental disease, etc." A similar listing by Habuto and Sawada stated that "same-sex love" of the first, second, third, and sixth types was not "pathological" (*byōteki*), and that the first two should be seen merely as an "abnormal" (*ijō*) manifestation of repressed cross-sex desire.[117] Such characterizations typically envisioned the male *dōseiaisha* as an inserter rather than insertee, his "active" role reconcilable with a masculine gender identity as well as erotic attraction toward females, and serving as a functional equivalent of male-female coitus or, alternatively, an escalated form of masturbation. Here, in other words, the *nenja* and the "roughneck" found their medical reincarnation.

The view that "same-sex love" was in many instances an acquired trait also raised the possibility of its prevention or cure. Edo-period writers had seldom spoken of "curing" *shudō*, since they did not regard it in a pathological light. At most, the *nyodō* faction in erotic debates had sought to influence their opponents' behavior through rhetorical persuasion, while their opponents attempted to woo their allegiance by the same means. With

---

116. Sawada, *Shinpi naru dōseiai*, 2:115–117.
117. Habuto and Sawada, *Hentai seiyokuron*, 104–107.

the rise of the medical model of *dōseiai,* however, sexologists began to devise practical therapies and social policies for inducing "normal" (that is to say, exclusively male-female) sexual behavior. While sexologists generally saw acquired cases of *dōseiai* as standing the best chance of prophylaxis or treatment, some asserted that even the congenital *dōseiaisha* might be rescued from a morbid future if the stimuli that brought his or her "latent" tendencies to the surface could be eradicated.

To begin with, sexologists advocated an easing of strict sex segregation, particularly among the young. For this reason, they were among the earliest supporters of coeducation, as well as the abolition of dormitories, seeking to dilute the rugged homosocial atmosphere that had fostered the Meiji "roughneck."[118] Kure Shūzō characterized coeducational schooling as the next best alternative to sending a child with a "disposition" for "same-sex love" to a neuropathic hospital (one of the most prestigious of which he himself headed).[119] Many sexologists also called for sex education and a general lifting of the veil of secrecy around sexuality, believing that this would serve to attenuate excessive curiosity about erotic matters, impart "appropriate" knowledge of the dangers involved, and prevent an irrational "fear of the opposite sex" from forming.[120] Outside the school, too, sexologists demanded greater opportunities for young men and women to socialize, although Habuto and Sawada warned in the same breath that regulatory authorities must remain vigilant lest such new freedoms corrupt "public morality" (*fūki*). The latter authors, both of whom began their publishing careers in the Meiji period, were among the most moralistic of their cohort, recommending, in addition to the above measures, the rejection of "unhealthy" (*fukenzen*) ideas, the proscription of lust-inciting "temptations" such as the European-style solicitation of partners through newspaper want ads, the propagation of moral and religious ideas, the imposition of legal strictures, the inculcation of "wholesome manners" (*ryōshū bizoku*), and, above all, a Meijiesque strengthening of "self-denial" (*kokkishin*).[121]

Sexologists cited a gradual rise in the age of marriage as another factor

118. Habuto and Sawada, *Hentai seiyokuron,* 340, 343–344, 348–349; Sakaki Yasusaburō, *Seiyoku kenkyū to seishin bunsekigaku* (Jitsugyō no Nihonsha, 1919), 182; Sawada, *Shinpi naru dōseiai,* 2:186–187, 192–193, 197–198; Yoneyama Tatsuo, "Dōseiai o kataru," *Kyūdai ihō* 6 (1932): 42.

119. Kure, "Dōsei no ai," 27.

120. Habuto and Sawada, *Hentai seiyokuron,* 342–343, 349–350; Kurimoto Tsunekatsu, "Seinen danjo ni sei kyōiku o hodokosu koto wa nani ga yue ni hitsuyō ka," *Sei,* June 1921, 12–19; Sawada, *Shinpi naru dōseiai,* 2:189–192, 198–199.

121. Habuto and Sawada, *Hentai seiyokuron,* 340–341, 349; Sawada, *Shinpi naru dōseiai,* 2:187–189, 198. Erotic want ads from males seeking other males appear in

behind the spread of *dōseiai* in contemporary society, and, as we have seen in the case of Fukushima, prescribed prompt nuptials by way of cure.[122] Here again, Morita was a noteworthy exception, claiming that, for all except the "pseudo" *dōseiaisha*, marriage to the opposite sex was "perverted" (*hentaiteki*), causing suffering to both individuals and, through heredity, to their offspring as well. To force the *dōseiaisha* to wed for the sake of "social morality" (*shakaiteki dōgi kannen*) was, in his words, "hypocrisy."[123] In practice, however, "social morality" imposed formidable pressures toward marriage, so that the reportedly high percentage of Western *dōseiaisha* who remained single throughout their adult lives sometimes astonished Japanese observers.[124] In a society that generally regarded love and matrimony as separate issues and equated the latter with responsible adulthood, Morita's rejection of what Habuto and Sawada called "marriage therapy" (*kekkon ryōhō*) was distinctly radical. Two decades later, a prominent sexologist could still announce with no sense of hypocrisy that he felt it his "mission" (*shimei*) to help the male *dōseiaisha* at least to reach the point where he could receive a "proper wife" (*chantoshita okusan*) and keep male lovers on the side.[125]

For the neurasthenic *dōseiaisha*, who was dysfunctional with the opposite sex for ostensibly neurological reasons, sexologists advised "recuperative therapy" (*setsuyō ryōhō*), in which the subject was expected to regain a "healthy" erotic desire by maintaining a regimen of moderate exercise, bland food, relaxation, change of scenery, and avoiding venues, such as schools or concerts, where members of his or her own sex congregated.[126]

Japanese newspapers at least as early as 1925, for an example of which see Mimura Tokuzō, "Aru tokui seikakusha no kokuhaku," *Hanzai kōron*, June 1933, 118.

122. See also Habuto and Sawada, *Hentai seiyokuron*, 337–339, 346–347; Katō, "Seiyoku no jiyū to seigen," 434–435, 437–439; Sawada, *Shinpi naru dōseiai*, 2:183–185, 196.

123. Morita, *Dōseiai no kenkyū*, 212–224.

124. See, for instance, Sakaki Yasusaburō, *Kawarimono* (Jitsugyō no Nihonsha, 1912), 111, which characterizes lifelong bachelorhood/spinsterhood as a sign of mental disease.

125. "<Tengoku ka jigoku ka> Danshi dōseiaisha no tsudoi," *Ningen tankyū*, January 1951, 79. The speaker was the psychologist Takahashi Tetsu, on whose life and career see Saitō Yozue, *Sekusorojisuto Takahashi Tetsu* (Seikyūsha, 1996); <Shin bungei tokuhon> Takahashi Tetsu* (Kawade shobō, 1993); Suzuki Toshibumi, *Sei no dendōsha: Takahashi Tetsu* (Kawade shobō, 1993).

126. Habuto and Sawada, *Hentai seiyokuron*, 345–347; Komine, *Dōseiai to dōsei shinjū*, 98; Sawada, *Shinpi naru dōseiai*, 2:195–196.

A number of authorities also prescribed hypnosis, although acknowledging its limitations in severe or congenital cases.[127] To males who sought a means of stimulating desire for the opposite sex, Sawada recommended testosterone injections, while Tanaka advocated testicle transplants, provided a willing and healthy donor could be found.[128] Morita, on the other hand, was skeptical of all attempts to treat *dōseiai*, declaring that human effort was powerless against the designs of "nature."[129]

Nevertheless, the belief that "same-sex love" might be cured was, if anything, strengthening around the time Morita wrote, owing in part to the influence of psychoanalytic theory. While Freud's "talking cure" itself never achieved the popularity in Japan that it did in the West, the psychoanalytic model of "same-sex love" had by midcentury made significant inroads into Japanese discourse, not simply as a reflection of its ascendance abroad, but also because it resonated in certain respects with native views. Freudian theory lent additional support to an acquired etiology for "same-sex love," which, from the beginning, had sat more comfortably with Japanese sexologists than explanations (such as Hirschfeld's) stressing purely congenital factors. Most early twentieth-century sexologists acknowledged both modes of causation, their relative importance varying with the author, yet over time the balance shifted subtly toward the acquired view.

Moreover, sexologists pinpointed the crucial moment of acquisition increasingly early in the individual's lifetime, echoing the Freudian notion that "same-sex love" constituted a form of arrested psychological development determined primarily by childhood influences. As early as 1919, the psychiatrist Sakaki Yasusaburō pointed out that many so-called innate (*seirai*) *dōseiaisha*, when examined closely, might be found to have experienced some traumatic incident early in their lives, the nature of which they did not always remember as adults, but which could still be coaxed to the surface with the help of a professional.[130] By 1936, even Sawada had adopted a quasi-Freudian perspective, asserting that a small but to him significant number of the *dōseiaisha* whom he had studied had been brought up single-handedly

127. Habuto and Sawada, *Hentai seiyokuron*, 345; Komine, *Dōseiai to dōsei shinjū*, 98; Ōtsuki Kenji, *Ren'ai seiyoku no shinri to sono bunseki shochihō* (Tōkyō seishin bunsekigaku kenkyūjo, 1936), 228; Sakaki, *Seiyoku kenkyū*, 175–176; Sawada, *Shinpi naru dōseiai*, 2:194–195.

128. Sawada Junjirō, "Seiteki hanmon kaiketsu," *Sei to ren'ai*, July 1921, 147; Tanaka, *Ai to zankoku*, 230–239.

129. Morita, *Dōseiai no kenkyū*, 224.

130. Sakaki, *Seiyoku kenkyū*, 176.

by a member of the same sex, thereby forming an overly strong attachment to this parent figure.[131]

As developed by the Viennese school, the psychoanalytic model maintained that such early maladjustments might be overcome later in life through the dynamic interaction of psychoanalyst and analysand. A magazine article in 1932 went so far as to announce that "modern medicine" had finally "conquered" (*seifuku*) "same-sex love," the purported success of such European therapists as Wilhelm Stekel in curing *dōseiaisha* having conclusively demonstrated that Hirschfeld was mistaken about its congenital origins.[132] Yet, for numerous cultural reasons, psychoanalysis as a clinical practice did not prosper in Japan to the extent that it did in the West, so that even Ōtsuki Kenji, who translated Freud's selected works, recommended that, because psychoanalysis took too much time, the postadolescent *dōseiaisha* would be better served by turning to hypnosis.[133]

Another familiar aspect of the Freudian model was its insistence upon the latent universality of "same-sex love" in all humans. While this view was in a sense an elaboration of the "compound sex" trope on a purely psychological level, it also blended with a long-standing reluctance in Japanese discourse to characterize the capacity for erotic relations with the same sex as a factor that radically and irrevocably differentiated one segment of the population from the rest, as did the "intermediate sex" trope of Hirschfeld and Morita. In addition, by siting "same-sex love" (or at least "two-sex love") as a normative stage in psychological development, its appearance prior to and in fact necessary for that of "cross-sex love," Freudian theory echoed the Edo-period conceptualization of male-male erotic behavior as preceding and in many instances superseded by male-female ties, as well as the Meiji association of male-male sexuality with the world of adolescence. Persons who exhibited "same-sex love" beyond their adolescent years had, according to this interpretation, failed to achieve the emotional maturity that an exclusively cross-sex pattern of erotic behavior signaled, just as "social morality" denied them full recognition as adults until they entered into male-female marriage.

Conversely, the perception of "same-sex love" as in most instances a passing phase created a temporary zone within whose boundaries erotic desires and (to a lesser extent) practices between members of the same sex could

131. Sawada, *Seiai jinsei*, 244.

132. Ikuno Shin'ichi, "Bakuroshō dōseiai o seifuku shita bankin igaku," *Hanzai kagaku*, April 1932, 51–56.

133. Ōtsuki, *Ren'ai seiyoku no shinri*, 228.

be classified as relatively healthy and "normal" (*jōtai*). According to the educator Ichikawa Genzō, this period fell between the ages of thirteen and seventeen in males—interestingly, a time span roughly identical with some of the narrower definitions of the Edo-period "youth."[134] Even Sawada acknowledged that he had several times experienced a "mild" (*keido*) variety of "same-sex love" in his adolescence, providing readers with a detailed description of the other parties' ages, physical types, characters, and the degree of intimacy that he had established with them.[135] If even a sexologist could admit to such feelings, then clearly "same-sex love" was not a fatal disease.

DISSECTING THE PAST, DIAGNOSING THE PRESENT

The contours of the "same-sex love" model as it took shape in twentieth-century Japan did not simply replicate Western sexual cartographies, but also were subtly molded by older conceptions of male-male (as well as female-female) sexual behavior—as we saw, for instance, in Sawada's etiological inventory. Japanese sexologists had at their disposal a wealth of textual information regarding such behavior in former eras of their country's history, a circumstance that enabled them to introduce "same-sex love" as a phenomenon whose roots extended as deeply into the Japanese past as that of the West, thereby reinforcing the model's claims to universal applicability.[136] This textual wealth they delved into freely, helping to rescue its store of knowledge from the silencing effects of Meiji "civilization." Ironically, the success of the latter can be gauged from the admission of Yasuda Tokutarō, an internist and social reformer, that he first learned the history of *shudō* by reading German works, the information they contained deriving in large part from Iwaya Sazanami.[137] At the same time, by mobilizing historical texts and personalities to flesh out the new construct of "same-sex love," sexologists provided male-male sexual behavior with labels that denizens of the eras in question would themselves not have recognized and rationales that they might not have understood. In this way, just as the past informed the present, so did the present inform the past.

134. Ichikawa Genzō, "Sei kyōikuron," *Sei*, September 1920 (zōkan), 30.
135. Sawada, *Shinpi naru dōseiai*, 1:21–30.
136. Japanese explorations of male-male sexuality in the historical West date at least as far back as an 1877 discussion of Roman prostitution in *Baiin enkakushi* (trans. Inagaki Ginji, 3 vols. [Keishōkaku], 3:11) but remain outside the scope of the present survey.
137. Yasuda Tokutarō, "Dōseiai no rekishikan," *Chūō kōron*, March 1935, 147.

The task of charting Japan's erotic past was by no means a new one. Meiji writers had engaged in it as part of the process earlier described as "museumification," as their Edo-period forebears had done in constructing a history of *shudō*. Prior to the twentieth century, however, such accounts seldom relied upon medical explanations or terminology. An 1887 book titled *Nihon jōkō no hensen* (Vicissitudes of Passion in Japan), for instance, explained the prevalence of male-male erotic ties during the Edo period as the outcome of a struggle between "nature" (*ten, shizen*), which favored love (*jōai*) between men and women, and a misogynistic "feudal system" that discouraged it. In a fashion that Foucault would have described as hydraulic, the deflected urge, implicitly gendered as masculine, had channeled itself instead into erotic relations with *bishōnen*, a choice that the book's author—the future novelist, poet, and Christian preacher Miyazaki Koshoshi—characterized as both "irrational" (*furi*) and "unspeakable" (*iu ni shinobizaru*). Since the Restoration, Miyazaki observed, such "hideous customs" had received their just condemnation, and, with the exception of such backward areas as Kyushu, even persons born in the Edo era had come to reform themselves.[138]

In asserting that the "instruments of passion change with time," Miyazaki's etiology stressed cultural and moral factors over biological destiny. By contrast, within the medicalized framework of "same-sex love," early twentieth-century sexologists began to subject male-male erotic practices of the Edo and earlier periods to a sort of retrospective dissection, seeking to ground the sexual behavior of the past in a present-day understanding of physiology and psychology. It was this impulse that prompted Habuto and Sawada to hypothesize, for example, that Satsuma warriors had, through their habitual indulgence in *nanshoku*, passed on a hereditary predisposition for "same-sex love" to their descendants. The "heroes" (*eiyū*) of old emerged in this view as congenitally tainted "urnings," to employ the term one author used to describe Hirata Sangorō and Yoshida Ōkura, the valiant samurai lovers immortalized in *Shizu no odamaki*.[139] Most writers, however, classified warrior *shudō*, along with its vestiges among latter-day Kyushuites, as belonging to the "customary" or "regional" variety of "same-sex love"—a type of "pseudo" *dōseiai* that was acquired as the result of imitation, "vainglory" (*kyoei*), or environmental influence, rather than be-

138. Suekane Naokichi [Miyazaki Koshoshi], *Nihon jōkō no hensen* (Banseidō, 1887), 76–88.
139. Hamao Shirō, "Dōseiai kō," *Fujin saron*, September 1930, 138.

ing inbred, and even Habuto and Sawada vacillated between the two etiological modes.[140] Yasuda similarly pointed out that such figures as the first
Tokugawa shogun, Ieyasu, despite having engaged in male-male sexual practices, could not properly be regarded as "pathological" (*byōnin*), since they
were equally capable of erotic relations with women.[141] Indeed, the relatively
permeable barrier between *nanshoku* and *joshoku* in the Edo period often
made it difficult to classify historical figures neatly in terms of "cross-sex
love" and "same-sex love," leaving sexologists little choice but to pronounce
them "psychic hermaphrodites."[142]

It was the samurai elaboration of *shudō* that most disturbed sexologists,
both because it elevated an ostensibly "unnatural" and "perverse" form of
behavior over the sexological norm, and because it implied a harmony between masculine gender identity and male-male sexual practices that the
dōseiai model disavowed. Friedländer's turn-of-the-century claims regarding the relationship between Japan's military might and southwestern
"pederasty" thus prompted vociferous rebuttals from Japanese sexologists.
Habuto and Sawada faulted Friedländer on a number of grounds, maintaining that many military heroes had eschewed male-male sexual practices;
that such warriors frequently pursued erotic relations with women; that
their fighting capacities, far from being related to their erotic pursuits, were
for the most part an inherited trait; that indulgence in male-male sexual
practices in fact posed a danger to warriors' health; and that the Japanese
had been a martially gifted people long before *nanshoku* became widespread.[143] Tanaka, too, charged Friedländer with a flawed understanding of
history, arguing that, by construing male-male sexual practices as the source
of martial vigor and not as a by-product of peculiar political and military

---

140. Habuto and Sawada, *Hentai seiyokuron*, 342; Hino Mitsuo, ed., "<Gojū-
nenkan no vēru o nuida kisho> Kōmurō Shujin-cho *Bishōnenron, ichimei dōsei shikijōshi*," pt. 1, *Erochika*, October 1970, 220–221; Nakamura, *Hentai seikakusha zakkō*, 69; Sawada, *Shinpi naru dōseiai*, 1:15–16; 2:117; Sugita Naoki, *Kindai bunka to
sei seikatsu*, Sei kagaku zenshū, no. 2 (Bukyōsha, 1931), 519; Yoneyama, "Dōseiai o
kataru," 42.

141. Yasuda, "Dōseiai no rekishikan," 148. Regarding other Tokugawa rulers, Itō
Gingetsu (<*Rimenkanteki*> *Isetsu Nihonshi* [Hakuundō shoten, 1909], 288–292)
portrays the fifth shogun Tsunayoshi's fondness for *bishōnen* as an indication of
"mental disease," while Mitamura Engyo ("Tsukiyo no sandai shōgun," in *Mitamura Engyo zenshū*, 1:59) suggests that this "perverse" trait had been inherited from
Tsunayoshi's father, the third shogun Iemitsu.

142. See, for example, Sawada's description of Saikaku as a "psychic hermaphrodite" in *Shinpi naru dōseiai*, 1:71.

143. Habuto and Sawada, *Hentai seiyokuron*, 316–324.

conditions, he had reversed the true relationship of cause and effect.[144] A 1913 text coauthored by the urologist Kitagawa Seijun and the folklorist Fujisawa Morihiko took another tack, contending that the *bishōnen* who served as erotic objects in *shudō* were not the strong and virtuous types that Friedländer imagined, but rather assumed the ways of "weak-willed women," shaving their eyebrows, powdering their faces, wearing women's clothing, and seeking to win the favor of patrons by virtue of their looks.[145] In this way, the ideological tension existing in Germany between Friedländer's masculinizing and Hirschfeld's feminizing paradigms of male-male sexuality found distant echoes on Japanese battlefields.[146]

The commercialized *shudō* culture of the Edo period also provided fertile ground for the sexological imagination. Habuto and Sawada asserted, without any statistical evidence, that *kagema* had rarely lived past the age of twenty-five, offering this allegation as proof that male-male sexual activity, particularly if an acquired practice, posed a dire threat to human health.[147] (Perhaps the authors confused the fact that some Edo-period texts cited twenty-five as the upper limit of youth with mortal, rather than professional, demise.) Tanaka, on the other hand, saw in the *kagema* the most likely evidence that Hirschfeld's "sexual interstages" had existed among the Edo-period population, suggesting that a significant number of male prostitutes had been congenital "effeminates" who harbored an innately "inverted" sexual desire, or, because their customers included females as well, at least exhibited "two-sex love." Tanaka acknowledged that, in suggesting that the *kagema* chose his profession in order to satisfy his own sexual urges, he contradicted Edo-period authors who assumed that the insertee role in male-male intercourse was devoid of erotic pleasure, but German sexology evidently seemed to him a more reliable guide to reconstructing the past than native textual tradition.[148] By 1947, a Freudian perspective had crept

144. Tanaka Kōgai, "Dōseiai ni kansuru gakusetsu ni tsuite," pt. 2, *Hentai seiyoku*, April 1924, 171–172.

145. Kitagawa Seijun and Fujisawa Morihiko, *Shikijō shisō no kaibō* (Ryūseidō, 1913), 235–236.

146. For more on this ideological tension, see Oosterhuis and Kennedy, *Homosexuality and Male Bonding*.

147. Habuto and Sawada, *Hentai seiyokuron*, 298.

148. Tanaka, "Danseikan ni okeru dōseiai," 116; Tanaka, "Dōseiai ni kanseru gakusetsu," pt. 2, 170; Tanaka, "Joseiteki danshi," 59–60; Tanaka, "Joseiteki danshi (andoroginī, Androgynie)," 209; Tanaka Kōgai, "Nanshoku ni kansuru shiteki oyobi bungakuteki kōshō," *Hentai seiyoku*, June 1924, 234–235; Tanaka Kōgai, *Ningen no seiteki ankokumen* (Ōsaka yagō shoten, 1922), 66. Sawada Junjirō ("Seiteki yūgi to baiin," *Sei*, January 1921, 50–51) divided *kagema* into three categories—

into interpretations of this figure, as when one writer claimed that many *kagema* had acquired their "sexual inversion" as the result of being repeatedly raped at a tender age, causing them to deviate from the "normal path" of psychosexual development.[149]

Sexologists were less convinced, however, that the behavior of the *kagema's* male customers constituted "true" *dōseiai*. Sakaki argued, for instance, that, while the *kagema* imitated women in his clothing and manners, the men who patronized him had retained their masculine identities, being mere "lechers" (*sukimono*) attracted by his feminine beauty. It was extremely rare, he maintained, for "inverts," at least of the "active" male variety, to take on the mental characteristics of the opposite sex.[150] Tanaka went one step further, asserting that, since prepubescent males and mature females shared many physical features in common, even a man with "ordinary" sexual desires could easily fall in love with a feminine-appearing boy's "gentleness" (*shiorashisa*), particularly if he had limited access to women, as in the case of Buddhist priests, or if, as with the *kagema's* samurai and townsman customers, he had simply grown sated with *joshoku*. The notion that it was in some sense "ordinary" for men to respond erotically to preadult males echoed the "beautiful boy" esthetic of Meiji and earlier times, but this attraction was now rationalized in biological terms and in a way that denied an autonomous basis for the *bishōnen's* charms apart from his resemblance to females.[151]

As the above example suggests, sexologists not only reshaped existing

---

"urnings," "psychic hermaphrodites," and those with "normal sexual desire"—depending upon whether their clients were men, men and women, or women exclusively. It should be noted, however, that there is little historical evidence for the institutionalized existence of the third variety of male prostitution in Edo-period Japan.

149. Hisamatsu Ippei, "Sodomī dan," *Ryōki* 3 (1947): 18.

150. Sakaki, *Seiyoku kenkyū*, 187–188. Similarly, the psychiatrist Sugita Naoki (*Kindai bunka*, 519) saw the behavior of the *kagema's* patrons as arising from "fashion" (*ryūkō*) rather than "deep psychological causes," while Saitō Tamao ("Danshi no seiyoku to daisan shigeki," *Kenkō jidai*, July 1931, 13), another medical doctor, employed the *kagemajaya* as an example of the "tertiary stimulation" of male sexual desire, which arose in a "perverse" manner from the existence of historically conditioned taboos.

151. Tanaka, "Danseikan ni okeru dōseiai," 115–116; Tanaka, "Dōseiai ni kanseru gakusetsu," pt. 2, 170–171; Tanaka, *Ningen no seiteki ankokumen*, 66. Tanaka held that, in the "orient," an effeminate "beautiful boy" had served as the ideal in male *dōseiai* from the earliest of times, whereas in the West (specifically Greece), the esthetic had originally revolved around a more masculine form of beauty and only later conformed to the Asian pattern. See "Danseikan ni okeru dōseiai," 108; *Ningen no seiteki ankokumen*, 44.

ideas about male-male sexuality on the basis of the new medical model, but, in doing so, made adjustments to that model so as to better conform with lo-cal understandings. Morita hinted at the creative aspect of this interaction when he wrote in 1931 that, if more Japanese engaged in serious research on "same-sex love," their findings might well surprise their foreign col-leagues.[152] While European knowledge of Japan's male-male erotic culture continued for the most part to rely uncritically on the turn-of-the-century revelations of Iwaya and Doriphorus, Japanese scholars themselves soon learned to challenge the assertions of Western authorities when these ap-peared to conflict with indigenous experience or textual tradition. Tanaka, for instance, rejected the opinion of the German neurologist Paul Möbius that "same-sex love" was rooted exclusively in congenital "degeneration," since this would imply that virtually the entire population of the Edo period had been organically impaired—a verdict about his ancestors that he was ob-viously unwilling to accept. "If Möbius had been familiar," he wrote, "with nanshoku as it was traditionally practiced in our country, he probably would not have voiced such an extreme view."[153] Sakaki, too, questioned the notion of "degeneration," citing the fact that many "great men and women" (ijin) of the past had exhibited "sexual inversion," both in Japan and elsewhere.[154]

While Tanaka and Sakaki sought through such historical observations to refine sexological understanding of "same-sex love," others harbored more profound objections toward the medicalization of Japan's erotic past. One such figure was Minakata Kumagusu, whose keen sense of historical and cultural diversity led him away from a facile acceptance of the medico-scientific model, which tended to stress the uniformity and predictability of erotic phe nomena, as in itself a sufficient vehicle for explaining sexual behavior. Mi-nakata's relativism is even more striking when one considers his lifelong interest in biology and early exposure to Western theories of "homosexu-ality." Yet the rapid changes in male-male erotic culture that Minakata had witnessed in his lifetime prevented him from embracing the latter uncriti-cally. Thus, in response to the German medical historian Julius Rosenbaum's suggestion that a proclivity toward male-male sexual practices among some peoples stemmed from an anal itch common in tropical climates, he scoffed that it was ludicrous to imagine that Japanese rectal conditions had suddenly improved with the Restoration. Minakata was acutely sensitive to the eth-

152. Morita, Dōseiai no kenkyū, 4–5.
153. Tanaka, "Danseikan ni okeru dōseiai," 116; Tanaka, "Dōseiai ni kanseru gakusetsu," pt. 2, 169–170; Tanaka, Ningen no seiteki ankokumen, 66.
154. Sakaki, Seiyoku kenkyū, 171–172.

nocentric nature of Western erotic cartographies, dismissing as "irresponsible" (*yoi kagen*), for example, the English scholar-adventurer Richard Burton's notion of a climatologically influenced "sotadic zone" in which male-male sexual practices were supposedly endemic, and which incorporated Japan monolithically into a vast geographic belt stretching eastward from the Mediterranean all the way across to the Americas. Instead of relying on the "pseudoscientific" (*ese kagakuteki*) theories of Western writers, who in any case did not always agree among themselves, it was wiser, the ethnographer Minakata concluded, to draw from history the lesson that the "spirit of the age" (*jisei*) and "custom" (*fūshū*) exerted a profound influence on sexual behavior.[155]

The elaboration of the "same-sex love" model involved not only a resurveying of Japan's erotic past, but also a new mapping of the present. Just as Edo-period writers perceived *shudō* as distributed unevenly across the social landscape, twentieth-century sexologists sought to chart the topographical features of "same-sex love" as currently practiced in their country. Sexologists characterized a number of social spaces as endemic sites of *dōseiai* in contemporary life, identifying these less on the basis of statistical research than on an impressionistic blend of common knowledge, casual observation, and textual familiarity. Given vastly changed social formations, the characters and institutions that populated this terrain naturally differed from those mentioned in Edo-period writings, but continuities and subtle modifications were also in evidence. While the Buddhist clergy and the kabuki demimonde lost the prominent place that *shudō* cartographers had once accorded them, their conspicuous profile in the older literature assured that they did not drop off the sexological map entirely. Instead of the temple and the theater, male-male sexuality was now seen to abide most typically in the school, and particularly among dormitory dwellers, whose "roughneck" habits Meiji journalism had done much to publicize. At the same time, Meiji penal reforms had brought the shadowy recesses of the prison, which *shudō* texts rarely mentioned, into public view, allowing the penitentiary to emerge as another archetypal site of *dōseiai*, along with other types of state-run disciplinary institution such as juvenile reformatories.

Taking the place of the samurai male of old on the sexological landscape was the modern soldier, no longer a hereditary class but, with the implementation of general conscription, a status that most able-bodied males at

155. Minakata, "*Ichidai otoko o yomu*," 4:19–21.

one point shared. It was widely acknowledged that male-male erotic practices were common in barracks life, as well as on the field of war, but until
the dismantling of Japan's armed forces after the Pacific conflict, the prestige
and political influence of the imperial army and navy were such as to discourage most sexologists from making overly explicit reference to this link.
The sensitivity surrounding this issue may be judged, for instance, from the
fact that the 1894 translation of Krafft-Ebing's *Psychopathia Sexualis*
omitted—albeit to little avail, since the edition was banned anyway—several
of the original's references to the military, such as the scandalous spectacle
of European soldiers hiring out their sexual services for money. Nevertheless, within its own ranks, the army occasionally approached the topic of male-
male sexuality in a surprisingly matter-of-fact way, as when the general staff
of the Japanese forces stationed in China after the Russo-Japanese War included in its official memoir of Beijing life a detailed description of the demimonde of male actor-prostitutes known as *xianggong* without feeling the
need to resort to the disapproving idiom of "civilized morality."[156] As noted
in the previous chapter, the imperial navy (*Yorozu*'s "buggery fleet"), too,
had by the early twentieth century earned a reputation as a breeding ground
for "same-sex love," as had the burgeoning merchant marine.

The townsman devotee of *shudō* found his equivalent on the sexological map of "same-sex love" not only among clerks and apprentices at traditional commercial establishments (in other words, the familiar figures of
the *bantō* and *detchi*), but among such new urban types as the industrial
laborer and the company employee. Among factory workers, it was sometimes claimed, male-male sexual relations were no less prevalent than
among students, although sexologists, including the socialist Morita, devoted far less effort to exploring their manifestations in proletarian culture than among the sons of the elite.[157] Habuto and Sawada wrote conde-
scendingly that since laborers, unlike students, were uneducated, they could
not understand the evils of *dōseiai* to which dormitory life exposed them,
while because they were poor, they could not afford the luxury of marriage. On the other hand, according to the authors, since white-collar workers possessed an education, they were less likely to turn to "same-sex love"
out of economic necessity than as the result of dissipation or misfortune

156. Shinkoku chūtongun shireibu, *Pekin shi* (Hakubunkan, 1908), 785–786.
157. For an ethnographic exploration of male-male erotic practices among the
prewar working class, see Akamatsu Keisuke, *Hijōmin no sei minzoku* (Akashi
shoten, 1991), 343–350.

in male-female romance.[158] Outside the urban environment, writers found male *dōseiai* lurking in such places as the mine, whose dark passageways, as we saw in a previous chapter, provided even convict laborers with opportunities for illicit sexual contact.

Thus, in various settings and among diverse social groups, sexologists discovered male-male erotic practices to be thriving in the present, rather than safely ensconced in the "museum" of history where Meiji writers had sought to embalm them. The association of the "same-sex love" model with an ostensibly "civilized" West helped to weaken the discursive link between male-male sexuality and "barbarism," and to reinscribe it within the realm of "civilization," albeit as part of the latter's "dark underside" (*rimen no ankoku*).[159] This gravitational shift was already evident in Kawaoka Chōfū's 1909 diatribe against *Vita Sexualis*, in which the author warned of the danger that, along with other "continental" ideas such as socialism and Mori's literary naturalism, Euro-American knowledge of male-male sexuality might one day become as familiar to Japanese schoolboys as to their Western counterparts.[160] Sexologists speeded this reorientation by christening "same-sex love" a "disease of civilization" (*bunmeibyō*), much like alcoholism and tuberculosis, whose incidence various trends in contemporary industrial society, such as later marriage and greater equality of the sexes, tended to encourage rather than diminish.[161] Faced at the same time with the increasing visibility of female-female sexual behavior—a topic that merits a separate study—early twentieth-century observers began to ask if "same-sex love" might not in fact be on the rise.[162]

158. Habuto and Sawada, *Hentai seiyokuron*, 192–193; Sawada, *Shinpi naru dōseiai*, 2:128–129.

159. Kitagawa Seijun and Fujisawa Morihiko, *Shikijō shisō*, 238–239.

160. Kawaoka Chōfū, "Gakusei no anmen ni wadakamareru nanshoku no ichidai akufū o tsūba su," *Bōken sekai*, August 1909, 78–79.

161. Habuto and Sawada, *Hentai seiyokuron*, 311, 337–339, 348; Sawada, *Shinpi naru dōseiai*, 1:128–129; 2:82, 183–185, 197.

162. For some examples of this new visibility, see Yukiko Hanawa, "Inciting Sites of Political Interventions: Queer 'n' Asian," *Positions* 4 (1996): 459–489; Pflugfelder, "'S' Is for Sister"; Jennifer Robertson, "Gender-Bending in Paradise: Doing 'Male' and 'Female' in Japan," *Genders* 5 (1989): 50–69; Jennifer Robertson, "The Politics of Androgyny in Japan: Sexuality and Subversion in the Theater and Beyond," *American Ethnologist* 19 (1992): 419–441; Jennifer Roberston, "Theatrical Resistance, Theatres of Restraint: The Takarazuka Revue and the 'State Theatre' Movement in Japan," *Anthropological Quarterly* 64.4 (1991): 165–177.

6 Pleasures of the Perverse

Male-Male Sexuality in Early Twentieth-Century Popular Discourse

Each of the three paradigms for understanding male-male sexuality examined in this study provided, in its respective era, a critical axis for distinguishing between "good" and "bad" varieties of sexual behavior. The disciplinary model of *shudō* (or *shikidō* more generally) set up, for example, a continuum between the "sophisticated" and the "boorish," in between which lay an infinite range of more minute discriminations. In this paradigm, it was not the gender of one's partner that determined the quality of a given sexual interaction but the esthetic and ethical circumstances of its execution. While the Meiji regime of "civilized morality" constructed an analogous dichotomy between "civilization" and "barbarism," it distinguished itself from the earlier paradigm by uniformly relegating all forms of male-male erotic behavior to the negative end of the spectrum, along with most varieties of male-female sexual interaction outside the confines of state-sanctioned marriage. Finally, in the medico-scientific model of sexuality that gained widespread acceptance in the early twentieth century, sexual behavior came to be classed in terms of "normality" (*jōtai*) and "perversion" (*hentai*), with "same-sex love" (*dōseiai*), in both its male and female forms, figuring among the latter's most typical manifestations. The allegedly "objective" and scientific nature of this taxonomy only superficially masked the subjective ethical judgments that it entailed.

While the "normality"/"perversion" dichotomy was in theory absolute, its conceptual clarity nevertheless blurred a bit at the edges when practically applied. We have seen, for example, in the previous chapter, how early twentieth-century Japanese sexologists like Tanaka Kōgai were loath to consign their ancestors en masse to the ignominious status of "perverts" simply because the textual record provided evidence of widespread male-male

sexual practices in former times. When in 1935 the sexologist Yasuda Tokutarō described same-sex crushes among contemporary schoolgirls, he similarly noted that it was at times difficult to distinguish "scientifically" between "normal" and "perverse" behavior.[1] The possibility that some forms
of "same-sex love" might in fact be "normal" found seeming confirmation
not only in the nonpathologizing manner in which earlier native discourses
had represented them, but also in more recent theories, such as those of
Freud, that framed them as a necessary, or at least harmless, part of psychosexual development.

If it was not always easy for sexologists to separate the "normal" from
the "perverse," it must have been even less so for the reading public who
looked to them for edification. Indeed, the titles of various books, magazines,
and articles published in the 1920s and 1930s give the impression not only
that "perversion" was ubiquitous, but that the connotations of the term were
not entirely negative. Such journals as *Hentai seiyoku* (Perverse Sexual Desire), *Hentai shinri* (Perverse Psychology), *Hentai chishiki* (Perverse Knowledge), and *Hentai shiryō* (Perverse Materials) catered not only to a professional audience, but to a popular one clearly more attracted than repelled
by the "perverse" nature of their contents, while the title of a multivolume
series like *Hentai jūnishi* (Twelve Perverse Histories) left it tantalizingly
unclear whether "perversion" described the subject or the object of the inquiry. In the realm of popular discourse, the label of the "perverse" did not
always carry the same degree of stigma that it did in the medical context
that gave it birth.[2] Indeed, insofar as popular sexologists sought to reach a
mass audience, their own writings often straddled, and thus illustrated the
interdependence of, the two domains.[3] As the notion of the "perverse"
filtered rapidly from medical into popular discourse, it came to figure not
only as the target of condemnation and cure, but at the same time as an ob-

1. Yasuda Tokutarō, "Dōseiai no rekishikan," *Chūō kōron*, March 1935, 150–151.
On same-sex attachments among early twentieth-century schoolgirls and the discourses surrounding them, see my "'S' Is for Sister: Schoolgirl Intimacy and 'Same-
Sex Love' in Early Twentieth-Century Japan," in *Gendering Modern Japanese History*, ed. Barbara Molony and Kathleen S. Uno (Cambridge: Harvard University
Press, forthcoming).
2. This is one of the central themes of Akita Masami's *Sei no ryōki modan: Nihon hentai kenkyū ōrai* (Seikyūsha, 1994). Akita, however, makes little reference to
male-male sexuality.
3. On the popularization of sexology in early twentieth-century Japan, see Sabine
Frühstück, *Die Politik der Sexualwissenschaft: Zur Produktion und Popularisierung
sexologischen Wissens in Japan, 1900–1941*, Beiträge für Japanologie, no. 34 (Vienna: Institut für Japanologie, Universität Wien, 1997).

ject of consumption and celebration, and, as we shall soon see, a subject that could speak for itself.

It was by providing a new language for speaking about sexuality that sexology made its most far-reaching impact upon popular discourse of the early twentieth century. With respect to male-male sexuality, this medicalized idiom allowed the legitimate articulation of what the Meiji regime of "civilized morality" had deemed "unspeakable." Naturally, it was not so much that the "unspeakable" had literally been left unspoken. The protocols of "civilized" discourse had permitted its utterance, but had sought to confine it to certain marginal contexts, such as the historical past, the geographical periphery, and the world of adolescence, and only if its moral propriety was simultaneously disavowed. Furthermore, the euphemizing idiom of "civilized morality" made little qualitative distinction between differing forms of "uncivilized" behavior.

By contrast, the language of sexology offered a complex vocabulary for articulating sexual behavior that was, or at least claimed to be, morally neutral. To speak of "same-sex love," for example, did not immediately elevate the speaker to a loftier ethical plane than those who indulged in it, as had, implicitly, such "civilized" euphemisms as "wicked deeds" and "barbarous practices." Rather, it put the speaker in a cognitive position akin to that of the doctor or scientist, whose ostensible task was the mere observation of natural phenomena, divorced from moral evaluation. The objectifying gaze of science allowed the subject to describe even himself or herself in "neutral" sexological terms, as did Sawada Junjirō, for instance, when he detailed for readers the various forms of "same-sex love" that he had experienced in his lifetime, or earlier, when Mori Ōgai depicted his autobiographical character Kanai Shizuka in *Vita Sexualis* as a sort of "urning" manqué. The sexological idiom made it possible to describe "same-sex love" not only from within the psychological recesses of the speaking subject, but in all corners of the external world, in keeping with the principle that the domain of natural law, and consequently of scientific investigation, knew no legitimate bounds. The margins to which "civilized" discourse had confined the representation of male-male sexual behavior could thus no longer contain its signifying potential: "perversion" spread, as it were, all over the map.

Early twentieth-century writings charted a complex geography of "perversion." While "civilized" discourse had envisioned a largely undifferentiated realm of "barbarous" sexual practice, the scientific gaze, whether wielded by sexologists or litterateurs, delighted in surveying and subdividing the terrain of nonnormative sexual behavior. "Same-sex love" was one in a long list of such "perversions," counting among its neighbors erotic phenomena ranging from fetishism and sadomasochism, which were constructs of equally recent coinage, to more arcane aberrations such as pygmalionism (the erotic desire for statuary) and "metatophism" (where the wife became the more assertive partner in a marital relationship).[4] The domain of "same-sex love" was furthermore segmented by a wide array of internal distinctions, the majority of them binary oppositions: male versus female, active versus passive, congenital versus acquired, true versus "pseudo," permanent versus temporary, complete versus partial, simple versus compound, and so forth. While the lexicon of *shudō* had indeed been vast, its descriptive possibilities were seldom so precisely and analytically defined.

The proliferation of "perversions" opened up, at the same time, new possibilities of pleasure. I mean this not only in the obvious sense that individuals might sample the convenient inventory of erotic practices that sexological and popular writings provided. Rather, the pleasures of "perversion" revolved equally around such acts as knowing, speaking, and seeing. The sexologist, for example, derived pleasure from his (and very rarely her) ability to categorize the different varieties of sexual behavior according to an authoritative conceptual scheme, thus demonstrating his superior knowledge. Likewise for the popular writer, the license that the sexological idiom gave to speak of "perversion" in a public forum sanctioned new forms of narrative pleasure, as well as new commercial opportunities. For both their audiences, the discourse on "perversion" transformed the sexual behavior of others into a spectacle for consumption as well as a vehicle for self-understanding. To the extent that readers perceived a difference between the described behaviors and their own, it helped to reassure them of their own "normality." Yet even if they recognized themselves within the pages of the text, the discomfiting awareness of their "perversion" might be offset to some degree by the epistemological security that derived from occupying a place within a larger signifying chain, as well as the possibility of speaking from a subject position that, while stigmatized, was nevertheless

---

4. For descriptions, respectively, of pygmalionism and "metatophism," see Satō Kōka, "Seiyokugaku goi," pt. 2, *Hentai shiryō*, June 1927, 61–66; Sugita Naoki, "Seiyoku oyobi sono ijō," *Bungei shunjū*, March 1931, 202. I have been unable to locate a Western-language account of the latter phenomenon, and so have had to guess at the original spelling.

publicly acknowledged. For many readers, no doubt, the spectacle of "perversion" offered a zone in which such distinctions of subject and object were less starkly drawn, the scopophilic delight of viewing the "perverse" shading subtly off into a vicarious enjoyment of its ecstasies.

Nowhere was the "perverse" more spectacularly celebrated and commodified than in the cultural phenomenon known as *ero-guro-nansensu*. Generally associated with the late 1920s and early 1930s, this formula refers to the conspicuous fascination with the "erotic," the "grotesque," and the "nonsensical" that pervades the popular culture of that era. Each of the three elements implied a perversion, as it were, of conventional values. The celebration of the "erotic" (*ero*) in its myriad forms constituted a rejection of the Meiji dictum that sexuality was unsuited for public display or representation unless it conformed to the narrow standards of "civilized morality." The elevation of the "grotesque" (*guro*) betrayed a similar disregard for prevailing esthetic codes, with their focus on traditional canons of beauty and concealment of the seamier sides of existence. Finally, the valorization of the "nonsensical" (*nansensu*) signaled a discontent with the constraining nature of received moral and epistemological certitudes. The fact that each of these words derives from a European language hints at the degree to which Japanese popular culture had become embedded by the early twentieth century in a global context wherein related (though never entirely identical) sociocultural phenomena were shared among industrial capitalist societies and discourses flowed with relative ease across national borders.[5]

In the present chapter, I use the *ero-guro-nansensu* formula (abbreviated henceforth as *ero-guro*) to designate a more general configuration of popular culture that, far from being restricted to the decade beginning in the mid-1920s, took shape earlier in the Taishō (1912–1926) period and persisted even through the tumultuous war years and their aftermath. In many respects, I would argue, it continues to characterize Japan even today. One element of this configuration was a tacit alliance between, on the one hand, a medico-scientific understanding of sexual phenomena that stressed their biologically rooted nature and susceptibility to objective evaluation, and on the other, an impulse, grounded in consumer capitalism, to put them on display less for scientific reasons than because of their profit-generating pos-

---

5. For a useful analysis of early twentieth-century popular culture, see Miriam Silverberg, "Constructing a New Cultural History of Prewar Japan," in *Japan in the World*, ed. Masao Miyoshi and H. D. Harootunian (Durham: Duke University Press, 1993), 115–143.

sibilities. The various pleasures that I have described above may be seen as nodal points in this larger grid of knowledge and power. Although the subsequent discussion focuses specifically on the ways in which male-male sexuality fit into this cultural nexus, it may shed some light as well on that era's construction of female-female and other sexualities.

THE PERVERT SPEAKS

When exactly did popular sexology become "popular"? The Edo period had produced a wealth of commercial texts devoted to the "way of eros" (*shikidō*), albeit the disciplinary paradigm that undergirded them differed in many respects from the medico-scientific model of sexuality referred to here as sexology. Nevertheless, by the time that sexological theories began to circulate on a large scale in the Meiji period, readers had long been accustomed to seeing the discussion of sexuality in print, and to parting with their cash in order to partake of its pleasures. In this sense, early Meiji sexological works dealing with the "creative organs" and sexual electrodynamics were the direct descendants of such late Edo-period popular erotic manuals as *Shikidō kinpishō* despite their radically differing conceptual vocabularies. Nevertheless, the reign of "civilized morality" made it more difficult than it had been in Edo times to publish works with explicit sexual content for fear of violating stringently enforced "obscenity" provisions, as well as more general canons of respectability.

With the growing legitimation of sexology as a branch of science in the early decades of the twentieth century, popular writings on sexuality experienced a renewed boom. It was not so much that Meiji writers had avoided erotic topics altogether—one can hardly imagine such a literature—as that they had framed their narratives as existing principally for other ends, such as moral elevation, intellectual edification, and artistic appreciation. The rise of sexology, however, licensed new forms of narrative that did not hesitate to name sexuality as their main concern, whether they issued from the pens of doctors or of laypersons. Moreover, in the context of increasingly universal literacy, the continued growth of the publishing industry, and the expansion of a leisured middle class, popular works now reached an audience of heretofore unparalleled proportions. Habuto Eiji and Sawada Junjirō's 1915 *Hentai seiyokuron* (On Perverse Sexual Desire), for example, was so successful as to receive no less than eighteen printings over the course of a decade. It is not difficult to imagine, as does the historian Donald Roden, that "the more Habuto, Sawada, and others exposed the dangers of aberrant relations, the more bored, urban middle-class readers turned to their books as a recreational escape from the very 'civilized' norms the 'doctors' said they were upholding."[6]

Among the alleged "dangers" described by Habuto and Sawada were those of male-male sexuality, on which the authors expatiated at length in their tome. The popularity of this and similar works contributed to increasing public familiarity with the medico-scientific model of "same-sex love" and its vocabulary. Indeed, it was during the 1910s that the term "same-sex love" itself, which forensic pathologists and other authorities since the Meiji period had translated from European languages in a bewildering variety of forms (Habuto and Sawada, for example, still use the somewhat cumbersome *dōseikan seiyoku* or "sexual desire between [members of] the same sex"), began to appear colloquially as *dōseiai*, which became more or less standard by the following decade. Habuto and Sawada's work illustrates, furthermore, the growing length that explicit narratives of male-male sexual behavior, recuperated by a newly legitimized sexology from the constraints of a "civilized" discourse that had sought their marginalization and euphemization, might now take: its section on "same-sex love" (both male and female) ran a full 260 pages.

Books devoted exclusively to male-male sexuality—or, following the new paradigm of "same-sex love," to male-male and female-female behaviors combined—also emerged from a long silence. A prominent example is Kōmurō Shujin's 1911 *Bishōnenron*, already discussed in chapter 4, although strictly speaking, its appearance dates from the very end of the Meiji period. Kōmurō Shujin's volume nonetheless illustrates the way in which medico-scientific knowledge of male-male eroticism (the work's alternate title, significantly, is *Dōsei shikijōshi*, "A History of Same-Sex Lust") lent a measure of respectability to a type of narrative that, far from emphasizing the need for cure, dwelt almost lovingly on the phenomena described, as, for example, in passages that graphically detail the physical and mental pleasures that anal intercourse held for the inserter—sections that the publisher felt it wiser to excise.[7] That the work was intended for a general audience is reflected in the fact that advertisements for it appeared not in medical journals but in the titillating pages of Miyatake Gaikotsu's *Kono hana* (This Flower), an antiquarian magazine devoted to the study of woodblock prints and of Edo-period popular culture more generally. Since the author

6. Donald Roden, "Taishō Culture and the Problem of Gender Ambivalence," in *Culture and Identity: Japanese Intellectuals during the Interwar Years*, ed. J. Thomas Rimer (Princeton: Princeton University Press, 1990), 45–46.

7. Kimoto Itaru, <*Hyōden*> *Miyatake Gaikotsu* (Shakai shisōsha, 1984), 641–642.

would not give his consent to the publisher's proposed deletions, however, the work circulated only in unauthorized form, indicating the degree of tension that still prevailed, as it would continue to do in later decades, between a censorship apparatus that Meiji bureaucrats had designed for the purpose of "civilizing" morality and a consumer-oriented press that continually tested its boundaries.

Comparable to, and indeed in many ways derivative of, Kōmurō Shujin's work was the 1928 *Nanshoku kō* (Study of *Nanshoku*), by Nakano Masato (writing under the pseudonym Hanabusa Shirō).[8] Like Kōmurō Shujin, Nakano brought together under the guise of amateur scholarship a wide range of textual materials relating to male-male sexuality, from *Nihongi* and Saikaku to Greek and Chinese classics to contemporary newspaper reports—the discursive regimes that originally produced them often at odds with one another. While well-versed in the vocabulary and concepts of Western sexologists such as Krafft-Ebing and Albert Moll, Nakano was a journalist rather than a doctor, serving as a sort of right-hand man to the flamboyant publisher of *ero-guro* literature Umehara Hokumei. The tenor of his prose is therefore not so much excoriatory or therapeutic as spectatorial and even consumeristic, as when the author ends a discussion of male prostitutes in the Edo period by speculating that, if such youths were to line the nighttime streets of Japan in the present day and age, most men, even if not "perverts," would surely want to try out their services "at least for an evening."[9] Not surprisingly perhaps, Nakano's work was promptly banned, as was a translation of Moll's observations on female-female sexuality that he published in the following year as *Dōseiai no shujusō* (The Many Faces of Same-Sex Love).[10]

In addition to books, many writings on male-male sexuality from the early twentieth century are to be found in the periodical press. The magazine was a favorite forum of sexologists, several of whom, including Sawada and Tanaka Kōgai, edited their own publications. Beginning in 1922, for exam-

8. Hanabusa Shirō [Nakano Masato], *Nanshoku kō* (Hassōdō shoin, 1928). The author provides addenda and errata in "Jicho nanshoku kō no ayamari ni tsuite," <Kokon> *Momoiro sōshi*, November 1928, 63–64.

9. Hanabusa, *Nanshoku kō*, 67.

10. Hanabusa Shirō [Nakano Masato], trans., *Dōseiai no shujusō*, Tankikan zuihitsu, no. 4 (Bungei shijōsha, 1929). Other early twentieth-century monographs on "same-sex love" are Morita Yūshū, *Dōseiai no kenkyū* (Chiba: Jinsei sōzōsha, 1931); Sawada Junjirō, *Shinpi naru dōseiai* (Kyōekisha shuppanbu, 1920; this is a variant edition of the work cited in chap. 5, n. 60). Hanabusa further explores the topic of "same-sex love" in "Petchi ruiza sono ta," *Hanzai kagaku*, December 1930, 75–79.

ple, Tanaka authored virtually single-handedly the monthly *Hentai seiyoku*, which appeared under the auspices of the Japanese Society for Psychiatric Medicine, founded in 1917 by Nakamura Kokyō. In it, Tanaka character- ized his writings as a "scholarly diversion" (*gakumonteki dōraku*), thereby distancing himself from Sawada and Habuto, to whom he referred with somewhat mocking reverence as "grandees of sexology" (*seigaku taika*).[11] Tanaka's was only one of a host of periodicals devoted to sexuality to appear during the 1910s and 1920s: titles incorporating the character for sex (*sei*) alone include *Sei*, *Seiron* (Sexology), *Shin sei* (New Sex), *Sei kōron* (Sex Re- view), *Sei to ai* (Sex and Love), *Sei to ren'ai* (Sex and Love), *Sei to shakai* (Sex and Society), *Seiyoku to jinsei* (Sexual Desire and Humanity), *Sei no kenkyū* (Sexual Research), and *Sei no chishiki* (Sexual Knowledge), not to mention *Sekkusu*, which is simply a transliteration of the English word. Other journals, such as those published by Umehara and his cohort Nakano, placed the "erotic" on an equal footing with the "grotesque" and the "non- sensical," appropriating the sexological idiom but making little pretense of a scientific mission. Whatever their stripe (such distinctions were often blurred), erotic magazines met with frequent censorship and generally did not survive for very long, but we should read this fact less as a reflection of their marginality than of the persistence and depth of market demand.

The proliferation of such periodicals also reflects the sense of timeli- ness that issues of sexuality held—or, more precisely, that these journals constructed—for readers and for society at large. As Sawada wrote in the inaugural issue of his magazine *Sei*, there were few aspects of society that were unrelated to the "sexual problem" (*sei mondai*), a notion that echoed such topics of contemporary debate as the "woman problem" (*fujin mondai*) and the issue of socioeconomic inequality, commonly referred to as the "so- cial problem" (*shakai mondai*). Sawada envisioned his journal as an ongo- ing forum for the discussion and eventual solution of the "sexual problem," providing enlightened guidance to educators, ethicists, religious authorities, legalists, and public policymakers.[12] Letters from readers make it clear, how- ever, that many enjoyed no such position of authority, but were attracted first and foremost by the racy nature of the contents. In what Roden calls one of the "great ironies" of early twentieth-century sexology, "What started out as prescriptive literature quickly lost the blessings of educators and police and thus descended into the underground culture."[13]

11. Tanaka Kōgai, "Shippitsu o oete," *Hentai seiyoku*, December 1924: 284.
12. "*Sei* hakkan no ji," *Sei*, January 1920, 1–2.
13. Roden, "Taishō Culture," 46.

It is the process by which popular culture came to embrace a medico-scientific understanding of sexuality that will concern us in the present chapter. Erotic magazines provide a useful entry point for considering this question precisely because of their ambiguous position at the interstices of medical and popular discourse. Neither purely medical, because their commercial viability depended upon a broader audience, nor purely popular, because they typically invoked the professional authority of experts, they form a hybrid space in which the language of sexology provided a sort of unifying idiom. Although doctors and scientists were among their most prominent contributors, the medium in which they wrote obliged them to present their ideas in ways that were accessible to general readers, thereby bridging the gap between medical concepts and existing modes of erotic understanding. Other writers could boast no scientific training, but merely welcomed the opportunity that such journals offered to discuss sexuality in a public forum, even if it meant sprinkling their prose with medical terminology. The result was a multiplicity, if not a cacophony, of voices.

Among the voices that made themselves heard for the first time in such journals was that of the "pervert." For males who had experienced or desired sexual contact with other males, the medical model of sexuality provided a mode of interpreting their behavior and feelings—that is to say, a subjectivity—that differed significantly from those that went before it. *Shudō* texts, for example, had helped construct the subjectivities of *nenja* and *wakashu*, molding the one into an erotic connoisseur and the other into a pliant sexual object. Whereas the narrative perspective of such texts had often converged with that of the *nenja*, the voice of the youth was often little more than a product of the author's wishful imagination, the desires and feelings of youths themselves seldom receiving direct expression in published prose (although poetry and letters might conceivably tell a different story). During the Meiji period, the voices of both *nenja* and *wakashu* ceased to appear with any frequency or authority in the pages of the popular text. The subjectivity that Meiji popular discourse inculcated was instead a "civilized" one, which suffered male-male eroticism only as the object of its disapproving gaze, associating it with certain marginalized "others" who in turn helped to define the subject itself: the old Japanese as opposed to the new, the regional as opposed to the national citizen, the immature adolescent versus the responsible adult. It was unthinkable within the discursive space of "civilization" for the "roughneck" to speak on his own behalf, except perhaps in a retrospective mode in which the subject stood alienated from his former self.

By making sexual behavior of all varieties a legitimate object of scientific inquiry, sexology afforded the male-male erotic subject new opportunities to speak and to be heard. While "perversion" was, from a medical perspective, undesirable, the medico-scientific model affirmed its material existence by planting it deep within the recesses of human physiology and psychology. Human sexual behavior was seen to reflect a basic "sexual personality" (*seiteki jinkaku*), which, although varying from individual to individual, fell into a limited number of objectively determinable categories.[14] By offering an authoritative taxonomy of sexual types, sexologists invited their audience to locate themselves within this conceptual framework and to claim one of its subjectivities, be it "normal" or "perverse," as their own. At the same time, paradoxically, the positing of diverse "sexual personalities" encouraged an increased attention to the particularity of the individual. The articulation of personal sexual feelings and experiences to which sexology gave license—indeed, upon which it greatly depended—stood in an ambivalent relationship to the sexological model itself. On the one hand, it might help bolster the validity of this model and of the definitions provided by sexologists, and on the other, it might serve to illustrate the ineffable variety of erotic experience (always greater than the ability of a given model to capture it) and thus prompt further refinement of that model or even challenge some of its basic premises.[15] During the early twentieth century, these conflicting impulses of generalization and individuation, of objectification and subjectivization, would play themselves out in various ways.

The "pervert," and specifically that newly classified species, the male *dō-seiaisha*, was spoken about before he himself spoke. In sexological writings, he first appears as a case history, in which the doctor described his symptoms and their supposed etiology and cure from his own position of superior knowledge. Many such case examples derived from Western sources, since psychiatry as a clinical practice possessed much shallower roots in Japan than in Europe and North America. Krafft-Ebing's nineteenth-century patients, for instance, continued to enliven the pages of Japanese sexology well into the following century. When it came to native examples, however, it was easier for sexologists in Japan to comb through contemporary newspa-

14. On the notion of "sexual personality," see Habuto Eiji and Sawada Junjirō, *Hentai seiyokuron* (Shun'yōdō, 1915), 93.

15. That popular discourse exerted a significant influence upon medico-scientific understandings of sexuality, and not simply the other way around, was acknowledged by the sexologist Sugita Naoki ("Seiyoku oyobi sono ijō," 190) when he remarked that "we [doctors] frequently draw various sorts of material and learn in other ways from the teachings of those engaged in literary activities."

pers and journals, or else to dissect the textual legacy of the past, than to await clinical visits from help-seeking "perverts," whom "social morality" discouraged from making intimate revelations about themselves and their families to outsiders.[16] Erotic magazines offered an alternative means of access to doctors and other experts that had the advantage of protecting the subject's anonymity. Often this interaction took the form of a confessional letter, in which the "pervert" told his own story, partly in search of remedy, but partly, one suspects, also for the sheer pleasure of the telling. The subsequent discussion will focus on letters found in two popular-sexology journals, Sawada's *Sei* and Tanaka's *Hentai seiyoku*, which date from the early 1920s.

Such first-person narratives allow us to hear the "pervert" speaking in his own voice, if not necessarily his own language. They inscribe the process by which some individuals who experienced sexual desire for members of the same sex came to internalize the sexological idiom and the new subjectivity that it entailed. Correspondents were quick to identify themselves according to a medico-scientific taxonomy, describing themselves as *dōseiaisha* ("congenital" or otherwise), "effeminate" or "evirated" males, possessors of a "perverse sexual desire" or "abnormal psychology," and so forth— categories with which their reading of these magazines, together with other contemporary sources, had made them familiar. "Since first taking this magazine [*Hentai seiyoku*] into my hands, I have gradually come to be aware of the fact that I am a *dōseiaisha*," wrote Y.K. of Kobe in 1923.[17] For some, the internalization of the sexological model involved a negative perception of their own condition and a desire for medical intervention. A twenty-eight-year-old who signs his letter Deformed Male (Fugu no Otoko) confided to Sawada, for example, that his "unnatural lust" (*fushizen na shikijō*) for men and lack of interest in women caused him great anxiety over the impending prospect of marriage, and wondered if there was any cure for his "disease." In response, Sawada wrote that his correspondent's "inverted sexual desire" (*tōsaku seiyoku*) seemed to him to be of a relatively mild variety that would likely disappear upon contracting a suitable marriage or through hypnosis, further recommending his recently published tract "The Mys-

16. Case histories of Japanese *dōseiaisha* often emerged not from freely sought therapy, but from less than voluntary circumstances, as when police or judicial authorities called in doctors to make a medical evaluation of persons in their custody. See, for example, Sugie Kaoru, "Hidōteki sodomiya no ichirei," *Sei*, October 1920 (zōkan), 171–176.

17. YK-sei, "Dōseiaisha no kurushimi," *Hentai seiyoku*, May 1923, 238.

tery of Same-Sex Love" (*Shinpi naru dōseiai*)—available, he adds, at two yen and sixty sen for the two-volume set.[18] In this interchange, we see Sawada subtly substituting an up-to-date clinical vocabulary ("inverted sexual desire") for the correspondent's somewhat quaintly Meijiesque terminology ("unnatural lust"), as well as blatantly illustrating the way in which scientific and commercial interests colluded.

Other letters show their writers appropriating the medical model and its vocabulary, but not entirely on doctors' terms. While Deformed Male accepted the premise that he was "diseased," many correspondents took pains to stress that they were physically healthy and "normal" despite their supposedly pathological condition. Nor was "same-sex love" a source of crippling anxiety for all: a reader who gives his name as Shibamichi Toshio, for example, describes himself unabashedly as a "worshiper" (*sūhaisha*) of *dōseiai*, waxing eloquent about a "boy" (*shōnen*) whom he loves so much "as to need not even life itself," or about former lovers for whom he would be willing to "endure any form of hardship."[19] Like Shibamichi, Shōyūsei, too, stressed the "self-sacrificing" (*kenshinteki*) nature of "same-sex love," maintaining that it could serve as a boon to "society and nation."[20] Both writers echoed earlier discourses that had extolled the ethical merits of *shudō*. While correspondents willingly, at times almost gleefully, imparted detailed information about their genital exploits (much of which is regrettably censored), they simultaneously emphasized the richness of their emotional lives, as if to underscore the fact that "same-sex love" was as much about "love" as it was about "sex." The tone of such accounts as Shibamichi's and Shōyūsei's is noticeably unapologetic, suggesting that the medical model's gloomy perception of "same-sex love" had not taken hold completely over their writers' subjectivities, which continued to be informed by other, less negative strains of discourse as well as their own personal experiences. What Shōyūsei felt "sad and lonely" about, significantly, was not his "perverse" inclinations per se, but the fact that advancing age was not likely to allow him the type or frequency of pleasures that he once enjoyed.[21]

While the medical model produced new forms of knowledge about male-male sexuality, it also raised the possibility of contestation over who would control and articulate that knowledge. The emergence of the male *dōseiaisha* as a speaking subject, rather than the spoken-about object that he had con-

18. "Dokusha yori," *Sei*, September 1920, 47.
19. "Dokusha no koe," *Sei*, January 1921, 134.
20. Shōyūsei, "Watakushi no taiken shitsutsu aru dōseiai," *Sei*, June 1921, 108, 110.
21. Shōyūsei, "Watakushi," 109.

stituted as a case history, challenged even the all-knowing authority of the sexologist himself. Shibamichi, for instance, wrote that the psychology of male-male sexuality that Sawada had found so "mysterious" he himself understood "completely," and offered to treat the eminent sexologist to dinner. The cause of his own suffering, as Shibamichi saw it, was not his "abnormal psychology" (*ijō na shinri*) so much as the lack of a "friend to whom he could tell his story" (*kataru tomo*)—a legacy, as it were, of the silencing operations of "civilized morality."[22] Despite sexology's pathologizing view of "same-sex love," therefore, individuals who engaged in "uncivilized" sexual behavior sometimes saw the sexologist as their most sympathetic listener.

This desire of the male *dōseiaisha* to tell his story was directed not only at sexologists, or at the general public before whose eyes he bared his confessional narrative, but also at others like himself. While Deformed Male had wondered whether "there are other people in this world who possess such an unnatural lust," those more familiar with sexological writings (such as the work that Sawada recommended), as well as with the published confessions of other *dōseiaisha*, were aware that there indeed were, and in some cases turned to sexologists to help them seek one another out. Shōyūsei proposed that it would be a "beneficial thing for scholarship" (*gakujutsujō yūeki na koto*) to bring a number of *dōseiaisha* like himself together in a single room and have them talk about their experiences, although it is easy enough to imagine that scientific progress was not the only benefit that entered his calculations.[23] The fact that Tanaka specifically discouraged readers of his journal from writing to him for the names and addresses of *dōseiaisha* likewise suggests the potential that sexology held to create horizontal connections among "perverts," thereby multiplying their opportunities for pleasure.[24] (It is conceivable that blackmail provided a motive for such inquiries as well.) While "organizations" and "clubs" of the sort proposed by A. in 1923 would not emerge for several decades, sexological journals facilitated a certain amount of communication among individuals who viewed themselves as *dōseiaisha*, regardless of the region where they resided. Readers of *Hentai seiyoku*, for example, used the pages of the magazine to debate such topics as whether it was appropriate for a male *dōseiaisha* to enter into matrimony with a woman. One of them, the aforementioned A., went so far as to recommend the legalization of same-sex marriage, responding to a newspaper account that an official in the Japanese colonial adminis-

22. "Dokusha no koe," 134.
23. Shōyūsei, "Watakushi," 110.
24. Tanaka, "Shippitsu o oete," 284.

tration of Taiwan had condemned such unions among the aboriginal population there.[25]

A more extended version of the confessional narrative may be found in
the writings of Watanuki Rokusuke, which appeared in the pages of such magazines as Nakamura's *Hentai shinri* and Umehara's *Hentai shiryō* during
the 1920s.[26] Adding only a barely fictionalized veneer to his personal experiences, Watanuki recounted erotic intrigues with both men and women with
a candor imaginable only under the legitimating auspices of sexology. In a
1923 article titled "My Perverse Psychology," Watanuki, who pursued a
fifteen-year career as an army officer before making his debut as a professional writer, described the various partners—ranging from fellow military
men to fishers, farmers, artists, local politicians, and construction workers, to
a wealthy Chinese merchant at the time of the Russo-Japanese War—with
whom he had experienced "same-sex love," as well as attributing similar
proclivities to his father. While classifying both his father and himself sexologically as "[psychic] hermaphrodites" (*ryōseiguyūsha*), he rejected the
pejorative overtones of the term "perversion," writing that the capacity for
such feelings existed in everyone, and it was only a question of whether or
not they awakened and took a concrete form. Nor did Watanuki's recently
professed Catholicism prompt him to repudiate the "God-given" nature of
his sexual desires: while claiming that he was "currently in the process" of
giving up the "impure" (*fuketsu*) pleasure of physical intercourse with other
males, he vowed he would continue to cherish the more "beautiful" aspects
of *dōseiai*, as his subsequent writings more than amply demonstrate.[27]

Watanuki's works provide illustration of the expanding variety of male-
male erotic behaviors and subjectivities that the new idiom of sexology
helped to articulate. While *shudō* texts had codified a strict division between

25. A-sei, "'Joseiteki danshi' o yonde," *Hentai seiyoku*, March 1923, 130; Tenkōsei, "Hangyakusha no sakebi," *Hentai seiyoku*, January 1923, 45–47; TK-sei, "Danshi dōseiaisha no kekkon ni tsuite," *Hentai seiyoku*, March 1923, 138–140. Additional opinions appeared in the previous (1922) volume of the magazine, but I have
not had the opportunity to examine them.

26. See, for example, Watanuki's following works: "Akisame ni saku dariya,"
<*Kokon*> *Momoiro sōshi*, December 1928, 80–94; "Aku no miryoku," *Hentai shin-
ri*, July 1926, 108–115; "Aru onna no isshō," *Hentai shinri*, August 1926, 63–68;
"Dōkei no hi: Aru chūseisha no nayami," *Hentai shinri*, September 1926, 102–105;
"Shizuka naru fukushū," *Hentai shiryō*, April 1928, 106–127. Watanuki was also
the author of several books, including <*Chōhen shōsetsu*> *Sensō* (Shūhōkaku, 1924);
<*Sōsaku*> *Reiniku o mitsumete* (Shizensha, 1923); <*Tantei shōgun*> *Akashi Mo-
tojirō: Nichiro sensō chōhō hishi*, Kiroku bungaku sōsho, no. 4 (Kawade shobō, 1937).

27. Watanuki Rokusuke, "Watakushi no hentai shinri," *Hentai shinri*, May 1923,
557–567.

the sexually penetrating *nenja* and the penetrated youth, privileging the subjectivity of the former, the notion of "same-sex love" could accommodate
a broader range of erotic combinations (so long as both parties were of the
same sex), thereby opening up new narrative perspectives. Even though
Watanuki was already in his forties when he began publishing, the erotic
subjectivity that he elaborated through his autobiographical prose was not
that of the youth-admiring *nenja*, although this is the role for which his
age would have ideally suited him under the disciplinary norms of *shudō*,
but one that prized the beauty of adult males even older than himself (one
postwar writer characterizes him as a "gerontophile").[28] Not only do Watanuki's texts embody a virile gaze, therefore, but the object of that gaze is
virile as well. Regarding sexual practice, Watanuki's characters express the
desire not to penetrate but rather to be penetrated: they are "passive" *dōseiaisha* in sexological terms, yet none the less aggressive in their pursuit
of sexual gratification. It is from the rather unlikely pen of a middle-aged
writer, then, that we hear the male erotic object, with his sexually penetra-
ble body, making himself heard, no longer simply as the target of others'
desire, as with the *wakashu* of the *shudō* text or the "beautiful boy" of Meiji
writings, but as a desiring subject in his own right. The emergence of this
narrative voice in popular discourse closely parallels the rise of the sexological model in the medical realm, which regarded erotic desire as innate
in all individuals (and not simply the *nenja* partner in the male-male erotic
couple), endowing each with a distinct "sexual personality."

Readers of sexology journals similarly gave voice to sexual desires and
subjectivities that had not found expression under preceding discursive
regimes. Like Watanuki, many viewed themselves as "passive" in sexological terms, even if their age fell outside the narrower boundaries of Edo-
period "youth." Some, like Shōyūsei, reported switching between "active"
and "passive" roles depending on their partner, or even engaged recipro-
cally in both with the same individual, implicitly ignoring the strict division that *shudō* convention had imposed between *nenja* and *wakashu*.[29]
Shōyūsei's reference to "mutual" (*sōgoteki*) sexual practices (the exact na-

28. Hanei Ryōtei, "Chomei Sodomu no hitobito: Kindai kara gendai made no
tenbō," *Fūzoku kitan*, January 1961, 82. For Watanuki's ideals of masculine and feminine beauty, see his response to the magazine survey "Suki na otoko, suki na onna,"
<Kokon> *Momoiro sōshi*, February 1928, 31–32.

29. Shōyūsei, "Watakushi," 109. By the late 1940s, a slang term—*donden*
(roughly, "flip-flop")—had come into existence to designate those who played both
inserter and insertee roles in male-male sexual activity. See Sumi Tatsuya, *Danshō
no mori* (Hibiya shuppansha, 1949), 134.

ture of which censorship unfortunately obscures) presents a contrast, too, with the tendency of sexologists to distinguish rigidly between sexual "activity" and "passivity," analogous in their minds to biological maleness and femaleness, thus revealing a gap between an idealized taxonomy and actual sexual practice. Some individuals, in other words, did not fit neatly into the categories that sexology provided. Such was the case as well when a perplexed A. wrote to Tanaka to ask whether he belonged to the "masculine" or "feminine" variety of male *dōseiaisha*—a dichotomy that Tanaka had introduced in the previous issue of the magazine—since his "retiring" (*hishakōteki*) and "impractical" (*jitsumu ni tekisezaru*) nature betrayed a "feminine" disposition, while his above-average hirsuteness and musculature were unmistakably "masculine."[30]

Despite heavy government and self-imposed censorship, confessional letters and other early twentieth-century accounts make reference to sexual acts that had received little attention in the pages of the *shudō* text. An erotic lexicon from the late 1920s, for instance, describes fellatio as a practice taking place not only between men and women, but also among "urnings." The author reproduces an exchange that allegedly occurred in Kyoto's Maruyama Park, in which a "pale-faced" man befriends a young student on a park bench, gradually steers the conversation toward the topic of "same-sex love," and finally asks him if he may play his "bamboo flute" (*shakuhachi*)—a colloquial expression for fellatio.[31] While statistical data on male-male sexual behavior do not exist for the period covered by this study, an informal survey published in 1952 suggests that many males had experienced mutual masturbation, or had either masturbated or been masturbated by another.[32] I do not mean to imply, of course, that such acts as male-male masturbation and fellatio never took place before the twentieth century, but only that the rubric of "same-sex love," with its exclusive focus on the sex of the parties involved, embraced a broader repertory of sexual practices than the hierarchical structure and esthetic sensibilities of *shudō* had allowed representation of. A., the earlier-mentioned reader of Tanaka's *Hentai seiyoku*, in fact expressed a positive aversion (*ken'o*) to anal intercourse, which had been central to the *shudō* repertory, although he nevertheless recognized himself as a *dōseiaisha*.[33]

30. A-sei, "'Joseiteki danshi' o yonde," 129–130.
31. Satō Kōka, "Seiyokugaku goi," pt. 1, *Hentai shiryō*, November 1926, 65.
32. Takahashi Tetsu, *Jinseiki: Nihon interigenchiya issenmei no zangeroku*, vol. 1 (Amatoriasha, 1952), 56, 57, 59, 111, 127–130.
33. A-sei, "'Joseiteki danshi' o yonde," 130.

Erotic magazines like *Sei* and *Hentai seiyoku* were not the only medium through which the sexological model gained popular currency. General-interest journals also devoted prominent coverage to the "sexual problem," much as they had earlier helped to publicize the "social problem" and the "woman problem." Discussions of sexuality were also a staple feature of women's magazines, to the extent that women's rights activists launched a campaign in 1928 to rid their pages of unwholesome confessional narratives and exposés, issuing a call for increased self-restraint on the part of publishers as well as stricter government censorship.[34] Although the gender of their audience prompted women's magazines to pay closer attention to "same-sex love" among women than among men, the fact that sexology drew an analogy between the two likely helped familiarize female readers with medical thinking on male-male sexuality. Nor was the latter seen as a "problem" for men alone. The prominent neurologist Kure Shūzō opened an article on "same-sex love" in a 1920 issue of *Fujin gahō* (Ladies' Pictorial), for instance, by appealing to women in their role as mothers to gain an understanding of this topic so as to prevent their "beloved sons and daughters from falling victim to this dread disease."[35]

In the realm of literature as well, the influence of the "same-sex love" model extended far beyond Watanuki's prose. While Watanuki achieved only a modest reputation in his time, and is barely remembered today, there are few canonical figures of the early twentieth-century literary stage who did not deal at some point in their writings with "same-sex love," whether in its male or female form.[36] In chapter 4, for example, we examined the portrayal of male-male sexuality in Mori Ōgai's *Vita Sexualis*, which appeared, only to be banned a month later, in 1909. Significantly, Mori was himself a doctor, and had received part of his medical training in Germany. In addition to yielding valuable insights into the erotic culture of Meiji "roughnecks," Mori's novel provides an early example of a literary work deeply informed by emerging medical conceptions of "sexual desire" (*seiyoku*), the likes of which would proliferate in the ensuing decades of the early twentieth century.

As his title indicates, Mori frames his work as a chronicle of the sexual life of one individual, recording the "steps by which sexual desire appears

34. Maruoka Hideko and Yamaguchi Miyoko, eds., *Kindai Nihon fujin mondai nenpyō*, vol. 10 of *Nihon fujin mondai shiryō shūsei*, ed. Maruoka Hideko et al., 10 vols. (Domesu shuppan, 1975–1981), 133.

35. Kure Shūzō, "Dōsei no ai," *Fujin gahō*, October 1920, 25.

36. For useful bibliographic resources, see Iwata Jun'ichi, *Nanshoku bunken shoshi* (Toba: Iwata Sadao, 1973); Kakinuma Eiko and Kurihara Chiyo, eds., *Tanbi shōsetsu gei bungaku bukkugaido* (Byakuya shobō, 1993).

in human life and the ways in which it affects that life."[37] Although the narrator, Kanai Shizuka, is deeply "suspicious" of the psychiatric view that "every aspect of a man's life is tinged with sexual desire," his attempt to describe his own erotic development from the age of six bears a striking resemblance to the sexological case history, just as the title of the manuscript echoes Krafft-Ebing's *Psychopathia Sexualis*.[38] While certain aspects of Mori's work recall such Edo-period narratives as Saikaku's *Life of an Amorous Man*—which follows, for example, a similar chronological format, beginning in the subject's childhood—its clinical terminology marks it unmistakably as a product of the twentieth century. In writing his novel, Mori was deeply influenced by the rising literary school of naturalism, which stressed the need for candor in describing sexual phenomena, albeit Mori at the same time criticized naturalists' single-minded preoccupation with the flesh (as a good Meijiite, he did not wish to lose sight of the spirit) and deterministic tendencies. The appearance of Mori's work probably did more, however, to further the ascendance of naturalism and of explicit narratives of "sexual desire" in general than to hinder them—not least, ironically, because of its notorious banning. Not only was Mori a "member of the educated circle governed by the law of prudery" (as Kanai describes himself in the novel)—a respectable citizen, in other words, of the world of "civilized morality"—but, as surgeon general of the imperial army, he was himself a high government official, thereby compounding the scandal of the incident.[39]

Mori's work is significant also in that it portrays male-male sexuality from a first-person perspective. In this respect it is closer to a confessional narrative than a case history in the strict sense—albeit, ironically, its author was himself a doctor. While the theme of male-male sexuality occupies only the early chapters of the work, thereby mirroring the emerging medical view of "same-sex love" as constituting an early stage in psychosexual development, and although the narrator specifically disavows his psychological credentials as an "urning," instead stressing his lack of sexual desire in any form, Mori's first-person representation of male-male eroticism foreshadows a growing tendency among early twentieth-century writ-

37. Mori Ōgai, *Wita sekusuarisu*, in *Ōgai zenshū*, ed. Kinoshita Mokutarō et al., 38 vols. (Iwanami shoten, 1971–1975), 5:89 (trans. Kazuji Ninomiya and Sanford Goldstein under the title *Vita Sexualis* [Rutland, Vt.: Tuttle, 1972], 28 [whence the quotation]).

38. Mori, *Wita sekusuarisu*, 5:87 (Ninomiya and Goldstein, *Vita Sexualis*, 26 [whence the quotation]).

39. Mori, *Wita sekusuarisu*, 5:178 (Ninomiya and Goldstein, *Vita Sexualis*, 152 [whence the quotation]).

ers to give "same-sex love" a subjective voice. In the genre of the "I novel" (*shishōsetsu*), of which Mori's work is often considered an early example, the "I" of the narrator not infrequently overlapped with the "I" of the author himself (or herself), just as the life history of *Vita Sexualis*'s Kanai bears a striking resemblance to the biographical details of Mori's own life—a fact likely not lost on many of Mori's readers. The future Nobel Prize winner Kawabata Yasunari went so far, in his 1948 work *Shōnen* (Boy), as to weave an entire novel out of actual diary entries, letters, and other compositions recording his love for a fellow schoolboy during the 1910s.[40]

While, in the case of such authors as Mori and Kawabata, male-male sexuality constitutes at best a subtheme within the larger corpus of their work, other litterateurs accorded it a more central importance. One of the most prolific writers on this subject was Inagaki Taruho, whose reputation as an author of "pure literature" (*junbungaku*) gave him a somewhat more respectable standing in literary circles than the "mass author" (*taishū sakka*) Watanuki.[41] Inagaki could nevertheless at times be quite explicit in his references to male-male sexuality, and came close to being banned on at least one occasion.[42] Instead of Watanuki's burly soldiers and fishermen, it was the adolescent male who served as Inagaki's erotic ideal.[43] In his stories, Inagaki frequently portrays "same-sex love" in a schoolboy setting, drawing upon his upbringing in early twentieth-century Kobe. For Inagaki, who was eleven years old at the close of the Meiji period, the *bishōnen* esthetic of that era provided a source of fascination and nostalgia that would inform much of his subsequent writing.

Inagaki was keenly aware of the rapid changes in erotic culture and discourse that had taken place since his childhood. He recalled in later years how the "*bishōnen* mood" that permeated close to a half century of Meiji culture had gradually faded under the influence of Taishō liberalism, with

40. Kawabata Yasunari, *Shōnen*, in *Kawabata Yasunari zenshū*, ed. Yamamoto Kenkichi et al., 37 vols. (Shinchōsha, 1980–1984), 10:141–255.

41. Many of Inagaki's writings on male-male erotic themes are collected in vols. 2 and 3 of *Inagaki Taruho taizen*, ed. Hagiwara Sachiko and Kawahito Hiroshi, 6 vols. (Gendai shichōsha, 1969–1970), and in *Shōnen tokuhon* (Ushio shuppansha, 1986). On Inagaki's life and work, I have also consulted *Bessatsu shinpyō* 10.1 (1977; special issue titled "Inagaki Taruho no sekai"); Inagaki Taruho and Inagaki Shiyo, *Taruho to Taruho* (Chūsekisha, 1986); Inagaki Taruho et al., *Taruho jiten* (Ushio shuppansha, 1975); Nakano Kaichi, *Inagaki Taruho no sekai* (Hōbunkan shuppan, 1984); Shirakawa Masayoshi, *Inagaki Taruho* (Tōjusha, 1976).

42. Inagaki Shiyo, *Otto Inagaki Taruho*, in *Taruho to Taruho*, 432.

43. See, for example, Inagaki Taruho, "Shin inu tsurezure," in *Inagaki Taruho taizen*, 2:80–81.

its more permissive attitude toward youthful sexuality, while the "advance of the Viennese school" (that is to say, Freudianism) had rendered into a thing of the past the simpler lyricism of such works as Kōmurō Shujin's *Bishōnenron*.[44] A considerable portion of Inagaki's writing during the 1920s and 1930s was devoted to the task of forging an esthetic of young male beauty (*shōnenbi*) more suited to the current age. "For the sake of a new civilization," comments one of his characters—modeled, apparently, after one of Inagaki's Western schoolteachers in Kobe—in a 1930 essay, "a new and liberalistic *shōnenbi* must be born."[45] In Inagaki's writings, the *shōnenbi* ideal emerges not only as a central element of traditional Japanese estheticism (*tanbishugi*), but as consonant also with such contemporary global artistic currents as futurism (a school by which Inagaki himself was strongly influenced), equally at home in the twentieth-century urban landscape as in the native past.[46] In the eyes of one of his characters, the unshorn forelocks of the Edo-period youth thus appear, with little sense of anachronism, to be a consummate embodiment of the quality of "it" marketed by the Hollywood actress Clara Bow.[47]

Inagaki's works stand in a complex and ambivalent relationship to the ascendance of the medical model. On the one hand, Inagaki was versed in a wide variety of Western authorities on "same-sex love," including Krafft-Ebing and Freud, and made frequent use of sexological vocabulary. On the other, he felt that the Freudian idiom of "inversion" was implicitly "negative" (*shōkyokuteki*), and himself preferred the term "boy love" (*shōnen'ai*) to "same-sex love" because of his predominant concern with male-male, rather than female-female, sexuality and his predilection for the "classical" (*tenkeiteki*) pattern of age-structured relations.[48] Inagaki strove less for the negation of the medical model, one might say, than for its estheticization. His 1926 short story "Uranism" (Tentai shikōshō), for example, conveys little of the clinical sense of that term, but rather the author's lifelong fascination with the celestial heavens from which the etymology of both "urning" and "uranism" derives.[49] Similarly, while Inagaki voiced reservations

44. Inagaki Taruho, "Miyatake Gaikotsu no *Bishōnenron*," in *Inagaki Taruho taizen*, 2:344–345.

45. Inagaki Taruho, "Shōnen tokuhon: Esseifū na seisaku," in *Shōnen tokuhon*, 56.

46. Inagaki Taruho, "Kamonohashiron," in *Inagaki Taruho taizen*, 2:147; Inagaki Taruho, "Shin inu tsurezure," 2:79; Inagaki Taruho, "Shōnen tokuhon," 55–56.

47. Inagaki Taruho, "Shōnen tokuhon," 66.

48. Inagaki Taruho, "Shin inu tsurezure," 2:80–81; Inagaki Taruho, "Shōnen tokuhon," 58.

49. Inagaki Taruho, "Tentai shikōshō," in *Inagaki Taruho taizen*, 1:96–106.

about the negative implications of Freudian terminology, Freud's notion of a deeply ingrained anal eroticism would become the cornerstone of his post-war erotic philosophy.[50]

The *bishōnen* esthetic whose passing Inagaki lamented naturally did not disappear overnight under the influence of the medical model. Inagaki himself mentions a number of Taishō-period authors who continued to celebrate the beauty of the adolescent male in their works, including such poets and writers of fiction as Murayama Kaita and Yamazaki Toshio.[51] In a 1921 essay, the novelist and national socialist Ozaki Shirō went so far as to assert approvingly that an "artistic demand" had lately arisen in Japan for a "new way of the *bishōnen*" (*atarashii bishōnendō*). As the nation's "artistic life" grew richer, Ozaki predicted, new forms of "*bishōnen* worship" (*bishōnen sūhai*) would take the place of an outmoded *nanshoku* that, together with the "way of the warrior" (*bushidō*), had disintegrated or ossified since the Meiji era. While Ozaki did not venture to speculate as to the contours of this new "way," the fact that he associated it both with contemporary esthetic currents and with the emerging notion of "perverse sexual desire" suggests not only that the "same-sex love" construct depended as much upon literature as medicine for its articulation, but that, from a nonmedical perspective, it might still receive a surprisingly positive evaluation.[52]

In envisioning a constructive social role for "same-sex love" in the future, Ozaki echoed the claims of the work of the British socialist Edward Carpenter (whom Ozaki refers to as a "champion" of *dōseiai*), as did Inagaki, whose 1930 essay quoted Carpenter's belief that "same-sex love" would contribute to the cultural progress of humankind.[53] A Japanese translation of Carpenter's *The Intermediate Sex* had appeared in the feminist literary journal *Safuran* (Saffron) as early as 1914, and in book form five years later.[54]

---

50. Inagaki introduces Freud's concept of *Analerotik* as early as his 1930 essay "Shōnen tokuhon" (58, 64–65).

51. Inagaki Taruho, *Shōnen'ai no bigaku*, in *Inagaki Taruho taizen* 3:256–476. For representative works by these authors, see Murayama Kaita, *Murayama Kaita zenshū*, ed. Yamamoto Tarō (Yayoi shobō, 1963); Yamazaki Toshio, *Bidō*, vol. 1 of *Yamazaki Toshio sakuhinshū*, ed. Ikuta Kōsaku, 3 vols. to date (Kobe: Sabato yakata, 1986–).

52. Ozaki Shirō, "Bishōnen no kenkyū," *Kaihō*, April 1921, 539–540.

53. Inagaki Taruho, "Shōnen tokuhon," 60; Ozaki, "Bishōnen no kenkyū," 539–540.

54. Aoyama Kikue, trans., *Chūseiron*, pts. 1–3, *Safuran*, May 1914, 1–22; June 1914, 130–153; July 1914, 55–76; Sakai Toshihiko and Yamakawa Kikue, trans., *Josei chūshinsetsu/Dōseiai* (Arusu, 1919).

In his preface to the latter, the socialist Sakai Toshihiko saw fit to add the caveat that the work's translator, the feminist and fellow socialist Yamakawa (née Aoyama) Kikue, did not endorse all of Carpenter's opinions on the subject.[55] While cryptic as to what aspects of Carpenter's thinking Yamakawa found objectionable, Sakai's note of caution subtly conveys the ambivalence with which many Japanese socialists and other leftist writers of the early twentieth century approached the topic of "same-sex love."

One of most outspoken of socialist authors on the subject was Morita Yūshū, whose sexological writings we have already encountered in the previous chapter. It is important to note that, while Morita vehemently denounced the persecution of *dōseiaisha*, his attitude toward "same-sex love" fell considerably short of a Carpenteresque affirmation. Morita was a firm advocate of "free love" (*jiyū ren'ai*), by which he meant unrestricted freedom of erotic interaction between the two sexes. If impediments to this freedom had not arisen in the first place, Morita maintained, the "abominable [*ken'o subeki*] phenomenon of *dōseiai*" would likely never have emerged. While accepting Hirschfeld's and others' view that in many individuals "same-sex love" was a congenital trait, he argued in Lamarckian fashion that the social injustices of the past, chief among them the system of private property, had been responsible for implanting this "perversion" in such persons' veins.[56] Morita was familiar with the theories of the German ethnologist Heinrich Schurtz, who viewed erotic alliances among youths in antiquity as a form of masculine revolt against primitive matriarchy (from a Marxian perspective, it must be kept in mind, the latter constituted a more equitable form of society), and speculated that present-day *dōseiai*—at least among males—might represent a legacy of this process.[57] Sakai Toshihiko, too, linked male-male sexual relations with the emergence of patriarchy and private property, arguing that the institutions of monogamy and female seclusion in ancient Greece had been responsible for such "corrupt" (*fuhai*) and "unnatural" (*fushizen*) side effects as prostitution, adultery, and *nanshoku*.[58] Although Morita's and Sakai's analyses

55. Sakai Toshihiko, "Hashigaki," in *Josei chūshinsetsu/Dōseiai*, 2.

56. Morita Yūshū, *Jiyū ren'ai hiwa* (Heibonsha, 1930), 265–275.

57. Morita, *Dōseiai no kenkyū*, 50; Morita Yūshū, *Hentai seiyoku hiwa* (Heibonsha, 1930), 5; Morita Yūshū, *Jiyū ren'ai to shakaishugi*, Shakai mondai sōsho, no. 7 (Bunka gakkai shuppanbu, 1925), 71–98. Similarly, the left-leaning sexologist Yasuda Tokutarō ("Doseiai no rekishikan," 149) viewed the rise of the *chigo* cult in medieval Japan as a masculine assault upon women's role as shamans, which had survived as a vestige of primitive matriarchy.

58. Sakai Toshihiko, *Danjo tōsōshi* (Eisendō shoten, 1920), 81–84.

focused on the historical, and specifically the European, past, their implication was that once contemporary Japanese society had solved the "social problem," the "sexual problem"—and perhaps even *dōseiai* itself—would also disappear.

To expose the inequities of the current social system, thus helping to generate support for socialism, was one of the objectives of the proletarian literary movement, which enjoyed its heyday during the 1920s and 1930s. In the writings of this school, as in the works of Morita and Sakai, "same-sex love" offered a convenient emblem for the structural defects of contemporary society. Perhaps the most famous practitioner of proletarian literature, Kobayashi Takiji, provides a classic example of this approach in his 1929 novel *Kani kōsen* (Factory Ship), which portrays the deplorable working conditions that prevail on a Japanese crab-processing ship fishing the icy waters off Kamchatka. The contract laborers aboard this all-male vessel are described by Kobayashi as "tortured by sexual desire," having been "unnaturally" deprived for months on end of female contact. Their thwarted eros manifests itself in ribald stories, songs, and pornography, in "self-abuse" (*jitoku*), and finally in "night crawling" (*yobai*) to fourteen- or fifteen-year-old factory hands, with whom they rendezvous in such dank and gloomy settings as between fishing nets or in a dingy storeroom, and whose reluctance they manage to overcome with a few pieces of caramel.[59] It is not the exploitation of the young factory hand by his senior shipmates to which Kobayashi seeks to draw attention, however, but rather of both parties by monopoly capitalism, which bears in the author's view the responsibility for creating such dehumanizing conditions in the first place.

Not all of proletarian literature, however, portrayed "same-sex love" in such purely physical terms, or with such blatantly doctrinaire ends. The 1934 short story "Rōkō" (Squalid Alleyways), for example, by Kataoka Teppei—who, it should be noted, had officially recanted his socialism during a prison stay two years earlier—offers a far more emotionally nuanced approach to the topic.[60] The chief male characters in the story are Sugita and his roommate Yamazaki (twenty-six and twenty years of age respectively at the be-

59. Kobayashi Takiji, *Kani kōsen*, in <*Teihon*> *Kobayashi Takiji zenshū*, ed. Eguchi Kiyoshi et al., 15 vols. (Shin Nihon shuppansha, 1968–1969), 4:35–37 (trans. Frank Motofuji under the title *The Factory Ship*, in *"The Factory Ship" and "The Absentee Landlord"* (Seattle: University of Washington Press, 1973), 32–33.
60. Kataoka Teppei, "Rōkō," *Chūō kōron*, June 1934, (sōsaku) 1–41. For Kataoka's views on female "same-sex love," see his "Josei fuan to dōseiai," *Kaizō*, March 1935, 78–84.

ginning of the narrative), who eke out a meager living peddling a fermented beverage (*amazake*) on the streets of Tokyo, and whom Kataoka describes as having been involved in an "unnatural relationship" (*fushizen na kankei*) since meeting two years earlier on a bench in Asakusa Park. The plot revolves around the intrusion into their drab lives of a female character, Torii Masuko, who eventually wins Yamazaki's affection. In poignant detail, Kataoka portrays both the jealousy that Yamazaki's "betrayal" wreaks upon Sugita, and the peculiar mix of guilt and resentment with which Yamazaki comes to regard his former lover. While Yamazaki thus moves in sexological terms from "same-sex love" to "cross-sex love," Sugita continues in his erotic pursuit of other males, and when last we hear of him he has formed a "special intimacy" (*tokubetsu na naka*) with a cross-dressing male prostitute, Chiyo-chan, whom he befriends in the backstreets of Osaka's Tennōji district.

Kataoka's story closes with the reflections of the character Tanno Orizō, who, like Kataoka himself, is an author of proletarian fiction. Upon learning that Sugita is a "male pervert" (*hentaisei no otoko*), Tanno is at first astonished, yet his surprise soon gives way to admiration for Sugita's decision to take up a job as a metalworker in a Kyushu factory, thereby leaving behind his "lumpenproletariat" existence for the life of a "steeled laborer." "Perverted or not, Sugita is a man with beautiful human emotions," Tanno reflects. While Kataoka's, like Kobayashi's, work is informed—the author's prison conversion notwithstanding—by socialist ideals, the former's willingness to entertain "beauty" and "perversion" in the same character, indeed in the same sentence, conveys a sense of the emotional complexity and human dignity of "same-sex love" that is difficult to detect in the latter author.

Kataoka's story serves to illustrate three commonly recurring tropes of early twentieth-century popular discourse on male-male sexuality. First, the "squalid alleyways" of the title links "same-sex love" with a vaguely "grotesque" urban environment. The cities of early twentieth-century Japan, and particularly the metropolises of Tokyo and Osaka, saw the emergence of a new subculture of male-male eroticism, the outlines of which begin to reveal themselves in popular discourse during the 1920s.[61] We shall have oc-

61. More local research is needed in order to determine the extent to which similar subcultures developed outside Tokyo and Osaka and the specific forms that they may have taken there. According to Inagaki Taruho ("Shōnen tokuhon," 61), male-male cruising areas could be found in Kyoto by 1930 (regarding Kyoto, see also Satō Kōka's account cited in n. 31 above), while, in 1948, Minami Takao ("Danshō ni kansuru ni-san no seishin igakuteki kōsatsu to sono shakai to no kanrensei ni tsuite,"

casion before the end of this chapter to revisit the benches of Asakusa Park and the backstreets of Tennōji. Second, like Kataoka's character Chiyo-chan, prostitutes were frequently portrayed as central actors in this subculture, embodying an "inverted" trope of male-male sexual behavior whose roots were neither exclusively medical nor popular. Third, in alluding to Chiyo-chan's friend, the notorious murderer Hana-chan, Kataoka drew upon, at the same time that he further strengthened, a conceptual association between male-male sexuality and criminality that the following section will explore in greater detail.

ERO-GURO NANSHOKU

Popular discourse had, of course, long associated male-male sexuality with criminal behavior. In Edo-period texts, the pursuit of *shudō*, particularly among sword-wielding samurai, gave rise to frequent duels, vendettas, murders, and other infringements of public peace and order. It was the conflict between the demands of the "way," on the one hand, and the norms of the community and polity, on the other, that endowed these accounts with their dramatic tension, just as it provided Edo-period lawmakers with a motive for the enactment of perisexual legislation. When early Meiji officials proscribed male-male anal intercourse, they shifted the focus of the legal gaze from such perisexual behaviors to genital acts. Nevertheless, the conceptual connection between sexual and social transgression remained alive in popular discourse—as we saw, for example, in the turn-of-the-century panic over the "decadent student." Ironically, this connection persisted despite the fact that the penal code after 1882 did not criminalize male-male sexual acts per se.

By the early twentieth century, criminal, like sexual, behavior had become the object of a rising scientific discipline. Criminology, like sexology, viewed social phenomena from a deeply biologized and medicalized perspective, positing criminal acts as a manifestation of physiological or psychological anomaly, or, alternatively, of a larger social pathology. Furthermore, many authorities saw criminality and sexuality as inherently related: as Sawada Junjirō put it in 1923, "There is no crime, large or small, that can-

---

in *Dōseiai to dōsei shinjū no kenkyū*, by Komine Shigeyuki and Minami Takao [Komine kenkyūjo, 1985], 277) reports the existence of a "network" of male prostitution extending as far as Kyushu. For a 1934 reference to organized male-male prostitution in Kyushu, see Furukawa Makoto, "The Changing Nature of Sexuality: The Three Codes Framing Homosexuality in Modern Japan," trans. Angus Lockyer, *U.S.-Japan Women's Journal, English Supplement* 7 (1994): 107.

not be traced to the lust that lies hidden beneath its surface."[62] Again like sexology, criminology was as much a part of mass culture as it was a professional discourse. The scientific study of criminal behavior lent legitimacy to a broader narrative exploration (one is tempted almost to say a celebration) of crime that was intended to entertain popular audiences no less than to provoke readers' moral indignation, filling the coffers of the publishing industry in the process. Bizarre crimes and colorful criminals had long provided a favorite topic of popular discourse, but gained a new allure in the early twentieth century as embodiments of the "grotesque," as well as the "erotic," aspects of human existence.

This conceptual association of male-male sexuality with criminality helps to explain why the first extended scholarly attempt to trace the history of *nanshoku* in Japan should have appeared in the pages of a popular-criminology magazine. Iwata Jun'ichi's *Honchō nanshoku kō* (Study of *Nanshoku* in Our Realm) was serialized in *Hanzai kagaku* (Criminal Science) from August 1930 to October 1931, its chronological narrative drawing to a premature close following the medieval era.[63] Interestingly, Iwata's study contains little mention of crime per se, whether according to the legal standards of the periods he examined or that in which he wrote. Rather, the author combines a rigorous empirical methodology (seldom relying, for example, on secondary sources) with an engaging prose style to produce a historical survey of remarkably high caliber given the forum in which it appeared. Iwata also contributed articles on *nanshoku* to such magazines as *Hanzai kōron* (Crime Review) and *Tantei shōsetsu* (Detective Story), yet he was by no means a criminologist, nor much interested in the topic of crime itself. Initially, Iwata had hoped to publish his research in the general-interest journal *Chūō kōron* (Central Review), but it was the popular criminology press, with its fascination for the "grotesque" and "erotic," that provided the more welcoming venue for his work, much as Iwata may have privately disparaged *ero-guro* journalists.[64]

Iwata's eclectic interests ranged from painting (he had apprenticed un-

62. Sawada Junjirō, *Seiyoku hanzai* (Kindai no kekkonsha, 1923), (jijo) 1.
63. *Honchō nanshoku kō* is reprinted, together with other writings, in Iwata Jun'ichi, *Honchō nanshoku kō* (Toba: Iwata Sadao, 1974), 1–168. Installments eight through eleven of *Honchō nanshoku kō* originally ran under the title "Muromachi jidai nanshokushi." Portions of Iwata's study are translated in Tsuneo Watanabe and Jun'ichi Iwata, *The Love of the Samurai: A Thousand Years of Japanese Homosexuality*, trans. D. R. Roberts (London: GMP, 1989).
64. Edogawa Ranpo, "Dōseiai bungakushi ni tsuite: Iwata Jun'ichi-kun no omoide," in *Honchō nanshoku kō*, n.p.; Iwata Jun'ichi to Minakata Kumagusu, 2

der the celebrated illustrator Takehisa Yumeji) to popular fiction (using the pen name Kanae Yukijirō) to the ethnography of his native Mie prefecture (as a member of Shibusawa Keizō's "Attic Museum," he published, among other treatises, a study of that region's *ama* or female divers).[65] In *Honchō nanshoku kō*, Iwata drew upon literary and other sources to depict *nanshoku* as spreading outward over the centuries from the monastic population to courtiers, samurai, and eventually to commoners, borrowing these familiar tropes of laicization and popularization from Edo-period writers on *shudō*. Publication of his study sparked a decade-long correspondence with Minakata Kumagusu, who, invoking a typical Meiji dualism, was critical of what he saw as his younger colleague's excessive attention to the "sexual" (*seiyokujō*) aspects of *nanshoku* to the neglect of the "spiritual" (*shinreijō*), and would provide him over the years with valuable bibliographic, ethnographic, and philological guidance.[66] Iwata, too, made an effort to distinguish between "same-sex love" (*dōseiai*) and "same-sex sexual desire" (*dōsei seiyoku*), yet was all too keenly aware that the historical sources he drew upon did not always differentiate clearly between the two.[67] His contribution to the historiography of male-male eroticism in Japan lies not only in *Honchō nanshoku kō* and other articles that he published during his lifetime, but in various writings that saw the light of day only after his death in 1945, including his correspondence with Minakata, two important lexicons, and an extensive bibliography of *nanshoku*-related works that, in deference to the Edo-period anthologist Kitamura Kigin, he dubbed *Nochi no iwatsutsuji* or "A Latter-Day Rock Azalea."[68]

The person responsible for introducing Iwata to the popular-criminology

September 1931, *Minakata Kumagusu nanshoku dangi: Iwata Jun'ichi ōfuku shokan*, ed. Hasegawa Kōzō and Tsukikawa Kazuo (Yasaka shobō, 1991), 94 (trans. William F. Sibley in "Morning Fog [Correspondence on Gay Lifestyles]," in *Partings at Dawn: An Anthology of Japanese Gay Literature*, ed. Stephen D. Miller [San Francisco: Gay Sunshine, 1996], 169).

65. For biographical information on Iwata, see Edogawa, "Dōseiai bungakushi"; Edogawa Ranpo, "*Honchō nanshoku kō* ni tsuite," in *Honchō nanshoku kō*, n.p.; Iwata Sadao, "Bōfu Iwata Jun'ichi," in *Minakata Kumagusu nanshoku dangi*, 412–433; Tsukikawa Kazuo, "Iwata Jun'ichi ryakunenpu," in *Minakata Kumagusu nanshoku dangi*, 434–437.

66. Minakata Kumagusu to Iwata Jun'ichi, 25 August 1931, *Minakata Kumagusu zenshū*, ed. Iwamura Shinobu et al., 12 vols. (Heibonsha, 1971–1975), 9:47.

67. Iwata Jun'ichi to Minakata Kumagusu, 16 August 1931, *Minakata Kumagusu nanshoku dangi*, 37 (Sibley, "Morning Fog," 144).

68. These writings may be found in *Minakata Kumagusu nanshoku dangi; Iwata Jun'ichi, Honchō nanshoku kō; Iwata Jun'ichi, Nanshoku bunken shoshi*. Sibley translates three of Iwata's letters in "Morning Fog."

press was, appropriately enough, the mystery writer Edogawa Ranpo, with whom Iwata had shared a more than decade-long friendship.[69] While Edogawa was an avid collector of *shudō* texts and collaborated with Iwata in his bibliographic research, his expertise extended equally to Western writings on "same-sex love," as well as to the emerging field of psychoanalysis. Edogawa was particularly fascinated by the Victorian intellectual John Addington Symonds (who had also made a strong impression upon Minakata), not only, it would appear, because of Symonds's defense of "sexual inversion," but also because Symonds's personal life seemed riddled by the same mysteries and contradictions that made up the stuff of good detective fiction. In 1933, Edogawa went so far as to contribute an article titled "J. A. Symonds's Secret Passion" to the journal *Seishin bunseki* (Psychoanalysis), speculating, among other things, that Symonds's "same-sex love" was related to his single-handed upbringing by his father, that one of Symonds's recurring dreams about a disembodied finger indicated a repressed memory of his father's penis, and that Symonds's writings represented a "sublimation" (*shōka*) of his "urning" nature.[70] Edogawa's penchant for the mysterious and criminal, as well as his grounding in Western sources, also reveal themselves in the fact that his most extended treatment of male-male eroticism in historical Japan revolves around a seventeenth-century murder and love-suicide incident that he learned of, ironically enough, through reading Edward Carpenter.[71]

In Edogawa's fiction, male-male sexuality plays a particularly prominent role in the 1929–1930 mystery tale *Kotō no oni* (Demon of the Lonely Isle). One of the central figures in this work is Moroto Michio, variously described in the narrative as a "pervert" (*henshitsusha*), a "sexual invert" (*seiteki*

69. Edogawa, "Dōseiai bungakushi," n.p.; Iwata Jun'ichi to Minakata Kumagusu, 27 August 1931, *Minakata Kumagusu nanshoku dangi*, 83–84.

70. Edogawa Ranpo, "J. A. Shimonzu no hisoka naru jōnetsu," in *Edogawa Ranpo zenshū*, 25 vols. (Kōdansha, 1978–1979), 17:71–100. Edogawa also discusses Symonds in "Shimonzu, Kāpentā, Jīdo," in *Edogawa Ranpo zenshū*, 17:66–68. The "secret passion" of Walt Whitman held a similarly mysterious fascination for Edogawa. See "Hoittoman no hanashi," in *Edogawa Ranpo zenshū*, 17:61–66.

71. Edogawa Ranpo, "Mokuzuzuka," in *Edogawa Ranpo zenshū*, 17:55–61. For Carpenter's rendering of the incident (drawing in turn upon the German ethnographer Friedrich Karsch-Haack), see Edward Carpenter, *Intermediate Types among Primitive Folk: A Study in Social Evolution*, 2d ed. (London: Allen, 1919), 151–155. *Shudō*-related slayings and suicides of the Edo period provided ready fodder for the early twentieth-century popular-criminology press, for examples of which see Miyagawa Mangyo, "Yushima yawa," pt. 9 of a series titled "Edo jidai no seiteki hanzai," *Hanzai kagaku*, February 1931, 63–72; "Nanshoku adauchi bidan," *Hanzai kōron*, October 1932, 164.

tōsakusha), a "man who is unable to love the opposite sex" (*isei ni koishienai otoko*), or, in the character's own words, a member of a "different race" (*ijin-shu*). Although the narrator has previously described him as a "born woman-hater" (*seirai onnagirai*), Moroto is made to reveal midway through the story that his "same-sex love" likely stems from early childhood, when his mother, or at least the person whom he believed to be so at the time, lavished upon him a blatantly sexual attention, causing him to subsequently view all women as "unclean"—an unmistakably Freudian twist on the familiar figure of the *onnagirai*. While Moroto's "perversion," like the hunchbacks, Siamese twins, and other anomalies of nature who fill the novel's pages, undoubtedly contributes to the uncanny atmosphere of the work, it does not have the result of alienating him fully from the narrator, Minohara—nor, one must assume, from audiences either. Although Minohara cannot return or even understand the "strange love" that Moroto has entertained for him since their student days, he teams up with his "odd friend" in order to solve a string of murders, forming one of the more unconventional pairs of sleuths in the detective-story genre. A curious mix of attraction and repulsion binds Minohara to his partner: at one point in the story, the narrator-protagonist imagines himself a woman in Moroto's arms, while elsewhere in the work he flees panic-stricken from his embraces.[72]

"Same-sex love" similarly functions as an emblem of the mysterious and criminal in the work of Edogawa's friend and fellow detective-fiction writer Hamao Shirō, a hereditary nobleman who enjoyed the distinction of serving in the House of Peers. Hamao, too, was well versed in such Western authorities on "homosexuality" as Krafft-Ebing, Carpenter, Hirschfeld, and the British sexologist Havelock Ellis, claiming that there was "nothing worth looking at" among Japanese writings on the subject.[73] While Edogawa did not hesitate, in a 1926 magazine essay, to describe his male-male erotic experiences as a middle-school student in late-Meiji Nagoya, Hamao was less given to this style of autobiographical confession, reportedly remarking to Edogawa that such memories as the latter had divulged in his article were not to be bandied about lightly but rather to be privately cherished.[74] Male-male sexuality nevertheless surfaces as a recurring theme in Hamao's writings, notably in the 1929 short story "Akuma no deshi" (Devil's Apprentice). Like Kataoka and Edogawa, Hamao constructs his narrative around a pair of males who have been involved in an erotic attachment in their

---

72. Edogawa Ranpo, *Kotō no oni*, in *Edogawa Ranpo zenshū*, 4:5–173.
73. Hamao Shirō, "Dōseiai kō," *Fujin saron*, September 1930, 142.
74. Nakajima Kawatarō, "Kaidai," in *Edogawa Ranpo zenshū*, 16:233.

younger days, one of them moving on later in life to "cross-sex love," the other remaining mired, as it were, in his "perversion." Ironically, it is the sexologically "normal" character, Shimaura Eizō, who appears as the criminal in the story, while the perennial "woman-hater" Tsuchida Hachirō pursues a respectable career as a public prosecutor—a position, interestingly, that Hamao himself once occupied in real life. Shimaura attributes his descent into crime (he has attempted to poison his wife) to his former schoolmate Tsuchida, whom he blames for having initiated him in their student days into a "diabolical philosophy" that found its textual underpinnings in such mystery authors as Edgar Allan Poe (Edogawa Ranpo's namesake, incidentally) and such authorities on "same-sex love" as Krafft-Ebing and Carpenter.[75]

A conceptual link between male-male sexuality and crime gained reinforcement not only through the fiction of Edogawa and Hamao, but also from real-life events and their journalistic representation. Already in the Meiji period, newspapers had played up this connection in their coverage of a highly publicized 1902 incident in which an eleven-year-old boy was found strangled on the streets of Tokyo, a piece of flesh mysteriously cut out of his buttocks. Although forensics experts could find no evidence of anal penetration, police focused their investigative efforts on the "decadent student" population of the city—who, as one newspaper informed its readers, were "the most intimately connected with *keikan*"—and at one point detained a Kagoshima male known for abducting "beautiful boys" as well as being an accomplished thief and swindler (he was eventually released).[76] Newspapers followed what they dubbed the "buttock-flesh" (*denniku*) incident with a voracious curiosity, although the alleged perpetrator, whose guilt to this day remains disputed, did not emerge for several years. While the purported motive had little to do with anal intercourse, but rather with an obscure medical remedy involving the consumption of human flesh, the incident nonetheless serves to illustrate the way in which journalism contributed to a public perception of male-male sexuality as a bizarre and sometimes criminal aberration.[77] Its echoes appear in a male-male erotic context as late as Oguri Mushitarō's 1936 mystery novel *Madōji* (Devil Boy), an eerie tale

75. Hamao Shirō, "Akuma no deshi," *Shin seinen*, April 1929, 168–198.
76. Umehara Hokumei, ed., <*Meiji Taishō*> *Kidan chinbun daishūsei*, 3 vols. (Bungei shijōsha, 1929–1931), 3:166.
77. For details of the incident, see Koishikawa Zenji et al., *Hanzai no minzokugaku: Meiji Taishō hanzaishi kara* (Hihyōsha, 1993), 69–84; Umehara, *Kidan chinbun*, 3:155–167.

that involves not only "same-sex love" but also one of its fellow "perversions," pygmalionism.[78]

By the 1930s, however, new figures had emerged to take the place of the turn-of-the-century "decadent student" in the criminal iconography of "perversion." We have already encountered one such figure in Kataoka's short story "Rōkō," which alludes to Chiyo-chan's friend S., alias Hana-chan, whom Kataoka describes as a "renowned" murderer.[79] Most contemporary readers, no doubt, would have had little trouble guessing that Kataoka referred to Shaji Hisaichi, known also by his stage name Hanayagi Biraku, who had made headlines less than a year before the story's publication. Although the murder in question had taken place in 1928, it had gone undiscovered until the fall of 1933, when a trunk belonging to Shaji was found by police to contain a severed male head. Upon his arrest, Shaji, who was a performer of female roles (*onnagata*) in a traveling stage troupe, confessed that the skull was that of his former lover Matsumoto Takezō, whom he had killed in the aftermath of a jealous quarrel. At the time of the murder, Shaji was not only living with Matsumoto, but also serving as a concubine to a German trader from Kobe, as well as peddling his charms professionally in the neighborhood of Osaka's Tennōji Park. After killing Matsumoto, Shaji had concealed his lover's head in a jar that he took with him when he moved from place to place, intending eventually to bury it on Mount Kōya—a highly appropriate venue in view of its centuries-long textual association with male-male eroticism. The "grotesque" nature of the crime, its theatrical milieu, and the "perverse" passions that it reflected offered a veritable field day for journalists. So great was the publicity surrounding the incident, apparently, that it got in the way of the police's investigative efforts, resulting in a temporary ban on newspaper coverage.[80]

By weaving Shaji, however briefly, into his narrative, Kataoka was able to link his fictional character Sugita with an urban subculture of male-male eroticism that the Shaji incident and *ero-guro* journalism in general had recently brought into public view. Even the fact that Sugita originally met his younger lover Yamazaki on a bench in Asakusa Park takes on a new meaning in this light. It hardly seems a coincidence that, in Inagaki's 1930 essay,

78. Oguri Mushitarō, *Madōji* (Shirokuro shobō, 1936).
79. Kataoka, "Rōkō," 41.
80. On Shaji, see Shimokawa Kōshi et al., *Josō no minzokugaku* (Hihyōsha, 1994), 111–128.

Asakusa appears at the top of a list of places in Tokyo where males could initiate sexual encounters with other males.[81] Public spaces like parks, sidewalks, and restrooms offered a relatively safe opportunity for strangers to strike up a conversation while maintaining their own anonymity; recall, for example, the "bamboo flute" exchange cited earlier in this chapter, whose setting was a bench in Kyoto's Maruyama Park.[82] By 1930, Inagaki could point to half a dozen sites in the city of Tokyo alone that enjoyed a reputation as male-male cruising areas. While it is unclear how long they had played such a role, we may note that Shaji reportedly met his German trader at one of these locations, Hibiya Park, as early as 1920. It was Asakusa, however, that gained the greatest notoriety among the prewar reading public, due in part to the emergence of what a 1930 article in *Hanzai kagaku* (the same popular-criminology journal that published Iwata's historical survey) dubbed the "new *kagema*," who made Asakusa Park one of his main places of business.[83]

By referring to the new figure as a *kagema*, Mimura Tokuzō, author of the article, drew a parallel between the contemporary world of male prostitution and that of the Edo period, which has been described in earlier chapters of this study.[84] And indeed, continuities are clearly in evidence. To begin with, Tokyo's "new *kagema*" plied his trade not too far from the old, in an entertainment district near the historical center (*shitamachi*) of the city. It was to Asakusa, in fact, that the shogunate had removed the "evil" theaters of Edo during its Tenpō reforms of the 1840s. And like their Edo-period predecessors, some among the "new *kagema*" enjoyed a connection to the stage—appearing, for example, as *onnagata* in traveling theater troupes, as was the case with Shaji. Just as the Edo-period culture of male prostitution had eastern and western hubs in Edo and Kamigata (today's Kansai region) respectively, counterparts of Tokyo's "new *kagema*" could be found in the Kansai metropolis of Osaka, where Asakusa's equivalent was the Tennōji area, haunt of Kataoka's fictional character Chiyo-chan, and especially the

81. Inagaki Taruho, "Shōnen tokuhon," 61.

82. For another park-bench encounter, set in Tokyo's Ueno Park around 1931, see Ishihara Ryō et al., "Modan Tōkyō ero fūkei," *Gendai no esupuri* 188 (1983): 140–141.

83. Mimura Tokuzō, "Shin Tōkyō kagemadan," *Hanzai kagaku*, July 1931, 127–133.

84. The cultural historian Ema Tsutomu made a similar connection in a 1935 essay ("Otoko no josō, onna no dansō," in *Ema Tsutomu chosakushū*, ed. Izutsu Gafū et al., 12 vols. [Chūō kōronsha, 1975–1978], 9:208) when he labeled such prostitutes the "new *wakashu* of the Shōwa era" (*Shōwa no shin wakashu*). Shōwa is the reign name for the period extending from 1926 to 1989.

working-class neighborhood known as Kamagasaki, where some 160 male prostitutes reportedly made their living in 1933.[85] The two milieux, like their Edo-period antecedents, were in various ways interconnected: individuals such as Shaji moved freely between them, and it appears that certain sub-cultural styles, such as the professional use of women's clothing, which is reported to have first become standard in the Osaka area, continued to flow in an easterly direction.[86] The *kagemajaya*, too, found a twentieth-century reincarnation in the inn (*ryokan*) for male prostitution: Mimura reports the existence of two such establishments near Asakusa, offering the services of over 50 male prostitutes combined.[87]

The "new *kagema*" and his predecessor also shared a somewhat murky legal status. The social researcher Ishizumi Harunosuke, for example, wrote that, while to be an "urning" was an "antisocial act" (*hanshakaiteki kōi*) in itself, male prostitution such as could be found in Asakusa Park represented an "even greater crime."[88] As we have seen, however, the penal code of 1907, like the Tokugawa bakufu's *Kujikata osadamegaki* before it, made no specific mention of male prostitution. Police authorities nonetheless regarded such activities as a matter of concern, and made various attempts to regulate or eradicate them. In 1930, for example, police officials in the Osaka precinct incorporating Kamagasaki reportedly drew up a list of well-known "habitués of passive *nanshoku*" (*hinanshoku jōshūsha*) in order to facilitate "regu-lating public mores" (*fūzoku torishimari*) as well as to "prevent sexual of-fenses."[89] Sweep-ups appear to have taken place periodically, but because male prostitution was not technically a crime, authorities could do little more than to issue a reprimand.[90] In a fictional account from 1933, we find au-thorities cutting off the tresses of one cross-dressing fourteen-year-old male prostitute so as to make him less attractive to potential clients—an in-triguing, if entirely extralegal, echo of Edo-period tonsorial policy—yet it is uncertain how frequently this practice occurred in actual life.[91] Despite

85. Minami, "Danshō ni kansuru," 272; Minami Takao, "Otoko-onna no hana-shi," in *Dōseiai to dōsei shinjū no kenkyū*, 298.

86. Sumi, *Danshō no mori*, 48–49.

87. Mimura, "Shin Tōkyō kagemadan," 128.

88. Ishizumi Harunosuke, "Hentai kojiki no seiteki hanzai," *Hanzai kagaku*, Oc-tober 1931, 170.

89. Hirai Sōta, "Ōsaka senshōshi," *Hanzai kagaku*, December 1930, 141. That the "effeminist" (*effeminisuto*) was dangerous less because he engaged in criminal acts himself than because he incited them in others was the viewpoint also of Nakano Masato (Hanabusa, "Petchi ruiza," 78).

90. Morino Tatsuzō, "Otoko ni kobi o uru otoko," *Hanzai kōron*, May 1932, 219.

91. Takeda Rintarō, "Kamagasaki," *Chūō kōron*, March 1933, (sōsaku) 64.

the ostensible legality of their activities, the inhabitants of the demimonde, like their Edo-period forebears, often took care to maintain an official front as members of more respectable professions (in Osaka, light entertainment [*yūgei kaseginin*] and sewing are said to have been most common), while the inns that Mimura describes evidently looked from the outside like perfectly ordinary hostelries.[92]

The clandestine nature of the new demimonde cannot be explained simply in terms of legal penalties, for few such strictures actually existed. Rather, it should be regarded as an effect of "social morality," whose policing operations functioned independently of legal discourse. While the "new *kagema*" and his world stood at the very heart of "civilized" society, they contravened many of that society's norms, and were constrained to resort to various strategies of self-concealment in order to survive in less than friendly surroundings. It is for this reason that I employ the term "subculture" in referring to this milieu, seeking to emphasize its marginality vis-à-vis mainstream culture (which is not to say that the subculture did not interact in significant ways with popular culture more generally). Despite the various continuities enumerated above, therefore, the "new *kagema*" stood in a vastly changed cultural position from his Edo-period namesake, who, although despised in official ideology, was a highly conspicuous and widely celebrated presence in popular discourse. Now, conversely, while legal discourse had little direct impact upon the "new *kagema's*" livelihood, it was popular discourse that reinforced his isolation from the rest of society.

Popular writings construed the male-male erotic subculture of the contemporary cityscape as a shadowy and secret world, the existence of which was barely known to or even suspected by outsiders. Mimura opens his article, for instance, by asserting that "readers may find it difficult to believe" that the inns he is about to describe might be found in the "shadows" of a mature capitalist society.[93] The narrative stance of such texts was thus to expose to the gaze of an unfamiliar public the workings of an elaborate subculture that existed under their very noses, yet remained largely hidden to all but the initiated. The ranks of the initiated overlapped to a large extent with the sexological category of the male *dōseiaisha*, for whom such knowledge was seen as virtually instinctual—for, as one writer put it, *dōseiaisha* had a sort of "sixth sense" about one another, forming a kind of "unorga-

92. Morino, "Otoko," 218–219.
93. Mimura, "Shin Tōkyō kagemadan," 127.

nized secret club" (*musoshikiteki himitsu kurabu*).[94] For those outside the club, the printed word offered an alternate means of acquiring this knowledge, albeit the access in question was voyeuristic rather than participatory. In this respect, early twentieth-century writings on the "new *kagema*" differed fundamentally from *shudō* texts, which had likewise dispensed a knowledge of male-male erotic culture, yet typically with the expectation that it would prove of practical benefit to the reader, or at least to the male audience whom it directly addressed. The character of that knowledge was now portrayed, moreover, not in terms of an ascending scale of sophistication, but of a descent into "perversion" and "grotesquerie."

Significant changes may also be seen in representations of the male prostitute. While popular discourse of the Edo period had painted the *kagema* as a mere object of male erotic desire, early twentieth-century writings endowed his latter-day equivalent with a distinct "sexual personality"— namely, that of the "passive" *dōseiaisha*. The "new *kagema*" of popular accounts was, in other words, a "pervert" as much as a prostitute, his sexual desire no less real and implacable a force than that of his patron. Two associated changes accompanied this representational shift. First, since the presumed orientation of the "new *kagema*'s*" desire lay exclusively toward males, early twentieth-century accounts seldom portray male prostitutes who entertain clients of both sexes, as popular writers (and artists) of the Edo period had often done. Whether such types of prostitution no longer existed or whether popular accounts simply ignore them is a difficult matter to judge in the absence of other evidence. Second, now that the male prostitute was perceived as a desiring subject in his own right, the distinction between amateur (*jiwakashu*) and professional (*uriwakashu*) that had been so fundamental to the Edo-period taxonomy of the "youth" grew increasingly blurred. The fact that the infrastructure of male-male prostitution was now less formally organized than in the Edo period added to the arbitrariness of the distinction, so that it was possible for the professional demimonde to blend almost imperceptibly into the larger male-male erotic subculture with which it shared many of the same public spaces. A 1932 account gives a sense of the ambiguity of this position, apparently of benefit to some of those who occupied it, when it reports that many of the "new *kagema*" insisted when questioned by police that their solicitation of sexual partners constituted a "diversion" (*tanoshimi*) rather than a livelihood—both of

94. Ifukube Takateru, "Dōseiai e no ichikōsatsu," *Hanzai kagaku*, January 1932, 293.

which were, in any case, perfectly legal.[95] In like vein, Mimura describes one individual, the son of a well-to-do banker, who pursued his calling out of "perversity" (*hentaisei*) rather than profit, turning over the money that he received to the inn where the encounter took place.[96] By the same token, since sexual acts in parks and other open-air places fell under the category of "public obscenity" (*kōkyō waisetsu*), punishable regardless of the gender of the parties involved, even informal sexual contacts occasionally required a certain expenditure of money for their consummation, if only in order to secure a cheap room.[97]

Popular discourse associated the "new *kagema*'s" insertee role in sexual intercourse not only with "passive" sexual desire, but also with a feminine gender identity. Take, for example, the character referred to as "Josō" in Takeda Rintarō's 1933 short story "Kamagasaki." While biologically male, "Josō" is described as "conducting himself in all aspects of daily life as a woman," employing feminine first-person pronouns and speech, and wearing women's clothing (the literal meaning of the term *josō*), makeup, and hairstyle. Few of the fictional character's clients therefore suspect that he is anything but a female prostitute—even, apparently, after engaging in sexual activity with him. For the narrator, the thrill with which "Josō" describes putting on women's garments offers clear "evidence" that his occupation has caused him to fall victim to an "incurable case of inversion" (*sukuubekarazaru tōsakushō*). "Josō," in other words, has already progressed irrevocably far along Krafft-Ebing's scale of "effemination": he even hopes to give birth to a child in order to become a more "complete woman."[98] Similarly, the character Aiko in the banned 1931 novel *Ero-guro danshō nikki* (*Ero-guro* Diary of a Male Prostitute) finds happiness by giving up his Asakusa-based life of prostitution and becoming "wife" to one of his former clients.[99]

Such representations clearly bear the imprint of medical discourse, and in particular the sexological trope of "inversion." At the same time, older influences from the realm of popular culture may also be detected. One of these is the theatrical tradition of the *onnagata*, who since the Edo period had performed femininity not only onstage, but sometimes in real life as well. Although it is unlikely that more than a small minority of the "new

95. Morino, "Otoko," 218–219.
96. Mimura, "Shin Tōkyō kagemadan," 133.
97. Inagaki Taruho, "Shōnen tokuhon," 63. For the law on "public obscenity," see Naikaku kanpōkyoku, ed., *Hōrei zensho*, annual pub. (Naikaku kanpōkyoku, 1887–), 1907 vol., (hōritsu) 98.
98. Takeda Rintarō, "Kamagasaki," 64–65.
99. Nagareyama Ryūnosuke, *Ero-guro danshō nikki* (Sankōsha, 1931).

kagema" (like their Edo-period predecessors) actually appeared onstage, popular writings often played up this link. The publicity of the Shaji case, for example, was enhanced by the fact that Shaji himself already possessed a modest reputation as an *onnagata* in the Kansai area. The association of acting, especially of female roles, with prostitution had, of course, enjoyed a long tradition in popular culture. Nevertheless, popular discourse made little connection between the *onnagata*'s occupation and his sexual desires before the rise of the sexological model cast him in the new role of *dōseiaisha*.

The process by which medical discourse on "same-sex love" helped to reshape existing notions about male-male sexuality reveals itself at the same time in shifting colloquial usage. Many Japanese of the early twentieth century would probably have described such characters as "Josō" and Aiko (Mimura's "new *kagema*") as *okama*, a noun literally meaning "pot." The pot, like the chrysanthemum, had served since Edo times as a familiar metaphor for the anus—the phrase "digging a pot" (*kama o horu*), for instance, meaning to play the inserter role in anal intercourse. During the Edo period, it is important to note, the term *kama* or *okama* (adding the honorific prefix *o-*) had denoted little more than a specific body part, or, in its verbal form, a particular sexual act. This usage remained prevalent well into the Meiji era. In a 1906 magazine article titled "Argument against *Okama*," for example, the target of the author's attack (a refutation of Benedict Friedländer's thesis that "pederasty" encouraged martial valor) is a type of act—something that is "carried out" (*okonawareta*)—rather than a class of persons.[100]

By the 1920s and 1930s, however, the term *okama* had typically come to signify a distinct type of individual: a male who enjoyed "passive" sexual intercourse with men, who exhibited feminine gender traits, and who often received money or some other form of remuneration for his sexual favors (as reflected in the cognate *okamayasan*, literally meaning "pot seller"). It was as if a particular orifice and its penetrative possibilities had come to define the individual's entire being. The *okama*, in other words, was a popular counterpart of the "passive" and "effeminate" male *dōseiaisha*, so that one 1927 source gives the word as a colloquial equivalent for the sexological term "urning."[101] Yet because popular discourse invested the label of *okama*, its honorific prefix notwithstanding, with distinctly pejorative connotations, male prostitutes and their patrons reportedly preferred to use their own sub-

100. Tsukiyosei, "Hiokamaron," *Marumaru chinbun* 1595 (1906): 4.
101. Satō, "Seiyokugaku goi," pt. 2, 92.

cultural vocabulary, including such designations as *gata* (a corruption of *on-nagata*) in prewar Osaka and *gorensan* (of less certain derivation) in post-war Tokyo.[102]

If the "new *kagema*" had one foot in Edo, the other rested in a popular culture that shared many features with other highly urbanized, industrial capitalist societies of the early twentieth century. While Mimura likened Tokyo's male prostitutes to their Edo-period predecessors, Inagaki Taruho compared them to their contemporary colleagues in such European cities as Berlin and Paris, with whom the Japanese public was familiar from sexological sources and other popular writings.[103] The reader of a 1917 Japanese translation of Henry de Halsalle's *Degenerate Germany* (published origi-nally in 1916 in England), for example, learned that some two thousand "*bishōnen* streetwalkers [*tsujigimi*]" could be found in Berlin alone.[104] Morita himself had seen a number of such individuals during his stay in Germany during the late 1910s, and mentions them several times in sub-sequent writings.[105] Such accounts painted the male prostitute as a charac-teristic, albeit "degenerate," feature of contemporary urban life, whether he walked Berlin's Friedrichstrasse or the sidewalks of Tokyo's Ginza (an-other cruising area on Inagaki's 1930 list). Much as the disappearance, at least from public view, of male prostitution in the Meiji period had provided a symbol of Japan's entry into the comity of "civilized" nations, its reemer-gence in the early decades of the twentieth century served, ironically, as proof that Japan did not lag culturally behind the other global powers.

The 1931 visit of Magnus Hirschfeld provided further confirmation of Japan's sexologically advanced status. Although Iwaya Sazanami and Do-riphorus had offered Western authorities a rudimentary knowledge of Japan's male-male erotic culture several decades earlier in the century, Hirschfeld was the first prominent Western sexologist to make the long jour-ney himself. One of the items on his Tokyo itinerary was Asakusa Park, where he hoped to see one of the "new *kagema*" at first hand.[106] The re-sulting excursion ranks as one of the most bizarre episodes in the annals of Euro-Japanese sexological exchange, rivaled only perhaps by Iwaya's turn-of-the-century banquet with Hirschfeld's Scientific-Humanitarian Com-

102. Morino, "Otoko," 217; Sumi, *Danshō no mori*, 53.
103. Inagaki Taruho, "Shōnen tokuhon," 60–61.
104. Dainihon bunmei kyōkai, trans., *Ankokumen no Doitsu* (Dainihon bunmei kyōkai, 1917), 220–221.
105. Morita, *Dōseiai no kenkyū*, 154, 184; Morita, *Hentai seiyoku hiwa*, 177.
106. The following account is based on Mimura Tokuzō, "Aru kagema no ichishi-tai: Hirushuferudo hakase o annai shite," *Hanzai kagaku*, June 1931, 222–235.

mittee, described previously. Hirschfeld's guide to the park was Mimura
Tokuzō, whose article of the prior year had drawn his attention to the new
phenomenon. Accompanying them were a certain "professor," whose name
Mimura discreetly omits in his account of the evening's activities, and
Tanaka Naoki, the editor of *Hanzai kagaku*, which devoted extensive cov-
erage to Hirschfeld's visit.

Thus it came about that Mimura found himself wandering the rainy
paths and copses of Asakusa Park one April night in search of a *"kagema"*
to submit to the scrutiny of the German doctor. Leaving the others behind,
Mimura casually struck up a conversation with a twentyish young man (Mimura's account does not provide a name) whose well-groomed features and
"somehow feminine" way of speaking left him "no doubt" that he was indeed a *kagema*. When asked by Mimura where his "colleagues" (*nakama*)
were, and whether he would take Mimura back to his lodgings, the young
man protested that he had no such "colleagues," and that Mimura erred in
thinking him a "professional" (*shōbainin*).[107] Nevertheless, he agreed to accompany Mimura to a nearby restaurant to continue their conversation.
Mimura was finally able to convince the young man to meet with Hirschfeld,
but not until he had ordered him three bottles of sake and a side dish, as
well as handing over a small sum of cash. By this time, however, Hirschfeld
had returned to his hotel, pleading exhaustion, and the painstakingly negotiated encounter never took place. Indeed, Hirschfeld does not even mention it in his published memoir of the journey.[108]

I have introduced this vignette not only for comic relief, but also because
it serves to illustrate some of the slippage that might occur between the gen-
eralizing impulses of popular and sexological discourse on the one hand and
the diversity of individual experience on the other. Even Mimura's confident
prose cannot fully mask this slippage, since the author has conveniently
recorded (we can only hope with some degree of accuracy) the young man's
words. It is entirely conceivable, for example, that the young man was indeed no "professional," but rather on the lookout for a casual sexual encounter, albeit not averse to accepting food and money from a well-heeled

107. Mimura's use of the term *nakama* is perhaps related to *ikken nakama*, a
subcultural designation for male prostitutes used in Tokyo during the late 1940s (see,
for example, Sumi, *Danshō no mori*, 53).

108. Hirschfeld did, however, visit Hibiya Park, whose subculture he described
as "the most animated and romantic I have ever encountered," reminding him of
"certain places in the Berlin Zoölogical Garden." See Magnus Hirschfeld, *Men and
Women: The World Journey of a Sexologist*, trans. O. P. Green (New York: Putnam's,
1935), 31.

and obviously desperate stranger. As one contemporary author noted, journalists often conflated *dōseiaisha* with persons who engaged in "*kagema*-like activities," although the latter represented only the most "decadent" (and hence the most journalistically interesting) among their cohort.[109] For Mimura, the world of the "new *kagema*" divided neatly into prostitutes and their clients, yet, in practice, the line between prostitution and cruising was undoubtedly more blurred, with many possible levels of subcultural participation. While Mimura could interpret the young man's protests only as a form of protective dissimulation ("His mouth may have denied it, but his attitude and way of speaking completely revealed that he was [a *kagema*]"), nothing except Mimura's professional authority as a journalist prevents us from giving his words greater credence. Ultimately, of course, we will never know what went on in the young man's mind, since Mimura's account has fixed him for posterity as the object, rather than the subject, of its discourse. From the perspective of the young man himself, things may have seemed quite different. He might easily have asked himself, for example, who was more "perverse": himself, taking a leisurely stroll in the park after a movie, or the stranger who had asked to accompany him to his lodgings, courted his favor with liquor and money, and sought to introduce him to an aging foreigner?

WAR AND AFTERMATH

As it turned out, Hirschfeld never returned to Germany after his extended voyage. The Nazi regime that had risen to power during his absence harbored a profound hostility toward the sexological establishment, and in 1933 ransacked Hirschfeld's Institute for Sexual Science. "Homosexuality," too, was a target of Nazi enmity, being associated, as the historian George Mosse has shown, with unmanliness in males, political conspiracy, eugenic impurity, and Judaism (Hirschfeld was himself Jewish).[110] Yet, as we have seen in chapter 3, legal measures designed to eradicate male-male sexual behavior did not emerge in wartime Japan as they did in fascist Germany. The launching of hostilities against China in 1931 set Japan on a political and diplomatic course that would bring it into alliance with Hitler and eventually to military defeat, but state policy toward "same-sex love," in both its male and fe-

109. Ifukube, "Dōseiai e no ichikōsatsu," 293. Similarly, Hamao ("Dōseiai kō," 141) suggested that the widespread notion that male prostitutes played only the "passive" role in male-male sexual relations was a misconception.

110. George L. Mosse, *Nationalism and Sexuality: Middle-Class Morality and Sexual Norms in Modern Europe* (Madison: University of Wisconsin Press, 1988).

male forms, remained basically unchanged throughout what Japanese historians commonly refer to as the "fifteen years' war." Although further comparative work is necessary, some factors that deserve consideration in explaining the relatively benign stance of wartime authorities in Japan toward male-male sexuality include the greater compatibility of male-male erotic behavior with hegemonic masculinity within the prevailing gender system, the absence of an organized movement of *dōseiaisha*, the lesser implication of notions of "same-sex love" with theories of race and heredity, and a long association of male-male eroticism with martial valor.

Still, the militarism of the 1930s and early 1940s had a muting effect upon *ero-guro* culture on the whole, driving it underground if not entirely out of existence. As public discourse came increasingly to revolve around the war effort, the celebration of erotic pleasure, particularly of a "perverse" variety, came to be seen as an unpatriotic form of self-indulgence. As Iwata observed in a letter to Minakata in 1937, the trend of the times (*jisei*) was such that people no longer felt free to publish "with an open mind" (*kyoshin de*) on the topic of male-male sexuality. At the time, Iwata was hoping himself to launch a journal devoted to the study of *nanshoku*, but had to abandon the idea because of hesitation among his planned backers, as well as spiraling paper prices as the result of wartime inflation.[111] Minakata warned Iwata that even the title he intended to give the magazine (*Azunai kenkyū*), which prominently featured a term (*azunai*) that the imperial chronicle *Nihongi* had used to describe a divinely punished transgression (see chapter 2), might be interpreted as "seditious" (*fuon*).[112] Iwata decided to "wait until the times change" to carry through with his project, but, as fate would have it, neither he nor Minakata would outlive the war.[113] Although Iwata underwent interrogation at the hands of the Special Higher Police (Tokkō) at least once during the early 1940s, this incident evidently had little to do with his interest in male-male eroticism but instead resulted from his frequent ethnographic forays into the countryside, Iwata's scholarly inquiries into local conditions having raised suspicions that he might be a spy.[114] Indeed, at the time of his death, Iwata was busy helping to catalogue the prime

111. Iwata Jun'ichi to Minakata Kumagusu, n.d. (postmarked 5 April 1937), *Minakata Kumagusu nanshoku dangi*, 320–321; Iwata Jun'ichi to Minakata Kumagusu, 21 August 1937, *Minakata Kumagusu nanshoku dangi*, 323.

112. Minakata Kumagusu to Iwata Jun'ichi, 31 January 1937, *Minakata Kumagusu zenshū*, 9:69.

113. Iwata Jun'ichi to Minakata Kumagusu, 21 August 1937, *Minakata Kumagusu nanshoku dangi*, 323.

114. Iwata Sadao, "Bōfu Iwata Jun'ichi," 428–429.

minister's library in preparation for its evacuation from Tokyo—a position not likely to be entrusted to an official persona non grata.

Even as Japan's military involvement escalated, male-male sexuality did not disappear entirely from the printed page. In the academic realm, for example, a relatively candid and unstigmatizing discussion of *nanshoku* was possible even at the height of the Pacific conflict, so long as it appeared in such contexts as "national literature" (*kokubungaku*) or the historical ethnography of Japan's colonial empire.[115] On a more popular level, Watanuki Rokusuke had no difficulty blending male-male eroticism with nationalistic and imperialistic concerns in his fictionalized 1937 biography of Akashi Motojirō, an intelligence officer active around the time of the Russo-Japanese war, whom Watanuki (himself a veteran of that earlier imperial conflict) describes as preferring "lovable old men" (*kawaii jīsan*) to the erotic charms of women.[116] His fellow author Inagaki Taruho continued to publish stories with male-male erotic themes as late as 1939, but thereafter turned his writing efforts to books primarily for young male readers on aviation and astronomy—the other two, besides anal eroticism, of the "three As," as he was wont to call them, that characterize his work thematically—which were presumably more in line with state objectives.[117]

Although postwar critics such as Yamazaki Masao have emphasized the interrelationship of *nanshoku*, "emperor-system ideology," and the imperial military forces, it should not be imagined that officials in wartime Japan would have explicitly acknowledged any such linkage.[118] On the contrary, public references to male-male sexuality within the ranks of the army and navy were generally taboo. In an unpublished study compiled during the early 1940s, for example, the physician and social researcher Komine Shigeyuki speculated that newspapers routinely quashed reports of "same-sex suicide" (*dōsei shinjū*) among soldiers or sailors for fear of riling military officials.[119] While *shudō* literature had devoted prominent attention to such demonstrations of mutual loyalty among warriors, glorifying them as a mark of samurai honor, the "perverse" implications with which sexology had imbued

115. See, for example, Gotō Tanji, *Chūsei kokubungaku kenkyū* (Isobe kōyōdō, 1943); Kawatake Shigetoshi, *Kabukishi no kenkyū* (Tōkyōdō, 1943); Mishina Shōei, *Chōsen kodai kenkyū, daiichibu: Shiragi karō no kenkyū* (Sanseidō, 1943).

116. Watanuki Rokusuke, *Akashi Motojirō*, 16.

117. Inagaki Taruho, "Fevaritto," in *Inagaki Taruho taizen*, 2:122–140; Inagaki Taruho, "Reidio no uta," in *Inagaki Taruho taizen*, 2:114–121.

118. Yamazaki Masao, *Mishima Yukio ni okeru nanshoku to tennōsei* (Gurafik-kusha, 1971).

119. Komine Shigeyuki, *Dōseiai to dōsei shinjū no igakuteki kōsatsu*, in *Dōseiai to dōsei shinjū no kenkyū*, 215.

them, along with their connotations of insubordination to authority, which recall the preoccupation with horizontal integration found in Edo-period law, made them by now a far too sensitive subject for representation. This is not to say that erotic bonds between males were not common within the armed forces—indeed, postwar accounts cite the imperial army and navy as the site of many men's first experience with *dōseiai*—but rather that popular discourse offers little in the way of contemporary testimony.

With the end of the conflict and the beginning of American Occupation (1945–1952), constraints on the public representation of sexuality inherited from earlier years relaxed somewhat, although they would never disappear entirely—as continued controversy over "obscene" publications to this day attests. Since Occupation officials were far more concerned with the expression of militarist, anti-American, or, in later years, communist sentiments than with the representation of erotic pleasure, censorship of sexually explicit writings grew more liberal than at any time since the early years of Meiji. In addition to espousing the virtues of freedom of speech and of enterprise, Occupation authorities brought with them a quintessentially American belief in scientific progress (including an increasingly Freudianized sexology), thus reinforcing both pillars—commercial and scientific—of what I have referred to as *ero-guro* culture. Although partially silenced during the war years, this culture had never been entirely erased, as its ability to reemerge so soon after the war itself bears powerful testimony to. Indeed, in an era of material deprivation and ideological disillusionment, the "erotic" and the "grotesque" held, if anything, an even more compelling allure.

With a receptive audience and relaxed censorship, commercial publications dealing with sexuality proliferated. Erotic magazines, for example, witnessed their biggest boom since the 1920s. Many were fly-by-night operations, known colloquially as *kasutori zasshi* or "moonshine magazines" because of their amateurish quality and tendency to collapse after three editions (*sangō*; homophonous with "three cups"), and made little pretense of any social value beyond entertainment.[120] Others sought a greater measure of respectability by portraying their mission as one of disseminating scientific (if nonetheless titillating) knowledge about sexuality to the reading public, such as the highly successful *Ningen tankyū* (Exploration of Humanity), founded in 1950, which promoted itself as a "sexology magazine for the cultured" (*bunkajin no sei kagakushi*). In such popular-sexology journals, as in their prewar forebears, "same-sex love" and the other "perversions" formed

120. For a detailed history of *kasutori zasshi*, see Yamamoto Akira, *Kasutori zasshi kenkyū: Shinboru ni miru fūzokushi* (Shuppan nyūsusha, 1976).

the subject of numerous articles, many of them penned by doctors or other professional experts. It would not be until the appearance of *Adonisu* (Adonis) in 1952, and hence outside the scope of this study, that we find a magazine devoted entirely to the topic of male-male sexuality, with a significant portion of its contributors identifying themselves as *dōseiaisha*.

With the end of the war, the male-male erotic subculture that had first caught the attention of *ero-guro* journalists during the 1920s was quick to reemerge into public view—now, indeed, more conspicuous than ever. Within half a year of the surrender, male prostitutes could be found in Tokyo's Ueno Park, which soon replaced nearby Asakusa in notoriety as a site for such activities.[121] Similarly, in Osaka, a magazine article from late 1947 reports that more than sixty male prostitutes made a living in the backstreets of Sannōchō, where they had relocated from a burned-out Kamagasaki.[122] Cross-dressing had increasingly become the professional norm, so that the casual observer might easily mistake a male prostitute for one of the unlicensed female streetwalkers known as *panpan* (from the American expression "pom-pom girl") whose numbers swelled during the Occupation. Indeed, according to numerous accounts, it was precisely because of the confusion between the two that male prostitutes were able to snag many of their customers.

Naturally, not all participants in this subculture of male-male eroticism were professionals, nor was prostitution the only form of commercial activity to be found in their midst. Even before the war, a small number of establishments had catered, if only clandestinely, to a clientele of male *dōseiaisha*, including the inns described in Mimura's account and a café about which the ethnographer Akamatsu Keisuke reports hearing rumors in prewar Osaka.[123] By 1948, we read of a tea shop in Tokyo's Shinjuku district (another emerging subcultural center, and today a veritable epicenter) where "peculiar"-looking men gathered to exchange erotic looks and conversation under the watchful eye of a similarly "afflicted" owner, enjoying the freedom to dress and speak as they wished in the security that a "special place for special people only" alone afforded.[124] Nevertheless, such establishments were forced to maintain a measure of secrecy in order to shel-

121. Minami, "Danshō ni kansuru," 278, 280.

122. Ōsaka Saburō, "Nanshoku kaidō o yuku," *Ryōki*, October 1947, 14.

123. Akamatsu Keisuke, *Hijōmin no sei minzoku* (Akashi shoten, 1991), 349. Akamatsu cannot confirm, however, the validity of the rumors. For two prewar Tokyo establishments allegedly catering to "sodomites" (*sodomaito*), see Uo Daigaku, "Oyama gyōjōki," *Hanzai kagaku*, August 1931, 73–76.

124. Minami, "Otoko-onna no hanashi," 299.

ter themselves from curious and unfriendly outsiders, and it was not until the 1950s that the phenomenon of the "gay bar" (an expression transplanted to Japan around the same time) emerged more fully into the open.

Precisely because of its half-hidden nature, the subculture of male-male eroticism that resurfaced under the Occupation provided a favorite topic for the expository efforts of postwar journalists. The July 1949 issue of the "moonshine magazine" *Bakuro* (Exposé), for example, treated readers to a detailed report on the male prostitutes of Ueno, alleging that they had formed a "union" of *okama*—a symbol, as it were, of postwar democratic liberties—that would help to solve the "population problem," another topic of contemporary debate.[125] Some magazines opened their pages to the confessions of male prostitutes themselves, inviting them to share with reporters the details of their "topsy-turvy lives," as one such article was titled, in the form of a roundtable discussion (*zadankai*).[126] The increasingly visible figure of the male prostitute also adorned the columns of postwar newspapers, typically in connection with some form of crime or violence, as had been the case with Shaji in the prewar era, including a 1946 episode in which one Osaka prostitute killed another in a dispute over turf, or a 1947 incident in which a Tokyo prostitute, angered by harassment of his profession, struck a high police official.[127] The subculture of male-male prostitution made its appearance, too, in postwar books, including writings by Kabiya Kazuhiko and Sumi Tatsuya's 1948 novel *Danshō no mori* (Grove of Male Prostitutes), which was produced also as a stage play featuring a genuine member of the demimonde in one of the lead roles.[128]

For all this publicity, the male prostitute continued to stand at the margins of mainstream culture, the operations of popular discourse itself help-

125. Kurumada Kingo, "Tōkyō okama (danshō) kumiai tanbōki," pt. 4 of a series titled "Shinpan Mito kōmon man'yūki," *Bakuro*, July 1949, 35–38.
126. See, for example, "Danshō no sekai," *Zadan*, January 1949, 36–45; "Danshō wa kataru: Sakasama jinsei," *Gekkan yomiuri*, October 1950, 53–57.
127. Ōsaka, "Nanshoku kaidō o yuku," 14; Shimokawa Kōshi, *Shōwa seisōshi*, 3 vols. (Dentō to gendaisha, 1980–1981), 2:106.
128. Kabiya Kazuhiko, *Chijō meian* (Nihon shuppan haikyū, 1948); Sumi, *Danshō no mori*. The guise of the prostitute is of course not the only one in which the male *dōseiaisha* appears in postwar literature. The year 1949 saw the publication, for example, of Mishima Yukio's debut novel, *Kamen no kokuhaku* (in *Mishima Yukio zenshū*, ed. Saeki Shōichi et al., 36 vols. [Shinchōsha, 1973–1976], 3:161–352 [trans. Meredith Weatherby under the title *Confessions of a Mask* (New York: New Directions, 1958)]), whose narrator tells the story of his gradual awakening as an "invert" (*tōsakusha*), much in the manner of a sexological confession, but makes no reference to an organized subculture. Since the bulk of Mishima's work lies outside the chronological scope of this survey, I have omitted him from the discussion.

ing to maintain a respectable distance between the two. The majority of readers, remarked one contemporary observer, Minami Takao, viewed him either with "curiosity" (*kōki*) or "condescension" (*keibetsu*), yet in any case as belonging to a "different world than us" (*wareware to wa bessekai*).[129] Curiosity seems to have fueled much of the publicity that surrounded him— a disposition that thrived precisely at the borderline between the hidden and revealed, the known and the unknown. Thus, even as journalists and popular writers exposed his shadowy world to public view, they paradoxically sought to preserve some of its aura of secrecy—as if the reader alone enjoyed privileged access to it—thereby reaffirming its essential otherness. This other "world" existed not only apart from that of the presumed reader (Minami's "us"), but on an implicitly inferior plane, whether he or she referred to it in the sexological language of "perversion" or using the vernacular epithet of *okama*. Nevertheless, this condescension was on the whole more self-satisfied than it was overtly hostile, so that, even among Minami's imaginary readership, the nightly goings-on at Ueno Park could provide a "topic of light conversation" (*karui wadai*).[130]

Although male prostitution had taken place before the war, and indeed for many centuries, it is telling that Minami depicts it as a quintessentially *après-guerre* phenomenon. In his capacity as a psychiatrist, Minami had performed clinical observations upon some twenty cross-dressing male prostitutes who plied their trade in Ueno Park, declaring them to be "sexual inverts" (although he could detect little evidence of any physical feminization and found that many, in fact, were capable of sexual relations with women) and "psychopaths."[131] At the same time, he, like many of his contemporaries, viewed their emergence as symptomatic of a more general social malaise, a product of the "instability" (*fuantei*), both ideological and economic, that the war had left in its wake.[132] The cross-dressing male prostitute served in this way as a symbol of a "defeated nation" (*haisenkoku*), much like his colleague the *panpan*, who similarly suffered her body to be penetrated by external forces. Minami and other authors were fond of noting that many such males had acquired their "perversion" while serving in the now disbanded

129. Minami, "Otoko-onna no hanashi," 296.
130. Minami, "Otoko-onna no hanashi," 296.
131. Minami describes his findings in "Danshō ni kansuru"; "Danshō no seishin igaku: Dansei josei no seikaku ni kanren shite," in *Dōseiai to dōsei shinjū no kenkyū*, 288–295; "Dōseiai: Sono kōsatsu to shori," in *Dōseiai to dōsei shinjū no kenkyū*, 283–287; "Otoko-onna no hanashi."
132. Minami, "Danshō ni kansuru," 272.

imperial army and navy, so that their descent into prostitution served metaphorically to recapitulate the emasculation of Japan's surrender, the humiliation of its occupation, and the confusion that surrounded its role in the postwar era.

CODA: HISTORICIZING MALE-MALE SEXUALITY IN JAPAN

In presenting the *dōseiaisha* as a symbol of postwar disorder, Minami voiced a theme that would appear many times in writings on the subject in following decades. Yet Minami's attempt to weave a historical context for male-male sexuality linked him with an enterprise that stretched backward over centuries. Whether perceived as a gift from Kūkai, a vestige of Sengoku misogyny or Genroku decadence, or the legacy of war and occupation, male-male sexual behavior had long provided an object of historical argument and speculation in Japan. In closing this study, it may be fitting therefore to reflect once more on the various interarticulations of history and male-male eroticism that have emerged in the course of the preceding chapters.

Minami's comments on the contemporary prevalence of male-male sexuality had numerous and diverse predecessors. Ihara Saikaku, for example, had glowingly described in the late seventeenth century the "excitement and titillation" that moneyed urban males could find in an increasingly commercialized culture of *shudō*. Yet even in emphasizing the up-to-dateness of these pleasures, he, like many other authors of the Edo period, possessed a sense of their embeddedness in a long and ongoing history. No less a historian than a poet of male-male eroticism, Saikaku envisioned the boundaries of the "way of youths" as extending far back into antiquity, in Japan as well as in more distant places. The disciplinary paradigm encouraged this exercise of the historical imagination by its very nature, since the legitimacy of a "way" gained credence precisely from its transmission in the past from authoritative sources. In its popular construction, *shudō* was a universal path, but also one with a specific linearity in time and space. While the narratives of origin that Saikaku and others spun in their works may not satisfy the positivist canons of latter-day historians, Edo-period writers nonetheless commonly acknowledged that male-male erotic behavior held a significant place in their history.

By the Meiji period, the generation of Saikaku had literally become history itself. Its textual productions now formed part of a historical record that was available to a newer cohort of writers on male-male sexuality—indeed, one that the champions of "civilized morality" could not easily ignore. Rather than denying the prior existence of male-male erotic relations in Japan, late nineteenth-century authors typically repudiated them from the standpoint of a reformed present. Precisely two centuries after Saikaku elevated Genroku "excitement and titillation" in his 1687 *Great Mirror*, Miyazaki Koshoshi (writing as Suekane Naokichi), chronicler of the "vicissitudes of passion," could thus declare with equal approbation that his fellow countrymen had virtually succeeded in eradicating the "hideous custom" of *nanshoku* over the two decades since the Meiji Restoration. "Civilized" writers such as Miyazaki sought to distance contemporary Japanese from their "barbarous" cultural and textual heritage by sealing male-male eroticism behind the protective glass of history. History served in this instance not to legitimate but to discredit male-male sexual practices, yet its relevance to the present, if only as a constitutive "other," was unmistakable.

Among sexologists of the early twentieth century, the written record of male-male eroticism in Japan offered another set of uses. The universal authority that sexologists claimed for the physiologically and psychologically rooted model of "same-sex love" that they constructed and popularized through their writings dictated that the categories and modes of sexual behavior they described reveal themselves in diverse times and places. Written accounts of male-male eroticism in Japan over many centuries furnished abundant material for such textual dissection. Just as an orientalized Japan came to figure prominently in Euro-American mappings of the global distribution of "perversion," so too the native past provided Japanese sexologists with a vast and eminently chartable territory for elaborating the new medico-scientific knowledge.[133] For early twentieth-century sexologists, male-male sexual practices in Japan's past and present were linked not only through heredity, as Habuto Eiji and Sawada Junjirō argued, but because both partook of a scientifically catalogued phenomenon believed to follow fixed principles transcending time and space. Whereas the Meiji author Miyazaki, seeking to divorce "barbarous" past and "civilized" present, had posited a diametric opposition between history and nature, his successors in the early twentieth century regarded both as interchangeable sources of scientific truth.

The present study has offered yet another narrative of male-male eroticism in Japanese history. The preceding chapters have explored three paradigms that shaped the meaning of male-male sexuality across three inter-

133. For examples of Euro-American ethnographic representation, see the numerous references to Japan in Rudi C. Bleys, *The Geography of Perversion: Male-to-Male Sexual Behavior outside the West and the Ethnographic Imagination, 1750–1918* (New York: New York University Press, 1995).

locking realms of Japanese discourse between the seventeenth and the mid–twentieth centuries. This narrative has drawn upon many of the same textual resources as the above sets of authors, as well as upon the writings of these authors themselves. Its aim, however, has been neither to offer a legitimating tradition for certain modes of erotic practice (in the manner of Saikaku), nor to pass moral judgment upon the conduct of others (like Miyazaki), nor to identify regularities within the diverse spectrum of human sexual behavior (like Habuto and Sawada). The divergent ways in which cultural authorities within the same geographic space have mapped male-male eroticism over the course of several centuries cannot help but undermine such unidimensional and totalizing interpretations. My goal instead has been to highlight the embeddedness of desires themselves within shifting constellations of cultural meaning. The apparent materiality of sexual practices and the seeming insubstantiality of erotic discourses are in the end not so easily distinguishable. Rather than assuming that the textual archive reflects in any simple fashion the realities of sexual behavior in the past, historians of sexuality must strive to understand the ways in which it has helped to organize larger systems of cultural knowledge and thus to produce the conditions under which human subjects, with complex desires, created and experienced their own realities.

By the same token, texts are more than disembodied words, possessing a materiality that persists in the face of censorship and denial. Meiji authorities may have tried to ban the works of Saikaku, for example, but he continues to live today in part because the enduring culture of print that he and his contemporaries helped solidify in the seventeenth century has rendered such attempts at bureaucratic obliteration Sisyphean. Thus, when a far-right propagandist in late twentieth-century Japan denounces the prevalence of "same-sex love" among postwar Japanese males as a deplorable sign of American cultural influence, he fights an uphill battle, since, ironically, the very library that houses his work preserves many earlier indigenous representations.[134] At best, the writer in question can only hope to construct a new historical narrative of male-male eroticism in Japan through the time-honored medium of the printed word—little realizing that through this act he proves himself heir to a much older legacy.

---

134. Sugawara Michinari, *Dōseiai* (San'aku tsuihō kyōkai, n.d.). A copy of this undated, but likely early-1970s, pamphlet may be found in the National Diet Library in Tokyo.

Bibliography

Aikikusei. "Ōsaka no kagema." *Kono hana* 11 (1910): 19.

Akaeboshi. Edo shunjū 1 (1976): 38–43.

Akaeboshi. In *Tokugawa bungei ruijū,* ed. Hayakawa Junzaburō, 12 vols., 12:420–426. Kokusho kankōkai, 1914–1916.

Akamatsu Keisuke. *Hijōmin no sei minzoku.* Akashi shoten, 1991.

———. *Sonraku kyōdōtai to seiteki kihan: Yobai gairon.* Gensōsha, 1993.

———. *Yobai no minzokugaku.* Akashi shoten, 1994.

———. *Yobai no seiairon.* Akashi shoten, 1994.

Akita Masami. *Sei no ryōki modan: Nihon hentai kenkyū ōrai.* Seikyūsha, 1994.

Akita Ujaku. "Dōsei no koi." *Waseda bungaku,* June 1907, 32–46.

Anayoshi. *Hōshin kōwa.* In *Sharebon taisei,* ed. Mizuno Minoru et al., 31 vols., 9:289–301. Chūō kōronsha, 1978–1988.

Anrakuan Sakuden. *Seisuishō.* In *Hanashibon taikei,* ed. Mutō Sadao and Oka Masahiko, 20 vols., 2:3–211. Tōkyōdō, 1975–1979.

Aoki Nobuharu. *Yūsei kekkon to yūsei danshu.* Ryūkinsha, 1941.

Aoyama Kikue, trans. *Chūseiron.* Pts. 1–3. *Safuran,* May 1914, 1–22; June 1914, 130–153; July 1914, 55–76. Translation of *The Intermediate Sex,* by Edward Carpenter (1908).

Aoyama, Tomoko. "Male Homosexuality As Treated by Japanese Women Writers." In *The Japanese Trajectory: Modernization and Beyond,* ed. Gavan McCormack and Yoshio Sugimoto, 186–204. Cambridge: Cambridge University Press, 1988.

Arai Hakuseki. *Kijinron.* In *Nihon shisō taikei,* ed. Ienaga Saburō et al., 67 vols., 35:145–181. Iwanami shoten, 1970–1982.

Arakawa Hidetoshi, ed. *Tenpō kaikaku machibure shiryō.* Yūzankaku, 1974.

Araki, James T. "*Sharebon*: Books for Men of Mode." *Monumenta Nipponica* 24 (1969): 31–45.

A-sei. "'Joseiteki danshi' o yonde." *Hentai seiyoku,* March 1923, 129–130.

Aston, W. G., trans. *Nihongi: Chronicles of Japan from the Earliest Times to A.D. 697.* London: Allen, 1956.

Azuma no Kamiko. *Fūryū hiyokudori.* In *Edo jidai bungei shiryō,* ed. Hayakawa Junzaburō et al., 5 vols., 5:81–133. Kokusho kankōkai, 1916.

Baijōken. *Yodarekake.* In *Edo jidai bungei shiryō,* ed. Hayakawa Junzaburō et al., 5 vols., 4:1–64. Kokusho kankōkai, 1916.

Bartholemew, James R. *The Formation of Science in Japan: Building a Research Tradition.* New Haven: Yale University Press, 1989.

Befu, Harumi. "Village Autonomy and Articulation with the State." In *Studies in the Institutional History of Early Modern Japan,* ed. John W. Hall and Marius B. Jansen, 301–314. Princeton: Princeton University Press, 1968.

Bessatsu shinpyō 10.1 (1977).

"Bidō no heifū." *Yomiuri shinbun,* 13 July 1889, 4.

Bleys, Rudi C. *The Geography of Perversion: Male-to-Male Sexual Behavior outside the West and the Ethnographic Imagination, 1750–1918.* New York: New York University Press, 1995.

Bock, Felicia Gressitt, trans. *Engi-shiki: Procedures of the Engi Era.* 2 vols. Sophia University, 1970–1972.

Boswell, John. *Christianity, Social Tolerance, and Homosexuality: Gay People in Western Europe from the Beginning of the Christian Era to the Fourteenth Century.* Chicago: University of Chicago Press, 1980.

Botai Michian. *Senryū Yotsumeya kō.* Taihei shooku, 1983.

Botsman, Dani V. "Punishment and Power in the Tokugawa Period." *East Asian History* 3 (1992): 1–32.

Bowers, John Z. *When the Twain Meet: The Rise of Western Medicine in Japan.* Henry E. Sigerist Supplements to the Bulletin of the History of Medicine, n.s., no. 5. Baltimore: Johns Hopkins University Press, 1980.

Braisted, William Reynolds, trans. *Meiroku Zasshi: Journal of the Japanese Enlightenment.* Cambridge: Harvard University Press, 1976.

Brundage, James A. *Law, Sex, and Christian Society in Medieval Europe.* Chicago: University of Chicago Press, 1987.

"Byakkotai no ōkō." *Yorozu chōhō,* 6 March 1899, 3.

Cabezón, José Ignacio. "Homosexuality and Buddhism." In *Homosexuality and World Religions,* ed. Arlene Swidler, 81–101. Valley Forge, Pa.: Trinity International, 1993.

Callahan, Caryl Ann, trans. *Tales of Samurai Honor,* by Ihara Saikaku. Monumenta Nipponica Monograph no. 57. Sophia University, 1981.

Caron, François, and Joost Schouten. *A True Description of the Mighty Kingdoms of Japan and Siam.* Ed. C. R. Boxer. Trans. Roger Manley. London: Argonaut, 1935.

Carpenter, Edward. *Selected Writings.* Ed. David Fernbach and Noël Greig. Vol. 1, *Sex.* London: GMP, 1984.

Charpentier, Adrien, ed. *Codes et lois pour la France, l'Algérie, et les Colonies.* 7th ed. Paris: Marchal, 1903.

Chauncey, George, Jr. "From Sexual Inversion to Homosexuality: The Changing Medical Conceptualization of Female Deviance." In *Passion and Power:*

Sexuality in History, ed. Kathy Peiss and Christina Simmons, 87–117. Philadelphia: Temple University Press, 1989.

Ch'en, Paul Heng-chao. *The Formation of the Early Meiji Legal Order: The Japanese Code of 1871 and Its Chinese Foundation.* Oxford: Oxford University Press, 1981.

Chidarumasei. "Nanshoku ni yoru fukakai no shinri." *Sei,* April 1920 (zōkan), 134–137.

Childs, Margaret H. "*Chigo Monogatari:* Love Stories or Buddhist Sermons?" *Monumenta Nipponica* 35 (1980): 127–151.

——— [Margaret Helen Childs]. *Rethinking Sorrow: Revelatory Tales of Late Medieval Japan.* Michigan Monograph Series in Japanese Studies, no. 6. Ann Arbor: Center for Japanese Studies, 1991.

Choi Park-Kwang. "Japanese Sexual Customs and Cultures Seen from the Perspective of the Korean Delegation to Japan." In *Imaging/Reading Eros: Proceedings for the Conference, Sexuality and Edo Culture, 1750–1850,* ed. Sumie Jones, 76–78. Bloomington: East Asian Studies Center, Indiana University, 1996.

Cohen, Stanley. *Folk Devils and Moral Panics: The Creation of the Mods and Rockers.* 2d ed. Oxford: Robertson, 1980.

Cooper, Michael, ed. *They Came to Japan: An Anthology of European Reports on Japan, 1543–1640.* Berkeley: University of California Press, 1965.

Dainihon bunmei kyōkai, trans. *Ankokumen no Doitsu.* Dainihon bunmei kyōkai, 1917. Translation of *Degenerate Germany,* by Henry de Halsalle (1916).

———, trans. *Hentai seiyoku shinri.* Dainihon bunmei kyōkai, 1913. Translation of *Psychopathia Sexualis,* by Richard von Krafft-Ebing (1886).

"Daiyonjūgō rairai mondō tsukiyo no kama o nuku no kotae." *Marumaru chinbun* 45 (1878): 711–712.

Dandō Shigemitsu. *Keihō kōyō kakuron.* Sōbunsha, 1964.

Danly, Robert Lyons, trans. "Flyboys," by Ihara Saikaku. In *Partings at Dawn: An Anthology of Japanese Gay Literature,* ed. Stephen D. Miller, 93–95. San Francisco: Gay Sunshine, 1996.

"Danshō no sekai." *Zadan,* January 1949, 36–45.

"Danshō wa kataru: Sakasama jinsei." *Gekkan yomiuri,* October 1950, 53–57.

"Daraku shōnen Byakkotai no shūkō." *Yorozu chōhō,* 25 March 1899, 3.

Dazai Osamu. "Omoide." In *Dazai Osamu zenshū,* 13 vols., 1:22–60. Chikuma shobō, 1957–1972.

De Bary, Wm. Theodore, trans. *Five Women Who Loved Love,* by Ihara Saikaku. Rutland, Vt.: Tuttle, 1956.

"The Defect in the Criminal Code." *Eastern World,* 27 May 1899, 7.

"Degenerated Tokyo Students." *Yorozu chōhō,* 26 May 1899, 2.

"Degeneration of Students." *Yorozu chōhō,* 18 May 1899, 2.

Denbu monogatari. In *Nihon koten bungaku zenshū,* ed. Akiyama Ken et al., 51 vols., 37:121–141. Shōgakkan, 1970–1976.

Dokai kōshūki, ed. Kanai Madoka. Jinbutsu ōraisha, 1967.
"Dokusha no koe." *Sei*, January 1921, 133–136.
"Dokusha yori." *Sei*, September 1920, 45–48.
Dokushō Koji. "Danshō." *Edo kaishi*, November 1889, 58–63.
Dōmoto Masaki. <*Zōhoban*> *Nanshoku engekishi*. Shuppansha, 1976.
Dore, R. P. *Education in Tokugawa Japan*. London: Routledge, 1965.
Drake, Christopher. "Mirroring Saikaku." *Monumenta Nipponica* 46 (1991): 513–541.
Duberman, Martin Bauml, et al., eds. *Hidden from History: Reclaiming the Gay and Lesbian Past*. New York: NAL, 1989.
Durham, Valerie. "Meiji shoki no dokufumono ni okeru akujo zōkei no retorikku." Pts. 1 and 2. *Tōkyō keizai daigaku jinbun shizen kagaku ronshū* 86 (1990): 220–242; 88 (1991): 90–108.
Edamatsu Shigeyuki et al., eds. *Meiji nyūsu jiten*. 9 vols. Mainichi komyunikēshonzu, 1983.
Edogawa Ranpo. "Dōseiai bungakushi ni tsuite: Iwata Jun'ichi-kun no omoide." In *Nanshoku bunken shoshi*, n.p. Toba: Iwata Sadao, 1973.
———. "Hoittoman no hanashi." In *Edogawa Ranpo zenshū*, 25 vols., 17:61–66. Kōdansha, 1978–1979.
———. "*Honchō nanshoku kō* ni tsuite." In *Honchō nanshoku kō*, n.p. Toba: Iwata Sadao, 1974.
———. "J. A. Shimonzu no hisoka naru jōnetsu." In *Edogawa Ranpo zenshū*, 25 vols., 17:71–100. Kōdansha, 1978–1979.
———. *Kotō no oni*. In *Edogawa Ranpo zenshū*, 25 vols., 4:5–173. Kōdansha, 1978–1979.
———. "Mokuzuzuka." In *Edogawa Ranpo zenshū*, 25 vols., 17:55–61. Kōdansha, 1978–1979.
———. "Shimonzu, Kāpentā, Jīdo." In *Edogawa Ranpo zenshū*, 25 vols., 17:66–68. Kōdansha, 1978–1979.
Ejima Kiseki. *Fūryū kyokujamisen*. In *Hachimonjiyabon zenshū*, ed. Hasegawa Tsuyoshi et al., 14 vols. to date, 1:255–453. Kyūko shoin, 1992–.
———. *Keisei denjugamiko*. In *Shin Nihon koten bungaku taikei*, ed. Satake Akihiro et al., 68 vols. to date, 78:247–384. Iwanami shoten, 1989–.
———. *Seken musuko katagi*. In *Hachimonjiyabon zenshū*, ed. Hasegawa Tsuyoshi et al., 14 vols. to date, 6:13–69. Kyūko shoin, 1992–.
———. <*Shikidō taizen*> *Keisei kintanki*. In *Nihon koten bungaku taikei*, ed. Takagi Ichinosuke et al., 102 vols., 91:151–381. Iwanami shoten, 1957–1968.
———. *Ukiyo oyaji katagi*. In *Hachimonjiyabon zenshū*, ed. Hasegawa Tsuyoshi et al., 14 vols. to date, 7:447–512. Kyūko shoin, 1992–.
———. *Yahaku naishō kagami*. In *Hachimonjiyabon zenshū*, ed. Hasegawa Tsuyoshi et al., 14 vols. to date, 2:1–166. Kyūko shoin, 1992–.
———. *Yakei tabitsuzura*. In *Hachimonjiyabon zenshū*, ed. Hasegawa Tsuyoshi et al., 14 vols. to date, 2:453–541. Kyūko shoin, 1992–.
Elisonas, Jurgis. "Notorious Places: A Brief Excursion into the Narrative Topography of Early Edo." In *Edo and Paris: Urban Life and the State in the Early*

Modern Era, ed. James L. McClain et al., 253–291. Ithaca: Cornell University Press, 1994.

Ema Tsutomu. "Otoko no josō, onna no dansō." In *Ema Tsutomu chosakushū,* ed. Izutsu Gafū et al., 12 vols., 9:204–209. Chūō kōronsha, 1975–1978.

Emi Suiin. "Chizomezakura." In <*Tanpen shōsetsu*> *Meiji bunko,* ed. Ōhashi Shintarō, 18 vols., 17:1–42. Hakubunkan, 1893–1894.

Engishiki. In <*Shintei zōho*> *Kokushi taikei,* ed. Kuroita Katsumi et al., 66 vols., 26:1–1032. Yoshikawa kōbunkan, 1964–1967.

Enomoto Haryū. "Shitaya no konjaku." *Bungei kurabu,* August 1900, 177–181.

Faure, Bernard. *The Rhetoric of Immediacy: A Cultural Critique of Chan/Zen Buddhism.* Princeton: Princeton University Press, 1991.

Foucault, Michel. *Discipline and Punish: The Birth of the Prison.* Trans. Alan Sheridan. New York: Vintage, 1979.

———. *The History of Sexuality.* Trans. Robert Hurley. 3 vols. New York: Vintage, 1980–1988.

Friedländer, Benedict. "Dōseiteki jōkō ni tsuite." *Jinsei,* April 1906, 183–186.

Frühstück, Sabine. *Die Politik der Sexualwissenschaft: Zur Produktion und Popularisierung sexologischen Wissens in Japan, 1900–1941.* Beiträge für Japanologie, no. 34. Vienna: Institut für Japanologie, Universität Wien, 1997.

Fujikawa Yū. *Nihon igakushi.* Nisshin shoin, 1941.

Fujime Yuki. "The Licensed Prostitution System and the Prostitution Abolition Movement in Modern Japan." *Positions* 5 (1997): 135–170.

———. *Sei no rekishigaku: Kōshō seido dataizai taisei kara baishun bōshihō yūsei hogohō taisei e.* Fuji shuppan, 1997.

Fujimoto Kizan. <*Kanpon*> *Shikidō ōkagami,* ed. Noma Kōshin. Kyoto: Yūzan shobō, 1973.

Fujisawa Akie. *Maezu kyūjishi.* Nagoya: Sohotsunoya, 1935.

Fukuda Hideko. *Warawa no hanseigai.* Iwanami bunko, no. 33-121-1. Iwanami shoten, 1983.

Fukushima Masanori. *Sei no kunō to ankoku no seiwa.* Osaka: Ibundō, 1928.

Funaoka Einosuke. "Nanshoku ni tsuite." *Kokka igakkai zasshi,* May 1899, 1–5.

Furth, Charlotte. "Rethinking Van Gulik: Sexuality and Reproduction in Traditional Chinese Medicine." In *Engendering China: Women, Culture, and the State,* ed. Christina K. Gilmartin et al., 126–146. Harvard Contemporary China Series, no. 10. Cambridge: Harvard University Press, 1994.

Furukawa Makoto. "The Changing Nature of Sexuality: The Three Codes Framing Homosexuality in Modern Japan." Trans. Angus Lockyer. *U.S.-Japan Women's Journal, English Supplement* 7 (1994): 98–127.

———. "Ren'ai to seiyoku no daisan teikoku: Tsūzokuteki seiyokugaku no jidai." *Gendai shisō,* July 1993, 110–127.

"Furyō shōnen hishochi o nerau." *Tōkyō nichinichi shinbun,* 25 July 1913, 7.

Fūryūjin. "Mazu jinsukeshin o haisubeshi." *Marumaru chinbun* 738 (1890): 6.

"Gakusei no daraku." Pt. 1. *Yorozu chōhō,* 24 April 1901, 3.

"Gakusei no daraku." Pt. 1. *Yorozu chōhō,* 26 April 1901, 1.

"Gakusei no daraku." Pt. 2. *Yorozu chōhō,* 9 April 1899, 1.

"Gakusei no fūki mondai." *Nihon,* 28 February 1898, 2.

"Gakusei no hogo kantoku." *Yorozu chōhō,* 19 November 1899, 2.

Garon, Sheldon. *Molding Japanese Minds: The State in Everyday Life.* Princeton: Princeton University Press, 1997.

Genshin. *Ōjō yōshū.* Vol. 6 of *Nihon shisō taikei,* ed. Ienaga Saburō et al., 67 vols. Iwanami shoten, 1970–1982.

Godaidai goshikimoku. 6 vols. *Yonezawa shishi hensan shiryō* 7, 10, 13, 16, 17, 19 (1981–1987).

Goldberg, Jonathan. *Sodometries: Renaissance Texts, Modern Sexualities.* Stanford: Stanford University Press, 1992.

Goodich, Michael. *The Unmentionable Vice: Homosexuality in the Later Medieval Period.* Santa Barbara, Calif.: Ross, 1979.

Gordon, Andrew, ed. *Postwar Japan as History.* Berkeley: University of California Press, 1993.

Gotō Tanji. *Chūsei kokubungaku kenkyū.* Isobe kōyōdō, 1943.

Graham, A. C., trans. *The Book of Lieh-Tzǔ: A Classic of the Tao.* New York: Columbia University Press, 1990.

Grau, Günter, ed. *Hidden Holocaust? Gay and Lesbian Persecution in Germany, 1933–45.* Trans. Patrick Camiller. London: Cassell, 1993.

Greenberg, David F. *The Construction of Homosexuality.* Chicago: University of Chicago Press, 1988.

Guth, Christine M. E. "The Divine Boy in Japanese Art." *Monumenta Nipponica* 42 (1987): 1–23.

Habuto Eiji. *Fujin sei no kenkyū.* Jitsugyō no Nihonsha, 1921.

———. *Fujin seiyoku no kenkyū.* Shichōsha, 1928.

———. *Gendai fujin to seiyoku seikatsu.* Hakubunkan, 1922.

———. *Hentai seiyoku no kenkyū.* Gakugei shoin, 1921.

———. *Koi oyobi sei no shinkenkyū.* Hakubunkan, 1921.

———. *<Nanpito mo kokoroubeki> Seiyoku no chishiki.* Hōkōdō, 1924.

———. *Onna to sono seiteki genshō.* Gakugei shoin, 1921.

———. *Ryōsei no seiyoku oyobi sono sai.* Gakugei shoin, 1921.

———. *Seikan.* Meishōsha, 1927.

———. *Seishokki oyobi seiyoku zensho.* Seihōdō, 1926.

———. *Seishoku eiseihen.* Kateisha, 1907.

———. *Seiyoku to ren'ai.* Nihon hyōronsha, 1921.

———. *Tsūzoku seiyokugaku.* Nihon hyōronsha, 1920.

———. *<Wakaki danjo no kokoroubeki> Seiyoku no chishiki.* Seikōdō shoten, 1921.

Habuto Eiji and Sawada Junjirō. *Hentai seiyokuron.* Shun'yōdō, 1915.

Haeberle, Erwin J. "Swastika, Pink Triangle, and Yellow Star: The Destruction of Sexology and the Persecution of Homosexuals in Nazi Germany." In *Hidden from History: Reclaiming the Gay and Lesbian Past,* ed. Martin Bauml Duberman et al., 365–379. New York: NAL, 1989.

Hagiwara Akihiko, ed. *<Chūkai> Satsuma biwa kashū.* Kagoshima: Ryūyōkai, 1965.

Haifū yanagidaru shūi. In *Nihon meicho zenshū: Edo bungei no bu,* ed. Ishikawa Torakichi et al., 31 vols., 26:753–864. Nihon meicho zenshū kankōkai, 1926–1929.

"Haiyū to fujin." Pt. 17. *Yorozu chōhō,* 13 May 1900, 3.

Hall, Ivan Parker. *Mori Arinori.* Cambridge: Harvard University Press, 1973.

Hall, John Carey. *Japanese Feudal Law.* Washington: University Publications of America, 1979.

Halperin, David M. "Historicizing the Subject of Desire: Sexual Preferences and Erotic Identities in the Pseudo-Lucanian Erôtes." In *Foucault and the Writing of History,* ed. Jan Goldstein, 19–34. Oxford: Blackwell, 1994.

———. "'Homosexuality': A Cultural Construct (An Exchange with Richard Schneider)." In *One Hundred Years of Homosexuality and Other Essays on Greek Love,* 41–53. New York: Routledge, 1990.

———. "One Hundred Years of Homosexuality." In *One Hundred Years of Homosexuality and Other Essays on Greek Love,* 15–40. New York: Routledge, 1990.

Hamada, Kengi, trans. *The Life of an Amorous Man,* by Ihara Saikaku. Rutland, Vt.: Tuttle, 1964.

Hamano Senzō, ed. *Kaika shinsen yanagidaru.* Hamano Senzō, 1880.

Hamao Shirō. "Akuma no deshi." *Shin seinen,* April 1929, 168–198.

———. "Dōseiai kō." *Fujin saron,* September 1930, 136–142.

Hanabusa Shirō [Nakano Masato], trans. *Dōseiai no shujusō.* Tankikan zuihitsu, no. 4. Bungei shijōsha, 1929. Translation of various writings by Albert Moll.

———. "Jicho nanshoku kō no ayamari ni tsuite." <Kokon> *Momoiro sōshi,* November 1928, 63–64.

———. *Nanshoku kō.* Hassōdō shoin, 1928.

———. "Petchi ruiza sono ta." *Hanzai kagaku,* December 1930, 75–79.

"Hanami ni tsuite no fūzoku torishimari." *Yorozu chōhō,* 2 April 1899, 3.

"Hanami zuii." *Yorozu chōhō,* 9 April 1899, 2.

"Hanamiren iyoiyo anshin subeshi." *Yorozu chōhō,* 11 April 1899, 2.

Hanasaki Kazuo. *Edo no kagemajaya.* Miki shobō, 1980.

———. *Fūryū tebako no soko.* Taihei shooku, 1980.

Hanawa, Yukiko. "Inciting Sites of Political Interventions: Queer 'n' Asian." *Positions* 4 (1996): 459–489.

Hane, Mikiso, ed. *Reflections on the Way to the Gallows: Rebel Women in Prewar Japan.* Berkeley: University of California Press, 1988.

Hanei Ryōtei. "Chomei Sodomu no hitobito: Kindai kara gendai made no tenbō." *Fūzoku kitan,* January 1961, 80–84.

Hanpō kenkyūkai, ed. *Hanpōshū.* 14 vols. Sōbunkan, 1959–1975.

Harafuji Hiroshi. "*Han* Laws in the Edo Period with Particular Emphasis on Those of Kanazawa *Han.*" *Acta Asiatica* 35 (1978): 46–71.

———. *Keijihō to minjihō.* Bakuhan taisei kokka no hō to kenryoku, no. 4. Sōbunsha, 1983.

Haraguchi, Torao, et al., trans. *The Status System and Social Organization of*

Satsuma: A Translation of the Shūmon Tefuda Aratame Jōmoku. Honolulu: University Press of Hawaii, 1975.

Hardacre, Helen. *Marketing the Menacing Fetus in Japan.* Berkeley: University of California Press, 1997.

Harootunian, H. D. "Late Tokugawa Culture and Thought." In *The Cambridge History of Japan,* ed. John W. Hall et al., 5 vols. to date, 5:168–258. Cambridge: Cambridge University Press, 1988–.

———. *Things Seen and Unseen: Discourse and Ideology in Tokugawa Nativism.* Chicago: University of Chicago Press, 1988.

Hasegawa Kōzō and Tsukikawa Kazuo, eds. *Minakata Kumagusu nanshoku dangi: Iwata Jun'ichi ōfuku shokan.* Yasaka shobō, 1991.

Hashiguchi Mitsuru. *Kagoshima-ken hōgen jiten.* Ōfūsha, 1987.

Hayashi Jiken. *Zassetsu nōwa.* In *Nihon zuihitsu taisei,* ed. Hayakawa Junzaburō et al., 81 vols.; 2d ser., 8:351–409. Yoshikawa kōbunkan, 1973–1979.

Hayashi Yoshikazu. *Edo ehon besutoserā.* Shinchōsha, 1991.

———. *Enpon Edo bungakushi.* Kawade shobō, 1991.

———. <*Enpon kenkyū*> *Zoku Utamaro.* Enpon kenkyū sōsho, no. 3. Yūkō shobō, 1963.

Hekma, Gert. "'A Female Soul in a Male Body': Sexual Inversion as Gender Inversion in Nineteenth-Century Sexology." In *Third Sex, Third Gender: Beyond Sexual Dimorphism in Culture and History,* ed. Gilbert Herdt, 213–239. New York: Zone, 1994.

Henderson, Dan Fenno. "The Evolution of Tokugawa Law." In *Studies in the Institutional History of Early Modern Japan,* ed. John W. Hall and Marius B. Jansen, 203–229. Princeton: Princeton University Press, 1968.

Herdt, Gilbert. *Same Sex, Different Cultures: Gays and Lesbians across Cultures.* Boulder, Colo.: Westview, 1997.

———, ed. *Third Sex, Third Gender: Beyond Sexual Dimorphism in Culture and History.* New York: Zone, 1994.

Hino Mitsuo, ed. "<Gojūnenkan no vēru o nuida kisho> Kōmurō Shujin-cho *Bishōnenron, ichimei dōsei shikijōshi.*" Pts. 1 and 2. *Erochika,* October 1970, 216–243; November 1970, 208–228.

Hinsch, Bret. *Passions of the Cut Sleeve: The Male Homosexual Tradition in China.* Berkeley: University of California Press, 1990.

Hioki Norio et al., eds. *Nihon hanrei taisei.* 26 vols. Hibonkaku, 1936.

Hiraga Gennai. *Fūryū Shidōken den.* In *Nihon koten bungaku taikei,* ed. Takagi Ichinosuke et al., 102 vols., 55:153–224. Iwanami shoten, 1957–1968.

———. <*Nanshoku saiken*> *Mitsu no asa.* In *Nihon shomin bunka shiryō shūsei,* ed. Geinōshi kenkyūkai, 16 vols., 9:101–111. San'ichi shobō, 1973–1978.

———. *Nenashigusa.* In *Nihon koten bungaku taikei,* ed. Takagi Ichinosuke et al., 102 vols., 55:33–94. Iwanami shoten, 1957–1968.

———. *Nenashigusa kōhen.* In *Nihon koten bungaku taikei,* ed. Takagi Ichinosuke et al., 102 vols., 55:95–151. Iwanami shoten, 1957–1968.

Hiraga Seijirō. *Kanmei hōigaku.* Kinbara iseki shoten, 1899.

Hirai Sōta. "Ōsaka senshōshi." *Hanzai kagaku*, December 1930, 135–141.

Hirata Atsutane. *Kokon yōmi kō*. In <*Shinshū*> *Hirata Atsutane zenshū*, ed. Hirata Atsutane zenshū kankōkai, 21 vols., 9:71–358. Meicho shuppan, 1976–1981.

Hiratsuka Yoshinobu. *Nihon ni okeru nanshoku no kenkyū*. Ningen no kagakusha, 1983.

Hirosue Tamotsu. *Henkai no akusho*. Heibonsha, 1973.

———. <*Shinpen*> *Akubasho no hassō*. Chikuma shobō, 1988.

Hirschfeld, Magnus. "Gendai ni okeru seibyōrigaku no chiho." *Hanzai kagaku*, June 1931, 236–241.

———. *Men and Women: The World Journey of a Sexologist*. Trans. O. P. Green. New York: Putnam's, 1935.

Hisamatsu Ippei. "Sodomī dan." *Ryōki* 3 (1947): 18–21.

Honpu Yasushirō. *Satsuma kenbunki*. In *Nihon shomin seikatsu shiryō shūsei*, ed. Miyamoto Tsuneichi et al., 32 vols., 12:353–423. San'ichi shobō, 1968–1984.

Hopper, Helen M. *A New Woman of Japan: A Political Biography of Katō Shidzue*. Boulder, Colo.: Westview, 1996.

Hori Tatsuo. "Kao." In *Hori Tatsuo zenshū*, ed. Nakamura Shin'ichirō et al., 11 vols., 1:267–288. Chikuma shobō, 1977–1980.

———. "Moyuru hō." In *Hori Tatsuo zenshū*, ed. Nakamura Shin'ichirō et al., 11 vols., 1:207–222. Chikuma shobō, 1977–1980.

Hosokawa Genshi. "Kokin wakashu no jo." In *Misonoya*, ed. Ōta Nanpo. Ed. Hayakawa Junzaburō et al., 4 vols., 4:479–482. Kokusho kankōkai, 1917.

Hozumi Nobushige, ed. *Goningumi hōkishū*. Yūhikaku, 1930.

———. *Goningumi seidoron*. Yūhikaku, 1921.

Hozumi Shigetō, ed. *Goningumi hōkishū zokuhen*. 2 vols. Yūhikaku, 1944.

Huang, Ray. *1587, a Year of No Significance: The Ming Dynasty in Decline*. New Haven: Yale University Press, 1981.

Huussen, Arend H., Jr. "Sodomy in the Dutch Republic during the Eighteenth Century." In *Hidden from History: Reclaiming the Gay and Lesbian Past*, ed. Martin Bauml Duberman et al., 141–149. New York: NAL, 1989.

Ichikawa Genzō. "Sei kyōikuron." *Sei*, September 1920 (zōkan), 29–33.

Ifukube Takateru. "Dōseiai e no ichikōsatsu." *Hanzai kagaku*, January 1932, 290–293.

Ihara Saikaku. *Kōshoku gonin onna*. In *Nihon koten bungaku zenshū*, ed. Akiyama Ken et al., 51 vols., 38:305–423. Shōgakkan, 1970–1976.

———. *Kōshoku ichidai onna*. In *Nihon koten bungaku zenshū*, ed. Akiyama Ken et al., 51 vols., 38:425–583. Shōgakkan, 1970–1976.

———. *Kōshoku ichidai otoko*. In *Nihon koten bungaku zenshū*, ed. Akiyama Ken et al., 51 vols., 38:97–303. Shōgakkan, 1970–1976.

———. *Nanshoku ōkagami*. In *Nihon koten bungaku zenshū*, ed. Akiyama Ken et al., 51 vols., 39:309–597. Shōgakkan, 1970–1976.

———. *Saikaku okimiyage*. In *Nihon koten bungaku zenshū*, ed. Akiyama Ken et al., 51 vols., 40:509–627. Shōgakkan, 1970–1976.

————. *Yorozu no fumihōgu.* In *Nihon koten bungaku zenshū,* ed. Akiyama Ken et al., 51 vols., 40:263–377. Shōgakkan, 1970–1976.

Iijima Hosaku. *Kagetsu zuihitsu.* Toyamabō, 1933.

Ijiri Matakurō Tadasuki. *Nyake kanjinchō.* In *Zoku gunsho ruijū,* ed. Hanawa Hokinoichi and Ōta Tōshirō, 82 vols., 33b:19–20. Zoku gunsho ruijū kankōkai, 1957–1969.

Ikeda Tamotsu, ed. *Kaika yanagidaru.* Vol. 1. N.p., n.d.

Ikegami, Eiko. *The Taming of the Samurai.* Cambridge: Harvard University Press, 1995.

Ikuno Shin'ichi. "Bakuroshō dōseiai o seifuku shita bankin igaku." *Hanzai kagaku,* April 1932: 51–56.

Imamura Yoshitaka and Takahashi Hideo, eds. *Akita-han machibureshū.* 3 vols. Miraisha, 1971–1973.

Imanishi Makoto. "<Shiryō honkoku> Matsudaira bunko *Nyake chōrō monogatari.*" *Yamanobe no michi* 9 (1962): 73–78.

Inagaki Ginji, trans. *Baiin enkakushi.* 3 vols. Keishōkaku, 1877. Translation of unidentified work.

Inagaki Shiyo. *Otto Inagaki Taruho.* In *Taruho to Taruho,* by Inagaki Taruho and Inagaki Shiyo, 195–452. Chūsekisha, 1986.

Inagaki Taruho. "Fevaritto." In *Inagaki Taruho taizen,* ed. Hagiwara Sachiko and Kawahito Hiroshi, 6 vols., 2:122–140. Gendai shichōsha, 1969–1970.

————. *Inagaki Taruho taizen.* Vols. 2 and 3. Ed. Hagiwara Sachiko and Kawahito Hiroshi. 6 vols. Gendai shichōsha, 1969–1970.

————. "Kamonohashiron." In *Inagaki Taruho taizen,* ed. Hagiwara Sachiko and Kawahito Hiroshi, 6 vols., 2:142–149. Gendai shichōsha, 1969–1970.

————. "Minakata Kumagusu chigo dangi." In *Inagaki Taruho taizen,* ed. Hagiwara Sachiko and Kawahito Hiroshi, 6 vols., 2:400–465. Gendai shichōsha, 1969–1970.

————. "Miyatake Gaikotsu no *Bishōnenron.*" In *Inagaki Taruho taizen,* ed. Hagiwara Sachiko and Kawahito Hiroshi, 6 vols., 2:340–398. Gendai shichōsha, 1969–1970.

————. "Nanshoku kō yodan." In *Minakata Kumagusu zenshū,* ed. Iwamura Shinobu et al., 12 vols., 9:617–623. Heibonsha, 1971–1975.

————. "Reidio no uta." In *Inagaki Taruho taizen,* ed. Hagiwara Sachiko and Kawahito Hiroshi, 6 vols., 2:114–121. Gendai shichōsha, 1969–1970.

————. "Shin inu tsurezure." In *Inagaki Taruho taizen,* ed. Hagiwara Sachiko and Kawahito Hiroshi, 6 vols., 2:76–92. Gendai shichōsha, 1969–1970.

————. *Shōnen tokuhon.* Ushio shuppansha, 1986.

————. "Shōnen tokuhon: Esseifū na seisaku." In *Shōnen tokuhon,* 46–72. Ushio shuppansha, 1986.

————. *Shōnen'ai no bigaku.* In *Inagaki Taruho taizen,* ed. Hagiwara Sachiko and Kawahito Hiroshi, 6 vols., 3:256–476. Gendai shichōsha, 1969–1970.

————. "Tentai shikōshō." In *Inagaki Taruho taizen,* ed. Hagiwara Sachiko and Kawahito Hiroshi, 6 vols., 1:96–106. Gendai shichōsha, 1969–1970.

Inagaki Taruho and Inagaki Shiyo. *Taruho to Taruho.* Chūsekisha, 1986.

Inagaki Taruho et al. *Taruho jiten*. Ushio shuppansha, 1975.

Inaoka Masafumi. *Bishōnen*. Osaka: Shinshindō, 1900.

Inoue Suguru et al., eds. *Sekushuariti no shakaigaku*. Iwanami kōza gendai shakaigaku, no. 10. Iwanami shoten, 1996.

Iro monogatari. In *Kanazōshi shūsei*, ed. Asakura Haruhiko and Fukuzawa Akio, 18 vols. to date, 4: 177–197. Tōkyōdō, 1980–.

Irokawa Daikichi and Gabe Masao, eds. *Meiji kenpakusho shūsei*. 5 vols. to date. Chikuma shobō, 1986–.

"Iroko to iu otoko." *Kono hana* 10 (1910): 18.

Ise Sadaharu. *Yamato kotohajime seigo*. In *Ekiken zenshū*, ed. Ekiken kai, 8 vols., 1:811–898. Ekiken zenshū kankōbu, 1910–1911.

Ishihara Ryō et al. "Modan Tōkyō ero fūkei." *Gendai no esupuri* 188 (1983): 135–142.

Ishii Ryōsuke, ed. *Kinsei hōsei shiryō sōsho*. Rev. ed. 3 vols. Sōbunsha, 1959.

———, ed. *Oshiokirei ruishū*. 16 vols. Meicho shuppan, 1971–1974.

Ishikawa Ichirō. *Edo bungaku zokushin jiten*. Tōkyōdō, 1989.

Ishikawa Kiyotada. *Jitsuyō hōigaku*. Nankōdō, 1900.

Ishimoto, Shidzué. *Facing Both Ways: The Story of My Life*. Stanford: Stanford University Press, 1984.

Ishizuka Hōkaishi. *Okaba yūkaku kō*. In *Mikan zuihitsu hyakushu*, ed. Mitamura Engyo, 12 vols., 1:17–189. Chūō kōronsha, 1976–1978.

Ishizumi Harunosuke. "Hentai kojiki no seiteki hanzai." *Hanzai kagaku*, October 1931, 168–172.

Itō Gingetsu. <*Rimenkanteki*> *Isetsu Nihonshi*. Hakuundō shoten, 1909.

Itō Sei. *Nihon bundanshi*. 18 vols. Kōdansha, 1953–1973.

Itō Shigure. "Keibatsu to seiyoku." *Ningen tankyū*, May 1951 (zōkan), 97–103.

Itō Tadashi. *"Ējanaika" to kinsei shakai*. Kōsō shobō, 1995.

Iwanami dairoppō. 1992 ed. Iwanami shoten, 1992.

Iwata Jun'ichi. "Bishōnen Fuwa Bansaku no koi." In *Honchō nanshoku kō*, 240–252. Toba: Iwata Sadao, 1974.

———. "Edo kagema no matsuro." In *Honchō nanshoku kō*, 212–224. Toba: Iwata Sadao, 1974.

———. "Haijin Bashō no dōseiai." In *Honchō nanshoku kō*, 253–267. Toba: Iwata Sadao, 1974.

———. *Honchō nanshoku kō*. Toba: Iwata Sadao, 1974.

———. *Nanshoku bunken shoshi*. Toba: Iwata Sadao, 1973.

———. "Yadoba no kagemajaya." In *Honchō nanshoku kō*, 200–212. Toba: Iwata Sadao, 1974.

———. Letter to Minakata Kumagusu, 16 August 1931. *Minakata Kumagusu nanshoku dangi: Iwata Jun'ichi ōfuku shokan*, ed. Hasegawa Kōzō and Tsukikawa Kazuo, 35–41. Yasaka shobō, 1991.

———. Letter to Minakata Jun'ichi, 27 August 1931. *Minakata Kumagusu nanshoku dangi: Iwata Jun'ichi ōfuku shokan*, ed. Hasegawa Kōzō and Tsukikawa Kazuo, 83–89. Yasaka shobō, 1991.

———. Letter to Minakata Kumagusu, 2 September 1931. *Minakata Kuma-*

gusu nanshoku dangi: Iwata Jun'ichi ōfuku shokan, ed. Hasegawa Kōzō and Tsukikawa Kazuo, 94–97. Yasaka shobō, 1991.

———. Letter to Minakata Kumagusu, 15 July 1935. *Minakata Kumagusu nanshoku dangi: Iwata Jun'ichi ōfuku shokan,* ed. Hasegawa Kōzō and Tsukikawa Kazuo, 297–301. Yasaka shobō, 1991.

———. Letter to Minakata Kumagusu, 21 August 1937. *Minakata Kumagusu nanshoku dangi: Iwata Jun'ichi ōfuku shokan,* ed. Hasegawa Kōzō and Tsukikawa Kazuo, 322–324. Yasaka shobō, 1991.

———. Letter to Minakata Kumagusu, n.d. (postmarked 5 April 1937). *Minakata Kumagusu nanshoku dangi: Iwata Jun'ichi ōfuku shokan,* ed. Hasegawa Kōzō and Tsukikawa Kazuo, 319–321. Yasaka shobō, 1991.

Iwata Sadao. "Bōfu Iwata Jun'ichi." In *Minakata Kumagusu nanshoku dangi: Iwata Jun'ichi ōfuku shokan,* ed. Hasegawa Kōzō and Tsukikawa Kazuo, 412–433. Yasaka shobō, 1991.

Iwaya Sazanami. "Hi-hakase to watashi." *Hanzai kagaku,* January 1932, 215–219.

———. "Nanshoku no benkai." *Chūō kōron,* March 1909, 75.

———. *Watakushi no konjaku monogatari.* Waseda daigaku shuppanbu, 1928.

———. *Yōkō miyage.* 2 vols. Hakubunkan, 1903.

Jones, Sumie, ed. *Imaging/Reading Eros: Proceedings for the Conference, Sexuality and Edo Culture, 1750–1850.* Bloomington: East Asian Studies Center, Indiana University, 1996.

Jordan, Mark D. *The Invention of Sodomy in Christian Theology.* Chicago: University of Chicago Press, 1997.

K.O. *<Jitsuroku shikeishūtachi no sei> Zoku saraba waga tomo.* Tokuma shoten, 1981.

Kabiya Kazuhiko. *Chijō meian.* Nihon shuppan haikyū, 1948.

"Kadai." *Marumaru chinbun* 1502 (1904): 29–30.

Kaempfer, Engelbert. *The History of Japan, Together with a Description of the Kingdom of Siam, 1690–92.* Trans. J. G. Scheuchzer. 3 vols. Glasgow: MacLehose, 1906.

Kageura Tsutomu, ed. *Matsuyama-han hōreishū.* Kondō shuppansha, 1978.

Kagoshima-ken kyōiku iinkai, ed. *Kagoshima-ken kyōikushi.* Maruyama gakugei tosho, 1976.

Kagoshima-shi gakusha rengōkai, ed. *<Satsuma hekouta> Shikon.* Kagoshima: Shun'endō, 1970.

Kaibara Yoshifuru. *Yamato kotohajime.* In *Ekiken zenshū,* ed. Ekiken kai, 8 vols., 1:689–810. Ekiken zenshū kankōbu, 1910–1911.

Kakinuma Eiko and Kurihara Chiyo, eds. *Tanbi shōsetsu gei bungaku bukkugaido.* Byakuya shobō, 1993.

Kanbashi Norimasa. *Kagoshima kuruwa monogatari: Urakaidō onna no rekishi.* Maruyama gakugei tosho, 1989.

Kasumi Nobuhiko. *Meiji shoki keijihō no kisoteki kenkyū.* Keiō gijuku daigaku kenkyūkai sōsho, no. 50. Keiō tsūshin, 1990.

Kataoka Teppei. "Josei fuan to dōseiai." *Kaizō*, March 1935, 78–84.

———. "Rōkō." *Chūō kōron*, June 1934, (sōsaku) 1–41.

Katayama Kuniyoshi and Eguchi Jō. *Saiban igaku teikō.* 2 vols. Shimamura Risuke, 1888.

Katayama Kuniyoshi et al. *<Zōho kaitei> Hōigaku teikō.* 4 vols. Shimamura Risuke, 1891–1897.

Katayama Masao, trans. *Danjo to tensai.* Dainihon tosho, 1906. Translation of *Geschlecht und Charakter,* by Otto Weininger (1903).

Katō Tokijirō. "Seiyoku no jiyū to seigen." *Katō Tokijirō senshū,* ed. Narita Ryūichi, 433–441. Kōryūsha, 1981.

Katō Yoshikazu. "Tessō yawa." *Hanzai kagaku,* February 1932, 146–149.

Katz, Jonathan Ned. *The Invention of Heterosexuality.* New York: Dutton, 1995.

Kawabata Yasunari. *Shōnen.* In *Kawabata Yasunari zenshū,* ed. Yamamoto Kenkichi et al., 37 vols., 10:141–255. Shinchōsha, 1980–1984.

Kawade Masumi. "Kagoshima-shi to Shichikō." In *Kinenshi,* 324–330. Kagoshima: Daishichi kōtō gakkō kinen shukugakai, 1926.

Kawamura Kunimitsu. *Otome no shintai: Onna no kindai to sekushuariti.* Kinokuniya shoten, 1994.

———. *Sekushuariti no kindai.* Kōdansha sensho mechie, no. 86. Kōdansha, 1996.

Kawamura Taichi. *Shimazu Masa-jo kaishinroku.* Yokohama: Kinrindō, 1891.

Kawaoka Chōfū. "Gakusei no anmen ni wadakamareru nanshoku no ichidai akufū o tsūba su." *Bōken sekai,* August 1909, 67–79.

Kawatake Shigetoshi. *Kabukishi no kenkyū.* Tōkyōdō, 1943.

Kawazoiyanagi. In *Nihon meicho zenshū: Edo bungei no bu,* ed. Ishikawa Torakichi et al., 31 vols., 26:865–936. Nihon meicho zenshū kankōkai, 1926–1929.

Keichū Koji. *Taihei hyaku monogatari.* In *Tokugawa bungei ruijū,* ed. Hayakawa Junzaburō, 12 vols., 4:318–372. Kokusho kankōkai, 1914–1916.

Keisai Eisen. *<Keichū kibun> Makura bunko hoi.* In *Nihon seiten taikan,* ed. Takahashi Tetsu, 2 vols., 1:93–124. Nihon seikatsu shinri gakkai, 1954.

Kennedy, Hubert. *Ulrichs: The Life and Works of Karl Heinrich Ulrichs, Pioneer of the Modern Gay Movement.* Boston: Alyson, 1988.

Ketelaar, James Edward. *Of Heretics and Martyrs in Meiji Japan: Buddhism and Its Persecution.* Princeton: Princeton University Press, 1990.

"Kii no henshōsha." *Yorozu chōhō,* 18 February 1901, 3.

Kikuchi Shunsuke, ed. *Tokugawa kinrei kō.* 6 vols. Yoshikawa kōbunkan, 1931–1932.

———, ed. *Tokugawa kinrei kō kōshū.* 6 vols. Yoshikawa kōbunkan, 1931–1932.

Kimoto Itaru. *<Hyōden> Miyatake Gaikotsu.* Shakai shisōsha, 1984.

———. *Onanī to Nihonjin.* Intanaru shuppan, 1976.

Kimura Motoi et al., eds. *Hanshi daijiten.* 8 vols. Yūzankaku, 1988–1990.

Kimuro Bōun. *Kanokomochi.* In *Nihon koten bungaku taikei,* ed. Takagi Ichinosuke et al., 102 vols., 100:349–386. Iwanami shoten, 1957–1968.

"<Kingindōhai kenshō mondai> Seinen gakusei o fuhai daraku seshimuru mottomo nikumubeki yūwaku no jibutsu goko o tōhyō no kekka." *Bōken sekai*, September 1909, 7.

Kinkin Joshi. *Jokeikun*. In *Nihon seiten taikan*, ed. Takahashi Tetsu, 2 vols., 2:97–124. Nihon seikatsu shinri gakkai, 1954.

Kinmonth, Earl H. *The Self-Made Man in Meiji Japanese Thought: From Samurai to Salary Man*. Berkeley: University of California Press, 1981.

Kitagawa Morisada. *Morisada mankō*. Ed. Asakura Haruhiko and Kashikawa Shūichi. 5 vols. Tōkyōdō, 1992.

Kitagawa Seijun and Fujisawa Morihiko. *Shikijō shisō no kaibō*. Ryūseidō, 1913.

Kitamura Kigin. *Iwatsutsuji*. In *Kanazōshi shūsei*, ed. Asakura Haruhiko and Fukuzawa Akio, 18 vols. to date, 5: 349–369. Tōkyōdō, 1980–.

Kobayashi Takiji. *Kani kōsen*. In *<Teihon> Kobayashi Takiji zenshū*, ed. Eguchi Kiyoshi et al., 15 vols., 4:3–89. Shin Nihon shuppansha, 1968–1969.

Kōda Rohan. *Higeotoko*. In *Rohan zenshū*, ed. Kagyūkai, 44 vols., 5:273–393. Iwanami shoten, 1978–1980.

Kodama Yoshio. *<Zuihitsushū> Gokuchū gokugai*. Ajia seinensha, 1942.

Koikawa Shunchō. *Mudaiki*. In *Edo no parojī ehon*, ed. Koike Masatane et al., 4 vols., 1:113–148. Gendai kyōyō bunko, nos. 1037–1040. Shakai shisōsha, 1980–1983.

Koishikawa Zenji et al. *Hanzai no minzokugaku: Meiji Taishō hanzaishi kara*. Hihyōsha, 1993.

Koizumi Eiichi. *Berurin yawa*. Waseda daigaku shuppanbu, 1925.

Kōke Yoshio. *<Shinpan> Keihō kōwa*. Chikura shobō, 1949.

<Kokkei shinbun furoku> Nihon shinkeihō. N.p., n.d.

Kokuritsu shiryōkan, ed. *Tsugaru-ke osadamegaki*. Shiryōkan sōsho, no. 3. Tōkyō daigaku shuppankai, 1981.

"Kokuso no torikeshi." *Yorozu chōhō*, 21 October 1898, 3.

Kōman Sensei. *Rokuchō ichiri*. In *Sharebon taisei*, ed. Mizuno Minoru et al., 31 vols., 12:55–65. Chūō kōronsha, 1978–1988.

Komine Shigeyuki. *Dōseiai to dōsei shinjū no igakuteki kōsatsu*. In *Dōseiai to dōsei shinjū no kenkyū*, by Komine Shigeyuki and Minami Takao, 11–265. Komine kenkyūjo, 1985.

Komori Yōichi. "Nihon kindai bungaku ni okeru nanshoku no haikei." *Bungaku* 6.1 (1995): 72–83.

Kon Tōkō. *Chigo*. Ōtori shobō, 1947.

Konishi Jin'ichi. *Michi: Chūsei no rinen*. Nihon no koten, no. 3. Kōdansha, 1975.

———. "Michi and Medieval Writing." Trans. Aileen Gatten. In *Principles of Classical Japanese Literature*, ed. Earl Miner, 181–208. Princeton: Princeton University Press, 1985.

Konoe Nobuhiro. *Inu tsurezure*. In *Kanazōshi shūsei*, ed. Asakura Haruhiko and Fukuzawa Akio, 18 vols. to date, 4: 3–26. Tōkyōdō, 1980–.

Konta Yōzō. *Edo no hon'yasan: Kinsei bunkashi no sokumen*. NHK bukkusu, no. 299. Nihon hōsō shuppan kyōkai, 1977.

————. *Edo no kinsho.* Edo sensho, no. 6. Yoshikawa kōbunkan, 1981.

Kōseishō. *Isei hyakunenshi.* 3 vols. Kōseishō imukyoku, 1976.

Kōseishō yobōkyoku. *Kokumin yūseihō gaisetsu.* Kōseishō yobōkyoku, 1940.

Kōshaku Maeda-ke henshūbu, ed. *Kaga-han shiryō.* 18 vols. Ishiguro Bunkichi, 1929–1958.

Kōshokken Ariwara no Narihira. *Kōshoku tabimakura.* In *Nihon seiten taikan,* ed. Takahashi Tetsu, 2 vols., 1:9–59. Nihon seikatsu shinri gakkai, 1954.

Krauss, Friedrich S. *Das Geschlechtleben in Glauben, Sitte, und Brauch der Japaner.* Beiwerke zum Studium der Anthropophyteia, no. 2. Leipzig: Deutsche, 1907.

Kumakura Isao. "Bunmei kaika to fūzoku." In *Bunmei kaika no kenkyū,* ed. Hayashiya Tatsusaburō, 569–592. Iwanami shoten, 1979.

Kumazawa Banzan. *Shūgi washo.* In *Nihon shisō taikei,* ed. Ienaga Saburō et al., 67 vols., 30:7–356. Iwanami shoten, 1970–1982.

Kure Shūzō. "Dōsei no ai." *Fujin gahō,* October 1920, 24–27.

Kurimoto Tsunekatsu. "Seinen danjo ni sei kyōiku o hodokosu koto wa nani ga yue ni hitsuyō ka." *Sei,* June 1921, 12–19.

Kurozukin [Yokoyama Kendō]. "Gashu no bishōnen." *Chūō kōron,* January 1912, 130–137.

Kurumada Kingo. "Tōkyō okama (danshō) kumiai tanbōki." Pt. 4 of a series titled "Shinpan Mito kōmon man'yūki." *Bakuro,* July 1949, 35–38.

Kusai Koenosuke. "Dainiketsu no setsu." *Marumaru chinbun* 213 (1881): 3110–3111.

"Kyōku." *Marumaru chinbun* 169 (1880): 2702–2703.

"Kyōku." *Marumaru chinbun* 217 (1881): 3186–3187.

"Kyōku." *Marumaru chinbun* 223 (1881): 3282–3283.

"Kyōku." *Marumaru chinbun* 294 (1882): 4416–4417.

"Kyōku." *Marumaru chinbun* 343 (1883): 5166–5167.

"Kyōku." *Marumaru chinbun* 381 (1883): 5794–5795.

"Kyōku." *Marumaru chinbun* 1201 (1899): 22.

Kyōto daigaku Nihon hōshi kenkyūkai, ed. *Hanpō shiryō shūsei.* Sōbunkan, 1980.

Kyōto machibure kenkyūkai, ed. *Kyōto machibure shūsei.* 15 vols. Iwanami shoten, 1983–1989.

Laderrière, Mette. "Yoshizawa Ayame (1673–1729) and the Art of Female Impersonation in Genroku Japan." In *Europe Interprets Japan,* ed. Gordon Daniels, 233–238. Tenterden, Kent: Norbury, 1984.

LaFleur, William R. *The Karma of Words: Buddhism and the Literary Arts in Medieval Japan.* Berkeley: University of California Press, 1983.

————. *Liquid Life: Abortion and Buddhism in Japan.* Princeton: Princeton University Press, 1992.

Lauritsen, John, and David Thorstad. *The Early Homosexual Rights Movement (1864–1935).* New York: Times Change, 1974.

Leavell, James B. "The Policing of Society." In *Japan in Transition: Thought and Action in the Meiji Era, 1868–1912,* ed. Hilary Conroy et al., 22–49. Rutherford, N.J.: Fairleigh Dickinson University Press, 1984.

Leupp, Gary P. *Male Colors: The Construction of Homosexuality in Tokugawa Japan*. Berkeley: University of California Press, 1995.

—— [Gary Leupp]. "Male Homosexuality in Edo during the Late Tokugawa Period, 1750–1850: Decline of a Tradition?" In *Imaging/Reading Eros: Proceedings for the Conference, Sexuality and Edo Culture, 1750–1850*, ed. Sumie Jones, 105–109. Bloomington: East Asian Studies Center, Indiana University, 1996.

Levenson, Joseph R. *Confucian China and Its Modern Fate*. Vol. 3, *The Problem of Historical Significance*. Berkeley: University of California Press, 1965.

Lu, David J., ed. *Japan: A Documentary History*. Armonk, N.Y.: Sharpe, 1997.

McClain, James L. *Kanazawa: A Seventeenth-Century Japanese Castle Town*. New Haven: Yale University Press, 1982.

McClellan, Edwin. *Woman in the Crested Kimono: The Life of Shibue Io and Her Family Drawn from Mori Ōgai's "Shibue Chūsai."* New Haven: Yale University Press, 1985.

McEwan, J. R. *The Political Writings of Ogyū Sorai*. Cambridge: Cambridge University Press, 1962.

Maeda Ai. "*Shizu no odamaki kō*." *Ōgai* 18 (1966): 21–27.

Maeda Chōhachi, ed. *Niijima ryūninchō*. Niijima Honson: Niijima kyōdokan, 1941.

Marra, Michele. "The Development of Mappō Thought in Japan." *Japanese Journal of Religious Studies* 15 (1988): 25–54, 287–305.

Marran, Christine. "'Poison Woman' Takahashi Oden and the Spectacle of Female Deviance in Early Meiji." *U.S.-Japan Women's Journal, English Supplement* 9 (1995): 93–110.

Marshall, Byron K., trans. *The Autobiography of Ōsugi Sakae*, by Ōsugi Sakae. Berkeley: University of California Press, 1992.

Maruki Sado [Hata Toyokichi]. "Chūkansei Hirushuferudo." *Hanzai kagaku*, June 1931, 220–221.

Maruoka Hideko and Yamaguchi Miyoko, eds. *Kindai Nihon fujin mondai nenpyō*. Vol. 10 of *Nihon fujin mondai shiryō shūsei*, ed. Maruoka Hideko et al., 10 vols. Domesu shuppan, 1976–1977.

Matsuda Osamu. *Hanamoji no shisō: Nihon ni okeru shōnen'ai no seishinshi*. Peyotoru kōbō, 1988.

Matsueda Itaru. "Jō no nandō: Minakata Kumagusu 'zaibei shokan' bekken." *Yasō* 15 (1985): 108–125.

Matsui Junji, trans. *Eibei hankanritsu*. Matsui Chūbei, 1879.

Matsui, Midori. "Little Girls Were Little Boys: Displaced Femininity in the Representation of Homosexuality in Japanese Girls' Comics." In *Feminism and the Politics of Difference*, ed. Sneja Gunew and Anna Yeatman, 177–196. Boulder, Colo.: Westview, 1993.

Matsui Shōyō. "Bōkokuron." Pt. 4. *Yorozu chōhō*, 18 April 1899, 1.

Matsumoto Yasuko. *Danjo seishoku kenzenhō*. Chūō kangofukai, 1900.

Matsunaga, Daigan, and Alicia Matsunaga. *The Buddhist Concept of Hell*. New York: Philosophical Library, 1972.

Matsuo Bashō. "Hokku hen." In *Nihon koten bungaku taikei,* ed. Takagi Ichinosuke et al., 102 vols., 45:3–280. Iwanami shoten, 1957–1968.

Matsuura Seizan. *Kasshi yawa,* ed. Yoshikawa Hanshichi. Kokusho kankōkai, 1910.

———. *Kasshi yawa zokuhen,* ed. Yoshikawa Hanshichi. 3 vols. Kokusho kankōkai, 1911.

Meijer, M. J. "Homosexual Offenses in Ch'ing Law." *T'oung Pao* 71 (1985): 109–133.

Miller, Stephen D., ed. *Partings at Dawn: An Anthology of Japanese Gay Literature.* San Francisco: Gay Sunshine, 1996.

Mimura Tokuzō. "Aru kagema no ichishitai: Hirushuferudo hakase o annai shite." *Hanzai kagaku,* June 1931, 222–235.

———. "Aru tokui seikakusha no kokuhaku." *Hanzai kōron,* June 1933, 113–118.

———. "Shin Tōkyō kagemadan." *Hanzai kagaku,* July 1931, 127–133.

Minakata Kumagusu. "Gekka hyōjin: Keizu funran no hanashi." In *Minakata Kumagusu zenshū,* ed. Iwamura Shinobu et al., 12 vols., 3:268–306. Heibonsha, 1971–1975.

———. "Ichidai otoko o yomu." In *Minakata Kumagusu zenshū,* ed. Iwamura Shinobu et al., 12 vols., 4:5–62. Heibonsha, 1971–1975.

———. "Onna o wakashu ni daiyō seshi koto." In *Minakata Kumagusu zenshū,* ed. Iwamura Shinobu et al., 12 vols., 2:440–444. Heibonsha, 1971–1975.

———. Letter to Nakayama Tarō, 8 August 1931. *Minakata Kumagusu zenshū,* ed. Iwamura Shinobu et al., 12 vols., 9:5–13. Heibonsha, 1971–1975.

———. Letter to Iwata Jun'ichi, 20 August 1931. *Minakata Kumagusu zenshū,* ed. Iwamura Shinobu et al., 12 vols., 9:14–45. Heibonsha, 1971–1975.

———. Letter to Iwata Jun'ichi, 25 August 1931. *Minakata Kumagusu zenshū,* ed. Iwamura Shinobu et al., 12 vols., 9:46–48. Heibonsha, 1971–1975.

———. Letter to Iwata Jun'ichi, 7 September 1931. *Minakata Kumagusu zenshū,* ed. Iwamura Shinobu et al., 12 vols., 9:52–55. Heibonsha, 1971–1975.

———. Letter to Iwata Jun'ichi, 16 September 1931. *Minakata Kumagusu zenshū,* ed. Iwamura Shinobu et al., 12 vols., 9:65–69. Heibonsha, 1971–1975.

———. Letter to Iwata Jun'ichi, 20 September 1931. *Minakata Kumagusu zenshū,* ed. Iwamura Shinobu et al., 12 vols., 9:70–78. Heibonsha, 1971–1975.

———. Letter to Iwata Jun'ichi, 27 September 1931. *Minakata Kumagusu zenshū,* ed. Iwamura Shinobu et al., 12 vols., 9:78–82. Heibonsha, 1971–1975.

———. Postcard to Iwata Jun'ichi, 5 May 1932. *Minakata Kumagusu zenshū,* ed. Iwamura Shinobu et al., 12 vols., 9:126–127. Heibonsha, 1971–1975.

———. Letter to Iwata Jun'ichi, 29 October 1932. *Minakata Kumagusu zenshū,* ed. Iwamura Shinobu et al., 12 vols., 9:129–134. Heibonsha, 1971–1975.

———. Letter to Iwata Jun'ichi, 7 November 1932. *Minakata Kumagusu zenshū,* ed. Iwamura Shinobu et al., 12 vols., 9:134–142. Heibonsha, 1971–1975.

———. Postcard to Iwata Jun'ichi, 1 February 1933. *Minakata Kumagusu zenshū,* ed. Iwamura Shinobu et al., 12 vols., 9:174. Heibonsha, 1971–1975.

———. Postcard to Iwata Jun'ichi, 25 April 1933. *Minakata Kumagusu zenshū,* ed. Iwamura Shinobu et al., 12 vols., 9:180–181. Heibonsha, 1971–1975.

———. Letter to Iwata Jun'ichi, 19 January 1934. *Minakata Kumagusu zenshū*, ed. Iwamura Shinobu et al., 12 vols., 9:230–232. Heibonsha, 1971–1975.

———. Letter to Iwata Jun'ichi, 7 October 1936. *Minakata Kumagusu zenshū*, ed. Iwamura Shinobu et al., 12 vols., 9:260–262. Heibonsha, 1971–1975.

———. Letter to Iwata Jun'ichi, 31 January 1937. *Minakata Kumagusu zenshū*, ed. Iwamura Shinobu et al., 12 vols., 9:267–271. Heibonsha, 1971–1975.

———. Letter to Iwata Jun'ichi, 14 June 1938. *Minakata Kumagusu zenshū*, ed. Iwamura Shinobu et al., 12 vols., 9:288–291. Heibonsha, 1971–1975.

———. Letter to Nakamatsu Morio, n.d. *Minakata Kumagusu zenshū*, ed. Iwamura Shinobu et al., 12 vols., 7:117–132. Heibonsha, 1971–1975.

Minami Takao. "Danshō ni kansuru ni-san no seishin igakuteki kōsatsu to sono shakai to no kanrensei ni tsuite." In *Dōseiai to dōsei shinjū no kenkyū*, by Komine Shigeyuki and Minami Takao, 272–282. Komine kenkyūjo, 1985.

———. "Danshō no seishin igaku: Dansei josei no seikaku ni kanren shite." In *Dōseiai to dōsei shinjū no kenkyū*, by Komine Shigeyuki and Minami Takao, 288–295. Komine kenkyūjo, 1985.

———. "Dōseiai: Sono kōsatsu to shori." In *Dōseiai to dōsei shinjū no kenkyū*, by Komine Shigeyuki and Minami Takao, 283–287. Komine kenkyūjo, 1985.

———. "Otoko-onna no hanashi." In *Dōseiai to dōsei shinjū no kenkyū*, by Komine Shigeyuki and Minami Takao, 296–300. Komine kenkyūjo, 1985.

Mishima Yukio. *Kamen no kokuhaku*. In *Mishima Yukio zenshū*, ed. Saeki Shōichi et al., 36 vols., 3:161–352. Shinchōsha, 1973–1976.

Mishina Shōei. *Chōsen kodai kenkyū, daiichibu: Shiragi karō no kenkyū*. Sanseidō, 1943.

"Mitabi Sōryū gidan no koto." *Yorozu chōhō*, 11 March 1900, 3.

Mitamura Engyo. "Choichoi no honzon." In *Mitamura Engyo zenshū*, ed. Mori Senzō et al., 28 vols., 12:178–189. Chūō kōronsha, 1975–1983.

———. "Dōseiai no iseika." In *Mitamura Engyo zenshū*, ed. Mori Senzō et al., 28 vols., 14:366–379. Chūō kōronsha, 1975–1983.

———. "Edo ni sukunai onnagata." In *Mitamura Engyo zenshū*, ed. Mori Senzō et al., 28 vols., 12:212–233. Chūō kōronsha, 1975–1983.

———. "Kan'eiji no Ueno." In *Mitamura Engyo zenshū*, ed. Mori Senzō et al., 28 vols., 8:296–353. Chūō kōronsha, 1975–1983.

———. "Ningenbi no kyōsō." In *Mitamura Engyo zenshū*, ed. Mori Senzō et al., 28 vols., 12:167–178. Chūō kōronsha, 1975–1983.

———. "Onnagata seijuku no jōken." In *Mitamura Engyo zenshū*, ed. Mori Senzō et al., 28 vols., 12:199–211. Chūō kōronsha, 1975–1983.

———. "Ryūyō no kenkyū." In *Mitamura Engyo zenshū*, ed. Mori Senzō et al., 28 vols., 12:344–354. Chūō kōronsha, 1975–1983.

———. "Ryūyō no mochinushi." In *Mitamura Engyo zenshū*, ed. Mori Senzō et al., 28 vols., 12:354–359. Chūō kōronsha, 1975–1983.

———. "Tsukiyo no sandai shōgun." In *Mitamura Engyo zenshū*, ed. Mori Senzō et al., 28 vols., 1:53–59. Chūō kōronsha, 1975–1983.

Mitsuo Sadatomo. *Kōbō Daishi ikkan no sho*. *Kinsei shomin bunka* 13 (1952): 13–24.

Miura Gorō. *Kanju shōgun kaikoroku.* Seikyōsha, 1925.
Miyagawa Mangyo. "Yushima yawa." Pt. 9 of a series titled "Edo jidai no sei-teki hanzai." *Hanzai kagaku,* February 1931, 63–72.
Miyahiro Sadao. *Kokueki honron.* In *Nihon shisō taikei,* ed. Ienaga Saburō et al., 67 vols., 51:291–309. Iwanami shoten, 1970–1982.
———. *Minka yōjutsu.* In *Kinsei chihō keizai shiryō,* ed. Ono Takeo, 10 vols., 5:263–320. Yoshikawa kōbunkan, 1931–1932.
Miyatake Gaikotsu. *Futanari kō.* In *Miyatake Gaikotsu chosakushū,* ed. Tanizawa Eiichi and Yoshino Takao, 8 vols., 5:320–394. Kawade shobō, 1985–1992.
———. *Kitai ryūkōshi.* In *Miyatake Gaikotsu chosakushū,* ed. Tanizawa Eiichi and Yoshino Takao, 8 vols., 4:319–454. Kawade shobō, 1985–1992.
———, ed. *Meiji kibun.* In *Miyatake Gaikotsu chosakushū,* ed. Tanizawa Ei-ichi and Yoshino Takao, 8 vols., 1:5–306. Kawade shobō, 1985–1992.
Monbushō sōmukyoku, ed. *Nihon kyōikushi shiryō.* 9 vols. Monbushō sō-mukyoku, 1890–1892.
Mori Ōgai. "Gaijō no koto o rokusu." In *Ōgai zenshū,* ed. Kinoshita Mokutarō et al., 38 vols., 29:154–156. Iwanami shoten, 1971–1975.
———. *Wita sekusuarisu.* In *Ōgai zenshū,* ed. Kinoshita Mokutarō et al., 38 vols., 5:83–179. Iwanami shoten, 1971–1975.
Moriguchi Kōji. "Tosa hansei kōki ni okeru 'chiin' kō: Wakazamurai no 'koi' no shūzoku." *Tosa shidan* 200 (1997): 45–52.
Morino Tatsuzō. "Otoko ni kobi o uru otoko." *Hanzai kōron,* May 1932, 217–220.
Morishima Nakayoshi. *Bankoku shinwa.* 5 vols. Edo: Suwaraya Ichibei, 1789.
———. *Kōmō zatsuwa.* In *Bunmei genryū sōsho,* ed. Kokusho kankōkai, 3 vols., 1:450–486. Taizansha, 1940.
Morita Yūshū. *Dōseiai no kenkyū.* Chiba: Jinsei sōzōsha, 1931.
———. *Hentai seiyoku hiwa.* Heibonsha, 1930.
———. *Jiyū ren'ai hiwa.* Heibonsha, 1930.
———. *Jiyū ren'ai to shakaishugi.* Shakai mondai sōsho, no. 7. Bunka gakkai shuppanbu, 1925.
———. "Sakutōkyōsha to shite no shijin Hoittoman." *Seiron,* July 1928, 58–63.
Moriya Takeshi. *Murashibai: Kinsei bunkashi no susono kara.* Heibonsha, 1988.
Morohashi Tetsuji. *Dai Kanwa jiten.* Rev. ed. 13 vols. Taishūkan, 1984–1986.
Morooka Son. "'Otokogirai' to 'onnagirai' to sono chiryōhō." *Kenkō no tomo,* April 1932, 14–19.
Morris, Ivan, trans. *Five Women Who Chose Love.* In *The Life of an Amorous Woman and Other Writings,* by Ihara Saikaku, 53–118. New York: New Directions, 1969.
———, trans. *The Life of an Amorous Woman.* In *The Life of an Amorous Woman and Other Writings,* by Ihara Saikaku, 119–208. New York: New Directions, 1969.
Mosse, George L. *Nationalism and Sexuality: Middle-Class Morality and Sex-*

ual Norms in Modern Europe. Madison: University of Wisconsin Press, 1988.

Motofuji, Frank, trans. *The Factory Ship,* by Kobayashi Takiji. In *"The Factory Ship" and "The Absentee Landlord,"* 1–83. Seattle: University of Washington Press, 1973.

Motoori Uchitō. *Senja kō.* In <Zōho> *Motoori Norinaga zenshū,* ed. Motoori Seizō, 13 vols., 12:145–195. Yoshikawa kōbunkan, 1926–1928.

———. *Wakanoura tsuru shō.* In <Zōho> *Motoori Norinaga zenshū,* ed. Motoori Seizō, 13 vols., 12:247–517. Yoshikawa kōbunkan, 1926–1928.

Mulvey, Laura. "Visual Pleasure and Narrative Cinema." *Screen* 16.3 (1975): 6–18.

Murakami Akio, trans. *Sei to seikaku.* Arusu, 1925. Translation of *Geschlecht und Charakter,* by Otto Weininger (1903).

Murakami Nobuhiko. *Meiji joseishi.* 4 vols. Rironsha, 1969–1972.

Murata Seiichi. "<Tokui nanshoku kō> Shimaya no bantō." *Kitan kurabu,* February 1954, 166–169.

Murata Tenrai and Saitō Masaichi. *Seiyoku to jinsei.* Bunkōdō shoten, 1912.

Murayama Kaita. *Murayama Kaita zenshū.* Ed. Yamamoto Tarō. Yayoi shobō, 1963.

Mushanokōji Saneatsu. "Kare." In *Mushanokōji Saneatsu zenshū,* ed. Inagaki Tatsurō et al., 18 vols., 1:3–17. Shōgakkan, 1988–1991.

Mutamagawa. In *Nihon meicho zenshū: Edo bungei no bu,* ed. Ishikawa Torakichi et al., 31 vols., 26:1–290. Nihon meicho zenshū kankōkai, 1926–1929.

Mutō Sadao. *Edo kobanashi jiten.* Tōkyōdō, 1965.

Nagareyama Ryūnosuke. *Ero-guro danshō nikki.* Sankōsha, 1931.

Nagoya shiyakusho. *Nagoya shishi: Fūzoku hen.* Nagoya: Nagoya shiyakusho, 1915.

Naikaku kanpōkyoku, ed. *Hōrei zensho.* Annual pub. Naikaku kanpōkyoku, 1887–.

Naikaku kirokukyoku, ed. *Hōki bunrui taizen.* 88 vols. Hara shobō, 1980.

Naimushō keihokyoku, ed. *Tokugawa jidai keisatsu enkakushi.* 2 vols. Keisatsu kenkyū shiryō, nos. 6 and 7. Naimushō keihokyoku, 1927.

Naitō Chisō. *Tokugawa jūgodaishi.* 12 vols. Hakubunkan, 1892–1893.

Nakahara Keizō. "Saikin furyō shōnen shōjo monogatari." *Chūō kōron,* December 1929, 149–158.

Nakajima Kawatarō. "Kaidai." In *Edogawa Ranpo zenshū,* 25 vols., 16:233–237. Kōdansha, 1978–1979.

Nakamura Kokyō. "Dōseiai no kaibō." *Fujin kōron,* June 1932, 435–438.

———. *Hentai seikakusha zakkō.* Hentai bunken sōsho, no. 3. Bungei shiryō kenkyūkai, 1928.

Nakano Kaichi. *Inagaki Taruho no sekai.* Hōbunkan shuppan, 1984.

Nakazawa Shin'ichi. "Kaidai: Jō no sekusorojī." In *Minakata Kumagusu korekushon,* ed. Nakazawa Shin'ichi, 5 vols., 3: 7–57. Kawade shobō, 1991–1992.

Nankai no Sanjin. *Nanshoku yamaji no tsuyu*. Vol. 6 of *Hihon Edo bungakusen*, ed. Yoshida Seiichi et al., 10 vols. Nichirinkaku, 1988–1989.

"Nanshoku adauchi bidan." *Hanzai kōron*, October 1932, 164.

Nattier, Jan. *Once upon a Future Time: Studies in a Buddhist Prophecy of Decline*. Nanzan Studies in Asian Religions, no. 1. Berkeley: Asian Humanities, 1991.

Needham, Joseph, et al. *Science and Civilisation in China*. 14 vols. to date. Cambridge: Cambridge University Press, 1954–.

Ng, Vivien W. "Ideology and Sexuality: Rape Laws in Qing China." *Journal of Asian Studies* 46 (1987): 57–70.

Nihon hōigakkai, trans. *Shikijōkyō hen*. Hōigakkai, 1894. Translation of *Psychopathia Sexualis*, by Richard von Krafft-Ebing (1896).

Nihon shoki. Vol. 1 of <*Shintei zōho*> *Kokushi taikei*, ed. Kuroita Katsumi et al., 66 vols. Yoshikawa kōbunkan, 1964–1967.

Ninomiya, Kazuji, and Sanford Goldstein, trans. *Vita Sexualis*, by Mori Ōgai. Rutland, Vt.: Tuttle, 1972.

Nishiki Bunryū. <*Naniwa chōja*> *Karanashi daimon yashiki*. In *Kindai Nihon bungaku taikei*, ed. Nonaka Jirō et al., 25 vols., 4:347–434. Kokumin tosho, 1926–1929.

Nishizawa Ippū. *Gozen Gikeiki*. In *Kindai Nihon bungaku taikei*, ed. Nonaka Jirō et al., 25 vols., 4:63–213. Kokumin tosho, 1926–1929.

———. *Onna daimyō Tanzen nō*. In *Kindai Nihon bungaku taikei*, ed. Nonaka Jirō et al., 25 vols., 4:215–346. Kokumin tosho, 1926–1929.

———. *Yakei tomojamisen*. In *Edo jidai bungei shiryō*, ed. Hayakawa Junzaburō et al., 5 vols., 2:315–353. Kokusho kankōkai, 1916.

Noguchi Takejirō. <*Onko chishin*> *Edo no hana*. Hakubunkan, 1890.

Noguchi Takenori and Paul Schalow. "Homosexuality." In *Kōdansha Encyclopedia of Japan*, 9 vols., 3: 217–218. Kōdansha, 1983.

Noma Kōshin. "Kaisetsu." In *Nihon shisō taikei*, ed. Ienaga Saburō et al., 67 vols., 60:373–399. Iwanami shoten, 1970–1982.

———. "Kaisetsu." In *Nihon koten bungaku taikei*, ed. Takagi Ichinosuke et al., 102 vols., 91:3–43. Iwanami shoten, 1957–1968.

Nomura Kanetarō. *Goningumichō no kenkyū*. Yūhikaku, 1943.

Nosco, Peter. *Remembering Paradise: Nativism and Nostalgia in Eighteenth-Century Japan*. Harvard-Yenching Institute Monograph Series, no. 31. Cambridge: Harvard University Press, 1990.

Oda Makoto. *Ichigo no jiten: Sei*. Sanseidō, 1996.

Ogawa Wataru. *Shigure sōshi*. Iinuma Sekiya, 1935.

Ōgokudō no Arittake. *Shikidō kinpishō*. Ed. Fukuda Kazuhiko. 2 vols. Ukiyoe gurafikku, nos. 2 and 3. KK besutoserāzu, 1990–1991.

Oguri Mushitarō. *Madōji*. Shirokuro shobō, 1936.

Ogyū Sorai. *Seidan*. In *Nihon shisō taikei*, ed. Ienaga Saburō et al., 67 vols., 36:259–445. Iwanami shoten, 1970–1982.

Ōhara Torao. *Nihon kinsei gyōkeishi kō*. 2 vols. Keimu kyōkai, 1943.

Oikawa Shigeru and Yamaguchi Seiichi. *Kyōsai no giga*. Tōkyō shoseki, 1992.

Oka Rokumon. *Zaioku waki*. Vols. 1 and 2 of *Zuihitsu hyakkaen*, ed. Mori Senzō et al., 15 vols. Chūō kōronsha, 1980–1981.

Oka Takurō, ed. *Nihon kindai keiji hōreishū*. 3 vols. Shihō shiryō bessatsu, no. 17. Shihōshō hishoka, 1945.

Okabe Tōhei. "Azunai kō." In *Ōō hitsugo*, ed. Nonoguchi Takamasa. In *Nihon zuihitsu taisei*, ed. Hayakawa Junzaburō et al., 81 vols.; 1st ser., 9:160–164. Yoshikawa kōbunkan, 1973–1979.

Okada Chōtarō. *Nihon keihōron*. Yūhikaku, 1894.

Okada Hajime, ed. <*Haifū*> *Yanagidaru zenshū*. 13 vols. Sanseidō, 1976–1984.

———. *Senryū suetsumuhana shōshaku*. 2 vols. Yūkō shobō, 1955.

Okamoto Kisen. *Sawamura Tanosuke akebono sōshi*. Vol. 11 of *Meiji bungaku meicho zenshū*, ed. Yamaguchi Tsuyoshi et al., 12 vols. Tōkyōdō, 1926–1927.

Omi Aya and Sakurai Yoshinari. "Kumoi Tatsuo den." In <*Tōhoku ijin*> *Kumoi Tatsuo zenshū*, ed. Omi Aya and Sakurai Yoshinari, (furoku) 1–19. Tōyōdō, 1894.

Ōmori Kaiin. "Rōgokunai no shūjin seikatsu." *Hanzai kōron*, July 1932, 170–175.

Ono Seiichirō. *Keihō kōwa*. Yūhikaku, 1932.

Ooms, Herman. *Tokugawa Village Practice: Class, Status, Power, Law*. Berkeley: University of California Press, 1996.

Oosterhuis, Harry, and Hubert Kennedy, eds. *Homosexuality and Male Bonding in Pre-Nazi Germany: The Youth Movement, the Gay Movement, and Male Bonding before Hitler's Rise: Original Transcripts from "Der Eigene," the First Gay Journal in the World*. New York: Harrington Park, 1991.

Origuchi Shinobu. "Kuchibue." In *Origuchi Shinobu zenshū*, ed. Origuchi hakase kinen kodai kenkyūjo, 32 vols., 24:1–78. Chūō kōronsha, 1965–1968.

Ortolani, Benito. *Das Kabukitheater: Kulturgeschichte der Anfänge*. Monumenta Nipponica Monograph no. 19. Sophia University Press, 1964.

Ōsaka Saburō. "Nanshoku kaidō o yuku." *Ryōki*, October 1947, 14–15.

Ōsaka-shi, ed. *Meiji Taishō Ōsaka shishi*. 8 vols. Nihon hyōronsha, 1933–1935.

Ōsaka-shi sanjikai, ed. *Ōsaka shishi*. 7 vols. Osaka: Ōsaka-shi sanjikai, 1911–1915.

Ōsawa Koresada. *Kibi onko hiroku*. Vols. 6–10 of *Kibi gunsho shūsei*, ed. Tanaka Seiichi and Morita Keitarō, 10 vols. Kibi gunsho shūsei kankōkai, 1921–1932.

Ōsugi Sakae. *Jijoden*. Kaizōsha, 1948.

Ōta Nanpo. *Ichiwa ichigen*. Supp. vols. 1–5 of *Nihon zuihitsu taisei*, ed. Hayakawa Junzaburō et al., 81 vols. Yoshikawa kōbunkan, 1973–1979.

———, ed. *Misonoya*. Ed. Hayakawa Junzaburō et al., 4 vols. Kokusho kankōkai, 1917.

Ōtorii Sutezō and Sawada Junjirō. *Danjo no kenkyū*. Kōfūkan shoten, 1904.

Otowaan Shujin [Ōhashi Matatarō]. "Otoko no ude." *Bungei kurabu*, April 1896, 91–161.

Ōtsuki Kenji. *Ren'ai seiyoku no shinri to sono bunseki shochihō*. Tōkyō seishin bunsekigaku kenkyūjo, 1936.

Ozaki Kyūya. "Oden Mitsu Segawa no sankaku kankei." *Edo nanpa kenkyū* 2 (1925): 49–63.

———. "Oden Mitsu Segawa no sankaku kankei ni okeru seikaku naru bunken." *Hentai shiryō*, December 1927, 65–78.

Ozaki Shirō. "Bishōnen no kenkyū." *Kaihō*, April 1921, 534–540.

Padgug, Robert A. "Sexual Matters: On Conceptualizing Sexuality in History." In *Hidden from History: Reclaiming the Gay and Lesbian Past*, ed. Martin Bauml Duberman et al., 54–64. New York: NAL, 1989.

Pflugfelder, Gregory M. Review of *Male Colors: The Construction of Homosexuality in Tokugawa Japan*, by Gary P. Leupp. *Monumenta Nipponica* 53 (1998): 276–280.

———. "'S' Is for Sister: Schoolgirl Intimacy and 'Same-Sex Love' in Early Twentieth-Century Japan." In *Gendering Modern Japanese History*, ed. Barbara Molony and Kathleen S. Uno. Cambridge: Harvard University Press, forthcoming.

———[Guregorī M. Furūguferudā]. *Seiji to daidokoro: Akita-ken joshi sanseiken undōshi*. Domesu shuppan, 1986.

———. "Strange Fates: Sex, Gender, and Sexuality in *Torikaebaya Monogatari*." *Monumenta Nipponica* 47 (1992): 347–368.

Plant, Richard. *The Pink Triangle: The Nazi War against Homosexuals*. New York: New Republic, 1986.

"Prevalence of Unnatural Crimes amongst Tokyo Students." *Eastern World*, 20 May 1899, 6.

"Prevalence of Unnatural Crimes amongst Tokyo Students." *Yorozu chōhō*, 23 May 1899, 2.

Ravina, Mark. *Land and Lordship in Early Modern Japan*. Stanford: Stanford University Press, forthcoming.

Rector, Frank. *The Nazi Extermination of Homosexuals*. New York: Stein, 1981.

Reischauer, A. K., trans. "Genshin's Ojo Yoshu: Collected Essays on Birth into Paradise." *Transactions of the Asiatic Society of Japan*, 2d ser., 7 (1930): 16–97.

Robertson, Jennifer. "Gender-Bending in Paradise: Doing 'Male' and 'Female' in Japan." *Genders* 5 (1989): 50–69.

———. "The Politics of Androgyny in Japan: Sexuality and Subversion in the Theater and Beyond." *American Ethnologist* 19 (1992): 419–441.

———. "The Shingaku Woman: Straight from the Heart." In *Recreating Japanese Women, 1600–1945*, ed. Gail Lee Bernstein, 88–107. Berkeley: University of California Press, 1991.

———. "Theatrical Resistance, Theatres of Restraint: The Takarazuka Revue and the 'State Theatre' Movement in Japan." *Anthropological Quarterly* 64.4 (1991): 165–177.

Roden, Donald. "Baseball and the Quest for National Dignity in Meiji Japan." *American Historical Review* 85 (1980): 511–534.

———. *Schooldays in Imperial Japan: A Study in the Culture of a Student Elite*. Berkeley: University of California Press, 1980.

———. "Taishō Culture and the Problem of Gender Ambivalence." In *Culture and Identity: Japanese Intellectuals during the Interwar Years*, ed. J. Thomas Rimer, 37–55. Princeton: Princeton University Press, 1990.

Rubin, Jay. *Injurious to Public Morals: Writers and the Meiji State*. Seattle: University of Washington Press, 1984.

Rucinski, Jack, trans. "Les joues en feu," by Hori Tatsuo. In *The Shōwa Anthology: Modern Japanese Short Stories*, ed. Van Gessel and Tomone Matsumoto, 2 vols., 1:28–37. Kōdansha International, 1985.

"Ryūyō-kun." *Yorozu chōhō*, 6 February 1897, 1.

Saeki Junko. *Bishōnenzukushi*. Heibonsha, 1992.

———. "'Ren'ai' no zenkindai, kindai, datsukindai." In *Sekushuariti no shakaigaku*, ed. Inoue Suguru et al., 167–184. Iwanami kōza gendai shakaigaku, no. 10. Iwanami shoten, 1996.

Saga monogatari. In *Muromachi jidai monogatari shūsei*, ed. Yokoyama Shigeru and Matsumoto Ryūshin, 15 vols., 5:336–352. Kadokawa shoten, 1973–1988.

Saigiku Sanjin [Jōno Denpei]. *<Sannin kyōkaku> Kagema no adauchi*. Junseidō, 1899.

Saiseiki. In *Nihon shomin bunka shiryō shūsei*, ed. Geinōshi kenkyūkai, 16 vols., 9: 113–130. San'ichi shobō, 1973–1978.

Saitō Ryūzō. *Genroku sesōshi*. Hakubunkan, 1905.

Saitō Shōzō. *Edo kōshoku bungakushi*. Seikō shoin, 1949.

Saitō Tamao. "Danshi no seiyoku to daisan shigeki." *Kenkō jidai*, July 1931, 11–13.

Saitō Yozue. *Sekusorojisuto Takahashi Tetsu*. Seikyūsha, 1996.

Sakai Shizu. *Nihon no iryōshi*. Tōkyō shoseki, 1982.

Sakai Toshihiko. *Danjo tōsōshi*. Eisendō shoten, 1920.

———. "Hashigaki." In *Josei chūshinsetsu/Dōseiai*, trans. Sakai Toshihiko and Yamakawa Kikue, 1–2. Arusu, 1919.

Sakai Toshihiko and Yamakawa Kikue, trans. *Josei chūshinsetsu/Dōseiai*. Arusu, 1919. Translation of *Pure Sociology*, by Lester Ward (1903), and *The Intermediate Sex*, by Edward Carpenter (1908).

Sakaki Yasusaburō. *Kawarimono*. Jitsugyō no Nihonsha, 1912.

———. *Seiyoku kenkyū to seishin bunsekigaku*. Jitsugyō no Nihonsha, 1919.

Sakuragi Menzō. "Josō no hentai otoko o tōte sono sei shinri o kiku." *Kenkō jidai*, January 1932, 96–99.

Sasakawa Tanerō. *Genroku jiseishō*. Hakubunkan, 1901.

Sasanoya. "Nanshoku." Pt. 1. *Fūzoku gahō*, September 1893, 11–13.

———. "Nanshoku." Pt. 5. *Fūzoku gahō*, February 1894, 18–19.

Sato, Barbara Hamill. "The *Moga* Sensation: Perceptions of the *Modan Gāru* in Japanese Intellectual Circles during the 1920s." *Gender and History* 5 (1993): 363–381.

Satō Kōka. *Jinrui hiji kō*. Bungei shiryō kenkyūkai, 1929.

———. "Seiyokugaku goi." Pts. 1 and 2. *Hentai shiryō*, November 1926 and June 1927 issues.

————. *Senryū hentai seiyokushi.* Onko shobō, 1927.

Satomi Ton. *Kimi to watashi.* In *Satomi Ton zenshū,* 10 vols., 1:85–201. Chikuma shobō, 1977–1979.

Sawada Junjirō. *Hentaisei to kyōraku.* Sekai ryōki zenshū, no. 9. Heibonsha, 1932.

————. *Ren'ai to seiyoku.* Kōbundō, 1922.

————. *Seiai jinsei.* Isseidō shoten, 1936.

————. "Seikan ijō no byōri oyobi shinri." Pt. 1. *Sei,* February 1921, 31–36.

————. "Seiteki hanmon kaiketsu." *Sei to ren'ai,* July 1921, 146–148.

————. "Seiteki yūgi to baiin." *Sei,* January 1921, 50–55.

————. *Seiyoku hanzai.* Kindai no kekkonsha, 1923.

————. *Shinpi naru dōseiai.* Kyōekisha shuppanbu, 1920.

————. *Shinpi naru dōseiai.* 2 vols. Tenkadō shobō, 1920.

Schalow, Paul Gordon. "The Invention of a Literary Tradition of Male Love: Kitamura Kigin's *Iwatsutsuji.*" *Monumenta Nipponica* 48 (1993): 1–31.

———— [Pōru Sharō]. "Josei no 'nanshokuron.'" *Bungaku* 6.1 (1995): 67–71.

————. "Kūkai and the Tradition of Male Love in Japanese Buddhism." In *Buddhism, Sexuality, and Gender,* ed. José Ignacio Cabezón, 215–230. Albany: State University of New York Press, 1992.

————. "Male Love in Early Modern Japan: A Literary Depiction of the 'Youth.'" In *Hidden from History: Reclaiming the Gay and Lesbian Past,* ed. Martin Bauml Duberman et al., 118–128. New York: NAL, 1989.

————. "Spiritual Dimensions of Male Beauty in Japanese Buddhism." In *Religion, Homosexuality, and Literature,* ed. Michael L. Stemmeler and José Ignacio Cabezón, 75–94. Gay Men's Issues in Religious Studies Series, no. 3. Las Colinas, Tex.: Monument, 1992.

————, trans. *The Great Mirror of Male Love,* by Ihara Saikaku. Stanford: Stanford University Press, 1990.

Screech, Timon [Taimon Sukurīchi]. *Ō-Edo ijin ōrai.* Trans. Takayama Hiroshi. Maruzen bukkusu, no. 36. Maruzen, 1995.

Sedgwick, Eve Kosofsky. *Between Men: English Literature and Male Homosocial Desire.* New York: Columbia University Press, 1985.

"*Sei* hakkan no ji." *Sei,* January 1920, 1–2.

Seigle, Cecilia Segawa. *Yoshiwara: The Glittering World of the Japanese Courtesan.* Honolulu: University of Hawaii Press, 1993.

Seikanbō Seiwa. *Kaidan toshiotoko.* In *Tokugawa bungei ruijū,* ed. Hayakawa Junzaburō, 12 vols., 4:448–491. Kokusho kankōkai, 1914–1916.

Seki Yuidō. *Danjo kōgō tokushitsu mondō.* Takebe Takisaburō and Kimura Inosuke, 1886.

"Senryū." *Marumaru chinbun* 88 (1878): 1405–1406.

"Senryū." *Marumaru chinbun* 98 (1879): 1566.

Setagaya Uboku. "Shina no ryūyōheki." *Kōgai,* June 1926, 16–24.

Shibayama Hajime. *Edo nanshoku kō: Akusho hen.* Hihyōsha, 1992.

————. *Edo nanshoku kō: Shikidō hen.* Hihyōsha, 1993.

Shigematsu Kazuyoshi. *Nihon keibatsushi nenpyō.* Yūzankaku, 1972.

―――. *Zukan Nihon no kangokushi.* Yūzankaku, 1985.
Shimizu Sadao. *Jitsuyō saiban igaku.* N.p.: Eimeikan, 1890.
Shimokawa Kōshi. *Shōwa seisōshi.* 3 vols. Dentō to gendaisha, 1980–1981.
Shimokawa Kōshi et al. *Josō no minzokugaku.* Hihyōsha, 1994.
<Shin bungei tokuhon> Takahashi Tetsu. Kawade shobō, 1993.
Shin sayoarashi. In *Nihon meicho zenshū: Edo bungei no bu,* ed. Ishikawa Tora-
    kichi et al., 31 vols., 9: 719–756. Nihon meicho zenshū kankōkai, 1926–1929.
Shinkoku chūtongun shireibu. *Pekin shi.* Hakubunkan, 1908.
Shinpen Aizu fūdoki. Vols. 30–34 of *Dainihon chishi taikei,* ed. Ashida Ijin et
    al., 40 vols. Yūzankaku, 1929–1933.
"Shinsho ryakuhyō." *Yorozu chōhō,* 30 October 1901, 1.
Shin'yūki. In *Nihon shisō taikei,* ed. Ienaga Saburō et al., 67 vols., 60:7–25.
    Iwanami shoten, 1970–1982.
Shirakawa Masayoshi. *Inagaki Taruho.* Tōjusha, 1976.
Shirakawa-shi, ed. *Shirakawa shishi.* 6 vols. to date. Shirakawa: Shirakawa-shi,
    1989–.
Shitō Masataka. *Sendai rukeishi.* Sendai: Hōbundō, 1980.
Shively, Donald H. "*Bakufu* versus *Kabuki.*" In *Studies in the Institutional His-
    tory of Early Modern Japan,* ed. John W. Hall and Marius B. Jansen, 231–261.
    Princeton: Princeton University Press, 1968.
Shizu no odamaki. Ichikawa Teishirō, 1885.
Shōgaku tosho. *Nihon hōgen jiten.* 3 vols. Shōgakkan, 1989.
Shohōken. *Shinjū ōkagami.* In *Kinsei bungei sōsho,* ed. Hayakawa Junzaburō
    et al., 12 vols., 4:181–233. Kokusho kankōkai, 1910–1912.
Shoku Nihongi. Vols. 12–15 of *Shin Nihon koten bungaku taikei,* ed. Satake
    Akihiro et al., 68 vols. to date. Iwanami shoten, 1989–.
Shōsaiō. *Gengenkyō.* In *Sharebon taisei,* ed. Mizuno Minoru et al., 31 vols.,
    3:303–313. Chūō kōronsha, 1978–1988.
Shōsei. "Meijiza." *Yorozu chōhō,* 13 March 1899, 1.
Shōyūsei. "Watakushi no taiken shitsutsu aru dōseiai." *Sei,* June 1921,
    108–110.
Shūkin Joshi. *Onna isha.* Seikōkan, 1902.
Shunroan Shujin. *Edo no shikidō: Seiai bunka o himotoku kindan no ezu to
    kosenryū.* 2 vols. Yōbunkan shuppan, 1996.
"Shūto shūto o korosu." *Yorozu chōhō,* 7 October 1900, 3.
Sibalis, Michael David. "The Regulation of Male Homosexuality in Revolu-
    tionary and Napoleonic France, 1789–1815." In *Homosexuality in Modern
    France,* ed. Jeffrey Merrick and Bryant T. Ragan, Jr., 80–101. New York: Ox-
    ford University Press, 1996.
Sibley, William F., trans. "Morning Fog (Correspondence on Gay Lifestyles),"
    by Minakata Kumagusu and Iwata Jun'ichi. In *Partings at Dawn: An An-
    thology of Japanese Gay Literature,* ed. Stephen D. Miller, 135–171. San Fran-
    cisco: Gay Sunshine, 1996.
Silverberg, Miriam. "Constructing a New Cultural History of Prewar Japan."

In *Japan in the World,* ed. Masao Miyoshi and H. D. Harootunian, 115–143. Durham: Duke University Press, 1993.

———. "The Modern Girl as Militant." In *Recreating Japanese Women, 1600–1945,* ed. Gail Lee Bernstein, 239–266. Berkeley: University of California Press, 1991.

Smith, Henry D., II. "The History of the Book in Edo and Paris." In *Edo and Paris: Urban Life and the State in the Early Modern Era,* ed. James L. McClain et al., 332–352. Ithaca: Cornell University Press, 1994.

Sōgi. *Chigo kyōkun.* In *<Shinkō> Gunsho ruijū,* ed. Hanawa Hokinoichi et al., 24 vols., 14:161–165. Naigai shoseki, 1928–1937.

Sōma Hiroyoshi. *<Eisei> Danjo hōten.* Keibunkan, 1908.

"Sōryū gidan no koto." *Yorozu chōhō,* 7 March 1900, 3.

Sotozaki Mitsuhiro. *Nihon fujinron shi.* 2 vols. Domesu shuppan, 1986–1989.

Statler, Oliver. *Shimoda Story.* New York: Random House, 1969.

Steakley, James D. *The Homosexual Emancipation Movement in Germany.* New York: Arno, 1975.

Stein, Edward, ed. *Forms of Desire: Sexual Orientation and the Social Constructionist Controversy.* Garland Gay and Lesbian Studies, no. 1. New York: Garland, 1990.

Suekane Naokichi [Miyazaki Koshoshi]. *Nihon jōkō no hensen.* Banseidō, 1887.

Sugawara Michinari. *Dōseiai.* San'aku tsuihō kyōkai, n.d.

Sugie Kaoru. "Hidōteki sodomiya no ichirei." *Sei,* September 1920 (zōkan), 171–176.

Sugimoto. *Shimeshigoto amayo no takegari.* In *Edo no bidō o tanoshimu: Seiai bunka no tankyū,* ed. Shunroan Shujin, 63–75. Miki shobō, 1995.

Sugimoto, Masayoshi, and David L. Swain. *Science and Culture in Traditional Japan,* A.D. 600–1854. M.I.T. East Asian Science Series, no. 6. Cambridge: MIT Press, 1978.

Sugita Naoki. "Hentai seiyoku no shujusō." *Kenkō no tomo,* January 1932, 2–7.

———. *Kindai bunka to sei seikatsu.* Sei kagaku zenshū, no. 2. Bukyōsha, 1931.

———. "Seiyoku oyobi sono ijō." *Bungei shunjū,* March 1931, 190–204.

Suisaishi. *Zatto ichiran.* In *Sharebon taisei,* ed. Mizuno Minoru et al., 31 vols., 26:239–261. Chūō kōronsha, 1978–1988.

"Suki na otoko, suki na onna." *<Kokon> Momoiro sōshi,* February 1928, 24–33.

Sumi Tatsuya. *Danshō no mori.* Hibiya shuppansha, 1949.

Suweyo-Iwaya [Iwaya Sazanami]. "Nan-šo-k' (die Päderastie in Japan)." *Jahrbuch für sexuelle Zwischenstufen* 4 (1902): 265–271.

Suzuki Kura. *<Meiji gonin dokufu no hitori> Shimazu Masa kaishin jitsuroku.* Yōmanrō, 1895.

Suzuki Toshibumi. *Sei no dendōsha: Takahashi Tetsu.* Kawade shobō, 1993.

Suzuki Toshio. *Edo no hon'ya.* 2 vols. Chūkō shinsho, nos. 568, 571. Chūō kōronsha, 1980.

Symonds, John Addington. *Male Love: A Problem in Greek Ethics and Other Writings.* Ed. John Lauritsen. New York: Pagan, 1983.

———. *The Memoirs of John Addington Symonds.* Ed. Phyllis Grosskurt. New York: Random House, 1984.

Taigasha Kihō. *Sanzen sekai iro shugyō.* In *Tokugawa bungei ruijū,* ed. Hayakawa Junzaburō, 12 vols., 3:257–290. Kokusho kankōkai, 1914–1916.

Takada Giichirō. *Hentai iwa.* Chiyoda shoin, 1936.

———. *Hentai seiyoku kō,* Sei kagaku zenshū, no. 12. Bukyōsha, 1931.

———. *Hentai seiyoku to hanzai, hanzai to jinsei.* Kindai hanzai kagaku zenshū, no. 1. Bukyōsha, 1929.

———. *Tōseijutsu.* Hakubunkan, 1928.

Takada Mamoru. *Edo gensō bungakushi.* Heibonsha, 1987.

Takagi Shunsuke. *Ējanaika.* Kyōikusha rekishi shinsho Nihonshi, no. 93. Kyōikusha, 1979.

Takahashi Katsuhiko. *Shinbun nishikie no sekai: Takahashi Katsuhiko korekushon yori.* PHP kenkyūjo, 1986.

Takahashi Tetsu. *Jinseki: Nihon interigenchiya issenmei no zangeroku.* Vol. 1. Amatoriasha, 1952.

Takamure Itsue. *Josei no rekishi.* Vols. 4 and 5 of *Takamure Itsue zenshū,* ed. Hashimoto Kenzō, 10 vols. Rironsha, 1965–1967.

Takaratsu Shusō [or Niimi Masatomo]. *Mukashi mukashi monogatari.* In *Zoku Nihon zuihitsu taisei,* ed. Mori Senzō and Kitagawa Hirokuni, 24 vols., supp. vol. 1:31–67. Yoshikawa kōbunkan, 1979–1983.

Takeda Akira. *Kyōdaibun no minzoku.* Kyoto: Jinbun shoin, 1989.

Takeda Rintarō. "Kamagasaki." *Chūō kōron,* March 1933, (sosaku) 53–76.

Takemura Tamio. *Haishō undō: Kuruwa no josei wa dō kaihō sareta ka.* Chūkō shinsho, no. 663. Chūō kōronsha, 1982.

Takeshiba Kisui. *Kami no megumi wagō no torikumi.* In *Nihon gikyoku zenshū,* ed. Ihara Seiseien et al., 50 vols., 32: 356–417. Shun'yōdō, 1929.

Takizawa Bakin. *Kinsesetsu bishōnenroku.* Ed. Miura Osamu. 2 vols. Yūhōdō shoten, 1913–1917.

Tamenaga Shunsui. <*Seishi jitsuden*> *Iroha bunko.* Ed. Miura Osamu. Yūhōdō shoten, 1913.

Tametō Gorō. *Taishō shin risshiden.* Dainihon yūbenkai, 1921.

Tanaka Kōgai. *Ai to zankoku.* Osaka: Fukuinsha shoten, 1925.

———. "Danseikan ni okeru dōseiai." *Nihon oyobi Nihonjin* 792 (1920): 107–116.

———. "Danseiteki joshi (ginandorīru)." *Hentai seiyoku,* March 1924, 104–110.

———. "Dōseiai ni kansuru gakusetsu ni tsuite." Pts. 1 and 2. *Hentai seiyoku,* March 1924, 117–121; April 1924, 169–172.

———. "Joseiteki danshi." *Hentai seiyoku,* February 1923, 49–60.

———. "Joseiteki danshi (andoroginī, Androgynie) no hanashi." In *Ki chin kai,* 204–209. Hōmeidō shoten, 1953.

———. "Joshi no danseika no byōriteki gen'in ni kansuru chiken hoi." *Hentai seiyoku,* December 1924, 255–257.

———. "Joshi no danseika no gen'in ni kansuru shinchiken." *Hentai seiyoku,* July 1924, 1–7.

———. "Josō suru hentai otoko to dansō suru hentai onna no hanashi." *Kenkō jidai*, December 1931, 108–112.

———. *Ki chin kai*. Hōmeidō shoten, 1953.

———. "Nanshoku ni kansuru shiteki oyobi bungakuteki kōshō." *Hentai seiyoku*, June 1924, 195–235.

———. *Ningen no seiteki ankokumen*. Ōsaka yagō shoten, 1922.

———. "Onna ni narisumashita otoko: Seiyoku tentōshō no ichirei." *Hentai seiyoku*, June 1925, 303–309.

———. "Onnagirai." In *Ki chin kai*, 144–148. Hōmeidō shoten, 1953.

———. "Shippitsu o oete." *Hentai seiyoku*, December 1924, 283–284.

———. "Tasei henshin no gen'in ni kansuru gakusetsu ni tsuite." *Hentai seiyoku*, March 1925, 105–113.

Tanizaki Jun'ichirō. "Akubi." In *Tanizaki Jun'ichirō zenshū*, 28 vols., 1: 299–329. Chūō kōronsha, 1966–1971.

———. "Itansha no kanashimi." In *Tanizaki Jun'ichirō zenshū*, 28 vols., 4:377–452. Chūō kōronsha, 1966–1971.

———. *Yōshō jidai*. In *Tanizaki Jun'ichirō zenshū*, 28 vols., 17:41–253. Chūō kōronsha, 1966–1971.

Tan'o Yasunori. "Honchō nanshoku bijutsu kō." *Hikaku bungaku nenshi* 26 (1990): 164–188.

Taoka Reiun. *Sūkiden*. In *Taoka Reiun zenshū*, ed. Nishida Masaru, 3 vols. to date, 5: 415–743. Hōsei daigaku shuppankyoku, 1969–.

"Teikoku kaigun to Yamamoto Gonnohyōe." Pt. 2. *Yorozu chōhō*, 3 July 1899, 1.

"Teikoku kaigun to Yamamoto Gonnohyōe." Pt. 4. *Yorozu chōhō*, 6 July 1899, 1.

"<Tengoku ka jigoku ka> Danshi dōseiaisha no tsudoi." *Ningen tankyū*, January 1951, 70–83.

Tenkōsei. "Hangyakusha no sakebi." *Hentai seiyoku*, January 1923, 45–47.

Tenshū Koji [Nishimura Tenshū]. "Satsuma shinjū." *Miyako no hana*, 15 February 1891, 1–22.

Teramoto Kaiyū. *Kabato kangoku shiwa*. Tsukigata, Hokkaido: Tsukigata-mura nanajūshūnen kinen sonshi hensan iinkai, 1950.

Tezuka Yutaka. *Meiji keihōshi no kenkyū*. Vols. 4–6 of *Tezuka Yutaka zenshū*, ed. Fujita Hiromichi and Terasaki Osamu, 10 vols. Keiō tsūshin, 1982–1994.

TK-sei. "Danshi dōseiaisha no kekkon ni tsuite." *Hentai seiyoku*, March 1923, 138–140.

Tomita Koreyuki. *Okushū kikō*. In *Nanbu sōsho*, ed. Ōta Kōtarō et al., 11 vols., 6:481–516. Morioka: Nanbu sōsho kankōkai, 1927–1931.

Torigoe Miyoshi, trans. *Gōkan kensatsuhō*. Matsui Chūbei, 1879.

Totman, Conrad. *Early Modern Japan*. Berkeley: University of California Press, 1993.

Toyoda Takeshi et al., eds. *<Aizu-han> Kasei jikki*. 16 vols. Yoshikawa kōbunkan, 1975–1990.

Tsubouchi Shōyō. *<Ichidoku santan> Tōsei shosei katagi*. Vol. 1 of *Meiji bungaku meicho zenshū*, ed. Yamaguchi Tsuyoshi et al., 12 vols. Tōkyōdō, 1926–1927.

Tsuchiya Megumi. "Chūsei jiin no chigo to warawamai." *Bungaku* 6.1 (1995): 40–49.

Tsuchiya Terumi. "Keimushonai no sei no nayami." *Seiron,* December 1928, 62–63.

Tsukioka Settei. *Onna dairaku takarabako. Kinsei shomin bunka* 19 (1953): 7–31.

Tsukiyosei. "Hiokamaron." *Marumaru chinbun* 1595 (1906): 4.

Tsunoda, Ryusaku, et al., eds. *Sources of Japanese Tradition.* New York: Columbia University Press, 1958.

Ubukata Toshirō. *Meiji Taishō kenbunshi.* Chūō kōronsha, 1978.

Ueno Chizuko. "Kaisetsu." In *Nihon kindai shisō taikei,* ed. Katō Shūichi et al., 24 vols., 23:505–550. Iwanami shoten, 1988–1992.

Ujiie Mikito. *Bushidō to erosu.* Kōdansha gendai shinsho, no. 1239. Kōdansha, 1995.

———. *Edo no shōnen.* Heibonsha, 1989.

———. "From Young Lions to Rats in a Ditch." In *Imaging/Reading Eros: Proceedings for the Conference, Sexuality and Edo Culture, 1750–1850,* ed. Sumie Jones, 115–118. Bloomington: East Asian Studies Center, Indiana University, 1996.

———. *Fugi mittsū: Kinjirareta koi no Edo.* Kōdansha sensho mechie, no. 88. Kōdansha, 1996.

Ulrichs, Karl Heinrich. *The Riddle of "Man-Manly" Love: The Pioneering Work on Male Homosexuality.* Trans. Michael A. Lombardi-Nash. 2 vols. Buffalo, N.Y.: Prometheus, 1994.

Umehara Hokumei, ed. *Meiji seiteki chinbunshi.* 3 (?) vols. Bungei shiryō kenkyūkai, 1926–?.

———, ed. *<Meiji Taishō> Kidan chinbun daishūsei.* 3 vols. Bungei shijōsha, 1929–1931.

Uno Kōji. "Futari no Aoki Aizaburō." In *Uno Kōji zenshū,* ed. Hirotsu Kazuo et al., 12 vols., 3:196–241. Chūō kōronsha, 1978–1979.

Uo Daigaku. "Oyama gyōjōki." *Hanzai kagaku,* August 1931, 73–76.

Urushiya Ensai. *Nanshoku kinometsuke.* In *Mikan chinpon shūsei,* ed. Sobu Fukurō and Imaoka Yoshio, 4 vols., 3:57–253. Koten hozon kenkyūkai, 1933–1934.

Van der Meer, Theo. "The Persecutions of Sodomites in Eighteenth-Century Amsterdam: Changing Perceptions of Sodomy." In *The Pursuit of Sodomy: Male Homosexuality in Renaissance and Enlightenment Europe,* ed. Kent Gerard and Gert Hekma, 263–307. New York: Harrington Park, 1989.

Van Gulik, R. H. *Sexual Life in Ancient China: A Preliminary Survey of Chinese Sex and Society from ca. 1500 B.C. till 1644 A.D.* Leiden: Brill, 1974.

Vance, Carole S. "Social Construction Theory and Sexuality." In *Constructing Masculinity,* ed. Maurice Berger et al., 37–48. New York: Routledge, 1995.

Varner, Richard E. "The Organized Peasant: The *Wakamonogumi* of the Edo Period." *Monumenta Nipponica* 32 (1977): 459–483.

Vitiello, Giovanni. "Taoist Themes in Chinese Homoerotic Tales." In *Religion, Homosexuality, and Literature,* ed. Michael L. Stemmeler and José Ignacio Cabezón, 95–103. Gay Men's Issues in Religious Studies Series, no. 3. Las Colinas, Tex.: Monument, 1992.

"Wakashu no jishitsu." *Kono hana* 18 (1911): 19.

Waseda daigaku Tsuruta monjo kenkyūkai, ed. *Nihon keihō sōan kaigi hikki.* Waseda daigaku toshokan shiryō sōkan, no. 1. 6 vols. Waseda daigaku shuppanbu, 1976–1977.

Washburn, Dennis. "Manly Virtue and the Quest for Self: The *Bildungsroman* of Mori Ōgai." *Journal of Japanese Studies* 21 (1995): 1–31.

Watanabe Shin'ichirō. "Kagemajaya hanjōki." *Kokubungaku: Kaishaku to kanshō,* February 1975 (zōkan), 90–106.

Watanabe Tsuneo. "Kindai, dansei, dōseiai tabū." Pt. 1 of "Bunmei oyobi tōsaku no gainen." *Kōchi daigaku gakujutsu kenkyū hōkoku: Jinbun kagaku* 29 (1980): 27–45.

———. "'Sekai himitsu' to kannōsei no shisutemu: Bunmei no shinsō ni hisomu 'danseisei no zeijakusa.'" *Dorumen* 3 (1990): 6–25.

Watanabe, Tsuneo, and Jun'ichi Iwata. *The Love of the Samurai: A Thousand Years of Japanese Homosexuality.* Trans. D. R. Roberts. London: GMP, 1989.

Watanuki Rokusuke. "Akisame ni saku dariya." <*Kokon*> *Momoiro sōshi,* December 1928, 80–94.

———. "Aku no miryoku." *Hentai shinri,* July 1926, 108–115.

———. "Aru onna no isshō." *Hentai shinri,* August 1926, 63–68.

———. <*Chōhen shōsetsu*> *Sensō.* Shūhōkaku, 1924.

———. "Dōkei no hi: Aru chūseisha no nayami." *Hentai shinri,* September 1926, 102–105.

———. "Shizuka naru fukushū." *Hentai shiryō,* April 1928, 106–127.

——— <*Sōsaku*> *Reiniku o mitsumete.* Shizensha, 1923.

———. <*Tantei shōgun*> *Akashi Motojirō: Nichiro sensō chōhō hishi.* Kiroku bungaku sōsho, no. 4. Kawade shobō, 1937.

———. "Watakushi no hentai shinri." *Hentai shinri,* May 1923, 557–567.

Watanuki Yosaburō. <*Enju tokushi*> *Fujin to danshi no eisei.* Shanhai shinchisha Tōkyō bunkyoku, 1905.

Wawrytko, Sandra A. "Homosexuality and Chinese and Japanese Religions." In *Homosexuality and World Religions,* ed. Arlene Swidler, 199–230. Valley Forge, Pa.: Trinity International, 1993.

Weatherby, Meredith, trans. *Confessions of a Mask,* by Mishima Yukio. New York: New Directions, 1958.

Weeks, Jeffrey. *Coming Out: Homosexual Politics in Britain, from the Nineteenth Century to the Present.* London: Quartet, 1977.

Wigen, Kären. "Mapping Early Modernity: Geographical Meditations on a Comparative Concept." *Early Modern Japan* 5.2 (1995): 1–13.

Wile, Douglas. *Art of the Bedchamber: The Chinese Sexual Yoga Classics, Including Women's Solo Meditation Texts.* Albany: State University of New York Press, 1992.

Wilson, William Scott, trans. *Hagakure: The Book of the Samurai,* by Yamamoto Tsunetomo. Kōdansha International, 1979.

Wolff, Charlotte. *Magnus Hirschfeld: A Portrait of a Pioneer in Sexology.* London: Quartet, 1986.

"Yaban gakusei no torishimari." *Yorozu chōhō,* 16 February 1898, 2.

Yamada Bimyō. *<Shintai shika> Wakashu sugata.* Kōun shooku, 1886.

Yamaguchi-ken monjokan, ed. *Yamaguchi-ken shiryō.* 4 vols. to date. Yamaguchi: Yamaguchi-ken monjokan, 1973–.

Yamamoto Akira. *Kasutori zasshi kenkyū: Shinboru ni miru fūzokushi.* Shuppan nyūsusha, 1976.

Yamamoto Hirofumi. *Junshi no kōzō.* Sōsho shi no bunka, no. 19. Kōbundō, 1994.

Yamamoto Seikichi. *Gendai no furyō seinen, tsuketari furyō joshi.* Shun'yōdō, 1914.

Yamamoto Seinosuke, ed. *Senryū Meiji sesōshi.* Makino shuppan, 1983.

Yamamoto Tsunetomo. *Hagakure.* In *Nihon shisō taikei,* ed. Ienaga Saburō et al., 67 vols., 26:213–579. Iwanami shoten, 1970–1982.

Yamamoto Yoshio. *Saiban igaku.* Shimamura Risuke, 1886.

Yamamura Saisuke. *Seiyō zakki.* 4 vols. Edo: Suzuki bun'enkaku, 1848.

Yamashita Seizō. *Kakke no rekishi: Bitamin hakken izen.* Tōkyō daigaku shuppankai, 1983.

Yamauchi Toyoaki et al., eds. *Yamauchi-ke shiryō: Dainidai Tadayoshi-kō ki.* 4 vols. Kōchi: Yamauchi jinja hōmotsu shiryōkan, 1980–1981.

Yamazaki Toshio. *Bidō.* Vol. 1 of *Yamazaki Toshio sakuhinshū,* ed. Ikuta Kōsaku, 3 vols. to date. Kobe: Sabato yakata, 1986–.

Yamazaki Yoshishige. *Gimonroku.* In *Zoku enseki jisshu,* ed. Ichijima Kenkichi et al., 2 vols., 2:361–378. Kokusho kankōkai, 1908–1909.

———. *San'yō zakki.* In *Nihon zuihitsu taisei,* ed. Hayakawa Junzaburō et al., 81 vols.; 2d ser., 6:63–162. Yoshikawa kōbunkan, 1973–1979.

<Yanagidaru yokō> Yanaibako. In *Shodai senryū senkushū,* ed. Chiba Osamu, 2 vols., 2:5–143. Senryū shūsei, nos. 5 and 6. Iwanami shoten, 1986.

Yanagigori. In *Shodai senryū senkushū,* ed. Chiba Osamu, 2 vols., 2:145–181. Senryū shūsei, nos. 5 and 6. Iwanami shoten, 1986.

Yarō kinuburui. Kinsei shomin bunka 13 (1952): 25–39.

Yasuda Tokutarō. "Dōseiai no rekishikan." *Chūō kōron,* March 1935, 146–152.

Yasumaru Yoshio. "'Kangoku' no tanjō." In *Bakumatsu Meijiki no kokumin kokka keisei to bunka hen'yō,* ed. Nishikawa Nagao and Matsumiya Hideharu, 279–312. Shin'yōsha, 1995.

YK-sei. "Dōseiaisha no kurushimi." *Hentai seiyoku,* May 1923, 238–239.

Yoneyama Tatsuo. "Dōseiai o kataru." *Kyūdai ihō* 6 (1932): 38–42.

"Yorozu kogoto." *Yorozu chōhō,* 8 March 1900, 3.

Yoshida Hanbei. *Kōshoku kinmō zui.* In *Kōshokumono sōshishū,* ed. Yoshida Kōichi, 2 vols., 1:49–122. Kinsei bungei shiryō, no. 10. Koten bunko, 1968.

———. *Nanshoku masukagami.* In *Kōshokumono sōshishū,* ed. Yoshida Koichi, 2 vols., 1:265–338. Kinsei bungei shiryō, no. 10. Koten bunko, 1968.

Yoshida Kōu. *<Akuji kaishun> Shimazu Omasa no rireki*. Osaka: Taikadō, 1888.

Yoshida Setsuko, ed. *Edo kabuki hōrei shūsei*. Ōfūsha, 1989.

Yoshii Bantarō.*<Jitchi ōyō> Saiban igakuron*. Taihōkan, 1887.

Yoshinaga Toyomi. *Tosa-han hōseishi*. Izumi shuppan, 1974.

Yoshitake Teruko. *Nyonin Yoshiya Nobuko*. Bungei shunjū, 1982.

"Yotabi Sōryū gidan no koto." *Yorozu chōhō*, 12 March 1900, 3.

Yūbin hōchi shinbun, 30 April 1881.

<Yunootōge magojakushi> Nanshoku taiheiki. In *Edo no ehon: Shoki kusazōshi shūsei*, ed. Koike Masatane et al., 4 vols., 4:35–52. Kokusho kankōkai, 1987–1989.

Zwilling, Leonard. "Homosexuality As Seen in Indian Buddhist Texts." In *Buddhism, Sexuality, and Gender*, ed. José Ignacio Cabezón, 203–214. Albany: State University of New York Press, 1992.

Index

A., 299–300, 302

Abortion, 150

Acolytes (*chigo*), 74–75, 196, 263, 264, 308n. *See also* Buddhist clergy

Acquired same-sex love, 268, 271–277, 278–279

Active/masculine and passive/feminine construction, 261–267, 272, 301–302, 321–322, 323

Actor evaluation books, 45n, 58

Actor-prostitutes: changing professional norms of, 58, 90–91; in domains, 134–135, 138–141; kabuki imitators, 118–120; *kagema* (see *Kagema*); military and, 284; segregation of, 116–118, 143, 155, 156; shaven forelocks of, 115–116; as symbol of sophistication, 69. *See also* Kabuki

Adolescence: Edo-period concept of (*see* Youth); juvenile delinquents, 224–225; male-male sexuality associated with, 211–212, 223–224, 263–264, 276–277, 288, 295; Meiji conception of, 211–212; students (*see* Student culture and sexuality)

Adonisu (Adonis), 330

Adoption, 180n

Adultery: and Edo-period legal discourse, 106, 109, 126–127; and Meiji legal discourse, 149–150, 165, 187. *See also* Marriage

Adulthood: medico-scientific model and, 263

Age: assumed to structure male-male sexuality, 18, 159, 166–168, 175–176, 252–253, 262, 267; Confucianism and, 103; of consent, 127, 159, 161n, 162, 163, 168–169, 171, 178, 181; consent constrained by hierarchies of, 217; of *kagema*, 280; of marriage, and same-sex love, 273–274, 285; medico-scientific model and, 252–253, 263, 267; of *nenja*, 36–37; prisons and hierarchy of, 185; reckoning of, 30n; of youth, defining, 30–34, 91, 116n, 252–253, 276–277, 280

Ainu, 4n, 6n

Aizu, 128n, 133, 138, 143, 161, 213, 219n

Akamatsu Keisuke, 330

Akashi Motojirō, 328

Akita (prefecture), 140

Akita Ujaku: "Dōsei no koi," 231

"Akuma no deshi" (Devil's Apprentice, Hamao Shirō), 315–316

Alcoholism, 285

Alternate attendance system, 136

Anal intercourse: anus, qualities of, 237; criminalization of, Meiji, 153,

Anal intercourse *(continued)*
   158–168, 183–187, 192; insertee
   assumed not to enjoy, 41–43, 55–
   56, 75, 167, 262, 268–269; *kawatsurumi* as term for, 86; *keikan* as
   term for, 159, 161–162, 162n;
   legalization of, Meiji, 168–182,
   190–191, 192; lubricants, 239;
   male-female, 159, 231n; medical
   discourse and, Edo period, 236–240;
   medical discourse and, Meiji, 240–
   241, 246–248; *nenja* as penetrating
   partner in, 37, 38, 41; noncriminal
   status of, Edo period, 158; noncriminal status of, Meiji, 158; and
   prison regulation, 183–189, 190–
   192; as quintessential practice of
   shudō, 41; rape (*see* Rape)
Ānanda, 86
Anayoshi, 59n
Androgyny, 256–257
Angyūsai: *Kari tsūshō kō*, 67
Anrakuan Sakuden: *Seisuishō*, 75, 104n
Aomori, 136. *See also* Hirosaki
Apprentices and shop boys, 43, 79,
   158n, 196, 238, 284
Ārāḍa Kālāma, 86
Arashi Daishi, 195n
"Argument against *Okama*" (Tsuki-
   yosei), 323
Arima, 239n
Ariwara Narihira, 88, 89
Ars erotica/scientia sexualis dichotomy,
   6–7, 10, 13
Asakusa, 195n, 310, 311, 317–318,
   319, 322, 324–326, 330
Asano Yoshinaga, 236
Azuma no Kamiko: *Fūryū hiyokudori*,
   40n, 61, 72–74, 80, 87n, 91, 104n,
   109n, 236n
Azunai, 99–100, 327

Baijōken: *Yodarekake*, 30n, 31n, 41n,
   51n, 64, 87
Bakufu. *See* Shogunal legislation
Bakuro (Exposé), 299
Ball and chain, 186–187, 191

Bamboo flute (*shakuhachi*): 302, 318
Bandō Mitsugorō III, 38n
Baseball, 257n
Bashō. *See* Matsuo Bashō
Bathhouses, regulation of, 147
Beautiful boys (*bishōnen*): in Meiji popular discourse, 194, 205, 209, 218,
   221, 225–234, 263, 281, 301, 305
Beauty: Edo-period ideals of, 35–36,
   54, 81; Meiji conception of, 226–
   227, 228–229; twentieth-century,
   301n, 306, 307; Western ideals
   of, 281n; of youths and females,
   comparability of, 35–36, 39, 54,
   228–229, 255–256, 281
Beriberi, 237
Bestiality, 100, 170, 172
Besu, 65
Biology: behavior as originating in
   body, 3, 269; etiology of same-sex
   love and, 269–270; male-female
   sexuality considered mandated by,
   21, 241, 243–244, 253; sex dichotomy and, 252, 253; unnatural acts
   and, 240–242, 243–244; youths and
   females compared in terms of, 281;
   zoological sexuality and, 240–242,
   243, 260
Bisexuality: as construct, 5, 252. *See
   also* Psychic hermaphrodism; Two-
   sex love
Bishamonten, 50, 67
Bishōnen (beautiful boys): in Meiji
   popular discourse, 194, 205, 209,
   218, 221, 225–234, 263, 281, 301,
   305
Bishōnen (Beautiful Boys, Inaoka
   Masafumi), 205n, 227
Bishōnenron (On the Beautiful Boy,
   Kōmurō Shujin), 225–227, 229–
   230, 248, 249, 263, 292, 306
Blackmail, 299
Blind (*zatō*), 73
Bloch, Iwan, 245n, 271
Body: signs of male-male sexual
   behavior, 174–175, 177, 246, 247;
   as source of behavior (*see* Biology)

Boissonade, Gustave, 169n, 170–171, 178n, 180, 181
Boorishness: ostentation and, 78; peasantry and, 80–81; samurai and, 73; as term, 81; townsman youths and, 79
Boys' literature, 227–228
Boys' theater, 228
Britain, 162, 258n
Brotherhood and loyalty oaths, 40–41; Edo-period legal discourse and, 108–109, 125–126, 127–132, 137, 185, 329; female version of, 190; flesh rituals, 41, 52, 90, 91; Meiji medical discourse and, 247–248; permanence of, 41; samurai class and, 71, 90, 91, 328
Buddhism: cross-dressing and, 151–152; and desire, 25; end of the law, *shudō* and, 91–92; insertee, and causes of desire for position of, 268; medical discourse and, 240; Meiji attacks on and reforms of, 198–199, 204; nativist observations of, 89, 101; priests and monks as terms in book, 26n; six paths of being (*rokudō*), 67–68, 241; texts of, and male-male sexuality, 64, 67–68, 86, 101; as way, 28, 82–83. *See also* Religion; Shinto
Buddhist clergy: celibacy and, 91, 101–102, 198–199, 242; Christian missionaries and, 65; connoisseurship of, 26; erotic texts and, 46; extended youth status and, 34; and *joshoku*, 101; Kūkai (*see* Kūkai); lay population as succeeding, in *shudō* prevalence, 90, 91, 313; legal discourse and, 102, 107–108, 155, 156, 198–199; literacy and, 46; marriage of, 198–199; medico-scientific view of, 199, 272, 281, 283; misogyny of, 74, 85, 94; prostitution and, 75–76, 101–102, 195n, 281; and public tolerance, 173, 199; in *senryū*, 91, 94, 101, 102, 195n, 197–198, 236n, 237; *shudō* texts and, 26, 47, 50–51, 61, 73–76, 91, 239–240
Buke shohatto, 110, 124
Bunjaku, 216
Burton, Richard, 283
Bushidō, 90. *See also* Samurai class
Butaiko, 68–69
Byakkotai, 219–220, 225

Callahan, Caryl, 71
Calligraphy, 28
Capitalism: proletarian literary movement and, 309
Capital punishment: Buddhist clergy and, 102; Chinese use of, 162; of convicts, 182; in domains, 125, 126, 127–128, 138, 140–141; European use of, 154, 162; prostitution and, 154
Caron, François, 97, 99
Carpenter, Edward, 259, 307, 314, 315, 316
Censorship: during wartime, 327–328; in Edo period, 200; failures of, 335; in Meiji period, 20, 199–201, 226n, 249, 284, 291, 292–293, 303, 304, 335; relaxing of, 329; in twentieth century, 292–293, 294, 301–302, 322, 329
Cherry-viewing, 152
Chidaruma (Bloodstained Bodhidharma), 201, 227
Chigo (acolytes), 74–75, 196, 263, 264, 308n. *See also* Buddhist clergy
Chigokasegi, 209
Chigo kyōkun (Precepts for Acolytes, Sōgi), 52, 74
Chigo monogatari, 46, 74, 85n, 89
Chigo no sōshi (Book of Acolytes), 28, 46, 74, 239
Chigouta, 209
Chiin. See Friendship
Chikamatsu Monzaemon, 70
Childhood, congenital same-sex love and, 257
Children's ditties, 196
Child Welfare Law, 157n

China: civilized morality and, 161–162; in Edo-period imagination, place of, 63–64; laws of, as influence, 106, 127, 159n, 161–162, 163, 172, 184; legitimization of *shudō* texts and, 63–64, 84–85, 86; male-male sexuality in, 63–64, 65, 243n, 284; medical discourse of, 235–236
Chōnin. See Townsman class
Chōshū. *See* Hagi
Christianity and male-male sexuality, 2, 42n, 65, 66, 98–99, 102, 104–105, 124n, 165–166, 170, 180, 201, 246, 271, 272, 300
Chrysanthemums, 85n, 164, 198, 200n, 209n, 323
Chūō kōron (Central Review), 312
Citong, 85n
Civilization: barbaric past cast in opposition to, 204; reinscription of same-sex love in, 285; as term, 20, 146–147
Civilized morality: Chinese influence on, 161–162; defined, 20, 147–148; enforcement of (*see* Legal discourse, Meiji; Popular discourse, Meiji); journalism and, 163, 219–220; and medical discourse, Meiji, 246; native context for, 146–148; as paradigm, 8, 19–20, 286; relativization of, 233–234; Western influence on (*see* The West)
Civil law, 149, 180
Climate theories, 171, 282–283
Clothing: prisons and, 185; regulation of, 115n, 121, 137, 151–153, 155, 258; roughnecks as defined by, 215, 216, 219, 221; youth as defined by, 33. *See also* Cross-dressing
Cohen, Stanley, 218, 221
Coming-of-age ceremony (*genbuku*), 33, 34
Commercialization: of publishing (*see* Publishing industry); of sexuality (*see* Prostitution)
Commercial sector: male-male sexuality and, 196–197, 284–285. *See also* Townsman class
Compound sex trope, 260–261, 276
Concubinage: and marriage, 38, 40; as protected, 106; protections nullified, 149, 172
Condoms, 244
Confucianism: ethical schema of, 102–104; legal discourse and, 104, 106, 111, 117n, 130, 132, 143; medical discourse and, 246; scholars of, in *shudō* texts, 73; *shudō* and, 55, 56, 103, 104, 131–132; socioeconomic hierarchy of, 70, 73, 80, 116–117, 143, 145, 148; as way, 28
Confucius: male-male sexuality and, 85–86
Congenital same-sex love, 226, 257, 268–271, 272, 273, 275, 276, 278, 282, 308
Connoisseurship: of Buddhist clergy, 26; of *nenja*, 56–59, 61, 295
Consent: age of, 127, 159, 161n, 162, 163, 168–169, 171, 178, 181; coerced, 178, 179; as concept, 181; lack of (*see* Rape; Violence); prisons and, 192; school environments and, 217
Conspiracy (*totō*), 129–132, 144, 185
Constructionism, 3–4
Contraception, 150, 244
Control culture, 221
Country of Rear-Lovers, 66n
Courtesans. *See* Prostitution, female
"Courtesans Are Better; No, Actors Are Better" (Ihara Saikaku), 59, 61, 80
Criminology, 311–314
Cross-dressing: female, 151–153, 190, 265n; legal discourse and, 151–153, 166–168, 258; medico-scientific model and, 257–258, 265; new *kagema* and, 322, 330; in *shudō* texts, 33n; twentieth-century journalism and, 265
Cross-sex love (*iseiai*): and compound sex trope, 261, 276; as excluding

same-sex love, 252, 267; as norm, 21, 252, 273; repressed desire for, 272; as term, 21, 251–252; two-sex love as normative in development of, 276. *See also* Male-female sexuality

Daikokuya Kodayū, 65n
Daimyo: laws governing, 110, 124; medico-scientific view of, 266, 272; pages of, 127–128, 129n, 136–137, 266. *See also* Domains
Daishin'in, 165, 166n, 174n, 178n, 187n
Danshoku. See *Nanshoku*
Danshō no mori (Grove of Male Prostitutes, Sumi Tatsuya), 331
Dazai Osamu, 223
Decadent students, 218–225, 311, 316, 317
Deformed Male (Fugo no Otoko), 297, 298, 299
Degenerate Germany (Henry de Halsalle), 324
Degeneration, 261, 263, 269, 282, 324
Denbu monogatari (Boors' Tale), 31, 47, 60, 61, 73, 80, 104n, 238, 266
"Denouncing the Great Evil of *Nan-shoku* That Lurks beneath the Surface of Student Society" (Kawaoka Chōfū), 229, 230, 285
Dildos, 23n, 177
Disciplinary paradigm. See *Shudō*, as a way
Discourse: hybrids of, 13–14; masculine as subject in, 14, 24, 25, 27, 30, 248n; realms of (*see* Legal discourse; Medical discourse; Popular discourse)
Divorce, 149–150
Dō. See *Way*
Domains, 11, 105, 124–125; bakufu control of, 110, 124, 136; commercialized *shudō* and, 134–143, 144; early Meiji administration of, 158; legal discourse in, 102, 124–142, 144–145, 158; names of, 124n; power structures in, 127–132

Donden, 301n
Doriphorus, 173, 199, 250, 282, 324
Dōseiai: as term, 248, 251–252, 292. *See also* Same-sex love
Dōseiai no kenkyū (Study of Same-Sex Love, Morita Yūshū), 260
Dōseiai no shujusō (The Many Faces of Same-Sex Love, Albert Moll), 293
Dōseiaisha: as identity, 261, 271, 297
"Dōsei no koi" (Love for the Same Sex, Akita Ujaku), 231
Double suicide. *See* Love suicide

Eastern World, 172–173, 177
Economic power: and access to publications, 24, 54
Edayoshi Saburōzaemon, 128
Edogawa Ranpo, 314–315
Edo period: censorship in, 200; China and, 63–64; forensic medicine during, 175; legal discourse of (*see* Legal discourse, Edo period); medical discourse of, 235–240, 241, 243, 244; Meiji museumification of, 206, 219, 278, 285, 334; polity of, 11, 105; popular discourse of (see *Shudō* texts); population registers of, 150n; as term, 15, 16–17, 18
Education. *See* Schools; Student culture and sexuality
Effemination: of beautiful boys, 229–230; effeminists, 319n; inversion trope and, 255–258, 280, 322, 332
Egalitarianism: and *shudō*, 37, 82
Eguchi Jō, 177
Ejaculation, 42n, 105, 165–166, 174, 236
Ejima (lady-in-waiting), 122
Ejima Kiseki, 53; *Keisei kintanki*, 62, 94, 243; on natural facility for *shudō*, 268n; on outcasts, 141n; on Shinto gods, 100n; on transition to male-male erotic behavior, 38n; on woman-haters, 40, 79–80

Electricity and coitus, 245–246
Ellis, Havelock, 7, 315
Ema Tsutomu, 318n
Enma, 68, 197
Environment. *See* Acquired same-sex
    love
Erections, 43n, 247
Ero-guro culture: crime and mystery
    and, 311–317; male-male erotic
    subculture and, 317–321, 330–333;
    postwar, 329–330; prostitution and,
    318–326, 330, 331–333; as term,
    290; and war, 327–329
Ero-guro danshō nikki (*Ero-guro*
    Diary of a Male Prostitute,
    Nagareyama Ryūnosuke), 322
Erotic debate, 57, 59–63, 272; audience
    of, 80; and Buddhism, 74, 80;
    household demise and, 104n; and
    jealousy, 40n; on reproductive
    function, 243; as world cultural
    tradition, 59–60
Eroticism: as term, 6
Etō Shinpei, 167
Eugenics, 179
Euphemisms. *See* Male-male sexual-
    ity, terms for
Europe. *See* The West
Evil places (*akusho*), 117–118, 120,
    137, 142–143, 223n
Eviration. *See* Effemination
Evolutionary theory, 243–244, 261

Family: acquired same-sex love and,
    275–276; social morality and,
    180–181. *See also* Marriage
Fecal matter, 174, 237, 238
Fellatio, 41n, 174, 302
Female-female sexuality: Buddhism
    and, 101; causes of, 272; current
    legal status of, 179–180; dildos and,
    23n, 177; legal discourse and, Edo
    period, 104, 176; male-male sexu-
    ality as isolated from, 23, 27, 60,
    104; male-male sexuality as parallel
    with, 21, 248, 303; in popular dis-
    course, Meiji, 189, 190; prisons and,

176, 182n, 183, 189–192; regulation
    of, Meiji, 168, 175, 176–177, 178,
    189–192; regulation of, Western,
    258n; same-sex love construct and,
    14, 175, 248, 252, 254, 287, 292,
    293, 303, 309n; visibility of, 285
Female-male sexuality. *See* Male-
    female sexuality
Females, 253; adultery laws and, 106,
    126–127, 149–150; anatomy of,
    244; as domestic laborers, 93;
    family structures as regulating,
    181; gender regulation of, 150–153;
    hatred of (*see* Misogyny); honor
    and, 72; humor and, 27, 29–30, 39,
    59n, 104n, 195n; masculinity of,
    152, 257; as samurai, 44n, 72; sexual
    relations with (*see* Female-female
    sexuality; Male-female sexuality);
    and *shudō* texts, 53–54; youths
    compared with, 35–36, 39, 54, 228–
    229, 255–256, 281
Femininity: of males (*see* Effemina-
    tion; Gender); of West, 250. *See
    also* Masculinity
Fetishism, 32, 289
First Higher School, 221
Flower arrangement, 28, 29, 49, 198
Fly boys (*tobiko*), 138–141, 143, 144
Folk medicine, 237–239
Folkways, *shudō* relegated to, 210
Forelocks: concealment of shaven,
    115–116, 119; regulation of, 33–34,
    115–116, 121, 122, 123; twentieth-
    century beauty ideals and, 306;
    youth as defined by, 32, 33–34
Forensic pathology, 13–14, 174–177, 254
Fornication, Meiji regulation of, 159,
    162
Foucault, Michel, 236; and *ars erotica/
    scientia sexualis* dichotomy, 6–7,
    10, 13; and hydraulic model of
    sexuality, 278; on prisons, 183;
    and transformation of sexual
    categories, 2
Four estates, 70, 73, 80, 116–117, 143,
    145, 148

France, 161–163, 168, 170–171, 172, 324
Free love, 308
Freud, theories of. *See* Psychoanalytic theory
Friedländer, Benedict, 250, 251, 279–280, 323
Friendship: Meiji period and, 231, 233; *shudō* and, 103, 129–131
Fudō, 67
Fujian, 64
Fujimoto Kizan, 69
Fujin gahō (Ladies' Pictorial), 303
Fujisawa Morihiko, 280
Fukiyachō, 117
Fukuda (family), 176–177
Fukuda Hideko, 189–190, 192
Fukui, 140n
Fukushima (prefecture), 133, 134, 207n. *See also* Aizu; Shirakawa (Fukushima)
Fukushima Masanori, 268, 274
Fukuzawa Yukichi, 149
Funai, 138
Furth, Charlotte, 235
Furuichi, 47n
Fūryū hiyokudori (Stylish Pair of Wing-Sharing Birds, Azuma no Kamiko), 40n, 61, 72–74, 80, 87n, 91, 104n, 109n, 236n
Fūryū sangokushi (Stylish Romance of the Three Kingdoms, Nishizawa Ippū), 62
Fuwa Bansaku, 88, 204n

Gakusha, 208n
Gata, 324
Gay bars, 330–331
Geisha: entertaining with *kagema*, 59n; female clientele of, 190; as supplanting *kagema*, 156–157, 195
Gender: active/masculine and passive/feminine construction, 261–267, 272, 301–302, 321–322, 323; of beautiful boys, 228–230, 280; compound sex trope, 260–261, 276; difference, erotic attraction

dependent on, 261–262; intermediate sex trope, 258–260, 261; inversion trope and, 255–258, 261, 280, 281, 314–315, 322; kabuki regulation and, 113–114, 115–116; medico-scientific model and, 253–254, 255–268, 279–280; men-women (*otoko-onna*), 166–167, 264–265; of *nenja*, 37, 39; regulation of, Edo period, 113–114, 115–116, 152–153; regulation of, Meiji, 150–153, 166–168, 190; of *wakashu*, 34–36, 228, 229, 262, 263–264
Gender differences: in adultery prosecution, 106, 126–127, 149–150; in education, 214; in family controls, 181; in literacy, 24, 46
Gengenkyō (Sutra of Opaque Wisdom, Shōsaiō), 33n, 43, 60n, 62, 66, 68n, 79
Genroku era, 95, 219, 333, 334
Genshin, 67–68
Germany: *Ehrenrat* of, 221; influence of, on medical discourse, 247, 249–251, 259–260, 269, 280, 282; Japanese influence on research of, 249–251, 282; laws of, 168, 172, 179, 258n; of the Nazis, 179, 264n, 326
Geschlecht und Charakter (Otto Weininger), 260
Gifu, 140n
Ginza, 324
Giri. See Honor
Gojū, 208, 211, 213
Gonpachi, 126–127
Gorensan, 324
Great Deity of *Shudō*, 100n
Great Mirror of Male Love, The (Ihara Saikaku), 24, 29; age variance of *nenja* in, 36; on contemporary *shudō*, 89, 334; extended youth portrayed in, 34, 116n, 256, 264; influence of, 47, 48; legitimacy invoked for, 51, 100–101; on lovesickness, 240n; misogyny in, 66; multiple editions

Great Mirror of Male Love (continued)
of, 46; samurai class and, 70, 76, 80,
91, 129n; and schools, 212n; townsman class and, 76, 77–78, 80, 91;
youths and females contrasted in,
35, 61–62
Greece, 2, 25, 59, 60n, 233, 250, 272,
281n, 293, 308
Guo Ju, 85, 197n

Habuto Eiji, 140n, 254, 257, 258, 263n,
264n, 271, 272, 273, 274, 278–279,
280, 284–285, 291–292, 294, 334,
335
Hachiman, 140n
Hagakure (In the Shadow of Leaves,
Yamamoto Tsunetomo), 47, 48,
76–77, 128–129, 167
Hagi, 129–130, 211, 215
Hair: gender regulation and, 151, 153,
258, 319; and *shudō* (*see* Forelocks)
Hakujin, 94
Halperin, David, 3, 59–60
Halsalle, Henry de, 324
Hamao Shirō, 278n, 315–316, 326n
Han. *See* Domains
Hanabusa Shirō. *See* Nakano Masato
Hanai Ume, 190n
Hanayagi Biraku. *See* Shaji Hisaichi
Hand-holding, 189
Hand signals, 217
Han dynasty, 84, 243n
Haniwari, 253n. *See also* Intersexuality
Hanzai kagaku (Criminal Science),
312, 318
Hanzai kōron (Crime Review), 312
Harootunian, Harry, 243
Hatchōbori, 156
Hatto no jōmoku, 127–128
Hayashi Jiken, 84, 86
Hekogumi, 207–208, 213
Hell, 67–68
Hemorrhoids, 175, 238, 240, 244n,
264n
Henderson, Dan, 109, 145
Hentai chishiki (Perverse Knowledge),
287

Hentai jūnishi (Twelve Perverse
Histories), 287
Hentai seiyoku (Perverse Sexual
Desire), 287, 297, 299–300, 302,
303
Hentai seiyokuron (On Perverse
Sexual Desire, Habuto Eiji and
Sawada Junjirō), 254n, 257–258,
263n, 264n, 271, 272, 273, 274,
278–279, 280, 284–285, 291–292
Hentai shinri (Perverse Psychology),
287, 300
Hentai shiryō (Perverse Materials),
287, 300
Heredity: and beautiful boys, 226;
eugenics, 179; same-sex love and,
226, 269, 278, 308, 327
Hermaphrodism. *See* Intersexuality
Hermaphrodism, psychic, 252, 267,
279, 300. *See also* Two-sex love
Heterosexuality: as term, 5, 25, 252
Hibiya Park, 318, 325n
Hidō, 28n, 64, 86
Higeotoko (Man with a Beard, Kōda
Rohan), 205
Hikaru Genji, 88
Hinsch, Bret, 84, 87–88
Hirado, 32n, 269
Hiraga Gennai: class background of,
70; and decline of *shudō*, 91–92, 93,
95; on erotic debate, 60; *Mitsu no
asa*, 65, 93, 135n, 138, 139;
Nenashigusa, 68, 197, 257;
Nenashigusa kōhen, 68, 69, 89,
91–92, 241n; on *shudō* origins, 87n
Hirata Atsutane, 89, 242
Hirata Sangorō, 209–210, 227, 278
Hirosaki, 125n, 136, 137
Hiroshima, 138–139, 143
Hirschfeld, Magnus, 173, 249–250,
259–260, 264n, 270, 276, 280, 315,
324–326
Hisaya, 140–141
Hokkaido, 6n, 69, 147n, 185, 186, 191
Holland: Dutch learning (*rangaku*), 65,
66, 67, 244; sodomy trials in, 154
Home Ministry, 165, 200

Homosexuality: as construct, 175,
214–215, 248; and erotic debate,
59–60; same-sex love as influenced
by concept of, 175–176, 248, 251; as
term, 4–5, 12, 23–25, 29, 30; terms
used in book (*see* Female-female
sexuality; Male-male sexuality;
Same-sex love; *Shudō*)
Honchō nanshoku kō (Study of
Nanshoku in Our Realm, Iwata
Jun'ichi), 312–313
Honor: and domain power structures,
128–129; of household, and sexual
behavior, 169–170, 180–181;
maturity and, 31; prisoners' codes
of, 191; samurai code of, 70–72,
76–77, 204, 328; of townsman
class, 76–77
Honpu Yasushirō, 208–209
Hood, Edward, 245
Hori Tatsuo, 223
Hormones, 253, 270
Hosoi Heishū, 132
Hotei, 134n
Household registry system (*koseki*),
150, 153, 170
Hsia dynasty, 85
Huang, Ray, 17
Humor: and Buddhist clergy, 75, 91,
94, 101, 102, 195n, 197–198, 236n,
237; criminality of anal intercourse, 163–164; on extended
youth, 34; female ignorance of
shudō, 104n; females as usurping
male prerogatives, 27, 29–30;
gender of *kagema*, 36n, 259n;
male-male sexuality between
adults, 33n; of Meiji period,
194–203. See also *Senryū*
Hyōjōsho, 108–109
Hypnosis, 178, 179, 275, 276
Hysteria, 238, 257

Ibaragi, 166
Ichigaya, 101
Ichikawa Genzō, 277
Iemitsu. *See* Tokugawa Iemitsu

Ieyasu. *See* Tokugawa Ieyasu
Ihara Saikaku: censorship of, 200, 335;
didacticism of, 53; erotic debate
and, 35, 59, 60–61, 80; *Great
Mirror of Male Love* (see *Great
Mirror of Male Love, The*); history
and, 333–334; *Kōshoku ichidai
otoko*, 29, 36–37, 39, 139, 184n,
304; nativism of, 87; as psychic
hermaphrodite, 279n; and Shinto
gods, 100n; *Yorozu no fumihōgu*,
239–240
Ikken nakama, 325n
Ikushima Daikichi, 122n
Ikushima Shingorō, 122
Illustrations, censorship of, 201
Imperial Diet, 148
Importuning, 111–112, 116, 143
Inaba Kotoji, 164n, 166–168, 265
Inagaki Taruho, 217n, 226n, 305–307,
310n, 317–318, 324, 328
Inaoka Masafumi: *Bishōnen*, 205n,
227
Incense peddlers (*kōguuri*), 123, 140,
141
Incest, 170, 171, 172, 268
India: and *shudō* origins, 64, 65, 85–86
Individuals: identity as same-sex love
person, 261; juridical status of, 181;
legal identity of, 150; sexology and,
296
Infanticide, 150
Inoue Kenkichi, 184–185
I novels (*shishōsetsu*), 305
Insertee: assumed to lack desire, 41–43,
55–56, 75, 167, 262, 268–269, 301;
beautiful boys in Meiji popular
discourse, 194, 205, 209, 218, 221,
225–234, 263, 281, 301, 305; as
desiring subject, 42n, 262–263,
300–301, 321–322; of Edo period
(*see* Youth); health of, 238–239,
244n, 246–247; as immune to
prosecution for rape, 168, 184;
medico-scientific model and,
261–266; physical signs of, 174–
175, 246; of West, 226, 263

Inserter: of Edo period (see *Nenja*);
health of, 229, 230, 236–238,
246–247; medico-scientific model
and, 261–262, 265–268; Meiji
roughnecks, 133, 212–225, 227,
229, 230, 272, 283, 303; physical
signs of, 174, 246; popular
discourse and, Meiji, 230
Institute for Sexual Science, 264n, 326
Interfemoral intercourse, 41n, 241,
245–246
Intermediate Sex, The (Edward
Carpenter), 307
Intermediate sex trope, 258–260, 261
Intersexuality, 150–151, 166, 253n,
259n; and same-sex love, conflation
of, 270; and sex dichotomy, 252,
253; sex reassignment and, 270
Inu tsurezure (Mongrel Essays in
Idleness, Konoe Nobuhiro), 41n,
43, 51, 78–79, 90, 91, 241n, 262
Inversion trope, 177, 255–258, 261,
280, 281, 314–315, 322, 331n, 332
Iroha bunko (Library of ABCs,
Tamenaga Shunsui), 96
Iroko, 154, 205
Iro monogatari, 30n, 61, 62, 85, 89
Iseai, as term, 21, 251–252. *See also*
Cross-sex love
Ise shrine, 47n, 107
Ishida Mitsunari, 229
Ishikawa (prefecture), 125. *See also*
Kanazawa
Ishikawa Kiyotada, 175
Ishinpō (Essential Medical Prescrip-
tions, Tanba Yasuyori), 235
Ishizuka Hōkaishi, 93, 120
Ishizumi Harunosuke, 319
Isle of Dwarves, 66n
Isle of Men, 66
Isle of Women, 66
Italy, 66. *See also* Rome
Iwata Jun'ichi, 44, 59n, 134–135, 232,
312–313, 327–328
Iwatsutsuji (Rock Azalea, Kitamura
Kigin), 88–89, 313

Iwaya Sazanami, 223, 250, 264n, 277,
282, 324
Izanagi, 87, 242
Izanami, 87, 242
Izawa Banryō, 86

Jahrbuch für sexuelle Zwischenstufen,
250
Jakarta, 65
Jakudō. See *Nyakudō*
Japan: American Occupation of, 6n,
17, 329–333; defined for purposes
of study, 6n; languages of, 4n;
study of sexuality in, 7–8
Japanese Society for Psychiatric
Medicine, 294
"J. A. Symonds's Secret Passion"
(Edogawa Ranpo), 314
Jie, 85
Jigamiuri, 123n
Jinkyo, 236, 247
Jiru, 84
Jitsugokyō, 50–51
Jiwakashu, 59, 321
Jōno Denpei: *Kagema no adauchi*,
121n, 205–206
Jōruri, 26n
Joshoku: Buddhist warnings against,
101; in decline, 91–92, 94–95; as
eclipsing *nanshoku*, 38–39; as elemental dyad, 235–236, 242–243;
female evocations of *shudō*, 30,
119, 253; kabuki and, 113–114,
115; moral panic and, 222–223;
and Sino-Japanese medicine,
235–237; as term, 25, 27; of
twentieth century (*see* Cross-
sex love). *See also* Male-female
sexuality
Journalism: criminality and male-male
sexuality in, 316–317; criminalization of anal intercourse and, 163,
164; cross-dressing coverage in,
265; gender enforcement and, 153;
humor in, 202; and moral panic
over roughnecks, 218–223; non-

criminalization of male-male
sexual acts and, 172–173; personal
ads in, 273; postwar male-male
erotic subculture and, 331–332;
regulation of, 200; sexological case
studies drawn from, 296–297; and
shizoku, 204
Juvenile delinquents, 224–225

Kabato prison, 185, 188
Kabiya Kazuhiko, 331
Kabuki: actor evaluation books, 45n,
58; bakufu regulation of, 112–120;
censorship of, Meiji, 201; domain
regulation of, 137–138, 139–140;
medico-scientific view of, 283;
men's, 115; playbooks as excluded
from study, 26n; prostitutes and
(*see* Actor-prostitutes); prostitution
as closely aligned with, 78, 93, 116;
rise of, 90; *shudō* themes in, 113–
114, 201, 205n; theater district,
segregation into, 116–118, 143,
155, 156, 318; *wakashu*, 112, 113–
114, 115; women's, 113. *See also*
Prostitution
Kabukiko, 114, 123, 141
Kabukimono, 130
Kaempfer, Engelbert, 97, 99, 135, 239
Kagema: adult careers of, 157n, 264;
age of, 280; in children's song,
196n; decline of, 93, 95, 156–157,
194–196; entertaining with geisha,
59n; erotic subjectivity of, 42n,
262, 280–281; females as imper-
sonating, 30, 119, 253; health of,
238, 280; as intersexed, 36n, 259n;
male/female clientele of, 34, 38,
121–122, 155–156, 264, 280;
medico-scientific view of, 280–
281; new, of twentieth century,
318–326; popular image of, Meiji,
227; regulation of, Edo period,
119–121, 154–156; as term, 120,
141. *See also* Actor-prostitutes;
Prostitution

Kagemajaya (teahouses): decline of,
93, 156–157, 194–195; in domains,
134–136, 155; Meiji descendants of,
195n; publishing industry and, 58;
regulation of, 120–122, 134–136,
154–156; samurai class and, 122,
137; Shinto and, 101; twentieth-
century reincarnation of, 319
Kagema no adauchi (*Kagema's*
Vendetta, Jōno Denpei), 205–206
Kagema onna, 30, 119, 253
Kagerō, 141
Kageyama Hideko. *See* Fukuda
Hideko
Kagoshima, 206–211, 221, 224, 316.
See also Satsuma
Kai, 158n
Kaibara Yoshifuru: *Yamato kotoha-
jime*, 86, 87
Kaitei ritsuryō, 153, 159–167, 176,
181, 184, 186, 187, 198
Kakusuke, 125
Kamagasaki, 319, 330
"Kamagasaki" (Takeda Rintarō), 322
Kameyama, 102n, 125n
Kana books (*kanazōshi*), 46–47
Kanae Yukijirō. *See* Iwata Jun'ichi
Kana script, 83–84
Kanazawa, 102n, 125–126, 138
Kan'eiji, 156n, 157, 239
Kangokuhō, 191n
Kangokusoku, 183, 188–192
Kani kōsen (Factory Ship, Kobayashi
Takiji), 309
Kansei reforms, 155, 200n, 213
Kappa, 68, 197
Karanashi daimon yashiki (Mansion
of the Great Quince Gate, Nishiki
Bunryū), 78
Kari keiritsu, 158
Kari tsūshō kō (Treatise on Trade with
the Flowery Quarters, Angyūsai),
67
Karma, 190, 240, 268, 269
Karsch-Haack, Friedrich, 250
Kasei jikki, 133

Kasette, 209
Kataoka Teppei: "Rōkō," 309–311, 315, 317
Katō Eijirō, 164
Katō Tokijirō, 266n
Katsuki Genzō, 126
Katsumi Sōsuke, 125
Kawabata Yasunari, 223, 305
Kawachi Nagano, 135
Kawade Masumi, 208n
Kawanabe Kyōsai, 201
Kawaoka Chōfū: "Denouncing the Great Evil of *Nanshoku* That Lurks beneath the Surface of Student Society," 229, 230, 285
Kawaramono, 117
Kawatsurumi, 86
Keihō, 149, 152, 157n, 159n, 168–182, 187, 188, 198n, 201, 224
Keihō sōsho, 127
Keikan: as term, 159, 168, 172, 183–184. *See also* Anal intercourse
Keisei kintanki (Courtesans Must Not Have Short Tempers, Ejima Kiseki), 62, 94, 243
Keishichō, 183
Kidnapping, 107
Kikuchi Ryūkichi, 186
Kinji, 107–109
Kinkin Joshi, 232n, 248n
Kinosaki, 239n
Kinsesetsu bishōnenroku (Modern Narrative of Beautiful Boys, Takizawa Bakin), 96, 227
Kinship metaphors: female-female sexuality and, 189–190; medico-scientific model and, 261–262; of *shudō* (*see* Brotherhood and loyalty oaths)
Kishōken Kōyūshi: *Yarō jitsugokyō*, 50–51, 68n
Kissing, 41n
Kitagawa Morisada, 95
Kitagawa Seijun, 280
Kitamura Kigin: *Iwatsutsuji*, 88–89, 313
Kobayashi Kenkichi, 186, 187

Kobayashi Takiji: *Kani kōsen*, 309, 310
Kobe, 225, 297, 305, 306, 317
Kobikichō, 117
Kōbō Daishi. *See* Kūkai
Kōbō Daishi ikkan no sho (Book of Kōbō Daishi, Mitsuo Sadatomo), 50, 51, 237, 241
Kōchi, 127–128, 204n, 210, 230–231
Kō chigo shōgyō hiden (Expounding the Sacred Doctrine of Acolytes Secretly Transmitted), 50, 52
Kodama Yoshio, 191
Kōda Rohan: *Higeotoko*, 205
Kōdō, 141
Kodomoya, 120–121, 156
Kō Eiichi, 163n
Kōguuri. See Incense peddlers
Kōha: as term, 214, 224. *See also* Roughnecks and smoothies
Koikawa Harumachi, 91n
Kojiki (Record of Ancient Matters), 87
Kōjimachi, 101
Kojima Jinzaburō, 184
Kōjōkan, 213n
Kōke Yoshio, 180
"Kokin wakashu no jo" (Hosokawa Yūsai), 51
Komamonouri, 123n
Komatsubara Eitarō, 222–223
Komine Shigeyuki, 123n, 328
Kōmurō Shujin: *Bishōnenron*, 225–227, 229–230, 248, 249, 263, 292, 306
Kongō, 67
Konishi Jin'ichi, 28, 43, 63
Konoe Nobuhiro: *Inu tsurezure*, 41n, 43, 51, 78–79, 90, 91, 241n, 262
Kono hana (This Flower), 206n, 292
Konpira shrine, 139
Korea, 6n, 63, 85, 152n, 248
Kōriyama, 32n
Kōsei ritsuryō kō, 159n
Kōshokken Ariwara no Narihira, 90n
Kōshoku ichidai otoko (Life of an Amorous Man, Ihara Saikaku), 29, 36–37, 39, 139, 184n
Kotohira, 139

Kotō no oni (Demon of the Lonely Isle, Edogawa Ranpo), 314–315

Kōya, Mount, 33n, 34, 42n, 83, 135, 232, 241n, 243n, 317

Kozōritori, 111, 122–123

Krafft-Ebing, Richard von, 7, 229, 249, 252n, 255, 256, 269, 284, 293, 296, 304, 315, 316

Krauss, Friedrich, 250

Kujikata osadamegaki, 106–109, 125, 158, 319

Kūkai: as beautiful boy, 88n; and continent, 64, 67, 85; and end of the law, 91; legitimization of *shudō* texts and, 50–51; as patron of *shudō*, 68, 83–84, 333; as repopularizer, 87; resentment of, 75

Kumamoto, 69, 125n, 127, 147n, 159n, 160–161, 164, 210

Kumazawa Banzan, 241n

Kurama shrine, 50

Kure Shūzō, 269n, 273, 303

Kyōgen, 33n, 68n

Kyōhō era, 92, 95, 200n

Kyoto: male-male erotic subculture and, 302, 310n, 318; regulation of *shudō* culture, 110, 113, 123–124, 155n, 156n, 158n; sophistication and, 69

Kyūkeihō. See *Keihō*

Kyushu, 29, 48, 69, 138, 167, 191, 210, 215, 269, 278, 310, 311n. *See also* Kagoshima; Kumamoto; Nagasaki; Saga; Satsuma

Laborers, 186, 265, 284–285, 309, 310

Law enforcement: of Meiji period (*see* Police); mutual surveillance, 141, 144–145, 164

Legal discourse: defined, 10–11, 98; hybrids involving, 13–14; male-female analogies in, 107–109, 127, 159n

Legal discourse, Edo period: Confucianism and, 104, 106, 111, 117n, 130, 132, 143; and disciplinary paradigm, 19, 98, 111, 131–132; diversity of, 105, 124, 142–145; of domains (*see* Domains); early Meiji survival of, 158; female prostitution and, 94, 106, 110, 120, 140, 141, 155, 156; gender regulation, 113–114, 115–116, 152–153; and love suicide (*see* Love suicide); and male-female sexuality, 106–109, 126–127; peasant knowledge of, 141–142; perisexual focus of, 105, 142, 181; and prostitution, male, 110–124, 134–144, 154–157; religion and, 98–105; shogunal legislation (*see* Shogunal legislation)

Legal discourse, Meiji: and anal intercourse (*see* Anal intercourse); censorship, 200–201; centralization and, 145, 147, 148–149; Chinese influences on, 159n, 161–162, 163, 172, 184; and civilized paradigm, 19–20, 147–148, 192, 193; and class, 148–149, 159–160, 166–168, 169, 181; and female prostitution, 148n, 150, 157; forensic pathology, 173–177; gender regulation, 150–153, 166–168, 190; identity of individuals, 150; male-female sexuality and, 149–150, 159n, 163, 168, 178–179, 187; and marriage, 149–150; popular discourse and, 163–164, 172–173, 198, 200–201; and prisons, 164n, 165–166, 182–192; and prostitution, male, 157; and religion, 198–199; and reproduction, 150; roughnecks and, 224; social morality and, 180–181, 192; Western influences on, 146, 147, 148, 149, 153–154, 161–163, 168, 169n, 170–171, 172, 177

Legal discourse, twentieth century: new *kagema* and, 319–320; sexologists' faulty grasp of, 258n; wartime, 179, 326–327

Legal discourse, Western, 98–99, 106, 154, 162, 170–171, 172, 173, 179, 258n, 271, 326; as influence on Meiji legal discourse, 146, 147, 148,

Legal discourse *(continued)*
149, 153–154, 161–163, 168, 169n, 170–171, 172, 177
Legitimization of *shudō* and texts, 49–53, 64, 83–89, 100–101, 333
Lesbianism. *See* Female-female sexuality
Leupp, Gary, 5n, 137n
Literacy: constituency of, 44, 46–47; gender differences in, 24, 46; Meiji expansion of, 20; and sexology, dissemination of, 291
Love: as term, 25, 107n, 231
Love suicide *(shinjū)*: female-female sexuality and, 177; popular sexology and, 314; shogunal law and, 107–109; as term, 107n; theater and, 114
Lubricants, 239
Lucid Mirror of Nanshoku (Yoshida Hanbei), 37n, 42n, 52–53, 54, 55–56, 57, 58, 71, 72, 79, 81, 90–91

McClain, James, 138
Madōji (Devil Boy, Oguri Mushitarō), 316–317
Maeda Otoki, 176–177
Maezu, 135, 143
Magazines, 194–203, 293–295, 297, 303, 329–330
Mahāmaudgalyāyana, 86
Maiko, 119n
Male: as term, 253
Male-female sexuality: commercialized *(see* Prostitution, female); debates on *(see* Erotic debate); decline of male-male erotic culture and, 93–95, 209; of Edo period (see *Joshoku*); as elemental dyad, 235–236, 242–243; medical discourse and, Meiji, 240, 246; men-women *(otoko-onna)* and, 167, 265; as norm, 21, 252, 273; patriotism and, 247–248; popular discourse and, Meiji, 203, 222–223, 278; regulation of, Edo period, 106–109, 126–127; regulation of, Meiji, 159n,

163, 168, 178–179, 187, 198–199; same-sex love as precluding, 252, 267; *shudō* not precluding, 38–39, 59–60, 103–104, 242–243, 252, 267, 276, 279; smoothies vs. roughnecks and, 214–216, 219, 222–223. *See also* Cross-sex love
Male gaze, 35n. *See also* Virile gaze
Male-male sexuality: between adults, 33n; civilized paradigm of *(see* Legal discourse, Meiji; Popular discourse, Meiji); and criminality, 311–317; disciplinary paradigm of (see *Shudō*, as a way); of Edo period (see *Shudō*); female authors and, 248n; female-female sexuality as isolated from discourse of, 23, 27, 61, 104; female-female sexuality as parallel with, 21, 248, 303; as focus of book, 4; legal discourse and *(see* Legal discourse); medico-scientific paradigm of *(see* Medico-scientific model of sexuality); as practice vs. essence, 39–40; of Satsuma Kagoshima, 206–211, 272, 278; symbols of, 85, 88–89, 164, 197, 198, 200n, 209n, 225–226, 323; as term of book, vs. homosexuality, 4–5; terms for *(see* Male-male sexuality, terms for); of twentieth century (see Same-sex love); urban subculture of, 317–326, 330–333; zoological evidence of, 240–242. *See also* Homosexuality
Male-male sexuality, terms for: from China, 4n, 24, 64, 161, 216; euphemisms/slang, 197, 197n, 202, 210, 215, 262, 301n, 323–324, 325n; homosexuality, 4–5, 12, 23–25, 29, 30; Inagaki Taruho and, 306; in Kagoshima, 209; *keikan*, 159, 168, 183–184; medico-scientific model and, 4n, 251–252, 261–262, 292, 323; *nanshoku*, 24–26, 131–132, 183–184, 232; *shudō* (see *Shudō*)

Male supremacy, 251–252

Mamushi no Omasa, 190n

Mañjuśrī (Monju), 67, 85

Marriage: adoption as alternative to, 180n; adultery (*see* Adultery); age of, and same-sex love, 273–274, 285; of clergy, 198–199; and concubinage, 38, 40; conjugal duties, 55, 103–104, 243, 264, 274; as cure for same-sex love, 268, 273–274; *joshoku* as expected career following, 38, 40, 106, 149, 172; male-male-female love triangles and, 38n; male-male sexuality as complement to, 38–39, 103–104; patriotism and, 247–248; regulation of, Meiji, 149–150; rejection of, 39–40; same-sex, and unions, 129–130, 180n, 249, 299–300; of samurai, 93–94

Martial arts: in Edo period, 28, 29, 71n; roughnecks and, 216

Marumaru chinbun ("Maruchin"), 194–203

Maruyama Park, 302, 318

Masculinity: active/masculine and passive/feminine construction, 261–267, 272, 301–302, 321–322, 323; capacity for loving youths as inherent in, 39, 266, 268; of females, 151–153, 190, 257; hierarchy of, and *shudō*, 18, 37, 252–253; insertees and, 35, 228–229; military prowess and male-male eros, 208, 216, 250, 279–280, 327; roughnecks vs. smoothies and, 212–225, 227, 229, 230, 272, 283, 303; *shudō* and, 34–36, 39, 228, 229, 262, 263–264, 266, 279. *See also* Femininity; Gender

Masse. See Buddhism: end of the law

Masturbation: Edo-period views of, 42n, 86; females and, 177 (*see also* Dildos); Meiji medical authorities and, 173–174, 175, 241, 245, 246, 247; mutual, 42n, 177, 302

Matriarchy, 308

Matsudaira Sadanobu, 134, 155

Matsui Masakata, 164, 204

Matsumae, 69

Matsumoto Takezō, 317

Matsumoto Tasaburō, 185

Matsumoto Yasuko, 247–248

Matsuo Bashō: on changing sexual habits, 38, 39; class background of, 70; on youths and females, comparability of, 35

Matsushiro, 102n

Matsuura Seizan, 207–208, 269

Matsuyama, 132, 133, 161, 213

Medical discourse: defined, 11–13; of Edo period, 235–240, 242, 243, 244; folk medicine, 237–239; hybrids involving, 13–14; of Meiji period (*see* Medical discourse, Meiji); Sino-Japanese medicine, 235–237, 240, 242; of twentieth century (*see* Medico-scientific model of sexuality); of the West (*see* Medico-scientific model of sexuality, Western)

Medical discourse, Meiji, 240–242; and anal intercourse, 174–175, 246–248; biology and (*see* Biology); and legal discourse, 173–177; and male-male sexuality, 173–176, 229–230, 240–242, 243–251; and popular discourse, 226, 229–230; Western influence on, 12–13, 175, 176, 214–215, 243–245, 246, 247, 248–251; zoological sexuality and, 240–242, 243

Medico-scientific model of sexuality: age and, 252–253, 263, 267; contestation over, 298–299; cross-sex love and (*see* Cross-sex love); estheticization of, 306–307; global dimensions of, 13; and heredity (*see* Heredity); history as dissected by, 277–285, 334; as paradigm, 21–22, 286; popular discourse based on (*see* Popular sexology); popularization of, 7, 12–13, 291–292; and

Medico-scientific model of sexuality
(continued)
  regional same-sex love, 210; researchers of, 254–255; resistance
  to, 233–234; same-sex love and (*see*
  Same-sex love); sex/gender system
  of, 251–254, 255–268; terms associated with, 25; and the West (*see*
  Medico-scientific model of sexuality, Western)
Medico-scientific model of sexuality,
  Western: case studies drawn from,
  247, 296; influence of, 232, 233,
  247, 249–251, 259–261, 269, 275–
  277, 280–281, 285; Japanese influence on research of, 249–251,
  277, 282; and Meiji period, 175,
  176, 214–215, 243–245, 246, 247,
  248–251; popular sexology and,
  293, 303, 304, 306–307, 314, 315;
  resistance to, 282–283
Meiji period: censorship in, 20, 199–
  201, 226n, 249, 284, 291, 292–293,
  303, 304, 335; centralization and,
  19–20, 145, 147, 148–149, 193;
  defined, 18, 146; government
  personnel of, 210–211; legal discourse of (*see* Legal discourse,
  Meiji); medical discourse of (*see*
  Medical discourse, Meiji); morality
  and (*see* Civilized morality);
  popular discourse of (*see* Popular
  discourse, Meiji); prostitution in,
  decline of, 194–196
Memoirs, 223
Menstruation, 72–73, 256–257
Men-women (*otoko-onna*), 42n,
  166–168, 264–265
Metatophism, 289
Michel, Louise, 260
Michi. See Way
Middle class, growth of, 291
Mikkaichi, 135–136
Military: male-male eros as empower-
  ing to, 208, 216, 250, 279–280, 327;
  navy, 211, 227n, 284, 328, 332–333;
  preparatory schools, 217–218; pros-

titution and, 284, 332–333; as site of
  male-male erotic practice, 283–284,
  328–329. *See also* Samurai class
Mimura Tokuzō, 318–319, 320, 322,
  323, 324, 325–326
Minakata Kumagusu, 42n, 134n,
  135–136, 195n, 199, 204n, 217,
  226n, 232–234, 262, 266, 268,
  282–283, 314; Iwata Jun'ichi and,
  232, 313, 327
Minami Takao, 310n, 332–333
Minamoto Yoshitsune, 50n, 88, 229
Mines, 186, 285
Ming dynasty, 64, 127, 243n
Minors: adults vs., dichotomy of, 181;
  criminal liability of, 163; obscene
  acts with, 162, 168–169, 170, 171,
  172, 174, 190–191, 224
Mirror, as symbol, 53
Misaki, 225n
Mishima Yukio, 331n
Misogyny, 39–40; Buddhism and, 74,
  85, 94; of Confucian doctrine, 74;
  extremes of, 269; in Ihara Saikaku,
  66, 256; medico-scientific model
  and, 251, 260, 267–268, 272;
  popular sexology and, 315, 316;
  samurai class and, 72–73, 93–94,
  204, 207, 216, 256, 267–268, 333;
  of townsman class, 40, 79–80
Mitamura Engyo, 94n, 279n
Mito, 43
Mitsudō, 28
Mitsu no asa (Hiraga Gennai), 65, 93,
  135n, 138
Mitsuo Sadatomo: *Kōbō Daishi ikkan
  no sho*, 50, 51, 237, 241
Miura Gorō, 217–218
Miyagawachō, 67n
Miyahiro Sadao, 242, 243
Miyajima, 138–139, 143
Miyaoi Sadao. *See* Miyahiro Sadao
Miyatake Gaikotsu, 292
Miyauchi, 139, 140
Miyazaki Koshoshi, 278, 334
Mizuno Tadakuni, 155
Möbius, Paul, 282

Moga, 258
Moll, Albert, 293
Monju (Mañjuśrī), 67, 85
Monks: as term in book, 26n. *See also*
    Buddhist clergy
Monma Chiyo, 180n
Monogamy, 40–41, 149–150
Moonshine magazines (*kasutori
    zasshi*), 329, 331
Moral panic, student culture and,
    218–224
Mori (domain), 213
Mori Arinori, 149
Mori Ōgai: on female-female
    sexuality, 177n; and male-male
    unions, 249; *Vita Sexualis*, 214–
    215, 217, 229, 259, 285, 288,
    303–305
Morioka, 102n, 125n
Mori Ranmaru, 88, 227
Morita Yūshū, 201n, 251n, 254n, 255,
    256–257, 260, 270–271, 274, 275,
    282, 284, 308–309
Motoori Uchitō, 42n, 95, 100n, 242n
Mukashi mukashi monogatari (Tales
    of Long Long Ago, Takaratsu
    Shusō or Niimi Masatomo), 92, 93,
    111n
Municipal decrees (*ofuregaki*),
    109–124, 143–144, 154–156
Murayama Kaita, 307
Murayama Sakon, 114
Murder: popular sexology and, 314,
    316–317; prison violence and, 185;
    shudō oaths and, 125–126. *See also*
    Love suicide
Museumification, 206, 219, 278, 285,
    334
Mushanokōji Saneatsu, 223
Music, 209–210
Mystery genre, 314–317

Nachi, Mount, 34
Nagasaki, 63, 65, 124n, 225, 227
Nagoya, 122n, 125n, 134n, 135, 143,
    225, 315
Nakajima Kanjūrō, 126

Nakamura Kokyō, 294, 300
Nakanishi Gen'emon, 126
Nakano Masato, 265n, 293, 294,
    319n
Nandō, 233
Nankai no Sanjin, 44, 46, 53; *Nan-
    shoku yamaji no tsuyu*, 33n,
    44–45, 56, 63–64, 65, 68–70, 73,
    76–77, 79–80, 81–82, 100n
Nanpa, as term, 214, 224. *See also*
    Roughnecks and smoothies
Nanshoku, 24–26, 131–132, 183–184,
    232; pronounced *danshoku*, 163n,
    184n; term used in book (see
    Shudō)
Nanshoku kinometsuke (*Nanshoku*
    Pickled in Young Pepperleaf Brine,
    Urushiya Ensai), 40n, 49, 50, 67,
    72, 85, 86, 87, 129n
Nanshoku kō (Study of *Nanshoku*,
    Nakano Masato), 293
Nanshoku masukagami (Lucid Mirror
    of *Nanshoku*, Yoshida Hanbei),
    37n, 42n, 52–53, 54, 55–56, 57, 58,
    71, 72, 79, 81, 90–91
Nanshoku ōkagami. See *Great Mirror
    of Male Love, The*
Nanshoku taiheiki, 51
Nanshoku yamaji no tsuyu (Nankai
    no Sanjin), 33n, 44–45, 56, 63–
    64, 65, 68–70, 73, 76–77, 79–80,
    81–82, 100n
"Nan-šo-k' (die Päderastie in Japan)"
    (Iwaya Sazanami), 250, 264n, 277,
    282, 324
Naoemon, 127, 145
Napoleonic law, 162, 170–171, 179
National Eugenics Law, 179
Nativism: criticism of *shudō*, 99–100,
    101; on desire for anal penetration,
    42n; histories of *shudō*, 86–89, 95,
    99–100; and male-female sexuality
    as norm, 242, 243
Naturalism, 285, 304
Navy, 211, 227n, 284, 328, 332–333
Nenashigusa (Rootless Grass, Hiraga
    Gennai), 68, 197

Nenashigusa kōhen (Rootless Grass, a Sequel; Hiraga Gennai), 68, 69, 89, 91–92, 241n

Nenja: age of, 36–37; as audience of *shudō* texts, 54–57; brotherhood bonds and (*see* Brotherhood and loyalty oaths); connoisseurship of, 56–59, 61, 295; medico-scientific equivalent of, 265–268, 272; municipal decrees governing, 111–112; as relative status, 39, 266; of samurai class, 71, 90; socioeconomic status and, 37–38, 82; as term, 36, 39; and woman-hating (*see* Misogyny). See also *Shudō*; Youth

Neurasthenia, sexual, 247, 274–275

Newspapers. *See* Journalism

Night crawling (*yobai*), 149, 309

Nihongi (Chronicles of Japan), 86, 99–100, 101, 293

Nihon jōkō no hensen (Vicissitudes of Passion in Japan, Miyazaki Koshoshi), 278, 334

Niigata, 208

Niimi Masatomo: *Mukashi mukashi monogatari*, 92, 93, 111n

Ningen tankyū (Exploration of Humanity), 329

Nishikawa Joken, 67

Nishiki Bunryū: *Karanashi daimon yashiki*, 78

Nishizawa Ippū: *Fūryū sangokushi*, 62; on salesboys, 135n; *Yakei tomojamisen*, 32, 37n, 42n, 61, 62, 85, 87n, 242n

Nitobe Inazō, 221

Nobility: as *shudō* text authors, 47, 78–79

Nochi no iwatsutsuji (A Latter-Day Rock Azalea, Iwata Jun'ichi), 313

Noguchi Takenori, 88

Noma Kōshin, 29

Nō theater, 50n, 114, 118

Nyake, 46n, 61n, 75. See also *Shudō*

Nyake kanjinchō (Subscription Book on Behalf of *Nyake*, Ijiri Matakurō

Tadasuki), 26–27, 28, 30n, 45–46, 64n

Nyakudō: as term, 28, 64. See also *Shudō*

Nyodō: as term, 27, 57–58; term used in book (*see Joshoku*). *See also* Prostitution, female

Nyoshoku. See *Joshoku*

Obscene acts: as term, 168, 177, 188n. *See also* Legal discourse, Meiji

Obscenity, as term, 174n, 200

Ochiai Yoshichika, 153n

Oda Nobunaga, 62, 88, 128, 227

Odawara, 135n

Oden, 38n

Ofuregaki (municipal decrees), 109–124, 143–144, 154–156

Oguri Mushitarō: *Madōji*, 316–317

Ogyū Sorai, 117n

"Ōharae no norito," 100

Okabe Tōhei, 99–100, 101

Okada Zenkichi, 184

Ōkagami, 51

Okama, 323–324, 332

Ōkawa Kazuma, 201n, 227

Okayama, 108n, 128n, 136, 139, 140, 144, 158n, 213n

Okinawa, 6n

Okitsu, 135, 239

Ōkubo Toshimichi, 211

Okuni, 113

Onnagata, 81, 114, 122n, 195n, 250, 264, 317, 318, 322–323, 324

Onnagirai. See Misogyny

Ooto, 153, 167, 258

Organizations and clubs for same-sex love people, 271, 299, 319–320

Orientalism, 6–7, 10–11, 13, 249–251, 334

Origuchi Shinobu, 223

Osaka: male-male erotic subculture in, 310–311, 330; new *kagema* and, 318, 319, 320, 324, 330, 331; regulation of *shudō* culture, 110, 113, 123–124, 155n, 156n;

roughnecks and, 225; sophistication and, 69
Ōsugi Sakae, 223
Ōta Nanpo, 88n
Otokogirai, 272
Otoko-onna, 42n, 166–168, 264–265
Otokozuki, 33n
Ōtorii Sutezō, 270
Ōtsuki Kenji, 276
Outcasts, 73, 116–117, 141, 182
Ōwakashu, 34n
Ozaki Shirō, 307

Pages, 43, 196, 204n; in legal discourse, 112, 126, 127–128, 137, 181; in popular discourse, Meiji, 227; in *shudō* texts, 32, 34, 73, 88, 92, 93, 109n, 129n, 266; and theater, 201n
Panpan, 330, 332
Passive/feminine and active/masculine construction, 261–267, 272, 301–302, 321–322, 323
Patriarchy, 55, 149, 170, 171, 180, 263, 308
Peasantry: education of, 213n; legal discourse and, 139–142, 144–145, 158n, 181; mutual surveillance and, 141, 144–145; sexual latitude enjoyed by, 149; as *shudō* text audience, 48, 52; in *shudō* texts, 80–81, 139. *See also* Socioeconomic status
Peddlers: of fan paper (*jigamiuri*), 123n; of incense (*see* Incense peddlers); of sundry goods (*komamonouri*), 123n
Pedophilia, 267
Peerage, 159–160, 161n, 315
Peers' School, 250
Periodization, 14–18
Perverse, meaning of, 21–22, 286–290, 296
Philippines, 65n
Physicians: in *shudō* texts, 73, 237n
Play, culture of, 243

Poe, Edgar Allan, 316
Poetry: as way, 28
Police: cross-dressing regulation by, 152; establishment of, 164–165, 181; and Iwata Jun'ichi, 327; and new *kagema*, 317, 319, 321–322, 331; and prisons, 183; and sexological case histories, 297n; and youth culture, 221–222, 316
Popular discourse: and civilized paradigm, 20; defined, 9–10, 26; and disciplinary paradigm (see *Shudō*, as a way); of Edo period (see *Shudō* texts); hybrids involving, 13–14; and medico-scientific model of sexuality, 21–22; Meiji (*see* Popular discourse, Meiji); samurai as distorted in, 70; of twentieth century (*see* Popular discourse, twentieth century; Popular sexology). *See also* Journalism; Publishing industry
Popular discourse, Meiji, 193–194; adolescence, male-male sexuality perceived to be limited to, 211–212, 223–224, 276, 288, 295; beautiful boys (*bishōnen*), 194, 205, 207, 209, 211, 218, 221, 225–234, 263, 281; censorship of, 20, 199–203, 226n, 291, 292–293, 303, 304, 335; and criminalization of anal intercourse, 163–164; desire vs. practice in, 230–233; Edo-period discourse compared to, 193, 333–334; and geographical marginalization, 206–211; history, male-male sexuality as relegated to, 203–206, 210, 219, 285, 334; and legal discourse, 163–164, 172–173, 198, 200–201; and medico-scientific model, 226, 229–230; the press (*see* Journalism); prostitution and, 205–206, 227; roughnecks and smoothies, 212–225, 227, 229, 230, 272, 283, 303; *senryū*, 194–203; sexology compared to, 288; voice in, 295

Popular discourse, twentieth century: criminology, 311–314; *ero-guro* culture (see *Ero-guro* culture); on prisons, 192; sexology (*see* Popular sexology)

Popular sexology: audience for, 287, 289–290, 291–294, 296, 329; defined, 13–14, 291, 295; forms of, 291–295, 303–311, 329–330; language of, 288–289, 292; male-male erotic subculture and, 317–326, 330–333; perverse, meaning of, 21–22, 286–290, 296; pleasures presented by, 289–291; sexual repertory expanded in, 302; voices in, of experts, 295, 296–297; voices in, of readers, 294, 301–302; voices in, of subject, 288, 295–296, 297–301, 304–305

Population: debate on, 331; reproduction control and, 150

Pots: as metaphor, 197n, 323

Poverty, 78–79, 153, 284, 309–310

Pregnancy, male, 243n, 322. *See also* Reproduction

Priests: as term in book, 26n. *See also* Buddhist clergy

Prisons: civilized morality and, 20, 182, 192; of Edo period, 182–183, 184n, 188; medico-scientific view of, 272, 283; panoptic model of, 183, 186; in popular discourse, 184n, 189–190, 192; power relations and male-male sexuality in, 182–183, 185, 187, 188–189, 191; regulation of, Meiji, 164n, 165–166, 182–192; rituals of, 182–183, 184, 188; slang, 197n

Problem in Greek Ethics, A (John Addington Symonds), 233

Proletarian literary movement, 309–311

Prostitution: Buddhist clergy and, 75–76, 101–102, 195n, 281; changing importance of, 90–91; class and regulation of, 143–144; decline of, 92–93, 95, 155–157, 194–196; in domains, 134–143, 158; female (*see* Prostitution, female); health issues in, 237, 238, 280; incense peddlers (*kōguuri*), 123, 140, 141; of *jiga-miuri*, 123n; of *komamonouri*, 123n; medico-scientific view of, 280–281; military and, 284, 332–333; and popular discourse, Meiji, 205–206, 227; and popular discourse, twentieth century, 310, 311, 318–326, 330, 331–333; postwar, 330, 331–333; regular patrons in, 40; regulation of, Edo period, 110–124, 134–144, 154–157; regulation of, Meiji, 157; regulation of, twentieth century, 157, 319–320; rivalries with female prostitution, 59n, 62; salesboys, 135, 239; as separate world, 66–67; *shudō* texts and, 57–59; socioeconomic status and, 37; as term, 27n; terms for, 141–142, 318, 323–324; townsman class and, 77–79, 119; of twentieth century, 318–326, 330, 331–333; youth status as extended for, 34. *See also* Actor-prostitutes; *Kagema*

Prostitution, female: decline and, 91–92, 94–95; evocation of *shudō* in, 30, 119, 253; female-female sexuality and, 272; health issues in, 238; *nyodō* as signifying, 27, 57–58; postwar, 330, 332; regulation of, Edo period, 94, 106, 110, 120, 140, 141, 155, 156; regulation of, Meiji, 148n, 150, 157, 208; rivalries with male prostitution, 59n, 62

Prostitution Prevention Law, 157

Psychic hermaphrodism, 252, 267, 279, 300. *See also* Two-sex love

Psychoanalytic theory, 275–277, 280–281, 287; and popular sexology, 306–307, 314, 315, 329

Psychopathia Sexualis (Richard von Krafft-Ebing), 249, 252n, 284, 304

Publishing industry: and criminology,

312; growth of, and cultural production of meaning, 10, 16, 28–29, 44–59; growth of, and dissemination of sexology, 291; *shudō* texts (see *Shudō* texts); as urban, 47. *See also* Censorship

Pygmalionism, 263, 289, 316–317

Qing dynasty, 106, 161, 162, 163

Racial theory, 171, 327
Rape: domain laws and, 127, 145; gang violence and, 133, 180; importuning regulations, 111–112, 116, 143; insertee as immune to prosecution for, 168, 184; and *kagema*, 281; Meiji legal discourse on, 158n, 159, 160, 161n, 162, 163, 164, 168–169, 184; as outside *shudō*, 79; in prisons, 184; statutory, 127, 161n, 162, 163, 168–169, 171, 178, 181. *See also* Violence
Ravina, Mark, 11, 132
Religion: cross-dressing and, 151–152; erotic debate as influenced by, 62–63; legitimacy of *shudō* and, 49–51, 83–84, 85–86; and medical discourse, Meiji, 246; *nanshoku* as term and, 25–26; syncretism, 62–63; terms used in book, 26n; of West, 2, 42n, 62, 65, 98–99, 102, 124n, 170, 180, 201, 246, 271, 272, 300. *See also* Buddhism; Buddhist clergy; Confucianism; Shinto
Reproduction: Edo-period views of, 243; Meiji control of, 150; Meiji views of, 243–244, 246, 247–248
Roads, 135, 136, 140
Robertson, Jennifer, 152
Rock azalea, 88–89, 313
Rod chains, 186, 187
Roden, Donald, 217, 291–292, 294
"Rōkō" (Squalid Alleyways, Kataoka Teppei), 309–311, 315, 317
Rokudō, 67–68, 241
Rome, 2, 6, 66, 277n
Rosenbaum, Julius, 282

Roughnecks and smoothies, 133, 212–225, 227, 229, 230, 272, 283, 303
Russia, 65n, 66n
Russo-Japanese War, 250, 284, 328
Ryukyu, 4n, 6n
Ryūyō, 200n, 216, 230

Sadomasochism, 289
Safuran (Saffron), 307
Saga, 48, 128, 167
Saga monogatari (Tale of Saga), 84
Saigō Takamori, 211
Saikaku. *See* Ihara Saikaku
Saiken, 58, 79, 93
Sain, 163
Saiseiki, 55n
Saitō Tamao, 281n
Sakaichō, 117
Sakai Toshihiko, 308–309
Sakaki Yasusaburō, 274n, 275, 281, 282
Śākyamuni, 82–83, 85–86
Salesboys, 135, 239. *See also* Peddlers
Same-sex love (*dōseiai*): as acquired, 268, 271–277, 278–279; Buddhist clergy as practitioners of, 199, 272, 281, 283; causes of, 268–272; compound sex trope of, 260–261, 276; as congenital, 226, 257, 268–271, 272, 273, 275, 276, 278, 282, 308; degeneration and, 261, 263, 269, 282, 324; erotic subjectivities in, range of, 300–301; as excluding cross-sex love, 252, 267; female-female sexuality and, 14, 175, 248, 252, 292, 303; gender and (*see* Gender); homosexuality construct as influence on, 175–176, 248, 251; intermediate sex trope of, 258–260, 261; inversion trope of, 177, 255–258, 261, 280, 281, 314–315, 322; latent universality of, 276; men-women (*otoko-onna*) and, 264–265; new *kagema* as embodying, 321–322; as pathology, 248–249; personal identity of, 261; popular sexology and (*see* Popular sexology); prevention and cure

Same-sex love (continued)
of, 272–276; pseudo vs. true, 271;
psychoanalytic theory and, 275–
277; as psychosexual stage of development, 276, 287, 304; regional,
210, 278–279; restructuring of
medical knowledge and, 12–13;
rights and organizations related to,
249, 260, 270–271, 299; sex/gender
system and, 251–254, 255–268;
shudō compared to, 252–253, 255–
256, 262–265, 266–269, 272–273;
as term, 175, 248, 251–252, 292,
306. See also Female-female
sexuality; Homosexuality; Male-
male sexuality
Same-sex unions, 129–130, 180n, 249,
299–300
Samurai class: brotherhood and (see
Brotherhood and loyalty oaths);
class structure and, 70; country-
dwelling, 73; decline of shudō and,
92, 93–94; double loyalties of, 127–
132, 144; education of, 212–213;
hierarchy of, 73; honor and, 70–
72, 76–77, 204, 328; as marriage/
family model in Meiji period, 149;
masculinity ideals of, 216, 279;
medico-scientific view of, 279–280;
in Meiji period (see Shizoku); and
misogyny, 72–73, 93–94, 204, 207,
216, 256, 267–268, 333; moderation
of sexuality and, 110, 111, 136; and
popular discourse, Meiji, 204–205;
roughnecks and style of, 216–218;
Satsuma/Kagoshima and, 207–
211; as succeeding Buddhist clergy
in shudō practice, 90; teahouse
attendance by, 122, 137; as term,
44n; theater and prostitution regulation and, 114, 118, 137, 144; townsman shudō compared with, 71–72,
76–77, 238n; violence and, 71–72,
76–77, 125–126, 128–133, 138, 144,
145, 204, 213, 217, 218, 311; warrior
morale (shiki), 208. See also Socioeconomic status

Sandal bearers (kozōritori), 111,
122–123
Sanjō Sanetomi, 201
Sannōchō, 330
Sanogawa Ichimatsu, 67
Santo Kyōden, 67
Sasanoya, 206
Satomi Ton, 223
Satsuma, 6n, 206–211, 213, 221–
222, 247, 272, 278. See also
Kagoshima
Satsuma habit, 210, 211, 221, 250
Sawada Junjirō: on criminology,
311–312; and medico-scientific
model, 254, 255, 257–258, 261,
263, 264n, 269–270, 271, 272, 273,
274, 275–276, 277, 278–279, 280,
284–285; and popular sexology,
288, 291–292, 293, 294, 297–298,
299, 334, 335; same-sex love
experiences of, 277, 288
Schalow, Paul, 14n, 24, 25, 38n, 47n,
50, 88
Schools: and age hierarchy, 217;
central system, establishment of,
160, 208, 212, 213–214; coeducational, 273; keikan incidents in,
160; medico-scientific view of,
273, 283; sex segregation in, 212;
student culture in (see Student
culture and sexuality)
Schopenhauer, 247
Schurtz, Heinrich, 308
Scientific-Humanitarian Committee,
249–250, 259–260
Scotland, 162
Sedgwick, Eve, 16
Segawa Kikunojō II, 69
Segawa Kikunojō V, 38n
Segregation: curing same-sex love
and, 273; female-female sexuality
and, 176; of kabuki actors, 116–
118, 143, 155, 156; in prisons, 176,
191; in schools, 212
Sei (Sex), 255, 294, 297–298, 299,
301–302, 303
Sei, as term, 253n

Seigle, Cecilia, 57n, 94–95
Sei kōron (Sex Review), 294
Sei no chishiki (Sexual Knowledge), 294
Sei no kenkyū (Sexual Research), 294
Seiron (Sexology), 294
Seishin bunseki (Psychoanalysis), 314
Seisuishō (Rousing Laughter, Anrakuan Sakuden), 75, 104
Sei to ai (Sex and Love), 294
Sei to ren'ai (Sex and Love), 294
Sei to shakai (Sex and Society), 294
Seiyoku to jinsei (Sexual Desire and Humanity), 294
Seiyō zakki (Miscellaneous Jottings on the West, Yamamura Saisuke), 66
Sekkusu (Sex), 294
Semen: conjugal duties and, 243; evidence of, 165–166, 174; and health, 236, 238n, 244
Sendai, 126, 138, 158n
Sengoku, 15, 95, 105, 163, 205, 216, 333
Senpe(-don), 209
Senryū: apprentices and shopboys in, 79, 196, 238; and bedchamber medicine, 235; Buddhist clergy, 91, 94, 101, 102, 195n, 197–198, 199n, 236n, 237; females in, 27, 29–30, 39, 59n, 195n; about *kagema*, 34, 36n, 80, 238; of Meiji period, 194–203
Seppuku, 71, 76, 126n. See also Suicide
Seventh Higher School, 208n
Sex dichotomy, 251, 252, 253, 261–262. *See also* Gender
Sex education, 273
Sex equality, 285
Sexological model. *See* Medico-scientific model of sexuality
Sexology: as term, 244. *See also* Medico-scientific model of sexuality
Sexual, as adjectival term, 6n
Sexual categories, construction and historicity of, 1–9
Sexual desire: as biological instinct, 3, 21, 253, 303–304

Sexual interstages theory, 259–260, 270, 280
Sexuality: as discourse vs. practice, in study, 8–9; as term, 5–6
Sexual neurasthenia, 247, 274–275
Sexual orientation, 3, 5, 253, 270
Sexual personality, 296, 301, 321
Sexual practices: anal intercourse (*see* Anal intercourse); anilingus, 41n; fellatio, 41n, 174, 302; interfemoral intercourse, 41n, 241, 245–246; masturbation (*see* Masturbation); vaginal coitus, 41, 235–236, 242–243. *See also* Female-female sexuality; Male-female sexuality; Male-male sexuality
Sexual problem, 294, 303, 309
Shaji Hisaichi, 317, 318, 319, 323, 331
Shanghai, 241, 243
Sharebon, 59n, 66–67
Shiba, 101, 120, 121, 139, 156
Shibamichi Toshio, 298, 299
Shibata, 125n
Shibayama Hajime, 33n, 82, 93
Shibusawa Keizō, 313
Shichinosuke, 107
Shijōgawara, 75, 117
Shikazō, 111
Shikidō: debates on (*see* Erotic debate); sophistication vs. boorishness and, 57, 69, 286; as term, 29. See also *Joshoku*; *Shudō*
Shikidō kinpishō (Court Record of *Shikidō* Secrets, Ōgokudō no Arittake), 237–238, 291
Shikoku, 127, 132, 136, 138, 139, 153, 167, 206. *See also* Kōchi; Matsuyama; Tokushima
Shimabara, 115n
Shimane, 213
Shimaya, 196–197
Shimazu Masa, 190
Shimizu (city), 135
Shimizu Sadao, 175–176
Shinbunshi jōrei, 200
Shinga Sōzu, 88
Shinjū. *See* Love suicide

Shinjuku, 330

Shinpa, 256

Shinritsu kōryō, 158, 161, 198

Shinroku, 107

Shin sayoarashi (New Storm at Night), 68

Shin sei (New Sex), 294

Shintaishi, 227

Shinto: clergy in *shudō* texts, 73; cross-dressing and, 151–152; god of hemorrhoids, 238; male-female sexuality and, 99; male-male sexuality and, 99–102; medical discourse and, 246; prostitution and shrines, 47n, 101, 120, 139, 140; *shudō* texts and, 52, 73, 100–101; syncretism and, 62–63; terms of book and, 26n; as way, 28. *See also* Buddhism; Nativism; Religion

Shin'yūki (Record of Heartfelt Friends), 30–31, 32, 34, 35, 46, 47, 51, 56, 103n, 240

Shiobara, 265n

Shiragiku, 88

Shirakawa (Fukushima), 134–135, 155

Shirakawa (Kumamoto). *See* Kumamoto

Shizoku: Edo-period and earlier predecessors to (*see* Samurai class); penalties designated for, 159–160, 161n, 166n; status accorded to, 159, 204

Shizu no odamaki (Humble Bobbin), 209–210, 216, 278

Shizuoka, 107

Shogunal legislation, 105–106, 143–144; and domains, control of, 110, 124, 136; municipal decrees, 109–124, 143–144, 154–156; penal law, 102, 106–109, 158, 319; sexual moderation and, 110–112

Shoguns: medico-scientific view of, 266, 279; as *wakashu*, 37–38. *See also* Daimyo

Shōheikō, 212–213

Shohōken, 108n

Shoku Nihongi (Chronicles of Japan, Continued), 86

Shōnen: as term, 215

Shōnen (Boy, Kawabata Yasunari), 305

Shōnen'ai, 306

Shōsaiō: *Gengenkyō*, 33n, 43, 60n, 62, 66, 68n, 79

Shōtoku Taishi, 88

Shōwa period, 318n

Shōyūsei, 298, 299, 301–302

Shudō: as *ars erotica*, 7; brotherhood and (*see* Brotherhood and loyalty oaths); class structures and (*see* Socioeconomic status); commercialized (*see* Prostitution); Confucianism and, 55, 103–104, 131–132; debates on (*see* Erotic debate); decline of, 83, 91–95, 203–204, 231; derivation of term, 26–27; egalitarianism and, 37–38, 81–82; exclusivity and, 40; as friendship, 103, 129–131, 231; laicization of, 90, 91, 313; legal regulation of (*see* Legal discourse, Edo period); male-female sexual activity as compatible with, 38–39, 59–60, 103–104, 242–243, 252, 267, 276, 279; medical discourse and, 235–240, 242, 243, 244; men-women (*otoko-onna*) and, 265; misogyny and (*see* Misogyny); religion and (*see* Religion); *senryū* imagery of (see *Senryū*); sexual practices of, 41–43, 302; term as used in book, 26n; as term, contested, 131–132; as term, homosexuality vs., 29, 30, 43; as term, obsolescence of, 95, 231; transmission of norms of (see *Shudō* texts); youth and (*see* Youth). *See also* Homosexuality; Male-male sexuality; Same-sex love

Shudō, as a way, 18–19, 27–29, 43, 48–49, 51–53; decline of, 83, 91–95; domain governments and, 131–132; legal discourse as recognizing, 111, 112; legitimacy of, 83–89;

marketing of, 57–58; new way, 307; reclaiming of, 231–234; shifts in views of, 89–95

Shudō monogatari (Tales of *Shudō*). See *Shin'yūki*

Shudō texts: audience and viewpoint of, 46–49, 53–59, 71–72, 295, 300–301; authors of, class origins, 47, 70, 76, 92; defined, 44; didactic genre of, 52–53; domain regulation and, 135; erotic debate (*see* Erotic debate); geographical visions of, 63–69; illustrations in, 44, 45, 47; Kyushu in, 69, 207–208; as legacy, 95–96; legitimizing strategies used in, 49–53, 64, 83–89, 100–101, 333; loyalty and, 129n; Meiji censorship and expurgation of, 200, 335; nativism and, 86–89; peasantry and, 48, 52, 80–81, 139; popular sexology compared to, 295, 300–301; and prostitution, 57–59; publishing industry and production of meaning in, 10, 16, 28–29, 44–59; urban perspective of, 69, 81, 139. *See also* Publishing industry

Shudōzuki, 38, 39

Shūkin Joshi, 246–247, 248n

Shuppan jōrei, 200

Slang. *See* Male-male sexuality, terms for

Smoothies, 212–225

Socialists: proletarian literary movement, 309–311; views of same-sex love, 307–311

Social morality: of Edo period, 144–145; legal discourse and, 180–181, 192; and male-male erotic sub-culture, 320; and marriage, 274, 276; and rights of same-sex love persons, 271

Social problem, 294, 303, 308–309

Society of Jesus, 124n

Socioeconomic status: barriers of, texts as breaking, 46–47, 48, 81–82; barriers of, theater as breaking, 118, 122, 138; differentiation of

legal penalties by, Meiji, 159–160, 161n, 166n, 169, 181; and educational opportunities, 212, 214, 218; egalitarianism of *shudō* and, 37–38, 81–82; legal unit of, 44n; legislative differences and, Edo period, 109, 143–145; leveling of, Meiji, 145, 148, 169, 181; medico-scientific views of, 284–285; ostentation as challenge to, 78; and popular sexology, 291–292; and sexual moderation, 110–111, 143; of *shudō* text authors, 47, 70, 76, 92; structure of Edo period, 70, 73, 80, 116–117. *See also* Peasantry; Samurai class; Townsman class

Sodom and Gomorrah, 66, 99

Sodomy. *See* The West

Sōgi: *Chigo kyōkun*, 52, 74

Sojun, 108–109

Sokokura, 238

Song dynasty, 243n

Sōryū gidan, 220

Sotadic zone, 283

Southwestern periphery, 69, 206–211, 215, 222, 250, 279

Spain, 65n

Species, propagation of, 244, 247

Spirituality: *shudō* and, 28, 233. *See also* Religion

Stekel, Wilhelm, 276

Stick medicines, 239

Storm (sutōmu), 217

Student culture and sexuality, 214; beautiful boys, 218, 221, 225–234, 263, 281; of Edo period, 132–133, 212–213; journalism and, 218–223; legal discourse and, 160–161, 164, 172, 224; roughnecks and smooth-ies, 212–225, 227, 229, 230, 272, 283, 303; violence and, 132–133, 212–213, 217–221, 225, 227. *See also* Schools

Subari, 75

Suekane Naokichi. *See* Miyazaki Koshoshi

Sugawara Michinari, 180n, 335

Sugita Naoki, 281n, 296n
Suicide, 99, 190. *See also* Love suicide; Seppuku
Sumi Tatsuya: *Danshō no mori,* 331
Sunpu, 107
Sutra of the Remembrance of the True Law, 67
Symonds, John Addington, 233, 314

Tachi, 262
Taigasha Kihō, 68n
Taihei hyaku monogatari (Hundred Tales from an Age of Great Peace, Keichū Koji), 74
Taira Atsumori, 88
Taishō period, 290, 305, 307
Taiwan, 299–300
Takada Giichirō, 219n, 251, 254, 258
Takahashi Tetsu, 274
Takaratsu Shusō: *Mukashi mukashi monogatari,* 92, 93, 111n
Takeda Rintarō: "Kamagasaki," 322
Takehisa Yumeji, 313
Take/Takejirō, 152
Takijirō, 182
Takizawa Bakin: *Kinsesetsu bishōnen-roku,* 96, 227
Tamenaga Shunsui: *Iroha bunko,* 96
Tanaka Kōgai, 254, 270, 275, 279–280, 281, 282, 286–287, 293–294, 297, 299, 302
Tanakaya Kiemon, 126–127
Tanba Yasuyori: *Ishinpō,* 235
Tang dynasty, 63, 219n
Tanizaki Jun'ichirō, 219n, 220, 223
Tanizaki Seiji, 220
Tantei shōsetsu (Detective Story), 312
Taoka Reiun, 204n, 230–231
Tea ceremony, 28, 49
Teahouses. See *Kagemajaya*
Tennōji, 310, 311, 317, 318
Tenpō reforms, 149n, 152–153, 155–156, 200n, 318
Testicle transplants, 275
Testosterone injections, 275
Theater: boys', 228; kabuki (*see* Kabuki); *kyōgen,* 33n, 68n; *jōruri,*

26n; new *kagema* and, 318; nō, 50n, 114, 118; *shinpa,* 256
Third genders, 36
Three countries (*sangoku*), 64
Tobiko. See Fly boys
Tōkaidō, 135
Tōke seihō jōjō, 130
Tokugawa Iemitsu, 115n, 279n
Tokugawa Ieyasu, 15, 65, 279
Tokugawa Mitsukuni, 43
Tokugawa period. See Edo period
Tokugawa Tsunayoshi, 279n
Tokugawa Yoshimune, 154
Tokushima, 128n, 136–137, 138
Tokyo English Academy, 214
Tomita Eikichi, 186–187
Tomoe Gozen, 72
Tomogui, 23n
Tōsei shosei katagi (Spirit of Present-Day Students, Tsubouchi Shōyō), 201n, 215–217, 230
Totsugawa, 239n
Tottori, 102n, 125n, 140
Townsman class: in domains, 126–127, 133, 134n, 141; imagery of, as enduring, 196–197; misogyny of, 40, 79–80; municipal decrees and, 109, 111, 143–144; and popular discourse, Meiji, 205–206; prostitution and, 77–79, 119; samurai *shudō* compared to, 71–72, 76–77, 238n; as term, 44n, 76. *See also* Commercial sector; Socioeconomic status
Townswomen: as term, 44n
Toyama, 32n
Toyokichi, 182
Toyotomi Hidetsugu, 88
Toyotomi Hideyoshi, 64n
Tradition: construction of, 87–89
Tribadie, 176
Tsubouchi Shōyō: *Tōsei shosei katagi,* 201n, 215–217, 230
Tsuchiura, 166
Tsunayoshi. See Tokugawa Tsunayoshi
Tsūwasan, 238

Tuberculosis, 285
Two-sex love (*ryōseiai*): *kagema* and, 280; as normative stage, 276; as term, 252. *See also* Bisexuality; Psychic hermaphrodism

Ubukata Toshirō, 219n, 221–222, 223
Uchimura Kanzō, 173
Ueno, 157, 318n, 330, 331, 332
Uesugi Harunori, 132
Ujiie Mikito, 93–94, 133
Uke, 262
Ulrichs, Karl, 249, 255, 259
Umehara Hokumei, 293, 294, 300
Uno Kōji, 223
"Uranism" (Inagaki Taruho), 306
Uriwakashu, 141n, 321
Urningin, 259
Urnings, 215n, 259, 278, 281n, 288, 302, 304, 306, 314, 319, 323
Urushiya Ensai, 53; *Nanshoku kinometsuke*, 40n, 49, 50, 67, 72, 85, 86, 87, 129n
Ushiwaka. *See* Minamoto Yoshitsune

Venereal disease, 174, 195n, 247, 264n
Violence: in domains, 125–133; female-female sexuality and, 176–177, 189–190; of gangs, 133, 180; importuning and, 111–112, 116, 143; kabuki and, 113, 114, 138; Meiji obscene-acts regulation and, 168, 169, 178; in prisons, 185, 189–190; rape (*see* Rape); rough-necks and, 133, 217–221, 227; samurai and, 71–72, 76–77, 125–126, 128–133, 138, 144, 145, 204, 213, 217, 218, 311; *shudō* rivalries sparking, 40; townsman class and, 76–77
Virile gaze, 35–36, 39, 228, 301
Virility: defined, 35
Visual representations, 44, 46, 47, 147, 153n, 199n, 201, 227, 312–313; as outside scope of study, 9n. *See also* Woodblock prints

Vita Sexualis (*Wita sekusuarisu*, Mori Ōgai), 214–215, 217, 229, 259, 285, 288, 303–305
Vocabvlario da lingoa de Iapam, 65

Waisetsu no kōi, 177. *See also* Obscene acts
Waisetsu no shogyō, 168. *See also* Obscene acts
Wakamatsu, 133, 213
Wakaonnagata, 264n
Wakashu: as term, 26–27, 141. *See also* Youth
Wakashudō. See Shudō
Wakashugata, 264n
Wakashugirai, 39, 268n
Wakashugurui, 112, 181, 241n
Wakashu jorō, 119n
Wakashu sugata (Youthful Figures, Yamada Bimyō), 227
Wakashuzuki, 39, 267
Wakayama, 42n, 125n, 137, 158n, 204n, 232
Warring States. *See* Sengoku
Warrior class. *See* Samurai class
Watanabe Chiyomatsu, 188
Watanabe Tsuneo, 35n, 228n
Watanuki Rokusuke, 300–301, 303, 305, 328
Watanuki Yosaburō, 241, 242, 243–244, 247, 260
Watsuji Tetsurō, 221n
Way (*michi/dō*), 28, 48–49, 63; codi-fication and marketing of, 28–29; ending of, 82–83; *shudō* as (*see* Shudō, as a way)
Way of youths. *See Shudō*
Wealth: conspicuous consumption, 78, 122; *shudō* culture and, 77, 78
Weininger, Otto, 260–261
The West: beauty ideals and, 227, 281n; Edo-period knowledge of, 64–66; as feminine, 250; forensic pathology of, 174, 175–176, 177; global culture and, 290; Japanese influence on research of, 249–251, 277, 282; in judgement of Japanese

The West (continued)
culture, 65, 146, 157n, 172–173,
222; legal discourse of (see Legal
discourse, Western); love ideals
and, 25, 231; medical discourse
of (see Medico-scientific model
of sexuality, Western); military
technologies of, 211; orientalizing
by, 6–7, 10–11, 13, 249–251, 334;
poetry of, 227; racial theory, 171;
religion of, and male-male sexuality, 2, 42n, 65, 66, 98–99, 102,
104–105, 124n, 165–166, 170, 180,
201, 246, 271, 272, 300; sodomy
concept and legislation, 2, 65, 66,
97, 98, 102, 104–105, 124n, 160,
165–166, 170; as term, 2n
Westphal, Karl, 255
Whitman, Walt, 314n
Wita sekusuarisu (Vita Sexualis, Mori
Ōgai), 214–215, 217, 229, 259, 285,
288, 303–305
Woman-haters (onnagirai). See
Misogyny
Woman Land, 66
Woman problem, 294, 303
Women's magazines, 303
Women's rights movement, 268
Woodblock prints: censorship of, 201;
of Edo period, 26, 38, 59n; Meiji
period and, 196, 197, 206, 292

Xenophobia, 139, 202
Xianggong, 284

Yagizawa Kiyokichi, 265n
Yakei tomojamisen (Friendly Sha-
misen of Actors and Courtesans,
Nishizawa Ippū), 32, 37n, 42n, 61,
62, 85, 87n, 138n, 242n
Yakushi, 67
Yamada Bimyō: Wakashu sugata, 227
Yamagata, 130, 133, 207n. See also
Yonezawa
Yamaguchi, 129, 215. See also Hagi
Yamamoto Gonnohyōe, 211

Yamamoto Tsunetomo: Hagakure, 47,
48, 76–77, 128–129, 167
Yamato kotohajime (Origins of
Things Japanese, Kaibara Yoshi-
furu), 86, 87
Yamazaki Masao, 328
Yamazaki Toshio, 307
Yamazaki Yoshishige, 93n, 95, 96
Yarō: as term, 115, 141. See also
Actor-prostitutes
Yarō bōshi, 115–116
Yarō jitsugokyō (True Word Teaching
on Actor-Prostitutes, Kishōken
Kōyūshi), 50–51, 68n
Yasuda Tokutarō, 277, 279, 287, 308n
Yasui Sokken, 236–237
Yin-yang, 236, 240, 245, 261
Y.K., 297
Yodarekake (Bib, Baijōken), 30n, 31n,
41n, 51n, 64, 87
Yokachigo, 209
Yokohama, 157n, 172, 195, 202
Yokoyama Kendō, 227n
Yonezawa, 130–132, 133, 213n
Yorozu chōhō, 172–173, 218, 219–220,
221, 222, 284
Yorozu no fumihōgu (Myriad Letter
Scraps, Ihara Saikaku), 239–240
Yoshichō, 91, 102, 120, 121n, 156, 163,
194, 195, 205
Yoshida Hanbei: Kōshoku kunmo zui,
43n, 238n; Lucid Mirror of Nan-
shoku, 37n, 42n, 52–53, 54, 55–56,
57, 58, 71, 72, 79, 81, 90–91
Yoshida Ōkura, 209, 278
Yoshida Rokunosuke, 140–141
Yoshimune. See Tokugawa Yoshimune
Yoshiwara, 58, 62, 94, 102, 120, 155.
See also Prostitution, female
Yoshiya Nobuko, 180n
Yoshizawa Ayame, 264n
Youth (wakashu): ages defining, 30–
34, 91, 116n, 252–253, 276–277,
280; anal penetration and (see
Anal intercourse); clothing and
(see Clothing); coming-of-age

ceremony (*genbuku*), 33; de-
eroticization of, 228n; females
compared with, 35–36, 39, 54,
228–229, 255–256, 281; gender
construction of, 34–36, 228, 229,
262, 263–264; lovers of (see
Nenja); lovesickness and, 240;
motivations of, 55–56; new, of
Shōwa era, 318n; secondary sex
characteristics of, 32; socioeconomic status and, 37–38; texts as

instructing, 54–56. *See also* Forelocks; Insertee; *Shudō*
Youth culture. *See* Student culture
and sexuality
Yushima, 59n, 101, 109n, 120, 139,
156–157, 163, 194, 195–196

Zatto ichiran (General Overview,
Suisaishi), 66
Zhou dynasty, 85n
Zoological sexuality, 240–242, 243, 260

Compositor:	Integrated Composition Systems
Text:	10/13 Aldus
Display:	Aldus
Printer and binder:	Thomson-Shore, Inc.